Belize

DISCARD

Northern
Cayes
p83

Northern
Belize
p133

Belize
District
p54

Tikal & Flores
(Guatemala)
p241

Cayo
District
p156

Southern
Belize
p194

Paul Harding, Ray Bartlett, Ashley Harrell

PLAN YOUR TRIP

ON THE ROAD

**RED-FOOTED BOOBY BIRD,
HALF MOON CAYE P130**

**MASK TEMPLE (P142),
LAMANAI**

CAYE CAULKER P112

Contents

Welcome to Belize

With one foot in the Central American jungles and the other in the Caribbean Sea, pint-sized Belize is packed with islands, adventure and culture.

Reefs & Cays

Belize Barrier Reef is the second largest in the world, after Australia's, and with more than 100 types of coral and some 500 species of tropical fish, it's pure paradise for scuba divers and snorkelers. Swimming through translucent seas, snorkelers are treated to a kaleidoscope of coral, fish, whale sharks and turtles, while divers go deeper, investigating underwater caves and walls and the world-renowned Blue Hole.

Add to this island life on the sandy cays, where you can spend your days kayaking, windsurfing, stand-up paddleboarding, swimming, fishing or lazing in a hammock, and you've got a perfect tropical vacation.

In the Jungle

Inland, a vast (by Belizean standards) network of national parks, wildlife sanctuaries and protected areas offers a safe haven for wildlife, which ranges from the industrious parades of cutter ants to tapirs, noisy howler monkeys, or the shy jaguar. Birders aim their binoculars at some 570 species, which roost along the rivers and lagoons and in the broadleaf forest. Keen-eyed visitors who take the time to hike can easily spot spider monkeys, peccaries, coatimundis, *gibnuts* and green iguanas.

In the Land of the Maya

Belize is home to one of the world's most mysterious civilizations – the ancient Maya. The Cayo District and Toledo's Deep South are peppered with archaeological sites that date to the Maya heyday (AD 250–1000), where enormous steps lead to the tops of tall stone temples, often yielding 360-degree jungle views. Explore excavated tombs and examine intricate hieroglyphs, or descend into natural caves to see where the Maya kings performed rituals and made sacrifices to their underworld gods.

Action & Adventure

Whether you're scuba diving the Blue Hole, ziplining through the jungle canopy, rappelling down waterfalls or crawling through ancient cave systems, Belize is a genuine adventure. Head to Cayo District where you can tube or canoe through darkened underground river systems or hard-core spelunk in renowned Actun Tunichil Muknal cave. Ziplining is virtually an art form in Cayo and Southern Belize where you can sail through the jungle at half a dozen locations. Horseback riding is well organized and hiking is superb in national parks, such as Mayflower Bocawina National Park, Cockscomb Basin Wildlife Sanctuary, Shipstern Nature Reserve and Río Bravo.

Why I Love Belize

By Paul Harding, Writer

Belize is a bit Latin America, a bit Caribbean, and just a little bit British (the language is a giveaway) but it all works beautifully. I love the low-key, laid-back nature of the people and the seamless mix of cultures that make up the street life, music, food and festivals – Belizean, Creole, mestizo, Garifuna, Maya and even Mennonites and expats. I love that you can be snorkeling on the barrier reef one day and hiking in the jungle the next. And I love that Belize still feels just a little undiscovered...but perhaps not for long.

For more about our writers, see p320

Above: Caye Caulker (p112)

Belize

N 0 ————— 50 km
0 ————— 25 miles

ELEVATION

1050ft
900ft
750ft
600ft
450ft
300ft
150ft
1ft

Ambergris Caye
Fine dining and easy access to the reef (p85)

Shark Ray Alley
Face-to-face encounters with underwater predators (p91)

Caye Caulker
Ultimate Belizean chill-out destination (p112)

Altun Ha
The most accessible of Belize's ancient ruins (p76)

Crooked Tree Wildlife Sanctuary
Bird-attracting lagoon (p73)

Lamanai
Ancient ruins overlook a jungle lagoon (p140)

Community Baboon Sanctuary
Cheeky howler monkeys (p71)

Belize Zoo
Rescued Belize wildlife (p80)

Nohoch Che'en Caves
Experience archaeology by cave tube (p163)

CARIBBEAN SEA

18°N

MEXICO

Chetumal
Consejo
Subteniente López
Santa Elena
Sergio Butrón Casas
Santa Rita
Corozal Town
Cerros
Douglas
San Pablo
Yo Creek
Cuello
La Union
Blue Creek
La Milpa
Chan Chich
Gallon Jug
Uaxactún

Rocky Point
Sarteneja
Chetumal Bay
Shipstern Nature Reserve
Shipstern Lagoon
COROZAL DISTRICT
Progresso
San Estevan
Orange Walk Town
Shipyard
Indian Church
Crooked Tree
Lamanai
Rio Bravo Conservation & Management Area
ORANGE WALK DISTRICT
Rancho Dolores
Bermudian Landing
Community Baboon Sanctuary
Burrell Boom
Belize Zoo
La Democracia
BELMOPAN

Río Hondo
New River
Old Northern Hwy
Philip Goldson Hwy
Maskall
Altun Ha
Crooked Tree Wildlife Sanctuary
Philip Goldson International Airport
Ladyville
Hattieville
Belize River
Northern Lagoon
Gales Point Nature Reserve
Nohoch Che'en Caves
George

Ambergris Caye
San Pedro
Shark Ray Alley
Caye Caulker Marine Reserve
Caye Caulker
Caye Chapel
Cayo Espanto
Hick's Cayes
Drowned Caye
St George's Caye
Belize City
Gallows Point Reef
Turneffe Atoll
Blackbird Caye
Central
Northern Caye
Blue Hole Natural Monument
Lighthouse

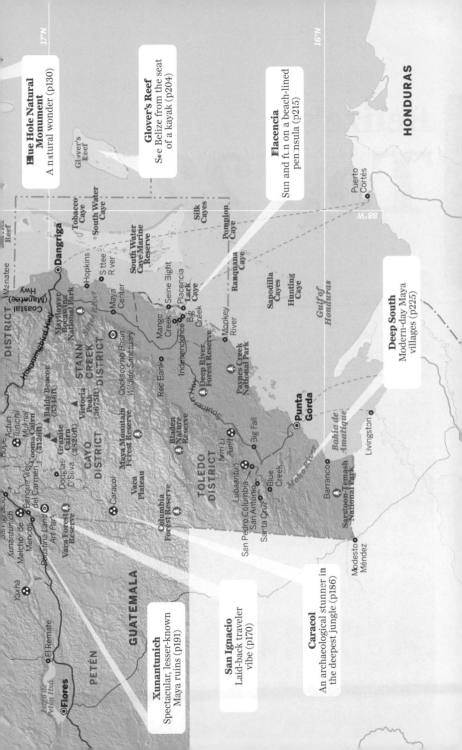

Blue Hole Natural Monument
A natural wonder (p130)

Glover's Reef
See Belize from the seat of a kayak (p204)

Placencia
Sun and fun on a beach-lined peninsula (p215)

Deep South
Modern-day Maya villages (p225)

Xunantunich
Spectacular, lesser-known Maya ruins (p191)

San Ignacio
Laid-back traveler vibe (p170)

Caracol
An archaeological stunner in the deepest jungle (p186)

HONDURAS

GUATEMALA

PETÉN

17°N

16°N

BELIZE DISTRICT

STANN CREEK DISTRICT

CAYO DISTRICT

TOLEDO DISTRICT

Gulf of Honduras

Bahía de Amatique

Belize's
Top 22

Diving the Blue Hole

1 The sheer walls of the Blue Hole Natural Monument (p130) drop more than 400ft into the blue ocean. Although it is partly filled with silt and natural debris, the depth still creates a perfect circle of startling azure that is visible from above. The wall of the Blue Hole is decorated with a dense forest of stalactites and stalagmites from times past. A school of reef sharks and the odd hammerhead keep divers company as they descend into the mysterious ocean depths.

Kayaking Glover's Reef

2 Lying like a string of white-sand pearls, Glover's Reef (p204) consists of half a dozen small islands surrounded by blue sea as far as the eye can see. Its unique position, atop a submerged mountain ridge on the edge of the continental shelf, makes it an ideal place for sea kayaking, both between the islands and around the shallow central lagoon. Get a kayak with a clear bottom and you're likely to see spotted eagle rays, southern stingrays, turtles and countless tropical fish swimming beneath as you paddle.

MATTEO COLOMBO / GETTY IMAGES ©

2

HENRY GEORGI / GETTY IMAGES ©

Ambergris Caye

3 Also known as La Isla Bonita, Ambergris Caye (p85) is the ultimate tropical paradise vacation destination (and that's what Madonna thought, too). Spend your days snorkeling the reef, kayaking the lagoon or windsurfing the straits; pamper yourself at a day spa or challenge yourself at a yoga class; ride a bike up the beach or take a nap at the end of your dock. After the sun sets, spend your evenings enjoying the country's most delectable dining and most happening nightlife in San Pedro.

Garifuna Culture

4 Garifuna culture is strong in Southern Belize and its most obvious cultural impression is music and drumming. Dangriga and Punta Gorda both have opportunities to study drumming and drum-making with Garifuna drum masters, while the Garifuna village of Hopkins (p205) is a hotbed of drumming for most of the year, especially around full moon nights. Garifuna Settlement Day (November 19) is an event not to be missed, particularly in Hopkins or Dangriga. Tasty Garifuna cuisine can also be found at shack restaurants in these communities. Bottom: Hopkins

Caye Caulker

5 A brisk breeze is almost always blowing (especially between January and June), creating optimal conditions to cruise across the water on sailboat, windsurfer or kiteboard. The world's second-largest barrier reef is just a few miles offshore, beckoning snorkelers and divers to frolic with the fish. The mangroves teem with life, inviting exploration by kayak. All these adventures await, yet the number-one activity on Caye Caulker (p112) is still swinging in a hammock, reading a book and sipping a freshly squeezed fruit juice. Paradise.

Altun Ha

6 You've drunk the beer, now it's time to visit the ruins that inspired the Belikin beer-bottle label. The most accessible of Belize's ancient ruins, Altun Ha (p76) displays 10 different structures dating from the 6th and 7th centuries, and it was also the site of some of the richest archaeological excavations in Belize, although the artifacts have long since been removed. You'll get your exercise climbing to the tops of the temples to take in the surrounding jungle panorama.

Xunantunich

7 Xunantunich (p191) isn't Belize's biggest or oldest archaeological site, but it's still one of the most impressive, especially for its remarkable hieroglyphics. After taking a hand-cranked ferry across the Mopan River, you'll walk through bird- and butterfly-filled jungle, until you reach a complex of temples and plazas that dates back to the early Classic Maya Period. Once there, you can explore a number of structures, and even climb to the top of 130ft-high El Castillo for a spectacular 360-degree view of the surrounds.

BRODIE COMPUTES INC / GETTY IMAGES ©

Belize Carnival

8 This is not the usual pre-Lenten extravaganza that takes place in other parts of the Caribbean in anticipation of the fasting season. In the 1970s, Belizeans started celebrating their own Carnival (p60) in September, as a spicy addition to the national holidays. Revelers don outrageous costumes and take to the streets in Orange Walk, Corozal Town and especially Belize City. In a flurry of movement, music and color, neighborhood camps design floats and wear costumes that depict local cultures and customs.
Left: Detail of Carnival costume

Lamanai

9 Spanning all phases of ancient Maya civilization, the ruins at Lamanai (p140) are known for their stone reliefs, impressive architecture, and the marvelous setting overlooking the New River Lagoon and surrounded by some of Northern Belize's densest jungle. Arrive at this outpost by boat, allowing upclose observation of birds and wildlife along the New River. On site, hear the roar of the howler monkeys while climbing the steep facade of the High Temple and admiring the Mask Temple's deformed face.
Top right: Mask Temple (p142)

Snorkeling Shark Ray Alley

10 Local fisherfolk used to come to Shark Ray Alley (p91) to clean their catch, and their discards would attract hungry nurse sharks and southern stingrays. As a result these predators have long become accustomed to the sounds of boat motors, which now bring snorkelers rather than fishers. Shark Ray Alley is the top snorkeling destination in Hol Chan Marine Reserve, a shallow, protected part of the Belize Barrier Reef that harbors an amazing diversity of colorful coral and other marine life.

Crooked Tree Wildlife Sanctuary

11 Belize is for the birds. Nowhere is that statement truer than at Crooked Tree (p73), a fishing and farming village centered on a lagoon. The wetlands attract hundreds of bird species, including dozens of migrants who stop on their way north or south. Birding is best during the drier months (February to May), when the lagoon dries up and the birds congregate around the puddles. Expert guides will lead you by boat or on foot to spot and identify your feathered friends. Top: Bare-throated tiger heron

Jungle Hiking

12 If it is off-the-beaten-path you are after, take a hike in one of Belize's many protected areas, such as Mayflower Bocawina National Park (p200) or Cockscomb Basin Wildlife Sanctuary. With jungle, mountains, waterfalls, swimming holes and even some small Maya ruins, you'll feel like you've left civilization and the 21st century behind. Off the tourist trail, you'll be sharing the park with countless birds, mammals, reptiles and, no doubt, a resident squad of black howler monkeys. Bottom: Mayflower Bocawina National Park

Maya Villages

13 To experience Maya life firsthand, trek through the villages of Belize's rural Toledo District, where ancient and contemporary Maya culture exist side by side, and rituals and folklore play an important role in everyday life. From the ancient ruins of Lubaantun (p237) to the cultural circuit through Big Falls, San Miguel and San Pedro Columbia, your trek will take you through some of Belize's most beautiful villages and allow you time to interact with a people whose civilization once surpassed Rome in political influence and grandeur.

Caracol

14 Step out of the modern world and into the ancient realm at Belize's largest Maya site, where you'll spend the day wandering through a city that once rivaled Tikal in political influence and, for many, is more impressive today. Standing in the central area of temples, palaces, craft workshops and markets, you'll feel the power and glory of ancient Caracol (p186). At 141ft, Caana (which means Sky Place) is still the tallest building in Belize. In addition to being the country's pre-eminent archaeological site, Caracol also teems with jungle wildlife. Bottom: Caana

13

14

CANNON PHOTOGRAPHY LLC / ALAMY ©

CHRISTOPHE BARBOCK / SHUTTERSTOCK ©

Nohoch Che'en Caves

15 Floating through a darkened cave river on an inflated tube with a helmet flashlight is a remarkably calming experience. Delve even further into the bowels of the earth with an experienced guide to discover some remarkable cave systems and subterranean rivers known as Caves Branch. At the Nohoch Che'en Caves (p163) you'll float through an underground network, experiencing wonders unseen in the world above. For more adventure, there are jungle ziplining courses, nature trails and ATV (All Terrain Vehicle) trails nearby.

Hummingbird Highway

16 Arguably Belize's most beautiful stretch of road, the winding Hummingbird Hwy (p164) offers unparalleled views of the Maya Mountains as it passes through jungles, citrus orchards and tiny villages. The Hummingbird also offers plenty of reasons to stop for a few hours and there are some fine upmarket lodges and budget guesthouses along the way. Explore St Herman's Cave, hike the jungle loop trail, take a dip in the crystal-clear Blue Hole, zipline through the jungle or rappel down Angel Falls.

Placencia

17 It's hardly off the beaten path, but at the end of a long peninsula there's a reason so many feet beat the path to Southern Belize's most popular beachside resort village. Placencia (p215) is just too chilled out to not spend some time kayaking, sailing or simply walking barefoot on the beach by day, and drinking rum cocktails by night. As for dining, it has most of Southern Belize's best restaurants and freshest lobster. Get here by road, sea ferry or the Hokey Pokey water taxi.

Hopkins

18 Halfway between the hustle of Dangriga and the tourist vibe of Placencia lies slacked-out Hopkins (p205), a low-key Garifuna village where life hasn't changed much in decades. Children walk the town's one street selling their mothers' freshly baked coconut pies and chocolate brownies; local men catch fish by day and play drums at night; and the pace of life is pleasantly slow. The beach is slender but on a fine day the view out across the Caribbean is sublime.

Community Baboon Sanctuary

19 The 'baboons' at this sanctuary (p71) are not really baboons, but rather black howler monkeys, an endangered species in Central America. The 'sanctuary' is not exactly a protected area, but more a network of private properties where the howlers live. Thanks to this community-based, grass-roots effort, property owners have agreed to preserve their land for the benefit of the resident monkeys. Although the sanctuary encompasses about 20 sq miles, guides take tourists to a small area where the welcoming troop allows for up-close observation of the funny monkeys.

Belize Zoo

20 Even people philosophically opposed to the concept of caged creatures will approve of this humane, earthy and educational zoo (p80). As a halfway house and rehabilitation center for injured, orphaned and rescued Belizean jungle animals, the Belize Zoo is a fabulous and friendly place to get a good look at the dozens of species of indigenous animals and birds that are difficult to spot in the wild. The zoo hosts myriad educational programs for kids and adults, including a festive birthday party for April the tapir; the tapir is the national animal of Belize.

Bottom right: Jaguar

Half Moon Caye Natural Monument

21 Part of the Lighthouse Reef Atoll, Half Moon Caye (p130) provides a nesting ground for the rare red-footed booby bird. Thousands of these waterfowl make their homes in the treetops, alongside the frigate bird and 98 other species. Dive the Half Moon Caye Wall (or snorkel the shallows); enjoy a beach picnic; then hike across the island and climb the observation platform to get a good look at the booby birds. Sea turtles also lay their eggs on the southern beaches. Top: Red-footed booby birds

San Ignacio

22 Western Cayo's main town (p170) is a relaxed and vibrant community from where you can organize any activity in the region. Saturday is the main market day, where locals sell their produce and wares, but on any day of the week you can chill at a traveler cafe on pedestrian Burns Ave, listen to live music at the Bamboo Bar, stroke green iguanas at San Ignacio Resort Hotel or simply plan your next foray to Mountain Pine Ridge, Caracol or Guatemala. Some of the best-value accommodation in Belize is right here.

21

22

Need to Know

For more information, see Survival Guide (p297)

Currency
Belize Dollar (BZ$)

Languages
English, Kriol, Garifuna, Spanish

Visas
For most nationalities, visas are issued upon entry for up to 30 days.

Money
ATMs are widely available; credit cards are accepted at most hotels, restaurants and shops.

Mobile Phones
Local SIM cards can be used in most unlocked international cell phones with the notable exception of phones from some operators in the US.

Time
GMT/UTC minus six hours

When to Go

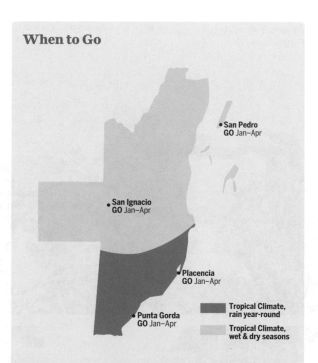

- San Pedro
  GO Jan–Apr

- San Ignacio
  GO Jan–Apr

- Placencia
  GO Jan–Apr

- Punta Gorda
  GO Jan–Apr

■ Tropical Climate, rain year-round

■ Tropical Climate, wet & dry seasons

High Season
(Dec–Apr)

➡ Expect sunny skies and warm days from January to April.

➡ Accommodations prices increase by 30% to 50%.

➡ Extra-high 'peak' prices from mid-December to mid-January; reservations are essential during this period.

Shoulder
(Nov & May)

➡ Chance of dry days in November and hot and humid in May.

➡ Fewer tourists and lower prices.

➡ Most attractions open across the region.

Low Season
(Jun–Oct)

➡ Heavy rainfall from June to mid-November, especially at night.

➡ Hurricanes possible between August and October.

➡ Few tourists; prices for accommodations drop significantly though some places close down.

Useful Websites

Belizean Journeys (www.belizeanjourneys.com) Online magazine covering life and nature in Belize.

Belize Tourism Board (www.travelbelize.org) Official tourism board site.

Belize Forums (www.belizeforum.com/belize) User forum discussing all topics Belizean.

Belize Explorer (www.belizeexplorer.com) Budget accommodations and travel advice.

Lonely Planet (www.lonelyplanet.com/belize) Destination information, hotel bookings, traveler forum and more.

Important Numbers

Belize has no regional, area or city codes. Dial a seven-digit local number from wherever you are in the country.

Belize's country code	501
Directory assistance	113
Emergency	90, 911
International access code	00
Operator assistance	115

Exchange Rates

Australia	A$1	BZ$1.47
Canada	C$1	BZ$1.54
Europe	€1	BZ$2.31
Guatemala	Q1	BZ$0.27
Japan	¥100	BZ$1.83
Mexico	M$1	BZ$0.10
NZ	NZ$1	BZ$1.33
UK	UK£1	BZ$2.58
USA	US$1	BZ$2

For current exchange rates, see www.xe.com.

Daily Costs

Budget: Less than BZ$120

➡ Camping or dorm bed: BZ$10–40

➡ Double room in a budget hotel: BZ$50–120

➡ Street-food stalls or self-catering: BZ$3–10

➡ One hour bus ride: BZ$5

Midrange: BZ$120–500

➡ Double room with private bathroom: BZ$120–350

➡ Dinner and drinks at local restaurants: BZ$15–35

➡ Adventure and caving activities: BZ$75–200

➡ Taxis/golf-cart hire: BZ$20–80

Top End: More than BZ$350

➡ Luxury accommodations per double: from BZ$350

➡ Fancy restaurants in resort areas: BZ$30–50

➡ Transportation by rental car or organized shuttles: BZ$80–100

➡ Shopping, day spas, private tours: from BZ$100

Opening Hours

Outside of banks, phone companies and government offices, you'll find most opening hours to be flexible. Restaurants and bars keep longer hours during high season, but will also close early if they wish (if business is slow etc).

Banks 8am to 3pm Monday to Thursday and 8am to 4pm or 4:30pm Friday

Pubs and Bars Noon to midnight (or later)

Restaurants & Cafes 7am to 9:30am (breakfast), 11:30am to 2pm (lunch) and 6pm to 8pm (dinner)

Shops 9am to 5pm Monday to Saturday, some open Sunday

Arriving in Belize

Philip Goldson International Airport (Belize City) Many hotels and resorts offer airport shuttles. Taxis into town cost BZ$50 for one to two passengers and BZ$60 for three to four passengers. No public buses serve the facility.

Main Bus Terminal (Belize City) Long-distance buses from Mexico arrive at the main bus terminal, which is a short distance from downtown Belize City – although walking is not recommended. Taxis wait outside the terminal and charge BZ$7 to downtown hotels or the water-taxi terminals.

International Departures Dock (San Pedro) Boat services from Mexico arrive at this facility in downtown San Pedro. Collective minivan taxis meet boats and charge BZ$7 around town. Rates to hotels outside the center are negotiable.

Getting Around

Air Maya Island and Tropic Air fly between all major towns in Belize. Planes are small, flights are short and fairly affordable.

Bus Most public travel in Belize is done by bus. All towns are serviced by one or more of a bewildering variety of private bus services, and you can usually flag down a bus on the highway.

Boat Caye Caulker and Ambergris are serviced by ferries from Belize City, and there is also a boat from Corozal to Ambergris with a possible Sarteneja stop.

Car Driving is on the right. All major highways are paved, but few have decent shoulders and painted dividing lines. Speed bumps are common but not all are marked.

For much more on **getting around**, see p308

see p308

First Time Belize

For more information, see Survival Guide (p297)

Checklist

➡ Make sure your passport has at least six months to run and check whether you need a visa

➡ Arrange for appropriate travel insurance

➡ Book accommodations, for your first two nights at least

➡ Check the local weather forecast at www.hydromet.gov.bz

➡ Find out whether your cell phone will work in Belize

What to Pack

➡ PADI (or equivalent) certification card if you're a diver

➡ Insect repellent – available locally but if you have a favorite brand/strength, bring it!

➡ Prescriptions or specialized medicines

➡ Mask, snorkel and reef shoes

➡ Binoculars for birdwatching and wildlife spotting

➡ Driver's license if you plan to hire a car

Top Tips for Your Trip

➡ Book island accommodations in advance, especially in high season. Many lodges offer free boat transfers for guests.

➡ Build some flexibility into your itinerary; you might find remote attractions such as caves closed if it's too wet, or accommodations on your island of choice booked out.

➡ Avoid driving at night. Highways are unlit, speed bumps unmarked and you risk hitting a local wandering on the road.

➡ Bring US dollars in currency along with your credit/debit cards. Some banks won't touch euros or other foreign currencies.

What to Wear

Belize is informal, so leave the suits and cocktail dresses at home, even if visiting fancy resorts. It's also hot and/or humid year-round, so heavy clothing is out. On the coast and cays, beachwear such as shorts, skirts, T-shirts or light cotton shirts is perfect. Bikinis are fine on the beach but inappropriate in towns and villages – a sarong is a useful covering. Bring lightweight long pants and a long-sleeved shirt to guard against biting insects and cool evenings. A lightweight raincoat or poncho is handy, though an umbrella is better. Sandals or flip-flops are ideal by the beach; in the jungles you'll need sturdy shoes or hiking boots if you plan on doing a lot of walking.

Sleeping

Lodges and Resorts The top level of accommodations in Belize are the remote jungle lodges and swish coastal island resorts, where the location is part of the attraction.

Cabins and Cabañas These range from rustic to luxurious and offer a level of privacy as they're free-standing.

Guesthouses Affordable, welcoming, found in most towns and villages. Often family-run.

Holiday rentals Apartments, villas and houses that can be booked online.

Money

The Belizean dollar (BZ$) is pegged to the US dollar at two to one (BZ$1 = US$0.50). Nearly every business in Belize accepts US dollars and prices are often quoted in US dollars at resorts and hotels – always check in advance whether you're paying in Belize dollars or US dollars.

ATMs are widely available; credit cards are accepted at most hotels, restaurants and shops.

Bargaining

Bargaining is not common in Belize with the notable exception of outdoor souvenir markets, where everything is negotiable. When business is slow, it's possible to obtain a discount on hotel rooms, golf-cart rentals and other tourism services, although this is usually limited to a quick back-and-forth rather than hard-edge bargaining.

Tipping

Tipping is not obligatory but is always appreciated if guides, drivers or servers have provided you with genuinely good service. Some hotels and restaurants add an obligatory service charge to your check (usually 10%).

Hotels Not needed but baggage porters appreciate a small gratuity.

Restaurants Round up the check between 5% and 10%.

Taxis Tips are not expected.

Tour Guides In high-volume areas, tour guides are used to receiving tips.

Languages

English is the national language of Belize. Spanish is widely spoken, especially in the far north and south, and you'll also hear Kriol and Garifuna.

Etiquette

Dress Apart from formal occasions, such as going to church, dress in Belize is generally very casual even when heading out to eat or for drinks. However, Belize remains a conservative nation and very revealing outfits may be frowned upon in some areas.

Greetings Don't be shy about making eye contact and greeting strangers on the street. Belizeans are friendly! The most common greeting is the catch-all 'Aarait?' ('Alright?'), to which you might respond 'Aarait, aarait?'

Queues Belizeans for the most part are firm in respecting queues. Where there is a turn system for services, respect the order. This is especially important at taxi ranks; while you may not be able to see a physical line, the drivers know whose turn it is, so ask before jumping into a vehicle.

Eating

Belize's national cuisine (p283) is rice and beans with chicken or fish; in the main tourist resorts and cities you'll find a good range of international food. Bookings are only required at fancy places in high season and at resort restaurants.

Street Food Places like San Ignacio, Orange Walk and Placencia have cheap street food such as tacos, quesadillas and *salbutes*, or barbecue with rice and beans.

Restaurants A restaurant in Belize covers everything from a shack serving Belizean dishes to a smart place at a resort. Many remote lodges and island resorts include meals (since there's nowhere else to eat!).

If You Like...

Sun & Fun

This is the Caribbean, so you'll more than likely spend at least a few days soaking up some rays and dipping your toes in the turquoise blue. Best time: January to April.

Caye Caulker The ultimate chill-out destination, with a laid-back village vibe and easy access to the sea. Don't miss Koko King. (p112)

Ambergris Caye If busy San Pedro is too much, head to one of the North Island resorts or seek out Secret Beach. (p85)

Placencia Beach-lined peninsula offering ample opportunities for swimming, sunning, snorkeling, scuba diving and offshore island experiences. (p215)

Hopkins Narrow but inviting beaches, village vibe and much less tourist traffic than nearby Placencia. (p205)

Diving & Snorkeling

Life under the sea is dramatic and diverse, from the fantastical coral formations and the kaleidoscopic fish that feed there to the massive and sometimes menacing creatures that lurk in deeper waters.

Glover's Reef On the reef, offering some of the most pristine diving and snorkeling opportunities in Belize. (p204)

Blue Hole Natural Monument Seen from the sky, this national landmark is a perfectly round, perfectly blue bull's eye. (p130)

Turneffe Atoll Attracts huge congregations of cubera snappers, horse-eye jacks, spadefish, reef sharks and king mackerel. (p128)

Hol Chan Marine Reserve Shallow waters offer excellent conditions for snorkeling, especially at Shark Ray Alley, but divers will be thrilled by the shipwreck at Amigos Wreck. (p86)

Caves

The erosive action of water on the relatively soft limestone of the Maya Mountains has produced numerous underground rivers and caves. Many of the caves were ritual sites for the ancient Maya, as they were considered to be close to the underworld.

Actun Tunichil Muknal Unforgettable caving experience, where you will see firsthand the evidence of the Maya rituals. (p168)

Nohoch Che'en Caves Branch Archaeological Reserve Combines the mystery of spelunking with river-rafting through an underground network of caves. (p163)

Barton Creek Cave Remote Barton Creek is one of the few caves you can canoe through. (p179)

Blue Creek Cave A remote cave in the Deep South where you and your guide might have the place to yourself. (p240)

Wildlife

Wildlife is the star of the show in Belize, thanks to conservation of the forests and reefs, where 25% of the land area is protected. From monkeys to manatees, you can see these creatures in their natural habitat.

Belize Zoo This amazing, privately funded zoo houses wildlife that has been injured or rescued throughout the country. (p80)

Community Baboon Sanctuary Get up close and personal with black howlers at this community-based, grassroots monkey refuge. (p71)

Swallow Caye Wildlife Sanctuary As many as 30 West Indian manatees inhabit these shallow waters southwest of Caye Caulker. (p113)

Cockscomb Basin Wildlife Sanctuary Also known as the jaguar reserve, this is a fine place for birdwatching and perhaps a jaguar sighting. (p41)

Birds

Birders know Belize. For everyone else with a spare pair of binoculars there are 570 resident and migratory species, inhabiting the shores of the rivers and lagoons or deep in the forest. Outstanding.

Crooked Tree Wildlife Sanctuary The lagoon is home to hundreds of bird species, including jabiru storks. (p73)

Red Bank Home to the spectacular scarlet macaw, which feasts on the forest fruits from December to March. (p225)

Río Bravo Conservation & Management Area Spot birds as varied as the collared aracari, oscillated turkey, rufous hummingbird and turkey vultures. (p144)

Cockscomb Basin Wildlife Sanctuary Jaguars might be hard to spot, but birds are everywhere in this celebrated sanctuary. (p41)

Outdoor Adventure

Come to Belize for action and adventure, to mount seemingly insurmountable temples, to dive to the ocean's darkest depths, and to feel the sticky heat of the jungle and the salty air of the sea.

Deep South Toledo's Deep South features lush jungles, crystal-clear swimming holes, waterfalls and Maya ruins. (p225)

Glover's Reef Islands ideal for hopping. Kayak the limpid waters,

Top: Xunantunich (p191)

Bottom: Manatee, Caye Caulker (p112)

admiring the prolific marine life from above. (p204)

Cayo District Around San Ignacio there are opportunities for hiking, horseback riding, caving and visiting Maya ruins. (p156)

Shipstern Conservation & Management Area Hiking trails, wildlife spotting and a boat trip on the lagoon make Shipstern an excellent adventure. (p153)

Eco-chic Resorts

Ecotourism was practically invented here. Belize offers myriad ways for travelers to tread lightly and go off-grid, from beach resorts powered by solar energy to jungle lodges built from reclaimed hardwoods.

Black Rock Lodge Sweet base for a jungle adventure, surrounded by towering cliffs and protected national park. (p190)

Chan Chich Lodge Chan Chich sits on 200 sq miles of private wildlife preserve on the Guatemalan border. (p145)

Turneffe Atoll Resorts on Blackbird Caye are taking steps to preserve the spectacular environment of the atoll. (p129)

Belize Boutique Resort & Spa In a secluded spot north of Belize City, this resort takes the eco jungle-lodge-and-spa concept to papmering extremes. (p75)

Cayo Espanto Private island resort with maximum attention to detail. (p128)

Maya Ruins

For almost 3000 years the ancient Maya civilization flourished in Belize, building towering temples as tribute to their god-like rulers. The remains of these once-mighty city-states are scattered throughout the country and are prime for exploration.

Xunantunich One of Cayo's prettiest Maya ruins, and definitely among the easiest to get to. (p191)

Caracol Once the most powerful kingdom of the Maya world, Caracol covers a vast, jungle-clad area. (p186)

Lamanai Ruins at Lamanai are among the oldest and the largest Maya sites in the country. (p140)

Lubaantun Among the most complete of Toledo's Maya ruins,

Lubaantun is easy to reach. (p237)

Altun Ha With its immaculate central plaza, Altun Ha is still a small but spectacular site north of Belize City. (p76)

Music

A rich diversity is evident in the music of Belize, where you'll hear rhythms and instruments representing Creole and calypso, Maya and Garifuna.

Maroon Creole Drum School Learn traditional drum crafting and playing at Emmeth Young's drum school in Punta Gorda. (p227)

Fido's Among the best places to see live music in San Pedro, Fido's has bands nightly. (p108)

Black & White This restaurant doubles as a cultural center, and occasionally hosts Garifuna drumming traditions. (p104)

Placencia On weekends the village rocks to the sounds of *punta rock*, reggae and Garifuna drumming. (p215)

Hopkins Garifuna drumming most nights and weekly live music at the excellent Driftwood Beach Bar. (p205)

Month by Month

January

Although the dry season hasn't officially started, the post–New Year holidays bring a huge influx of people and an increase in prices. Visitors might see some rain, but (hopefully) not enough to spoil their good time.

✵ New Year

Burrell Boom hosts a longstanding New Year's Day horse race. Hundreds of spectators cheer on the cyclists who ride from Corozal to Belize City as part of the Krem Annual New Year's Day Classic (www.krembz.com). The biggest NYE party is in San Pedro.

February

The dry season is here, so enjoy sunny skies and warm temperatures day after day. Prices for accommodations remain relatively high.

🏃 Birding

Lagoons and rivers begin to dry up and birds become easier to spot, as they congregate around the limited remaining water sources. Migration also significantly increases the number of species you might tick off your list. Prime birdwatching conditions continue through to May.

✵ El Gran Carnaval de San Pedro

This festival takes place mainly in San Pedro with music, dancing, costumes, parades and church services. (p95)

🏃 Closing of the Lobster Season

The lobster's mating and spawning season is from mid-February to mid-June. Belize respectfully gives the crustaceans some privacy, closing the season for trapping lobsters on February 15.

✵ Sidewalk Art Festival

Arts, craft and street music along the beachfront Sidewalk path in Placencia. (p218)

March

The dry season rolls on and tourists and residents enjoy perfect blue skies and warm temperatures. Take care to minimize water usage.

🏃 Baron Bliss Day

On March 9 (or the closest Monday), Belize pays tribute to its greatest benefactor. Part of Bliss' legacy is a trust that funds an annual boat race in Belize City, and other towns follow suit by hosting smaller races and regattas. (p60)

🏃 La Ruta Maya Belize River Challenge

Participants from all walks of life join teams to compete in this grueling, four-day canoe race (www.larutamaya.bz). Following the original trade and transport route, the race runs along the Macal and Belize Rivers from San Ignacio to Belize City. (p70)

April

The weather is dry and it's beginning to get hot, especially in the southern parts of the country. Expect extra crowds during the weeks before and after Easter.

Holy Week

Various services and processions are held in the week leading up to Easter Sunday. Good Friday and Easter Monday are official state holidays, so most businesses are closed all weekend.

May

Humidity increases and the dry season gradually turns to wet toward the end of May, but this can be a good time to travel with fewer tourists.

✕ Chocolate Festival of Belize

This food and cultural festival in Punta Gorda pays homage to Maya chocolate and music. (p228)

June

Dry season becomes humid season in June, though showers are short and often at night. Visitors who can tolerate a few raindrops will enjoy the peaceful atmosphere and lower prices.

✕ Lobster Season Reopens

Lobster season reopens on June 15 and the coastal towns and fishing villages

Top: Garifuna Settlement Day

Bottom: Chocolate Festival of Belize

celebrate! Food festivals take place in Caye Caulker, San Pedro and Placencia, with music, drinking and plenty of seafood. See also www.sanpedrolobsterfest.com and www.placencia.com.

July

The humidity has really kicked in; expect short, sharp heavy showers.

☆ Belize International Film Festival

Screens films from Central America and the Caribbean in Belize City, with additional screenings in Placencia. Traditionally held in July but moved to October in 2016 and November in 2018. See www.belizefilmfestival.com for updates.

August

Weather is hot, humid and usually wet, wet, wet. Belizeans are on the lookout for hurricanes and tourists make themselves scarce.

📷 Costa Maya Festival

People with Maya in their blood or in their souls come from all parts of Central America and Mexico to celebrate Maya coastal culture in San Pedro. See also www.internationalcostamayafestival.com.

September

It's the height of hurricane season, but it's also the most festive month in Belize, which celebrates its national holidays with gusto.

📷 September Celebrations

The holidays commence on the Battle of on September 10, with ceremonies and celebrations around the country. For the next 10 days, Belize hosts carnival parades and fun competitions. The celebrations culminate with outdoor concerts on September 21, Independence Day. (p60)

November

The rain starts to let up. As temperatures drop in the northern hemisphere around Thanksgiving, the trickle of tourists turns into a steady stream.

📷 Garifuna Settlement Day

A celebration of one of the country's richest minority cultures, November 19 commemorates the Garifuna arrival on Belizean soil in 1832. The country gets down with lots of drumming, dancing and drinking, especially in Dangriga, Hopkins and Punta Gorda, where celebrations may last several days and feature a 'coming ashore' ceremony. (p197)

December

December still brings some rain, but not enough to deter the many travelers who want to spend their holidays in the tropics. Most lodgings are extra expensive in the last two weeks of the month.

📷 Christmas Day

Belizeans celebrate Christmas much like North Americans, decorating their houses with colorful lights weeks ahead. Most people spend Christmas Day sharing meals with family and friends. In some places, festivities continue until January 6, when Garifuna *jonkonu* dancers go from house to house.

Itineraries

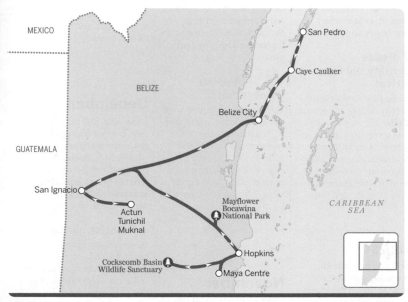

 Belize in a Week

If time is short you can either spend it relaxing in one place or plan carefully and experience the best of Belize. This short itinerary covers the best of Belize, allowing time for beaches, islands and inland adventure.

Start in **Belize City** but head straight to the water taxi terminal and book a ticket to laid-back **Caye Caulker** or more upbeat **San Pedro** on Ambergris Caye. Either place makes a good base for exploring the reef. After two or three days on the cays, return to Belize City and catch the bus straight to **San Ignacio**. This relaxed traveler town in Cayo District is the base for visiting Actun Tunichil Muknal cave, Caracol, Xunantunich, Barton Creek Cave and more. If you only have time for one, we recommended **Actun Tunichil Muknal cave**. Track back down the Hummingbird Hwy to **Hopkins** for some beach time and Garifuna drumming. Finish with a tour up to **Mayflower Bocawina National Park** for a day of hiking to waterfalls and ziplining through the jungle. Alternatively, visit the chocolate factory at **Maya Center** and make the excellent detour into the 'jaguar reserve' of **Cockscomb Basin Wildlife Sanctuary**.

 ### The Whole Enchilada: From Corozal to Punta Gorda

4 WEEKS

This itinerary starts in the quaint mestizo town of **Corozal**, just south of the Mexican border. Spend one day in **Orange Walk Town**, where you can cruise the New River and explore the Maya ruins at **Lamanai**. Then head east to the small fishing village of **Sarteneja** for some amazing wildlife watching at **Shipstern Conservation & Management Area**.

From Sarteneja, catch the fast ferry to **San Pedro**. Stay on either **Ambergris Caye** or **Caye Caulker**, but allow yourself at least four days to chill out in a hammock, kayak out to the reef, frolic with the fish and feast on fresh seafood.

When you head back to the mainland, don't bypass the animal-lovers' sights outside **Belize City** in the Belize District, including the **Community Baboon Sanctuary** and the **Belize Zoo**. If you're into birds, spend a night or two around the **Crooked Tree Wildlife Sanctuary**. Further west in Cayo, base yourself in or around **San Ignacio** and take four or five days experiencing regional adventures, whether it be delving deep into the caves at **Actun Tunichil Muknal** or **Barton Creek**, horseback riding, climbing the tall temples at **Caracol** or **Xunantunich**, or all of the above.

By now you have been away from the Caribbean for way too long, so spend a few days in the coastal village of **Hopkins** to absorb some Garifuna rhythms. From here, you can hike the beautiful jungle trails at **Mayflower Bocawina National Park** or **Cockscomb Basin Wildlife Sanctuary**. From **Dangriga**, arrange a boat out to **Tobacco Caye** for a day of snorkeling on the reef.

Head south to **Placencia** to enjoy lovely sandy beaches, lively bars and lots of water sports. If time permits, indulge your tropical-island fantasies with a week-long stay at **Glover's Reef**, which has an irresistible low-key vibe and brilliant diving and snorkeling. Finish up in **Punta Gorda**, the southernmost town in Belize from where you can explore the Deep South.

Top: Caye Caulker
(p112)

Bottom: Hiking trail
to Blue Creek Cave
(p240)

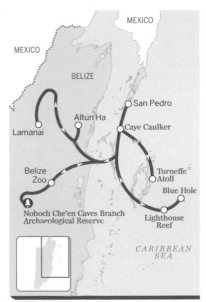

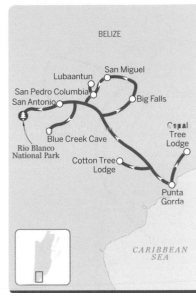

1 WEEK Northern Lights

If you only have a week to spare, make a base on one of the Northern Cayes, where you have access to an impressive range of activities on land and sea.

Choose laid-back **Caye Caulker** or busier **San Pedro**, as they are closest to the mainland. From here, you can take snorkel or dive trips to **Turneffe Atoll** and **Lighthouse Reef**, the latter home to the amazing **Blue Hole**.

You can also use either of these islands as a base for day trips to the mainland. Spend a day in the Belize District to visit **Belize Zoo** or the Maya ruins at **Altun Ha**.

It's an easy trip to eastern Cayo District, where you can go cave-tubing in the **Nohoch Che'en Caves Branch Archaeological Reserve** or ziplining through the forest canopy. You can also head north to the Maya ruins at **Lamanai**, enjoying a peaceful boat ride on the New River along the way.

5 DAYS Deep South

Exploring Belize's Deep South can take just a couple of days, but to truly appreciate the village life, allow five days.

Punta Gorda is a chilled-out, slightly ramshackle coastal town and a natural spot to begin your trek. There are budget digs in PG but if you'd like to experience some luxury, book yourself in at **Cotton Tree Lodge** or **Copal Tree Lodge**. The true beauty is in exploring the villages, chocolate-making enterprises and cultural tours out of PG. One of the best circuits is from **Big Falls**, then head off the highway to **San Miguel**, where you can stay with a local family before moving on to **San Pedro Columbia**, which you can use as a base to explore nearby **Lubaantun**. Later, head to the small Maya village of **San Antonio**, detouring for a hike and a swim at beautiful **Río Blanco National Park**, or caving at **Blue Creek Cave**.

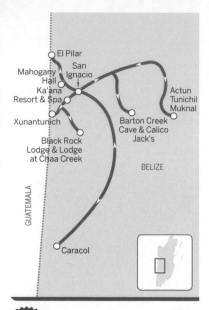

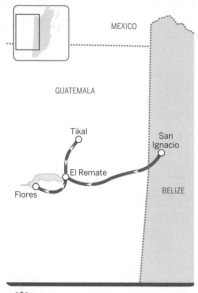

3 DAYS Wild West

If beaches and diving aren't your thing, head west to the caves, hikes and Maya ruins of Cayo district.

Start at the traveler-oriented **San Ignacio** to get a feel for the town, visiting the Maya site of Cahal Pech and the green iguanas at San Ignacio Resort Hotel. San Ignacio has plenty of good budget hotels and restaurants, so save your money for a night at one of the excellent ecolodges in the region. Arrange a tour to explore the amazing ritual cave of **Actun Tunichil Muknal**, and/or the superb Maya ruins at **Caracol**, either of which will take up all of your second day. A third option is canoeing through **Barton Creek Cave** and ziplining at **Calico Jack's**.

On your third day, wake up early and do a half-day trip to either **Xunantunich** or **El Pilar** before checking into one of the better hotels or ecolodges in western Cayo: **Mahogany Hall** is closest to El Pilar, while the fabulous **Ka'ana Resort & Spa** is closer to Xunantunich. Other stand-outs include **Black Rock Lodge** and the **Lodge at Chaa Creek**.

5 DAYS A Jaunt Into Guatemala

Across the border and within easy reach lie the glory and splendors of the ancient Maya world: ancient ruins surrounded by lush rainforests, and a few really lovely towns thrown in for good measure. Taking it all in would take months, so we suggest a five-day compromise.

Leaving San Ignacio on the morning of the first day, head directly to **El Remate**. The lakefront town makes a lovely base and has accommodations in all budget ranges. Head to **Tikal** early the next morning and spend the day exploring this fascinating ancient Maya city. Having made arrangements to spend the night at one of Tikal's three hotels, you can enjoy the sunset from the top of Temple IV at your leisure. Spend the first half of the third day exploring Tikal further (it's worth it) before heading back to El Remate to relax.

On your remaining days, hang out in **Flores** and soak up the town's island ambience, perhaps taking a half-day trip to one of the parks, villages or smaller ruins that are in the area.

Plan Your Trip
Diving & Snorkeling

Belize is a world-class destination for diving and snorkeling – after all, the world's second-longest barrier reef parallels the country's entire coastline. From north, central and south cays to stunning offshore atolls, whatever your level of underwater experience you'll find a place to explore and indulge in Belize.

Northern Cayes

The two main centers in this northern sector of the barrier reef are Ambergris Caye and Caye Caulker, both of which are a short flight or boat ride from Belize City.

Ambergris Caye is the largest offshore island and the most developed, so it attracts most of the visiting divers. Many choose Ambergris for the variety and quality of its accommodations and nightlife, though it is pretty relaxed compared with other Caribbean destinations. Many of the accommodations along the shoreline have their own dive shops onsite. Ambergris also has the only two hyperbaric chambers in Belize.

Caye Caulker, a few miles to the south of Ambergris Caye, is smaller and more laid-back, but also a popular choice. Although prices are generally lower on Caye Caulker than Ambergris, this does not apply to snorkeling and diving, perhaps due to the choices being more limited. (There are only a handful of dive shops on Caulker.)

It is also possible to dive the northern reefs and the atolls on a daily basis from a base in Belize City, where there are currently two major dive operators.

The barrier reef is only a few minutes by boat from either island. Diving here is quick and easy, though visibility is not always prime and the water can be

When to Go
December to July

What to Read
Lonely Planet *Diving & Snorkeling: Belize*

Reef Creature Identification and Reef Fish: Florida, Caribbean, Bahamas by Paul Humann and Ned Deloach

www.scubadivingbelize.com

www.ambergriscaye.com/diving

Best for Snorkeling
Hol Chan Marine Reserve (p86), Northern Cayes

Shark Ray Alley (p91), Northern Cayes

Long Caye (p131), Glover's Reef Atoll

Best for Diving
Blue Hole Natural Monument (p80), **Half Moon Caye Natural Monument** (p131), Lighthouse Reef

Turneffe Elbow (p128), Turneffe Atoll

Long Caye (p131), Glover's Reef Atoll

somewhat surging. Some divers will put up with a longer boat ride to get better visibility and drop-off clarity. Most of the dive shops offer similar deals in terms of the sites they visit and the prices of their packages. All of the dive shops take boats out to Turneffe and Lighthouse Reef Atolls.

Hol Chan Marine Reserve

At the southern end of Ambergris Caye, Hol Chan Marine Reserve (p86) was established more than two decades ago. The profusion of marine life is a testament to the reserve's success. A lot of Hol Chan Marine Reserve is shallow and in many cases the sites are better for snorkeling, but divers have the opportunity to explore a sunken ship at Amigos Wreck. Although the reef is fishier in the south of this section, the north holds more formations, with deep spur-and-groove cuts and interesting terrain.

Central Cayes

Close to the big city but far enough away to be another world apart, the small isles and resorts on the Central Cayes are idyllic and convenient for barrier reef divers. They're normally not as busy as the reefs further north; it is quite possible to go the whole day and not see another dive boat.

If you're staying on the mainland, Hopkins is a good base from which to explore the Central Cayes. A boat ride to the dive sites is about 30 minutes on good days. Beautiful on sunny, calm days with sandy flats, reefs and old staghorns peeking above the surface, the dives are done in the deep passes in the middle of the reef. Nearby are nine passes or cuts; the dive involves a descent to between 35ft and 55ft and then a swim along the deep drop-off looking for denizens.

Alternatively, depart from Dangriga for the resorts on the Central Cayes. Tobacco Caye is a tiny 5-acre island only 10 miles from Dangriga, with the only genuine budget accommodations and one dive outfit at Reef Lodge. This cay sits right on the edge of the barrier reef, provides excellent snorkeling, and is one of the few beach-diving locations in Belize. South Water Caye is a little larger and offers more expensive accommodations, but also sits on the crest of the barrier reef, offering beach diving and spectacular snorkeling.

South Water Caye Marine Reserve

Encompassing both Tobacco Caye and South Water Caye, this 62-sq-mile marine reserve protects a unique reef system. A visitor permit (BZ$10) is required but dive and snorkel tour operators will include this.

There is a variety of reef topographies to be explored, ranging from shallow-water coral gardens to spur-and-groove formations, and, of course, the drop-offs from the reef edge. A little further south, the spurs and grooves change to what is known locally as a double-wall reef system. Here there are two separate systems, the first of which slopes sharply seaward from depths of 40ft down to 120ft. This is followed by a wide sand channel with isolated coral outcrops and pillars, and then a second coral reef rising to 60ft before it plunges over the wall beyond scuba-diving depths.

LIVE-ABOARD BOATS

If you are a truly dedicated diver wanting to maximize the number of dives during your trip, then choosing a live-aboard boat is the only way to go. Your 'hotel' moves with you to the dive site, which gives you the opportunity to dive four or five times a day, including night dives. The boats that operate in Belizean waters are comfortable and well equipped, and will even pamper you with hot showers on the dive deck and warm towels to wrap up in. All boats depart from Belize City and operators organize all ground transfers for you. Live-aboard boats in Belize include the *Belize Aggressor III* and *IV* (www.aggressor.com). A seven-night all-inclusive package costs from BZ$6000 per person.

Top: Snorkeling,
Ambergris Caye (p85)

Bottom: Coral,
Tobacco Caye (p201)

LEARNING TO DIVE
....

Have you ever wondered what it would be like to swim along a spur-and-groove reef system, to tunnel through underwater caves or to peer over a drop-off into the blue and watch schools of fish cruise by? Your trip to Belize is a great opportunity to find out. Learning to dive is not as difficult as you might think, and most of the larger dive centers offer 'Discover Scuba' to see if the sport appeals to you.

The Professional Association of Diving Instructors (PADI) system is the most popular certification program worldwide. The first step is the basic Open Water Diver qualification, which usually requires three days of instruction. It is possible to complete the full three-day program while you are in Belize, or you might undertake your basic theory training close to home and complete your dives in Belize under the PADI referral system. Courses include equipment. A Discover Scuba course costs around BZ$350 with two dives, and a three-day PADI Open Water certification course is BZ$900.

Belize's best spots for novice divers include the following:

➡ Mexico Rocks, off Ambergris Caye
➡ Hol Chan Cut, south of Ambergris Caye
➡ Half Moon Caye Wall, in Lighthouse Reef
➡ Faegon's Point and Tobacco Cut, near Tobacco Caye
➡ Long Caye Lagoon and Long Caye Cut, Glover's Reef
➡ Any site near Placencia
➡ Silk Cayes or Mosquito Caye South, near Placencia

Southern Cayes

The Southern Cayes have developed into a diving hot spot, with excellent sites around the Silk Cayes and Laughing Bird Caye. The base for these dives is the popular resort town of Placencia. The sandy peninsula has some of the best beaches in Belize, while laid-back restaurants and a wide range of accommodations make it an excellent base. Dive shops are scattered around town, as well as being connected with specific resorts.

Gladden Spit & Silk Cayes Marine Reserve

The northernmost point of the southern reef area constitutes the Silk Cayes Marine Reserve. Blue-water action takes the form of whale sharks, bull sharks, hammerheads, dolphins and shoaling fish, all due to the seasonal spawning of cubera snapper. Looking for whale sharks in blue water is hard work, however, and not always fruitful (especially since they are night feeders). But from April to June, the spawning snappers attract the whale sharks and other predators into Gladden Spit, which is only about 12 miles off the barrier reef.

All year round, dives in the Silk Cayes can produce sightings of spotted eagle rays, turtles, moray eels, southern stingrays, large grouper, barracuda, king mackerel, dolphins and several shark species, as well as many smaller tropical reef fish and invertebrates. Manta rays appear with more frequency during winter months when the water temperatures drop, starting in December and January.

The reef table here is much wider and so it takes a little longer to reach the barrier reef by boat; however, the numerous islands with large expanses of coral reef and connecting channels between them are a bonus, providing a host of alternative dive and snorkeling sites on the way to and from the reef.

Laughing Bird Caye Faro Reef System

Laughing Bird Caye appears to be all that is left of another submerged atoll, its approximately 2.5 acres of land seemingly diminishing with passing storms and wave action. The cay got its name from the many laughing gulls that once nested here, but most of their nesting areas have since been swallowed by the rising sea. Pelicans and osprey still use the island as nesting grounds, as do sea turtles. Laughing Bird Caye is one of Belize's national parks and a part of the Belize Barrier Reef Reserve System World Heritage Site, which includes the island and surrounding reefs.

Within the faro is a system of patch reefs and coral ridges bursting with luxuriant hard-coral growth and a variety of sponges and soft coral. The tremendous diversity of fish and invertebrate life in the inshore waters around the island make them ideal for both snorkeling and diving. There are several dive sites at the north and south of the island, all with basically the same marine life and terrain, although in the north it is possible to go a bit deeper.

Offshore Atolls

There are only four atolls in the Caribbean and three of them are right here off the coast of Belize. All three – Turneffe Atoll, Lighthouse Reef and Glover's Reef – lie offshore from the barrier reef, rising from great depths to just a few feet above sea level. You can dive them on day trips from the main islands, choose one of the atoll-based resorts or take a live-aboard boat that concentrates on diving the atolls.

Turneffe Atoll

Turneffe Atoll is the largest of the offshore trio and comprises a series of islands that runs north–south. Here you will find an area dominated purely by mangrove islands, where juveniles of every marine species are protected until they make their way into the wider waters. Sand flats, shallow gardens and life-filled walls are all highlights of Turneffe dives.

The Elbow is the most beloved Turneffe dive site, with its enormous schools of pelagic fish and pods of dolphins. Although suffering from overfishing in the past, the Elbow has bounced back thanks to the efforts of local resorts. Visibility varies widely depending mostly on the wind direction. A lot of wave action can stir things up in the mangroves, carrying nutrients into the water and reducing visibility. But more often, the deep water around the atolls guarantees excellent visibility and some of the most thrilling wall-diving you'll find anywhere.

RESPONSIBLE DIVING

Please consider the following tips when diving and help preserve the ecology and beauty of reefs:

➡ Never use anchors on the reef, and take care not to ground boats on coral.

➡ Avoid touching or standing on living marine organisms or dragging equipment across the reef. Polyps can be damaged by even the gentlest contact. If you must hold on to the reef, only touch exposed rock or dead coral.

➡ Be conscious of your fins. Even without contact, the surge from fin strokes near the reef can damage delicate organisms. Take care not to kick up clouds of sand, which can smother organisms.

➡ Practice and maintain proper buoyancy control. Major damage can be done by divers descending too fast and colliding with the reef.

➡ Take great care in underwater caves. Spend as little time within them as possible as your air bubbles may be caught within the roof and thereby leave organisms high and dry. Take turns to inspect the interior of a small cave.

➡ Resist the temptation to collect or buy coral or shells, or to loot marine archaeological sites (mainly shipwrecks).

➡ Ensure that you take home all your rubbish and any litter you may find as well. Plastics in particular are a serious threat to marine life.

➡ Avoid feeding fish. Rules are in place to prevent tour operators chumming or feeding fish.

➡ Minimize your disturbance of marine animals. Never ride on the backs of turtles.

ISRAEL MORAN / SHUTTERSTOCK ©

Top: Scuba diving, Half Moon Caye (p130)

Bottom: Boca del Rio (Christ of the Abyss; p90)

The northwest site moorings such as Sandy Slope and Amber Head normally sit in 35ft to 40ft of water and the reef becomes a spur-and-groove system that leads to a vertical wall. This drops to a sandy shelf around 100ft to 120ft at most sites, then falls off again past sport-diving limits. The northwest side is protected from the occasional strong eastern and southeastern winds that sometimes blow in.

When the wind shifts to the north-northwest, blowing down from the US Gulf, conditions are better to dive on the east side, at sites such as Grand Bogue II and Front Porch. This reeftop and wall starts a bit deeper, in the 40ft to 60ft range, and is known for being less of a slope and quite sheer in some spots. The reeftop also has interesting swim-throughs and some tight spurs and grooves.

Being the closest atoll to the coast, Turneffe is a quick trip from Ambergris Caye and Caye Caulker, although there are also resorts on Blackbird Caye (part of Turneffe Atoll).

Lighthouse Reef

At about 50 miles offshore, Lighthouse Reef is the atoll that lies furthest to the east. Lighthouse Reef is probably the best-known atoll in Belize and it is certainly the most popular, due to the Blue Hole. While this icon of Belize diving makes the atoll a major attraction, it is really the stunning walls, many swim-throughs and superb blue water that make it a favorite with both longtime, experienced Belize divers and complete novices.

Lighthouse Reef is home to Half Moon Caye Natural Monument (p131), a national park managed by the Belize Audubon Society, where a colony of rare red-footed boobies can be observed up close. There are a few fantastic dive sites nearby, such as Aquarium and Painted Wall. Other sites in the vicinity include the coral-covered Long Caye Wall.

Dive boats go out to Lighthouse Reef from both Ambergris and Caye Caulker, but the easiest way to see these sites is via a live-aboard boat. The commute from site to site is minimal, and divers can take advantage of early-morning dives and fascinating night dives. Alternatively, there are a few small lodges on Long Caye, while camping is allowed on Half Moon Caye.

> ### SURF SAFARI BIG FIVE
> → Shark
> → Stingray
> → Barracuda
> → Moray eel
> → Octopus

Glover's Reef

In Southern Belize, divers will find the third of the Belizean atolls. Of the three, Glover's Reef sees the least amount of human contact and remains largely unexplored. Glover's Reef Atoll was named after the 17th-century pirate John Glover, who used the islands as a base for raids against treasure-laden Spanish galleons heading to and from the Bay Islands of Honduras.

First recognized as a bird sanctuary in 1954, it has long been atop the conservation list, getting various conservation designations in 1978 before finally being declared a complete marine reserve in 1993, then a Unesco World Heritage Site in 1996. There is a marine research station on Middle Caye and the remains of an ancient Maya settlement are being studied on Long Caye.

Located about an hour's boat ride from the mainland, Glover's Reef rises from abyssal depths of well over 2000ft; indeed, a dive site located midway between Long Caye and Middle Caye is known as The Abyss. Oval in shape, the reef is comprised of more than 700 patch reefs within a 100-sq-mile lagoon. Just to the south is one of the Caribbean's deepest valleys, where depths reach 10,000ft.

There are several rustic outpost resorts here for divers and fishers, each occupying its own island and offering an ecofriendly existence. Otherwise, there is day-boat diving from Hopkins and Placencia, and live-aboard boats occasionally cruise this far south.

The chance of seeing dolphins, mantas and whale sharks keeps adventurous divers coming back for more. The spectacular walls and hard-coral formations are just a few minutes from the islands that fringe the eastern side of the atoll. If you get the chance, dive the west side of the atoll as well to explore some wonderful swim-throughs and caves.

Plan Your Trip
Belize Outdoors

Forget museums and galleries – Belize is all about the great outdoors. Despite its small land area, an extraordinary variety of national parks and wildlife and marine reserves provides an incredible stage for the adventure traveler, whether diving, hiking or caving.

When to Go

Fishing May to July (also year-round)

Kayaking December to May

Sailing & Windsurfing February to April

Caving January to April

Hiking & Horseback Riding January to May

Resources

Destinations Belize (www.destinationsbelize.com) is a Placencia-based travel agency with useful information on fishing in Belize, including fish guides, tide charts and fishing location descriptions.

Cruising Guide to Belize and Mexico's Caribbean Coast, by Freya Rauscher, provides comprehensive information for anyone navigating these complicated waters.

Best For...

Fishing Ambergris Caye (p85)

Kayaking Glover's Reef Atoll (p204)

Sailing Placencia (p215)

Windsurfing Caye Caulker (p112)

Caving Actun Tunichil Muknal (p168)

Hiking Cockscomb Basin Wildlife Sanctuary (p213), Shipstern Conservation & Management Area (p153)

Horseback Riding Cayo (p181)

Hiking

In Belize, hiking usually means guided walks in search of birdlife, as well as other flora and fauna. Many lodges have access to trails on their own or nearby properties that you can walk by yourself, but more often lodge walks are with a guide who will show you the animals and plants along the way. Several places offer night walks. Lodges with access to hiking trails include the following:

Chan Chich Lodge (p145) Chan Chich is set on 130,000 acres of protected land and the lodge maintains 9 miles of trails for birding and wildlife-watching, with or without a guide.

Macaw Bank Jungle Lodge (p183) Located on 50 beautiful acres in the foothills of the Maya Mountains, Macaw Bank is ripe for exploration, and includes a trail along the eponymous river.

Black Rock Lodge (p190) Trails departing from the lodge have enticing names like Mountain Summit, Vaca Falls and Vista Loop, promising challenging climbs, waterfalls and wonderful views.

Blancaneaux Lodge (p185) Guided hikes include an early-morning bird walk and a late-night 'jaguar quest,' as well as an all-day jungle trek and a special orchid-hunting walk.

Lodge at Chaa Creek (p190) The 365-acre nature reserve here features the Macal River and a Rainforest Medicine Trail.

Many of the nature preserves and national parks also have well-developed and well-maintained jungle trail networks that you can walk with or without guides:

Cockscomb Basin Wildlife Sanctuary (p213) The well-marked hiking trails are excellent for birding and wildlife-watching, though you'll be very lucky to spot a jaguar.

Mayflower Bocawina National Park (p201) It's only 11 sq miles, but it contains about 7 miles of hiking trails (including the access road) to jungle, mountains, waterfalls and Maya ruins.

Shipstern Conservation & Management Area (p153) There is a short nature trail that circles the visitors center, but a real appreciation of Shipstern requires taking a longer guided hike to Xo-Pol or along Thompson Trail.

Río Bravo Conservation & Management Area (p144) The country's largest protected area has a network of hiking trails and ranger roads; walks depart from both of the field stations.

Río Blanco National Park (p239) In the Deep South, this 105-acre preserve has marked nature trails and a spectacular waterfall.

Caving

The karstic geology of parts of western Belize has produced many extensive and intricate cave systems, which are fascinating, challenging and awesome to investigate. To the ancient Maya, caves were entrances to Xibalba, the underworld and residence of important gods. Many Belizean caves today still contain relics of Maya ceremonies, offerings or sacrifices, and this archaeological element makes cave exploration doubly intriguing. One of the few caves in the country that you can enter without a guide is St Herman's Cave, but even there you are required to take a guide if you want to go more than 300yd into the cave.

The most thrilling caves that are in the west of the country include Actun Tunichil Muknal (p168), with its evidence of human sacrifice; Barton Creek Cave (p179), which you explore by canoe; Che Chem Ha (p193), with its vast array of ancient pottery; and the caves in the Nohoch Che'en Caves Branch Archaeological Reserve (p163).

WHAT'S IN YOUR BACKPACK

Whether you're planning to hike or horseback ride for an hour or for a day, it's best to be prepared. Be ready for the hot sun, voracious mosquitoes or sand flies, the bird sightings and the ever-present possibility of finding a swimming hole.

➡ Water
➡ Hat, sunscreen and sunglasses
➡ Camera
➡ Tropical-strength insect repellent
➡ Binoculars
➡ Swim gear
➡ Lightweight travel towel

Careful Caving

➡ Remember that caves and their contents are extremely fragile. Don't disturb artifacts or cave formations, and try to avoid tours with large groups of people.

➡ For your own well-being, check the physical demands of a cave trip beforehand.

➡ Remember that some caves are subject to flash floods during rainy periods.

➡ An extra flashlight and a spare set of batteries is never a bad idea.

➡ If you have claustrophobic tendencies or are terrified of the dark (or bats), there is no shame in admitting that caves are not for everyone!

Horseback Riding

Belize has an active equestrian community. A growing number of lodges offers rides to their guests and – in some cases – nonguests.

Backpackers Paradise (p154) Backpackers has some of the cheapest horseback riding in the country; it's also one of the few places that will let you ride without a guide (as long as you know how!).

Banana Bank Lodge (p164) Near Belmopan, Banana Bank is a highly recommended lodge with a well-tended stable of 100-plus horses, where you can enjoy anything from a two-hour ride to a multiday riding package.

DUARTE DELLAROLE / SHUTTERSTOCK ©

Top: Horseback riding, Stann Creek District (p196)

Bottom: Kayaking, Glover's Reef (p204)

Cotton Tree Lodge (p234) In the Deep South near Punta Gorda, Cotton Tree offers horseback riding trips for guests and nonguests.

Sweet Songs Jungle Lodge (p190) Provides all levels of horseback riding, ranging from a short one-hour excursion to the Belize Botanic Gardens, to a longer journey to Cristo Rey Falls (with river crossings).

Hanna Stables (p189) Long-running Hanna's offers horseback riding trips from a ride around San Lorenzo farm to the popular half day tour to Xunantunich.

Outback Trails (p205) This independent ranch near Hopkins runs morning and afternoon trail rides for all levels.

MET Outfitters & Lodge (p181) This rustic resort operates individual rides and riding-based holidays that combine lowland jungles and Mountain Pine Ridge.

Ziplining

Ziplining – flying through the jungle canopy in a harness attached to a fixed cable – is immensely popular in Belize. These days operators must adhere to strict safety standards so the quality and competition is high. Associated activities include ATV riding, rock climbing and waterfall rappelling. Some of the best courses:

Angel Falls Belize Xtreme Adventures (p165) One of the newest in Belize, just off the Hummingbird Hwy.

Calico Jack's (p181) Well-established nine-run, 15-platform zipline and canyon swing near San Ignacio.

Zipline Canopy Tour (p164) The closest zipline course to Belize City is just outside Nohoch Che'en Caves reserve.

Bocawina Adventures (p201) At Mayflower Bocawina National Park, one of the most thrilling adventures in Belize features ziplining and waterfall rappelling.

Mayan Sky Canopy Tour (p213) This new course just off the southern highway is convenient to both Placencia and Hopkins.

Big Falls Extreme Adventures (p235) Smaller operation in Toledo District with river tubing to boot.

Kayaking

The translucent waters of the Caribbean are as inviting for kayakers as they are for divers and snorkelers. It's amazing how much underwater life is visible from above the surface, and you can enjoy snorkeling and birdwatching as you go.

If you fancy some kayaking, consider staying at one of the resorts or hotels on the Placencia peninsula or Ambergris Caye, many of which provide free kayaks for guests. At San Pedro, Caye Caulker, Hopkins, Placencia village and Punta Gorda, you can rent a kayak for anywhere between BZ$30 and BZ$60 per day. Glover's Atoll Resort (p204) rents out single/double touring kayaks by the week for BZ$290/450.

A number of Belize- and North America–based firms offer recommended kayaking holidays:

Belize Kayak Rentals (p197) If you want to go it alone on your kayaking expedition, this branch of Island Expeditions rents out kayaks from its base camp in Dangriga. Also provides weekly packages, which include a boat charter out to the cays.

Island Expeditions (p197) This ecologically minded Canadian company takes tours departing from Dangriga or Belize City, including week-long kayaking expeditions and inland trips, with either hiking in the jungle or visiting Maya ruins.

Seakunga Adventure (p218) Offers a variety of excellent kayaking tours, including both sea kayaking and river kayaking.

Slickrock Adventures (p204) These top-class water-sports holidays are based on Long Caye, Glover's Reef, and combine sea kayaking, surf kayaking, windsurfing, snorkeling and diving. Accommodations are in stilt cabanas.

Canoeing

Canoes are more common than kayaks on inland rivers, especially the Mopan and Macal Rivers near San Ignacio. Both have some rapids, so be sure to choose a stretch of river that's right for your level. Many lodge accommodations in the area rent out canoes, and tour outfits in San Ignacio will also take you out on guided trips.

LA RUTA MAYA BELIZE RIVER CHALLENGE

One morning in early March the waters of the Macal River beneath San Ignacio's Hawkesworth Bridge are the gathering place for a colorful flotilla of three-person canoes. They are assembled for the start of La Ruta Maya Belize River Challenge, a grueling four-day race down the Belize River to Belize City, where they arrive on Baron Bliss Day, a national holiday in memory of a great Belizean benefactor. From relatively humble beginnings in 1998, the race has grown into Central America's biggest canoe event, attracting international and Belizean teams.

Even though it's all downstream, this is no gentle paddle. The fastest teams cover the river's 170 or so winding miles from San Ignacio to Belize City in around 19 hours, while the slowest take around 36 hours. The race is divided into four one-day stages: Hawkesworth Bridge to Banana Bank Lodge near Belmopan (around 50 miles); Banana Bank to Bermudian Landing (60 miles including Big Falls Rapids); Bermudian Landing to Burrell Boom (35 miles); and Burrell Boom to Belcan Bridge, Belize City (25 miles).

In addition to being Belize's largest competitive sporting event, La Ruta Maya is an impressive conservation effort, as all proceeds are donated to local environmental efforts to revitalize and sustain Belizean waterways. Check out www.larutamaya.bz.

One of the most unusual canoe trips is the underground river through Barton Creek Cave (p179). Another nice place to use a canoe is the bird paradise of Crooked Tree Lagoon (p73).

Sailing

A day's sailing on crystal-clear Caribbean waters, with a spot of snorkeling or wildlife-watching topped with an island beach BBQ, is a near-perfect way to spend a day. Tours depart from San Pedro, Caye Caulker or Placencia.

Some of these companies offer multiday sailing and camping trips, as well as popular boozy sunset and moonlight cruises. Raggamuffin Tours (p119) and Blackhawk Sailing Tours (p119) both do relatively economical island-hopping sails to Turneffe Atoll, Lighthouse Reef and Placencia.

On longer sailing trips you can reach not only Belize's hundreds of islands but also the attractive Guatemalan ports of Lívingston and Río Dulce, the Honduras' Bay Islands and much of the rest of the eastern Caribbean. Several companies offer charters out of Hopkins, Placencia and San Pedro:

Under the Sun (p205) The Lodge Hopper's Special is an outstanding eight days of Caribbean cruising on an 18ft Hobie Cat, with plenty of stops for snorkeling, fishing, kayaking and hammocking.

Catamaran Belize (p92) A reliable charter company that rents out a swanky 35ft catamaran for customized day-trips.

Island Dream Tours (p92) Offers sailing aboard a spacious motorized catamaran including sunset booze and dinner cruises.

Moorings (p216) Luxury catamaran with customized bareboat (self-charter) sailing from Placencia. Or you can hire a skipper. It's based at Laru Beya marina, 4 miles north of Placencia.

(p207) This Hopkins-based outfit operates custom half- and full-day boat charters for up to five people, including snorkeling, fishing and island-hopping.

Fishing

This angler's paradise is home to 160 miles of barrier reef, hundreds of square miles of flats, and dozens of jungle-lined rivers and lagoons – all of which teem with a great variety of fish. The best months are May through July, with their hot sunny weather, though every species has its ideal time and place. Spin fishing, fly-fishing and trolling can all be enjoyed year-round.

Tarpon, snook and jacks inhabit the estuaries, inlets and river mouths, while bonefish, permit and barracuda are found out in the lagoons and flats. The coral reefs support grouper, snapper and jacks, and the deeper waters beyond are home to sailfish, marlin, pompano, tuna and bonito. The flats off the cays and mainland raise realistic hopes of the angler's 'Grand Slam': permit, tarpon and bonefish all in one day. Catch-and-release is the norm for these fish and for most snook. Check with your guide or hotel about the regulations for your area and season.

The most popular fishing bases are in the Northern Cayes, especially San Pedro and Caye Caulker, but there are also fishing outfits in Sarteneja and Belize City.

For tarpon and bonefish, Belize's southern waters, from Placencia to Punta Gorda, are gaining in popularity. It's easy to charter a boat in places such as Glover's Reef, Hopkins, Placencia and Punta Gorda.

River fishing for big tarpon, snook, cubera snapper and 35lb to 100lb goliath grouper is also possible year-round. The Sibun and Belize Rivers and Black Creek are the most frequently fished rivers, but the Deep, Monkey, Temash and Sarstoon Rivers in the south are good, too.

Lodges and guides may have equipment to rent but it's best to bring your own tackle. Fishing charters start from around BZ$800 a day.

Windsurfing & Kitesurfing

With a light-to-medium warm easterly breeze blowing much of the time and the barrier reef offshore to calm the waters, conditions on Caye Caulker and Ambergris Caye are ideal for windsurfing. Regulars here boast occasional runs of 10 miles. Beware the boat traffic though, especially at San Pedro. Mellower beaches can be found in Hopkins, home to a small but dedicated group of windsurfers. Winds are biggest (typically 10 to 17 knots) from February through April.

Kitesurfers can do introductory courses on Ambergris Caye or Caye Caulker. If you are a dedicated kitesurfer, you can rent gear from the same operators and head

out on your own adventure – there's even a rescue boat if you go too far!

Kitexplorer (p117) Provides kitesurfing lessons and rentals on Caye Caulker.

Stand-up Paddleboarding

Stand-up paddleboarding is gaining popularity, not only in the calm Caribbean Sea but along rivers that drain into it. San Pedro, Caye Caulker and Hopkins all have SUP operators who run tours and rent out boards. In Hopkins you'll find tours down the Sittee River and night tours to see the bizarre bioluminescence.

Bigsup Belize (p92)

Barefoot Fisherman Expeditions (p119)

Hopkins Stand-up Paddleboarding (p210)

River-Tubing

River-tubing, where you float down the river in an inflated rubber ring, is a popular pastime in Belize. Depending on the current, it's more relaxing than canoeing or kayaking – naturally you only float downstream and the only technique you need to know is how to avoid getting beached, eddied or snagged on rocks while continuing to face the right direction.

The Mopan River near San Ignacio is a popular spot for river-tubing, as is the Río Grande at Big Falls in Toledo District. Most lodges offer tubes and transportation for their guests, or you can rent tubes at the river's edge and go it alone.

The best of all Belizean tubing adventures is the float in and out of a sequence of caves on the Caves Branch River inside the Nohoch Che'en Caves Branch Archaeological Reserve (p163). People come on day trips from all over Belize for this. Book a tour or just show up and hire a guide at the entrance.

Plan Your Trip
Travel with Children

Belize has some special ingredients for a family holiday. It's both affordable and safe, especially compared to other Caribbean destinations, and it's small and easy to navigate. Belizeans are famously friendly, and traveling with kids will often break down barriers between tourists and residents, sometimes opening doors to local hospitality.

Best Regions for Kids

Belize District
Many of the Belize District activities and attractions are designed with the cruise-ship passenger in mind. Turns out that cruisers and kids have some of the same criteria: fun stuff that's easy to reach and easy to enjoy in a limited time frame.

Northern Cayes
The boat ride itself is a sort of adventure. Once you reach these paradisiacal islands, the adventure continues with swimming, snorkeling, sailing, kayaking and more traditional beach fare.

Cayo District
Older kids especially will enjoy the wild west and all of its jungle activities.

Belize for Kids

Fun & Games

Attractions in Belize – sea life, exploring caves, climbing ruins, watching for birds, wildlife and bugs – will delight kids as much as grown-ups. Most tours and activities can easily accommodate children and teenagers, although they are generally not appropriate for toddlers and babies. With these wee ones, activities might be limited to playing on the beach, swimming in the sea and swinging in the hammock. That's not the worst vacation either.

Most towns and tourist destinations have parks and public beaches where your little ones can frolic with the locals. If your child speaks English, there'll be no language barrier to mixing with local kids.

Food

Your kids will probably be happy to eat most typical Belizean and Mexican foods, such as sandwiches, rice and beans, fried chicken, hamburgers and tacos. Bakery goods, pasta and pizzas are additional favorites. Tropical fruit smoothies are delicious and healthy.

Health

For the most part, Belize is safe and healthy for you and your family. Be cautious concerning insect bites, sunburn and, of course, water and sanitation.

Transportation

If you do not intend to do much traveling around the interior, consider going local. Public intercity transport is usually on old American school buses that have retired to Belize, so your kids will probably be familiar and comfortable (as long as the journey is not too long). Most car-rental companies can provide child seats – usually free of charge – but it's advisable to inquire when you make your reservation. Around the cays, most transportation is by boat, which is a fun activity in itself.

Children's Highlights
Action & Adventure

Caving As long as your kids are not afraid of the dark, they will be thrilled by cave-tubing at Nohoch Che'en Caves Branch Archaeological Reserve (p163) or canoeing into Barton Creek Cave (p179).

Maya Ruins All of the Maya ruins offer a chance for kids to run, climb and explore.

Horseback Riding Some Cayo lodges offer jungle horseback riding, including Banana Bank Lodge (p164) and Mountain Equestrian Lodge (p181).

Ziplining Ride Belize's fabulous ziplines across the jungle canopy at Mayflower Bocawina National Park (p201), Calico Jack's (p181) or Angel Falls Belize Xtreme Adventures (p165).

Belize District Besides hiking, biking, kayaking and horseback riding, Bacab Eco Park (p70) also has an amazing swimming pool.

Animal Encounters

Ambergris Caye Kids get a kick out of fish. Take them snorkeling at Hol Chan Marine Reserve (p86) near Ambergris Caye.

Belize District Sightings (and hearings) of the black howler monkey are practically guaranteed at the Community Baboon Sanctuary (p71).

Belize District Children love to get up-close-and-personal with the animals at the Belize Zoo (p80). Even teens are keen on the night safari.

San Ignacio Kids come face to face with some scaly monsters at the Green Iguana Exhibit (p171) at the San Ignacio Resort Hotel.

Beach Retreats

Around Placencia For traditional sun-and-sand activities like sandcastle-building, kite-flying and wave-wading, beaches are the best at Placencia or Hopkins.

Central Cayes Snorkeling and kayaking are on your doorstep at family-friendly Thatch Caye or budget-friendly Tobacco Caye.

Ambergris Caye Children's yoga classes are just the beginning of the fun at Ak'bol Yoga (p94).

Ambergris Caye The giant waterslide into the sea, floating trampoline and sailing classes are sure to keep little ones entertained at Caribbean Villas (p99).

Jungle Lodges

Hummingbird Hwy Many exciting land adventures can be delivered in one handy place at Ian Anderson's Caves Branch Jungle Lodge (p166).

Bullet Tree Falls Your family can sleep in a tree house at Parrot Nest Jungle Lodge (p188).

Cayo District Trek Stop (p192) is an affordable ecolodge with loads of kid-friendly fun.

Punta Gorda Explorers will get lost and found again in the jungle maze at Hickatee Cottages (p230).

Toledo District The cool cabins at Cotton Tree Lodge (p234) are connected by a jungle boardwalk.

Rainy-Day Destinations

Belize District Life-size replicas of Garifuna homesteads and logging camp scenes bring history to life at Old Belize (p78) outside of Belize City.

Cayo District Learn about the life cycle of the butterfly and play disc golf at Tropical Wings Nature Center (p192).

Top: Family beach time

Bottom: Snorkeling in San Pedro, Ambergris Caye (p87)

JENNIFER WAN / EYEEM / GETTY IMAGES ©

FOR YOUR BUDDING BIOLOGISTS

Several organizations offer excellent programs that combine adventure and education, designed specifically for the younger set.

Belize Zoo (www.belizezoo.org) Kids between 12 and 17 years old can attend Conservation Camp, a five-day program exploring the waterways and wildlife of the Sibun River.

Oceanic Society (www.oceanic-society.org) Your family (kids must be over 10 years) can join Oceanic Society biologists for a family field study, which combines science and snorkeling, to learn about dolphins, manatees and sea turtles.

International Zoological Expeditions (www.izebelize.com) The IZE family adventure explores the rainforest around Blue Creek in Toledo, and the sea and reef around South Water Caye.

Shipstern Conservation & Management Area (www.visitshipstern.com) This organization runs a 'ranger for a day' adventure that allows participants to accompany local staff as they go about their duties.

Toledo District At Ixcacao Maya Belizean Chocolate (p233) kids can learn how to make chocolate with plenty of tasting throughout the process.

Hopkins Kids will enjoy learning Garifuna drumming at Lebeha (p205) or other schools in the village.

Planning

When to Go

Kids are less likely to tolerate the tropical showers that occur often during the rainy season. Considering that Belize is an outdoor-activity sort of place, you're better off taking your children during the drier months (December to May).

Before You Go

Make sure your children are up-to-date on all their routine vaccinations such as chicken pox, tetanus and measles, in addition to any special vaccinations (p301) recommended for Belize.

What to Pack

In the towns and tourist destinations, grocery stores are stocked with basic necessities, but you are not guaranteed to find the exact brand your child is accustomed to, so make sure you bring enough supplies. Other more specialized children's items might be difficult to find.

Where to Stay

➜ Most hotels, lodges and resorts welcome children – some with special activities and even childcare. Many places allow children (usually under the age of 12) to stay for free or at a reduced rate. The icon 🌣 indicates accommodations that are family-friendly.

➜ Look for suites, cabins and condos that have the possibility of self-catering (eg in room kitchenette). Eating at 'home' is an easy way to save money on meals, to make sure everybody gets to eat what they want, and to avoid waiting for tables and the other hassles of dining out with children.

➜ Inquire in advance about the availability of high chairs and cribs at your accommodations. Some resorts and restaurants will be able to provide these upon request but it's worth finding out for certain so you can make alternative arrangements if necessary.

➜ Holiday rental sites such as Airbnb are a good option for booking houses or apartments.

Regions at a Glance

Belize's 9000 sq miles are crammed with diversity, most evident in the geographical contrast between the Caribbean Sea and interior jungle regions. The Northern Cayes and the coastal destinations in Southern Belize are prime destinations for diving, snorkeling and other water sports (not to mention hammock swinging and drinking rum cocktails); the dense forests of Cayo and Belize Districts and inland parts of Northern and Southern Belize are better for birding, wildlife-watching, caving, ziplining and other jungle adventures.

Ethno-cultural differences are also apparent between regions. The mestizo influence is greatest in Northern Belize, while the Maya and Garifuna cultures thrive in Southern Belize. Creole culture is most vibrant in Belize District.

Belize District

Birding
Wildlife
Maya Ruins

Feathered Friends

Crooked Tree Wildlife Sanctuary is undoubtedly the country's top destination for birds and for people who like to watch birds. The lagoon and its environs are home to some 276 species; don't forget your binoculars.

Furry Friends

'Friends' is the operative word here, since the wildlife is not quite as 'wild' as in other parts of the country. Nonetheless, the Belize Zoo is a fabulous place to meet and greet the native species. Sightings are guaranteed!

Maya Ruins

Altun Ha is significantly smaller than some of the country's other Maya sites, but it's still an impressive exhibit of ancient craftsmanship and labor. It's also well maintained and easy to access as a day trip from Belize City or the Northern Cayes.

p54

Northern Cayes

Activities
Food
Beaches

Under the Sea

Whether you're a certified diver or a novice snorkeler, the number-one reason to come to the Northern Cayes is to frolic with the fish and admire the colorful coral. This is world-class diving and snorkeling, accessible from any of the northern cays or outer atolls.

Fruits of the Sea

The proliferation of fancy resorts and hotels has at least one positive consequence: amazing food. Thanks to fresh seafood and talented chefs, Ambergris boasts the country's best (and most expensive) eating.

Lounging by the Sea

OK, we admit it: the cays do not have super-fine beaches. The coastline is dominated by mangroves and sea grass, instead of vast stretches of sand. But that doesn't mean it's not spectacularly beautiful, with picturesque docks providing plenty of places for swimming, sunbathing and hammock swinging.

p83

Northern Belize

Maya Ruins
Wildlife
Food

New River & Old Ruins

The beauty of Lamanai is not only that it's a vast, exquisite archaeological site (the country's second largest), but also that it's surrounded by lush rainforest and is accessible primarily by boat. The jungle river cruise combined with the exploration of the ruins makes this one of the most popular and rewarding ways to spend a day in Belize.

Where the Wild Things Are

It's a little-known fact that the wild things are actually in Northern Belize. The remote corners of Corozal and Orange Walk are home to two of the country's most pristine and best-protected nature preserves: Río Bravo and Shipstern Conservation & Management Areas.

Hot & Spicy

We can thank the mestizo and Mexican population for spicing up the cuisine in Northern Belize.

p133

Cayo District

Ecolodges
Maya Ruins
Activities

Eco-chic

When it comes to natural attractions, Cayo has everything (except the beaches!). The district's ecolodges are among the best in the country, taking full advantage of the region's natural splendors. From remote Black Rock Lodge to the exquisite Blancaneaux Lodge, you'll surely find a perfect setting for your jungle adventure.

Ancient Cities

For almost 3000 years, the ancient Maya civilization flourished in Belize, building towering temples as tributes to their godlike rulers. The remains of these once-mighty city-states are scattered throughout the country, with the most magnificent ones, including Caracol and Xunantunich, in Cayo.

Jungle Adventure

Spelunking, cave-tubing, ziplining, horseback riding, hiking, river kayaking, birdwatching and more make Cayo an adventurer's paradise. You'll get tired, wet and dirty, but you'll never get bored.

p156

Southern Belize

Beaches
Wildlife
Food

Sun & Sand

Mainland Hopkins and Placencia both have barefoot-perfect beaches but head out to any of Southern Belize's cays, where you can spend your days beachcombing, snorkeling, kayaking, fishing and, of course, lazing in a beachfront hammock.

Wild & Wonderful

Southern Belize is home to some of the country's finest nature reserves, including Cockscomb Basin Wildlife Sanctuary and Mayflower Bocawina National Park. Your chances of spotting stunning birds, reptiles and small mammals are very high, and you're almost guaranteed to hear the cacophony of howler monkeys.

Sweet & Spicy

Southern Belize is a great place to dine on traditional Garifuna and Maya dishes, not to mention amazing fresh seafood. Don't miss the chance to take a sampling tour of iconic Marie Sharp's (hot sauce) Factory.

p194

Tikal & Flores, Guatemala

Maya Ruins
Jungles
Activities

Archaeological Bliss

The spectacular ruins of ancient Tikal and Yaxhá are the reason most visitors come to the Peten region, but those with a serious interest in the Maya will want to explore further, visiting the many smaller (and not so small) sites that dot the landscape.

Into the Wild

The parts of this region that feature towns and paved roads are small by comparison with the vast majority of the area, which is covered in jungle and accessible only to those willing to trek by foot, horseback or helicopter; Peten is firmly on any off-the-beaten-path traveler's list.

Fun for All

There's more to this region than just the Maya ruins; activities include water sports on beautiful Lake Peten, hiking through nature reserves, ziplining across jungle canopies and exploring the beautiful island town of Flores.

p241

On the
Road

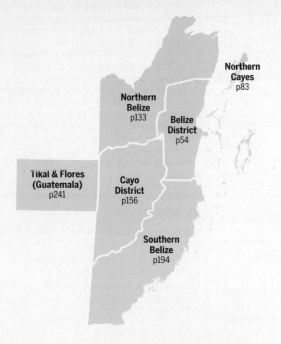

Belize District

Best Places to Eat

➡ Celebrity Restaurant (p65)

➡ Nerie's II Restaurant (p64)

➡ Belamari (p64)

➡ Belize Boutique Resort & Spa (p75)

➡ Cheers (p79)

➡ Crooked Tree Lodge (p74)

Best Places to Stay

➡ Belize Boutique Resort & Spa (p75)

➡ Beck's Bed & Breakfast (p74)

➡ Manatee Lodge (p82)

➡ Savanna Guesthouse (p80)

➡ Villa Boscardi (p61)

➡ Monkey Bay Wildlife Sanctuary (p79)

Why Go?

What a contrast is the district that shares its country's name! Belize District comprises 1600 sq miles at the heart of the nation, and includes its largest population center and some of its most pristine tropical environs.

Belize City gets a bad rap for its impoverished areas, some of which are plagued by crime and violence. But the seaside city also embodies the country's amazing cultural diversity, its neighborhoods packed with people, restaurants and shops that represent every ethnicity.

Beyond the city center, the gritty Caribbean urbanism crumbles, revealing a landscape of vast savanna that stretches to the north, dense tropical forest to the west, and lush marshland to the south. There's lots to see and do in Belize District – so much that a week-long visitor could spend the entire vacation here, sampling the country's Maya heritage, Creole culture and luxuriant wildlife, all within an hour's drive of the city.

When to Go

Mar Baron Bliss Day celebrations, including a sailing regatta and La Ruta Maya canoe race.

May The village of Crooked Tree goes nuts for a weekend during the annual Cashew Festival.

Sep Two weeks of Belize City festivities, including a carnival parade, music and dancing.

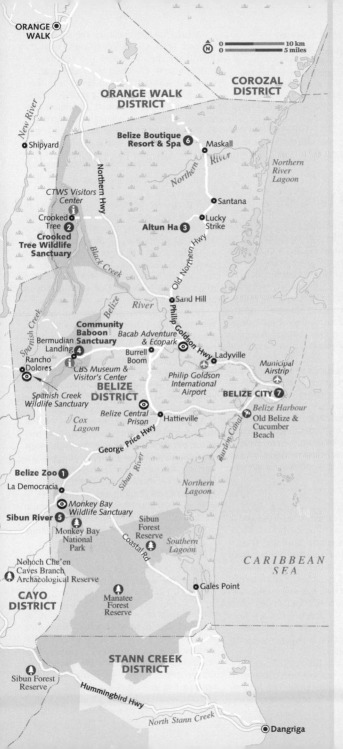

ORANGE WALK

New River

Shipyard

ORANGE WALK DISTRICT

COROZAL DISTRICT

Belize Boutique Resort & Spa ⑥
Maskall

Northern River

Northern River Lagoon

CTWS Visitors Center
Crooked Tree ②
Crooked Tree Wildlife Sanctuary

Northern Hwy

Santana
Lucky Strike
Altun Ha ③

Black Creek

Belize River
Spanish Creek

Sand Hill

Old Northern Hwy

Philip Goldson Hwy

Community Baboon Sanctuary
Bermudian Landing ④
Bacab Adventure & Ecopark
Burrell Boom
Ladyville

Municipal Airstrip

Rancho Dolores
CBS Museum & Visitor's Center

Spanish Creek Wildlife Sanctuary

BELIZE DISTRICT

Philip Goldson International Airport

BELIZE CITY ⑦

Belize Harbour

Cox Lagoon

Belize Central Prison
Hattieville

Burdon Canal

Old Belize & Cucumber Beach

George Price Hwy

Belize Zoo ①
La Democracia

Sibun River

Monkey Bay Wildlife Sanctuary

Sibun River ⑤
Monkey Bay National Park

Sibun Forest Reserve

Northern Lagoon

Coastal Rd

Southern Lagoon

CARIBBEAN SEA

Nohoch Che'en Caves Branch Archaeological Reserve

CAYO DISTRICT

Manatee Forest Reserve

Gales Point

STANN CREEK DISTRICT

Sibun Forest Reserve

Hummingbird Hwy

North Stann Creek

Dangriga

0   10 km
0   5 miles

Belize District Highlights

❶ Belize Zoo
(p80) Getting a first-hand introduction to the country's native species at this beloved rescue center

❷ Crooked Tree Wildlife Sanctuary
(p73) Relaxing in an authentic Belizean village and cruising the lagoon in search of the famous jabiru stork.

❸ Altun Ha
(p76) Exploring the Maya ruins that inspired Belikin beer labels and national banknotes.

❹ Community Baboon Sanctuary
(p71) Spending a night surrounded by the roar of black howler monkeys.

❺ Sibun River
(p79) White-water kayaking through the breathtaking habitat of fig trees, toucans and river otters.

❻ Belize Boutique Resort & Spa
(p75) Indulging in an afternoon of luxurious pampering in the jungle.

❼ Belize City (p56) Experiencing Belize's many local cultures and learning their histories at a top-notch museum.

ⓘ Getting There & Away

Belize District forms the central transport hub of the nation and is connected to other parts of the country by air, bus and boat. There are two airports in Belize City, as well as marine terminals for boat services to the Northern Cayes and a busy bus terminal serving destinations all over the country.

Travelers with their own transport are also likely to become fairly familiar with the district, as the country's two main highways intersect here.

BELIZE CITY

POP 61,760

Belize City is the historical (if no longer the actual) capital of the nation, making it an interesting place to spend a day or two. Its ramshackle streets are alive with colorful characters who represent every facet of Belize's ethnic make up, especially the Creoles. And while the urban scenery may involve the occasional fetid canal or run-down neighborhood, it also features handsome colonial houses, seaside parks, bustling shopping areas and sailboats that bob at the mouth of Haulover Creek.

You might find Belize City menacing, but you certainly won't find it dull. And while it doesn't top the list of Belize tourist destinations, visitors often admire the city's raffish charms and cultural vibrancy. Lately the government has gone to greater lengths to make tourists feel safe, with some success. But the city remains markedly less relaxed than the rest of Belize, and its reputation for poverty and crime persists.

History

Belize City owes its existence to the harbor at the mouth of Haulover Creek, a branch of the Belize River, down which the Baymen (early British woodcutters) floated lumber from their inland camps. After the rainy season, the Baymen would come to the coast to dispatch their lumber overseas and spend most of the proceeds on rum. Popular lore has it that the settlement – at first just a few huts surrounded by mosquito-ridden swamps – grew on a landfill of the Baymen's mahogany chips and rum bottles.

The settlement had little significance until 1779, when the Spanish briefly captured St George's Caye. 'Belize Town' then became and remained the British headquarters in Belize.

During the 19th century the town grew on both sides of Haulover Creek, with the British merchants' homes and buildings of the ruling elite clustered along and near the southern seafront. African slaves and their descendants lived in cabins further inland. By the 1880s the town had a population of around 5000; the great majority were Creoles descended from the British and their slaves, though whites still held all the power and wealth. Belize City witnessed most of the significant events on the long road to Belizean independence, including riots in 1894, 1919 and 1950.

The city was devastated by hurricanes in 1931 and 1961. It was 1961's Hurricane Hattie that spurred the government to build a new capital at Belmopan, 52 miles inland. This left Belize City, and particularly the Creole population, feeling neglected, which led to an increase in emigration by those seeking to escape the overcrowding, unemployment and poor sanitation.

Since the 1980s and 1990s, the city has been plagued by drug use and gang violence, which have contributed to tough conditions for the city's underemployed working class. Middle-class residential areas have developed on the northern and northwestern fringes of the city, while the central areas either side of Haulover Creek remain the country's cultural and commercial hub.

The 21st century has brought about a dramatic transformation – albeit in a tiny corner of the city. Cruise liners anchor off the coast of Belize City and with them come the day tourists, who head for 'Tourist Village' – a large purpose-built facility at the mouth of Haulover Creek. In 2018, Belize was poised to welcome 500,000 cruise-ship passengers to its Belize City and Harvest Caye cruise ports (up from zero at the turn of the millennium).

◉ Sights

Belize City's main historical sights are all located within walking distance of the Swing Bridge.

★ Goff's Caye   ISLAND

Some of the most spectacular snorkeling in Belize happens just a short swim off the powder-white sands of Goff's Caye, a tiny, uninhabited island just a 30-minute boat ride to the southeast of Belize City. With nothing but some coco palms and a couple of *palapa*-covered (open-air shelter with a thatched roof) picnic tables, the idyllic island sits right beside the Belize Barrier Reef and a healthy community of resident corals, lobsters, conch, stingrays, colorful fish and more.

★ **Museum of Belize** MUSEUM
(Map p62; ☎ 223-4524; www.nichbelize.org/museum-of-belize-and-houses-of-culture; Gabourel Lane; BZ$10; ⊙9am-5pm Tue-Thu, to 4:30pm Fri & Sat) This modern museum in the Fort George District provides an excellent overview of the story of Belize, told through exhibits housed in the country's former main jail (built of brick in 1857). Fascinating displays, historical photos and documents bear testimony to the colonial and independence eras, along with an exhibit on slave history and a new contemporary art gallery.

The Maya Treasures section, upstairs, is rather light on artifacts (most of Belize's finest Maya finds were spirited away to other countries) but there are some impressive examples of Maya jade, as well as some ceramics and sculpture. You'll also find plenty of informative models and explanations of the major Maya sites around the country. Other sections of the museum are devoted to Belize's coins and its insect life. The museum also has a good little gift shop.

★ **Swing Bridge** LANDMARK
(Map p62) This heart and soul of Belize City life, crossed by just about everyone here just about every day, is said to be the only remaining manually operated bridge of its type in the world. The bridge, a product of Liverpool's ironworks, was installed in 1923, replacing an earlier bridge that had opened in 1897.

These days it is rarely opened except to allow tall boats to pass in advance of serious storms, but if you're lucky, you might get to watch the procedure that brings vehicles and pedestrians in the city center to a halt.

The Swing Bridge is a favorite hangout for hustlers looking to part tourists from their valuables. You are likely to be approached by seemingly friendly sorts with outstretched hands asking, 'Where you from?' Be advised that the chances of said encounter resulting in a mutually beneficial cultural exchange are slim to none. Downstream from the bridge, Haulover Creek is usually a pretty sight, with numerous small yachts and fishing boats riding at anchor.

Image Factory GALLERY
(Map p62; ☎ 223-1493; www.imagefactorybelize.com; 91 North Front St; ⊙9am-5pm Mon-Fri) `FREE`

The country's most innovative and exciting art gallery stages new exhibitions and hosts regular book launches, usually of work by Belizean artists. Opening receptions are mostly held early in the month, out on the deck, which looks out on Haulover Creek.

Traveller's Heritage Center Museum MUSEUM
(☎ 223-2855; www.onebarrelrum.com; Mile 2 Philip Goldson Hwy; tour & tasting BZ$20; ⊙8am-5pm Mon-Fri) Out on the northern highway, this is an interesting little rum museum. You'll get to see the bottling process, learn how to make Belizean cocktails and sample the goods.

Digi Park LANDMARK
(Newtown Barracks Green; Map p58; Barrack Rd) A pleasant waterside recreation area complete with food huts selling local and international cuisine, a playground and a walled-in sandy area with water access, although you'd probably want to avoid swimming here. There is also a stage where concerts and cultural events are held.

Government House HISTORIC SITE
(House of Culture; Map p62; www.nichbelize.org; Regent St; BZ$10; ⊙9am-4pm Mon-Fri) Fronting the sea down at the end of Regent St, this handsome two-story wooden colonial mansion served as the residence of Britain's superintendents and governors of Belize from the building's construction in 1814 until 1996. At the time of research the building was undergoing renovation and was closed to the public but will once again serve as the Belizean House of Culture when work is complete.

The house, one of the oldest in Belize, is worth a visit for its historical exhibits, colorful displays of modern Belizean art, spacious colonial ambience and grassy gardens. It was here, at midnight on September 21, 1981, that the Union Jack was ceremonially replaced with the Belizean flag to mark the birth of independent Belize. Displayed in the gardens is the tender from Baron Bliss' yacht.

St John's Cathedral CHURCH
(Map p62; Albert St; ⊙8am-noon Mon-Fri, to 6pm Sat & Sun) Immediately inland of Government House stands St John's Cathedral, the oldest Anglican church in Central America. It was built by slave labor between 1812 and 1820 using bricks brought from Britain as ballast. Notable things to see inside are the ancient pipe organ and the Baymen-era tombstones

Belize City

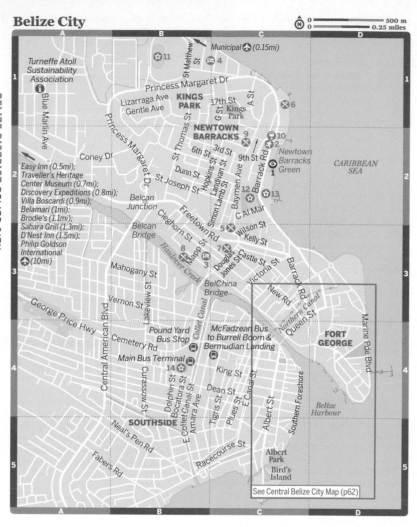

that tell their own history of Belize's early days and the toll taken on the city's early settlers.

Baron Bliss Tomb MONUMENT
(Map p62; Fort St) At the tip of the Fort George peninsula lies the granite Baron Bliss Tomb, the final resting place of Belize's most famous benefactor, who never set foot on Belizean soil while alive. Next to the tomb stands the **Fort George Lighthouse** (Map p62; Fort St), one of the many benefits the baron's munificence has yielded the country.

🏃 Activities

Although most divers and snorkelers base themselves out on the cays, it is actually quicker to access some of the best sites directly from Belize City. Some hotels in the city offer their guests diving and snorkeling outings, and you can also organize ocean or river fishing through Belize City adventure outlets.

Sit & Sip Pedal Tours CYCLING
(Map p58; ☎ 223-2453; www.belizepedaltours.com; cnr Barrack & Newton Barracks Rds; tours per person BZ$110, pub crawl per person from BZ$50; ☺ tours

Belize City

8:30am-4pm, pub crawl 9-10pm) Tour Belize City or crawl its pubs on a 15-seater 'bike bus' that leaves from the eponymous Sit & Sip lounge in the city's Newtown Barracks area. Private custom tours also available.

Diving & Snorkeling

The usual scuba destinations are the barrier reef, Turneffe Atoll Marine Reserve and Lighthouse Reef. Prices (excluding equipment) range from around BZ$250 for a two-tank dive at the barrier reef, to BZ$585 or so for a three-tank dive at Lighthouse Reef (usually including the Blue Hole).

Snorkeling day trips to the barrier reef start at around BZ$180 per person.

Fishing

Around Belize City, anglers have their choice of rivers, flats, channels, cays, mangrove islands and barrier reef. The most frequently hooked species include snook, permit, tarpon and bonefish, and trips start at around BZ$800 for four people.

Yoga

Om Shanti Belize YOGA
(Map p62; ☑610-0882, 227-2247; www.omshantibelize.com; 10 Fort St; per class BZ$25, packages available; ☺ see website for class schedule) A wonderful yoga studio and wellness center with an attached, delicious vegan cafe (p65), in a new waterfront location in Fort George. The teachers excel at what they do, offering several different types of yoga, including aqua yoga in a saltwater pool, along with tai chi classes, workshops and teacher training.

The spa offers all the usual massages, but also reflexology, reiki and biomagnetism.

Tours

Popular day-trip activities and destinations from Belize City include cave-tubing at Nohoch Che'en Caves Branch Archaeological Reserve in Cayo; visits to the Maya ruins at Lamanai in Orange Walk, Altun Ha, Xunantunich in Cayo and even Tikal in Guatemala; birding at Crooked Tree Wildlife Sanctuary; and viewing the animals at the Community Baboon Sanctuary or the Belize Zoo. Several hotels offer tours to their guests.

Many taxi drivers in town are part-time tour guides; they may give you a sales pitch as they drive you around the city. These cabbies/guides can be quite knowledgeable and personable and may suit you if you want a customized tour; in general prices for tours to regional attractions start from BZ$200 per day. Hotel staff can often make personal recommendations of cabbies known to them. Make sure your guide has a Belize Tourism Board (BTB) license.

Discovery Expeditions ADVENTURE
(☑671-0748; www.discoveryhelize.com; 5916 Manatee Dr, Buttonwood Bay) Specializes in mainland tours to Maya sites, national parks and caves, and offers zip-lining and river kayaking.

Sea Sports Belize ADVENTURE
(Map p62; ☑223-5505; www.seasportsbelize.com; 83 North Front St; ☺8am-5pm Mon-Fri, to 3pm Sat) A PADI dive shop that also specializes in wildlife-encounter tours, river cruises, barrier-reef snorkeling and manatee- and dolphin-spotting.

S&L Travel TOURS
(Map p62; ☑227-7593, 227-5145; www.sltravelbelize.com; 91 North Front St) A very reputable agency that offers half-day and full-day trips inland, as well as customized trip packages throughout and to Tikal in Guatemala. It specializes in birdwatching. Also offers air-conditioned internet access (BZ$6 per hour) from its office and does private airport transfers for BZ$40 for up to three people.

✿ Festivals & Events

September Celebrations CULTURAL
(◉ Sep 10-21) Starting on National Day and culminating on Independence Day, two weeks of city-wide patriotic celebrations keep the locals dancing in the streets. The Belize Carnival, a street festival held during this time, sees Belizeans don colorful costumes and dance to Caribbean beats.

Baron Bliss Day REGATTA
(◉ Mar 9) This public holiday involves a regatta in front of Fort George Lighthouse, among other festivities and events. It regularly coincides with the epic La Ruta Maya canoe race, which finishes in Belize City.

Belize International Film Festival FILM
(www.belizefilmfestival.com; ◉ Nov) Showcases films produced in Belize and in other Central American and Caribbean countries. Takes place at the Bliss Centre for the Performing Arts.

🛏 Sleeping

Accommodations are found both north and south of Haulover Creek. The top-end places are to the north, and most of the midrange and budget places are to the south. A few new spots have popped up near the regional airport.

TBG B&B B&B $
(Map p58; ☑ 632-2838; www.facebook.com/guillermo .alamina; St Luke St; r BZ$110; P ❋ 🛜) Tucked into the newer, largely residential Kings Park neighborhood, this five-room B&B is convenient for those flying into or out of Belize City's Municipal Airstrip. The digs are modern and well-appointed, and the kind owner prides himself on serving elaborate breakfasts, often including johnnycakes, fry jacks and fresh mango from the property's tree.

Sea Breeze Guest House GUESTHOUSE $
(Map p62; ☑ 203-0043; www.seabreeze-belize. com; 18 Gabourel Lane; r with/without bathroom BZ$60/50, tr with air-con BZ$80; ❋ 🛜) This little family-run guesthouse is a solid budget choice, although the razor wire surrounding the place makes it look like the owners are planning to withstand more than just the usual crime of Belize City – a zombie apocalypse, perhaps? The nine rooms are clean and comfortable for the price; and the Kalam family offers low-key but accommodating service.

The location in Fort George is safe, convenient and quiet – an easy walk from the water taxi or from the facilities at Tourist Village. The place lacks the hangout atmosphere of more popular backpacker places, but for functionality and value it's unbeatable.

BLISS OF BELIZE

Only Belize could have an annual holiday in honor of a national benefactor with a name like Baron Bliss. Born Henry Edward Ernest Victor Bliss in Buckinghamshire, England, in 1869 (the title 'Baron' was hereditary), Bliss was a man with a powerful love of the sea and of sailing. So much so, in fact, that he left his wife and his native land for the Caribbean in 1920, spending the next six years living aboard his yacht *Sea King II* off the Bahamas and Trinidad. After a bad bout of food poisoning in Trinidad, the baron took up an invitation from Belize's attorney general, Willoughby Bullock, to drop his anchor off the country on January 14, 1926.

Sadly, Baron Bliss' health took a decisive turn for the worse before he could leave his yacht; his doctors pronounced that the end was nigh. On February 17, 1926, the baron signed a will aboard the *Sea King II*, leaving most of his £1 million fortune to Belize. On March 9 he died. He had, apparently, fallen in love with Belize without ever setting foot on its soil.

The testament decreed that a Baron Bliss Trust be set up to invest his bequest, and that all income from it be used for the permanent benefit of Belize and its citizens, while the capital sum was to remain intact. No churches, dance halls or schools (except agricultural or vocational schools) were to be built with Bliss Trust moneys, nor was the money to be used for any repairs or maintenance to the Trust's own projects.

Over the decades the Baron Bliss Trust has spent more than US$1 million on projects such as the Bliss Centre for the Performing Arts (p66) and the Fort George Lighthouse (p58; beside which lies the baron's tomb), both of which are in Belize City; and several health centers and libraries around the country. An annual national holiday, Baron Bliss Day, is celebrated on or close to March 9, the anniversary of the good man's death.

Belcove Hotel   HOTEL $

(Map p62; ☑ 227-3054; www.belcove.com; 9 Regent St; r without bathroom BZ$65, r with bathroom & air-con BZ$93, deluxe d/tr with air-con BZ$104/115; � ✇) Secure and impeccably clean, the family-owned Belcove occupies a bright-yellow-and-burgundy building overlooking Haulover Creek. Staff is courteous and accommodating, and owner Myrna is deeply knowledgeable about the area. The central location is convenient to transport and the sights, while the balcony overlooking the creek is a great place to unwind.

Caribbean Palms Inn   GUESTHOUSE $

(Map p62; ☑ 227-0472; 26 Regent St; r from BZ$78-112; ✇✇) This downtown option on busy Regent St does not win any prizes for character but offers simple, affordable rooms with good mattresses in a central location. All have private bathroom, although some are a bit dark.

★ Villa Boscardi   B&B $$

(☑ 223-1691; www.villaboscardi.com; 6043 Manatee Dr, Buttonwood Bay; s/d BZ$185/225; ✇@✇✇) Set in a secure middle-class suburb, this guesthouse and its charming hosts will smooth away any stresses that Belize City's rougher edges might induce. The eight rooms are large and elegant, built with Belizean materials and decorated with fresh, bold colors and prints. Some rooms have kitchen facilities, while guests of the other rooms have access to a shared kitchen.

Breakfasts of eggs and pastries are served in the cozy sitting area, and in the backyard there's a newly installed pool/Jacuzzi with color-changing lights. The guesthouse is about 4 miles northwest of the city center, but there are at least five restaurants within walking distance and it's safe to walk there.

Bella Sombra Guest House Downtown   GUESTHOUSE $$

(Map p62; ☑ 631-8989; www.bella-sombra-guest-house-bz.book.direct; 36 Hydes Lane; s/d/tr BZ$100/140/180; ✇✇✇) A fantastic mid-range guesthouse bang in the middle of downtown with large, spotless modern rooms boasting good mattresses and all the mod-cons, including huge flatscreen TVs. Most rooms have a kitchenette with a sink, microwave and fridge while some have large writing desks. The rooftop terrace is a great place to drink a beer and watch the sunset. Advance reservations essential.

The friendly owners also run Bella Sombra King's Park, a more homey option targeted at long-term guests and located near the municipal airstrip.

D'Nest Inn   B&B $$

(☑ 223-5416; www.dnestinn.com; 475 Cedar St; s/d/tr incl breakfast from BZ$144/179/214; ✇✇) Your hosts Gaby and Oty have evidently put a lot of care into this retreat on the northern edge of town. The individually decorated rooms have four-poster beds, handmade quilts and plenty of Victorian-era antiques. Even more enticing, a lush garden beckons with blooming orchids and allamandas, singing birds and quiet corners.

If you're extra lucky, you may even spot a manatee in the adjoining canal. It's easy enough to travel the 3 miles into town by taxi or by bus, but in all honesty, you probably won't want to leave this tropical paradise.

Easy Inn   HOTEL $$

(☑ 223-0380; www.easyinnbz.com; Mile 2 Philip Goldson Hwy; s/d/ste BZ$120/140/160; ✇✇✇) It's hard to miss this bright-orange three-story hotel on the Philip Goldson Hwy offering spacious rooms with all the mod-cons. It's distinctly lacking in atmosphere but is reasonably priced for the city. A new suite offers a full kitchen.

Bakadeer Best Time Inn   GUESTHOUSE $$

(Map p58; ☑ 223-0659; 74 Cleghorn St; r BZ$109; ✇✇) This little guesthouse, set along a shady corridor a good distance back from the road, was purchased by a new owner in 2018 who has plans to upgrade and renovate much of the hotel. Service is professional, but the neighborhood feels somewhat dodgy, so avoid walking around here at night.

The owner will be providing a cheap shuttle to the airport and rental cars will also be available on site.

Coningsby Inn   GUESTHOUSE $$

(Map p62; ☑ 227-1566; 76 Regent St; r BZ$100; ✇@✇) A comfortable small hotel in an attractive colonial-style house, the Coningsby is recommended for attentive service and tight security. Rooms are fairly Spartan and show some wear, but there is plenty of inviting common space, including a breezy balcony. Also on offer: excellent breakfasts, laundry service and tours. The location offers easy access to downtown, but it can be noisy.

Central Belize City

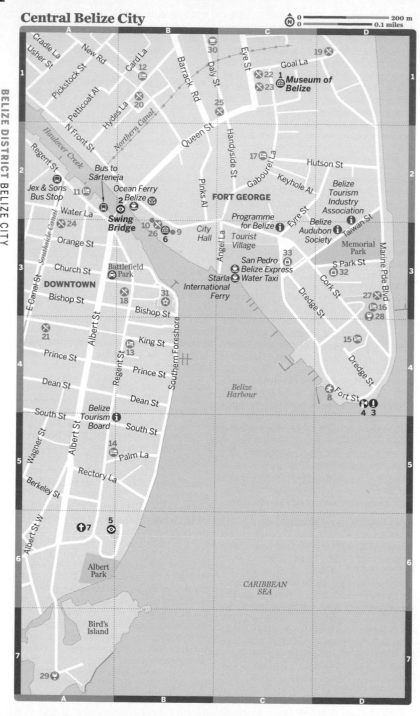

Central Belize City

Belize River Lodge LODGE **$$$**
(☑ 225-2002, in USA 888-275-4843; www.belizeriver
lodge.com; 2-night/7-night fishing all-incl package
(double occupancy) BZ$4121/10,631; ✳☎) Be-
lize's oldest fishing lodge remains one of its
best. Set in lush, tropical grounds close to
the airport, this gleaming mahogany gem
is a comfortable and convenient riverside
base for anglers. An included airport pick-up
involves a short boat ride, and trips to the
nearby river mouth, Caribbean sea and some
idyllic flats and mangrove-lined lagoons are
equally speedy.

Bonefish, tarpon, permit and snook
abound in close-by waters, and the lodge
provides top-notch guides and rental equip-
ment. There's also a Belize River Lodge out-
post on Long Caye.

**Radisson Fort George
Hotel** HOTEL **$$$**
(Map p62; ☑ 223-3333; www.radisson.com; 2 Marine
Pde Blvd; r BZ$545-621; ⓟ✳@☎⛱) Available
at the city's top hotel are 102 conservatively
decorated rooms with all the comforts. While
offering top international-class service, the
Radisson avoids the cultural detachment
that often comes with such packages, with
local woods, furnishings and decorations
conferring genuine Belizean character.

There are three classes of room: Club
Tower (the fanciest option, in a glass tower
where the marble-floored rooms all enjoy a
full sea view); Colonial (in the original hotel
structure, with fine wooden furnishings and
partial sea views); and Villa (the least expensive, across the street from the main hotel).
In addition to the two swimming pools, and
a few bars and restaurants, the hotel also has
a spa and its own dock. The hotel can help
organize tours and shuttles as well.

Great House GUESTHOUSE **$$$**
(Map p62; ☑ 223-3400; www.greathousebelize.
com; 13 Cork St; s/d BZ$374/408; ⓟ✳@☎) This
historic colonial-style mansion was built as
a private home in 1927 on a piece of prime
Fort George real estate. Nowadays, the Great
House features 16 graceful rooms that are
individually decorated, all with hardwood
floors and furniture, ceiling fans and floral
prints. Many perks assure your warm wel-
come, including fresh fruit and hot coffee
upon arrival.

The Great House is across the street from
the Radisson, so it offers easy access to the
big hotel's restaurants and services.

Princess Hotel & Casino HOTEL **$$$**
(Map p58; ☑ 223-2670; www.wyndhamhotels.com/
hotels/belize-city-belize; Barrack Rd, Kings Park;

s/d/ste incl breakfast BZ$275/296/333; P ❋ @
🛜 🖼) This six-story seafront hotel in the north of the city is also an entertainment and social center, with bustling public areas – in fact, a better place to visit for a bit of diversion than a place to stay. Rooms are ample and pretty much what you'd expect for the price at a seaside casino.

There's an excellent little coffee shop (and even a movie theater) downstairs.

✗ Eating

Most of the fancier restaurants are in the hotels in the Fort George and Newtown Barracks districts, north of the Swing Bridge; you'll find some reliable local restaurants in the commercial area south of the Swing Bridge. You can also chow down very happily at some of the bars around town.

★ Nerie's II Restaurant   BELIZEAN $
(Map p62; ☑ 223-4028; cnr Queen & Daly Sts; mains BZ$10-18; ⏰ 8am-10pm Mon-Sat, to 3pm Sun) Nerie's offers most accompaniments imaginable to rice and beans, including curried lamb, stewed cow foot, lobster and deer. Begin with a choice of soups, including chicken, *escabeche* (with chicken, lime and onions), *chirmole* (with chicken and a chilli-chocolate sauce) or cow foot, and finish with cassava pudding. Nerie's has another outlet – Nerie's I Restaurant – on the north side.

Dario's Meat Pies   BELIZEAN $
(Map p62; ☑ 605-0587, 203-5197; 33 Hydes Lane; meat pies BZ$1.25; ⏰ 5am-3pm Mon-Sat) Ask any local who makes the best meat pies and they'll tell you without hesitation, Dario's. Get in the line (which will probably wrap around the block) and choose from beef or chicken. They're also resold all over the country but it's best to buy them oven fresh at the source.

The fillings are piping hot – take care when biting through the crust. And Belizean pies are small, so grab a few.

Ice Cream Shoppe   ICE CREAM $
(Map p62; ☑ 223-1965; 17 Eve St; scoop BZ$4; ⏰ 11am-7pm Mon-Thu, to 9pm Fri-Sun; ❋ 🛜) When the heat hits 'unbearable' head to this boutique ice-cream parlor and cool off with delicious homemade ice cream in a variety of great flavors, including some starring local fruits sour sop and craboo. Order a few scoops and sit back and enjoy the air-con and fast wi-fi.

Nerie's I Restaurant   BELIZEAN $
(Map p58; ☑ 224-5199; 12 Douglas Jones St; mains BZ$10-18; ⏰ 7:30am-4:30pm Mon-Sat) One of two branches of this local institution serving up budget-friendly quality Creole food.

Ma Ma Chen Restaurant   TAIWANESE, VEGETARIAN $
(Map p62; ☑ 223-4568; 7 Eve St; mains BZ$5-13; ⏰ 10am-5pm Mon-Fri; 🖋) Looking for an antidote to meat-heavy Belizean cuisine? Look no further: Ma Ma Chen's is a genuine Taiwanese-style vegetarian restaurant, serving tofu, brown rice and vegetable dishes. The seating area is cozy and bright, and the meals are fresh, filling and healthy.

Brodie's   SUPERMARKET $
(Mile 3 Philip Goldson Hwy; ⏰ 8:30am-7pm Mon-Thu, to 8pm Fri, to 5pm Sat, to 1pm Sun) A large supermarket with a wide range of groceries that is a convenient place to stock up before a long trip. Has a **second location** (Map p62; 2 Albert St; ⏰ 8:30am-7pm Mon-Thu, to 8pm Fri, to 5pm Sat, to 1pm Sun) southeast of city center.

Marvas   BELIZEAN $
(Map p62; ☑ 207-4654; East Canal St; mains BZ$8-9; ⏰ 7am-8pm, to 6pm Sun) One of the few places that you'll always find open in downtown, Marvas prepares cheap Creole classics served with a huge plate of rice and beans. There's no sign and the dining room is a pretty basic affair, but you'll get to watch all kinds of local characters swing by for takeout. The fiery homemade hot sauce is legendary.

Dit's Restaurant   DINER, BAKERY $
(Map p62; ☑ 227-3330; 50 King St; snacks BZ$3, mains BZ$8-9; ⏰ 8am-5pm Wed-Sat, to 3pm Sun) It doesn't look like much but Dit's is a local favorite and a fine place to get rice-and-beans Belizean standards, sandwiches and Mexican dishes. On special occasions, it even serves up *salbutes* (a Belizean variation on the tortilla).

★ Belamari   INTERNATIONAL $$
(☑ 615-2075; 63 Seashore Dr; pasta BZ$21-34, mains BZ$26-65; ⏰ noon-10pm Tue-Thu, to 11pm Fri & Sat, to 10pm Sun) This open-air, seaside restaurant in Buttonwood Bay is a chic new spot for cocktails, and all the better if you make a meal of it. The menu spans several continents, with everything from Brazilian shrimp stew to mushroom chicken marsala to pork schnitzel. And though the kitchen's a bit pokey, the breezy dining area and ocean views are lovely.

★**Spoonaz Photo Cafe**   CAFE **$$**
(Map p62; ☏ 223-1043; www.facebook.com/
spoonazorlater; 89 North Front St; johnnycakes
BZ$2.25, mains BZ$10-25; ⊗7am-6pm Mon-Thu,
to 7pm Fri & Sat, to 2:30pm Sun; bar til 10pm) An
oasis in downtown Belize City, this cosmo-
politan cafe serves quality coffee as well as
paninis and sandwiches. There is a smart air-
conditioned lounge area inside but you really
want to be under the green cloth umbrellas
out the back watching the sailboats bobbing
on Haulover Creek and working your way
through the cocktail list.

The menu includes local specialties such
as rice 'n' beans and stewed chicken, and
there's a popular BBQ on Saturdays with
baby-back ribs, spicy, smoked chicken wings
and chili nachos.

Riverside Tavern   GRILL **$$**
(Map p58; ☏ 223-5640; 2 Mapp St; burgers BZ$15-
20, mains BZ$29-37; ⊗11am-10pm Mon-Sat) This
riverfront establishment has developed a
reputation for serving up the best hamburgers in Belize City, and its fried onion rings,
pastas and steaks are also on point. The
portions are large, and best devoured at an
outdoor table on the water, accompanied by
a local beer. Air-con lovers may prefer the
comfy dining room or bar, though.

Take a taxi here and back at night; the
'hood can be rough.

Om Shanti Cafe   VEGAN **$$**
(Map p62; ☏ 227-2247; www.omshantibelize.com/
cafe-and-gift-shop; 10 Fort St; mains BZ$10-20;
⊗8:30am-6:30pm Mon-Sat; ☏) 🌱 This fantas-
tic new vegan cafe in Fort George is just the
thing after a challenging Ashtanga class in
the attached yoga studio (p59), or a massage
at the wellness center, all set in a gorgeously
restored and repurposed waterfront abode.
Menu selections include papaya ceviche, ve-
gan nachos and vegan cashew cheese, and
the soups, natural juices and desserts are
also phenomenal.

Celebrity Restaurant   INTERNATIONAL **$$**
(Map p62; ☏ 223-7272; www.celebritybelize.com;
cnr Marine Parade Blvd & Goal Lane; mains BZ$16-
40; ⊗11am-11pm) We love Celebrity because it
is a semi-swanky place that is not inside a
hotel. The place has an extensive menu that
includes American favorites, such as steaks
and sandwiches, Mexican fare like fajitas and
quesadillas, plenty of pasta dishes and a few
Mediterranean surprises such as hummus,
kofta and kebabs.

That said, the chef's specialty is seafood –
and you are in Belize, after all – so why not
sample the lobster hollandaise or the heaping plate of conch ceviche? The ambience is
casual with a happening bar as you enter and
a large dining room further inside.

Chon Saan Palace   CHINESE **$$**
(Map p58; ☏ 223-7100; cnr Kelly & Nurse Seay
Sts; mains BZ$19.50-33; ⊗11am-11pm; ☏) The
Chon Saan has been beloved in Belize City
since it opened in the 1970s. The extensive
menu includes more than 200 items, includ-
ing plenty of fresh seafood (which you can
see swimming around the tanks). Favorite
dishes include chicken in cashew nuts, lob-
ster in black bean sauce and Singaporean-
style chow mein.

Sahara Grill   LEBANESE **$$**
(☏ 203-3031; Vista Plaza, Mile 3.5 Philip Goldson
Hwy; mains BZ$13-28; ⊗10am-2pm & 6-10pm
Mon-Sat) You wouldn't expect to find such
quality in a strip mall on the edges of town
but this unpretentious Lebanese diner is
popular among expats and visitors alike
for its variety of delicious Middle Eastern
delicacies.

Hour Bar   BELIZEAN **$$**
(Map p58; ☏ 223-3737; Barrack Rd; mains BZ$23-
45; ⊗11am-11pm Sun-Wed, to midnight Thu, to 1am
Fri & Sat) With a fantastic waterside location,
this large open-air restaurant is a great
place for a meal. It's also well worth sticking
around afterwards for a few drinks.

Sumathi Indian Restaurant   INDIAN **$$**
(Map p58; ☏ 223-1172; 19 Baymen Ave; mains
BZ$25-35; ⊗11am-10pm; ☏) Belize City's fa-
vorite Indian restaurant provides a solid
range of flavorsome curries, tandooris and
biryanis (spicy rice with meat or vegetables), with plenty of vegetarian options,
all in generous quantities. All curries are
served with rice and naan bread, and Bol-
lywood films on the TV intensify the mood.
It's not cheap but it's decent value for the
quality.

Stonegrill Restaurant   FUSION **$$$**
(Map p62; ☏ 223-3333; Radisson Fort George Hotel,
2 Marine Pde Blvd; mains BZ$30-46; ⊗11:30am-
9pm; ℗) At this thatched poolside restaurant
at the Radisson you get to grill your own
meal – steak, fajitas, shrimp, chicken satay
and the like – on super-hot volcanic stones.
It's fun, tasty and free of added fat.

BELIZE DISTRICT BELIZE CITY

🍷 Drinking & Nightlife

Top-end hotel bars are one focus of Belize City social life. It's more fun than it might sound, pulling in a range of locals, expats and tourists. The best of the city's nightlife is, fortuitously enough, located in the relatively safe Newtown Barracks area in the north of town.

★ Bird's Isle Restaurant   BAR
(Map p62; ☑ 207-6500; Bird's Island; ⊙ 10:30am-2:30pm Mon-Fri, 5:30pm-9pm Wed, to midnight Thu, to 10pm Fri, 10:30am-10pm Sat) Bird's Isle may be the best that Belize City has to offer. An island oasis at the southern tip of town, it manages to defy the urban grit that lies just a few blocks away. Locals and tourists alike flock to the *palapa* to partake of sea breezes, fresh-squeezed juice and cold beers.

It has fine views at sunset, but unfortunately at dusk it is engulfed by bloodthirsty mosquitoes – come early or late.

Club Elite   CLUB
(Map p58; Princess Hotel & Casino, Barrack Rd, Kings Park; ⊙ 10pm-4am Fri & Sat) Located inside the Princess Hotel complex this is the city's most fashionable disco, which (being Belize) is still a fairly casual affair. Dress up, but not too much.

Thirsty Thursdays   BAR
(Map p58; 164 Newtown Barracks; ⊙ 3pm-2am Wed-Sat) A favorite among the young crowd, this hip bar has a large balcony overlooking Digi park. There are early-bird drinks specials from 5pm to 9pm.

Moon Clusters Coffee House   CAFE
(Map p62; ☑ 203-0139; 25 Daly St; frozen coffee BZ$6; ⊙ 1-6pm Mon, 9am-6pm Tue-Sat) The coolest cafe in town, serving up great frappes, many types of espresso, and pastries, donuts and muffins. The space doubles as a gallery of brightly colored murals created by a local artist.

Baymen's Tavern   BAR
(Map p62; ☑ 223-3333; Radisson Fort George Hotel, 2 Marine Pde Blvd; ⊙ 8am-11pm) The main bar at the Radisson is friendly and sociable, with a pleasant outdoor deck.

Vogue Bar & Lounge   LOUNGE
(Map p58; Princess Hotel & Casino, Barrack Rd, Kings Park; ⊙ 6am-10pm) The lounge bar at the Princess gets lively on Friday nights when a mixed young crowd launches a new weekend.

☆ Entertainment

Main venues for spectator sports are the **MCC Grounds** (Map p58; cnr Barrack Rd & Calle Al Mar), for football and cricket; **Rogers Stadium** (Map p58; Dolphin St) for softball; and the **Marion Jones Complex** (Map p58; Princess Margaret Dr), which is used for various events.

Bliss Centre for the
Performing Arts   PERFORMING ARTS
(Map p62; ☑ 227-2110; www.nichbelize.org; Southern Foreshore) Operated by the Institute for Creative Arts, the revamped Bliss Centre has a fine 600-seat theater that stages a variety of events throughout the year. Look for concerts of traditional Belizean music and shows celebrating Belize and its culture. Annual events include the Belize Film Festival and the Children's Art Festival in May.

Princess Cinema   CINEMA
(Map p58; ☑ 223-2670; Princess Hotel & Casino, Barrack Rd, Kings Park; BZ$15) The two-screen Princess cinema shows first-run Hollywood films, though usually a bit later than their US release dates.

Princess Hotel & Casino   CASINO
(Map p58; Barrack Rd, Kings Park; ⊙ noon-4am Mon-Thu, to 6am Fri-Sun) The casino at the Princess Hotel is an informal and fun place to try to boost your budget, with roulette, poker and blackjack tables, plus hundreds of slot machines and a floor show with dancers kicking up their heels at 10pm. You need to show ID such as your passport or driver's license to enter (minimum age is 18).

🛍 Shopping

Schlocky souvenirs are in abundance at the Tourist Village and Tourist Village Flea Market, while Albert St and its side streets are the main local shopping corridors. Decent gift shops are situated within the Museum of Belize, the Radisson, the Princess Hotel and in Old Belize, outside the city.

Image Factory   ART, BOOKS
(Map p62; 91 North Front St; ⊙ 9am-5pm Mon-Fri) The shop at this hip art gallery has the country's best range of books, including international literature, and titles on Belizean and Caribbean society and history. There is also a fine collection of local art for sale.

National Handicraft Center   GIFTS & SOUVENIRS
(Map p62; 2 South Park St; ⊙ 8am-5pm Mon-Fri, to 4pm Sat) This store carries the best stock of high-quality Belizean arts and crafts at fair

prices. Attractive buys include shade-grown coffee and local chocolate, carvings in zericote and other native hardwoods, slate relief carvings of wildlife and Maya deities, and CDs of Belizean music.

Tourist Village
Flea Market   GIFTS & SOUVENIRS
(Map p62; Fort St; ☺8am-4pm, cruise-ship days only) On the street outside the Tourist Village, vendors set up tents and tables to sell their wares, which include T-shirts with snappy slogans, jewelry, woven bags and blankets, and plenty of carved wooden items. Quality varies widely and prices are negotiable.

This is one of the few places in Belize where vendors are not afraid to engage in the hard sell. On non-cruise days, the selection is limited, but you might find a few scattered tables.

ⓘ Information

DANGERS & ANNOYANCE
You'll likely spend most of your time in the commercial and Fort George districts, both of which are safe during daylight. However, note the following:

➜ Be wary of overly friendly strangers
➜ Don't flash signs of wealth
➜ Don't leave valuables in the hotel
➜ Don't use illicit drugs
➜ Avoid deserted streets
➜ The Southside district (south of Haulover Creek and west of Southside Canal) sees frequent, gang-related violent crime, but non-intergang crime (petty and violent) is also an issue.
➜ Stay on main roads or take taxis when going to or from bus terminals and stops.
➜ After dark, always take taxis and don't go anywhere alone.

Police maintain a fairly visible presence in the main areas frequented by tourists in Belize City, and will intervene to deter hustlers and other shady characters, but you can't rely on them to always be where you need them.

MEDICAL
Belize City has the best medical facilities in the country.
Karl Heusner Memorial Hospital (☎223-1671, 223-1548; www.khmh.bz; Princess Margaret Dr; ☺emergency services 24hr) is the city's largest public hospital.

Belize Medical Associates (☎223-0302; www.belizemedical.com; 5791 St Thomas St; ☺emergency services 24hr) is one of several good private facilities.

MONEY
All banks exchange US or Canadian dollars, British pounds and, usually, euros. Most ATMs are open 24 hours, though it's highly recommended that you visit them during daylight hours.
Belize Bank (60 Market Sq; ☺8am-3pm Mon-Thu, to 4:30pm Fri) The ATM is on the north side of the building. There is another **Belize Bank ATM** (North Front St) that is convenient for water taxis.
Scotia Bank (cnr Albert & Bishop Sts; ☺8am-3pm Mon-Thu, to 4:30pm Fri)

POST
Main Post Office (Map p62; ☎227-2201; North Front St; ☺8am-4pm Mon-Thu, to 3:30pm Fri)

TELEPHONE
Digi (☎223-1800; www.ivedigi.com; Regent St; ☺8am-5pm Mon-Fri) Pick up SIM cards for mobile devices at this downtown shop.

TOURIST INFORMATION
Belize Tourism Board (BTB; Map p62; ☎227-2420; www.travelbelize.org; 64 Regent St, Belize City; ☺8am-5pm Mon-Thu, to 4pm Fri) Pick up maps, magazines and all sorts of information relating to travel around Belize. This is also where you will find the cruise-ship schedule, which is published in a handy booklet.
Belize Tourism Industry Association (BTIA; Map p62; ☎227-1144; www.btia.org; 10 Taiwan St; ☺8am-noon & 1-5pm Mon-Thu, to 4pm Fri) The BTIA is an independent association of tourism businesses, actively defending 'sustainable ecocultural tourism'. The office provides leaflets about the country's regions, copies of its *Destination Belize* annual magazine (free), and information on its members, which include many of Belize's best hotels, restaurants and other tourism businesses. The website has lots of information.
Turneffe Atoll Sustainability Association (Map p58; ☎670-8272; www.turneffeatoll sustainabilityassociation.org; 1216 Blue Marlin Av, downstairs from OAS; ☺8am-5pm Mon-Thu, to 4pm Fri) Manages the Turneffe Atoll Marine Reserve.

ⓘ Getting There & Away

AIR
Belize City has two airports: Philip Goldson International Airport (BZE), which is 11 miles northwest of the city center off the Philip Goldson Hwy; and the Municipal Airstrip (TZA), around 2 miles north of the city center. All international flights use the international airport. Domestic flights on both local carriers are divided between the two airports, but those using the Municipal Airstrip are cheaper (often significantly).

The following airlines fly from Belize City:

American Airlines (www.aa.com) Direct flights to/from Miami, Dallas/Fort Worth, Charlotte and Los Angeles.

Avianca (www.avianca.com) Flights to/from San Salvador (El Salvador).

Copa Airlines (www.copaair.com) Flies to Panama City with connections all over Latin America and the Caribbean.

Delta Airlines (www.delta.com) Direct flights to/from Atlanta.

Maya Island Air (☑ 223-1403, 223-1140; www.mayaislandair.com; Belize City Municipal Airport) Operates flights to Dangriga, Placencia, Punta Gorda, San Pedro (Ambergris Caye) and Orange Walk. From the international airport, the airline also serves Corozal (Mexico).

Southwest Airlines (www.southwest.com) Offers good deals to Houston, Denver and Fort Lauderdale.

Tropic Air (☑ 224-5671; www.tropicair.com; Belize City Municipal Airport) Flights to Dangriga, Placencia, Punta Gorda, San Ignacio, Belmopan and San Pedro. From the international airport, the airline also serves Flores (Guatemala); Roatán (Honduras); and Cancún (Mexico).

United Airlines (www.united.com) Direct flights to/from Houston.

BOAT

There are two water-taxi companies on North Front St offering similar services to Caye Caulker and San Pedro. On Fridays, there's also a ferry to Dangriga that continues on to Honduras.

San Pedro Belize Express Water Taxi (Map p62; ☑ 223-2225; www.belizewatertaxi.com; Brown Sugar Mall, Front St) Professionally run water-taxi service with nine departures a day (approximately every hour from 8am to 5pm) to Caye Caulker (one way/return BZ$36/56, 45 minutes) and San Pedro (one way/return BZ$56/76, 1½ hours). Also operates one daily boat to and from Caye Caulker to Chetumal, Mexico (via San Pedro).

Ocean Ferry Belize (Map p62; ☑ 223-0033; www.oceanferrybelize.com; North Front St) Runs boat services to Caye Caulker (one way/return BZ$19/30, 45 minutes) and San Pedro (one way return BZ$29/50, 1½ hours) out of the old Caye Caulker Water Taxi terminal. Leaves Belize City for both destinations at 8am, 10:30am, 1:30pm, 3pm and 5:30pm.

Starla International Ferry (Map p62; ☑ 628-0976; Brown Sugar Mall, Front St) Leaves from the San Pedro Belize Express terminal at 9am on Fridays, stopping in Dangriga (BZ$160) before continuing on to Puerto Cortés, Honduras (an additional BZ$110). The whole trip takes 5½ hours. On Monday the boat makes a return trip, arriving in Belize City at 4:30pm.

BUS

Belize City's **main bus terminal** (Map p58; West Collet Canal St) is the old Novelo's terminal next to the canal which now sports a faded Rastafarian red, gold and green paint job. Most buses leave from here, although local buses within Belize District to destinations such as Ladyville and Burrell Boom leave from around the corner at the **Pound Yard bus stop** (Map p58; Cemetery Rd).

To judge from the barely legible, handwritten schedules that adorn the walls, the country's intercity bus system is utter chaos. Indeed, there are dozens of companies that ply the main routes out of Belize City – south to Punta Gorda, west to Benque Viejo del Carmen and north to Corozal. It's actually simpler than it seems, since plenty of buses ply the main routes and prices and service do not vary much between companies. Note that there are fewer departures on Sunday and the last buses leave earlier.

Belmopan (BZ$6, 1¼ hours, 52 miles) All southbound buses and all westbound buses pass through Belmopan. Many of the services to the south run express to Belmopan and then make stops after the capital. Any non-express bus heading to Belmopan can drop you anywhere along George Price Hwy.

Benque Viejo del Carmen (BZ$12, three hours, 80 miles) Buses depart every half hour from 5am to 9pm.

Bermudian Landing/Rancho Dolores (BZ$5 to BZ$8, one hour, 27 miles) **McFadzean buses** (Map p58; Amara Ave) depart from Amara Ave next to the school at 12:15pm, 3:25pm, 5pm, 5:20pm and 8pm. The 3:25pm and 5pm services continue to Rancho Dolores.

Burrell Boom (BZ$2.50 to BZ$4, 45 minutes, 20 miles) All buses to Bermudian Landing pass through Burrell Boom. There's also a direct bus to Burrell Boom from the Pound Yard bus stop at 4:50pm. Alternatively, catch any bus traveling along the Philip Goldson Hwy, get out at the Burrell Boom turnoff and hitch 3 miles to the village.

Cancún, Mexico (BZ$112, 10 hours, 320 miles) Mexican company ADO runs comfortable air-conditioned buses direct to Cancún from the main bus terminal at 11am and 7:30pm. It stops in Tulum, Playa del Carmen and Cancún airport before arriving at the Cancún bus terminal. Buy tickets in advance in the bus terminal.

Chetumal, Mexico (BZ$16, 3½ hours, 102 miles) Through buses to Chetumal leave every half hour or so from 5am to 11:30am. Alternatively, take one of the frequent northbound buses to Corozal, from where there is local transport to the border. An express, air-conditioned tourist service to Chetumal (BZ$50, three hours) leaves from the Brown Sugar Mall at 1:15pm.

Corozal (BZ$10, three hours, 86 miles) Buses run north to Corozal hourly from 5am until 7:30pm.

Crooked Tree (BZ$3.50, one hour, 36 miles) **Jex & Sons** (Map p62; Regent St) runs buses from the corner of Regent St W and W Canal St at 10:45am from Monday to Saturday, with two additional buses departing at 5pm and 5:20pm from the Pound Yard bus stop. You can also take any northern bus and hitch from the turnoff.

Dangriga (BZ$12, three hours, 107 miles) All southbound buses to Punta Gorda stop in Dangriga.

Flores, Guatemala Fuente del Norte runs a daily luxury bus to Flores (BZ$50, five hours, 145 miles) at 10am. Marlin Espadas runs a smaller bus on the same route at 1pm. Both services depart from the Brown Sugar Mall. From Flores there are connecting bus services to Guatemala City and and Pedro Sula, Honduras.

Mérida, Mexico (BZ$112, 10 hours, 343 miles) ADO runs an air-conditioned express bus direct to Mérida three to four times a week leaving from the main bus terminal at 7pm. Alternatively, take the Cancún bus and change once across the border in Quintana Roo.

Orange Walk (BZ$6, two hours, 57 miles) Hourly from 5am to 7:30pm; all buses to Corozal and Sarteneja stop in Orange Walk.

Punta Gorda (BZ$24 to BZ$28, six to seven hours, 212 miles) The terminus for the southern lines – the main one operated by James Bus Line. Buses depart hourly from 5:15am to 3:45pm.

San Ignacio (BZ$10, 2½ hours, 72 miles) All westbound buses to Benque stop in San Ignacio.

Sarteneja (BZ$15, 3½ hours, 96 miles) Light-blue buses depart from **Regent St** (Map p62; Regent St) just northwest of the Swing Bridge at 10:30am, noon, 1:45pm, 4pm and 5pm; runs express to Orange Walk.

CAR & MOTORCYCLE
The main roads in and out of town are the Philip Goldson Hwy (to the international airport, Orange Walk and Corozal), which heads northwest from the Belcan Junction, and the George Price Hwy (to Belmopan and San Ignacio), which is the westward continuation of Cemetery Rd. Cemetery Rd gets its name from the ramshackle Lord's Ridge Cemetery, which it bisects west of Central American Blvd.

🛈 Getting Around

Though many of the spots where travelers go are within walking distance of each other, it's always safest to take a taxi after dark.

CAR & MOTORCYCLE
Belize City has the heaviest traffic in the country, although it is usually only slow going for a short time in the morning and again in the evening. There's a limited one-way system, which is easy to work with. If you need to park on the street, try to do so right outside the place you're staying. Never leave anything valuable on view inside a parked car.

Car-rental firms in Belize include the following:

AQ Car Rental (222-5122; www.aqbelizecarrental.com; Philip Goldson Hwy; 8am-5pm) Locally run outfit that offers the best rates in Belize backed up by top-notch customer service. Free pick-up and drop-off service within city limits. There's another branch at Philip Goldson International Airport.

Budget (223-3986, 223-2435; www.budget-belize.com; Philip Goldson Hwy; 8am-5pm) There is also an office at Philip Goldson International Airport and another in Placencia.

Crystal Auto Rental (223-1600; www.crystal-belize.com; Philip Goldson Hwy; 7am-5pm) One of the best local firms; allows vehicles to be taken into Guatemala. There's another branch at Philip Goldson International Airport.

Euphrates Auto Rental (610-5752, 227-5752; www.ears.bz; 143 Euphrates Av, Southside; 6am-5pm Mon-Fri, to 3pm Sat) Local firm that offers some good deals.

Hertz (223-5395; www.hertz.com; 11A Cork St; 8am-4:30pm Mon-Fri) Also has a branch at Philip Goldson International Airport.

Thrifty (207-1271; www.thrifty.com; 715 Gibnut St; 8am-5pm Mon-Sat) Additional outlet at Philip Goldson International Airport.

TAXI
Taxis (Map p62) cost around BZ$10 for rides within the city, give or take; if it's a long trip from one side of town to the other, expect to be charged a bit more. Confirm the price in advance with your driver. Most restaurants and hotels will call a taxi for you.

NORTH OF BELIZE CITY

The recently renamed Philip Goldson Hwy is still referred to by many locals as the Northern Hwy. It stretches from Belize City and into Orange Walk District, passing by the communities of Ladyville and Burrell Boom (west of which you'll find the Community Baboon Sanctuary). At Sand Hill the road forks. To the west, the road continues to Orange Walk, passing the turnoff for the Crooked Tree Wildlife Sanctuary. To the east, the Old Northern Hwy leads to the Maya ruins of Altun Ha and a dreamy jungle resort and spa.

ℹ️ Getting There & Away

Most places in the region are connected to Belize City by infrequent bus services that usually leave the villages early in the morning and return in the late afternoon. There are no bus connections between villages on different side roads so travelers must either backtrack to Belize City or make their way out to the Philip Goldson Hwy and try to flag down a passing service.

Renting a vehicle is the best way to fully explore the region.

Burrell Boom

POP 2218

A tranquil and charming village, Burrell Boom occupies a quiet bank of the Belize River, just 19 miles north of Belize City and 3 miles west of the Philip Goldson Hwy. Founded in the 18th century, the village takes its name from the iron chains ('booms') that loggers extended across the river to trap the mahogany logs that were sent from further upriver. You can still see the boom and anchors on display in Burrell Boom Park in the village center.

Burrell Boom is a quick trip from the Community Baboon Sanctuary, but otherwise there are no big tourist draws in the immediate vicinity. Rather, the village's attraction is the exquisite natural setting, ideal for canoeing, birding and croc-spotting. Locals take advantage of the lush fruit trees and distill a huge variety of fruit wines, especially sweet berry and cashew wines.

🏃 Activities

Bacab Adventure & Eco Park   HIKING

(☑225-3537, 225-2587; www.bacabecopark.com; adult/child BZ$10/5, tour prices vary; ⏲10am-sunset; 🅟) 🗷 Part nature reserve, part theme park, Bacab is set on more than 500 acres of jungle through which hiking trails and waterways wind. While it's not a destination for hardcore naturalists, it's a great escape from Belize City, especially for families, who'll appreciate the green environs, huge swimming pool complete with waterfall and the opportunity to check out some animals.

While this place was established with the cruise-ship tourist in mind, days when the ships aren't in (schedules change all the time; call the front desk to find out) are absolutely serene.

A nature hike will reward observers with multiple bird sightings and perhaps a glimpse of resident howler monkeys or crocodiles. Adventurers might wish to explore the reserve on horseback (best scheduled a day in advance), by kayak or even by mountain bike. The staff is warm and friendly and service absolutely top-notch.

While Bacab is loads of fun, its goal is more complex, as management has undertaken an intensive reforestation effort, planting more than 25 species of native trees.

There is also a gift shop located onsite and a beautiful *palapa* restaurant that serves American, Caribbean and Belizean cuisine.

To get to Bacab, turn off the Burrell Boom road into Ridge Lagoon Estates and follow the signs. It claims to be open every day but has been known to close during inclement weather – call before trekking out here. Bring bug spray.

✨ Festivals & Events

La Ruta Maya   CANOEING

(⏲Mar) Burrell Boom comes to life every year in March, when this annual canoe race passes through. Contestants spend their third night on the banks of the river in town, making this an ideal location for observers to hunker down with a cold drink and watch the fun.

🛏️ Sleeping

While there is one fine resort in Burrell Boom there isn't much in the way of cheap accommodations around the village. Budget travelers might choose to stay down the road in Bermudian Landing.

Black Orchid Resort   RESORT $$$

(☑225-9158; www.blackorchidresort.com; 2 Dawson Lane; r BZ$300-600, ste BZ$642, villas BZ$773; 🅟❄🅰️🌐) 🗷 Attentive service and comfortable accommodations are the main draws at this classy riverside resort. Spacious rooms feature big beds made of mahogany; bedspreads are sprinkled lightly with hibiscus flowers. Mexican-tiled bathrooms and private balconies provide the perfect place to sip your morning coffee and listen to the birds awaken.

The verdant flower-filled grounds stretch down to the river, where complimentary canoes, kayaks and paddle boats are available for guests' use. (Bicycles are also free.) Other amenities include a nice restaurant and bar, a small gift shop and plenty of

HURRICANE WATCH

Hurricanes have long bedeviled the Belizean coast, leaving their marks in very visible ways. For example, the Split on Caye Caulker was created when Hurricane Hattie whipped through here in 1961. This is the same storm that motivated the Belizean government to build a new inland capital at Belmopan.

The effects of these tropical storms are not only physical: hurricane season is ingrained in the brains of the residents, who long remember the last evacuation and always anticipate the next one. Any visitor to Belize is likely to engage in at least one conversation about the most recent tempest (more, if it was a bad one). Here are a few of the lowlights from Belizean hurricane history:

Hurricane Five (1931) One of the deadliest seasons in Atlantic Coast hurricane history. Hurricane Five hit the coast of Belize on a national holiday, meaning that emergency services were slow to respond. The entire northern coast of the country was devastated, and around 2500 people were killed.

Hurricane Hattie (1961) This history-making hurricane killed 275 people and destroyed much of Belize City. Afterward, survivors apparently roamed the rubble-strewn streets in search of food and shelter. Many moved to refugee camps, which later morphed into permanent settlements – the origins of the town Hattieville. Hurricane Hattie provides the backdrop for Carlos Ledson Miller's novel *Belize* and Zee Edgell's *Beka Lamb*.

Hurricane Iris (2001) This devastating Category 4 storm made landfall in southern Belize, destroying many rural Maya villages and leaving upward of 10,000 people homeless. Off the coast south of Belize City, a live-aboard dive ship capsized, killing 20 people. Joe Burnworth recounts the tragic tale in his book *No Safe Harbor*.

Hurricane Richard (2010) This Category 1 hurricane made a direct hit on the tiny community of Gales Point severely damaging houses and isolating the village. The only loss of life on land was an expat American who was mauled by a jaguar which had escaped when a tree fell on its cage.

Hurricane Earl (2016) Some in Belize are still recovering from this Category-1 that forever altered the country's landscapes and caused upwards of US$100 million in damages. Around 80% of the homes in Belize District were flooded and countless structures on the cays and coastline were destroyed.

Recent scientific evidence suggests that the strength of hurricanes increases with the rise of ocean temperatures. So as our climate continues to change, countries such as Belize are likely to experience more-frequent and more-intense hurricane hits.

adventure tours. Bonus: free international airport transfers.

❶ Getting There & Away

Both Bacab Adventure & Eco Park and Black Orchid Resort will arrange transfers from Belize City (BZ$70) or from the international airport, so it's unlikely you will be dependent on public transportation. That said, six buses a day service Burrell Boom from Belize City (although some arrive late in the evening and head back very early in the morning). There are fewer buses on Saturday and one (or none) on Sunday. Alternatively, buses ply the Philip Goldson Hwy every half hour, so if you can get a lift from the village to the highway turnoff, you won't have to wait long.

Community Baboon Sanctuary

No real baboons inhabit Belize; but Belizeans use that name for the Yucatán black howler monkey (*Alouatta pigra*), an endangered species that exists only in Belize, northern Guatemala and southern Mexico and is one of the largest monkeys in the Americas. The Community Baboon Sanctuary (CBS; www.howlermonkeys.org; nature walk/river tour/villages tour BZ$14/28/50; ⊙ 8am-5pm) is a community-run, grassroots conservation operation that has engineered an impressive increase in the primate's local population.

CBS occupies about 20 sq miles, spread over a number of Creole villages in the

Belize River valley. More than 200 landowners in seven villages have signed pledges to preserve the monkey's habitat, by protecting forested areas along the river and in corridors that run along the borders of their property. The black howlers have made an amazing comeback here, and the monkeys now roam freely all around the surrounding area.

◉ Sights

CBS Museum & Visitor's Center   MUSEUM
(☑ 245-2009,245-2007,622-9624;baboonsanctuary @hotmail.com; Bermudian Landing; adult/child BZ$14/7; ☉ 8am-5pm; ℗) In a newly constructed building, CBS Museum & Visitor's Center has a number of good exhibits and displays on the black howler, other Belizean wildlife and the history of the sanctuary. Included with the admission fee is a 45-minute nature walk on which you're likely to get an up-close introduction to a resident troop of black howlers. Along the way the trained local guides also impart their knowledge of the many medicinal plants.

The center has also added horseback riding, cycling, kayaking and a butterfly farm to its list of activities, and sells maps (BZ$6) of local trails. There are nearly 200 bird species in the area to keep wildlife watchers busy.

Other activities that can be organized here include night hikes, canoe trips and croc-spotting tours. The center can also connect you with local homestays providing both food and lodging.

Note that there is a local business purporting to be the official visitor's center on the road into the village – the real version is right in front of the Bermudian Landing cricket oval.

🛏 Sleeping

The CBS Museum & Visitor's Center) can organize homestay accommodations (double including two meals per person BZ$90) in Bermudian Landing and the other villages participating in the sanctuary program. Conditions are rustic (not all places have showers or flush toilets), but there's no better way to experience Creole village life and support the community.

There are also private lodges in Bermudian Landing and some of the other villages.

Howler Monkey Resort   LODGE **$$**
(☑ 607-1571; www.howlermonkeyresort.bz; cabins BZ$250-270; ℗ ✳ 🛜 ⊠) 🖉 Ed and Melissa Turton's beautiful, rustic jungle lodge consists of eight cabins of varying size and proximity to the river, set on 20 jungle-filled acres above a bend in the Belize River. This is the place to come to hear the howler monkeys roar at night and watch birds, agouti, iguana and even the occasional crocodile roam during the day.

Ed and Mel are excellent wildlife guides (and chefs), and their resort has trails to explore, a canoe tour (BZ$80 per canoe) and even a river-fed swimming pool. Direct bookings include breakfast and dinner for two in the dining room.

Another surprisingly excellent feature of the Howler Monkey Resort is its bat house; that is, an old cabin that's been converted to a bat sanctuary. The benefit of this to visitors

---

THE MONKEY THAT ROARED

Listen! Up in the sky! It's a jet plane! It's a Harley Davidson! It's a Led Zeppelin! No, it's a howler monkey.

Just how loud is the vociferous simian? The howl of the howler monkey peaks at around 128 decibels, which is louder than a lion's roar, an elephant's trumpet or even a chainsaw. This makes the howler the loudest of all land animals. A hollowed-out bone in the throat gives the 20lb primate the anatomical ability to crank up the volume.

The male monkeys make all the noise. Howler troops, which number about a dozen members, are matriarchal. The females only need one or two mature males around to defend their preferred patch of rainforest from hungry rivals. So early in the morning and late in the afternoon, when the dominant male traipses up to his treetop trapeze to make his booming broadcast, *stay away!*

There are officially nine species of howler, but only one in Belize – the Yucatán black howler, which happens to be the largest. Belizeans refer to it as a baboon, but the baboon is an Old World monkey; the howler is strictly New World. Even if you do not see a howler monkey on your trip to Belize, you will likely hear one. Its haunting cry carries as far as 5 miles.

isn't obvious at first, but becomes so once you realize that the bats pay their rent by keeping the area nearly mosquito free.

Nature Resort   CABAÑAS **$$**
(☑610-1375, 223-6115; www.natureresortbelize .com; Bermudian Landing; cabañas s/d BZ$130/ 150, r with fan BZ$90; P ⊛) Right next to the CBS Museum & Visitor's Center, this little resort has six comfortable cabañas and five rooms in a lovely natural setting. There's a new restaurant, Drina's, which serves up decent Creole food (hours vary). It is managed remotely from Belize City and there is not always staff onsite, but you can make bookings through the Visitor's Center and online.

❶ Getting There & Away

Bermudian Landing is 27 miles northwest of Belize City and 9 miles west of Burrell Boom. Buses depart from the CBS Museum & Visitor's Center to Belize City (BZ$5 to BZ$8, one hour) very early in the morning with additional departures at noon and 3:30pm from Monday to Saturday. Buses leave Belize City from the corner of Amara Ave and Cemetery Rd at 12:15pm, 3:25pm, 5pm, 5:20pm and 8pm.

The CBS Museum & Visitor's Center arranges private transportation between Bermudian Landing and Belize City for BZ$80 round trip.

Crooked Tree

POP 1000

Founded in the early 18th century, Crooked Tree – 33 miles from Belize City – may be the oldest non-indigenous village in Belize. Apparently the area got its name from early logwood cutters who boated up Belize River and Black Creek to a giant lagoon marked by a tree that seemingly grew in every direction. These 'crooked trees' (logwood trees, in fact) still grow in abundance around the lagoon. Until the 3.5-mile causeway from the highway was built in 1984, the only way to get here was by boat, so it's no wonder life still maintains the slow rhythm of bygone centuries.

Crooked Tree village is the gateway to the eponymous wildlife sanctuary, quite possibly one of Belize's best birding areas. It's worthwhile for nature lovers and those seeking a peaceful rural community in a beautiful setting. Stay the night to be here at dawn, when the birds are most active.

⊙ Sights

Crooked Tree
Wildlife Sanctuary   NATURE RESERVE
(CTWS; www.belizeaudubon.org; BZ$8; ⊙8am-4:30pm) ✎ Between November and April, migrating birds flock to the lagoons, rivers and swamps of the massive Crooked Tree Wildlife Sanctuary, which is managed by Belize Audubon. The best birdwatching is in April and May, when the low level of the lagoon draws thousands of birds into the open to seek food in the shallows. That said, at any time between December and May, birdwatchers are in for hours of ornithological bliss.

Boat-billed and bare-throated tiger herons, Muscovy and black-bellied whistling ducks, snail kites, ospreys, black-collared hawks and all of Belize's five species of kingfisher are among some 300 species recorded here. Jabiru storks, the largest flying bird in the Americas, with wingspans of up to 8ft, congregate here year round but are particularly easy to spot in April and May.

At the entrance to the village, just off the causeway, stop by the CTWS Visitor Center (p75) to browse the interesting displays, books and information materials for sale. It's here that you'll be asked to pay your admission fee. The helpful, knowledgeable staff will provide a village and trail map, as well as information on expert local bird guides.

⚡ Activities

Walking Trails
A series of walking trails weave along the lakeshore and through and beyond the village. The CTWS Visitors Center supplies maps for self-guided exploration.

Boat Tours
Any of the local hotels can arrange a boat tour of the lagoon (up to four people BZ$200). Tours usually last three to four hours and it's best to plan for an early departure. This activity is particularly worthwhile from December to February, before the level of the lagoon has dropped off dramatically. Expert guides know which birds live in every nook and cranny of the swampland.

South of the lagoon, Spanish Creek and Black Creek harbor plenty of birds all year in their thick tree cover. Black Creek is also home to black howler monkeys, Morelet's crocodiles, coatimundi and several species of turtle and iguana; Spanish Creek gives access to Chau Hix, an ancient Maya site with a pyramid 80ft high.

✨ Festivals & Events

Crooked Tree Cashew Festival   FOOD & DRINK
(⊘May) Crooked Tree is home to a great number of cashew trees and this festival celebrates the cashew harvest in a big way, with music, dancing and lots of cracking, shelling, roasting and stewing of cashews, as well as the making of cashew cake, cashew jelly, cashew ice cream, cashew wine (not unlike sweet sherry) and cashew you-name-it.

🛌 Sleeping

Crooked Tree has developed excellent accommodations for such a small village, largely due to the pioneering efforts of intrepid birders. There's everything from camping and rustic cabañas to an upscale B&B.

Tillett's Village Lodge   GUESTHOUSE $
(☑ 662-1908, 607-3871; www.tillettvillage.com; r BZ$70-100, cabañas from BZ$100, lakeside cabins from BZ$200; P 🌣) The Tilletts are a Crooked Creek clan who have reared some of the most celebrated bird guides in the country. Their welcoming guesthouse is a good option for those that want to immerse themselves in village life. It has two basic cabañas and five simple rooms. Some have air-con while all feature comfortable beds, hot showers and local bird-themed artwork.

The thatched-roof upstairs rooms are more atmospheric than the concrete ones below, and the front yard area contains a little restaurant serving good Creole cooking (meals BZ$12 to BZ$20). The Tilletts also have a fully furnished two-bedroom house on the lagoon that sleeps up to six. When it's dry you can drive right to the door, but if it's raining you might have to reach it by boat.

A pioneering family in Belize's ecotourism field, the Tilletts offer tours around the area, including trips to Altun Ha, Lamani, Belize Zoo and elsewhere. They also lead horseback tours, nature walks and birding trips on the lagoon.

Tillett's is on the main street, 500yd north of the 'Welcome to Crooked Tree' sign.

Jacana Inn   HOTEL $
(☑ 604-8025, 620-9472; jacanainn5@gmail.com; per campsite BZ$20, s/d BZ$70/80, s/d with air-con BZ$90/100; 🛜) Run by the Nicholson family, this friendly hotel sits on a gorgeous spot on the banks of the northern lagoon. While it's still a work in progress, it offers 12 basic but comfortable rooms perfect for birders visiting Crooked Tree.

Mrs Nicholson will provide breakfast and lunch with advance notice (BZ$9 to BZ$14), and locally made wines are available for sale. Some rooms offer hot water, others do not. Laundry is available for BZ$10 per load.

★ Beck's Bed & Breakfast   B&B $$
(☑ 633-3398; www.becksbedandbreakfast.com; r BZ$196-327; P 🌣 🛜 🏊) Tucked into a five-acre plot in Crooked Tree's interior, this pine forest-shrouded B&B offers the town's most sumptuous digs. The colonial-style home contains just three guest rooms, tastefully and lavishly appointed, and a fully equipped kitchen where amicable host Becky whips up authentic Belizean breakfasts. Outside, a lovely courtyard leads to a relaxing swimming pool surrounded by greenery,

Becky can help arrange tours on the island and beyond, and she also serves a delectable three-course dinner on request (BZ$40).

Crooked Tree Lodge   CABAÑAS $$
(☑ 626-3820, 365-6611; www.crookedtreelodge-belize.com; campsites per person BZ$20, cabañas BZ$175-225; P 🛜) 🦟 Mick is a British pilot who served for years in Belize; Angie was born and bred in Crooked Tree. This kind couple has found their little plot of paradise in Crooked Tree and installed beautifully crafted wood cabañas, all with private porches overlooking the lagoon and providing perfect sunrise views. The self-service waterfront bar and open-plan dining room are wonderful and welcoming.

Homemade meals – served family-style – are moderately priced (BZ$20 to BZ$30) and delicious. Mick and Angie will also help you arrange tours or activities. The lodge provides reusable water bottles, and campers have access to the fridge.

Note that prices are per cabaña, some of which have various beds, and management is flexible with squeezing friends together in one room. The lodge is located at the north end of the village; cross the causeway and turn right at the 'Welcome to Crooked Tree' sign.

Bird's Eye View Lodge   HOTEL $$
(☑ 615-2846, 203-2040; www.birdseyeviewbelize.com; campsites per person BZ$20, s BZ$130-150, d BZ$200-300; P 🌣 🛜) Aptly named, this lodge is an great spot for viewing the waterfowl that inhabit the sanctuary's lagoon. Catering to birdwatchers for more than 15 years, the

lodge's 25 rooms are of ample size and include good beds, ceiling fans and Mexican-tile floors. The more expensive rooms upstairs have access to the balcony that yields lovely vistas over the lagoon.

Meals (BZ$30 to BZ$36) are served in a bright dining room. The lodge offers lagoon boat tours (BZ$250), nature walks with experienced bird guides (per person per hour BZ$20), horseback riding (per hour BZ$30) and canoe rental (per canoe per hour BZ$10). There is an onsite gift shop selling local village-made products, including cashew jam, hot sauce and fruit wines. The Bird's Eye View Lodge is about 1 mile south of the 'Welcome to Crooked Tree' sign.

❶ Information

CTWS Visitors Center (☑ 223-5004; ⊙ 8am-4:30pm) Check in here to pay your entrance to the Crooked Tree Wildlife Sanctuary on arrival in town. You only pay once – no matter how long you are going to stick around.

❶ Getting There & Away

To reach Crooked Tree village, turn off the Philip Goldson Hwy 33 miles north of Belize City and drive across the causeway into the village. The CTWS Visitor Center is immediately on the right. From the 'Welcome to Crooked Tree' sign, other posts will direct you to the various lodges.

Buses leave the village for Belize City (BZ$5, one hour) at 5am, 6am and 6:30am. They return from Belize City at 10:45am, 5pm and 5:20pm, with the first bus leaving from downtown on West Regent St and the afternoon services leaving from the Pound Yard bus stop near the main bus terminal.

Most hotels will arrange vehicle transfers from Belize City (BZ$170) or from the international airport (BZ$150). Alternatively, if your host is willing to fetch you from the Philip Goldson Hwy turnoff, you can take any northbound bus from Belize City.

Old Northern Highway

If you wish to get a sense of what Belize was like before the tourist boom, take a drive along the sleepy Old Northern Hwy, which forks off from the Philip Goldson Hwy about 20 miles north of Belize City. The road was a major thoroughfare during colonial rule, but these days it gets very little traffic, especially to the north of the Maya ruins at Altun Ha.

The Old Northern Hwy is now freshly paved – but still very narrow – from the Philip Goldson Hwy until the turnoff to Altun Ha. It's a scenic drive that traverses dense jungle dotted with tiny villages. North of Altun Ha, the quality of the road declines drastically, and north of Maskall it's all gravel.

Maskall is the only civilization of any note along the Old Northern Hwy, so there's rarely anybody to ask for help when you get a flat tire. Locals advise avoiding the northern part of this highway and, instead, to approach Altun Ha from the south (even if you are coming from northerly points such as Orange Walk or Corozal).

WORTH A TRIP

SPA IN THE JUNGLE

An oasis of luxury in the middle of dense broadleaf forest, **Belize Boutique Resort & Spa** (☑ 225-5555, in US 800-861-7001, in US 815-312-1237; www.belizeresortandspa.com; Mile 40.5 Old Northern Hwy; r BZ$460, junior ste BZ$540, ste BZ$850, villas BZ$1050-1250; ❰P ❄ 🛜 ❱) takes the jungle-lodge-and-spa concept to extremes of expensive pampering. Lush tropical grounds harbor individually designed rooms in a variety of African, Creole, Maya and even Gaudíesque styles – including honeymoon and 'fertility' suites, and a jungle tree house. All rooms are spacious, stylish and even a bit glamorous. There are two pools and a solar-heated mineral bath, waterfalls and romantic daybeds with privacy curtains. The elegant open-air restaurant serves good seafood, healthy salads and fresh-squeezed juices to guests as well as nonguests – reservations are required.

For active resort guests, there is a range of adventures and tours, including horseback riding and jungle excursions. But the main attraction here is the full range of decadent spa treatments and packages (BZ$190 to BZ$1030), including body scrubs, mud wraps and aromatherapy. The specialty is the Mood Mud Massage, that uses house-made scented or unscented 'mud' mixtures to revitalize the skin, relax the muscles and enhance the mood. The romantic Couples Mood Massage is popular with honeymooners.

The resort is about 2 miles north of Maskall village (13 miles north of Altun Ha).

◉ Sights

Altun Ha
RUINS

(www.nichbelize.org/altun-ha/; BZ$10; ☺8am-5pm) Altun Ha, the Maya ruins that have inspired Belikin beer labels and Belizean banknotes, stands 31 miles north of Belize City, off the Old Northern Hwy. While smaller and less imposing than some other Maya sites in the country, Altun Ha, with its immaculate central plaza, is still spectacular and well worth the short detour to get here.

The original site covered 1500 acres, but what visitors today see is the central ceremonial precinct of two plazas surrounded by temples.

The ruins were originally excavated in the 1960s and now look squeaky clean following a stabilization and conservation program from 2000 to 2004.

Altun Ha was a rich and important Maya trading and agricultural town with a population of 8000 to 10,000. It existed by at least 200 BC, perhaps even several centuries earlier, and flourished until the mysterious collapse of Classic Maya civilization around AD 900. Most of the temples date from around AD 550 to 650, though, like many Maya temples, most of them are composed of several layers, having been built over periodically in a series of renewals.

In Plaza A, structure A-1 is sometimes called the Temple of the Green Tomb. Deep within it was discovered the tomb of a priest-king dating from around AD 600. Tropical humidity had destroyed the garments of the king and the paper of the Maya 'painted book' buried with him, but many riches were intact: shell necklaces, pottery, pearls, stingray spines used in bloodletting rites, ceremonial flints and the nearly 300 jade objects (mostly small beads and pendants) that gave rise to the name Green Tomb.

The largest and most important temple is the Temple of the Masonry Altars (B-4) also known as the Temple of the Sun God. The restored structure you see dates from the first half of the 7th century AD and takes its name from altars on which copal was burned and beautifully carved jade pieces were smashed in sacrifice. This is the Maya temple that's likely to become most familiar during your Belizean travels, since it's the one depicted (in somewhat stylized form) on Belikin beer labels.

Excavation of the structure in 1968 revealed several priestly tombs. Most had been destroyed or desecrated, but one, tomb B-4/7 (inside the stone structure protruding from the upper steps of the broad central staircase), contained the remains of an elderly personage accompanied by numerous jade objects, including a unique 6in-tall carved head of Kinich Ahau, the Maya sun god – the largest well-carved jade object ever recovered from a Maya archaeological site. An illustration of the carving appears in the top-left corner of Belizean banknotes.

A path heading south from structure B-6 leads 600yd through the jungle to a broad pond that was the main reservoir of the ancient town.

At the entrance to the site there is a small museum featuring informative displays covering the history of Altun Ha and a full-scale model of the Kinich Ahau carving.

You can find licensed guides (BZ$20 per visitor) outside the museum building. While you don't need a guide to find your way around the site, their services are recommended as they can show you details you might otherwise miss.

Modern toilets, and drinks and souvenir stands are found near the ticket office, and the site has good wheelchair access.

Altun Ha

Ⓝ 0 ▬▬▬ 50 yds

Old Northern Hwy (2.4mi) ↑
Souvenir Ⓖ Shops
ⓘ Ticket Office
🏛 Museum
A-6
A-7
A-1 (Temple of the Green Tomb)
Plaza A
A-2
A-3
A-4
A-5
B-4 (Temple of the Masonry Altars)
B-1
Plaza B
B-2
B-3
B-5
B-6
Reservoir (0.3mi) ↘

ℹ Getting There & Away

Many tours run to Altun Ha from Belize City, Caye Caulker, or from San Pedro on Ambergris Caye.

To get here with your own vehicle, turn off the Philip Goldson Hwy 20 miles from Belize City at a junction signed 'Altun Ha,' then drive 11.5 miles along the newly paved Old Northern Hwy to Lucky Strike village, where another paved road heads off west to Altun Ha (2.4 miles).

Irregular buses serve Maskall from Belize City and will drop you at Lucky Strike. Heading back to the city, buses leave only in the early morning, so it makes a day trip to the ruins difficult. Traffic along the jungle-lined Old Northern Hwy tends to be light, so if you're hitchhiking prepare to wait.

WEST OF BELIZE CITY

Formerly the Western Hwy and still referred to as such by many locals, the George Price Hwy stretches from Belize City through the village of Hattieville, and on to Belmopan and Cayo District. This part of Belize District is mostly agricultural, offering wide vistas of farmland with glimpses of the Mountain Pine Ridge in the distance. At Hattieville, a good, paved road heads north through Burrell Boom to hook up with the Northern Hwy, which is an excellent way to avoid the city when driving around Belize District.

Old Belize

Located just 5 miles outside of Belize City, this strange museum and adventure park was designed to provide hurried cruise-ship tourists with a neatly encapsulated version of Belizean history and culture. Somebody soon realized that most cruisers were more interested in sun and fun, so they built a beach (with requisite restaurant and beach bar). As demand grew for more action, Old Belize added a giant water slide, a towering swing and a train ride through the museum.

If you are in Belize for one day (as most cruisers are), Old Belize is a place that you can sample a little bit of everything. If you

BELIZE DISTRICT OLD BELIZE

DON'T MISS

BELIZE CENTRAL PRISON

Only in a country as laid-back as Belize could a fully functioning prison also be considered a tourist attraction. It's the only prison in Belize (the name 'Hattieville' is to Belizeans what 'San Quentin' is to Americans) and, as such, it houses criminals of all stripes, from pickpockets to murderers. But don't come looking for some sort of American-style corporate-owned Supermax with imposing concrete walls topped with electrified razor ribbon. The 'Hattieville Ramada' (as it's called on the streets) looks more like a summer camp. Its main prison buildings are set back from the road and surrounded by farmland, where the prisoners work. So what makes the prison worth a visit?

Two words: gift shop. **Belize Central Prison** (Mile 2 Burrell Boom Rd, Hattieville; ⊙8am-3pm) has a gift shop that sells items from the reformatory's renowned woodshop. Inside the small shop (located on the road and outside of the actual prison itself) you'll find hand-carved walking sticks, traditional masks, religious icons such as crucifixes, statues depicting saints, a host of carved Jesus figures, and even beautifully crafted wooden doors. All items in the shop are meticulously crafted by the prisoners themselves from locally grown woods, including mahogany, teak and sandalwood. There's also a variety of smaller items, such as jewelry, cards, calendars, hammocks, clothing and other assorted knickknacks, all of which have been made by the prisoners.

This most unusual penal facility is part of the larger vision of an organization called the Kolbe Foundation, which took over the management of the once-notorious government prison and restructured it in a way that was more in line with the foundation's Christian philosophy. Rather than merely punishing criminals by sequestering them from society, the Kolbe approach focuses more on rehabilitation through education and development of skills. In addition to the various craft-making shops inside the prison, there are also a number of small-scale animal farms and gardening operations that supply some of the prison's food. One of the long-term goals of the foundation is for the prison to be self-sustainable; as such, all funds earned by gift-shop sales go back to the maintenance of the prison, meaning that your purchases directly assist in the rehabilitation of Belize's criminal element (who might otherwise wind up robbing you on your next visit to Belize).

happen to be here for longer, there are plenty of places where the history and culture, sun and fun, and action and adventure are more authentic and rewarding. You will, however, have to venture further than 5 miles outside of Belize City.

◉ Sights

Old Belize Exhibit   MUSEUM
(📱 222-4129; www.oldbelize.com; Mile 5 George Price Hwy; BZ$10; ⊘ 7:30am-4:30pm Tue-Fri, 9am-5pm Sat & Sun; P ♿) This is the original Old Belize, which manages to pack the country's entire ecological, archaeological, industrial and political history into a 15-minute mini-train ride through a museum. It starts in the rainforest, with reproductions of the tropical trees and limestone caves that you'll find (for real) just a few miles west. A Maya exhibit has reproductions of some temples and tombs, which you also might see (for real) just a few miles north of here.

The most interesting parts of the museum are the industry exhibits, which display some genuine artifacts, such as a sugarcane press and a steam-powered saw mill. There is also a reproduction of the interior of a Garifuna home, as well as a life-size model of a Belize Town street from the early 20th century.

Your trip through Old Belize ends at the gift shop, which is actually pretty well stocked with interesting knickknacks, including T-shirts, rum, chicle gum and Cuban cigars.

Kukumba Beach   BEACH
(📱 222-4129; www.oldbelize.com; Mile 5 George Price Hwy; BZ$20; ⊘ 7:30am-4:30pm Tue-Fri, 9am-5pm Sat & Sun) If you are desperate for some beach time but you can't leave the Belize City area, this artificial beach is not a terrible option. It's a 350ft stretch of sand dotted with thatched-roof huts surrounding an artificial lagoon. A massive waterslide – also known as Slippery Conch – drops from a 50ft platform into the lagoon and there is also a giant rope swing and a couple of water trampolines.

The friendly beach bar serves three fruity cocktails for the price of two, though they contain barely any alcohol. There are also showers and changing facilities.

Back in the 1950s this plot of land was owned by an American grower and trader, who exported all kinds of vegetables (including cucumbers) to the US. This port was used to package and load the produce-laden boats, and thus earned the name Kukumba Beach.

❶ Getting There & Away

Any westbound bus will drop you at the Old Belize entrance (BZ$2, 10 minutes from Belize City). A taxi will cost around BZ$30.

Monkey Bay

The Monkey Bay Wildlife Sanctuary stretches from the George Price Hwy to the Sibun River, encompassing tropical forest, savanna and riparian ecosystems while providing an important link in the biological corridor between coastal and inland Belize. Across the river is the remote Monkey Bay National Park, which together with the sanctuary creates a sizable forest corridor in the Sibun River Valley. The park and the sanctuary get their name from a bend in the river – called a 'bay' in Belize – noted for its resident black howler monkeys.

◉ Sights & Activities

Monkey Bay
Wildlife Sanctuary   WILDLIFE RESERVE
(📱 664-2731, 822-8032; www.monkeybaybelize.com; Mile 31.5 George Price Hwy; ⊘ 7am-5pm) 🍃 A natural, privately protected area just off one of the country's main highways, this 1070-acre wildlife sanctuary and environmental education center offers lodging and activities for casual travelers, as well as internship activities for those with a more long-term interest in Belize. A well-stocked library provides plenty of reference and reading matter on natural history and the country.

Activities center around the Sibun River, which attracts sweaty travelers (and other kinds of wildlife) to its inviting swimming hole. Around 250 bird species have been identified at the sanctuary. Larger wildlife, such as pumas, tapirs and coatimundi, have been spotted on the 2-mile track running down beside the sanctuary to the river. Guided jungle hikes from the lodge to the river cost BZ$55 for one to four visitors. Other activities include canoeing (BZ$122 per visitor) and trips to nearby Tiger Cave (BZ$142 per visitor). There are also guided birding hikes that vary in price.

In the dry season, guides take adventurers about 12 miles north to Cox Lagoon, which is home to jabiru storks, deer, tapir, black howlers and lots of crocodiles.

★ **Conservation Adventures**   KAYAKING
(📱 637-7406, in USA 503-512-0524; www.conservationadventures.wordpress.com; 2-day overnight trip

KAYAKING CLEAN-UPS

Kayaking down whitewater, surrounded by wildlife, is a rush like no other. And several years ago, naturalist Jes Karper began to wonder: why not pick up trash as you go? He's been paddling the rivers of Belize for two decades, but has recently turned his expertise towards a little something he likes to call Conservation Adventures.

The kayaking trips are fully customizable, with everything from tame, half-day trips down the Sibun River to white-water kayaking and overnight camping expeditions. The overnights can include jungle hammocks with bug nets and rain flys (or tents if the guests prefer them), along with masks, snorkels, drybags and cooking gear Jes uses to prepare the simple, healthy meals. These trips allow for excellent birdwatching and wildlife sighting in the early morning, and can also include paddling at sunset or under the full moon. The Sibun teems with toucans, egrets and kingfishers and howler monkeys can regularly be spotted.

In addition to collecting garbage on the rivers, Karper emphasizes environmental education on his trips, and his groups monitor the health of the riparian ecosystems they glide through. The operation is based west of Belize City, near the Monkey Bay Wildlife Sanctuary, but Conservation Adventures can guide you on rivers throughout the country. Discounts are available should guests opt for additional nights on the river or to bring their own camping equipment and food.

A six-hour trip down the Sibun River for 2/3-or-more people costs BZ$170/150 per person. An overnight camping trip for 2/3-or-more people is BZ$400/320 per person.

2/3-or-more people BZ$400/320 per person) Run by long-time expat, naturalist and paddling extraordinaire Jes Karper, these day and multi-day kayaking trips are notable for their emphasis on giving back while adventuring through some of Belize's most striking riparian environs. Trips involve education on the environment, cleaning up the river and monitoring its health.

Eli Miller WILDLIFE WATCHING
(☏ 625-3652; ell.miller41@gmail.com) An excellent licensed guide at Monkey Bay.

Tiger Cave CAVING
(per person BZ$142) This large, limestone cave on a private farm adjoining the Monkey Bay Wildlife Sanctuary can be explored on guided tours. The Mayan people once used it as a ceremonial cave, leaving pottery and sacrificial items, and it's also inhabited by false vampire bats, Yucatán banded geckos, tailless whip scorpions and more.

There's a relaxing 20-minute hike through the jungle to get to the cave.

🍽 Sleeping & Eating

Monkey Bay Wildlife Sanctuary LODGE **$**
(☏ 822-8032, 664-2731; www.monkeybaybelize.com; Mile 31.5 George Price Hwy; campsites per person BZ$22, bunkhouse per person BZ$60, r BZ$84, cabins BZ$190-240, 4-person houses BZ$175;

P ❄ @ 🛜 🛄) 🅿 Accommodations at the sanctuary range from camping out on raised platform decks to houses with full kitchens. All options have shared or private bathrooms with rainwater showers (some hot, some cold). It's a rustic but comfortable and affordable way to spend the night in the wild. There are also six private cabañas with views to the distant mountains.

The amenities demonstrate ecological principles in action, with biogas latrines (though there are also flush toilets) producing methane for cooking, rainwater catchment and partial solar energy. Buffet-style meals are served with advanced notice (breakfast BZ$24, lunch BZ$27, dinner BZ$30) and the lodge can cater to dietary restrictions and preferences.

Cheers AMERICAN, BELIZEAN **$$**
(☏ 822-8014; www.cheersrestaurantbelize.com; Mile 31.25 George Price Hwy; meals BZ$9-24; ⏰ 6am-8pm Mon-Sat, 7am-7pm Sun; P ❄) This large, airy and friendly restaurant serves hearty meals, including all-day breakfasts, roast-beef sandwiches and excellent Cuban tilapia. Naturally, rice, beans and stewed chicken are served as well. If you fancy spending the night, there are three simple but spacious cabañas (BZ$130) onsite convenient for an overnight if you are heading further west.

DON'T MISS

BELIZE ZOO

If most zoos are maximum-security wildlife prisons, then the **Belize Zoo** (☎625-3604, 822-8000; www.belizezoo.org; Mile 29 George Price Hwy; adult/child BZ$30/10; ⏰8:30am-5pm, last entry 4:15pm) is more like a halfway house for wild animals that can't make it on the outside. A must-visit on any trip to Belize District, the zoo has many animals you're unlikely to see elsewhere – several tapirs (a Belizean relative of the rhino) including a baby, *gibnuts*, a number of coatimundi (they look like a cross between a raccoon and a monkey), scarlet macaws, white-lipped peccaries, pumas and many others.

But what really sets Belize Zoo apart is that the zoo itself – and in some cases, even the enclosures of individual animals – are relatively porous. This means that the wildlife you'll see inside enclosures are outnumbered by creatures who have come in from the surrounding jungle to hang out, eat, or – just maybe – swap tales with incarcerated brethren.

Among the animals you'll see wandering the grounds (aka 'free runners') are Central American agoutis (also called bush rabbits), huge iguanas, snakes, raccoons, squirrels and jungle birds of all sorts.Take a night tour (one of the best ways to experience Belize Zoo, as many of the animals are nocturnal) and you'll be just as likely to see a *gibnut* outside enclosures as in. You'll also be able to hear ongoing long-distance conversations between the zoo's resident black howler monkeys and their wild relatives just a few miles away.

The story of the Belize Zoo began with filmmaker Richard Foster, who shot a wildlife documentary entitled *Path of the Raingods* in Belize in the early 1980s. Sharon Matola – a Baltimore-born biologist, former circus performer and former US Air Force survival instructor – was hired to take care of the animals. By the time filming was complete, the animals had become partly tame and Matola was left wondering what to do with her 17 charges. So she founded the Belize Zoo, which displays native Belizean wildlife in natural surroundings on 29-acre grounds. From these beginnings, the zoo has grown to provide homes for animals endemic to the region that have been injured, orphaned at a young age or bred in captivity and donated from other zoos.

Many of the animals in Belize Zoo are rescue cases, that is, wild animals that were kept as pets by individual collectors. The zoo makes every attempt to recondition such animals for a return to the wild, but only when such a return is feasible. In cases where return is impossible (as is the case with most of the zoo's jungle cats, who have long since forgotten how to hunt, or never learned in the first place), they remain in the zoo: perhaps not the best life for a wildcat, but better than winding up in some closet.

Sleeping

Savanna Guest House (☎615-6884; www.belizesavannaguesthouse.com; Mile 28.5 George Price Hwy; r incl breakfast BZ$154; 📶) Opened by Richard and Carol Foster, the naturalist filmmaker couple whose productions led to the creation of the original Belize Zoo, Savanna Guesthouse is a fascinating place to stay that sits on the site of the original animal exhibits where it all began. There are just three comfortable rooms, boasting lovely hardwood floors and opening out onto a screened balcony.

While the accommodations are top-notch, perhaps the best reason to choose Savanna is the fascinating hosts who attend their clients with a personal touch. Take a guided walk along the private nature trail, head into the studio to observe first-hand how nature documentaries are made, or just relax and enjoy their amazing tales of jungle shoots in far-flung places.

Tropical Education Center (☎625-8330; tec@belizezoo.org; Mile 29 George Price Hwy; campsites per person BZ$17, dm/s/d incl 2 meals BZ$70/120/150, guesthouses incl 2 meals s/d BZ$141/173; P 📶) Run by the Belize Zoo, these rural lodgings are set on 84 acres of tropical savanna with lush gardens and plenty of wildlife. Sleeping options run from dorm-style private rooms – you'll only share with those in your group – in the 'Savannah Castle' to neat, wooden forest cabañas on stilts.

🍷 Drinking & Nightlife

Lil Texas BAR

(📋 610-9691; Mile 31.75 George Price Hwy; mains BZ$11-24; ⏱ 8am-late) Lil Texas is the region's drinking hole of choice. It also serves American and Belizean cuisine in a distinctly Belizean setting – a mosquito-screened *palapa* house – drenched in pure American whimsy. The walls are covered in kitschy signs and bumper stickers, and there's a country music soundtrack.

Specialties include BBQ pork ribs (with 10 different sauces), as well as a couple of veggie options.

ℹ Getting There & Away

Any non-express bus doing the Belize City–Belmopan run will drop you at the sanctuary turnoff (around 220yd from the main entrance) or at Cheers (BZ$6, 50 minutes from Belize City).

ALONG THE COASTAL ROAD

The Coastal Rd – also known as the Manatee Hwy – heads south from the George Price Hwy, and runs parallel to the coast (appropriately enough) for 36 miles to the town of Dangriga. The Coastal Rd is dirt, which means it is slow going at the best of times, and sometimes impassable during the rainy season. Some car-rental companies advise against driving on the Coastal Rd, which is not really 'a shortcut to Placencia' as it is sometimes called.

ℹ Getting There & Away

There is no longer any bus service along the Coastal Rd so if you want to explore the area you'll need your own wheels. Bear in mind that many rental companies prohibit their vehicles from using this route, so check before heading out.

It's also possible to get to the region by boat charter from Belize City.

Gales Point

POP 350

There's off-the-beaten track, way-off-the-beaten track and then there's Gales Point, a village founded around 1800 by runaway slaves from Belize City. The traditional Creole enclave sits on a narrow peninsula that juts out about 3 miles into the Southern Lagoon, one of a series of interconnected lakes and waterways between Belize City and Dangriga. To the west, jungle-clad limestone hills rise above the plains, and to the east, a narrow stretch of forest and mangrove swamp separate the lagoon from the Caribbean Sea.

The striking natural beauty has long attracted intrepid travelers and nature enthusiasts. Gales Point is home to the highest concentration of West Indian manatees in the Caribbean, and the nearby beaches are Belize's primary breeding ground for hawksbill turtles. The 14-sq-mile Gales Point Wildlife Sanctuary offers some of the most amazing birdwatching opportunities in the country.

🏃 Activities

Nature tours bring most visitors to Gales Point, and for the majority of these you'll need to hire a guide with a boat; all accommodations can set you up with one (your hosts will certainly be able to connect you with a guide, if they aren't guides themselves). In addition to fishing, the lagoons surrounding Gales Point are specifically noted for birding, turtling and, of course, manateeing.

Visitors can also kayak the lagoon from Manatee Lodge. It's complimentary for guests and BZ$50 for non-guests.

Manatee-watching

Manatees graze on sea grass in the shallow, brackish Southern Lagoon, hanging out around the **Manatee Hole**, a depression in the lagoon floor near its east side that is fed by a warm freshwater spring. The manatees rise about every 20 minutes for air, allowing spectators views of their heads and sometimes their backs and tails. A 1½-hour manatee-watching boat trip costs around BZ$150 depending on group size. Manatee-watching can also be combined with other activities. (Swimming with the manatees is no longer permitted.)

Turtle-watching

Around 100 hawksbill turtles, which are protected in Belize, as well as loggerheads, which aren't, lay their eggs on the 21-mile beach that straddles the mouth of the Bar River, which connects the Southern Lagoon to the sea. For both species, this is one of the main nesting sites in the country. Turtle-watch outings (BZ$350 for up to four guests) involve a boat trip down the river, then a 4-mile nocturnal beach walk to look for nesting turtles. Note that this trip can be physically challenging, and the turtles can be elusive.

Birdwatching

In the Northern Lagoon, about 45 minutes from Gales Point by boat, is **Bird Caye**, a small island that is home to many waterfowl, including frigate birds, great egrets and toucans. It's possible to visit here on a combined trip with the Manatee Hole for around BZ$400. There are some other great birding spots closer to Gales Point, which can also be visited on the tour.

Fishing

Large tarpon quite often break the surface of the Southern Lagoon. You can also fish for snook, snapper, jack and barracuda in the lagoon and rivers. A half-/full day trip for up to three people costs around BZ$700/900.

🛌 Sleeping

Apart from one reasonably comfortable lodge, accommodations in Gales Point are very basic. Don't expect much more than four semisolid walls and a mattress.

Yellow Bell Guesthouse GUESTHOUSE **$**
(☑ 662-4649, 661-3094; r BZ$50) In front of the school near the entrance to town, Yellow Bell is the most comfortable of the cheapies. It offers homey rooms complete with worn rugs in a cute wooden house with yellow trim. Owner John Moore offers a variety of tours in his boat, including birdwatching, turtle-spotting and of course manatee observation (BZ$120 to BZ$160).

He's a self-described 'King of Tarpon' and also leads fishing trips in the Southern Lagoon and nearby rivers (half-/full day BZ$400/700).

Gentle's Cool Spot CABIN **$**
(☑ 665-5667, 668-0102; d/tr BZ$45/60; ▣) A quarter of a mile south of the tip of Gales Point, the accommodations includes three small rooms with cold-water showers, double beds, tiny windows and little else. Ms Gentle also does Creole meals (BZ$7) and hair braiding for BZ$40. Anyone with hair long enough to braid and an hour to kill is welcome.

Mr Gentle no longer runs tours himself, but they can organize trips with other local boat owners.

Ionie's B&B CABIN **$**
(☑ 245-8066, 651-5168; r BZ$25-35) A mile south of the tip of Gales Point, this B&B is run by friendly Ionie Samuels (also a justice of the peace, if you've got matrimony in mind). This house on stilts has dingy, simple rooms, fans and shared bathrooms with cold showers. Good-sized Belizean meals for under BZ$10.

★ Manatee Lodge HOTEL **$$**
(☑ 663-8870, 532-2400; www.manateelodge.com; r BZ$170, incl all meals BZ$260; ▣ 🛜) The only midpriced lodge in the area, Nancy Bailey's Manatee Lodge takes up the tip of the Gales Point peninsula and is situated in a beautiful garden surrounded on three sides by the Southern Lagoon. The eight rooms, spread over two floors, are spacious and comfortable, with bathtubs and lots of varnished wood.

There is a large sitting-reading room with a lovely, breezy veranda that overlooks the lagoon. There is also a dining room for guests of the lodge. The lodge is most popular with groups, individual travelers, nature lovers and fishermen. A wide range of activities is on offer, including basketball, volleyball and complimentary kayaks.

❶ Getting There & Away

Getting to Gales Point can be quite a mission. The village is located about 1 mile off the Coastal Rd; the turnoff is 22 miles off the George Price Hwy and 14 miles from the Hummingbird Hwy.

CAR

The Coastal Rd and the road into the village are unpaved and in fairly poor condition and some car-rental companies prohibit driving the route – check before you sign up. The village may be accessible in a normal car during the dry season. In the rainy season, the road floods and a 4WD is essential to avoid getting stuck in the mud.

BOAT

The best way to travel to or from Gales Point for those who can afford it is by boat via a network of rivers, canals and lagoons stretching from Belize City. The trip takes about two hours, and costs around BZ$500 for up to four people. Arrangements can be made through the Manatee Lodge.

BUS

There are no longer regularly scheduled buses to Gales Point.

Northern Cayes

Best Places to Eat

➡ Hidden Treasure (p106), San Pedro

➡ Hibisca by Habaneros (p126), Caye Caulker

➡ Wild Mango's (p106), San Pedro

➡ Robin's Kitchen (p106), Ambergris Caye

➡ Il Pellicano (p126), Caye Caulker

Best Places to Stay

➡ Matachica Beach Resort (p101), Ambergris Caye

➡ Jungle Cocoon (p121), Caye Caulker

➡ Ak'bol Yoga Resort (p101), Ambergris Caye

➡ Sea Dreams Hotel (p122), Caye Caulker

➡ Caye Casa (p98), San Pedro

Why Go?

Daydream a little. Conjure up your ultimate tropical island fantasy. With more than 100 enticing isles and two amazing atolls, chances are that one of Belize's northern cays can match this dream and make it a reality.

If you imagined stringing up a hammock on a deserted beach, there is an outer atoll with your name on it. Pining to be pampered? You can choose from an ever-growing glut of ritzy resorts on Ambergris Caye. San Pedro is prime for dancing the night away to a reggae beat, while Caye Caulker moves at a slower pace.

But the islands are only the beginning: only a few miles offshore, the Belize Barrier Reef flourishes for 190 awe-inspiring miles, offering unparalleled opportunities to explore canyons and coral, to come mask to snout with nurse sharks and stingrays, and to swim with schools of fish painted every color of the palette.

When to Go

Dec–Apr Peak tourist season, with warm, wonderful weather and much higher prices for accommodations.

Jun–Jul Opening of lobster season, which is celebrated with much fanfare on Ambergris and Caye Caulker.

Aug San Pedro holds Belize's biggest street party, the International Costa Maya Festival.

Northern Cayes Highlights

1 Ambergris Caye (p85) Availing yourself of the amazing aquatic activities – from sailing and paddleboarding to snorkeling and diving.

2 Caye Caulker (p112) Relaxing in a hammock or at the beach, resetting your internal clock to the island's languid rhythms.

3 Lighthouse Reef (p129) Descending into the darkness of the Blue Hole Natural Monument and exploring the nearby reefs and swim-throughs.

4 Shark Ray Alley (p91) Snorkeling alongside a wriggling pile of nurse sharks and stingrays.

5 Half Moon Caye (p131) Spying a rare red-footed booby on this castaway-cool cay.

6 Secret Beach (p104) Golf-cart adventuring to the island's new paradise, and bringing floaties for the tranquil turquoise water.

7 Swallow Caye Wildlife Sanctuary (p113) Catching sight of a West Indian manatee hovering in shallow waters.

8 Caye Caulker Forest Reserve (p112) Kayaking into the wilderness to investigate the impressive birdlife.

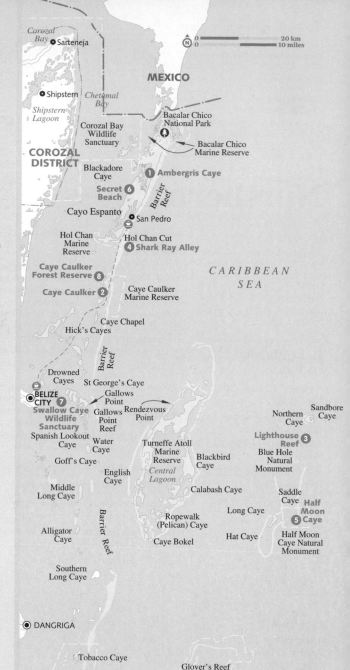

ℹ️ Getting There & Away

Flights usually serve San Pedro (on Ambergris Caye) and Caye Caulker, connecting them to each other, Belize City, Orange Walk, Belmopan, San Ignacio and Corozal, near the Mexican border. The airport on Caye Caulker was undergoing maintenance during research but was set to reopen late 2018, and Northern Caye's (Lighthouse Reef) airstrip was also out of service.

Regular passenger boats go from Belize City to San Pedro, and to Caye Caulker. No scheduled boats run to/from the outer islands, but most of the lodges located there provide transportation for their guests.

AMBERGRIS CAYE

POP 16,444

The undisputed superstar of Belize's tourism industry, 'La Isla Bonita,' strikes an impressive and perhaps even magical balance of large-scale tourism development with a fun, laid-back atmosphere. Sure it gets busy – especially in high season when a procession of golf carts clogs the narrow streets of the main town, San Pedro – but it's still the kind of place where it's acceptable to hold up traffic while you greet an old acquaintance.

Complaints about over-development aside, Ambergris Caye remains an archetypal tropical paradise where sun-drenched days are filled with fruity drinks and water sports. There are plenty of simple pleasures to be had, from riding a bike along a windswept beach path to wading in crystal clear waters. And the island's most valuable asset, the flourishing barrier reef a half-mile offshore, is the epicenter of the country's snorkeling and diving industries and the source of its most imaginative culinary scene.

History

Once the southern tip of the Yucatán Peninsula, Ambergris Caye was an important Maya trading post. Around 1500 years ago, in order to open up a better trade route between the Yucatán coast and mainland Belize, the Maya dug the narrow channel at Bacalar Chico that now separates Ambergris from Mexico.

As with their counterparts on the mainland, the local Maya inhabitants gradually retreated to the bush as contact with the Europeans became more frequent. Whalers in the 17th century probably gave the island its current name, which derives from the waxy gray substance used in perfume production that comes from the intestines of sperm whales. According to folklore, British, French and Dutch pirates used the island's many coves as hideouts when ambushing Spanish ships, so they may also be responsible for the title. Treasure troves have been discovered on the island, and gold coins and old bottles have been washed ashore – all evidence of pirates using the island for its fresh water, abundant resources and hidden coves. These swashbucklers turned into mainland loggers who partly depended on manatees and turtles from the northern cays for their survival.

Ambergris Caye was not significantly populated until the War of the Castes, when the war in the Yucatán first forced *mestizos*, and then Maya, across Bacalar Chico and onto the island. The town of San Pedro (named for Peter, the patron saint of fishermen) was founded in 1848.

Ownership of the island was bandied about between a group of wealthy British mainlanders. Finally, in 1869, James Hume Blake purchased the land for US$625 with the gold of his wife, Antonia Andrade, a rich Spanish refugee widow from the Yucatán. The Blake family converted much of the island to a coconut plantation, conscripting many of the islanders to work the land.

The coconut business thrived for less than a century. By the 1950s it had been all but destroyed by a series of hurricanes. In the 1960s, the Belize government forced a purchase of Ambergris Caye and redistributed the land to the islanders.

While the coconut industry declined, the island's lobster industry began to develop. The market for these crustaceans skyrocketed once refrigerated ships came to the island. San Pedro lobster catchers formed cooperatives and built a freezer plant on their island.

Perhaps inevitably, the waters close to Ambergris Caye were overfished. Fisherfolk looked to supplement their incomes by acting as tour, fishing and dive guides for the smattering of travelers who visited the island. Today, lobster stocks have partly recovered with the aid of size limits and an annual closed season, but tourism and real estate are the booming businesses on Ambergris.

◉ Sights

Bacalar Chico National Park & Marine Reserve

NATIONAL PARK

(day admission BZ$10) 🏞️ At the northern tip of Ambergris Caye, Bacalar Chico is a Unesco World Heritage Site made up of 41 sq miles of protected land and sea, accessible

Ambergris Caye

Back on the water, tour boats make snorkeling stops and motor through an ancient channel that was dug by seafaring Maya about 1500 years ago. Today the narrow channel separates Ambergris Caye from the Mexican mainland.

The coral is extra colorful around the reserve, as there is significantly less damage from boats and tourists. Besides the bountiful fish, there's a chance of seeing manatees, as well as green and loggerhead turtles. If the waters are calm, some tour boats go to Rocky Point, notable as one of the only places in the world where land meets reef.

The return trip hugs the east side of the island, and some boats make a final snorkeling stop at Mexico Rocks. Not all tour operators run trips to Bacalar Chico, due to the long travel distance, but Seaduced by Belize (p92) and Searious Adventures (p90) are two reliable options.

★ **Hol Chan Marine Reserve**   DIVE SITE
(☎ 226-2247; www.holchanmarinereserve.org; national park admission BZ$20) ✦ At the southern tip of Ambergris, the 6.5-sq-mile Hol Chan Marine Reserve is probably Belize's most oft-visited diving and snorkeling site. It offers spectacular coral formations, plus an abundance and diversity of marine life – not to mention its proximity to the cays. Hol Chan is Mayan for 'Little Channel,' which refers to a break in the reef known as Hol Chan Cut. The channel walls are covered with colorful corals, which support an amazing variety of fish life, including moray eels and black groupers.

Although the reef is the primary attraction of Hol Chan, the marine reserve also includes sea-grass beds and mangroves. The sea grass provides a habitat for nurse sharks and southern stingrays, which lend their name to Shark Ray Alley (p91). Snorkelers have the chance to get up close to both species, due mainly to the fact that the animals are used to getting fed by tour boats.

All dive operators and nautical tours offer trips to Hol Chan. For information and displays on marine life, visit the Hol Chan Visitors Center (p110).

House of Culture   CULTURAL CENTER
(Map p96; ☎ 226-5100; Almond St; ☉ 9am-5pm Mon-Fri) **FREE** Find out more about the fascinating culture found in San Pedro at this cultural center near the football field. Frequently changing displays celebrate local traditions and events such as Día de Muertos and Garifuna Settlement Day.

only via an hour-long boat ride from San Pedro. Upon arrival, visitors check in at the San Juan ranger station, where there is a small museum showcasing Mayan artifacts, and 11 miles of nature trails. Although sightings are infrequent, the area is home to crocodiles, white-tail deer, ocelots, pumas and jaguars.

Map labels:
0 — 1 km / 0 — 0.5 miles
Rojo Beach Bar (0.8mi); Matachica Beach Resort (0.9mi); Portofino Resort (1.7mi); X'tan Ha (3mi); Secret Beach (5mi)
Mexico Rocks (1mi)
Buena Vista Point
North Island
Water Taxi
Barrier Reef
San Pedro River
San Pedro Lagoon
See Central San Pedro Map (p96)
Coconut Dr
Entrada San Pedro
South Island
Sea Grape Dr
Hol Chan Marine Reserve (1.5mi)

Ambergris Caye

🏃 Activities

If you're into water sports, you'll be in ecstasy on Ambergris. San Pedro is awash with tour companies and individuals organizing scuba diving, snorkeling, windsurfing, sailing, kitesurfing, swimming and fishing trips.

Diving

Many hotels have their own dive shops that rent equipment, provide instruction and organize diving excursions. Numerous dive sites are within a 10- to 15-minute boat trip from San Pedro. Among the most popular (and affordable) is Hol Chan Marine Reserve, south of the island, and **Esmeralda** (Map p86) in front of the school.

Quoted prices sometimes don't include admission to the marine reserves, which is BZ$20 for Hol Chan, BZ$20 for Half Moon Caye (p131) and BZ$60 for the Blue Hole (p130). Many companies also quote prices without including equipment hire so make sure you confirm what is included.

A one-tank local dive including gear costs from BZ$100 to BZ$150; with two tanks it's from BZ$150 to BZ$200. Night dives are BZ$120 to BZ$140, including a headlamp. Three-day open-water dive courses cost about BZ$1100, including equipment. E-learning courses, which allow you to do the reading and tests online before your trip, have gotten popular, and cost around BZ$750 (plus the online course fees). A one-day Discover Scuba Diving course (offered by most of the dive shops) costs around BZ$320.

Day trips further afield to the Blue Hole and Lighthouse Reef (p129) (three dives) including park fees cost around BZ$700 while Turneffe trips (three dives) cost from BZ$500 to BZ$700.

There are lots of independent dive operators around town, many of whom also run snorkeling and even mainland tours. Prices are fairly similar but quality varies wildly; diving here is a big investment so it's worth shopping around and spending a little extra if necessary to go with a crew you're comfortable with.

★ Ecologic Divers   DIVING

(Map p96; ☑ 226-4118; www.ecologicdivers.com; 1-/2-/3-tank dives BZ$112/180/247) 🏊 High-end dive shop with great customer service and solid environmental credentials. It offers all the local dives, fishing expeditions and boat cruises. Management promises small groups, with one dive master to every six divers on all immersions. Also recommended for dive courses.

Packages to the Blue Hole including breakfast, lunch, drinks and park admission fees run at BZ$697 while Turneffe Atoll trips are BZ$540.

★ Neptune's Cove   DIVING

(Map p86; ☑ 652-3568, in USA & Canada 877-913-3364; www.neptunescovebelize.com; Corona del Mar dock; snorkeling trips from BZ$110, 2-tank dive from BZ$180, half-day reef fishing from BZ$600) Top-notch dive and snorkel shop that offers highly personalized experiences with knowledgeable local guides. Offers undersea adventures around the island and beyond, along with scuba certification courses, reef fishing and mainland tours. Specializes in smaller groups.

Belize Pro Dive Center   DIVING

(Map p86; ☑ 226-2092; www.belizeprodivecenter. com; Banyan Bay pier; 1-/2-tank dive BZ$101/169; ☺ 7am-6pm) Professionally run dive shop with two-tank reef dives and Hol Chan trips departing every morning, as well as offshore dives and dive courses.

Amigos del Mar Dive Shop   DIVING

(Map p96; ☑ 226-2706, in USA 800-882-6159; www.amigosdive.com; 1-/2-tank BZ$150/210) The island's largest scuba diving operation runs two local trips each day, one departing at 9am and another at 1:30pm. It also runs regular trips to the Blue Hole and Turneffe Atoll, as long as 10 people sign up.

Chuck and Robbie's   DIVING, SNORKELING

(Map p86; ☑ 226-4425; www.ambergriscayediving. com; Boca del Rio Dr; 1-/2-tank dive BZ$130/190, snorkeling BZ$100) A very popular dive shop with personalized attention and friendly staff who are serious about both safety and diver enjoyment. Also runs recommended snorkeling trips to sites all over the reef.

SeaStar Belize   DIVING

(Map p86; ☑ 226-3365; http://seastarbelize.com; Dive Bar; ☺ 7am-5pm) A boutique dive shop catering to groups and offering customized experiences, with occasional overnight diving and fishing trips to distant cays. When the diving is over, the boozing begins, and it often continues back at the Dive Bar (p108; which is under the same excellent ownership).

Scuba School Belize   DIVING

(Map p96; ☑ 226-2886; www.scubaschoolbelize. com; San Pedro Holiday Hotel dock; 1-/2-tank dive BZ$150/185) This center specializes in diver training and gets excellent reviews from newbies for the staff's patient and careful approach. Also on offer is a full range of dive and snorkel trips on the reef. An open-water course costs BZ$606, and an e-learning course is BZ$433.

Belize Diving Adventures   DIVING

(Map p86; ☑ 226-3082; www.belizediving adventures.net; ☺ 8am-5pm) Offers dive trips to the Blue Hole for BZ$695 (not including the BZ$80 park fee) and single-/ double-/triple-tank dives (including gear) for BZ$142/202/272. Discounted multi-day dive packages to various sites around the reef are a good deal. Fishing and land tours also available.

Ambergris Divers   DIVING

(Map p96; ☑ 226-2634; www.ambergrisdivers.com) This experienced local operator has three offices, with the main one located on a dock just east of Wahoo's Lounge. It runs trips all over the local reef and also to the offshore atolls. Two-tank dives run from BZ$150 to BZ$180 depending on gear rental and destinations, while Blue Hole trips are BZ$700.

Reef Adventures   DIVING

(Map p86; ☑ 226-2538; www.reefadventures .net; Wet Willy's Dock; 1-/2-/3-tank dives BZ$160/ 200/270) A friendly and laid-back dive shop specializing in diving and snorkeling trips to sites around the local reef. It runs snorkel trips (including gear and park fees) for BZ$100 and night dives for BZ$200 per person, and also offers fishing excursions (BZ$250 per person).

Island Divers Belize   DIVING

(Map p86; ☑ 226-4800; www.belizeislanddivers. com; Boca del Rio Dr; 1-/2-tank dive BZ$100/170)

LOCAL KNOWLEDGE

VOLUNTEERING ON THE NORTHERN CAYES

With two field operations in the Northern Cayes, the reputable, conservation-oriented **Oceanic Society** (☎ in USA 800-326-7491; www.oceanicsociety.org; St. George's Caye; family education program per person BZ$5000, voluntourism/snorkeling program per person BZ$6400) is a wonderful conduit for not only encountering marine creatures, but also studying them and giving a little something back.

The NGO has been running education and volunteer projects in Belize since 1991, though the programs are constantly evolving. Currently, there are two distinct opportunities for week-long experiences that occur several times throughout the year: an eco-snorkeling program on the Turneffe Atoll, and a student and family volunteer program based at the NGO's field station on St George's Caye.

At St George's Caye, visiting families and students are part of a research program that includes monitoring manatees, dolphins and sea turtles, as well as coral reef health and conch populations. The family program is available over a week (or two, if there's a demand) in August, and student groups are welcomed in May, June and November. Accommodations are rustic and dormitory-style, with each fan-cooled unit containing three bunk beds and a bathroom. All meals and research boat trips are included. Discounts are available for family groups with children under 16.

At the Turneffe Atoll, visitors take part in week-long, educational snorkeling tours in November, January and February. These include lectures on fish identification, coral reefs, and the effect of climate change on sea life. Biologists who specialize in sea turtles and marine mammals make presentations, and there's an included trip to the Blue Hole and Half Moon Caye. Lodgings at the wonderful Turneffe Flats Lodge (p129), meals, transport, guides and activities are all included, but gratuities and the Blue Hole/Half Moon Caye admission fee (BZ$80) are not.

With all programs, the Oceanic Society can arrange for trip extensions involving land-based tours such as jungle hikes, birdwatching, canoeing and visits to Mayan ruins. These can be customized based on your budget.

This knowledgeable and well-organized local dive outfit will tailor dives to individual client interests.

Ramon's Dive Shop   DIVING
(Map p96; ☎ 226-2071; www.ramons.com; Coconut Dr, Ramon's Village; 1-/2-tank BZ$112/180) One of the biggest dive shops on the island, this is a good place to arrange offshore dives as it usually has the numbers to get regular trips going. It also has snorkeling, fishing trips and Blue Hole excursions.

Snorkeling

The most popular destinations for snorkeling excursions include Hol Chan Marine Reserve (p86) and Shark Ray Alley (p91; BZ$90 including park fee) or Mexico Rocks (p90) and Tres Cocos (p90; BZ$100). Snorkeling operators usually offer two daily half-day trips (three hours, two snorkel stops), departing at 9am and 2pm.

Full-day snorkeling trips that run out to Bacalar Chico (p85) at the northern tip of Ambergris (six hours, three stops) go for around BZ$200.

Many dive boats take snorkelers along if they have room, but snorkelers sometimes get lost in the shuffle on dive boats, so you are better off joining a dedicated snorkel tour whenever possible. Unfortunately, snorkel tours do not often run to Blue Hole, so if you have your heart set on snorkeling around the edge of this World Heritage Site, you'll have to tag along with the divers.

Do not attempt to swim out to the reef from the island as fast boats are unlikely to spot you in the water. You can snorkel around a number of docks around San Pedro including the one at Ramon's Village, but do not venture out beyond the buoys. The docks do not support the extensive life that the reef does, but the snorkeling is free of charge.

Grumpy and Happy   SNORKELING
(☎ 226-3420, in USA 888-273-9226; www.grumpy andhappy.com) If you want to enjoy your time with the fish – without having to make conversation with other people – sign up with this husband-wife team who offer private, custom snorkel trips. They cater to

AROUND AMBERGRIS: WHERE TO DIVE & SNORKEL

Mexico Rocks

This snorkeling site (national park admission BZ$20), 15 minutes from San Pedro and with a maximum depth of just 8ft, is a unique patch of reef towards the northern end of the island. Visitors will enjoy the shallow cluster of corals, including the *Montastrea annularis* corals, which are unique to the Northern Shelf Lagoon. Many small invertebrates inhabit the turtle grass and coral heads, while abundant fish life includes grouper, snapper, grunts, filefish and more. Mexico Rocks was declared a marine park in 2015, and a BZ$20 park fee was introduced.

Boca del Rio (Christ of the Abyss)

The underwater terrain at Boca del Rio (Map p86), a half-mile northeast of San Pedro, is a spur-and-groove system, featuring rolling coral hills and sandy channels. This is one of the few sites with healthy staghorn coral as well as plate corals. Around 90ft, there are big coral heads, barrels and tubes, and turtles are often spotted here. A short swim away is a statue of St Peter that resembles Jesus, which gives this site its alternative name, 'Christ of the Abyss.'

Tres Cocos

Tres Cocos (Map p86) is a bit deeper than most dive sites around San Pedro, with coral heads rising up to 50ft and a wall with spurs that spill out from 90ft to 120ft, but there's also a shallow snorkeling area nearby. The marine life here is wonderful, with a thick growth of star corals, big plating corals, red rope sponges and soft sea whips, and gorgonians on the upper reaches of the spurs. The place is renowned for shoals of schooling fish, including snapper, horse-eye jack and spotted eagle rays.

Tackle Box Canyons

Located about a mile offshore from downtown San Pedro, this great site (Map p86) offers big, steep coral grooves. There are swim-throughs in many places along the drop-off on the way to the outer reef. Gray angels, redband and stoplight parrotfish, and blue chromis hang out along the outer wall, and it's not uncommon to spot marine turtles here.

special-needs snorkelers with prescription masks and easy-to-climb ladders. There is no storefront, so make arrangements by phone or online.

They also do private tours to Mayan ruins and caves on the mainland.

Searious Adventures SNORKELING, SAILING (Map p96; ☑ 636-3001, 226-4202; www.searious adventuresbelize.com) A long-running and respected outfit that offers a variety of adventures on the water and on the mainland. Combine snorkeling and sailing with the catamaran snorkel tour (BZ$146) which includes three snorkeling stops and a remote BBQ on the way from San Pedro town to Mexico Rocks.

Wildlife-watching

The most reliable offshore manatee-watching is off Swallow Caye (p113) near Belize City. Being a marine reserve, visitors are not permitted to enter the water and you'll spend the visit watching the animals surface.

Tours from Ambergris Caye usually include a lunch and snorkel stop, in addition to a cruise through the manatee habitat. This trip is slightly cheaper (and travel times are shorter) from Caye Caulker, where folk are also working on manatee conservation.

The all-day tour with Searious Adventures includes lunch and two snorkel stops, as well as a viewing of the manatees at Swallow Caye. The BZ$180 fee does not include park fees (adult BZ$10, child BZ$5).

With Seaduced by Belize (p92), you can see the manatees at Swallow Caye, have lunch at Goff's Caye (p56), feast at a beach BBQ and snorkel at Coral Gardens all for BZ$210.

When conditions are favorable, it's also possible to spot manatees frolicking in the channel between San Pedro and Caye Caulker. Here it's permitted to dive in and snorkel

Tuffy Canyons

Tuffy Canyons (Map p86), about 1.6 miles south of San Pedro, is marked by deep grooves and a long, narrow tunnel. This high-walled passage leads to an opening at 80ft to 90ft onto the reef drop-off. Look for some attractive sponges in the deeper reaches, and the occasional eagle ray or dolphin pod passing by. Marauding nurse sharks hang around the entire dive.

Cypress Garden

Due to chumming, this San Pedro **dive site** (Map p86) was once the spot to see nurse sharks and grouper. The feedings have stopped and the fish have moved elsewhere, but the site remains worthwhile for its pronounced undercuts that provide habitat for arrow crabs and shrimps, as well as drums of all sizes. The coral growth here includes flower coral, thin leaf lettuce coral and some rare pillar coral. There are also some good swim-throughs nearby.

Hol Chan Canyons

Four miles south of San Pedro, this site, part of the Hol Chan Marine Reserve, is famous for its dramatic canyons and ample sea life, including eagle rays, stingrays and shoaling schools of fish. The canyons are lined with large coral, which hides black snapper, chubs, schoolmasters and mutton snappers, as well as moray eels and channel crabs. Yellowtails are ubiquitous, but you might also spot tarpon. The dive maxes out at about 70ft.

Shark Ray Alley

Only snorkeling is allowed at this perennially popular spot, which is in a shallow part of the Hol Chan Marine Reserve. Shark Ray Alley was traditionally a place for local fishers to clean fish, and the creatures attracted to the fish guts soon became a tourist attraction. As the name implies, the area is known for the big southern stingrays and mooching nurse sharks that come right up to the boat when it first arrives. Horse-eye jacks also abound.

Esmerelda

Right in front of the town school, this 50ft to 75ft dive features a spectacular series of deep canyons covered with flourishing soft corals. There is an amazing variety of marine life in the area, including grouper, dolphins, nurse sharks, moray eels and eagle rays, not to mention an astonishing array of tropical fish.

alongside the animals. Local snorkel guides will know if there are any around and can organize trips to see them.

Swimming

Although there are some sandy beaches around the island, especially in front of big hotels, which truck in sand to furnish their waterfronts, San Pedro is not a classic Caribbean swim-from-the-shore destination. Sea grass at the water line makes entering from the sand unpleasant, so you'll mostly be swimming from piers in waters protected by the reef.

When you do this, watch carefully for boats: there's plenty to see down under if you snorkel, but you often can't see or hear if a boat is coming your way. Have someone look out for you.

Secret Beach (p104) is a wonderful place to swim, but it's quite a trek from San Pedro, while Ramon's Village Pier (p98) is the best spot in town. The further north or south you go on the island, the fewer people there are on the piers.

All beaches are public and most waterside hotels are generous with their deck chairs, but a proprietorial air is developing about the piers, which are also supposed to be public.

Fishing

San Pedro draws fishing enthusiasts who are anxious to take a crack at Belize's classic tarpon flats, which cover over 200 sq miles. The ultimate angling accomplishment is the Grand Slam: catching bonefish, permit (best from March to May) and tarpon (best from May to September) all in one day. In the reef, fishers get bites from barracuda, snapper, jacks and grouper.

Deep-sea fishing is less of a drawcard; most people are here for the reef. There are, however, stories of giant marlin caught out in the deep beyond.

Fishing is mostly on a catch-and-release basis, but your fishing guide might clean and cut your catch if you intend to eat it. In addition to fishing specialists, some of the dive shops also offer fishing trips.

Go Fish Belize FISHING
(Map p86; ☑ 226-3121, 636-3121; www.gofishbelize.com; Boca del Rio Dr) This experienced local operator offers flats fishing trips for tarpon, bonefish and permit, and reef fishing outings (half-day BZ$750, full day BZ$900). It also organizes night fishing (BZ$900) and combo fishing/BBQ/snorkeling outings (BZ$1000). Prices are per boat, with each boat holding four guests, except for the backcountry trip which holds two.

Tres Pescados FISHING
(Map p96; ☑ 226-3474; www.belizefly.com; Barrier Reef Dr; ☺ 10am-5pm) Purchase all the gear you need to go fly-fishing at the Ambergris flats or take a guided expedition (full day BZ$900). The fly shop also offers a variety of courses ranging from beginners to advanced fly-fishers.

Water Sports

Ambergris is ideal for wind-powered sports: the offshore reef means the waters are always flat, but there is no shortage of breeze to power your craft. The windiest time of year is between January and June, when the wind speed is usually between 12 and 20 knots.

San Pedro Watersports WATER SPORTS
(Map p96; ☑ 226-2888; www.sanpedrowatersports.com; ☺ 8am-5pm) Stop by this waterside kiosk for jet skis (BZ$200 per hour), paddleboards, hoverboards, flyboards and kayaks.

Bigsup Belize WATER SPORTS
(Map p86; ☑ 602-4447; www.bigsupbelize.com; Boca del Rio Dr; SUP rental per hour BZ$30; ☺ 8am-4pm) Offers stand-up paddleboard (SUP) rentals in addition to instruction and river tours through the mangroves.

Belize Parasail WATER SPORTS
(Map p96; ☑ 671-3866; www.belizeparasail.net; Fido's Dock; single/tandem flights BZ$170/340) For a panoramic view of the island, take to the air with a parachute pulled behind a speedboat at this parasailing outfit located on Fido's Dock. It also does private group tours on a pontoon boat (half-day/full day from BZ$500/1000) and is accommodating to guests with mobility issues and disabilities.

Castaway Caye WATER SPORTS
(Map p86; ☑ 671-3000; www.castawaycaye.com; Boca del Rio Dr, Wet Willy's Dock; parasailing BZ$200; ☺ 9am-5pm) A one-stop water-sports shop offering parasailing, jet-ski rental and tours (single/double BZ$538/378 per person), banana-boat rides and kayak trips. It also runs a popular new jungle tour involving a super-stretched SUV limo.

Sailing

Seaduced by Belize BOATING
(Map p96; ☑ 226-2254; www.seaducedbybelize.com; Tarpon St, Vilma Linda Plaza; ☺ 7am-6pm; ☑) Offers a range of sailing trips, including a sunset cruise and a full-day trip to Caye Caulker. Also runs good-value outings to spot manatees at Swallow Caye (BZ$210 plus a BZ$30 park fee), including lunch at Goff's Caye and snorkeling. Other tours include visits to Bacalar Chico and a recommended full-day trip to Robles Beach, complete with snorkel stops and beach BBQ.

Island Dream Tours BOATING
(Map p86; ☑ 615-9656; www.islanddreamtours.com; Sandbar Hostel's Dock; per person day cruise BZ$270, dinner cruise BZ$180, booze cruise BZ$130) Offers a variety of trips aboard a spacious motorized catamaran including snorkeling trips and epic sunset booze and dinner cruises.

Catamaran Belize BOATING
(Map p96; ☑ 621-7245; www.catamaranbelize.com; snorkel day-trip BZ$220) Reliable charter company that rents out a swanky 35-foot catamaran for customized day-trips, and also runs a booze and snorkeling cruise to Hol Chan, Shark Ray Alley and Caye Caulker. A buffet lunch is included, and the trip back offers a lovely sunset view.

Sirena Azul BOATING
(Map p96; ☑ 226-2326; www.bluetanginn.com; Sandpiper St, Blue Tang Inn) This lovely 40ft wooden yacht crafted from Belizean hardwoods operates out of the Blue Tang Inn and offers half-day snorkeling trips to Hol Chan for BZ$120 and sunset sailing cruises for BZ$110.

Biking

The North Island is a wonderful place for a cycle. With the breeze off the ocean and the palms shading your path, you can ride all the way up to Matachica Beach Resort and beyond. Just follow the sandy path that runs along the beach from the Reef Village Resort in Tres Cocos. There are a few places to stop for a fruit smoothie or an ice-cold Belikin beer along the way. Rent bikes from one of the shops in San Pedro town.

Day Spas & Yoga

If you have come to Ambergris Caye for a bit of rest and relaxation, you may want to schedule a massage at one of the waterside spas.

★ **Science & Soul Wellness** YOGA
(Map p86; ☑615-0089; www.scienceandsoul wellness.com; Mahogany Bay; yoga class from BZ$40, massage from BZ$180; ☺9:30am-6pm) This gorgeous and professionally run wellness center is a reason in itself to book at stay at Mahogany Bay, the posh new 'townlet' about 2.5 miles south of San Pedro. The yoga studio is the first in Belize to offer aerial classes, which cater to all levels of experience, and the instructors are top-notch.

Just Relax Massage MASSAGE
(Map p86; ☑666-3536; shirlenesantino@yahoo. com; Boca del Rio beachfront; ☺8:30am-6pm) Certified massage therapist Shirlene Santino runs a small beachfront day spa out of a lovely cloth tent. Shirlene specializes in Swedish, deep tissue and Belizean-style massage (using coconut oil and incorporating a variety of deep tissue toxin-releasing techniques). Beachfront massages are BZ$80 to BZ$100 per hour, and house calls are BZ$120 to BZ$140.

Sol Spa SPA
(Map p96; ☑226-2410; www.belizesolspa.com; Barrier Reef Dr, Phoenix Resort; ☺9am-5pm Mon-Sat) Sol Spa offers the whole range of body work and facial treatments, as well as yoga classes.

Oasis Spa MASSAGE
(Map p96; ☑631-6970; oasisspabelize@gmail.com; Fido's Dock; 30/60min massage from BZ$60/120; ☺9am-5pm) Head to this well-run spa for massages, manicures, body wraps, body scrubs, ear candling and facials. It's located over the water at the end of Fido's Dock.

Delmy's Unique SPA
(Map p96; ☑621-7470; Coconut Dr, Sunbreeze Hotel; massage from BZ$150; ☺9am-5pm) In addition to massages, this recommended spa also offers ear candling, facials, body scrubs, manicures and pedicures.

Ocean Essence SPA
(Map p86; ☑604-0766, 637-5014; www.ocean essencedayspa.com; Sea Grape Dr; 60/90min massage BZ$190/230; ☺9am-5pm) On a seaside dock a few minutes south of town, this tiny place wins the award for its location – literally *above* the water. In addition to ear candling (BZ$70), there are plenty of traditional treatments, as well as a romantic ocean-side couples massage. Located on the Caribbean Villas Hotel pier.

Massage by the Reef MASSAGE
(Map p96; ☑615-7725, 621-8025; Amigos del Mar Dock; massage per hour from BZ$80; ☺9:30am-7pm)

NORTHERN CAYES AMBERGRIS CAYE

CROCODILES IN PERIL

Crocodiles are having a tough time around Ambergris Caye, particularly because humans have been steadily encroaching on their habitat. One thing you can do to help support these magnificent (if terrifying) beasts is to go on a nighttime crocodile tour with the **American Crocodile Education Sanctuary** (ACES; Map p96; ☑623-7920; www.americancrocodilesanctuary.org; Esmeralda St; per person BZ$100; ☺6:45-9pm), a nonprofit that, for the last ten years, has been 'protecting people from crocs and crocs from people.'

Not only will you learn cool stuff (crocodiles sleep with one eye open!) but the admission fee will go toward helping ACES collect data to further assess the health of the local population, which consists of two species: Morelet's and the American crocodile. It's likely that at some point on your spooky cruise through the mangrove habitat, at least one pair of reptile eyes will glow orange in the guide's light. Lucky participants may even witness a crocodile wrangling or tagging event, which is part of the organization's research.

FYI, don't even think about feeding, touching or bothering a crocodile. It's also illegal to own them (or their parts) without permits and you can be fined up to BZ$500 for this type of offense. The tour leaves from the Office restaurant on the lagoon side of the island.

For a massage with a view head up to this friendly spot above the Amigos del Mar dive shop, with fantastic, uninterrupted panoramas along the full length of the reef in both directions. Every massage comes with a complimentary foot or back scrub.

Ak'bol Yoga YOGA

(Map p86; 226-2073, 626-6296; www.akbol.com; Mile 2.25, North Island; classes BZ$30; ⊙9am Mon-Sat, 10am Sun) With two open, thatch-roof yoga studios (one at the end of the dock), Ak'bol offers daily walk-in classes, in addition to the week-long yoga retreats that are scheduled throughout the year. The retreats vary in price, but always include seven nights accommodation, all buffet meals (minus one dinner) and all the yoga, with at least two classes offered per day.

🎓 Courses

Belizean Kitchen
Cooking Class COOKING

(Map p96; ☑615-1321; www.belizefoodtours.com; cnr Barrier Reef Dr & Pelican St; BZ$150; ⊙10:30am-1:30pm & 5:30-8:30pm Mon-Fri) Run by the wonderful people also behind Belize Food Tours (p95), this class feels like a holiday celebration with the large Belizean family that's welcomed you with open arms (and plenty of culinary expertise). Over three boozy hours, the group splits duties on everything from conch ceviche to sweet potato palm cake (a Garifuna specialty), or Belizean-style, fish-filled empanadas.

In addition to all the delicious food and bottomless rum drinks, there's also an interlude of traditional dancing.

Tours

Nautical Tours

Most nautical tours include snorkeling, swimming and sunning; full-day trips also include lunch, and often a beach BBQ. Tours to Caye Caulker and other nearby attractions are often run on sailboats, while those to more remote destinations, such as Bacalar Chico and Swallow Caye, are usually the domain of motor vessels.

El Gato BOATING

(☑602-8552; www.ambergriscaye.com/elgato; half-/full-day cruise BZ$120/200) Sail to Caye Caulker aboard the *El Gato*, stopping to snorkel if you like. Also offers sunset cruises.

Reef Runner Glass Bottom Boat BOATING

(Map p96; ☑602-0858; Barrier Reef Dr; half-day tour BZ$110; ⊙9am & 2pm; 🚻) Here's a way to get a look at the reef without getting wet (if you don't want to). The standard half-day trip visits Hol Chan and Shark Ray Alley. Snorkeling is optional. Children 11 and under can go for BZ$40.

FEEDING THE FISH

To feed or not to feed? That has long been the question, and finally there's a fairly straightforward answer. Don't do it.

For years, chumming has been common at Shark Ray Alley and other sites, as guides want to guarantee a good time for their guests. Fish feeds usually mean close-up views, more interaction and – sometimes – incredible photographs.

Purists argue that feeding changes a fish's natural behavior; it may alter their natural abilities to forage for food if they become dependent on humans. It certainly makes them more vulnerable to the hand that feeds them as, for example, the wrong kind of food can be harmful. For some people, fish feeds have a tinge of falseness, lessening the thrill of interacting with the creatures in their natural habitat.

This is one controversy that will undoubtedly continue as long as there are snorkel guides and dive masters who want to entertain their clients. But there has been a strong push in 2018 to end feeding at all sites other than Shark Ray Alley, and it's looking like the movement will succeed. Regardless, visitors should be aware that feeding can be dangerous: lurking barracuda can shred a hand in seconds, poor-sighted moray eels can leave an awful tear in the skin, and aggressive stingrays can give you a mean hickey. Do we even have to mention sharks?

These creatures are inherently dangerous and frequently present at fish-feeding sites. Ask the snorkel or dive operator if there will be a fish feeding taking place during your trip, and if the answer is yes, switch companies. That way you can come home with all of your digits intact.

Tanisha Tours BOATING
(Map p86; ☎ 226-2314; www.tanishatours.com; Hurricanes Bar; ⊕) This experienced local tour operator specializes in nature trips. Guide Daniel Nuñez takes his guests to the mouth of the Belize River to see manatees, then continues up the river for sightings of birds, crocodiles and plenty of howler monkeys. He also runs fishing trips and tours to Lamanai.

Mainland Tours

Many visitors to Belize use San Pedro as their base and make excursions by plane or boat to other parts of the country. Mainland trips are operated by many of the dive and boat-tour firms.

Altun Ha (p76), the closest Maya ruin to the cays, is one of the most popular day trips from San Pedro. Trips cost BZ$150 to BZ$220 and go by boat across the San Pedro Lagoon, up the Northern River to Bomba village and then by bus to Altun Ha. Some companies pair Altun Ha with a stop at the exotic Belize Boutique Resort & Spa (p75). The time here can be filled with lunch, then swimming or spa treatments (at extra cost).

If you're interested in seeing more wildlife, you might combine Altun Ha with a trip to the Community Baboon Sanctuary (p71), Crooked Tree Wildlife Sanctuary (p73) or Belize Zoo (p80), all in Belize District.

Altun Ha is lovely, but it doesn't have the importance or architectural variety of Lamanai (p140). If you want a closer look at Maya history and ruins, consider the Lamanai River Trip (BZ$270 to BZ$310), which takes you up the New River (lots of bird and croc spotting) to the spectacular ruins in Orange Walk. This is a great tour, but it makes for a long day trip in a variety of vehicles – ocean boat, van, river boat and then back again.

Another option is a cave-tubing adventure (BZ$300 to BZ$460) at Nohoch Che'en Caves Branch Archaeological Reserve (p163) in Cayo. Tours combine a river-tube float and a tour of a cave, where you'll see stalagmites and stalactites and possibly pottery shards and other evidence of the ancient Maya. At some point during the tour, the group spends a few spooky moments in total darkness. This tour is often packaged with a trip to the Belize Zoo or a zip-line tour at Jaguar Paw Resort.

Tours going west to San Ignacio, Xunantunich and Mountain Pine Ridge are available from San Pedro, but you'll spend most of the day getting to and from these sites. It's better to spend a few days in the west rather than trying to visit from the cays.

LA ISLA BONITA

When Madonna sang about her dreams of San Pedro, she was referring to the captivating capital of Ambergris Caye, which has since adopted the inevitable nickname 'La Isla Bonita.'

★ Belize Food Tours FOOD
(Map p96; ☎ 615-1321; www.belizefoodtours.com; cnr Barrier Reef Dr & Pelican St; food tours from BZ$124, cooking classes BZ$150) For a delicious introduction to all things yummy in Belize, hop on a fabulous food tour run by one of the island's pioneering families. The lunch tour, 'Belizean Bites,' and dinner tour, 'Savor Belize' both meander through San Pedro's mom-n-pop kitchens, sampling a wide variety of authentic dishes and drinks hailing from Belize's many cultural influences.

The company also offers a cooking class, and it's an absolute blast.

✪ Festivals & Events

Costa Maya Festival CULTURAL
(www.internationalcostamayafestival.com; ☉ Aug) During the first weekend in August, participants from all over Central America celebrate their shared heritage. The streets of San Pedro are filled with music, parades, dancing and drinking, culminating in a bodybuilding contest and the crowning of a festival queen.

El Gran Carnaval
de San Pedro CULTURAL
The weekend before Lent is a big party in San Pedro. The parades and costumes of more typical carnival celebrations are replaced with body-painting and flour-fighting – great fun to watch and even more fun to participate in.

San Pedro
Lobster Festival FOOD & DRINK
(www.sanpedrolobsterfest.com; ☉ Jun) The third week in June is dedicated to the spiny tail. San Pedro re-opens lobster season with a block party featuring live music, delicious seafood and the crowning of the Lobsterfest king and queen.

🛏 Sleeping

Accommodations on Ambergris Caye skew toward the high end, particularly outside of San Pedro, and the best spots tend to book

Central San Pedro

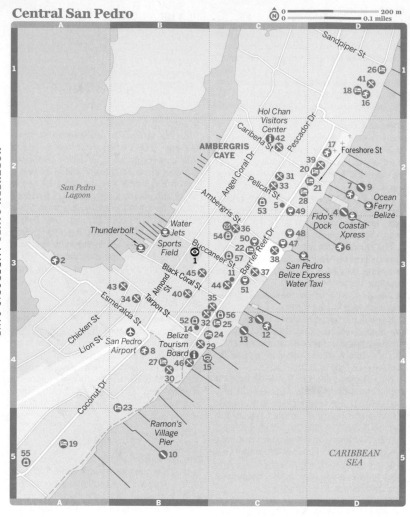

up fast in high season, between December and May. Almost all hotels accept major credit cards, though you may pay a surcharge. For apartments, suites and condominiums, check www.ambergriscaye.com.

🛏 San Pedro

While it's convenient and fun to be in the middle of the action, some of the places right in the town center can be noisy. If you are on a tight budget, you may have no other choice.

Sandbar   HOSTEL **$**
(Map p96; ☎ 226-2008; www.sanpedrohostel.com; Boca del Rio Dr; dm/r BZ$30/120; ❄ ☎) Rejoice! A tight budget no longer means having to bed down in a stifling room on a back street. San Pedro's only waterfront hostel is easily its best. The bright private rooms have big sliding doors leading onto a balcony with Caribbean vistas, while the air-conditioned dorms are well designed with privacy curtains and individual power sockets for each bed.

Guests can hang out on loungers by the water and use the wooden dock. Downstairs,

Central San Pedro

there is a happening sand-floored bar that serves great pizza.

Ruby's Hotel HOTEL **$**
(Map p96; ☎226-2063; www.rubyshotelbelize.com; Barrier Reef Dr; s/d BZ$54/87, r with air-con BZ$120; ❄️☎️) This white-with-red-trim hotel on the beach near Wild Mango's is a local landmark and budget favorite. Unfortunately the fan-cooled rooms themselves are pretty tired – but not bad value considering the price and location. Thin walls do little to block out the revelries of your neighbors, so you might as well join the party.

Hotel San Pedrano GUESTHOUSE **$**
(Map p96; ☎226-2054; julzlab@gmail.com; Barrier Reef Dr; r with fan/air-con BZ$82/105; ❄️☎️) There are no views from this 2nd-story, streetside hostelry, but you might catch the breeze from the balcony. Relatively spacious rooms have two or three beds, and the downstairs grocery store has some seriously delicious fresh fruit icy poles.

Pedro's Hotel HOSTEL, HOTEL **$**
(Map p86; ☎226-3825, 206-2198, 610-5526; www.pedroshotel.com; Sea Grape Dr; s/d without bathroom BZ$30/60, r with air-con BZ$120, deluxe BZ$140; ❄️☎️🏊) One of the cheapest budget options on the island, Pedro's is a longtime San Pedro party-hotel favorite. The original 'hostel' has tiny cell-like rooms with thin walls and shared bathrooms. The best accommodations are near the pool in the deluxe annex, which has 12 rooms featuring flat-screen TVs with 110-plus channels, air-con and en-suite bathrooms with hot showers.

Thomas Hotel
GUESTHOUSE $

(Map p96; ☎ 226-2061; Barrier Reef Dr; r with air-con BZ$93; ❄ 🗢) Rooms here are equipped with TV and minifridge. The comfy little balcony out back sports a wonderful view of the building next door. Bit pricey for the ambience.

Conch Shell Inn
HOTEL $$

(Map p96; ☎ 626-5202, 226-2062; www.ambergris caye.com/conchshell; Caribeña St; r downstairs/upstairs BZ$148/188; ❄ 🗢) This pink-and-white beauty on the beach offers excellent value smack dab in the middle of town. The 10 brightly tiled rooms are spacious and comfortable, and the upstairs ones have kitchenettes and hammocks hanging on the shared balcony. The sandy beach area is not great for swimming, but it is decked out with hammocks and lounge chairs from which to watch the comings and goings.

Air-conditioning is available for BZ$30 a night but the rooms are designed to take advantage of ocean breezes, so you probably won't need it.

Parham Plaza Hotel
HOTEL $$

(Map p96; ☎ 226-4565; www.parhamplaza.com; Barrier Reef Dr; r from BZ$150; P ❄ 🗢) On the site of one of San Pedro's original hotels, in front of the park right in the middle of town, this friendly new hotel has clean and comfortable rooms with air-conditioning. Rooms are fairly spacious and fit up to five guests, making them a good deal if you get a group together.

SARGASSUM SEAWEED

Since 2014, a unusually hefty bloom of sargassum seaweed has plagued the coast of Belize's northern cays and other areas of the Caribbean, choking shorelines and emitting a foul, sulfurous odor that tends to disgust people and even make them ill. In other extreme cases, large-scale die-offs of fish and other marine life have washed up on the islands' shores. Scientists believe warming ocean temperatures and agricultural runoff in South America are to blame, as they create ideal conditions for these thick mats of seaweed to proliferate. When choosing your hotel, particularly on Ambergris Caye, ask about the property's policy for raking up sargassum. Some establishments are more diligent than others.

Hotel del Rio
GUESTHOUSE, CABINS $$

(Map p86; ☎ 226-2286; www.hoteldelriobelize.com; Boca del Rio Dr; r BZ$120-150, cabañas BZ$180-300; ❄ 🗢) Just south of San Pedro River, this little lodge is in a perfect spot on a quiet stretch of beach, and provides easy access into town. Rooms vary in size and layout: most enticing are the fan-cooled, thatched-roof cabañas (sleeping two to four people), which have a central *palapa* that's ideal for socializing or swinging in a hammock.

★ Caye Casa
BOUTIQUE HOTEL $$$

(Map p86; ☎ 226-2880; www.cayecasa.com; Boca del Rio Dr; r BZ$250, ste BZ$325, villa from BZ$425; ❄ 🗢 🏊) At the quiet northern end of San Pedro town, Caye Casa stands out for its simplicity, sophistication and utter loveliness. The sweet colonial-style *casitas* (small cottages) and villas offer thatched-roof porches with wonderful sea views, fully stocked kitchens with stainless-steel appliances and limestone countertops, spacious tiled bathrooms and inviting king- and queen-sized beds.

The hosts go above and beyond to ensure their guests' comfort and convenience. Note the three-night minimum stay during peak periods.

Ramon's Village
RESORT $$$

(Map p96; ☎ 226-2071; www.ramons.com; Coconut Dr; r from BZ$337, ste from BZ$709; ❄ 🏊) Guests love the exotic, faux-jungle setting at this luxurious beach resort with a giant Maya mask known as 'Rey Ramon' overlooking the grounds. Thatched-roof cabañas are surrounded by lush greenery and flowering hibiscus and bougainvillea, allowing for plenty of privacy. Beachfront cabañas are front and center, with uninhibited Caribbean vistas; seaside cabañas are set back a bit.

Ramon's boasts one of the best beachfronts on the island, with a dock for swimming and lounge chairs for sunning. It's also got its own dive shop, tour office, beach yoga and fitness classes (BZ$45).

White Sands Cove
RESORT $$$

(Map p86; ☎ 226-3528, in USA 646-355-3623; www. whitesandscove.com; 1-bedroom condos BZ$430-510, 2-bedroom condos BZ$630-710; ❄ 🗢 🏊) If you want to get away from it all without giving up any of the comforts of home, White Sands Cove – 2.5 miles north of San Pedro – is for you. Condos are furnished with fully equipped kitchens and spacious living areas. The beach bar and freshwater pool are set up for optimal relaxation.

Active types can take advantage of the complimentary bikes and kayaks. White Sands receives rave reviews for above-and-beyond service.

Blue Tang Inn
GUESTHOUSE **$$$**

(Map p96; ☑ 226-2326, in USA 866-881-1020; www.bluetanginn.com; Sandpiper St; r BZ$350-530, deluxe ste BZ$560; ❄ 🛜 ⛱) Named for one of the brightest and most beautiful fish on the reef, the Blue Tang lives up to this enticing image. Each of the suites at this beachside retreat includes kitchen facilities, dining furniture and living space. Big windows and vaulted ceilings make some of the rooms seem even bigger than they are.

Many rooms have good sea views, but for the best views of all, make your way upstairs to the rooftop – one of the highest vantage points on the island – for the true 360-degree panorama.

Sun Breeze Hotel
HOTEL **$$$**

(Map p96; ☑ 226-2191; www.sunbreeze.net; 7 Coconut Dr; r BZ$458-596; ❄ 🛜) This hotel is a good choice for those looking for a little comfort by the sea, and offers a few newly upgraded rooms. Located just south of the Belize Tourism Board office, the Sun Breeze has clean and comfortable rooms, featuring two double beds, air-conditioning and hot showers, set around a spacious yard with a fine pool.

San Pedro Holiday Hotel
HOTEL **$$$**

(Map p96; ☑ 226-2014; www.sanpedroholiday.com; Barrier Reef Dr; r BZ$268-326, apt BZ$424; ❄ 🛜) The central location of this place is both a bonus and a shortcoming. Sure, there's great people-watching and easy access to everything, but this is a busy stretch of beachfront and it doesn't get much privacy. Nonetheless, it's a pretty little place, with intricate wooden trim adorning the porches and decks.

The wood-paneled rooms are not particularly spacious and are fairly simple, but they are clean and functional. The suites are not really much of an upgrade.

Changes in Latitudes
B&B **$$$**

(Map p96; ☑ 226-2986; www.changesinlatitudesbelize.com; 36 Coconut Dr; r incl breakfast from BZ$225; ❄ 🛜) Unique in San Pedro for its intimate atmosphere, this B&B is a short block from the beach. The six rooms are small but stylish, with wood and bamboo adding Belizean flair. All rooms overlook a well-tended garden with an exotic flower-covered pagoda – the perfect place for guests to sip fruity cocktails and swap snorkeling tales.

🛏 South of San Pedro

If you need a vacation from your vacation, get out of San Pedro. South of town, you can enjoy more peace and privacy, although you still have easy access to the restaurants and facilities in town. If you don't feel like making the trek (more than a mile in some cases), a few restaurants and bars cater to the southerners.

⭐Victoria House
RESORT **$$$**

(Map p86; ☑ 226-2067, in USA 800-247-5159; www.victoria-house.com; Sea Grape Dr; r from BZ$420, casitas BZ$710, villas BZ$900-4200; ❄ 🛜 ⛱) This elegant beach resort is one of the oldest on the island, but is meticulously maintained and shines like new. It's fronted by a beautiful, wide beach shaded by palms, while the grassy grounds center around two excellent pools. Rooms are in thatched-roof *casitas*, or colonial-style 'plantation' houses, with a sophisticated white-on-white scheme that oozes luxury.

Villas are fully furnished with a huge array of top-of-the-line mod cons. It's a bit of a trek into town but complimentary bicycles and four daily shuttles will help get you into town. Considering the beautifully landscaped gardens, huge variety of activities on tap, personalized service and highly touted restaurant and spa, you might never leave the resort!

Coral Bay Villas
HOTEL **$$$**

(Map p86; ☑ 226-3003, in USA 214-396-3215; www.coralbaybelize.com; Sea Grape Dr; r BZ$400; ❄ 🛜 ⛱) One of the best deals on the island, this attractive colonial-style hotel is set back from the ocean, leaving a wide, sandy swath shaded by coconut palms free for casual hammock swinging. Five deluxe condos are equipped with full kitchens, wireless internet access, cable TV and – lest you forget where you are – private verandas with sea views.

It's accessible to town but the beach gets very little foot traffic this far south, so it feels like you have the whole place to yourself. Bicycles and kayaks are available for guest use. There's an age minimum of 18 years.

Caribbean Villas Hotel
RESORT **$$$**

(Map p86; ☑ 226-2715; www.caribbeanvillashotel.com; Sea Grape Dr; r from BZ$294, suite BZ$424-534; ❄ 🛜 ⛱) Boasting one of the widest stretches of beach south of town and two pools, this well-run resort is good value especially for

NORTHERN CAYES AMBERGRIS CAYE

families, who'll love the El Diablo Aqua Park. It's got a giant slide into the sea, a 300ft zip-line to the beach and a couple of trampolines. The new sushi restaurant on the property is also recommended.

Rooms are simple but comfortable; go for one in the original concrete buildings – they have sea views and get more light than those in the new wooden structure. The suites are a particularly good deal with some holding up to six guests.

Mahogany Bay Village — RESORT $$$

(Map p86; ☎226-4817; www.mahoganybayvillage. com; r from BZ$412; [P][❄][🛜][🏊]) This new 60-acre resort 2.5 miles south of San Pedro is now the largest resort in Belize, and its glistening white colonial structures are an ode to British Honduras. Part of Hilton's Curio Collection, the 205-unit planned 'townlet' was still being erected at the time of research, but all of the biggest draws were complete.

There's the Bay Club and its sparkling pool, the Great House (a 22,000-sq-ft event center), the immaculate yoga studio (p93), the up-market sushi restaurant, the coffee shop, the local food stalls and the private island Beach Club, complete with overwater Bali-beds, a short boat ride away.

It's all breathtaking, and whether you opt for a single-room villa, a family cottage (with a bunk bed and pool) or a town home, rest assured that your surroundings and furnishings are made of sustainable hard-woods and locally crafted. Of course, before the resort existed, this area was a lagoon habitat for mangroves, fish and birdlife. Trade offs...

Xanadu Island Resort — RESORT $$$

(Map p86; ☎226-2814, in US 866-351-4752; www. xanaduislandresort.com; Sea Grape Dr; studios from BZ$515, 2-bedroom apt BZ$995; [❄][🛜][🏊]) 🌿 If being surrounded by greenery is a priority, it's hard to beat this resort set in lush trop-ical gardens alive with bird song. Right by the water south of town, rooms have an at-mosphere of rustic luxury and are fitted with every amenity. The thatched-roof cabañas are clustered around a hot tub and heated pool shaded by palm trees.

Bicycles, kayaks, paddleboards and snor-kel gear for local explorations are compli-mentary.

Diamond Lodge — BOUTIQUE HOTEL $$$

(Map p86; ☎226-4377; www.diamondlodgebelize. com; 2 Sea Grape Dr; r from BZ$400; [❄][🛜][🏊]) Just south of town and tucked away from

anything resembling grit, this darling new boutique hotel is adorned in contemporary furnishings, sophisticated art and a soothing blue-and-beige color scheme. The 10 well-appointed rooms in the rambling one-time residence are simultaneously lavish and homey, while the in-house chef and relaxing spa round out the amenities.

Pelican Reef Villas — HOTEL $$$

(Map p86; ☎226-4352, 226-2352, in USA 281-942-1103; www.pelicanreefvillas.com; Sea Grape Dr; 2-/3-bedroom ste from BZ$561/998; [❄][🛜][🏊]) At the far south reaches of San Pedro, this intimate resort is a tranquil option for those looking to escape the bustle of downtown without abandoning modern facilities and a touch of luxury. The rooms feature elegant furnishings and excellent kitchens and there is a pool with a cave-like sunken bar and a long dock sheltering an artificial reef that at-tracts interesting marine life.

Mata Rocks Resort — BOUTIQUE HOTEL $$$

(Map p86; ☎226-2336; www.matarocks.com; Sea Grape Dr; r BZ$340-390, ste BZ$445-480; [❄][🛜][🏊]) Modern and minimalist, this intimate 17-room hotel features contemporary design with hardwood or tile floors, stucco walls and high ceilings. Every room gets a bit of an ocean view, however the property is not par-ticularly big and it can feel a little crowded. Guests can enjoy the complimentary bikes and breakfast is included.

Note that this property has a four-night minimum stay in high season.

Corona del Mar — GUESTHOUSE $$$

(Map p86; ☎226-2055; www.coronadelmarhotel. com; Coconut Dr; r BZ$298-414; [❄][🛜][🏊]) This hotel consists of a small boutique property and the large concrete structure next door, and is a decent-value waterside option. The rooms in the original Corona building are better equipped than the run-down pool-side ones next door, but make sure you get an ocean view; the garden view ones don't get a breeze and should really be called 'road view.' There's a relaxing, attached restaurant and bar.

Banana Beach Resort — RESORT $$$

(Map p86; ☎226-3890; www.bananabeach.com; Sea Grape Dr; r BZ$294, ste poolside/oceanfront BZ$418/490; [❄][🛜][🏊]) This place may be too motel-like for some tastes and could certainly do with some cosmetic work, but while it is not elegant, it's reasonable value considering the waterside location. Rooms are in a big concrete building and are set either around two swimming pools or facing the water.

North Island

The North Island is where you should go if you really want to get away from it all. The resorts here are all top end and mainly accessible by boat; you can travel in and out by golf cart or car to at least 5 miles north of the bridge, but the island ferry is probably a more pleasant way to go.

★**Daydreamin' Bed & Breakfast** B&B $$
(Map p86; ☑601-3306; www.daydreaminbelize. com; Tres Cocos; BZ$185-200; ❄️🛜💺) With just four tidy cabins and a delicious cafe (p108) perched around a small, relaxing pool, this North Island getaway is easily one of Ambergris' most charming. The owner is an absolute class act, and her relaxed professionalism is palpable throughout the property. The elegant units are constructed from nine types of local hardwood, each featuring a unique design. Adults only.

★**Ak'bol Yoga Resort** RESORT $$
(Map p86; ☑626-6296, 226-2073; www.akbol.com; s/d BZ$80/116, cabañas BZ$333-380; 🛜💺) Yogis, rejoice! Ak'bol, or 'Heart of the Village,' is a sweet retreat in a near-perfect location about 1 mile north of town on the North Island. The seven colorful cabañas have delightful details, such as handcrafted hardwood furniture and mosaic sinks with conch shell faucets. Enjoy plantation-style shutters that open to the sea and mosaic tiled showers that are open to the sky.

Alternatively, save your cash and sleep in a hostel room with shared bathroom. Either way, you're free to enjoy the lush grounds and wonderful pool surrounded by greenery. The fabulous food at the breezy beach bar is worth a trip even if you're not staying here, as are the daily yoga classes in the studio surrounded by sea.

★**Matachica Beach Resort** RESORT $$$
(☑226-5010; www.matachica.com; Mile 5.5; r BZ$655-1725; P❄️🛜💺) Vying for the title of 'swankiest resort,' Matachica is extravagant, exotic and eclectic. This place is serious about the idea of tropical luxury, so down duvets and Frette linens cover the mosquito-netted beds, and each thatched-roof cottage boasts classic furniture and private patios...hung with hammocks, of course. The luxury villas have private terraces and outdoor hot tubs.

Other highlights include the excellent Mambo Restaurant (p105) and the indulgent Jade Spa.

Pur Boutique Cabanas BOUTIQUE HOTEL $$$
(Map p86; ☑226-2050, 630-4781; www.purboutique cabanas.com; r BZ$346-478; ❄️🛜💺) This cozy hotel consists of just six cabañas, a taco bar, and a lap pool and swim-up pool bar designed to encourage guests to make friends. Studio-style rooms offer relaxing verandas and are sumptuously appointed with high-end finishes, super-comfy linens and granite sinks. The kind owners could not be more enthusiastic about hosting. Free bicycles are available for guests.

Portofino Resort RESORT $$$
(☑226-5096; www.portofino.bz; Mile 6; beachfront cabañas BZ$738, ste from BZ$940, all-inclusive food & drink BZ$275; ❄️🛜💺) Who knew a thatched-roof cabin could be so chic? With high ceilings and elegant wood floors, huge picture windows, Mexican tiles and Guatemalan rugs, these lodgings are at once primitive and plush. The resort is professionally run and yet remains wonderfully intimate and has personalized check-in where guests can choose from a selection of handmade Belizean soaps.

The improved road means that the resort is now accessible from San Pedro by golf cart, although the water taxi remains the quickest way to arrive. Free pick-up on arrival and drop-off when checking out is included.

Cocotal Inn & Cabanas GUESTHOUSE $$$
(Map p86; ☑226-2097; www.oocotalbelize.com; Mile 2.5; r from BZ$250, casitas BZ$534, 2-bedroom apt BZ$610; ❄️🛜💺) A wonderful antidote to bland condos, the Cocotal has just half a dozen apartments offering a cool, colonial atmosphere with fans hanging from high mahogany ceilings, potted plants, tile floors and wicker furniture. The most charming option is the cupola-topped *casita* (apartment) with sunlight pouring through its skylights. It's all very secluded and sophisticated, and good value to boot.

Paradise on the Caye B&B $$
(☑615-2042; www.paradiseonthecaye.com; Secret Beach; r incl breakfast BZ$190; 🛜) Secret Beach's only accommodation offers just three fan-cooled, brightly colored stilted cabañas; one orange, one green and one teal. Two of the units are small, each with a four-poster queen bed and a little bathroom, while the third option is a family unit with bunk beds, a terrace and a sizable bathroom.

Tranquility Bay   RESORT $$$

(🛏 in USA 800-827-3319; www.tranquilitybayresort.
com; Bacalar Chico Marine Reserve; r from BZ$324;
❄🛜) For something completely different,
check out this far-flung resort situated within
the Bacalar Chico Marine Reserve. It's nothing too fancy, and there's nobody for miles,
but the point is that you can walk a couple
of hundred feet from your cabaña, strap on a
mask and snorkel, and boom, there's the reef.
It's ideal for families seeking a low-key vacay.

Accommodations include fully-equipped
one- and two-bedroom cabañas, a budget
suite and a 'prime minister's suite,' which is
gargantuan, with a great upstairs terrace.
The Aquarium seafood restaurant is on stilts
over the water, where eagle rays, tarpon and
bonefish tend to hang out at night. (This is an
ideal time to snorkel.)

It's possible to get here on a golf cart, but
it takes around two hours from San Pedro,
and much of the trip is on the sand. A ferry
transports most guests to and from San Pedro, and will bring day-trippers for around
BZ$30 each way.

X'tan Ha   RESORT $$$

(🛏 in USA 844-360-1553; www.xtanha.com; Mile 7.2;
casitas from BZ$426, villas from BZ$510; ❄🛜♨)
Fronted by a fine stretch of white sand this
low-key resort features neat wooden cabañas
trimmed with bright colors. Rooms strike a
good balance between amenities and tran-
quility. Just offshore there is a large expanse
of turquoise water free of seagrass or you can
take a dip in one of the two pools and watch
iguanas scurry around the grounds.

Some rooms are a little tight for space,
especially the bathrooms, but all are well
finished and have excellent facilities. Service
is top-notch throughout the resort and the
onsite restaurant serves quality meals.

Captain Morgan's Retreat   RESORT $$$

(Map p86; 🛏 226-2208; www.captainmorgans.com;
casitas/villas from BZ$418/518; 🅿❄🛜♨) After
a recent overhaul, old favorite Captain Mor-
gan's is once again competitive with some
of the newer luxury resorts on the island.
Among the many room types, the thatched
cabins with private porches overlooking the
sea are the most atmospheric. There are also
three swimming pools, each with their corresponding bar spread along the waterfront.

The onsite casino features slot machines,
blackjack and roulette (with plans for poker,
too). The resort was the filming location for

the first season of reality TV show *Temptation Island*; whether that inspires you or
scares you off will depend on what you're
looking for in Belize.

Finally, beware the time-share sales pitch!

El Pescador Lodge & Villas   RESORT $$$

(Map p86; 🛏 226-2398; www.elpescador.com; Mile
2.5; standard r BZ$550, 1-/2-/3-bedroom villas
BZ$800/1250/1700; ❄🛜♨) 🐾 With the at-
mosphere of a charming old-time fishing
lodge and amenities of a luxury hotel, this
42-acre property is a sweet retreat for anglers and adventurers. Set in an intimate,
colonial-style building, the sea-facing standard rooms have polished hardwood floors
and colorful hand-woven tapestries. The villas are nothing short of vast – perfect if you
have family or friends in tow.

Coco Beach   RESORT $$$

(Map p86; 🛏 226-4840; www.cocobeachbelize.com;
Mile 3.5; r/ste BZ$805/1265, casitas BZ$1035) If
you plan to spend a great deal of your trip
just lazing in your resort, this large luxury operation is a solid choice. All of the rooms are
spacious with modern appliances, big windows and elegant rattan furniture, but Coco
Beach's biggest selling point is its two large,
brilliant turquoise swimming pools, considered to be the best on the island.

The stretch of beach here is not the best
but there's an onsite activity center that organizes trips to the attractions around the
island and beyond. It's almost 4 miles north
of the bridge. You'll pay BZ$20 per person for
a boat or van transfer from either the airport
or the ferry drop-off.

Grand Caribe   RESORT $$$

(Map p86; 🛏 226-4726; www.grandcaribebelize.com;
Mile 2; 1-/2-bedroom condo from BZ$900/1100;
🅿❄🛜♨) One of the largest resorts on
the island, Gran Caribe has around 100
luxurious condos offering sea-views and
fitted out to the highest levels of comfort.
From massive flat-screen TVs to modern
American-style kitchens and private wireless routers, the suites have absolutely every
modern convenience and are all bright and
well furnished.

Las Terrazas   RESORT $$$

(Map p86; 🛏 226-4249; www.lasterrazasresort.
com; Mile 3.5; 1-bedroom villa BZ$830-1900,
2-bedroom villa BZ$1211-2282; ❄🛜♨) This
stylish resort has a slick, modern design
that is big on comfort and service. The

wide, coconut-shaded beach is a major selling point although the manicured resort grounds don't really connect with the surrounding environment. Suites are very well equipped and many boast private balconies with sea views.

✖ Eating

Although there are plenty of options for cheap street food, tacos and fry-jacks (deep-fried dough), at a sit-down place it's unlikely you'll pay less than BZ$50 per person – Ambergris Caye is easily the most expensive restaurant scene in Belize. That said, the island also offers the country's freshest seafood and most innovative chefs, so diners usually get their money's worth.

✖ San Pedro

For the budget-conscious traveler, several small cafes in the town center serve simple meals that are easy on the wallet. There are also several taco shops that open in the morning and again in the evening serving tasty cheap meals for under BZ$10.

★ **DandE's Frozen Custard** ICE CREAM $
(Map p96; ☎ 660-5966; www.dande.bz; Pescador Dr; ice cream from BZ$6; ⊗ 2-9:30pm; ☀) Don't be confused by 'frozen custard.' It's basically high-quality ice cream, made with eggs for extra richness, then churned as it freezes for dense creaminess. The flavors change frequently, often featuring local fruity flavors such as coconut, sour sop and mango. Alternatively you can't go wrong with 'not just' vanilla. DandE's also makes sorbet, but don't forego the frozen custard.

Belize Chocolate Company SWEETS $
(Map p96; ☎ 226-3015; www.belizechocolate company.com; Barrier Reef Dr; chocolates BZ$1-12, chocolate class per person BZ$15; ⊗ 8:30am-7pm Mon-Sat, 10:30am-4pm Sun; ☀ 🛜) Run by Chris and Jo Beaumont, the same couple who manufacture the amazing (and Ambergris-produced) Kakaw brand chocolate, this cafe serves up the finest cacao products on the island. There's also a new chocolate class, that includes learning about the history of cacao, making some chocolate and sampling the finished product. The 40-minute classes take place at 10:30am on weekdays.

Especially refreshing in this hot clime is the Chococino, an iced-chocolate drink made with French press coffee (BZ$10).

Neri's Tacos MEXICAN $
(Map p96; ☎ 605-1878; Tarpon St; tacos from BZ$0.35; ⊗ 5am-noon & 5-9pm) For seriously cheap and tasty eats, do as the locals do and head to Neri's, on the back side of the island, for delicious tacos, burritos, fry-jacks and *tostadas*. The large communal tables and laid-back family vibe mean you might make some new friends over dinner.

Pupuseria Salvadoreño SALVADORAN $
(Map p96; ☎ 226-3237; Pescador Dr; pupusas BZ$2.50-5, mains BZ$10-30; ⊗ 10am-10pm Wed-Mon) For something different that is both cheap and filling you can't go wrong with this Salvadoran-run *pupusa* shop. The *pupusas* (filled savory maize pancakes) are cooked on a hot plate on the street and brought into the pink-walled, open-air dining room. There is also a good selection of Mexican and local dishes.

My Secret Deli BELIZEAN $
(Map p96; ☎ 226-3223; Caribeña St; meals BZ$10-25; ⊗ 8am-3pm & 6-9pm Mon-Sat) This is one secret too good to keep, especially for the budget-conscious traveler looking for good bargain eats. This family-run eatery serves filling Belize favorites such as stewed chicken, steak and rice, and the lunch specials are particularly sought after. It gets busy but is worth waiting for a table.

Ruby's Café BAKERY $
(Map p96; ☎ 226-2219; Barrier Reef Dr; breakfasts BZ$2.50-8, pastries BZ$3-5; ⊗ 4.30am-5pm; ☀) This tiny place is packed with locals during the morning hours. Nobody can resist the sweet and sticky cinnamon rolls, chicken-filled johnnycakes, homemade banana cake, and hot tortillas filled with ham, cheese and beans. There is only one tiny table so grab your breakfast to go and find a shady spot on the beach.

Celi's Deli FAST FOOD $
(Map p96; ☎ 226-2103; Barrier Reef Dr; deli items BZ$1-8; ⊗ 5am-4pm) A fantastic find for breakfast or lunch, Celi's Deli serves great food to go – sandwiches, meat pies, burritos, tacos and homemade cakes.

Food Stands BELIZEAN $
(Map p96; Barrier Reef Dr; snacks BZ$5; ⊗ 6pm-3am) The fast food stands around the park are pretty average if you're sober, but are a tasty treat after the bars close when there's not much else open.

Black & White GARIFUNA **$$**
(Map p86; ☑605-2895; gariculenter@gmail.com; Villa Dr; mains BZ$20-35; ☺9am-9pm) Adorned in tropics-themed table cloths, local art and charming lattice, this little restaurant serves up Garifuna specialties including *hudut* (red snapper prepared in coconut milk with spices and pounded plantains) and cassava bread, the staple food of the group's ancestors. The restaurant doubles as a cultural center, and occasionally hosts educational performances involving Garifuna history, lifestyle and drumming traditions.

The performance is BZ$50 per person including a buffet, or BZ$40 without food. Call or email to find out when the next performance takes place.

Juice Dive HEALTH FOOD **$$**
(Map p96; ☑615-7395; www.facebook.com/juice dive; Pescador Dr; juice from BZ$16, mains from BZ$21; ☺7am-8pm; ☑) The first commercial cold-pressed juice operation in Belize also serves up all kinds of vegetarian and vegan delights: acai bowls, vegan nachos, wheat grass shots, you name it. The salads and wraps are particularly delicious and everything here is easy on the conscience, with biodegradable packaging and utensils made of plant fiber.

The family that owns the place is as kind as it is worldly.

Poco Loco's FOOD HALL **$$**
(Map p96; ☑226-4689; www.facebook.com/pg/PocoLocoBZ; Barrier Reef Dr; mains BZ$15-25; ☺7:30am-10pm; ☎☑) New, al fresco food court with build-your-own salads, crepes, specialty burgers, burritos, desserts and plenty of vegetarian and vegan options. There's also a bar, the Tipsy Toucan, and a charming, colorful seating area filled with plants and natural light.

El Fogón BELIZEAN **$$**
(Map p96; ☑671-1277, 206-2121; www.elfogonbelize. com; 2 Trigger Fish St; mains BZ$17-45; ☺11am-9pm Mon-Sat) At first glance the ambience doesn't seem to match the price tag at this backstreet eatery, but once the food arrives you'll be not too worried about the lack of chic design. El Fogón serves up wonderfully prepared classic Belizean Creole cuisine including plenty of fresh seafood cooked to perfection. The conch is especially tasty.

Elvi's Kitchen BELIZEAN **$$**
(Map p96; ☑226-2404, 226-2176; Pescador Dr; mains BZ$18-37; ☺11am-10pm Mon-Sat; ☑) This San Pedro institution has been around since the early days, serving up local specialties such as shrimp creole, fried chicken and conch *ceviche*. The funky tropical decor, loud marimba music and T-shirts for sale give it a cruise-line atmosphere, but it's a good place to sample some authentic and filling local cuisine.

Estel's Dine by the Sea BREAKFAST **$$**
(Map p96; ☑226-2019; www.ambergriscaye.com/estels; Buccaneer St; breakfast BZ$12-20, mains BZ$15-35; ☺6am-9pm; ☑) This long-standing breakfast favorite is basically an extension of the beach – complete with sandy floors and ocean breezes. Stop by for a breakfast burrito, some Mayan eggs or an eye-opening coffee.

SECRET BEACH

The island's worst-kept secret is a dreamy stretch of northwestern shoreline that has nonetheless retained the name Secret Beach. Getting here is a big part of the allure, as it requires a 45-minute golf cart ride north of San Pedro and across much of the North Island, over steamy lagoons and hauntingly beautiful mangrove swamps where crocodiles lurk.

The reward for your effort is an away-from-it-all kind of paradise that San Pedro once was, completely off-the-grid and featuring soft white sands, clear turquoise waters, yummy seafood shacks and as many tropical cocktails as you can slurp. The anchoring establishment out here is Wayne's World (p105), a restaurant and bar under the same ownership as the area's first (and only) lodgings, Paradise on the Caye (p101). Other highlights include the posh Maruba Beach Klub (p107) with its techno beats and brightly colored lounge pillows, and Blue Bayou (p107), a small, family-owned hideaway with partly-submerged picnic tables and a convivial vibe.

Paddleboards, kayaks and canoes are available for rent at Wayne's World, and there's also beach volleyball, cornhole and a wandering hair-braider. For the best bites at the beach, hit up the food shack Aurora's and try the BBQ grouper or fish tacos.

Breakfasts are served until 4pm but there are also sandwiches, burgers, fish and chips, and burritos on the chalkboard menu.

Wayne's World Bar & Grill GRILL **$$**
(Secret Beach; mains BZ$20-25; ⊙10am-5pm; 🛜) The pioneering restaurant at Secret Beach remains its most economical, offering wings, burgers, seafood, tacos, empanadas and more. It's set on a prime stretch of sand and also rents canoes, kayaks and paddleboards.

Melt SANDWICHES **$$**
(Map p96; ✒226-6358; Sandpiper St; meals BZ$10-30; ⊙7am-midnight; 🛜) A friendly waterside cafe specializing in artisan grilled-cheese sandwiches made with locally baked breads. There are 16 tasty varieties to choose from in addition to gourmet wraps and salads. Also has a good range of breakfast options. There's live music Monday, Wednesday and Friday, and karaoke on Tuesday, Thursday and Saturday.

Caramba! Restaurant BELIZEAN **$$**
(Map p96; ✒226-4321, 226-3850; www.caramba restaurantbz.com; Pescador Dr; burgers BZ$20-25, mains BZ$14-55; ⊙11am-10pm Thu-Tue; ✳🛜✒🍴) Caramba is a busy place due to its excellent food, fun atmosphere and attentive service. Mexican and Creole dishes focus on fresh fish and seafood cooked in at least 10 tasty ways. The tropical decor (including the staff's festive attire) enhances your seafood feast.

El Patio Restaurant & Grill BELIZEAN **$$**
(Map p96; ✒226-3898; Barrier Reef Dr; mains BZ$20-48; ⊙11am-10pm) Potted plants, a flowing fountain and a candlelit interior make this sand-floored *palapa* an inviting setting for a romantic dinner. Grilled meats and seafood are the specialty, accompanied by fresh-squeezed, thirst-quenching fruit juices or ice-cold Belikin beers.

O Restaurant INTERNATIONAL **$$$**
(Map p86; ✒226-4249; Las Terrazas, Mile 3.5, North Island; light meals BZ$18-30, mains BZ$34-62; ⊙7am-9pm) Located inside a high-end resort, this modern restaurant feels more Miami than Belize so it's no surprise that the menu goes beyond rice and beans to include everything from curry and risotto to Bailey's-infused chocolate sea urchin. It's pricey, but the quality fare hits the spot if you're looking for something different. Go for a table on the rooftop terrace.

Aji Tapas Bar & Restaurant MEDITERRANEAN **$$$**
(Map p86; ✒226-4047; North Island; tapas BZ$14-28, mains BZ$28-60; ⊙11am-9pm Fri-Sun, 5-9pm Mon, Wed & Thu; ✒) If you're in the mood for romance, book a table at this magical Mediterranean hideaway. Surrounded by swaying palms, the dining area is only steps from the sea. The menu features a few classic tapas (such as garlic shrimp or bacon-wrapped dates), as well as some delectable seafood dishes (including highly recommended paella). Personalized service completes the delightful experience.

There's also a pool, and the bar is open until 10pm on weekends. There are also accommodations now: the seven units are adorably furnished and decorated (from BZ$350). They have air-con, kitchenettes or kitchens, cable TV and wifi. Some have ocean views, others have lagoon views. Keep your eyes peeled for crocodiles.

Mambo Restaurant INTERNATIONAL **$$$**
(✒220-5011; www.matachica.com; Mile 5.5, Matachica Beach Resort; mains BZ$56-68; ⊙7am-10pm) The Matachica Beach Resort's award-winning restaurant is as eclectic and exotic as the resort itself. Although the restaurant specializes in Italian fare, with a fine selection of carpaccio and pasta, the menu does not skimp on fresh seafood or local seasonal produce. Plenty of good options for vegetarians, too.

While you are here, be sure to stroll around the grounds to thoroughly appreciate this tropical fantasy. Reservations required.

Portofino Restaurant EUROPEAN, CARIBBEAN **$$$**
(✒226-5096; www.portofino.bz; Portofino Resort; mains BZ$28-95; ⊙7-11am, 11:30am-4pm & 6-9pm) In a brilliant Belizean setting, European-Caribbean fusion cuisine at Portofino Restaurant makes perfect sense. The menu features freshly caught snapper, stone crab, lobster and other seafood prepared with diverse (and delectable) sauces. If you're feeling really romantic, inquire about private dining on the pier.

A complimentary shuttle boat leaves Fido's Dock at 6:30pm; reservations recommended.

Blue Water Grill INTERNATIONAL **$$$**
(Map p96; ✒226-3347; www.bluewatergrillbelize. com; Sun Breeze Beach Hotel, Coconut Dr; mains BZ$30-60; ⊙7am-9:30pm; ✒) It's hard to resist the huge open-air restaurant on this

beachfront property, and almost everybody who comes to San Pedro ends up eating here at some point. Few are disappointed. The menu is wide-ranging and includes some safe options, such as pizza and pasta, as well as more adventurous dishes with Asian and Caribbean flavors.

On Tuesday and Thursday it offers sushi. The place is always busy, but it's big so you probably won't have to wait for a table.

South of San Pedro

With the entrance of mega-resort Mahogany Bay, you can bet that the dining scene down south is being taken up a notch.

★Robin's Kitchen   JAMAICAN $$
(Map p86; ☑651-3583; Sea Grape Dr; mains BZ$14-25; ⊙7am-9pm Sun-Thu, to 5:30pm Fri, 6:30-9pm Sat) At this simple, small roadside restaurant south of town, Jamaican BBQ king Robin prepares the best jerk chicken and fish this side of Kingston. Dishes are spicy but with subtle flavors, and his sauces are also to die for. If you catch your own fish, Robin will prepare it for you any way you like and will only charge for sides.

He also prepares vegetarian dishes. It's a fair hike south of town, opposite the Royal Palms Resort, but well worth the trip.

Jambel Jerk Pit   CARIBBEAN $$
(Map p96; ☑226-3515; Barrier Reef Dr; mains BZ$16-30; ⊙7am-9pm; ▣) Right on the waterfront, this poolside place serves tasty Caribbean cuisine for lunch and dinner, but most come here for the excellent all-you-can-eat buffet (BZ$40) on Wednesday and Saturday (6pm to 9pm), when you can fill up with conch fritters, jerk chicken, jerk pork and spicy shrimp.

There's another location 5.5 miles north of the bridge at the site of the old Xamanek Resort.

★Wild Mango's   INTERNATIONAL $$$
(Map p96; ☑226-2859; 42 Barrier Reef Dr; mains BZ$20-48; ⊙11:30am-9pm Mon-Sat; ☑) Exuding a carefree, casual ambience (as a beachfront restaurant should), this open-air restaurant manages to serve up some of the island's most consistent and creative cuisine. With a hint of the Caribbean and a hint of Mexico, the dishes showcase fresh seafood, Cajun spices and local fruits and vegetables. The place is usually packed – come early or make a reservation.

★Hidden Treasure   CARIBBEAN $$$
(Map p86; ☑226-4111; www.hiddentreasure belize.com; 4088 Sarstoon St; mains BZ$29-68; ⊙5-9pm Wed-Mon; ☑) Living up to its name, Hidden Treasure is a gorgeous open-air restaurant in an out-of-the-way residential neighborhood (follow the signs from Coconut Dr). Lit by candles, the beautiful bamboo and hardwood dining room is the perfect setting for a romantic dinner, which might feature almond-crusted grouper, blackened snapper with bacon-wrapped shrimp, or pork ribs with a ginger pineapple BBQ glaze.

When you make your reservation, inquire about free transportation from your hotel.

Jyoto   JAPANESE $$$
(Map p86; ☑628-0100; www.facebook.com/ jyotorestaurant; Sea Grape Dr, Mahogany Bay; mains BZ$35-85; ⊙noon-2:30pm & 5-9:30pm Wed-Mon) Sure, there are sushi joints on Ambergris Caye. But this is the first upmarket Japanese establishment, and the classically trained and well-traveled Chef Toshiya has truly raised the bar. Traditional offerings include tempura, *gyoza* and *tataki,* while some fun Belizean takes on Japanese favorites include a miso soup with conch, or the wildly delicious ceviche roll.

There's also a good selection of sake, and even a sake-flavored ice cream for dessert.

Black Orchid   INTERNATIONAL $$$
(Map p86; ☑206-2441; www.blackorchidrestaurant .com; South Coconut Dr; mains BZ$40-60; ⊙3-9pm Tue-Sat) Fine dining in San Pedro is still a fairly relaxed affair, as demonstrated by this attractive restaurant in the deep south of the island that serves up high-quality meals made from fresh local ingredients in a semi-formal dining room. Alongside the fine cuts of beef, you'll also find pasta dishes and, of course, plenty of fresh seafood.

Burgers, sandwiches and light meals are served during the day. Reservations are recommended.

★Palmilla Restaurant   INTERNATIONAL $$$
(Map p86; ☑226-2067; www.victoria-house.com; Coconut Dr; mains BZ$48-78; ⊙7am-10pm; ▣☑) The classy, candlelit restaurant at Victoria House is the island's priciest, but also one of its best. Arrive before sunset to have a mojito on the veranda, then head into the white-tablecloth dining room to devour a cashew-crusted grouper or imported beef tenderloin. There's also a seasonal fish

market, involving fresh seafood that is handpicked by the chef at the hotel's dock.

Dishes are enormous, flavorful and artfully presented. Vegan and vegetarian options abound, and the wine list slays. At lunchtime you might prefer Admiral Nelson's Beach Bar, the hotel's casual, open-air cafe on the beachfront.

North Island

For a romantic evening out, travel up the coast by ferry for an exotic starlit evening at one of the North Island's excellent restaurants. You can expect unusual menus featuring excellent seafood dishes.

★ Truck Stop   FOOD HALL $$

(Map p86; ☑ 226-3663; www.truckstopbz.com; mains BZ$15-27; ☺ noon-9pm Wed-Sun; ☎ ☑) This absurdly cool shipping-container food park doubles as Ambergris Caye's entertainment hub, offering movie nights, adult spelling bees, live music, farmers markets and backyard games such as ping pong and cornhole. And there's a pool! And a bar! And a dock over the lagoon with a funny (but true) warning about crocodiles.

The colorful containers are dedicated to ice cream, Latin American food, Southeast Asian cuisine and New Haven–style pizza, and the food is all fresh and yummy, made with locally sourced ingredients. The owners are expat filmmakers who know how to make things amazing; expect this place to keep getting better and better. It's a mile north of San Pedro.

Rain   INTERNATIONAL $$$

(Map p86; ☑ 226-4000; www.rainbelize.com; Gran Caribe; mains BZ$40-85; ☺ 7am-10pm) The swankiest place to eat on the North Island is this smart rooftop restaurant in the Grand Caribe complex that serves sophisticated international plates with a view. Prices are some of the highest on the island, but both the service and quality of the dishes are up there. Try the chef's recommended wine-pairing menu.

🍸 Drinking & Nightlife

Most hotels have comfortable bars, often with sand floors, thatched roofs and reggae music. Bars open from late morning till late at night. If you are planning to have a drink, bring insect repellent to see you through dusk.

★ Blue Bayou   COCKTAIL BAR

(☑ 623-8051; www.facebook.com/pg/bluebayou belize; Secret Beach; ☺ 10am-5pm) Tucked away from the louder bars and restaurants, this is the locals' favorite at Secret Beach, mainly for the picnic tables partially submerged in the waist-deep, turquoise cove. It's easy to spend an entire day here, throwing back Belikins and feasting on delicious ceviche, whole jerk fish or curry venison. Cash only.

★ Stella's Sunset Wine Bar & Restaurant   WINE BAR

(Map p86; ☑ 602-5284; www.stellasmile.com; Mile 1, Tres Cocos; ☺ 4-9pm Mon-Wed, Fri & Sat, 8am-1pm Sun) Stella's is a classy but unpretentious wine bar set in a lovely garden on the edge of the San Pedro Lagoon that affords fine sunset views. Sit on lounge chairs under the trees or at a table in the *palapa* and work your way around two dozen different whites and reds.

There are also wine specials for those who don't have to drive their golf cart home. For eats there is a rotating menu of pizza, hamburgers and Caribbean-style fare, with appetizers available every night (mains BZ$20 to BZ$35). On Sunday morning it's all about the crepes and the eggs Benedict.

Rojo Beach Bar   BAR

(☑ 226-4012; www.rojolounge.com; ☺ noon-10pm Tue-Sat) This laid-back beach bar is way up north, but is a great stop on the way home from Secret Beach. Grab a frozen mojito and relax under the *palapa* or in the oceanfront pool, and snorkel off the dock. Bar games include beer pong, pool, giant Jenga and cornhole, and there's a friendly resident parrot.

Maruba Beach Klub   LOUNGE

(☑ 610-3775; Secret Beach; ☺ 9am-5pm) 🌿 The poshest spot on Secret Beach features flowing curtains, an upstairs spa, pulsating techno beats and beach recliners decked out in bright pillows. The Klub has solar-powered everything and a vegan-friendly menu featuring a meatless burrito bowl and a spinach veggie wrap (mains BZ$28 to BZ$35). Wash everything down with a mango-rita.

There's a complimentary ferry that leaves from the San Pedro lagoon at 11am and returns at 4:30pm each day. Call for reservations. Klub is a sister business of the also-fabulous Belize Boutique Resort & Spa (p75).

Crocs Sunset Sports Bar   BAR

(Map p86; ☑ 610-0026; ☺ 11am-11pm) A new go-to for sunset, this open-air, triple-decker bar has large-screen TVs and picture-perfect views over the lagoon.

Nook   BAR
(Map p96; Barrier Reef Dr; ⊙4-10pm Tue-Sun) Delicious sangria, funky cocktails, live music and original snacks are main draws at this new installment right across from the park. With its color-changing old-timey lamps and flowing, sheer curtains, it's got a bit of a gypsy aesthetic, and is under the same expat ownership as two equally fabulous bar-restaurants in Placencia.

Marbucks   COFFEE
(Map p86; Tres Cocos; ⊙7am-2pm) The North Island's only real coffee shop serves up all kinds of caffeinated beverages – both hot and cold – using quality Guatemalan beans (BZ$4 to BZ$15). Also sells excellent breakfasts. It's just off the main road, with the excellent B&B Daydreamin' (p101) attached.

Palapa Bar   BAR
(Map p86; ☑226-3111; www.palapabarandgrill.com; San Pedro; ⊙10am-11pm) This over-the-water *palapa*, a mile south of San Pedro bridge, serves burgers and tacos, and is a fantastic place for tropical drinks any time of day. No laws against drinking and floating, so when it's really hot you are invited to partake of a bucket of beers while relaxing in an inner tube. There's also live music and jam sessions on the weekends.

Dive Bar   BAR
(Map p86; ☑226-3365; www.divebarbz.com; North Island; ⊙7am-midnight) A chill beach bar where scuba divers tend to meet in the morning for breakfast and congregate in the evenings to discuss the day's adventures. The food and cocktails are top notch and the SeaStar Belize (p88) dive shop, under the same ownership, is next door.

Wayo's Beernet   BAR
(Map p86; ☑661-8271; Boca del Rio Dr; ⊙10am-midnight) You'll find a social crowd gathering at this laid-back bar on a pier off the pretty Boca del Rio waterfront just north of San Pedro's center. Pull up a stool at the well-stocked, *palapa* bar and enjoy the sea views.

Blue Marlins   BAR
(Map p96; Foreshore St; ⊙2pm-2am Thu-Sat, to midnight Sun-Wed) A popular pre-disco hangout, this small open-air bar with a plywood dance floor gets packed with locals and visitors alike. The soca and reggaeton soundtrack inside is set to maximum volume,

but there is also a large sandy area out front offering a more mellow experience.

Fido's   CLUB
(Map p96; ☑226-2056; www.fidosbelize.com; 18 Barrier Reef Dr; ⊙10am-midnight) This enormous *palapa* is decorated with seafaring memorabilia and attracts crowds for drinking, dancing and hanging out. There's plenty of seating, an extensive food menu and an ample-sized dance floor. Live music is on most nights at 9pm – classic and acoustic rock, reggae and the occasional record spin.

Jaguar's Temple Club   CLUB
(Map p96; www.jaguarstempleclub.com; Barrier Reef Dr; ⊙midnight-4am Thu-Sat) You can't miss this surreal Maya temple, complete with jaguar face, across from the central beachside park. The place does its very best to create a 'wild' atmosphere, with jungle dioramas setting the stage and lighting effects keeping it spooky.

Big Daddy's Disco   CLUB
(Map p96; Barrier Reef Dr; ⊙11pm-4am) Right next to San Pedro's church, this entertainment complex pulls a crowd once most of the bars around town have closed. There is a bar by the water and a cavernous disco behind.

Wahoo's Lounge   BEACH BAR
(Map p96; ☑226-2002; Barrier Reef Dr; ⊙11am-midnight) This otherwise innocuous sports bar has made a name for itself by hosting the weekly 'Chicken Drop' (6pm Thursday). Sort of like bingo with chickens, it gives new insight to the origin of the term 'chicken shit.' The sand is divided by numbered squares and a chicken is put in the middle of it; participants place bets on where it will drop its load. Give people enough alcohol and they are amused by anything.

Roadkill Bar   BEACH BAR
(Map p86; ☑628-6882; Coconut Dr; ⊙4pm-midnight Mon-Thu, from 11am Fri-Sun) Feels like a beach bar, but it's actually on the roadside a block back from the water. It's a welcoming place that is difficult to fly past without stopping for a drink. Karaoke on Wednesdays, dollar tacos on Tuesdays.

☆ Entertainment

Live music is rampant on Ambergris Caye, emanating from various bars and restaurants around the island every night of the week. Paradise Theater is great for a movie, Wahoo's Lounge continues to hold the infamous Thursday 'chicken drop,' and Truck Stop (p107) hosts super-fun events like adult spelling bees and game-show nights.

Paradise Theater CINEMA

(Map p86; ☑636-8123; www.facebook.com/paradisetheater; North Island; BZ$10; ⏰6-11:30pm Fri-Sun) A cinema and performing-arts center just north of the bridge, with two theaters, a concession stand and a full bar. One theater seats 300, the other 150, and both offer air-con and surround sound for the mostly first-run showings. Check what's playing on the Facebook page. Avoid the bridge toll by parking on the south side and walking across.

🔒 Shopping

Plenty of gift shops sell T-shirts, beachwear, hammocks, jewelry and ceramics. But there are also interesting boutiques, fancy gift stores, art galleries and woodwork shops. Prices are high but you might find unique and artistic souvenirs.

Sometimes artisans sell their woodwork and handicrafts from stalls on the street near the central park, and you can often find Maya merchants selling locally made handicrafts along the waterfront north of Fido's dock.

Belizean Breezes Soap Co GIFTS & SOUVENIRS

(Map p96; ☑226-4322; www.belizeanbreezes.com; Pescador Dr; ⏰9am-8pm Mon-Sat) New place that sells a variety of unique, natural products, from cupcake soaps to whipped shower butters. There are two locations, one on Barrier Reef Dr and one on Pescador Dr.

12 Belize GIFTS & SOUVENIRS

(Map p96; ☑670-5272; www.12belize.com; Tarpon St, Vilma Linda Plaza; ⏰9am-5:30pm Mon-Sat) If the cheesy offerings on the front street aren't really your style, head up the stairs to this small shop to find a selection of interesting, locally made gifts including handmade soaps, Mayan bags and local sauces.

Little Old Craft Shop ART

(Map p96; ☑634-7075; Coconut Dr; ⏰8am-8pm) Talented and friendly local artist Ricardo Zetina crafts beautiful jewelry and figurines, as well as wonderful wood carvings. If your purchase is too big for your suitcase he will arrange shipping for you.

Gallery of San Pedro, Ltd ART

(Map p96; ☑226-4304; www.thegallerysp.com; Pescador Dr; ⏰9am-6pm Mon-Sat, to 3pm Sun) Maintains the largest collections of paintings by Belizean artists in the country, in addition to a wide variety of other quality arts and crafts including tapestries, hammocks and masks, all from Belize.

Belizean Arts Gallery ART

(Map p96; www.belizeanarts.com; 18 Barrier Reef Dr; ⏰9am-10pm Mon-Sat) This is one of the country's best shops for local art and handicrafts, selling ceramics, wood carvings, Garifuna drums and antiques alongside affordable and tasteful knickknacks. You'll also find a decent selection of paintings by local and national artists. Rainforest-flora beauty products, including soaps, are on sale, too. It's inside Fido's.

San Pedro Originals ART

(Map p96; ☑226-4075; islandexcursion@btl.net; Barrier Reef Dr; ⏰10am-9pm) Displaying the works of nine local artists, this tiny gallery is chock-full of colorful island-inspired paintings. It arranges shipping.

Saul's Cigar Coffee House DRINKS

(Map p96; ☑627-1585; saul.nunez@me.com; Pescador Dr; ⏰9am-10pm; 🛜) Catering to all of your vices with a good selection of freshly roasted coffee beans, local rum creme (available for tasting) and cigars from all over the Caribbean. There's even free wi-fi so you can check your email.

Ambar FASHION & ACCESSORIES

(Map p96; ☑226-2824; 18 Barrier Reef Dr; ⏰9am-10pm Mon-Fri, to 9pm Sat, 10am-6pm Sun) Beautiful handmade jewelry in interesting and diverse styles, including plenty of options from the namesake stone. Custom designs made while you wait. It's inside Fido's.

ℹ Information

DANGERS & ANNOYANCES

Don't leave anything unattended in a golf cart that you're hoping to see later, especially in the center of San Pedro. And be sure to lock the steering wheel. The island isn't a dangerous place, but opportunistic theft is common.

EMERGENCY

Police	☑206-2022
Fire	☑206-2372

INTERNET ACCESS

Dominion's Internet Cafe (Barrier Reef Dr; per hour BZ$6; ⏰8:30am-10:30pm) Centrally located internet cafe.

MEDIA

Two rival media outlets keep readers informed about news and events.

Ambergris Today (www.ambergristoday.com) Online news service.

San Pedro Sun (www.sanpedrosun.com) Online news as well as weekly printed newspaper.

MEDICAL SERVICES

San Pedro has both private and public health facilities, but for serious conditions you would want to get to Belize City.

Hyperbaric Chamber (☎ 615-4288, 226-2851; belize@sssnetwork.com; Lion St; ⊙ 24hr) Center for diving accidents – it's in front of the Maya Island Air terminal.

Ambergris Hopes Medical Clinic (☎ 615-2998, 226-2660; Pescador Dr; ⊙ 8am-noon & 1:30-5pm & 7-9pm Mon-Fri, 8-9:30am Sat, 8-11am Sun) Private clinic with its own hyperbaric chamber.

San Carlos Medical Clinic, Pharmacy & Pathology Lab (☎ 226-2918, emergencies 627-3462; 28 Pescador Dr; ⊙ 7am-9pm) Private clinic treating ailments and performing blood tests.

San Pedro Policlinic (☎ 226-2536, emergency 660-2871; Sea Grape Dr; ⊙ in-patient services 8am-8pm Mon-Fri, to noon Sat; emergencies 24hr) A public health clinic with 24-hour emergency services.

MONEY

You can exchange money easily in San Pedro, and US dollars are widely accepted. Most accommodations accept card payment, but many restaurants are cash only.

Atlantic Bank (Barrier Reef Dr; ⊙ 8am-3pm Mon-Fri, 9am-noon Sat)

Belize Bank (Barrier Reef Dr; ⊙ 8am-3pm Mon-Thu, to 4:30pm Fri)

POST

Post Office (Map p96; Pescador Dr; ⊙ 8am-noon & 1-4:30pm Mon-Thu, to 4pm Fri)

TOURIST INFORMATION

Ambergris Caye (www.ambergriscaye.com) Excellent island information and a lively message board.

Tacogirl (www.tacogirl.com) Long-standing local blog on all things good in San Pedro and around Belize; coupons and other deals are sometimes on offer.

Belize Tourism Board (Map p96; ☎ 226-4532; Barrier Reef Dr; ⊙ 8am-noon & 1-5pm Mon-Fri) Goverment tourism office with limited practical information.

Hol Chan Visitors Center (Map p96; ☎ 226-2247; Caribeña St; ⊙ 8am-noon & 1-5pm Mon-Fri, 8am-noon Sat-Sun) Information and displays on marine life.

ⓘ Getting There & Away

AIR

The San Pedro airstrip is just south of the town center on Coconut Dr. The Tropic Air terminal is at the north end of the strip, right on Coconut Dr, while the Maya Island Air terminal is on the west side of the strip. All flights depart between 6am and 5pm.

Tropic Air (☎ 226-2012; www.tropicair.com; Coconut Dr) Hourly flights operate to/from Belize City's Philip Goldson International Airport (one way BZ$178, return BZ$315, 18 minutes), as well as around a dozen flights to the Belize City Municipal Airstrip, 12 miles closer to town (one way BZ$116, return BZ$206, 15 minutes). There are also four flights a day to Caye Caulker (one way BZ$106, return BZ$156, five minutes). Additional flights depart for Corozal (one way BZ$151, return BZ$267, 20 minutes, five daily), Orange Walk (one way BZ$172, return BZ$304, 20 minutes, three daily), Belmopan (one way BZ$255, return BZ$450, 40 minutes, three daily) and San Ignacio near the Guatemalan Border (one way BZ$310, return BZ$547, 55 minutes, three daily).

Maya Island Air (☎ 226-2485; www.mayaislandair.com; ⊙ 6:30am-6pm) Runs regular flights to Philip Goldson International Airport (20 minutes, one way BZ$146 to BZ$233, return from BZ$293 to BZ$464) and Belize Municipal Airstrip (20 minutes, one way BZ$83 to BZ$135, return BZ$166 to BZ$310) with some services stopping on Caye Caulker. Also has four or five flights daily to Corozal and one to Orange Walk. Check website for latest schedules.

BOAT

There are two water-taxi companies running the route between San Pedro and Belize City via Caye Caulker, both departing from docks on the reef side of the island.

San Pedro Belize Express Water Taxi (Map p96; ☎ 226-3535; www.belizewatertaxi.com; San Pedro public dock) runs services to Caye Caulker (one way BZ$30, return BZ$50, 30 minutes) and Belize City (one way BZ$40, return BZ$70, 1½ hours) at 6am, 6:30am, 7:30am, 8:30am, 10am, 11:30am, 1pm, 3pm and 4:30pm.

Ocean Ferry Belize (Map p96; ☎ 226-2033; www.oceanferrybelize.com; Caribeña Foreshore) runs regular boat services to Caye Caulker (one way BZ$19, return BZ$30, 30 minutes) and Belize City (one way BZ$29, return BZ$50, 1½ hours). Boats leave San Pedro at 6am, 8am, 10am, 1pm and 4pm.

Thunderbolt (Map p96; ☎ 631-3400; Black Coral St; one way/return BZ$50/90) operates a daily service between San Pedro and Corozal in northern Belize (one way BZ$50, return BZ$90, two hours) departing from behind the football field on the lagoon side of the island.

🛈 GETTING TO CHETUMAL (MEXICO) BY BOAT

Many travelers choose to exit Belize by sea using Water Jets or San Pedro Belize Express Water Taxi, which offer an efficient ferry service on alternating days between Caye Caulker, San Pedro and Chetumal (Mexico). Daily boats leave Caye Caulker at 7am and stop in San Pedro to pick up passengers and clear immigration. Though theoretically the boat should leave San Pedro by 8:30am, the immigration line can move more slowly than at land borders. In addition to the BZ$40 exit fee, passengers are charged a BZ$2.50 'facility usage fee.'

The trip between San Pedro and Chetumal takes around two hours. Once you've cleared immigration in San Pedro you'll be unable to leave the dock and must board the boat. There is usually a money changer hanging around to change your leftover Belizean currency into Mexican pesos or US dollars.

Upon entering the port of Chetumal, you'll be greeted by soldiers and your luggage will be inspected by drug-sniffing dogs before you are asked to pay the Mexican tourism tax of US$25 (M$533); save your receipt to avoid paying this tax again when exiting Mexico.

There are also departures every morning around 8am for Chetumal, Mexico (one way BZ$100 to BZ$110, two hours) from the **International Departures Dock** (Buccaneer St) on the lagoon side of town with companies **Water Jets** (Map p96; ☑ 226-2194; www.sanpedro-watertaxi.com; Buccaneer St) and San Pedro Belize Express Water Taxi taking turns to make the run.

🛈 Getting Around

You can walk into the center of town from the airport terminals in five minutes and the walk from the boat docks is even shorter.

Minivan taxis ply the streets looking for customers. Official rates are BZ$7 during the day and BZ$10 at night to anywhere in the town center. For hotels outside the center negotiate the rate before hopping in.

There is a small toll bridge over the San Pedro river. Pay a ridiculous BZ$5 for each 20m crossing on a golf cart. Bicycles cross for free.

BICYCLE

Many hotels and resorts provide bikes for their guests for a small fee or for free. Otherwise, you can rent a bike at a couple of places in town, such as **Beach Cruiser** (☑ 607-1710, 651-1533; solenyancona@gmail.com; Pescador Dr; per day BZ$18; ☺10am-7pm Mon-Thu, to 9pm Fri & Sat, to 5pm Sun).

BOAT

The **Coastal Xpress** (Map p96; ☑ 226-2007; www.coastalxpress.com; Amigos del Mar pier; per trip BZ$10-28, day pass BZ$50, week pass BZ$250; ☺5am-10pm) operates a regular scheduled passenger boat service between San Pedro town and the resorts on the North Island. Boats leave from the Amigos del Mar pier roughly every 2½ hours from 6am to 10pm. Charter services are also available to destinations outside their normal route or schedule. Tickets costs BZ$10 to BZ$28 depending on distance traveled, but if you are staying on the North Island you may want to consider a week-long pass (BZ$250).

Many resorts and restaurants also offer a water-shuttle service into town for clients.

GOLF CART

These days, traffic jams are not unusual in San Pedro due to the glut of golf carts cruising the streets. Note that some golf carts are battery-powered and others run on gas; the former being more ecologically sound and the latter having greater endurance. Expect to pay between BZ$100 and BZ$160 per day, although when things are slow you can negotiate a sizable discount. Most rental outlets will drop the cart off at your hotel.

NOLA Gulfkart Rentals (☑ 615-5278; www belizebuggies.com; Lion St; golf cart rental per day/week BZ$120/635; ☺8am-5pm Mon-Sat) A laid-back place with good prices and attentive service.

Island Adventures (☑ 226-4343; www island golfcarts.com; Coconut Dr; golf cart rental per day/week BZ$160/622) Has good new carts and a central location.

Moncho's Cart Rentals (☑ 226-4490; www. sanpedrogolfcartrental.com; 11 Coconut Dr; golf cart rental per day/week BZ$140/587; ☺8am-6pm) A professional operator with a large fleet of quality vehicles.

Polo's Golf Carts (☑ 226-2467; Barrier Reef Dr; golf cart per day/week BZ$100/500; ☺7am-7pm) On Barrier Reef Dr.

Rocks Golf Cart Rentals (☑ 629-4321, 226-2044; www.rocksgolfcartsbelize.com; Pescador Dr; golf cart rental per day/week BZ$100/450; ☺8am-midnight) Located inside the Rocks Grocery Store, significant discounts are available during slower times.

CAYE CAULKER

POP 2000

'No Shirt, No Shoes...No Problem.' You'll see this sign everywhere in Belize, but no place is it more apt than Caye Caulker. On this tiny island, where cars, too, are blissfully absent, dogs nap in the middle of the dirt road and suntanned cyclists pedal around them. The only traffic sign on the island instructs golf carts and bicycles to 'go slow,' and that directive is taken seriously.

In place of hassles, Caulker offers balmy breezes, fresh seafood, azure waters and a fantastic barrier reef at its doorstep. The easygoing attitude is due in part to the strong Creole presence on the island, which pulses to a classic reggae beat and is home to a small community of Rastafarians. This has long been a budget traveler's mecca, but in recent years tourists of all ages and incomes have begun to appreciate the island's unique atmosphere.

History

Caye Caulker was originally a fishing settlement. It became popular with 17th-century British buccaneers as a place to stop for water and to work on their boats. Like its neighbor Ambergris Caye, it grew in population with the War of the Castes. It was purchased in 1870 by Luciano Reyes, whose descendants still live on the island. Reyes parceled the land out to a handful of families, and to this day descendants of those first landowners still live in the general vicinities of those original parcels. These islanders were self-sufficient, exporting turtle meat until the turtle population was decimated.

During much of the 20th century, coconut processing, fishing, lobster trapping and boat building formed the backbone of the island's economy. Caulker was one of the first islands to establish a fishers cooperative in the 1960s, allowing members to receive fair prices for the lobster and other sea life pulled from their waters.

Caye Caulker remains a fishing village at heart, and fishing (as well as boat design and construction) continue. Tourism, which began as a small part of Caulker's economy in the late 1960s and 1970s (when small numbers of hippies found their way to the island), has become its prime economic mover, and the idea of Caulker without tourism would strike most Belizeans as ludicrous. Today, many islanders operate tourism-related businesses, but there are no plans for large-scale development. Caulker residents enjoy the slow rhythm of life as much as visitors do.

◉ Sights

★ Koko King
BEACH

(☑626-8436; www.facebook.com/KokoKingCaye Caulker; ⊗10am-midnight) For those looking to kick it on the soft white sand and in the docile sea, tropical cocktail in hand, surrounded by like-minded travelers, Koko King reigns supreme. It's an all-in-one sort of beach party, with a fully-stocked bar, a tasty Caribbean restaurant and a plethora of beach games and water toys – you can easily spend all day here.

Arriving involves a quick ferry trip (complimentary if you spend BZ$20 at the beach, which you prove with a wristband) or self-guided kayaking, paddleboarding or swimming adventure across the Split. If you get here early, it's worthwhile to rent a swing bed (BZ$50) or a shaded spot behind the beds (BZ$25). For true Koko King diehards, onsite We'Yu Boutique Hotel (rooms from BZ$200) opened in late 2018. Comes in handy when the place throws its famous full-moon parties.

Caye Caulker Forest Reserve
NATURE RESERVE

🌿 The northernmost 100 acres of the island constitute the Caye Caulker Forest Reserve, declared in 1998. Birdlife is prolific in the reserve, particularly wading birds, such as the tricolored heron, and songbirds, including the mangrove warbler. Somewhat rare species that can be spotted include the white-crowned pigeon, rufus-necked rail and black catbird. Inland lagoons provide habitat for crocodiles and turtles, five species of crab, boa constrictors, scaly tailed iguanas (locally called 'wish willies'), geckos and lizards.

The littoral forest on Caye Caulker is mostly red, white and black mangrove, which grows in the shallow water. The mangroves' root systems support an intricate ecosystem, including sponges, gorgonians, anemones and a wide variety of fish. Besides the mangroves, the forest contains buttonwood, gumbo-limbo (the 'tourist tree'), poisonwood, madre de cacao, ficus and ziracote. Coconut palms and Australian pines are not native to this region, but there is no shortage of them.

The forest reserve is an excellent, but very challenging destination for kayakers. You may prefer to paddle up the calmer, west side of the island to avoid strong winds and rough seas. There's also an excellent new tour with Richard's Adventures (p117) that brings intrepid guests along a 1-mile boardwalk through the crocodile habitat.

Swallow Caye
Wildlife Sanctuary
WILDLIFE RESERVE

(☑ 226-0567; www.swallowcayemanatees.org; adult/child BZ$10/5) 🐾 About 19 miles southwest of Caye Caulker, the vast Swallow Caye Wildlife Sanctuary spans nearly 9000 acres, including Swallow Caye and some parts of nearby Drowned Caye. Here the ocean floor is covered with turtle-grass beds, which support a small population of West Indian manatees.

After tireless efforts on the part of conservationists and guides, a wildlife sanctuary was established here in 2002. Swimming with manatees is forbidden by the Belizean authorities, and education programs dissuade boat operators from using their motors near the manatees and from speeding through the area (propeller injuries are one of the chief causes of manatee deaths). There is a permanent caretaker in these waters, although some complain that this is not enough to adequately enforce regulations.

Patient visitors are usually rewarded with several sightings of breaching and feeding manatees, often including a mother and calf swimming together.

Caye Caulker
Marine Reserve
NATURE RESERVE

🐾 Declared a marine reserve in 1998, the 61-sq-mile Caye Caulker Marine Reserve includes the portion of the barrier reef that runs parallel to the island, as well as the turtle-grass lagoon adjacent to the Caye Caulker Forest Reserve. It is rich with sea life, including colorful sponges, blue-and-yellow queen angel fish, Christmas tree worms, star coral, redband parrotfish, yellow gorgonians and more.

Between April and September, snorkelers and divers might even spot a turtle or a manatee. All local snorkel and dive operators lead tours to the Caye Caulker Marine Reserve.

The Split
BEACH

A narrow channel that splits Caye Caulker into two, the Split has deep waters free of seaweed, making it one of the island's best swimming areas. This is particularly true with the recent construction of a seawall, a wading area with picnic tables, a spa, restaurants and a kayak and paddleboard rental shop. The loud music and rowdy crowd at

the adjacent bar, Lazy Lizard (p126), will either enhance or dampen your experience, depending on what you're looking for.

🏃 Activities

Caulker's an ideal base for snorkeling and diving adventures at the nearby reef. The northern part of the island – a tempting destination for kayakers – is mostly mangroves, which are home to an amazing variety of birdlife. Other than that, all visitors should be sure to schedule in plenty of time for swinging in a hammock and enjoying the breeze (which is indeed a legitimate activity here).

Diving

There are enough top-class dive sites in the surrounding area to inspire divers of all levels to stick around for a while.

Common dives made from Caye Caulker include two-tank dives to the local reef (BZ$250 to BZ$280) and two-tank dives to check out the wide variety of aquatic life at Esmeralda off San Pedro (from BZ$310). You can also organize two-tank dives off Turneffe Atoll (from BZ$335) and three-tank trips to the Blue Hole Natural Monument and Half Moon Caye (from BZ$500 including park fees) but these are sometimes subcontracted out to bigger operators from San Pedro, so make sure you know who you are going with before you sign up.

Belize Diving Services
DIVING

(☑ 226-0143; www.belizedivingservices.com; Chapoose St; ⊙ 8am-6pm) Professional and highly recommended dive shop that runs PADI-certification courses and offers immersions around the local reefs, as well as offshore dives at Turneffe North and the Blue Hole. It also offers advanced technical dive training and organizes trips to local cave systems.

Snorkeling

It is possible to snorkel around the Split, but to really experience life under the sea it's necessary to sign up with a tour operator and go out to the reef.

The most popular destination for snorkeling trips is Hol Chan Marine Reserve (p86) and Shark Ray Alley (p91). Full-day tours cost BZ$120 to BZ$140 and visit several different snorkeling sites; some include a stop in San Pedro for lunch (not included in the price). Some trips also include a visit to a sunken barge near the northern tip of Caye Caulker and, in season, manatee spotting in the channel.

Caye Caulker

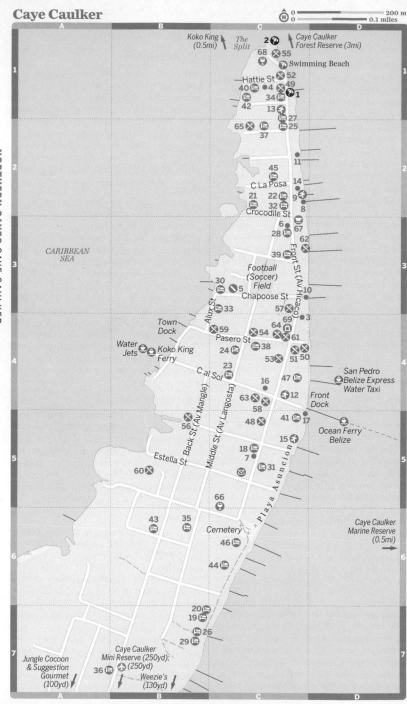

Even though it is only a short boat ride off-shore, only licensed guides are permitted to take snorkelers out to the reef, which helps protect this fragile ecosystem. To get the most out of your trip, it's important to hunt around for a quality guide – the best guides are knowledgeable about the reef and adept at spotting and identifying many hidden creatures.

**Stressless
Eco Friendly Tours**   SNORKELING, FISHING
(✆ 624-6064; www.stresslessecofriendlytours.com; Calle al Sol) ✐ This professional operation stands out in the crowded snorkeling market for its great customer service, focus on sustainability and passionate guides. It offers a condensed version of the classic Hol Chan/Shark Ray Alley trip, along with charter

WEDDINGS & HONEYMOONS

Getting married in Belize is popular and surprisingly easy and affordable. Most upscale resorts and hotels offer wedding packages and services, which simplifies the planning process enormously. For a more customized approach, there are a few wedding planners working in the most popular destinations – Caye Caulker, San Pedro, Hopkins and Placencia.

Legal Requirements

Five days, two passports and one justice of the peace. That's about all it takes to get married in Belize, which is one reason that destination weddings are becoming so popular here. Of course, the gorgeous setting doesn't hurt either.

The government bureaucracy that oversees such things is the **Belize General Registry** (✆ 227-7377; www.belizejudiciary.org; cnr Regent St & Treasury Ln; ⊘ 8am-noon & 1-5pm Mon-Fri). Here's what it takes to make your marriage legal:

➨ Obtain your application for a marriage license from the Register General (available by fax or in person).

➨ Complete the application and have it notarized by a justice of the peace (the Register General can provide contacts for JPs in your area).

➨ Both parties must be in Belize for three days before submitting your application to the Register General. Submit your application, along with photocopies of your passports showing your photograph and your arrival date. If either party has been married before, proof of divorce or widowhood is also required.

➨ For overnight service, the application costs BZ$500, plus a BZ$10 administrative fee. If you don't need expedited service, the fee is only BZ$200 plus administrative fee.

➨ When it's ready, pick up your marriage license and go get married!

➨ The marriage ceremony must be performed by a justice of the peace, a minister of a registered church or a boat captain. Two witnesses (one male and one female) must be present.

➨ After the ceremony, the marriage must be registered in the Belize Registry Department.

➨ Your marriage is legal and valid anywhere in the world. Congratulations!

Belizean Bliss

So you've decided to go the nontraditional route; now the fun begins! Here are a few ideas for a truly memorable and uniquely Belizean wedding:

Sunset Sail Charter a catamaran and exchange your vows as you sail off into the sunset together (literally and figuratively).

Private Island Belize has dozens of them; take over your very own island on your special day.

Maya Temple Exchange your vows atop the High Temple (no bloodletting or human sacrifice required).

Scuba Wedding Let the fish be your witnesses at an underwater affair.

Caye Caulker

Alternatively, half-day snorkeling trips visit the Caye Caulker Marine Reserve (BZ$70 to BZ$100) located just in front of the island, and include Coral Gardens, the Swash (a stand of coral near an opening in the reef where the current and swells attract a good variety of marine life) and Shark Ray Village (Caulker's own shark and ray habitat).

Some tour operators also take snorkel groups to Goff's Caye (p56) or the Turneffe Atoll if there is demand – these are longer trips that promise more pristine reefs and a greater variety of fish. Dedicated snorkel tours to Blue Hole and Lighthouse Reef are rare, although snorkelers are usually welcome to tag along with dive boats if space permits.

All of the tour operators in town take groups snorkeling, as do the sailing companies. Shop around for an operator you are comfortable with, and find out about group size and what is included before signing up.

excursions and trips to Goff's Caye. Some snorkeling trips conclude with sunset ceviche, rum punch and a beach bonfire.

Wildlife Watching

Tours are available to observe manatees in the Swallow Caye Wildlife Sanctuary (p113), and are followed by one or two snorkeling stops and a lunch break at Sergeant's Caye or Goff's Caye (p56). If you don't have any luck spotting manatees in the morning, the boat might return to Swallow Caye in the afternoon to give it another go. The tour usually lasts from 9am until 4pm and costs around BZ$170 per participant.

Note that visitors are not permitted to enter the water within the sanctuary and even if you are lucky enough to spot manatees you will possibly only see the animals briefly as they surface for air.

When temperatures are high, many manatees leave the mud around Swallow Caye and can be observed in the channel near to Caye Caulker, where you can get a better view of the majestic animals. When manatees are around, many companies offer a specialized manatee snorkeling trip (from BZ$100).

Richard's Adventures & Estuary Tours   WILDLIFE
(☑ 602-0024; Playa Asuncion; snorkeling & croc tour per person $BZ70) Local guide and conservationist Richard Castillo not only excels at spotting marine life around the reefs, but he is also the only guide who can bring guests to the new crocodile reserve within Caye Caulker Forest Reserve (p112.) He is part of the team that installed the 1-mile boardwalk through the mangrove swamp, and is a virtual encyclopedia on the habitat.

Ask him about the time Scarface the crocodile chased him on a paddleboard.

Sailing

Several companies organize day sailing trips, most of which visit two or three different snorkeling sites – usually around Caye Caulker Marine Reserve (p113) or Hol Chan Marine Reserve (p86). At around BZ$140 the price is similar to a regular snorkel tour, but the difference is that your journey will be wind powered. While it is a more pleasant way to travel, note that you'll probably spend more time traveling between sites and less time in the water. In general, the sailboats are large, meaning they can take larger groups than the little motorboats other tour operators might use.

In addition to the snorkeling trips, sailing companies also offer sunset cruises (BZ$70) and moonlight sailing trips. Island-hopping trips include overnight excursions to Lighthouse Reef or Turneffe Atoll, as well as multiday trips to the southern cays and Placencia (BZ$700). These tours usually involve one or two nights camping on the beach, as well as plenty of snorkel stops.

Swimming

Caye Caulker's official public beach is at the northern end of the village near the Split, but it's not much to look at, and visitors much prefer to get into the water at the tip of the Split itself. There, a new seawall was recently constructed and you can jump right into the deep water (off a diving platform, if you're bold!) or wade in a shallow area newly populated with wooden picnic tables under *palapas*. You can also snorkel around here, but beware of boats cruising through deeper water on the north shore.

Another dramatic improvement to the beach scene of Caye Caulker is Koko King, an oceanside club on a stretch of pristine sand just north of the Split. A boat taxi brings guests here at no charge if they spend BZ$20 at the bar or restaurant, and it's more than worth it for a glorious day of sun-tanning in a beach recliner and splashing around in the calm waters, tropical cocktail in hand.

It's also possible to swim off the end of the docks that line the east side of the island. Many of the docks are supposed to be public, but some hotel owners have become proprietorial, putting up gates to give privacy to their guests, who use the sun lounges and deck chairs provided.

The surf breaking on the barrier reef is easily visible from the eastern shore of Caye Caulker. Don't attempt to swim out to it, as powerful boats speed through these waters. Also be aware that crocodiles live around some parts of the west side of the island.

Water Sports

With an easterly wind blowing much of the time, and its shallow waters protected by the barrier reef, Caulker has superb conditions for windsurfing and kitesurfing, especially between November and July.

Kitexplorer   KITESURFING
(☑ 652-7308; www.kitexplorer.com; Front St; equipment rental per hour/half-day/full day BZ$120/200/300; ☺ 8am-6pm) Offers a two-hour introductory course (BZ$360) or a six-hour basic course (BZ$980), as well as equipment

rental. Also offers windsurfing classes and has stand-up paddleboards. Located at the northern end of the island near the Split.

★ Contour   WATER SPORTS
(☑ 615-8757; www.contourbelize.com; Front St; rentals per hour/half-day/full day BZ$25/60/80; ☺ 8am-6pm) This well-run shop brings something different to the world of Caulker aquatic recreation: taking visitors through mangroves or on sunset tours on paddleboards. It also rents out its equipment.

Fishing
Just about any skipper will take you fishing in the deep water, flats or reef, and it's cheaper from here than from Ambergris Caye. Grand Slams are not unusual (catching permit, tarpon and bonefish all in one day); other fish often caught include snook, barracuda, snapper and shark, usually on a catch-and-release basis. If you venture out for deep-sea fishing, look for wahoo, sailfish, kingfish, snapper, grouper, jacks, shark and barracuda.

Half-/full-day fly-fishing or deep-sea fishing trips for two to three people run at BZ$500/700. Do make a point of learning which fish are legal to keep, as there has recently been an issue with some visitors bringing back protected fish.

Hiking, Cycling & Birdwatching
Across the split on the north side, large swaths of natural areas are still untouched by the tourist boom. Particularly rewarding for exploration are the remote parts, including a newly opened crocodile sanctuary at the northern end of the island, within the Caye Caulker Forest Reserve (p112). Here, a raised, 1-mile boardwalk cuts through the mangrove forest, and its an excellent place to spot crocs and water birds, including rails, stilts and herons, as well as ospreys and mangrove warblers. Note that the mosquitoes here can be atrocious.

The southern part of the island is also relatively undeveloped, especially in the interior, despite the fact that houses are being built along the coastline south of the airstrip. A rough trail suitable for hiking or biking follows the perimeter of the southern tip, beginning and ending at the airstrip. The airstrip itself is flanked by swampy marshland, making it a fantastic place to spot birds, including the killdeer, the black-necked stilt, the common black hawk and herons of all kinds.

Just north of the airstrip, the Caye Caulker Mini Reserve is run by the Caye Caulker branch of the Belize Tourism Industry Association (BTIA). There is a short interpretative trail that runs through the littoral forest.

Spas & Yoga
After swimming, snorkeling and sunning, you may be in need of a little hands-on healing.

Healing Touch Day Spa   SPA
(☑ 206-0380; www.healingtouchbelize.com; Front St; ☺ 9am-7pm) Ms Eva McFarlane can take care of all your beauty and body needs, including manicures and pedicure; Reiki, reflexology, body scrubs, facials, aura cleansing and aromatherapy are also available. This was the first spa on the island.

★ RandOM Yoga   YOGA
(☑ 637-4109; www.randomyoga.com; Pasero St, above Namaste Cafe; ☺ 9am) A couple of floors above the Namaste Cafe (p124), this excellent, long-standing yoga studio offers daily, 9am classes and occasional sunset classes on an open-air platform with a distant ocean view. The donation-based and consistently high caliber classes are run by long-time island expat and top-notch owner/instructor Jessie Wigh. She and her husband also offer week-long retreats.

⟳ Tours
Although most tour operators have their own specialties, many offer similar versions of the same trips, with similar prices. Most tour operators work closely together, consolidating tours on slow days and juggling overflow at busier times. Snorkel gear, water and fruit are included in the price of most boat trips.

Aside from the boat tours, some companies also organize trips to the Belizean mainland, including those involving zip-lining, cave-tubing and visiting Maya sites at Lamanai and Altun Ha.

★ Anda De Wata Tours   ADVENTURE
(☑ 607-9394, 226-0640; www.snorkeladw.com; Front St) Does floating on an inner tube pulled behind a slow-moving boat sound like a dream come true? Anda De Wata's 90-minute sunset boat-and-float tour (BZ$70, all-you-can drink, rum punch included) may be your own personal paradise. The company also offers great snorkeling tours around local reefs, including complimentary professional photos, and flyovers to check out the Blue Hole.

Caveman Tours SNORKELING

(☑ 226-0367; www.cavemansnorkelingtours.com; Front St; half-/full-day trips BZ$70/130; ☺ 8:30am-6:30pm) Captain Caveman's guides offer extremely popular snorkeling trips throughout local waters, as well as manatee-watching expeditions and occasional private trips to Goff's Caye and Swallow Caye. The Captain is serious, safety conscious and very attentive to customer needs. His office is inside the handicraft market.

Blackhawk Sailing Tours BOATING

(☑ 607-0323, 662-4806; www.blackhawksailing tours.com; Front St) Locally owned and operated, Blackhawk offers sailing/snorkeling tours; overnight sailing trips, where guests sleep under the stars on sandy isles; and sunset reggae cruises complete with fresh ceviche.

Spearfishing Shack SNORKELING, FISHING

(Captain Jacob; ☑ 620-8821, 651-3925; Crocodile St; tours per person BZ$140) A favorite among backpackers, Captain Jacob and his crew lead full-day snorkeling and spearfishing tours around the Belize Barrier Reef.

Tsunami Adventures ADVENTURE, FISHING

(☑ 226-0462; www.tsunamiadventures.com; Calle al Sol; ☺ 8am-6pm) Bring home some barracuda, grouper or snapper on one of the many fishing tours run by this established local company. Tsunami also offers a wide range of other activities including flyovers of the Blue Hole, snorkeling trips, kayaking excursions, island-hopping sightseeing outings and tours on the mainland.

Anglers Abroad FISHING

(☑ 226-0602; www.anglersabroad.com; Hattie St) Experienced and professionally run outfit offering adventurous fishing trips throughout the region. Head to the office inside Sea Dreams Hotel to arrange your tour.

Frenchie's Diving DIVING

(☑ 226-0234; www.frenchiesdivingbelize.com; Front St) Well-regarded local dive operator offering a full range of dives throughout the region, including full-day trips (three dives) to Blue Hole/Turneffe (BZ$450/580), and half-day trips (two dives) to Esmeralda/Spanish Bay BZ$250/270. Night dives at Caye Caulker Marine Reserve cost BZ$150. It also runs overnight dive adventures, which include six immersions and a night on Half Moon Caye.

Raggamuffin Tours BOATING

(☑ 226-0348; www.raggamuffintours.com; Front St; ☺ 8am-6pm) Runs popular three-day sailing and camping trips to Dangriga departing every Tuesday and Friday that pass through some less-visited islands and areas of reef. Advance reservations are essential. Also runs snorkeling tours to Hol Chan, sunset sailing cruises and a half-day trip to the Caye Caulker Marine Reserve.

Carlos Tours SNORKELING

(☑ 600-1654, 226-0458; carlosayala10@hotmail. com; Front St; snorkeling day trips BZ$140; ☺ 11am & 1:30pm, ☑) Popular local guide Carlos and his son (also Carlos) run these snorkeling tours from a catamaran and offer high-quality underwater photographs to guests on a CD for BZ$30. Trips run to Hol Chan, Shark Ray Alley and Coral Gardens, and include a yummy lunch onboard.

Barefoot Fisherman Expeditions FISHING

(☑ 226-0405; www.barefootfishermanexpeditions. com; Front St) A serious operation dedicated to all kinds of fishing excursions, including catch-and-release sportfishing (half day BZ$500, full day BZ$800). It also rents kayaks and stand-up paddleboards.

Reef Watersports WATER SPORTS

(☑ 635-7219; www.reefwatersports.com; Front St) This high adrenaline outfitter right by the Split offers jet-ski rentals (BZ$140 per half hour, BZ$240 for an hour). It also offers various packages including wakeboarding and waterskiing. Check its website for package details.

E-Z Boy TOURS

(☑ 226-0349; www.ezboytoursbelize.com; Front St; ☺ 8am-6:30pm) Runs the full gamut of tours and activities, including snorkeling tours, sailing, manatee watching at Swallow Caye and half- and full-day deep-sea fishing trips (BZ$600/900).

★★ Festivals & Events

Lobsterfest FOOD & DRINK

Caulker hosts the original Northern Cayes Lobsterfest, which marks the opening of lobster fishing season on June 15, although the festival is usually held a couple of weekends later so there's enough lobster to go around. The streets are filled with *punta* (traditional Garifuna dance) drumming, Belikin beer and grilled lobster.

Other activities include a fishing tournament, canoe races, dance performances and – of course – the annual Lobster Festival Pageant.

🛏 Sleeping

Caulker offers an endless array of accommodations options, from budget digs to boutique hotels and charming rental properties. Golf-cart taxis meet boats upon arrival; if you don't have a reservation they will take you around to look at a few places to stay. It's best to book in advance if you're coming around Christmas or Easter.

🛏 Central Area

The majority of the budget-friendly options are along Front St, stretching from the water taxi docks up to the Split. There are also some good backpacker places and midrange options on the less-trafficked, western side of the island.

Yuma's House Belize HOSTEL $
(📞 206-0019; www.yumashousebelize.com; Front St; dm/s/d BZ$38/75/90; 🛜) This fun and freshly painted hostel is just a few steps from the water-taxi dock, giving it a prime location in the center of town and at the water's edge. It takes full advantage of the choice positioning with a dock for guests and a breezy, palm-shaded garden complete with hammocks and picnic tables from which to admire the view. Guests have access to a well-equipped kitchen.

Ocean Pearl Royale Hotel HOTEL $
(📞 226-0074; oceanpearl@btl.net; Park St; r with/without air-con BZ$95/70, cabañas BZ$120, apt BZ$120; ❄🛜) Located on a quiet side street, this small hotel is surrounded by sandy grounds strewn with palms and flowering trees that attract hummingbirds and other beauties. The five clean rooms are remarkably good value, with brightly painted walls and simple wood furnishings. A big, airy lobby offers space for guests to congregate and swap island stories.

Travellers Palm HOSTEL $
(📞 636-4871; Travellers Palm St; dm with fan/air-con BZ$26/32; ❄🛜) A new, banana-yellow hostel a bit south of the action is the best backpacker deal on the island. The four co-ed dorms are basic but adequate, and three offer air-con. There's also a single private room, and a sweet rooftop hangout spot featuring hammocks, a bar and a kitchen. The staff are super nice and kayaks are available to guests.

Sophie's Guesthouse GUESTHOUSE $
(📞 661-2715; besophiesguest@gmail.com; Almendra St; r BZ$74) This laid-back budget option

near the Split on the back side of the island has five simple but neat rooms in an elevated wooden house. It's close to all the action but in a supremely tranquil setting and there is a decent swimming spot just in front. All rooms share bathrooms.

Mara's Place GUESTHOUSE $
(📞 600-0080; maras_place@hotmail.com; Front St; d BZ$109; @🛜) The eight guest rooms spread over a number of two-story wooden cabañas are simple but spotless, and cramped but comfortable. Not exactly luxurious, they nonetheless include a few perks you would not expect, such as a private veranda complete with hammock, lightning-quick wi-fi and reading material.

There is a communal kitchen on the premises, and the main town beach is right across the street, where Mara also runs the Sip & Dip – the most popular place for waterside socializing among islanders and Belizean visitors.

Bella's Hostel HOSTEL $
(📞 626-8238, 226-0360; www.bellasinbelize.com; Crocodile St; dm with/without air-con BZ$35/25, r from BZ$65; 🛜) On the back side of the island, Bella's is a hideaway for the backpacker set, who appreciate the good-value dorms in the elevated wooden house. There is a chilled-out vibe here aided by laid-back management and good tunes. You are likely to see travelers sharing a meal in the kitchen, playing cards on the balcony and taking advantage of free rentals, such as canoes and bikes.

Jeremiah's Inn HOTEL $
(📞 625-2618; Front St; r BZ$67-72; ❄🛜) A good budget choice, fan-cooled rooms at this small hotel right on the main drag are comfortable enough (though somewhat spartan), surrounding a shared courtyard. A central location assures that you're never more than a stone's throw from Caulker's many aquatic attractions. There are some new air-con rooms, and more renovations are planned.

Tropical Oasis HOSTEL $
(📞 605-6779; karianne_mokkelbost@hotmail.com; Calle La Posa; dm BZ$25, cottages BZ$50) Basic but centrally located and well suited to hardy backpackers, this low-key place has a ramshackle, pastel collection of semi-open huts and dorms covered in mosquito mesh that lets in plenty of fresh air. There is also an outdoor kitchen, as well as hammocks hung around the ample yard, which contains three outdoor showers.

★**Jungle Cocoon** BUNGALOW **$$**
(☑630-8396; Av Mulche; r BZ$218; 🛜) Jungle-shrouded and dripping with character, this octagonal bungalow has got to be Caye Caulker's most romantic stay. The bedroom is spacious, with lovely hardwood flooring and tasteful art, but the bathroom is the real treat, offering a sitting area complete with a drum set, and lots of natural touches, including a live tree surrounded by conch shells.

Large windows on each of the bungalow's eight sides highlight the lush tropical land-scaping, and the adjacent private garden is an ideal spot to take morning coffee and baked goods from Suggestion Gourmet (p124), the property's fabulous restaurant.

Island Magic HOTEL **$$**
(☑226-0505; www.islandmagicbelize.com; Front St; r BZ$240-500; ❄🛜▦) Offering excellent value for its accommodations and amenities, Island Magic offers spacious, earth-toned rooms with fully equipped kitchens and dining areas on the 1st and 2nd floors, with more-expensive rooms offering glorious ocean views from private balconies on the 3rd and 4th floors.

The swanky swimming pool is an added bonus and the new restaurant and bar, Magic Grill, is delightful. Grab one of the hanging tables suspended beneath *palapas* on the sand. An attached tour company can hook you up with island and mainland excursions.

Blue Wave GUESTHOUSE **$$**
(☑206-0114; www.bluewaveguesthouse.com; Front St; r with/without bathroom BZ$120/64, deluxe BZ$170, cabañas BZ$200; ❄🛜) Look for the attractive log-cabin-style house overlooking Front St, and you'll know you've arrived at the Blue Wave, an inviting guesthouse with several different accommodation options. 'Deluxe' rooms are spacious and stylish, with air-con, TV, private bathrooms and breezy balconies. Beneath the owners' clapboard house, there are three cheaper, fan-cooled rooms with shared facilities.

Leeside Rooms GUESTHOUSE **$$**
(leesiderooms@gmail.com; Alux St; r from BZ$180; ❄🛜) This charming, small guesthouse offers a pair of elegant air-conditioned rooms with small verandas that overlook the water, as well as cheaper fan-cooled rooms upstairs. Located on the lagoon side behind the football field, there is less noise and less light than on Front St. The stylish interior design features high beds, tiled floors and walls hung with old maps.

Amanda's Place GUESTHOUSE **$$**
(Casita Cariñosa; ☑226-0547; www.cayecaulker casita.com; Front St; apt BZ$190, house BZ$200-390; ❄🛜▦) Amanda offers a variety of accommodations on leafy grounds with a nice pool a block from the beach. On one side of the property there is a modern three-bedroom *casita* with a rooftop terrace. The main building looks over the road to the water and has two art-filled studios with kitchenettes downstairs and a traditional Belizean-style apartment upstairs.

Caye Caulker Condos HOTEL **$$**
(☑226-0072; www.cayecaulkercondos.com; Front St; ste BZ$215-303; ❄🛜▦) Inside this attractive, salmon-colored concrete block on Front St sit eight sweet retreat suites. Each has a fully equipped kitchen, satellite TV and fancy bathrooms with romantic two-person showers made of stone. Suites each have a private balcony, and the rooftop terrace – with its 360-degree views – is a key selling point.

Caye Caulker Plaza Hotel HOTEL **$$**
(☑226-0780; www.cayecaulkerplazahotel.com; cnr Middle St & Calle al Sol; r BZ$164-192; ❄🛜) This 50-room hotel offers good amenities including private bathrooms with hot showers, cable TV, in-room safes and mini refrigerators. More-expensive rooms also have private balconies, while cheaper ones are on the ground floor. The beautiful rooftop terrace is open to all. Staff are friendly, and the location is central.

Rainbow Hotel HOTEL **$$**
(☑226-0123; www.cayecaulkerhotelbz.com; Front St; r BZ$200-230; ❄🛜) Bright blue paint, a couple of rainbows for decoration and up-graded rooms make this bunker-like concrete building relatively appealing. Bottom-floor rooms open right onto the street so you can sit out front and enjoy the street life. For privacy, choose a room on the top floor or rent one of the cottages (BZ$220 to BZ$250) at the back. All rooms have flat-screen TVs, mini fridges and coffee makers.

Costa Maya Beach Cabanas GUESTHOUSE **$$**
(☑226-0432; www.costamayabelize.com; Front St; r BZ$100-180, ste BZ$220-300; ❄🛜) This well-run guesthouse has a new building out the back with six spacious, air-conditioned suites featuring large fridges and two queen beds, as well as a large rooftop terrace. In front, the

cheaper original units can be a bit gloomy but each has a porch, perfect for catching sea breezes. Guests enjoy beach chairs, a swimming dock and complimentary canoes and bicycles.

Pancho's Villas
HOTEL $$

(☏ 226-0304; www.panchosvillasbelize.com; Pasero St; d with/without kitchenette BZ$190/130; ✳🛜) Resembling a big square wedding cake with lemon-yellow frosting, Pancho's Villas is a little out of place on this quiet side street. The building is decked out with all the modern amenities, such as kitchenettes, cable TV and the rest. It's not particularly stylish, but it's convenient and pretty good value.

De Real Macaw Guest House
GUESTHOUSE $$

(☏ 226-0459; www.derealmacaw.biz; Front St; r BZ$100-140, apt BZ$260; ✳🛜) All the rustic lodgings dotting the leafy grounds here are inspired by the jungle, from cabañas built from pimenta sticks to the beachfront rooms with thatched-roof verandas. The decor continues the theme with swinging hammocks and woven tapestries, but the rooms are also equipped with modern conveniences such as TVs, fridges and coffee makers.

The kind owner is a mother of six, and caters particularly to families.

★ Sea Dreams Hotel
B&B $$$

(☏ 226-0602; www.seadreamsbelize.com; Hattie St; r BZ$272, apt BZ$370-480; ✳🛜) A lovely guesthouse on the north side of the island, Sea Dreams offers a rare combination of easy access and sweet tranquility. Spend the day lounging around the Split, then retreat to the cozy accommodations just a few steps away. Original paintings by local artists adorn the colorful walls of the rooms and apartments, which are elegant and comfortable.

The small dock on the back side gives access to one of the best swimming areas on the island – it's deep, usually free of sea grass and affords glorious sunset views. For even better panoramas, head up to the rooftop lounge. Breakfast, bikes, paddleboards and canoes are all included.

★ Caye Reef
BOUTIQUE HOTEL $$$

(☏ 610-0240; www.cayereef.com; Front St; apt BZ$558-598; ✳🛜🏊) The six apartments at Caye Reef have been designed with the utmost attention to detail – from the original artwork hanging on the walls to the swinging hammocks hanging on the private balconies. Room prices rise with the floor, with the most expensive rooms on the third.

As comfortable and classy as they are, the apartments are not the main attraction to staying at Caye Reef: that would be the roof deck, complete with hammocks, hot tub and 360-degree sea views.

Weezie's
BOUTIQUE HOTEL $$$

(☏ 226-0603, in USA 970-376-2167; www.weezies cayecaulker.com; Av Mangle; r from BZ$281, cottages from BZ$368; ✳🛜🏊) A dreamy new addition to the southern stretches of Caye Caulker, with just a few hotel rooms and cottages offering a highly personalized experience. The rooms are clustered into dainty clapboard buildings surrounding luxe lap pools, while two blocks inland, three fully-equipped cottages also share a pool. All interiors are spacious, comfy and adorned in local hardwoods and art.

Iguana Reef Inn
RESORT $$$

(☏ 226-0213; www.iguanareefinn.com; Chapoose St; standard r BZ$358-398, deluxe r BZ$418-458; ✳🛜🏊) Set on sandy grounds fringed with palms, the Iguana Reef is both upscale and informal. It's the kind of place you can roam around barefoot by day, but you might dress up for dinner. Bamboo furniture, Mexican tapestries and local artwork adorn the jewel-toned rooms.

Outside, you can lounge poolside or pull up a lounge chair on the fantastic waterside area by the dock, which is now home to a small seahorse habitat that tour boats often stop in to visit.

At the end of the day, take your pick from the extensive menu of tropical cocktails at the beach bar and watch the sunset. A continental breakfast is included.

Seaside Cabanas
RESORT $$$

(☏ 226-0498; www.seasidecabanas.com; Calle al Sol; r BZ$258-358, ste BZ$398; ✳🛜🏊) Sun-yellow stucco buildings shaded by thatched-palm roofs exude a tropical atmosphere at this beachfront beauty. The interior decor features desert colors, rich fabrics and plenty of pillows. Most of the rooms occupy the main building facing the ocean; closer to the sea, the comfortable cabañas take advantage of the location with private rooftop decks and terrace hot tubs.

South of Town

South of the cemetery, Caye Caulker is noticeably quieter, with less foot traffic and mostly midrange options. The back streets to the south are known as 'Gringo Heights,' for this is where many expats have bought property and built houses, some of which are available for longer-term rentals via **Caye Caulker Vacation Homes** (📱 630-1008; www.cayecaulker rentals.com; Middle St).

Ignacio Beach Cabins
CABIN **$**

(📱 226-0175; Playa Asuncion; r BZ$45-100; 🛜) In the far south of town, Ignacio offers very basic waterfront lodging in weathered cabins on stilts. Here you are giving up a bit of comfort but the reward is tranquility; there is little foot traffic this far south, so it feels private and pristine. The cold-shower cabins all have easy access to the beach, but the pricier ones are at the water's edge, catching cool breezes.

★ Oasi
GUESTHOUSE **$$**

(📱 623-9401; www.oasi-holidaysbelize.com; Back St; apt BZ$190-210; 🅿🛜) 🏊 Set around blooming tropical gardens featuring an inviting pool, this excellent guesthouse has just four elegant apartments with lovely wide verandas (hung with hammocks, of course). Woven tapestries and warm hues enrich the interiors, which are equipped with full kitchens, sofas and quality bathrooms. There's also a small bar and Italian restaurant, Il Baretto (p126), that hosts lively concerts and events.

Hosts Luciana and Michael go above and beyond to ensure you enjoy your stay, offering expert opinions about local snorkel and dive trips. The guesthouse is away from town and just off the waterfront; it has free bikes available that make for easy outings. The place runs largely on solar power.

Colinda Cabanas
CABAÑAS **$$**

(📱 226-0383; www.colindacabanas.com; Playa Asuncion; r BZ$138-318; 🅿🛜) It's hard to miss Colin and Linda's brightly colored yellow-and-blue property, which sits south of the cemetery. Both the cabañas and suites are appointed with fridges, hot showers and comfy beds alongside value-adding extras such as coffee makers with a stash of gourmet Belizean coffee beans and binoculars for wildlife spotting. The suites have a full kitchen and air-conditioning.

Out the front there is a fine dock with a *palapa* throwing shade on a pair of swinging hammocks. Complimentary bicycles, kayaks and snorkeling equipment are available to guests.

Barefoot Beach Belize
GUESTHOUSE **$$**

(📱 226-0205; www.barefootbeachbelize.com; Playa Asuncion; r BZ$144-164, studio BZ$174, ste & cottages BZ$264; 🅿🛜) Painted in candy colors, this perky place is on a quiet stretch of beach at the southern end of the village. Suites and cottages have kitchens and living space, with direct access to beach breezes; rooms are smaller but still spacious, with fridges, air-con and coffee makers. The whole place has a tropical theme, with plenty of floral prints and sea-themed artwork.

Maxhapan Cabanas
CABIN **$**

(📱 226-0118, 610-4993; maxhapan04@hotmail.com; 55 Pueblo Nuevo; s/d/tr BZ$100/110/120; 🅿🛜) In an unexpected location south of town, Maxhapan has three sweet, yellow cabañas clustered around a sandy yard complete with an elevated *palapa* with hammocks and a bring-your-own bar, where guests can gather. Natural light floods the spotless, modern cabins, which are equipped with fridges, air-con and TV. Your host, Louise, guarantees your comfort and happiness.

The only drawback is that it's not on the water, which explains why it's such a bargain. Free bikes are a bonus.

Anchorage Resort
HOTEL **$$**

(📱 206-0304; www.anchoragebelizeresort.com; Playa Asuncion; r BZ$172; 🅿🛜) This is not the place to come for style or swank, but if you're in search of reasonably priced accommodations right by the water then it's a fairly good deal. The powder blue resort boasts one of the widest stretches of sand on the island and the rooms, while a little generic, are equipped with plenty of perks, such as king-size beds, cable TV and private balconies.

Tree Tops Guesthouse
GUESTHOUSE **$$**

(📱 226-0240; www.treetopsbelize.com; Playa Asuncion; r with/without bathroom from BZ$196/152, ste BZ$261; 🅿@🛜) For years Doris has been winning accolades for her hospitality and helpfulness. The spacious, cool and clean rooms are very comfortable and are decorated with original artistic touches. Set back from the beach, the three-story building is fronted by a pleasant palm-shaded garden, while a roof terrace with panoramic vistas towers over the treetops, giving the place its name.

There is also a sandy area by the waterside with recliners for guest use.

Tropical Paradise Hotel
RESORT **$$**

(📱 226-0124; www.tropicalparadise.bz; Front St; r BZ$140-165, cottages BZ$165, ste BZ$250-300; 🅿🛜) With an ideal location on the waterside just south of the cemetery, Tropical Paradise is Caulker's 'original beach resort.' It was one of the first places to clean a stretch of sand, furnish it with painted lounge chairs and entice guests with cocktails. There are more stylish places to stay, but these orange and yellow cottages still offer decent value.

🍴 Eating

Caulker is all about the creatures of the sea, with lobster season running from mid-June to mid-February, and conch season from October to June. There are plenty of street eats, too, from ad-hoc beachside grills to the island's famous 'Cake Lady', who shows up on Front St with a cart filled with amazing homemade cakes right around dusk.

Namaste Cafe   HEALTH FOOD $
(☑637-4109; Pasero St; salads & sandwiches BZ$12; ⊙7:30am-4:30pm Mon-Sat; 🛜) 🌿 From the hibiscus-lime kombucha and garlic-cilantro hummus to the chia pudding, this place absolutely oozes hippie goodness. The salads and sandwiches are fresh and healthy, this is also a lovely spot to relax with your feet in the sand, sipping some tea, after one of the excellent, donation-based yoga (p118) classes upstairs. Eco-conscious offerings include biodegradable takeaway containers.

Gelato Italiano   ICE CREAM $
(The Split; ice cream BZ$7-12; ⊙11am-6pm) Gelato Italiano serves up first-class ice cream to the island. Choose from a dozen varieties of genuine Italian gelato and head outside to pull up a stool on the long balcony overlooking the vivid blue Caribbean. The perfect way to cool off.

Errolyns House
of Fry Jacks   BELIZEAN $
(Middle St; BZ$1.50-6; ⊙6:30am-2pm & 6:30-9pm Tue-Sun) Who said Belize had to be expensive? Locals and travelers alike descend on this neat takeout hut to chow down on the island's best-value breakfast – delicious golden fry-jacks (deep-fried dough) filled with any combination of beans, cheese, egg, beef or chicken. Cheap, filling and delicious.

Amor Y Café   BREAKFAST $
(☑610-2397; Front St; breakfast BZ$6-12.50; ⊙6am-2pm; 🍴) There's no contest when it comes to the most popular breakfast spot on the island – this place is always busy, but you won't have to wait long for a table on the shaded porch overlooking Front St. Take your pick from freshly squeezed juices, scrambled eggs or homemade yogurt topped with fruit – and don't miss out on the freshly brewed coffee (with espresso ice cubes!).

If you have to pack a lunch, sandwiches are available to go.

Glenda's Café   BELIZEAN $
(☑226-0148; Back St; mains BZ$9-12; ⊙7am-1pm Mon-Fri) Glenda's serves traditional Belizean food in a clapboard house on the island's west side. It boasts some of the best breakfasts in town, from cinnamon rolls and orange juice to full cooked breakfasts of bacon or ham, eggs, bread and coffee. Burritos, tacos, sandwiches and chicken with rice and beans are offered for lunch. Arrive early for breakfast.

★ Caribbean Colors
Art Café   HEALTH FOOD $$
(☑605-9242; Front St; mains BZ$10-25; ⊙7am-2:30pm Fri-Wed; 🍴) What began as a gallery (p127) for owner and artist Lee Vanderwalker has morphed into a top-notch cafe. And the art's still on the walls. While you browse you can treat yourself to a coffee or a cool smoothie, then sit down for a fresh and healthy breakfast, salad or sandwich. There are lots of veggie and vegan options, too.

On Wednesdays there's a sushi menu, and during mango season, the chef prepares mouthwatering pancakes, salads and crumbles with the fruit.

Suggestion Gourmet   EUROPEAN $$
(☑630-8396; Av Mulche; mains BZ$20; ⊙7:30am-5pm & 6-8:30pm) Tucked into the jungle in the southern reaches of Caye Caulker, this delicious artsy little bistro is a local favorite thanks to head chef Frédéric Grandchamp's winning concept. Basically, he asks customers what they want, then finds a way to serve it (hence the restaurant's name). Certain menu items, such as rotisserie chicken, paella crevette and schnitzel, tend to recur.

Visit Facebook (search for 'Suggestion Gourmet') to contribute a suggestion or check the menu for the week, and don't miss the all-you-can-eat pizza night or the mango crumble dessert.

Blue Beard   FRENCH $$
(☑633-2234; mains BZ$10-25; ⊙9am-9pm Wed-Sun) This new bistro might look like another casual, sandy-bottomed eatery, but make no mistake. The Southern French fare is hearty and the chef knows just what to do with those tender hunks of filet mignon, that heavenly blue-cheese sauce and the accompanying ratatouille. Pair it with a French wine and end on French toast with salted butter caramel.

Wish Willy
BELIZEAN $$

(🖉671-5948, 660-7194; 40 Park St; mains BZ$20; ⊙6:30-10:30am & 5:30-11:30pm) An institution on Caye Caulker, the sandy front yard of dreadlocked local Maurice Moore is easily the most chilled-out spot for a mouthwatering Belizean meal. Yes, the tables are hopelessly tilted, and the service is island-slow, but the pulsating calypso beats and convivial atmosphere more than compensate. Best for a fry-jack and beans breakfast or a grilled seafood dinner.

Roy's Blue Water Grill
BELIZEAN $$

(🖉607-5166; Pasero St; mains BZ$18-35; ⊙5-10pm) Beloved local chef Roy is the brains behind this simple open-air restaurant just off the main drag. The menu features plenty of fresh seafood, including stone crab, coconut encrusted snapper and jerk lion fish, but there are also interesting chicken and pork dishes, all imbued with rich Caribbean flavors.

Belizean Flava
SEAFOOD $$

(🖉634-0922; Front St, above Barrier Reef Sports Bar & Grill; mains BZ$20-50; ⊙5:30-10pm) The island's most popular grill, and rightly so. Take your pick from the fantastic selection of lobster, snapper or conch, that will then be expertly grilled before being served up with tasty sides of your choice. Service is super friendly and there is a great, laid-back atmosphere – no doubt aided by the generous amounts of free rum punch.

Pasta per Caso
ITALIAN $$

(🖉602-6670; Front St; mains BZ$28; ⊙6-9pm Sat-Wed; 🖉) Pull up a stool at one of the long tables on the deck and dig into some of the best homemade pasta in Belize, prepared the traditional way by the Italian owner. There is usually one vegetarian and one non-veg sauce served with a healthy portion of one of the many varieties of fresh pasta made onsite. Garden fresh salads and parmesan plates also make an appearance.

Little Kitchen Restaurant
BELIZEAN $$

(🖉667-2178; off Luciano Reyes St; mains BZ$15-25; ⊙6-11am & noon-4pm & 6-10pm) Elba Flower's Little Kitchen is a 3rd-floor, open-air restaurant on Caulker's southwestern side serving traditional (yet artfully done) Belizean dishes such as curry shrimp, coconut red snapper and excellent conch fritters (just to name a few). Portions are big and it's outstanding value, although we have some concerns about immature lobsters on the menu – make sure yours is legal size.

Its unique vantage point makes it a fine spot to watch the sun go down with a cocktail made with local rum or a fresh juice.

Happy Lobster
SEAFOOD $$

(🖉226-0064; Front St; mains BZ$15-30; ⊙6:30am-9:30pm Wed-Mon; 🖉) The lobster at this Caulker institution is actually not that happy, but you will be after eating big plates of fresh fish, spiced with Creole flavoring or sweetened with coconut. The place also has lots of vegetarian options and a popular breakfast menu, and the front porch is a pleasant place to watch the activity on Front St.

Ana's Genie
MIDDLE EASTERN $$

(🖉605-3305; Front St; mains BZ$14-27; ⊙11am-8pm Sun-Fri) Nestled behind a couple of rental shops, this tiny restaurant doesn't look like much but grab a stool or a picnic table and enjoy great Middle Eastern cuisine prepared by the Belizean owner, who trained in Jordan. The hummus and baba ganoush are top notch.

Bambooze
SEAFOOD $$

(🖉636-0238; waterfront; mains BZ$14-25; ⊙noon-9:30pm; 🖉) In one of the best locations on the island, this casually cool bar and grill sits right on the waterside, with swings hanging from the rafters and tables set up in the sand. Besides the Cajun specialties, you can feast on a huge seafood burrito or a grilled fish sandwich, washed down with a fruit smoothie or a strong daiquiri. The bar usually stays open late.

Rose's Grill
SEAFOOD $$

(🖉226-0407; rosesgrillandbar@hotmail.com; Calle al Sol; mains from BZ$20-40; ⊙11am-4pm & 5-11pm Wed-Sun, 5-11pm Mon & Tue; 🖉) Take your pick from the fresh fish and lobster on display at this friendly streetside grill restaurant. Then head back to the shade of the *palapa* while they grill it for you. There are also pizza, pasta, meats and vegetarian options, and the family-style seating at big picnic tables makes for a lively atmosphere. In high season, make reservations.

Rainbow Grill & Bar
SEAFOOD $$

(🖉226-0281; waterfront; mains BZ$10-25; ⊙10:30am-9pm Tue-Sun; 🖉) Perched on a deck over the turquoise waters, this local favorite is evidence of Caulker's agreeable temperatures. By day, nibble on vegetarian plates, burgers, quesadillas, burritos and sandwiches. At night, fancier fare includes fish, shrimp, conch and lobster cooked how you like it, including simple lemon with butter, Jamaican jerk or Oriental-style.

Barrier Reef Sports
Bar & Grill INTERNATIONAL $$
(Front St; mains BZ$10-25; ⊘9am-midnight; 🛜) This unlikely spot is a no-holds-barred expat hangout but has surprisingly delicious food. If you don't like the multiple TVs blaring sports interviews into the atmosphere, take a seat out front and enjoy the breeze off the ocean.

★Il Pellicano ITALIAN $$$
(✐226-0660; Pasero St; mains BZ$25-42; ⊘5:30-9:30pm Tue-Sun) Head to the lagoon side of the island to find this wonderful garden restaurant preparing a small, but constantly changing, selection of outstanding classic Italian dishes including flavorful homemade pastas and the best pizza on the island. Accompany your meal with Italian wine served by the glass or bottle, and be sure to sample the excellent desserts.

★Hibisca
by Habaneros INTERNATIONAL $$$
(✐626-4911; cnr Front St & Calle al Sol; mains BZ$32-58; ⊘5:30-9:30pm Fri-Wed) Caulker's poshest restaurant is located in a brightly painted clapboard house in the center of town. Here chefs prepare gourmet international food, combining fresh seafood, meat and vegetables with insanely delicious sauces and flavors. Wash it down with a fine wine or a jug of sangria.

Sit in the funky bar and sip a fruity cocktail or enjoy the buzz and eat by candlelight at the tables on the veranda. Reservations are recommended in high season.

🍸 Drinking & Nightlife

Lazy Lizard BEACH BAR
(The Split; ⊘10am-11pm) The Lazy Lizard is described as a 'sunny place for shady people,' though most folks here tend to be attractive, young travelers, swimming about and sunbathing as they are plied with booze and cocktails. The bar's 2nd-story balcony offers spectacular views of the Split, and its cornhole tournaments, beach rugby games and full-moon parties are delightful.

Barrier Reef Sports
Bar & Grill SPORTS BAR
(✐226-0077; Front St; ⊘9am-midnight) Perennially popular with expats and international visitors alike, this waterfront beach bar serves fantastic international food and all kinds of drinks. There is often live music and major sporting events are shown on the many flat-screen TVs. It's pretty much the only place on the island that you are always guaranteed to find a social atmosphere.

Complimentary Fireball shots and rum punch flow nightly at 11pm, particularly if you're dancing.

I&I Reggae Bar BAR
(✐668-8169; Luciano Reyes St; ⊘4pm-1am Mon-Wed, to 2am Thu-Sat) I&I is the island's most hip, happening spot after dark, when its healthy sound system belts out a reggae beat. Its three levels each offer a different scene, with a dance floor on one and swings hanging from the rafters on another. The top floor is the 'chill-out zone,' complete with hammocks and panoramic views. A great place for a sunset drink.

Ice & Beans COFFEE
(✐662-5089; Front St; ⊘6am-6pm) If the heat is getting too much, pick up an iced coffee or iced tea at this friendly coffee shop and take a stool on the breezy balcony overlooking the water. It also sells delicious, fresh minidonuts. Be warned: they'll get you in with the free samples then you'll keep coming back for more.

☆ Entertainment

Il Baretto LIVE PERFORMANCE
(✐623-9401; Av Mangle; ⊘7:30pm Sat) On the leafy grounds of Oasi (p123), this classy little bar and performance space is an ideal venue to experience some of the talented local musicians and circus acts. Yes, the *palapa* can somehow hold an acrobat dangling on a silk. Also the espresso, wines, cocktails and juices are fabulous, and there's a small Italian menu.

🛍 Shopping

Caulker has a few shops selling T-shirts, beach gear and souvenirs, but this is not the best place for shopping. Keep your eye out for colorful paintings and handmade jewelry by local artists.

Little Blue Gift Shop GIFTS & SOUVENIRS

(☑ 637-4109; Front St; ⊙ 9am-6pm Mon-Sat) This excellent gift shop near the dock sells hand-crafted artisanal products made from local ingredients, including non-chemical bug spray made with coconut oil, and a variety of interesting works by artists from all over Belize.

Caribbean Colors ART

(☑ 605-9242; Front St; ⊙ 7am-2:30pm; 🛜) This shop stocks a collection of silk-screened fabrics, jewelry and paintings by the owner, artist Lee Vanderwalker, as well as pieces by other Belizean artists. The attached cafe (p124) is one of the island's best.

ℹ️ Information

DANGERS & ANNOYANCES

Take care with belongings left in hotel rooms – especially in some of the more rustic accommodations south of town – as room robberies are regularly reported. If your room doesn't lock properly, ask for another and make use of the hotel safe if one is available.

INTERNET ACCESS

Cayeboard Connection (☑ 206-0022; Front St; per hour BZ$12; ⊙ 9am-9pm) Internet access and printing; sells coffee and books.

LAUNDRY

Caye Caulker Coin Laundromat (Calle al Sol; per wash/dry cycle BZ$4; ⊙ 6am-6pm Mon-Sat, to noon Sun)

Marie's Laundry (☑ 206-0575; Middle St; per 8lb BZ$10; ⊙ 8am-8pm)

Ruby's Laundry (☑ 628-0868, 602-9298; Calle al Sol; per load BZ$15; ⊙ 8am-5pm Mon-Sat, to noon Sun)

MEDICAL SERVICES

There is a basic health center on the island but if you really need medical attention you're better off heading directly to Belize City.

Caye Caulker Health Center (☑ 226-0166, emergency 668-2547; ⊙ 8am-noon & 1-5pm Mon-Fri) Just off Front St, two blocks south of Calle al Sol.

MONEY

Atlantic Bank (Middle St; ⊙ 8am-3pm Mon-Fri, 9am-noon Sat) Has a pair of fairly reliable ATMs, although make sure you have some cash before you arrive in case they are out of service.

POST

Post Office (Estella St, Caye Caulker Health Center Bldg; ⊙ 8am-noon & 1-4:30pm Mon-Thu, to 4pm Fri)

TOURIST INFORMATION

GoCayeCaulker.com (www.gocayecaulker.com) General information for visitors.

Caye Caulker BTIA (www.cayecaulkervacation.com) The official site of the Caye Caulker branch of the Belize Tourism Industry Association (BTIA).

ℹ️ Getting There & Away

AIR

Caye Caulker's airstrip was closed during re-search, but set to reopen in late 2018. **Maya Island Air** (☑ 226-0012; www.mayaislandair.com) and **Tropic Air** (☑ 226-0040; www.tropicair.com) connect Caye Caulker with San Pedro and Belize City. The airline offices are at the southern end of the island.

BOAT

There are two companies running boats from Caye Caulker to Belize City and San Pedro.

Ocean Ferry Belize (☑ 226-0033; www.oceanferrybelize.com; Calle al Sol) runs boats from the main dock on Calle al Sol. Departs to Belize City (one way BZ$19, return BZ$30, 45 minutes) at 6:30am, 8:30am, 9am, 10:30am, noon, 1:30pm and 4:30pm. Boats to San Pedro (one way BZ$19, return BZ$30, 30 minutes) go at 8:45am, 11:15am, 2:15pm, 3:45pm and 6:15pm.

San Pedro Belize Express Water Taxi (☑ 226-0225; www.belizewatertaxi.com) departs from the pier in front of the basketball court. Service to San Pedro (one way BZ$18, return BZ$28) at 8:45am, 9:45am, 11:15am, 12:45pm, 2:15pm, 3:45pm, 4:45pm, 5:15pm and 6:15pm, and Belize City (one way BZ$18, return BZ$28) at 6:30am, 7am, 8am, 9am, 10:30am, noon, 1:30pm, 3:30pm and 5pm.

The docks are beside each other on the reef side of the island.

San Pedro Belize Express Water Taxi also runs a service to Chetumal, Mexico, every other day via San Pedro. **Water Jets** (☑ 206-0010; www.sanpedrowatertaxi.com; lagoon dock) runs the same service on alternate days.

ℹ️ Getting Around

Caulker is so small that most people walk every-where. A couple of golf-cart taxis hang out around Front St and charge BZ$5 to BZ$7 per short trip around town.

You can rent a golf cart at **Buddy's Golf Cart Rentals** (☑ 628-8508; buddysgolfvartrentals@gmail.com; Middle St; per hour/day/24hr BZ$25/100/150) but bicycle rental is far cheaper and just as fast a way to get around. You can rent bikes at grocery stores, tour operators and hotels.

OTHER NORTHERN CAYES

Cayo Espanto

The coconut-covered Cayo Espanto is just 3 miles or a seven-minute boat ride from San Pedro, but feels a world away. As the story goes, the island was christened Cayo Espanto or 'Phantom Caye' by local fishermen who claimed it was populated by *duendes* (mischievous Mayan pranksters). If fish and rum were left unguarded on this island, the mythical creatures apparently snatched them up.

It seems the *duendes* have since gone into retirement, because most modern visitors who set foot on this tropical paradise never want to leave. It's not uncommon for celebrities to frequent the island, which has hosted the likes of Robert De Niro, Harrison Ford and Tiger Woods. Leonardo DiCaprio loved it so much that he bought neighboring **Blackadore Caye** to build his own environmentally friendly island resort.

🛏 Sleeping

Cayo Espanto RESORT $$$
(✍ in USA 910-323-8355; www.aprivateisland.com; villas incl all meals from BZ$3006; ❄ 🛜 ❄) Billed as 'a private island,' this ultimate romantic retreat boasts seven delightful villas, each designed for maximum privacy and panoramic views. Each *casa* has a private dock complete with loungers under cloth umbrellas and private waterside plunge pools.

Luxurious and stylish yet unpretentious, the overall vibe here is shipwreck chic – the kind of outcome you'd expect if a couple of talented interior designers and architects had washed up along with Gilligan and his team.

Each villa has polished concrete or bright tile floors and king-size beds dressed in high-thread-count designer sheets. There is an abundance of comfortable cane furniture and the TVs and other mod-cons are carefully hidden in elegant wooden cupboards so as not to clash with the castaway vibe. Many rooms also have alfresco showers sheltered by coconut trees and mangroves.

The most unusual option is Casa Ventanas, which is perched out at the end of a long dock, surrounded by 360 degrees of crystal blue loveliness, while two-story Casa Estrella is extra spacious and affords fantastic views from the upstairs master bedroom.

One of the highlights of staying at Cayo Espanto is the exceedingly attentive service (all packages include the services of a personal 'houseman'). Prior to arrival, guests are invited to fill out a preferences survey, which is used to prepare for all aspects of the visit, including the menu. Chefs create artistic, delicious dishes according to your personal tastes and serve them in the privacy of your villa.

Turneffe Atoll

Belize's newest protected marine area, Turneffe Atoll, is the largest and most biologically diverse atoll in the Americas. At 30 miles long and 10 miles wide, the area is alive with coral, fish and large rays, making it a prime destination for diving, snorkeling and catch-and-release sport fishing. It was only in 2012 that environmental groups succeeded in protecting the 131,690-hectare area now dubbed the Turneffe Atoll Marine Reserve, and the Turneffe Atoll Sustainability Association in Belize City manages it.

The atoll is dominated by mangrove islands, the nurseries on which almost all marine life depends to ensure juvenile protection and biological productivity. Although the atoll is best known for its walls, there are also many shallow sea gardens and bright sand flats inside the reef that are excellent sites for novice divers and snorkelers. If you plan on going ashore, bring insect repellent.

🏃 Activities

Diving, snorkeling and catch-and-release fishing are all popular around the marine reserve. There are no fees to enter, but the Turneffe Atoll Sustainability Association (p67) accepts donations.

Diving

The best dive spots are in the southern reaches of the atoll, which are less visited by big dive boats, and have more live coral coverage and a wider variety of marine life.

Turneffe Elbow was for years the most popular site, until overfishing became an issue in 2014. Now protected, the site is again welcoming big schools of fish and predators in large numbers. Other sites include **Myrtle's Turtle**, named for the resident green turtle that appears annually, and **Triple Anchor**, marked by three anchors remaining from a wreck.

Fishing

Fishing enthusiasts are attracted by the flats, which are ideal for saltwater fly-fishing.

🛌 Sleeping

Lodging is available on the Turneffe Islands at all-inclusive resorts, which offer diving, snorkeling and/or fishing packages.

★ Turneffe Island Resort RESORT $$$

(🗹 in USA 713-236-7739, in USA 800-874-0118; www.turnefferesort.com; 4-night all-incl resort/diving/fishing packages (based on double occupancy) BZ$7604/10,754/12,555; 🌡@🛜🏊) At the southern tip of the atoll, the fanciest of the Turneffe resorts offers gorgeous cabañas with screened porches, wooden floorboards, and indoor and outdoor showers, all set amid coconut palms just yards from the beach. There's world-class diving within minutes of the resort, and it has even established its own timezone, allowing guests to capitalize on daylight hours.

In short, Hemingway would have approved, particularly because some of Belize's best tarpon fishing is also a three-minute boat ride away.

Another untold highlight is the camaraderie that tends to develop among guests, as the resort offers prime opportunities for the guests to bond over the day's activities at an intimate tiki bar and over delicious, communal meals.

Blackbird Caye Resort RESORT $$$

(🗹 in USA 866-909-7333; www.blackbirdresort.com; Blackbird Caye; 3-night resort/dive packages from BZ$2514/3550; 🌡🛜🏊) This large resort has a range of comfortable accommodations including thatched-roofed cabañas right on the sand, complete with screened porches strung with hammocks from which to admire the sea views. The resort offers complete snorkeling and dive packages, and is popular with kayakers as it has coral gardens, uninhabited islands and mangrove creeks all ripe for exploration.

There is a pool with Caribbean views, which comes in handy as the sea in front of the resort is not the best for swimming. Meals are served in a huge *palapa* restaurant near the main dock.

Turneffe Flats Lodge RESORT $$$

(🗹 232-9022, in USA 888-512-8812; www.tflats.com; Blackbird Caye; 3-night packages from BZ$1900; 🌡🛜🏊) 🤿 Although its principal fame is as a fishing retreat with expert guides, this

Blackbird Caye lodge also offers excellent dive trips that are less crowded than at other resorts (because the other guests are out fishing). Accommodations are in spacious, three-bedroom villas and duplex cabañas, each with a veranda and dramatic views of the waves crashing on the nearby reef.

The owners of the lodge are particularly active in local conservation efforts, and their snorkeling eco-tour, 'Atoll Adventure,' earns high marks with travelers

ℹ Getting There & Away

Of Belize's three coral atolls, the Turneffe Atoll is located the closest to the mainland and the most accessible.

It is usually visited by day trip, as it's within easy reach of Caulker, Ambergris and Belize City to the north, and Glover's Reef and Hopkins village to the south. Even Placencia dive boats occasionally make the trip to Turneffe Elbow, at the southern tip of the islands. On rough days it's favored by San Pedro dive operators because much of the trip can be made behind the barrier reef, protecting passengers from choppy open seas.

Turneffe Atoll resorts run a scheduled boat service to and from Belize City on Wednesday and Saturday. A private boat transfer costs around US$450 one way

Lighthouse Reef

At 50 miles from the mainland, Lighthouse Reef is the furthest of the three atolls from the coastline. But it is probably the most visited, thanks to the allure of the mysterious Blue Hole Natural Monument. While this icon of Belize diving makes the atoll a major attraction, it is the stunning walls, majestically adorned with swim-throughs, and clear blue water that make it a favorite of both longtime divers and complete novices.

In addition to Half Moon Caye and Long Caye, uninhabited islands in the atoll include Northern Caye, Sandbore Caye, Saddle Caye and Hat Caye, some of which are popular with mosquitoes and crocodiles.

🏊 Activities

Snorkeling, diving and fishing are the main diversions around this far-flung atoll.

Diving & Snorkeling

Besides the Blue Hole, there is no shortage of fantastic dive sites in Lighthouse Reef, including **Painted Wall**, named for the plethora of painted tunicates found here; the **Aquarium**, often visited as a second stop after

DON'T MISS

BLUE HOLE NATURAL MONUMENT

At the center of Lighthouse Reef is the world-famous **Blue Hole Natural Monument** (www.belizeaudubon.org; national park admission BZ$60; ⊙ 8am-4:30pm), an incomparable natural wonder and unique diving experience. It may not involve a lot of undersea life, but it remains a recreational diver's best opportunity for a heart-pounding descent into a majestic submarine sinkhole. The chance of spotting circling reef sharks and the occasional hammerhead further sweeten the deal.

In the 1970s, underwater pioneer Jacques Cousteau explored the sinkhole and declared the dive site one of the world's best. Since then the Blue Hole's image – a deep azure pupil with an aquamarine border surrounded by the lighter shades of the reef – has become a logo for tourist publicity and a symbol of Belize. The hole forms a perfect 1000ft-diameter circle on the surface and is said to be 430ft deep, but as much as 200ft of this may now be filled with silt and other natural debris.

Divers drop quickly to 130ft, from where they swim beneath an overhang, observing stalactites above and, sometimes a few reef sharks. Although the water is clear, light levels are low, so a good dive light will enable further appreciation of the rock formations. Because of the depth, ascent begins after eight minutes; the brevity of the dive may disappoint some divers. The trip is usually combined with other dives at Lighthouse Reef, and many divers will tell you that those other dives are the real highlight. But judging from its popularity – most dive shops make twice-weekly runs to the Blue Hole – plenty want to make the deep descent.

On day trips the Blue Hole will be your first dive, which can be nerve-racking if you're unfamiliar with the dive master and the other divers, or if you haven't been underwater lately. It may be worth doing some local dives with your dive masters before setting out cold on a Blue Hole trip. An alternative is to take an overnight trip to Lighthouse Reef, where there's a dive shop offering a livelier (and more athletic) Blue Hole experience.

Long Caye Diving Services owner Elvis Solis has been inside the Blue Hole more than 500 times, and has mapped out a unique course that he offers to small groups who are either staying at Itza Lodge, where the dive shop is based, or traveling independently. The dive begins on the northern stretch of the Blue Hole, drops to 130ft, and at around 80ft brings divers through a couple of small caves where squirrel fish and nurse sharks tend to lurk. The safety stop is a long one, around 25 minutes, and is achieved while circling the rim of the Blue Hole, where sea fans, sponges, turtles, barracudas and other reef dwellers can be spotted.

The coral around this shallow perimeter will appeal to snorkelers as well, though the trip is expensive trip and you'll probably have to tag along on a dive boat. Diving or snorkeling, the trip involves two hours each way by boat in possibly rough, open waters. There's a BZ$60 marine-park fee for visiting Blue Hole, and that is usually on top of the dive fees.

the Blue Hole; and the **Cathedral**, known for its amazing variety of sponges.

Half Moon Caye Wall is the best of the lot for its variety of coral formations along the wall and within canyons and swim-throughs. Of particular interest is a field of garden eels found on the sand flats near the wall.

Snorkelers don't despair: the shallows around the dive sites are interesting as well.

ⓘ Getting There & Away

Most visitors to Lighthouse Reef come on either a one-day dive trip or live-aboard dive excursion from San Pedro (on Ambergris Caye) or Caye

Caulker. Lodges on Long Caye run scheduled boat services from Belize City when there is demand.

Half Moon Caye

A nesting ground for the rare red-footed booby bird, the Half Moon Caye Natural Monument is the most visited of the Lighthouse Reef islands, and for good reason. Its palm-lined beaches are castaway-cool, its verdant, tropical interior nurtures a stunning array of life and its crystalline underwater surrounds are ideal for peeking in on coral and sea critters.

Rising less than 10ft above sea level, the cay's 45 acres hold two distinct ecosystems. To the west is lush vegetation fertilized by the droppings of thousands of seabirds, including some 4000 red-footed boobies, the magnificent frigate bird and 98 other bird species. The east side has less vegetation but more palms.

Loggerhead and hawksbill sea turtles, both endangered, lay their eggs on the southern beaches.

◎ Sights & Activities

★ Half Moon Caye
Natural Monument   NATURE RESERVE
(www.belizeaudubon.org; national park admission BZ$20; ⊘ 8am-4:30pm) Half Moon Caye Natural Monument is known first and foremost as providing nesting grounds for the rare red-footed booby bird, but the island's enchantments go far beyond that. There's also a lighthouse, excellent beaches and spectacular submerged walls that teem with marine flora and fauna. Underwater visibility can extend more than 200ft here.

A nature trail weaves through the southern part of the island to an observation platform that brings viewers eye level with nesting boobies and frigate birds. Along the path you'll see thousands of seashells, many inhabited by hermit crabs, and more than a few large iguanas.

The Belize Audubon Society has a visitors center where you must register and pay a BZ$20 park fee on arrival. If you're on a tour, your guide collects the park fee from each guest and pays for the group.

Island Expeditions   ECOTOUR
(☑ in US 1-800-667-1630; www.islandexpeditions.com) Based out of Canada, Island Expeditions runs the Kayaking, Reef and Rainforest Adventure Vacation through Belize, which includes a kayaking trip to Half Moon Caye. Check its website for more details.

🛏 Sleeping & Eating

Belize Audubon Society administers a basic campsite (BZ$20 per person) which is booked through the main office in Belize City. Visitors must bring the tents.

Alternatively there is a high-end base camp that is used by Island Expeditions for kayaking, snorkeling and diving adventures. It features heavy duty luxury tents on raised wooden floors with outdoor showers and compost toilets.

There are no restaurants on the island – bring all your food needs from the mainland in addition to plenty of water.

❶ Getting There & Away

Organized day trips on large dive boats, mainly from San Pedro and Caye Caulker, stop at Half Moon Caye on their way to/from the nearby Blue Hole. Live-aboard dive trips also frequently visit the island. Alternatively, it's a short boat ride from the lodges on nearby Long Caye.

Long Caye

Long Caye at Lighthouse Reef (www.belizeisland.com) is an idyllic private island of just 710 acres, with 210 set aside as a nature reserve. White sand beaches and coconut palms abound, and there are plans to develop part of the island as a resort.

Previously, the cay had a bit of a 'ghost island' feel about it, with few permanent residents, a couple of private homes and two laid-back accommodation options. The crumbling state of some of the infrastructure, including the western dock, adds to the feeling of an abandoned paradise.

That said, it is close to some of Belize's best diving sites, and a more spacious option than being holed up on a live-aboard dive boat. Overnighting here means you'll make it to the Blue Hole before the big dive boats arrive from San Pedro, to have the site to yourself.

☂ Activities

You can snorkel right from the shore, and there's a partly submerged old sugar cane barge with some interesting resident marine life, including seahorses. But the main reason to travel all the way to Long Caye is diving – some of Belize's best dive spots are a short boat ride away. Sport fishing is another highlight.

Long Caye
Diving Services   DIVING
(☑ 601-5181, in USA 305-600-2585; www.itzalodge.com/diving; Itza Lodge; per dive BZ$140) Based within Itza Lodge on Long Caye, this highly professional dive shop caters to both resort guests and independent clients who arrive on yachts, sailboats or cruise ships. The dive shop owner, Elvis Solis, has extensive experience diving the Blue Hole and has come up with an alternative way of exploring the iconic undersea sinkhole.

🛏 Sleeping

There are two lodges on the island, though at the time of research, one had recently changed ownership and was in the process of being renovated and converted into a resort. Advanced reservations are essential to ensure that the facilities are ready.

Itza Lodge   LODGE **$$$**

(☑ in USA 305-600-2585; www.itzalodge.com; 3-day resort package BZ$1470-2070; 📶) 🍃 The biggest place to stay on the island has 12 hardwood rooms with ocean views and private bathrooms in the main lodge and 12 smaller rooms with shared bathrooms in a smaller wing. Meals are served in a lovely thatched open-air dining room with views over the Caribbean to nearby Half Moon Caye.

The social heart of the lodge is the large common area which has a large map of the atoll painted on the floor and is filled with folk art and musical instruments from around the globe. There are stand-up paddleboards and kayaks for guest use, as well as a DVD collection for those quiet island evenings.

The new owner plans to construct a gift shop, spa, hot tub and tiki bar. Rooms will eventually have air-con, and prices may rise accordingly.

Huracan Diving Lodge   B&B **$$$**

(☑ in USA 954-802-5005; www.huracandiving.com; 4-night dive package s/d from BZ$3442/4208; 📶) 🍃 This small dive lodge is a sweet little escape with lots of dark stained wood and simple tropical decor. It's not right on the water, but is only a short walk away. There are five rooms all featuring king-size or twin beds draped in mosquito nets and colorful throw pillows. Delicious gourmet meals are served on the front deck.

The owner is an artist and his paintings can be found hanging throughout the property.

Packages include transportation by boat from Belize City, all meals and several days of glorious diving. Nightly rates are also available; check the website for current deals.

❶ Getting There & Away

Lodges on the island organize scheduled boat transport (US$250 return) on Wednesday and Saturday. This is sometimes included in package prices, and some guests may be able to convince dive operators to drop them on the island (usually for a considerable fee).

A private boat charter can be arranged from around US$650 one way. It's also possible to arrive by private helicopter transfer for around US$2000 per trajectory.

Northern Belize

POP 98,400

Best Places to Eat

➜ Maracas Bar & Restaurant (p140)

➜ Nahil Mayab (p140)

➜ Patty's Bistro (p149)

➜ Corozo Blue's (p150)

➜ Crabby's (p155)

Best Places to Stay

➜ Cerros Beach Resort (p153)

➜ Serenity Sands (p148)

➜ Chan Chich Lodge (p145)

➜ Almond Tree Resort (p149)

➜ Backpackers Paradise (p154)

Why Go?

As Cancún is the northern entry point into Belize from Mexico, many travelers save a chunk of change by flying in here and bussing or driving down to their final destination. Passing through the flat farmland and provincial towns of Northern Belize, relatively few are inspired to linger.

But this chilled-out stretch of Belize, entirely void of crowds, with unbeaten paths, abundant wildlife, fine Maya ruins and deserted beaches is well worth a look if you're seeking to get away from the scene further south. What's more, Corozal and Sarteneja, both attractive coastal towns, are easily accessible by boat from San Pedro.

Northern Belize comprises two districts: Corozal and Orange Walk, both traversed by the straight, flat Philip Goldson Hwy. Off the main road, adventurous travelers will find pretty fishing villages, pristine jungles, ancient Maya cities and anachronistic Mennonite communities.

When to Go

Jan–Apr The dry season opens up top trekking opportunities throughout the region.

Mar–Jun Spot flocks of water birds while cruising in a canoe on stunning Shipstern Lagoon.

Sep Residents from all over Belize come to party at Orange Walk's famous Carnival.

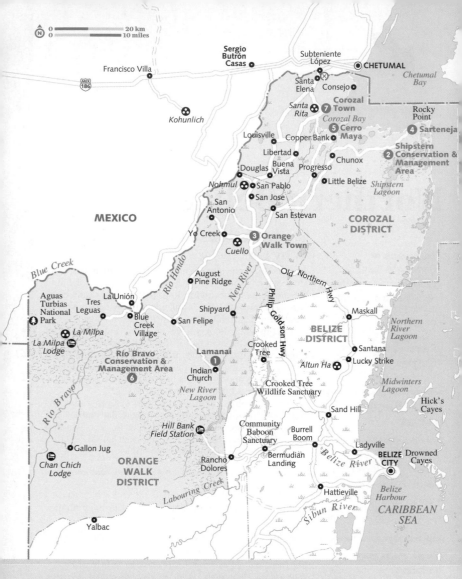

Northern Belize Highlights

1 **Lamanai** (p140) Taking a riverboat tour along the New River to these magnificent Maya ruins.

2 **Shipstern Conservation & Management Area** (p153) Spotting crocs and other lagoon inhabitants.

3 **Orange Walk Town** (p135) Tucking into the best street food in the north.

4 **Sarteneja** (p153) Chilling in this laid-back fishing town.

5 **Cerro Maya** (p152) Enjoying ocean views from this waterfront Maya temple.

6 **Río Bravo Conservation & Management Area** (p144) Discovering unexcavated ruins and undisturbed wildlife.

7 **Corozal Town** (p146) Soaking up the saltwater breezes while sipping cocktails.

History

Located on the eastern fringe of the ancient Maya heartland, Northern Belize supported many settlements through history without producing any cities of the size or grandeur of Caracol, which lies further south in Belize, or Tikal in Guatemala. It was home to important river trade routes that linked the interior with the coast: the north's major Maya site, Lamanai, commanded one of these routes and grew to a city of up to 35,000 people during the Maya peak, known as the Classic Period. The city at Lamanai continued to serve as a Maya center until the Spanish arrived in the 16th century.

Meanwhile, another city grew up further west at La Milpa. During the late Classic Period, La Milpa was home to 46,000 people, but archaeologists believe the city came to an abrupt end in the 9th century AD, possibly due to environmental and economic stresses brought on by drought.

A Spanish expedition into Northern Belize from the Yucatán in 1544 led to the conquering of many of the region's Maya settlements and, later, the creation of a series of Spanish missions distantly controlled by a priest at Bacalar in the southeastern Yucatán. Maya rebellion was fierce, and after a series of battles the Spanish were driven out of the area for good in 1640.

British loggers began moving into the region in search of mahogany in the 18th century. They encountered sporadic resistance from the now weakened and depleted Maya population, which had been ravaged by European-introduced diseases.

In 1847 the Maya in the Yucatán rose up against their Spanish-descended overlords in the War of the Castes ('Guerra de Castas' in Spanish), a vicious conflict that continued in diminishing form into the 20th century. Refugees from both sides of the conflict took shelter in northern British Honduras (as Belize was then called), with people of Spanish descent founding the towns of Orange Walk and Corozal, and the Maya moving into the forests and countryside. It wasn't surprising that intermittent hostilities took place in British Honduras. One group of Maya, the Icaiché, was repulsed from Orange Walk after fierce fighting in 1872. The border between Mexico and British Honduras was not agreed upon between the two states until 1893.

Caste War migrants from the Yucatán laid the foundations of modern Northern Belize by starting the area's first sugarcane plantations. Despite the sugar industry's many vicissitudes, it is now the backbone of the Northern Belize economy, with some 900 cane farms in the region.

ℹ Getting There & Away

The Philip Goldson Hwy links Belize City with the Mexican border via the region's two main towns, Orange Walk Town and Corozal Town. Several bus companies service the route, with some going as far as Chetumal, 7 miles into Mexico. Approximately 30 daily buses run each way from Belize City to Corozal Town and beyond. There are also daily buses connecting Orange Walk Town with Sarteneja (though the nicest way to get to Sarteneja is by boat from Corozal Town). There is a regular boat service that connects Corozal Town and Sarteneja with San Pedro on Ambergris Caye. Both Corozal Town and Orange Walk Town also have direct air links to San Pedro.

ORANGE WALK DISTRICT

POP 51,000

Orange Walk is one of the more spread out and thinly populated districts in Belize – most travelers are passing through on the Philip Goldson Hwy or heading to the main town of Orange Walk. Outside of this population center, most of the communities and attractions west of the highway are connected by a network of (mostly) unpaved roads linking farming communities.

Further west and to the south, these grid roads disappear entirely, and you're in what Belizeans refer to as 'deep bush,' the backwoods jungle country that makes up most of Orange Walk District. It's here you'll find the vast Río Bravo Conservation & Management Area and, further out still, the village of Gallon Jug and the ultra-exclusive Chan Chich Lodge. More accessible – particularly via the New River – is the unmissable Maya site of Lamanai.

Orange Walk Town

POP 13,700

Orange Walk Town is many things to many people: agricultural town, economic hub, Mennonite meeting place, street-food city... but it is not generally considered a tourist town. The town itself, just 57 miles from Belize City, doesn't have much to keep travelers around for more than a day or two, but it is the premier base from which to make the superlative trip to the ruins of Lamanai and longer excursions into the wilds of Northern Belize. Orange Walk has a fine location beside the New River, which meanders lazily along the east side of town, and there are a few very nice (and reasonably priced) hotels and restaurants for visitors who choose to hang around for a bit.

Sights

Nohmul RUINS

FREE For a taste of how Belize's many majestic ruins may have looked to early explorers before being excavated and landscaped, head to this vast jungle-covered Maya site just off the Philip Goldson Hwy. Meaning 'Great Mound' in Maya, Nohmul (noh-mool) was a town of 3000 people during the late Classic Period. The ruins – and Belize – made headlines in 2013 when a construction company bulldozed one of the site's main temples in order to obtain material for road construction.

Though the site is on private land, all pre-Colombian sites are protected under Belizean law. The construction company was convicted and fined BZ$24,000 in 2016. While the temple was damaged beyond repair, many other structures remain buried, forming jungle-covered outcrops surrounded by a sea of sugar cane. The ruins themselves aren't spectacular – at first glance they look just like a series of hills – but with some imagination and a sense of adventure it is a rewarding place to visit as you scramble up mounds sheltering untold archaeological riches below.

You'll almost certainly have the place to yourself, which adds to the sense of discovery. Scramble to the top of the lofty main tower from where, through the thick jungle, you'll catch glimpses over the endless sugar fields of Orange Walk District. Keep your eye out for exposed steps on the peaks of the mounds and a hidden, partially excavated section of walls that form a deep stone nook shaded by thick jungle.

From the northern edge of Orange Walk, drive 9.6 miles north on the Philip Goldson Hwy to the village of San Jose. Turn west at the north end of the village and drive 1.3 miles west to Nohmul. The site is not well marked so you'll probably have to ask for directions through the maze of sugar roads. A taxi from Orange Walk is about BZ$60, round trip.

Cuello RUINS

(☏320-9085; Yo Creek Rd; ☉9am-5pm) FREE Close to Orange Walk Town, Cuello (*kway-yo*) is one of the earliest-known settled communities in the Maya world, probably dating back to around 2400 BC, although there's not much left to show for it. Archaeologists have found plenty here, but only Structure 350, a nine-tiered pyramid, is of much interest to the non-expert. The pyramid was constructed around AD 200 to AD 300, but its lower levels date from before 2000 BC.

The site is on private property owned by Cuello Distillery, 4 miles west of Orange Walk (take San Antonio Rd out of town). It is not really open to the public, although the distillery usually allows access if you turn up during office hours. It's a good idea to call and make advance arrangements. A taxi to Cuello from Orange Walk costs about BZ$25, round trip.

Banquitas House of Culture MUSEUM

(☏322-0517; Banquitas Plaza; ☉8:30am-5:30pm Mon-Thu, to 4:30pm Fri) FREE The modern Banquitas House of Culture has an attractively displayed exhibit on Orange Walk's history. It's especially good on the local Maya sites, and has artifacts, maps and illustrations, as well as exhibits that change monthly. It's set in a pleasant, small, riverside park with an amphitheater.

Flagpole Plaza LANDMARK

(Arthur St) A small plaza behind the Town Hall that was once the site of Fort Cairnes, a British military post during the War of the Castes conflict.

Independence Plaza HISTORIC SITE

(Main St) This run-down plaza near the bridge over the New River marks the site of Fort Mundy, a strategic British military position.

Tours

Sugarcane and street tacos aside, the main reason travelers come to Orange Walk is to head out to the Maya ruins at Lamanai. Tour companies offer full-day trips (from 9am to 4pm) by riverboat that give visitors a chance to see the prolific birdlife along the New River and to learn about the history and archaeology at Lamanai. Any hotel can help make arrangements for this tour. The price includes a picnic lunch served by the New River Lagoon at the entrance to the temple complex. These companies usually require a minimum of four people to make the trip. You should probably reserve your place the day before, although you may be lucky on the morning you want to go.

Orange Walk Town

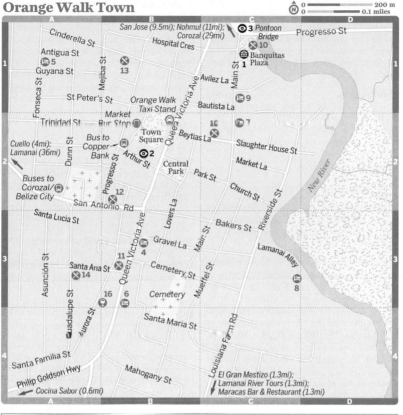

Orange Walk Town

◎ Sights
1 Banquitas House of Culture C1
2 Flagpole Plaza B2
3 Independence Plaza C1

🛏 Sleeping
4 Akihito Hotel B3
5 Casa Ricky's A1
6 D'Victoria Hotel B3
7 Hotel de la Fuente C2
8 Lamanai Riverside Retreat C3
9 St Christopher's Hotel C1

✕ Eating
10 Aegea Blue's C1
11 Juanita's B3
12 Lee's Chinese Restaurant B2
13 Loz B1
14 Nahil Mayab A3
15 Panificadora La Popular C2

🍷 Drinking & Nightlife
16 Hi 5 .... B3
Lamanai Riverside
Retreat .... (see 8)

Lamanai Eco Tours TOURS
(☎ 610-1753; www.lamanaiecotours.com; Mile 49.5 Philip Goldson Hwy) This experienced tour operator runs boat trips from near the Tower Hill Bridge just outside Orange Walk and has professional and attentive guides. Fishing and birding as well as Lamanai tours. Not to be confused with Lamanai Eco Adventures right next door.

Lamanai Eco Adventures TOURS
(☎ 610-2020; www.lamanaiecoadventures.com; Tower Hill Bridge; per person BZ$100; ⊙ tours 9:30am) One of several tour operators based by the toll bridge just south of Orange Walk, Lamanai Eco Adventures has good boats and its knowledgeable guides get top reviews.

Lamanai River Tours   TOURS

(☎ 322-2290; 1 Naranjal St; per person BZ$100) Located at El Gran Mestizo, this is the only Lamanai tour company based in Orange Walk Town. Its boat will pick you up at your hotel dock. Tour price includes admission and lunch at the site.

Reyes & Sons   TOURS

(☎ 610-1548, 322-3327; Tower Hill Bridge, Philip Goldson Hwy; per person BZ$100) Reyes & Sons keeps its boat docked by the Philip Goldson Hwy bridge over the New River, 5 miles south of town, but staff will pick you up at your hotel with advanced notice.

🛏 Sleeping

Orange Walk has a small range of reasonably priced, comfortable accommodations located both in the town center and out along the river.

St Christopher's Hotel   HOTEL $

(☎ 302-1064; www.stchristophershotelbze.com; 10 Main St; r with fan/air-con BZ$80/120; P ❄ 🛜) The flowering gardens and riverside setting make this otherwise nondescript hotel an attractive place to stay. The rooms themselves are spacious but plain. River-boat trips to Lamanai pick you up right from the hotel grounds and your hosts – the Urbina family – are attentive and welcoming, in a low-key, unassuming sort of way.

Casa Ricky's   GUESTHOUSE $

(☎ 634-3759; 39 Fonseca St; r BZ$45-70; 🛜) There's just a couple of basic rooms (the cheapest has a shared bathroom) and an apartment in this backpacker-friendly guesthouse with kitchen facilities and a relaxing garden. The young owner is helpful with local information and booking tours.

Akihito Hotel   HOTEL $

(☎ 302-0185; philosophy.dude@gmail.com; cnr Queen Victoria Ave & Gravel Lane; r with/without air-con BZ$65/45; ❄ @ 🛜) The cheapest of the bunch, the Akihito has a collection of very plain rooms with small bathrooms in a large concrete building on the main road. Most of the hotel was under renovation when we visited so should be much improved. The family who runs the hotel is very friendly and a treasure trove of local information.

El Gran Mestizo   RESORT $$

(☎ 322-2290; www.elgranmestizo.bz; 1 Naranjal St; dm BZ$30, cabañas BZ$130-160, family cabins BZ$200; P ❄ 🛜) If you don't mind being a little way out of the center, El Gran Mestizo is a fantastic little resort on the banks of the New River. The compact cabañas are cozy and equipped with fridge, TV, air-con and comfy beds, while the premium cabins have a full kitchen and split-level living. There's even an immaculate six-bed dorm for budget travelers.

All accommodations face the river but are set back in a garden. It's a great spot for those looking to be surrounded by nature but who want to be close to town. Free transfers to and from town are available to guests, and the onsite restaurant is one of the best in town. Boat trips to Lamanai operate from here.

Hotel de la Fuente   HOTEL $$

(☎ 322-2290; www.hoteldelafuente.bz; 14 Main St; r BZ$90-170, ste BZ$130-170; P ❄ 🛜) This family-run hotel is well located in the center of Orange Walk, but most of the rooms are situated in a new building that is set back from the hustle and bustle (and noise) of the road. The budget and standard rooms vary only by size and are probably the best value in town, while the suite is equipped with a full kitchen.

Lamanai Landings   HOTEL $$

(☎ 670-7846; Mile 51 Philip Goldson Hwy, Tower Hill; r BZ$160-200; ❄ 🛜) On the New River Lagoon about 7km south of Orange Walk, this hotel is perfectly placed for trips to Lamanai and a variety of other adventure tours. All rooms face the lagoon and have balconies, air-con, modern bathrooms and cable TV. The onsite *palapa* (open-air shelter with a thatched roof) restaurant is a great spot to enjoy the water views.

Lamanai Riverside Retreat   GUESTHOUSE $$

(☎ 302-3955; Lamanai Alley; r BZ$110-160; P ❄ 🛜) Located right on the New River in Orange Walk, this place has a popular riverside restaurant-bar and just three rustic wooden rooms, with breezy balconies, air-con and mosquito-netted beds. It's not the fanciest digs in town, but the jungle atmosphere and accommodating service are excellent.

The owner is involved in the cataloging and protection of the area's crocodile population, and will be glad to tell you all about the crocs and other animals that call the river home.

D'Victoria Hotel
HOTEL **$$**

(322-2518; 40 Queen Victoria Ave; r BZ$130-175; P ❄ 🛜 🏊) Rooms are clean but basic at this nondescript but popular hotel south of the center. The biggest selling point is the pool (nonguests BZ$5), which is a great option for cooling off in the Orange Walk heat.

🍴 Eating

Orange Walk is known for its street food. Surrounding the town plaza are tiny cafes, snack stalls, fruit stands and pushcarts offering a veritable smorgasbord of Northern Belizean and Mexican foods. Piped-in music and enticing aromas create an irresistible atmosphere, especially on Saturday afternoons. Everything is super cheap and hygiene standards are generally good.

Come n' Dine Restaurant
BELIZEAN **$**

(302-0311; Philip Goldson Hwy; dishes BZ$8-40; 6am-5pm) Unassuming and unexpected, this roadside restaurant serves some of the best Belizean food around. Located right next to the gas station on a crook of the Philip Goldson Hwy just a couple of miles south of town, it's well placed for road-trippers (but also worth the trip if you are staying in town). Look for excellent stews, steaks and stir-fries.

Juanita's
BREAKFAST, BELIZEAN **$**

(8 Santa Ana St; breakfast BZ$4-6, mains BZ$7-8; 6am-2pm) You can tell from the number of dedicated locals who flock to this place that the food here is satisfying. Simple, clean and very well priced, Juanita's serves eggs and bacon for breakfast, and rice and beans and other local favorites, such as cow-foot soup, during the rest of the day, along with coffee and cold beer.

Lee's Chinese Restaurant
CHINESE **$**

(11 San Antonio Rd; dishes BZ$8-25; 11am-midnight;) Orange Walk's most popular Chinese eatery, Lee's serves up a superior range of Hong Kong–style dishes. Aside from the blaring TV and the plastic tablecloths, the atmosphere is festive and welcoming, with the stylish dragon-theme decor kept cool by whirring ceiling fans. The menu is extensive, including excellent seafood and vegetarian options.

Panificadora La Popular
BAKERY **$**

(Beytias Lane; pastries BZ$2-8; 6:30am-8pm Mon-Sat, 7:30am-noon & 3-6pm Sun) Orange Walk's best bakery is always busy with locals helping themselves to sticky buns, cinnamon rolls, croissants and meat pies, all of which make for a perfect breakfast or lunch for the road.

Loz
ICE CREAM **$**

(3 Cinderella St; ice cream from BZ$2; 8am-9pm) This backstreet ice-cream parlor is a good place to cool off with slushies, frozen yogurt or just plain ice cream.

★ Aegea Blue's
INTERNATIONAL **$$**

(628-0090; Main St, Banquitas Plaza; mains BZ$18-40; 11am-11pm Wed-Sun) Aegea Blue's benefits from its lovely location on the New River and breezy garden setting. Like its sister restaurant in Corozal, the highlight here is the stone pizza oven but the menu has plenty of international dishes such as pasta, steaks and tacos, and Belizean standards.

The cocktail bar here is among the most civilized places in Orange Walk for an evening drink.

NORTHERN BELIZE ORANGE WALK TOWN

PARTY TIME, SPANISH STYLE

One of the more colorful features of multi-ethnic Belize is the diversity of feasts and celebrations. Holidays in Northern Belize reflect a strong Mexican influence, with old-style Catholic Spanish roots.

A Northern Belizean Christmas is a distinctive festival. While Maya are gearing up for animistic Deer Dances and Brits are planning Boxing Day football parties, the north gets ready for **Las Posadas**. The tradition is more than 400 years old, and is practiced still in Mexico and Guatemala as well. It is based on Mary and Joseph's unsuccessful search for accommodation – Las Posadas means the 'the lodging.' For nine days, beginning on December 16, people participate in candlelit processions, singing hymns, stopping at designated homes, in a loose re-enactment of the Bible story that culminates in a big Christmas Eve ceremony. In a secular spin-off to the tradition, Northern Belizeans still go around to each others' houses at Christmas time, being treated to holiday dishes, cakes and drinks.

The other big event in the north is **Orange Walk Carnival** held on Independence Day in September when the whole town turns out for dancing, parades and concerts.

Cocina Sabor BELIZEAN $$

(☑ 322-3482; Philip Goldson Hwy; mains BZ$15-45, light meals BZ$10-25; ⊙11am-10pm Wed-Mon) This welcoming place on the highway has a large menu of Belizean and international fare, from rice and beans to authentic pasta and flavorsome steak served in the spotless air-conditioned timber dining room. During the day it serves light meals such as burgers and wraps. Service is prompt and courteous, and there's a well-stocked bar.

Maracas Bar & Restaurant BELIZEAN $$

(☑ 322-2290; 1 Naranjal St; mains BZ$10-34; ⊙11:30am-10pm Wed-Sun, to 11pm Fri & Sat) For good eats in a fantastic natural riverside setting, take a taxi down to this restaurant at the El Gran Mestizo on the banks of the New River south of town. For the full experience pick a table in one of the waterside *palapas* and choose from Belizean, Mexican, seafood and international dishes on the ample menu.

There's also a full bar and cocktail list; bring bug spray if you want to dine outside.

Nahil Mayab BELIZEAN, MEXICAN $$

(☑ 322-0831; www.nahilmayab.com; cnr Santa Ana & Guadalupe Sts; mains BZ$14-25; ⊙11am-9pm Tue-Thu, to 11pm Fri & Sat; 🕿🖉) Decked in exotic greenery and faux Maya carvings, the dining room evokes the district's surrounding jungles, as does the pleasantly shaded patio. It's a fun, kitschy atmosphere in which to sample some Yucatecan-inspired food, such as *pibil* (pulled pork with onions and beans) or *poc chuc* (marinated pork loin).

Less adventurous eaters will appreciate the sandwiches, burgers, burritos, tacos and good old-fashioned rice and beans.

🍺 Drinking & Nightlife

Orange Walk is a town where farmers from all over Northern Belize (including the area's sizable Mennonite population) come to swap tales, sell produce and feast at Chinese restaurants, which also function as bars during the day when traditional nocturnal establishments are closed.

There are a couple of lovely bars surrounded by nature on the banks of the New River.

Lamanai Riverside Retreat BAR

(Lamanai Alley; ⊙8am-10pm) With its breezy deck and *palapa* tables with lovely river views, this restaurant-bar gets crowded on weekends. The menu is pretty extensive, but the place is recommended mainly for drinking and socializing.

Hi 5 CLUB

(Aurora St; ⊙7pm-5am Thu-Sun) Orange Walk's best late-night option, Hi 5 is in fact two venues, one with a lounge bar opening from 6pm onwards and an air-conditioned disco next door. The music is better in the bar but sooner or later all punters end up next door.

ℹ Information

Orange Walk lacks an official tourism information center, though most hotels do a pretty good job of providing local information.

Northern Regional Hospital (☑ 322-2072; Philip Goldson Hwy; ⊙emergency services 24hr) Located a half-mile north of the Pontoon Bridge on the northern edge of town.

ℹ Getting There & Away

BUS

Orange Walk is the major Northern Belize bus hub for buses plying the Corozal–Belize City route. There are half a dozen companies servicing this route and around 30 buses a day going in each direction. All long-distance buses, including services to Belize City, Corozal, Chetumal and Sarteneja, stop at the Dunn St **bus terminal** (Temporary Bus Station) west of the cemetery. It was supposed to be a temporary facility and locals are still waiting for a permanent bus station.

Buses to rural destinations around Orange Walk District, such as **Copper Bank** (Progresso St), leave from various points around the market. Schedules are subject to change, so ask in advance around the market or at your hotel.

Buses heading north from Orange Walk begin at 6:45am and run until around 9:15pm. Heading south to Belize City, buses begin at 4:45am and run until 8:30pm. The trip to Belize City takes around two hours, and costs BZ$5 to BZ$8; the trip to Corozal is slightly quicker and cheaper.

There are also direct services to Belmopan at 4:15am and 4:45am that bypass Belize City.

The bus to Indian Church near Lamanai (BZ$8, 1½ hours) departs from the **market** (St Peter's St, Market Square) at 3:45pm on Monday and Friday.

TAXI

Orange Walk Taxi Stand (Queen Victoria Ave) Taxis park by the town plaza.

Lamanai

One of the biggest and best excavated Maya sites in northern Belize, **Lamanai** (www.nichbelize.org; BZ$10; ⊙8am-5pm) lies 24 miles south of Orange Walk Town up the New River (or 36 miles by road). The ruins are known both for their impressive architecture and marvelous setting, surrounded by dense rainforest overlooking the New River Lagoon. The translation of the word *lamanai* – which means 'submerged crocodile' in Maya – gives a pretty good indication of the local residents of this jungle setting.

Bring plenty of bug spray – the jungle surrounding the ruins is home to vicious mosquitos.

History

Lamanai not only spans all phases of ancient Maya civilization but also tells a tale of ongoing Maya occupation and resistance for centuries after the Europeans arrived, equaling the longest known unbroken occupation in the Maya world. Lamanai was inhabited at least as early as 1500 BC, and was already a major ceremonial center, with large temples, in late Preclassic times.

It seems to have surged in importance (perhaps thanks to its location on trade routes between the Caribbean and the interior) around 200 or 100 BC, and its major buildings were mostly constructed between then and AD 700, although additions and changes went on up until at least the 15th century. At its peak it is estimated to have had a population of around 35,000.

When the Spanish invaded Northern Belize from the Yucatán in 1544, one of the most important of the missions they set up was Lamanai, where they had found a thriving Maya community. But the Maya never readily accepted Spanish overlordship, and a rebellion in 1640 left the Lamanai mission burned and deserted. Maya continued to live here until the late 17th or 18th century, when they were decimated by an epidemic, probably smallpox.

Archaeological excavations commenced as early as 1917, but large-scale digging, by David Pendergast of Canada's Royal Ontario Museum, only began in 1974. The painstaking work of uncovering more than 700 structures found here will take several lifetimes, not to mention huge amounts of funding.

◎ Sights

Arriving at Lamanai by boat, you'll first be brought to the small museum, which exhibits some beautiful pottery, and obsidian and jade jewelry. Then you'll head into the shady jungle, passing gigantic guanacaste (tubroos), ceiba and ramón (breadnut) trees, strangler figs, allspice, epiphytes and examples of Belize's national flower, the black

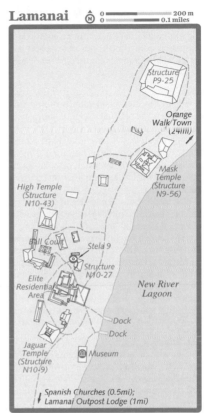

Lamanai

orchid. In the canopy overhead you might see (or hear) some of the resident howler monkeys. A tour of the ruins takes a minimum of 90 minutes, but can be done more comfortably in two or three hours.

Lamanai Museum   MUSEUM
(⊘8am-5pm) In the main administrative building where you pay your entrance fee, this small museum features artifacts unearthed throughout the Lamanai complex, including the original Stela 9 – the most detailed of three main carved stone slabs found here. In addition to pottery and jewelry, there are also some informative displays covering all aspects of Maya civilization.

Jaguar Temple   RUINS
This temple (Structure N10-9), fronting a 100yd-wide plaza, was built in the 6th century AD and modified several times up to at least the 15th century – a fine example of the longevity of the Lamanai settlement. The

stone patterning on the lowest-level turns depicts two cleverly designed jaguar faces, dating from the initial 6th-century construction. On the opposite (north) side of the plaza is a set of buildings that were used as residences for Lamanai's royal elite.

Stela 9   RUINS
North of the elite residential complex, this temple was the original site of the intricately carved standing stone erected in AD 625 to commemorate the accession of Lord Smoking Shell in AD 608 that is now on display in the site museum. A faithful replica has been placed in front of the temple in the original position.

The stone shows the leader in ceremonial regalia, wearing a rattlesnake headdress with quetzal feathers at the back, and holding a double-headed serpent bar diagonally across his body, with a deity emerging from the serpent's jaw at the top. The remains of five children – ranging in age from newborn to eight – were buried beneath the stela. Archaeologists believe the burial must have been highly significant, since offerings are not usually associated with the dedication of monuments.

Ball Court   RUINS
Not far west of Stela 9 is Lamanai's ball court, one of the smallest in the Maya world – but with the largest ball-court marker found yet! A ceremonial vessel containing liquid mercury, probably from Guatemala, was found beneath the marker.

High Temple   RUINS
North of the ball court, across a plaza shaded by trees, is Structure N10-43, the highest at Lamanai, which rises 125ft above the jungle canopy. Few large buildings in the Maya world were built as early as this one, which was initially constructed around 100 BC. You can climb to its summit for fabulous panoramas over the rest of Lamanai, the New River Lagoon, and plains and forests stretching out on all sides.

This grand ceremonial temple was built from nothing on a site that had previously been residential, which indicated a dramatic surge in Lamanai's importance at the time.

Mask Temple   RUINS
The Mask Temple (Structure N9-56) was begun around 200 BC and modified several times up to AD 1300. It has two 13ft stylized masks of a man in a crocodile headdress emblazoned on its west face to the north and south of the main stairs. Dating from about AD 400, these are considered some of the finest big masks in the Maya world.

What you actually see are fiberglass replicas that have been crafted in front of the original limestone masks in order to protect them. Deep within this building archaeologists found the tombs of a man adorned

---

CHURCHES OF LAMANAI

Lamanai is one of the few Maya sites in Belize with clearly identifiable Spanish colonial ruins within the indigenous city. The road from the southern entrance to the site passes what remains of a large stone church. These ruins provide evidence of the Spanish practice of demolishing indigenous structures and using the materials to create Christian places of worship.

The first church in Lamanai was constructed in 1544 on top of an existing Maya temple. Archaeologists believe that Spanish priests didn't reside permanently in Lamanai but rather visited as part of an established circuit of indigenous settlements.

While there is evidence that some of the residents of Lamanai embraced Christianity, including the discovery of a Christian burial site, overall the Maya of Lamanai didn't take kindly to the Spanish demolishing sacred places and imposing their beliefs, and burnt the church to the ground in 1610.

Not to be diverted from their mission, the stubborn Spanish built another, much larger church on the site – the famed Indian Church, which gives its name to the adjacent village. The scale and form of the church suggests that the Catholic leaders had grand plans for the Lamanai area.

The church continued to function until 1640 when a major Maya rebellion saw the community abandon Christianity and revert to an indigenous belief system. This time the church wasn't destroyed but rather reworked into a traditional place of worship, with the placement of a stela around the church entrance accompanied by an offering of zoomorphic figurines and animal bones.

with shell and jade jewelry, and a woman from almost the same date. The pair are thought to be a succession of leaders – perhaps a husband and wife, or brother and sister.

Spanish Churches RUINS

Some 400yd south of Jaguar Temple are the remains of the thick stone walls of two Spanish colonial churches, which were built by Maya forced labor from the remains of a temple. The southern church was built in 1544, and the northern one in the 1560s. Both were destroyed by the Maya, the second one in the 1640 rebellion.

Unknown to the Spanish, the Maya placed sacred objects such as crocodile figurines inside the churches while building them. A 300yd path opposite the churches leads to the partly overgrown remains of a 19th-century sugar mill, which some say directly contributed to the final abandonment of Lamanai by bringing new diseases into the area.

Tours

Most visitors approach Lamanai by guided river trip from Orange Walk Town, not just to avoid the long, unpaved road, but to take advantage of the river trip itself. The majority of tours set out from docks near the Tower Hill Bridge around 4 miles south of Orange Walk and cost BZ$80 to BZ$100 per person. Most companies will include a free vehicle transfer from Orange Walk on request. It's also possible to travel by boat all the way from downtown Orange Walk Town to Lamanai for BZ$100 per person; this version involves another 20 minutes on the New River.

Whichever tour you take, the boat ride is an opportunity to observe the river's prolific and colorful birdlife, as well as crocs, iguanas, monkeys and other wildlife. Most guides who do the 1½-hour trip are experts in local archaeology and ecology, making this tour a two-for-the-price-of-one experience. Besides the beautiful jungle and lagoon, the river voyage passes the Mennonite community of Shipyard before reaching the ruin site.

Most tours leave around 9am and return to Orange Walk around 3pm. Tours include lunch, which is usually served in the lagoon-side *palapas* at the archaeological site upon arrival.

Sleeping

For serious archaeology buffs it's worth staying the night in Indian Church village near the Lamanai site so you can explore it at your own pace before and after the tour groups have gone. There is one very basic guesthouse and one high-end lodge within walking distance of the site. Whichever you choose, having the ruins to yourself is worth the price tag/discomfort.

Guesthouse Olivia GUESTHOUSE $

(668-8593; Indian Church; r per person BZ$40) This no-frills guesthouse has the only cheap beds near the Lamanai site. Don't expect luxury, but rest easy knowing you'll have the archaeological site all to yourself in the morning. Call first to make sure there is a room ready. It's near the Lamanai turnoff in the heart of Indian Church.

Lamanai Outpost Lodge LODGE $$$

(670-3578, in USA 954-636-1107; www.lamanai. com; r from BZ$315;) For those who can afford it, this classy riverside lodge is the perfect option for fully exploring Lamanai. About 1 mile south of the ruins, the outpost is perched on a hillside just above the lagoon, and boasts panoramic views from its bar and gorgeous open-air dining room.

The 17 thatched-roof bungalows, each with fan, private bathroom and veranda, are lovely and perfectly suited to the casual jungle atmosphere. Two of the rooms have air-con. Packages include meals, transfers to/from Belize City and two guided small-group activities per day. The list of activities ranges from visiting the ruins to observing howler monkeys, sunrise canoeing and nocturnal crocodile encounters. Birding is big here: almost 400 species have been documented within 3 miles of the lodge.

Getting There & Away

If you decide to go without a guide, you can get to the village of Indian Church (next to Lamanai) from Orange Walk, but the bus goes only twice a week, on Monday and Friday. You'll need to find somewhere to spend a few nights while waiting for your return bus.

If you have a vehicle, Lamanai is a fairly straightforward one-hour drive from Orange Walk. Once you leave the highway, it's 20 miles along a reasonably good unpaved road passing farmland and the Mennonite communities of Guinea Grass and Shipyard.

Río Bravo Conservation & Management Area

If you're looking for true, wild tropical rainforest, this is it. Encompassing 406 sq miles in northwest Belize, the Río Bravo Conservation & Management Area (RBCMA) takes up 4% of Belize's total land area and is managed by the Belizean nonprofit organization **Programme for Belize** (PFB; Map p62; ☑ 227-5616, emergency phone 615-3900; www.pfbelize.org; 1 Eyre St; ☺8:30am-5pm) (PFB). The RBCMA harbors astonishing biological diversity – 392 bird species (more than two-thirds of Belize's total), 200 tree species and 70 mammal species, including all five of Belize's cats (jaguar, puma, ocelot, jaguarundi and margay). Río Bravo is said to have the largest concentration of jaguars in all of Central America.

Parts of the territory of the RBCMA were logged for mahogany and other woods from the 18th century until the 1980s, but distance and inaccessibility helped to ensure the survival of the forest as a whole. The area also contains at least 60 Maya sites, including La Milpa, the third-largest site in Belize.

History

Maya lived in this area as early as 800 BC. When Spanish expeditions first journeyed here the Maya were still using the same river trade routes, though by then their population was seriously depleted. Mahogany loggers moved into the area by the mid-18th century but were subject to intermittent attacks by the Maya for at least a century. By the late 19th century the Belize Estate and Produce Company (BEC) owned almost all of the land in northwestern Belize. The company carried out major timber extractions, floating mahogany and Mexican cedar out through the river system to the coast. With the advent of rail systems and logging trucks, operations flourished until overcutting and a moody market finally prompted the BEC to stop cutting trees in the early 1980s.

Intensive chicle tapping also took place throughout the 20th century, and you can still see slash scars on sapodilla trees throughout the RBCMA.

Belizean businessman Barry Bowen, owner of the Belikin brewery and the country's Coca Cola distribution rights, bought the BEC and its nearly 1100 sq miles of land in 1982. He quickly sold off massive chunks to Yalbac Ranch (owned by a Texan cattle farmer) and Coca Cola Foods. Meanwhile the Massachusetts Audubon Society was looking for a reserve for migrating birds. Coca Cola donated 66 sq miles to support the initiative (a further 86 sq miles followed in 1992), and Programme for Belize was created to manage the land. Bowen also donated some land, and PFB, helped by more than US$2 million raised by the UK-based World Land Trust, bought the rest, bringing its total up to today's 406 sq miles.

◉ Sights & Activities

At the RBCMA the PFB seeks to link conservation with the development of sustainable land uses. Programs include tree nurseries, extraction of nontimber products such as chicle, thatch and palm, experimental operations in sustainable timber extraction, and ecotourism.

La Milpa   RUINS
FREE In the northwestern corner of the RBCMA, La Milpa is the third-largest Maya site in Belize, believed to have had a population of 46,000 at its peak between AD 750 and AD 850. Its 5-acre Great Plaza, one of the biggest of all Maya plazas, is surrounded by four pyramids up to 80ft high. Now the structures are all covered with jungle and inhabited with howler monkeys, evoking the mystery and history of the ancient ruins.

Guides from the field station at La Milpa Lodge can accompany your hike to shed light on the function of the various structures, and to point out the stelae and other moss-covered artifacts that still remain in the area.

Birdwatching
Río Bravo is one of the country's prime birding areas. The conservation area may attract fewer birders than more accessible destinations such as Crooked Tree, but it attracts more birds – 392 species to be exact. Due to its remote location and vigilant protection measures, Río Bravo is home to dozens of species that are rarely spotted in other parts of the country. Case in point: in 2005 the RBCMA was selected as the release site for the restoration of the amazingly majestic and globally threatened harpy eagle. Although you're unlikely to spot a harpy eagle, other large avian species are not uncommon, including the ocellated turkey, the crested guan and the ornate hawk eagle. The open area around La Milpa Lodge attracts fly-catchers, mannekins, redstarts, orioles, tanagers, trogons and hummingbirds, so you can lounge in your hammock with your binoculars and

WORTH A TRIP

CHAN CHICH LODGE

Located in the middle of a 200-sq-mile private reserve in the far western corner of Orange Walk District, **Chan Chich Lodge** (☑ 223-4419, in USA 800-343-8009; www. chanchich.com; Gallon Jug; cabañas incl breakfast BZ$750-950, villas with air-con BZ$1300; P @ ⛱ ⛱) is one of Belize's original ecolodges. The supremely comfortable thatched cabañas are built from local hardwoods and surround the partly excavated ruins of an ancient Maya plaza and feature wooden slat walls that open up to the sounds of nature.

There is a swimming pool housed in a plant-filled conservatory and a variety of activities in the surrounding jungle, including horseback riding and canoeing.

The remote setting and pristine environs make Chan Chich a destination in and of itself: many bird and wildlife enthusiasts arrive via charter flight from Belize City and spend the whole of their Belize visit right here. Various packages can include meals, drinks, tours and activities.

watch the show. Alternatively, guides organize early-morning bird walks around the grounds.

🛏 Sleeping & Eating

La Milpa Lodge LODGE $$
(☑ 227-5617, 227-5616; www.pfbelize.org; s/d from BZ$212/350, without bathroom BZ$187/325; P 🛜) 🥘 The four lovely hardwood thatched cabañas at La Milpa Lodge are in tune with the natural surroundings and feature big comfortable beds, ceiling fans, spacious bathrooms, writing desks and power outlets. There are also fan-cooled dormitory-style rooms with shared bathrooms.

You may be able to connect to the slow internet in the restaurant area but don't plan on much more than sending emails. For full meals packages, add an additional BZ$130 per visitor to the prices.

Hill Bank Field Station LODGE $$
(☑ 227-5635, 227-1020; www.pfbelize.org; s/d BZ$212/350, without bathroom BZ$162/280; P @) 🥘 Guests at Hill Bank stay in spacious hardwood cabañas built on a clearing adjacent to the New River Lagoon. There are also ecologically sound dormitory-style accommodations that have shared bathrooms featuring composting toilets. Rooms have wide balconies with hammocks perfect for watching the abundant birdlife in the area. Add BZ$130 per visitor for meals packages.

ℹ Getting There & Away

Most visitors rent a vehicle to get to either field station. La Milpa is about one hour from Orange Walk Town (via Yo Creek, San Felipe, Blue Creek and Tres Leguas). Hill Bank is about two hours from Belize City (via Burrell Boom, Bermudian

Landing and Rancho Dolores), although it's also possible to travel from Orange Walk by road or boat via Lamanai.

Call Programme for Belize or check the website for detailed directions and advice on road conditions (the later stages of both trips involve sections on unpaved roads, which can be impassable after heavy rains). PFB can also help arrange transfers from Orange Walk, Belize City or Lamanai.

COROZAL DISTRICT

POP 47,440

The country's northernmost district, Corozal is wedged between Orange Walk District and the border. Its proximity to Mexico lends it a certain Spanish charm, and also offers easy access to travelers coming from Cancún or Chetumal. In recent years, Corozal has been 'discovered' by outsiders, who are racing to buy up the affordable seaside property and build retirement homes on their little plots of paradise. However, this district is still quite unknown to Belize-bound tourists, who don't often venture off the Philip Goldson Hwy.

Spread around Corozal Bay, Corozal is prettier and more compact than Orange Walk District, and most of the sights are well within striking distance – by boat or road – of Corozal Town itself.

ℹ Getting There & Away

Corozal District is the first taste of Belize for many travelers after crossing the border with Mexico at Santa Elena. Local buses and minivans connect the border with Corozal Town.

The main bus route between Corozal District and the rest of Belize runs the length of the Philip

Goldson Hwy, connecting Corozal Town with Belize City via Orange Walk Town. Another major bus line connects Belize City and Sarteneja via Orange Walk Town.

There is an airport south of Corozal Town with regular flights to and from San Pedro. It's also possible to travel between San Pedro and Corozal Town or Sarteneja by boat.

Corozal Town

POP 12,300

Just 9 miles south of Mexico and 29 miles north of Orange Walk Town, Corozal sits charmingly on the soapy-blue waters of Corozal Bay and has a vibe different from any other town in Belize, with its obvious Mexican influence. Most of the town's wealth comes from its position as a commercial and farming center, rather than from tourism. In fact, the town's fledgling tourism sector has been hit hard by the direct boat service between San Pedro and Chetumal, which has seen many travelers bypass Corozal altogether.

But Corozal remains a fine place to be a tourist as it escapes the holiday-ville atmosphere that haunts some of the other places in Belize. With ocean breezes, affordable hotels, fine food and easy access to the rest of the district, Corozal is worth a stop on the way to or from Mexico – if not as a detour from your Belizean itinerary when heading further south.

History

The ruins of the Postclassic Maya trading center, now called Santa Rita (probably the original Chetumal), lie beneath parts of modern Corozal. Across the bay, Cerros was a substantial coastal trade center in the Preclassic period.

Modern Corozal dates from 1849, when it was founded by Mexicans fleeing the War of the Castes. The refugees named their town Corozal after the Spanish word for cohune palm, a strong symbol of fertility.

For years Corozal had the look of a typical Mexican town, with thatched-roof homes. Then Hurricane Janet roared through in 1955 and blew away many of the buildings. Much of Corozal's wood-and-concrete architecture dates from the late 1950s. As in Orange Walk, the Corozal economy is based on sugarcane farming, although there's also quite a bit of trade with nearby Chetumal in Mexico as well.

⊙ Sights

★ Corozal House of Culture   HISTORIC SITE
(cnr 2nd St South & 1st Ave; ☺ 9am-5pm Mon-Fri) FREE Built in 1886, this fine old Spanish Colonial building once housed a bustling market beside the old customs house. It was one of only 11 buildings spared by Hurricane Janet in 1955. Today the historic building houses a cultural center and museum with exhibits of local artifacts. It's also a de facto tourist office; pick up a copy of the *Corozal Town Historical Walk* leaflet for a short self-guided stroll.

See the Facebook page at www.facebook.com/CHOCNICH for information about monthly events.

Santa Rita   RUINS
(BZ$10; ☺ 8am-6pm) Santa Rita was an ancient Maya coastal town that once occupied the same strategic trading position as present-day Corozal Town, namely the spot situated between two rivers – the Río Hondo (which now forms the Belize–Mexico border) and the New River (which enters Corozal Bay south of town). Much of Santa Rita remains unexcavated, but it is worth making a short excursion out of town to explore the site.

To reach the Maya site, head out of town on Santa Rita Rd. Continuing north on the main highway toward Mexico, turn left at the Super Santa Rita store. Some 350yd past the store you'll find a wooded area on the right and in its midst a partially restored pyramid offering an amazing view across the surrounding town to the bay. Apply liberal amounts of bug spray before making the trip. A taxi from downtown costs around BZ$5.

Corozal Museum   MUSEUM
(☏ 402-3314; 129 South End; admission by donation; ☺ hours vary) Called 'A Window to the Past,' the exhibit at this little museum focuses on the experience of the East Indian population, who arrived around 1838 as indentured servants working on the sugar plantations, but also features traditional items from other ethnic groups. It's located about a half-mile south of town right on the Philip Goldson Hwy.

There are other small cultural museums covering Maya and Garifuna culture in villages surrounding Corozal; contact the Corozal House of Culture for directions and to check when it's open.

Corozal Town

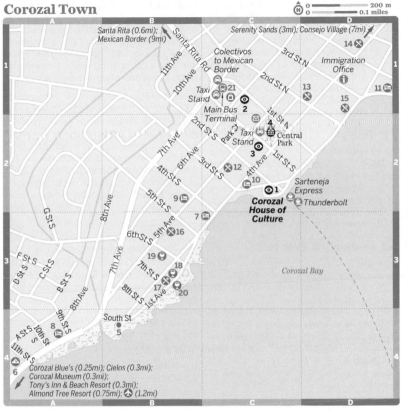

Corozal Town

Fort Barlee   HISTORIC SITE
(1st St North) At the center of town, this fort was built in 1849 by Caste War refugees for protection from attacks by hostile Maya. Only the remains of the brick corner turrets are still visible on the fort site.

Town Hall NOTABLE BUILDING
(1st St South; 9am-noon & 1-5pm Mon-Fri)
FREE A colorful and graphic **mural** by
Belizean-Mexican artist Manual Villamor
Reyes enlivens the lobby of the town hall. The
mural depicts episodes from Corozal history,
including the War of the Castes, with the talk-
ing cross and the fall of Bacalar; the flight of
refugees into British Honduras; the founding
of Corozal; and Hurricane Janet.

Tours

Our Island Tour TOURS
(633-9372, 633-0081; ourislandtours@yahoo.
com; 1st Ave) Offers a tour by boat to the ruins
at Cerro Maya (BZ$50 per person, minimum
three people), as well as fishing trips and other adventures. Call ahead as the office (a hut
on the waterfront) is often closed.

Festivals & Events

Art in the Park ART
(www.corozal.com/culture/artinpark; 5:30-10pm)
FREE On one Saturday of every month,
downtown Corozal hosts an outdoor art ex-
hibition and mini music festival, known as
Art in the Park. Artists congregate in Central
Park to display their wares, with paintings,
photography, woodwork and more. Music
is performed live or piped in over the loud
speakers and the whole town comes out to
socialize.

Sleeping

The best places to stay are along the coastal
strip, with water views: more upmarket resorts are south of town, while some decent
budget guesthouses are more central to town.
There's a camping ground here but no backpacker hostels.

Hotel Maya HOTEL $
(422-2082; hotelmaya@btl.net; 7th Ave, South
End; d BZ$85, s/d with air-con BZ$95/120;)
Run by the very friendly Rosita May, the
Hotel Maya is a long-time favorite of budget-
conscious travelers. Rooms are clean and
homey, and enlivened by colorful bedspreads
and paintings by local artists. Apartments are
available for long-term rentals. In addition to
being a licensed travel agent, Rosita is also a
great source of local information.

Hok'ol K'in Guest House GUESTHOUSE $
(422-3329; www.corozal.net; 89 4th Ave;
s/d/tr with fan BZ$77/104/109, with air-con
BZ$92/120/130;) With a Maya name
meaning 'rising sun,' this modern, well-run,

small hotel overlooking the bay may well be
the best value in town. The large, impeccably
clean rooms are designed to catch sea breezes. Each has two double beds, a bathroom
and a balcony with hammock. Hok'ol K'in
also has a cafe serving meals at reasonable
prices (breakfasts are particularly good).

Sea Breeze Guesthouse GUESTHOUSE $
(422-3051; 1st St Ave; s/d BZ$65/75, with air-con
BZ$95/110;) This secure two-story guest-
house at the north end of town faces Corozal
Bay, with a swimming jetty right out the front
and kayaks for rent. Rooms are compact but
clean and all with private bathroom – in the
sultry summer months it's worth paying extra for air-con. The upstairs common areas
are a great place to hang out with a cold beer.

Caribbean Village CAMPGROUND $
(422-2725; www.belizetransfers.com; 7th Ave;
campsite per person BZ$10, RV BZ$40;) This
seafront plot at the south end of town is the
place for campers or RVers. Lot spaces include all connections (water, electricity, sew-
age) and the camping ground has toilets and
cold showers. The owners are licensed travel
agents who rent vehicles (per day BZ$160),
run transfers and book tickets throughout
Central America.

Las Palmas Hotel HOTEL $
(422-0196, 602-5186; www.laspalmashotel
belize.com; 123 5th Ave; s/d/ste BZ$100/120/160;
) This centrally located hotel looks a
bit like a white wedding cake. Simple, clean
rooms have all the basics covered but are
distinctly lacking in character and seem a bit
pricey for what you get. There is plenty of gat-
ed parking onsite.

Serenity Sands B&B $$
(669-2394; www.serenitysands.com; 50 Serenity
Lane; d incl breakfast BZ$200-210, house BZ$220;
) Located about 3 miles north
of Corozal Town, this B&B is off the beaten
track, off the grid and out of this world. The
remote beachside setting – guests have free
use of the private beachfront pool – offers
the perfect combination of isolation and ac-
cessibility, and the four spacious upper-story
rooms are decorated with locally crafted fur-
niture and have private balconies.

For ultimate privacy there is also a bargain-
priced self-contained two-bedroom house
with kitchen for rent, situated behind the
main building.

Scrumptious breakfasts include home-
made pastries, fresh fruit and organic eggs

from the resident chickens. Aside from the delightfully serene setting and the top-notch service, the B&B has striven to reduce its environmental impact by preserving the local habitat, utilizing solar power and continuously improving waste management.

To reach Serenity Sands, drive north out of town onto Consejo Rd, and watch for the sign for the turn off. Alternatively, call the hotel and it'll arrange a taxi from town for BZ\$20.

★ Almond Tree Resort   RESORT $$
(☑422-0006; www.almondtreeresort.com; 425 Bayshore Dr; r BZ\$210-380; P🐕❄🀙🛜🏊) Tucked away on the bay south of town, Almond Tree is a gorgeous little 10-room resort and Corozal's most luxurious central offering. Most of the stylish suites have wonderful sea views, Caribbean-style furniture, Maya and Mexican artworks and modern bathrooms. Deluxe suites have full kitchenettes. The whole place is centered on lush grounds and a glorious swimming pool.

Home-cooked meals include seafood dishes, pasta and steaks. Turn onto Almond Dr a half-mile south of town, and follow the shoreline (and the signs) to Bayshore Dr.

Mirador Hotel   HOTEL $$
(☑422-0189; www.mirador.bz; cnr 4th Ave & 3rd St South; r BZ\$70-110, with air-con BZ\$100-140, ste BZ\$165-200; 🀙🛜🏠) Occupying a prominent corner block in Flatiron building style, the four-story Mirador is a local landmark. The staff are friendly and many rooms are enhanced by lovely ocean views and bright decor (ask for one of the nine bay-view rooms). The two-room suites are great for families or groups, while the rooftop patio affords tremendous views of the bay.

Tony's Inn & Beach Resort   RESORT $$
(☑422-2055, 422-3555; www.tonysinn.com; Almond Dr; s/d/tr BZ\$170/190/210, deluxe r BZ\$250; P🀙🏠) This southside resort is the largest in town, with uniform rooms on two floors surrounding a small garden. Spacious and comfortable rooms offer all necessities, such as hair dryers and cable TV, and there's free wi-fi throughout the property. The in-house restaurant Cielo's is a lovely seaside spot for food and drinks.

✖ Eating

Travelers who pass through Corozal on their way to Southern Belize may want to spend an extra day in Corozal just to eat some great food before heading out into the land

of stewed chicken and rice and beans. Check out the 2nd floor of the Gabrielle Hoare Market (p151) for cheap eats. Corozal's waterfront is the place to go for higher-end dining.

★ Wood House Bistro   ASIAN $
(☑636-0209; 1st Ave; dishes BZ\$9-30; ⊗noon-10pm Wed-Mon) Wood House is a real standout among the Chinese restaurants in Corozal (and Belize in general). The dining area is open air, with solid timber furniture, a Caribbean-style bar and a world music soundtrack. The food is eclectic, offering more than the usual fried chicken. Singapore-style noodles are especially good, as are the dumplings, spicy wontons and extensive seafood offerings. The bar generally stays open till midnight.

Patty's Bistro   BELIZEAN $
(cnr 2nd St North & 4th Ave; meals BZ\$8-20; ⊗10:30am-8pm, closed Sun; 🀙) This Corozal favorite retains its friendliness and commitment to good local food. The yellow walls are hung with hokey beach art, and the tables are covered in plastic tablecloths, but the atmosphere is so welcoming that the informal interior only adds to the charm.

The place is best known for its conch soup (BZ\$16), a thick potato-based chowder with vegetables, rice and chunks of conch meat, but more adventurous diners may want to go for the cow-foot soup (BZ\$10). You'll find more Mexican and Belizean fare on the menu, not to mention burgers, sandwiches and other standards.

Venky's Kabab Corner   INDIAN $
(☑402-0546; 5th St South; dishes BZ\$10-15; ⊗9am-9pm) Chef Venky is the premier – and, as far as we know, only – Hindu chef in Corozal, cooking excellent Indian meals, both meat and vegetarian. The place is not much to look at on the inside, in fact there is just one table that is usually covered in assorted clutter, but the food is excellent and filling.

Two main dishes and a few sides easily serve three people.

Scotty Bar & Bistro   INTERNATIONAL $
(☑422-0005; 41 First Ave; mains BZ\$10-30; ⊗noon-midnight Thu-Tue) This thatched sea-facing bar and restaurant is popular among locals, expats and visitors for its international menu of burgers, pasta, pizza, rice and beans and fresh fish. There's occasional live entertainment or DJs in the evenings.

RD's Diner
BELIZEAN **$**

(☑422-3796; 25 4th Ave; mains BZ$10-25; ☺8am-10:30pm, closed Sun; ❋) Rick and his staff go above and beyond to ensure a good time at this unassuming eatery. The interior might be nondescript but it's an excellent place to sample some local specialties such as *gibnut* (small, brown-spotted rodent) stew. Otherwise the menu offers a mix of Belizean, Mexican and straight-up continental fare, such as burgers, salads and fried seafood.

Al's Cafe
DINER **$**

(5th Ave; snacks BZ$1-2, mains BZ$6-8; ☺9am-4pm Mon-Sat & 6-9pm Sat) This tiny local place is one of several diners popular for tasty Mexican snacks and cheap daily lunch specials. Try the burritos with beans, chicken and cheese – and very hot habanero sauce!

Corozo Blue's
PIZZA, BELIZEAN **$$**

(☑422-0090; Philip Goldson Hwy; mains BZ$15-35; ☺10am-midnight Sun-Thu, 10am-2am Fri & Sat; ☎☑) The waterfront location at this semi-enclosed, stone-hewn restaurant and day resort is unbeatable, with indoor, beachfront and garden seating offering a great view of the bay. It's popular for the stone-oven wood-fired pizzas, late breakfasts and formidable steaks, but also burgers and Belize standards such as rice and beans and *ceviche*.

There's also a full bar and fresh juices – this is a fine place to come just for a sunset drink. Parents take note – Blue's also has a playground with swings and a jungle gym.

Cielos
INTERNATIONAL **$$**

(☑422-2055; www.tonysinn.com; Almond Dr; mains BZ$18-49; ☺11am-10pm) The waterfront restaurant at Tony's Inn offers a delightfully sophisticated setting and fine food served under a breezy *palapa* with dockside seating stretching out into the bay. Specialties include prime steaks, fajitas and pasta dishes such as creole shrimp. The bar offers a fine selection of tropical fruity cocktails and other drinks.

 ## Drinking & Nightlife

Corozal's best bars are found along the waterfront in town. For a sunset drink, the waterside hotels and restaurants on the southern edge of town serve up cold beers with a view.

Jam Rock
BAR

(☑402-2205; 1st Ave; ☺11am-midnight Wed-Mon) In a park right by the bay, this open-air watering hole catches plenty of breeze and is popular with expats and locals alike. Tasty meals are served from noon to 10pm, the bar is well stocked and there's a convivial tropical vibe.

Bay Breeze
BAR

(1st Ave; ☺noon-midnight Tue-Sun) Have a seat at this open-air bar and restaurant and enjoy the Corozal Bay breeze with a cold Belikin or an even colder margarita or piña colada. Also has an extensive list of cocktails.

Cactus Plaza
NIGHTCLUB

(6 6th St South; ☺6pm-late Fri-Sun) You can't miss this building, which looks a bit like a cross between a Christmas tree and a Mexican fruitcake. It's open late on weekends as a bar and nightclub, also serving Mexican snacks such as tacos (BZ$3 to BZ$5).

CONSEJO

About 7 miles north of Corozal, Consejo is a sweet small fishing village set on Chetumal Bay, offering little more than a pristine stretch of beach and lovely sunrise views. Bring a book and your binoculars and you might be content to stay here for quite a while.

There aren't many amenities for tourists in Consejo. But there is a handful of folks who like the place so much that they decided to stay, setting up a sort of outpost for expats at Consejo Shores at the southern end of the village.

Located around 2 miles northwest of Consejo, the family-run **Smuggler's Den** (☑629-9460; http://smugglersdenbelize.tripod.com; Consejo; r/bungalows/houses BZ$70/120/220; P☎) has spacious thatched bungalows with kitchenettes and a lounge area set around a grassy yard that runs down to a tranquil stretch of sand. The food here gets rave reviews, especially the owner's special roast beef; reserve ahead if you're a nonguest.

Buccaneer Palapa (☑604-0600; Consejo; mains BZ$9-18; ☺9am-9pm) is one of the few places in Consejo for a cold Belikin, bowl of *ceviche* or Mexican snacks such as tacos, tostados and nachos (try the lobster nachos in season).

🅰 Shopping

Gabrielle Hoare Market   GIFTS & SOUVENIRS
(6th Ave; ⊘ 6:30am-5:30pm Mon-Sat, to 3pm Sun)
Amid the fruit, vegetables and fish, you'll
also find a few local craftspeople selling art,
woodwork and tapestries. The 2nd floor has
stores selling food and locally made clothing.
You'll certainly find a greater selection further south (especially in the more tourism-
focused towns).

ℹ Information

MONEY

Atlantic Bank (cnr 4th Ave & 3rd St North;
⊘ 9am-4pm Mon-Fri) Has a reliable ATM accepting all major cards.

Belize Bank (cnr 5th Ave & 1st St North;
⊘ 9am-4pm Mon-Fri) Situated on the plaza; ATM
accepts most international credit cards.

Scotiabank (4th Ave; ⊘ 8am-3pm Mon-Thu,
to 4:30pm Fri) Currency exchange and cash
advances; ATM accepts all international cards.

POST

Post Office (5th Ave; ⊘ 8:30am-noon &
1-4:30pm Mon-Thu, to 4pm Fri) On the site of
Fort Barlee, facing the plaza.

TOURIST INFORMATION

Corozal House of Culture (p146) Can help with
local information, including a self-guided historical walking tour.

Immigration Office (🖉 402-0123; 4th Ave;
⊘ 8am-4pm Mon-Thu, to 3:30pm Fri) Provides
30-day visa extensions for most nationalities.

ℹ Getting There & Away

AIR

Corozal's airstrip (CZH) is a couple of miles south
of the town center in Ranchito. Taxis (BZ$10)
meet incoming flights. Both **Tropic Air** (🖉 226-
2012; www.tropicair.com; Airport, Ranchito) and
Maya Island Air (🖉 422-2333; www.mayaisland
air.com; Airport, Ranchito) fly in and out of Corozal with direct flights to San Pedro.

BOAT

Corozal is connected to Sarteneja and San Pedro
by regular boat. **Thunderbolt** (🖉 422-0026, 610-
4475; 1st Ave) is the town's main water-taxi service and while the advent of the Chetumal-to-San
Pedro boat has made this journey less popular,
crossing the border by bus and taking this boat is
significantly cheaper.

It leaves Corozal at 7am, returning from San
Pedro at 3pm, stopping at Sarteneja only on
request. The trip to Sarteneja takes 30 minutes
and costs BZ$25/50 one-way/return; San Pedro

ℹ **GETTING TO MEXICO:
COROZAL TOWN TO CHETUMAL**

Getting to the border The border
crossing at Santa Elena (Belize) and
Subteniente López (Mexico) is 9 miles
north of Corozal and 7 miles west of Chetumal. *Colectivos* (shared taxis) to the
border (BZ$5, 20 minutes) depart from
near the main bus stand in Corozal. Local
buses from Corozal to Chetumal stop at
the Nuevo Mercado (New Market), about
0.75 miles north of the town center.

At the border Travelers departing from
Belize by land have to pay a BZ$40 de-
parture tax; this includes both the exit
fee and a government-imposed conservation fee. Bus travelers, heading in either direction, have to get off the bus and
carry their luggage through customs.

Moving on Across the border, Mexican
colectivos and private taxis run into
Chetumal or you can arrange a private
taxi for BZ$60 from Corozal to the ADO
intercity bus terminal in Chetumal.

is two hours away and will cost you BZ$50/90
one-way/return.

Sarteneja Express (p155) is a water-taxi service connecting Corozal and Sarteneja on Monday, Wednesday, Friday and Saturday.

BUS

Corozal's **main bus terminal** is a key stop for
nearly all of the myriad bus lines that ply the Philip
Goldson Hwy down to Orange Walk and Belize
City. At last count, 30 buses daily were doing the
2½-hour run from Corozal Town to Belize City,
from 3:30am until 7pm; there are half a dozen
buses in the other direction on the 15-minute
run to the Mexican border, with the last coming
through around 4pm. There are a couple of very
early direct buses to Belmopan via Orange Walk
at 3am and 3:30am.

In Chetumal, Mexico, buses from Corozal stop
at the Nuevo Mercado (New Market), about 0.75
miles north of the town center. A taxi from the
Nuevo Mercado to the intercity bus station or
town center is around US$1. From Chetumal to
Corozal, buses leave from the north side of the
Nuevo Mercado from around 4:30am to 6pm.

There are two buses daily, except Sunday, from
Corozal to Copper Bank, leaving at 11am and
3:30pm.

TAXI

Colectivos (Corozal United Taxi Cooperative;
Santa Rita Rd) (shared taxis) to the Mexican

COROZAL FREE ZONE

Straddling the Belize–Mexico border at Santa Elena–Subteniente López, 9 miles north of Corozal Town, Corozal Free Zone (www.belizecorozalfreezone.com) is an experiment in global capitalism originally designed to boost the economy of Northern Belize by attracting Mexican shoppers and providing jobs for Belizeans. It's essentially a tax-free shopping district but it's bigger than most Belizean towns, with streets, gas stations, cafes, casinos and, of course, lots of shops selling knock-off brand-name gear, cheap alcohol and jewelry.

The catch, of course, is that you need to exit Belize in order to shop for a bargain. As a nonresident tourist you can shop in the free zone on your way out of the country (after leaving Belize customs) or on your way in (after clearing Mexican customs but before entering Belize). Shops are staffed by both Belizean and Mexican workers.

Unlike their Mexican counterparts, Belizeans can't just show up, shop and go home, due to restrictive import regulations and duties on the Belizean side of the border. In essence, the Free Zone is a bargain-basement shopping mall for consumers on the Mexican side of the border – one that Belizean customers can only utilize with some degree of bureaucratic wrangling.

Shoppers can get excellent deals on alcohol, household appliances and brand-name shoes and clothing but the duty-free goods are for sale for use outside of Belize; if you bring your loot back into Belize, you are obliged to pay all applicable taxes.

border depart for the Belizean immigration post (BZ$5, 20 minutes) from outside the main bus terminal from 7am to 7pm. Once you complete border formalities, Mexican *colectivos* and private taxis run into Chetumal. If you are in a hurry, these minivans will run a private transfer for BZ$25 to the border post or BZ$60 all the way to the ADO intercity bus terminal in Chetumal.

Regular city taxis charge around BZ$30 to the border or BZ$70 to the ADO bus terminal; you can find them outside Corozal Town's **main bus terminal** (Santa Rita Rd) or around **Central Park** (5th Ave).

Cerro Maya & Copper Bank

POP 500

The small fishing village of Copper Bank (called San Fernando on some maps) is set on the shores of a brackish lagoon known as Laguna Seca (which is anything but dry). The village is a tiny place with a lazy, hazy tropical charm but there's not much here to attract travelers other than as a wayside stop on the way to Cerro Maya or Sarteneja.

Although Copper Bank is only 9 miles from Corozal, it's isolated due to the poor condition of the roads and the necessity of crossing the New River by hand-cranked cable ferry. The Maya ruins at Cerro Maya (also known as Cerros) are 2.5 miles north, overlooking Corozal Bay; the New River and the surrounding jungles are ideal for fly-fishing, birdwatching and other outdoor adventures.

☉ Sights

Cerro Maya
RUINS

(Cerros; BZ$10; ⊙8am-5pm) The ruins at Cerro Maya make up the only Maya site in Belize that occupies beachfront property. It is composed of a series of temples built from about 50 BC. While the site is mostly a mass of grass-covered mounds, the center has been cleared and two structures are visible. Be warned: Cerro Maya can get very very buggy, especially during the rainy season; cover up and don't skimp on the bug spray!

In late Preclassic times, its proximity to the mouth of the New River gave Cerro Maya a key position on the trade route between the Yucatán coast and the Petén region. The temples are larger and more ornate than any others found in the area, and archaeologists believe Cerro Maya may have been taken over by an outside power at this time, quite possibly Lamanai. Cerros flourished until about AD 150, after which it reverted rapidly to small, unimportant village status.

Climbing **Structure 4** (a funerary temple more than 65ft high) offers panoramic views of the ocean and Corozal Town just across the bay. Northwest of this, **Structure 5** stands with its back to the sea. This was the first temple to be built and may have been the most important. Large stucco masks flanking its central staircase have been covered with modern replicas for protection but the new material looks out of place and the models are not as well executed as those at Lamanai.

Southwest of Structure 5, a third structure remains unexcavated, protected by an army of mosquitoes. Apparently Structure 6 exhibits a 'triadic' arrangement (one main temple flanked by two lesser ones, all atop the same mound), which is also found in Preclassic buildings at Lamanai and El Mirador in the Petén.

🛏 Sleeping

The closest accommodation is nestled on the edge of Corozal Day just to the east of Cerro Maya or across the lagoon on Orchid Bay.

★ Cerros Beach Resort RESORT, CABAÑAS **$$**
(623-9530, 623-9763; www.cerrosbeachresort. com; cabañas BZ$120; P) About 3.5 miles north of Copper Bank, on the coast and surrounded by jungle, this rustic little beach resort is a wonderfully remote spot. It has everything a great getaway should, including a top location on the crystal-blue side of Corozal Bay, fantastic ecofriendly facilities, and genuine, welcoming hosts.

The four beautiful, hardwood, thatched-roof cabañas are equipped with hot solar showers and come with free use of kayaks, bicycles and fishing gear. Just behind the accommodations there are nature trails and it's possible to walk to the Cerro Maya ruins through the bush. The recommended restaurant features many ingredients grown onsite in the organic garden, and the owner makes and bottles his own fruit wine.

The Thunderbolt boat service between San Pedro and Corozal will drop you at the resort if you have a group of four or more travelers.

Orchid Bay Resort RESORT **$$$**
(650-1925, in USA 1-800-973-2468; www. orchidbay.bz; Orchid Bay Rd; cabañas/condos BZ$350/500;) On a remote patch of coast across the water from Copper Bank, Orchid Bay is part holiday resort and part gated community where expats have purchased property. The thatched beachfront cabañas come with screened-in porches, full kitchen and all mod-cons, while the spacious two-bedroom condos would suit a family. The resort has a restaurant and small store.

Orchid Bay is a place for relaxation but there is also beach volleyball, kayaking, swimming and fishing tours to keep you busy.

ℹ Getting There & Away

An unpaved road runs from Corozal to Copper Bank, punctuated by a river that needs to be forded by a hand-cranked cable ferry, and on to Cerros. During the dry season you can pass in a regular vehicle but when it's wet you may need a 4WD.

Buses leave from near the pier in Corozal for Copper Bank (one hour) at 11am and 4pm, returning from Copper Bank at 1pm and 6:30pm.

Cerro Maya is about 2.5 miles north of the village of Copper Bank. Bus schedules to Copper Bank don't facilitate day trips to Cerros; if you don't have your own vehicle, you can organize a private boat transfer from Corozal (BZ$40 per person) or hire a taxi (costing around BZ$100 per vehicle including an hour wait at the site).

Sarteneja

POP 3500

If you came to Belize in search of sparkling blue waters, delicious fresh seafood, fauna-rich forests and affordable prices, look no further than Sarteneja (sar-ten-*eh*-ha). The tiny fishing and shipbuilding village, located near the northeastern tip of the Belizean mainland, is a charming base from which to explore both the nautical and jungle treasures of the region.

The village spreads just a few blocks back from its long, grassy seafront. It's a delicious place to chill out for a few days. From this lovely seaside setting, visitors can also head out to the Shipstern Conservation & Management Area and take birding, fishing and wildlife-watching trips all along the fabulous coast of Northern Belize, including to Bacalar Chico National Park & Marine Reserve, on the northern tip of Ambergris Caye.

◉ Sights

Stroll along the shoreline to admire the wooden sailboats that are still constructed and painted in workshops around town.

Shipstern Conservation & Management Area NATURE RESERVE
(660-1807; www.visitshipstern.com; BZ$10; 8am-5pm) Run by a nonprofit organization, this large nature reserve, which protects 43 sq miles of semideciduous hardwood forests, wetlands and lagoons and coastal mangrove belts, has its headquarters 3.5 miles southwest of Sarteneja on the road to Orange Walk. Lying in a transition zone between Central America's tropical forests and a drier Yucatán-type ecosystem, the reserve's mosaic of habitats is rare in Belize.

All five of Belize's wildcats and scores of other mammals can be found here, and its

250 bird species include ospreys, roseate spoonbills, white ibis and a colony of 300 pairs of American woodstorks, one of this bird's few breeding colonies in Belize.

Admission allows access to both a small museum and butterfly house at the headquarters, as well as a short botanical trail that leads to an observation tower over the treetops. There are several other longer hiking trails, including Thompson Trail, which goes to the shore of the lagoon and along which you may spot agouti and peccari in addition to plenty of bird species. It's accessible only in the dry season.

Of course, the best way to see the lagoon and its birdlife is by taking a full-day boat tour, which costs BZ$450 for up to three people (including lunch).

About a 40-minute drive from the headquarters, Xo-Pol has a treetop hide overlooking a large forest-surrounded pond where you might see crocodiles, waterfowl, peccaries, deer and tapirs. Half-day birding tours are BZ$70 per visitor. Rangers also take adventurers on overnight expeditions to Xo-Pol for BZ$250.

Another interesting tour is the 'Ranger Experience' where visitors accompany the reserve rangers on their daily rounds, assisting in patrols and research tasks.

Call ahead to check on conditions and book tours. Don't forget your long sleeves, pants and bug spray!

☞ Tours

Sarteneja Tour Guide
Association   ADVENTURE
(☑ 621-6465; North Front St; ⊙ 9am-5pm) A cooperative of enthusiastic young guides that rents kayaks (per hour/day BZ$10/50) and runs tours around Sarteneja and to the ruins at Cerro Maya. It also organizes boat trips to remote Bacalar Chico at the northern trip of Ambergris Caye (BZ$160 per visitor).

🛏 Sleeping

There are accommodations with sea views along the waterfront in town; nature lovers should check out the accessible rural places in the surrounding area. For information on Sarteneja homestays, call 669 4911.

Backpackers Paradise   CABAÑAS, CAMPGROUND $
(☑ 423-2016, 607-1873; www.cabanasbelize.word press.com; Bandera Rd; camping BZ$12, s/d/ tr BZ$45/55/60, cabañas BZ$50/66/70, family

house BZ$60/80/90; ☎) Peaceful, sustainable and affordable, this laid-back and rustic spot set on lush grounds is a 15-minute walk from the beach and is a good base for budget travelers. Apart from camping, there's a range of basic screened cabañas, some with private bathrooms, and two Mennonite-built free-standing houses sleeping four to six people.

The common area is a good place to meet other travelers, there's high-speed internet, a communal kitchen, horses and bicycles for rent, and plenty of other activities in the area. Meals are available. If you contact the owner Nathalie in advance, she will send a taxi (BZ$10) to meet your boat. If arriving by bus, get off at the 'Welcome to Sarteneja' sign at the entrance to town. Also offers secure vehicle parking for those looking to take the boat over to San Pedro.

Shipstern Nature
Reserve Bungalows   LODGE $
(☑ 660-1807; www.visitshipstern.com; Shipstern Conservation & Management Area; dm/s/d BZ$40/80/100) Located at the Shipstern Conservation & Management Area headquarters 3 miles out of town, these four bungalows are a great choice for visitors intending to take early nature tours or looking to be surrounded by wilderness. The air-con rooms have private bathroom and open out onto a screened porch for enjoying the sounds of the jungle.

There are also two spacious dormitories that make excellent-value budget accommodations. The large onsite restaurant serves all meals (BZ$10 to BZ$20) and can prepare takeout packages for those going on tours.

Fernando's Seaside
Guesthouse   GUESTHOUSE $
(☑ 423-2085; www.fernandosseaside.com; North Front St; d BZ$100; ✳☎) This colorful family-run hotel – one of Sarteneja's originals – has five spacious rooms, each with two double beds, private bathrooms with hot showers, and air-con. Go for one of the two at the front that have fine sea views. Meals are served and Fernando also arranges snorkeling, fishing and other trips around the area.

Mayra's Guest House   GUESTHOUSE $
(☑ 661-3262; North Front St; d BZ$50) Simple but clean and pleasant rooms face the Caribbean Sea at this homestay-style guesthouse. The host family can whip up meals on request.

WORTH A TRIP

LITTLE BELIZE

Located on the eastern shore of Progresso Lagoon, Little Belize is an Old Order Mennonite community of approximately 2000 residents. Among the more traditional Mennonite groups, these folks look as though they've come straight from the prairie, driving around in horse-drawn carriages, with men wearing broad-brimmed hats and overalls and women in long dresses and bonnets.

Like most Mennonite villages, Little Belize is an industrious place, with an economy thriving on farming. One of the largest employers in the village is Belize Exports Ltd, which grows papayas for export to North America.

Old Order Mennonites are typically an insular group, interacting with outsiders just enough to sell their wares. Tentatively opening itself up to rural tourism, Little Belize offers visitors a rare opportunity to get a closer look inside this enigmatic community. With advanced arrangements, visitors can tour the village in a horse-drawn buggy, visiting the papaya packing plant, a poultry farm, a wood workshop and other local industries. Make arrangements in advance through the Shipstern Conservation & Management Area. A visit to Little Belize can be combined with a visit to the mestizo community of Chunox and the Maya ruins at Cerros in a full-day tour for BZ$150.

Little Belize is a 40-minute drive from Sarteneja, Corozal or Orange Walk. There is no public transportation available, but the Shipstern Conservation & Management Area can organize transfers.

✗ Eating

Crabby's   BELIZEAN, SEAFOOD **$$**
(☑620-8358; 127 North Front St; mains BZ$8-27; ☺10:30am-3:30pm & 5:30-9pm Tue-Sun) Crabby's is in a welcoming thatched, open-sided restaurant and bar that ranks as Sarteneja's best, with a fine waterfront location and convivial vibe. The specialty is local seafood (try the lionfish burger with onion rings) but you'll also find Belizean classics, burgers, wings and fajitas. Saturday is barbecue day. Enjoy cocktails and ice-cold beers, with sunset happy hour from 5:30pm.

Martineja   AMERICAN **$**
(☑423-2021; North Front St; mains BZ$5-16, pizzas BZ$22-30; ☺8am-10pm Fri-Mon; 🛜) The place for pizza in Sarteneja, this garden terrace restaurant back from the waterfront is a great place to be on the weekend with a fun-loving local and expat crowd and regular entertainment. Along with the specialty lionfish and lobster pizzas, there's a generous menu of burgers, tacos, conch fritters and pasta.

ℹ Information

There are no ATMs in Sarteneja and not many businesses accept cards so bring plenty of cash.

ℹ Getting There & Away

BOAT
The **Sarteneja Express** (☑635-1655; North Front St; one-way/return BZ$15/25) ferry runs between Sarteneja and Corozal Town on Monday, Wednesday, Friday and Saturday, departing at 7am. From Corozal the boat leaves at 4pm. With advance notice, the **Thunderbolt** (☑610-4475, 631-3400) ferry between Corozal and San Pedro stops in Sarteneja daily. The ride to Corozal takes 30 minutes (BZ$25); to San Pedro it's 1½ hours at sea (BZ$50).

BUS
Four buses daily run between Belize City and Sarteneja (BZ$15, three hours) leaving from next to the Swing Bridge in Belize City at 10:30am, noon, 1:45pm, 4pm and 5pm. They return from Sarteneja at the unsociable hours of 3:30am, 4:30am, 5:30am and 6:30am. You can also pick them up in Orange Walk around 1½ hours after they depart from Belize City. No service on Sunday.

CAR & MOTORCYCLE
Sarteneja is 40 miles northeast of Orange Walk by a mostly unpaved all-weather road that passes through the village of San Estevan and the scattered Mennonite community of Little Belize. Drivers from Corozal Town can reach Sarteneja (43 miles) by driving to Copper Bank and then crossing the river and heading to the town of Chunox on the Orange Walk Town–Sarteneja road.

ℹ Getting Around

You can rent bicycles at guesthouses or at **Brisis Rental** (La Bandera St; per day BZ$10; ☺6am-6pm) in town.

Cayo District

POP 93,350

Best Places to Eat

➡ Running W Steakhouse (p177)

➡ Benny's Kitchen (p192)

➡ Ko-Ox Han-nah (p177)

➡ Guava Limb Cafe (p176)

➡ Caladium Restaurant (p161)

Best Places to Stay

➡ Black Rock Lodge (p190)

➡ Lodge at Chaa Creek (p190)

➡ Ian Anderson's Caves Branch Jungle Lodge (p166)

➡ Trek Stop (p192)

➡ El-Rey Hotel (p157)

Why Go?

Cayo District is Belize's premier adventure and eco-activity region. The lush environs of the Wild West are covered with jungle, woven with rivers, waterfalls and azure pools, riddled with caves and dotted with Maya ruins ranging from small, tree-covered hills to massive, magnificent temples. Cahal Pech, Xunantunich, El Pilar, and the mother of all Belizean Maya sites – Caracol – are all in Cayo.

Travelers leave the coast and head inland to tube through river caves, zipline over the jungle canopy or horseback ride through the Maya Mountains. From a base at San Ignacio or Belmopan – or one of the numerous outstanding jungle lodges – tour operators can easily get your adventure started. This region teems with nature, from botanic gardens and butterfly houses to primeval jungles and rainforests, where the only thing coming between you and the wildlife is a pair of binoculars.

When to Go

Jan–Mar Sun-drenched days, cooler nights and dry roads make these months a great time to explore Cayo.

Apr & May The height of the hot, dry season.

Jun–Nov Plenty of rain and muddy roads.

ⓘ Getting There & Away

AIR

There are two airstrips in Cayo District, both served by daily Tropic Air flights: Belmopan and the tiny Maya Flats airstrip about 7 miles from San Ignacio.

BUS

Buses run along the George Price Hwy between Belize City and Benque Viejo del Carmen, stopping in Belmopan and San Ignacio. For destinations in Southern Belize, change in Belmopan.

BELMOPAN

POP 19,460

Like many purpose-built capital cities around the world, Belmopan can seem a bit dull at first glance. Wide ordered streets, empty urban parklands and drab government buildings conspire to give it a desolate feel. The exception is the vibrant central market area, where cheap food stalls and incoming buses provide some welcome activity.

But this is the national capital, a major transport hub, a place to extend your visa and an easygoing university city with a decent range of restaurants. More importantly, it's a useful base for exploring nearby caves, national parks, the Hummingbird Hwy and most of the attractions in eastern Cayo.

History

Belmopan was conceived after Hurricane Hattie all but destroyed Belize City in 1961. Certain that a coastal capital would never be secure from further terrible hurricanes, the government decided to move and built the new capital here in 1971.

A grand new National Assembly was built to resemble a Maya temple and plaza, with government offices around it. Government needs have since outgrown these core buildings and an assortment of less-uniform government offices are spread out around the central green. Many government ministries and other organizations are based here, as are a few embassies, giving the place an unexpected international atmosphere.

⊙ Sights

The main market days are Tuesday and Friday, when stallholders come from all over the district to sell produce.

George Price Center for Peace & Development   MUSEUM

(☑822-1054; www.gpcbelize.com; Price Center Rd; ⊗8am-5pm Mon-Thu, to 4pm Fri) FREE This museum and conference center celebrates the life of Belize's beloved statesman and first prime minister after independence, George Price, who died in 2011. As well as photographs and information panels, there's an archive of documents and letters written by Price.

Belize Archives Department   ARCHIVES

(☑822-2247; www.archives.gov.bz; 26-28 Unity Blvd; ⊗8am-5pm, to 4:30pm Fri, closed 2nd & 4th Friday of the month) This local history collection is mainly a reading room and research facility with computers for public use. You can stop by and chat with the researchers on anything to do with Belizean history.

🛏 Sleeping

Belmopan suffers from a dearth of good budget accommodations but there are a few decent midrange places in town and more upmarket lodges located in the surrounding region.

★El Rey Hotel   HOTEL $

(☑822-3438; www.elreyhotel.com; 23 Moho St; s/d/tr from BZ$90/100/110, ste BZ$180/190/200; P❄🛜) Northeast of town, El Rey is Belmopan's best budget offering, an affordable and welcoming place with 12 plain, clean ground-floor rooms equipped with private bathroom, TV and wi-fi, plus one budget room available for BZ$70. All rooms have air-con, there's a small cafe and tours can be booked here.

★Hibiscus Hotel   HOTEL $$

(☑822-0400, 633-5323; www.hibiscusbelize.com; Market Sq; s/d BZ$110/120; ⊗reception from 2pm Mon-Sat; P❄🛜) 🌿 Close to Belmopan's lively market place, this neat little place has just six motel-style rooms. Comforts include king and twin-sized beds, flat-screen cable TV, bath tubs, and tea and coffee facilities. There's an eco angle – some of the profits go to support local avian conservation and rescue projects – and the decent Corkers restaurant and bar is upstairs.

Villa San Juan   B&B $$

(☑822-0958; www.villasanjuanbelmopan.com; 3639 Tangelo St; s/d BZ$180/210; P❄🛜🍽) The three comfortable rooms in this family-run Spanish-style villa orbit a homey communal lounge-dining area and overlook a large

Cayo District Highlights

1 **San Ignacio** (p170) Hanging out in this traveler-friendly town, especially for market day on Saturday.

2 **Hummingbird Highway** (p164) Bridging the gap between Cayo and coastal Southern Belize along the region's most scenic drive.

3 **Caracol** (p186) Exploring these remote and ancient Maya ruins.

4 **Actun Tunichil Muknal** (p168) Serious spelunking in Belize's most dramatic cave.

5 **Nohoch Che'en Caves Branch Archaeological Reserve** (p163) Cave-tubing, jungle ziplining and

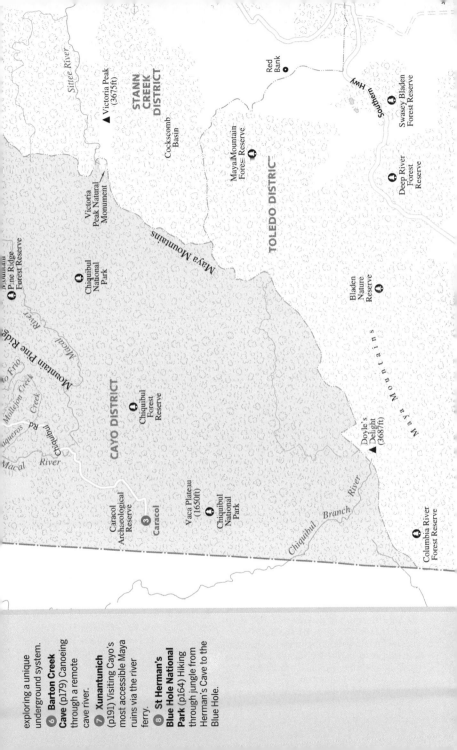

Sittee River

▲ Victoria Peak
(3675ft)

STANN CREEK DISTRICT

Red Bank

Cockscomb
Basin

Victoria
Peak Natural
Monument

Maya Mountain
Forest Reserve

Swasey Bladen
Forest Reserve

TOLEDO DISTRICT

Southern Hwy

Deep River
Forest
Reserve

Pine Ridge
Forest Reserve

Chiquibul
National
Park

Maya Mountains

Micael River

Bladen
Nature
Reserve

to Frio

Mountain Pine Ridge

Mollejon Creek

Creek

Chiquibul
Forest
Reserve

CAYO DISTRICT

Caracol
Archeological
Reserve

❸ Caracol

Vaca Plateau
(1650ft)

Chiquibul
National Park

Maya Mountains

▲ Doyle's
Delight
(3687ft)

Chiquibul Branch River

Columbia River
Forest Reserve

Macal River

vaqueros Rd

Chiquibul Rd

exploring a unique
underground system.

**❻ Barton Creek
Cave** (p179) Canoeing
through a remote
cave river.

❼ Xunantunich
(p191) Visiting Cayo's
most accessible Maya
ruins via the river
ferry.

**❽ St Herman's
Blue Hole National
Park** (p164) Hiking
through jungle from
Herman's Cave to the
Blue Hole.

Belmopan

in-ground pool. Rooms are individually decorated and furnished, with cable TV and air-con. It's in a quiet part of town near the hospital.

Bull Frog Inn HOTEL **$$**
(☏822-2111; www.bullfroginn.com; 25 Half Moon Ave; s/d BZ$180/213; P❋☎) The Bull Frog is a cheerful, if nondescript, place on the eastern edge of town. The 26 rooms are spacious and comfortable enough with cable TV, fridge and two double beds (kids under 12 years stay free). There's a playground and a popular restaurant and bar.

✗ Eating

The market area is the place for cheap eats and you'll find more restaurants strung out along the highway west of town.

⭐**Market Food Stalls** MARKET **$**
(Market Sq; from BZ$2; ☉6am-6pm) For a cheap meal, you can't beat the food stalls in the market square. They serve quick-fire Mexican snacks such as burritos and *salbutes* (mini-tortillas, usually stuffed with chicken), as well as Belizean standards such as beans and rice or cow-foot soup, or omelets and fry-jacks for breakfast.

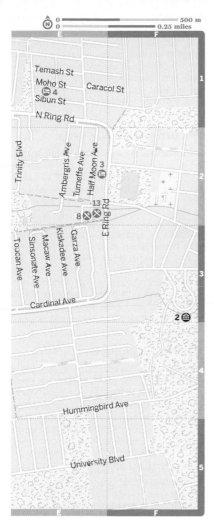

Belmopan

⊚ Sights

⊟ Sleeping

⊗ Eating

⊜ Drinking & Nightlife

⊛ Entertainment

Sat; 🕾) Scotchies is a Jamaican transplant serving smoky jerk chicken and pork, sausage, wings and ribs, along with sides such as mashed sweet potato, yam, breadfruit and Red Stripe beer. Dining is in a cool garden beneath one of the octagonal thatched *palapas* (open-air shelters with a thatched roof).

Casa Cafe   CAFE **$**
(📞822-2098; 43 Forest Dr; snacks BZ$3-10; ⊙8am-6pm; 🕾📶) With good coffee, waffles, ice cream and breakfast snacks, Casa is a great place to start the day. It also dishes up vegetarian Asian dishes such as egg rolls and noodles for lunch.

Wing Stop   AMERICAN **$**
(📞802-0048; 3896 Mountain View Blvd; meals from BZ$5; ⊙9am-midnight; 🕾) If wings are your thing, this is the place. Try buffalo (six pieces for BZ$10) or a range of flavors up to the mind-bendingly spicy 'atomic'. Also burgers, pizzas and carrot sticks. The semi open-air bar is convivial and claims to be open 24 hours if enough drinkers stick around. Happy hour is 5pm to 7pm.

★**Caladium Restaurant**   BELIZEAN, SEAFOOD **$**
(📞822-2754; Market Sq; mains BZ$5-35; ⊙7:30am-8pm Mon-Fri, to 7pm Sat; ❋) In the market area, the Caladium is regarded by many as Belmopan's best restaurant. The intimate dining room goes well with the menu of Belizean favorites, such as fried fish and coconut rice, stew beef and BBQ chicken. Well-made burgers sit comfortably alongside Belizean treats such as lobster creole.

Scotchies   JAMAICAN **$**
(📞832-2203; 7753 Hummingbird Hwy; mains BZ$7-15; ⊙11am-9pm Mon-Thu, to 9:30pm Fri &

Veggie Garden
VEGETARIAN $

(📋 602-1644; off Hummingbird Hwy; mains BZ$9-20; ⊙ 8am-6pm Mon-Fri, to 4pm Sat; 🛜🍴) This sweet Taiwanese vegetarian restaurant serves excellent ovo-lacto dishes (using eggs and dairy) from noodles to dumplings, as well as fresh juices and smoothies. It's down a lane off the Hummingbird Hwy on Belmopan's outskirts.

Moon Clusters
Coffee House
CAFE $

(📋 602-1644; 4 Shopping Center, E Ring Rd; coffee & drinks BZ$3-11; ⊙ noon-7pm Mon-Sat; ✳) The Aguilar family's excellent little old-school coffee shop serves some of the best java in Belize, from Cuban dark roast to the attitude adjustment, a five-shot espresso that will keep you up all night. It's all about the drinks here with a variety of smoothies and shakes, but it can whip up a quesadilla too.

Brodies
SUPERMARKET $

(Shopping Center, E Ring Rd; ⊙ 8am-7pm Mon-Sat, 9am-1pm Sun) Well-stocked supermarket with beer and wine.

Everest
NEPALI $$

(📋 600-8850; off Bliss Pde; mains BZ$15-20; ⊙ 8am-7:30pm; 🍴) Belmopan's (and probably Belize's) only Nepalese restaurant is in a welcoming blue shack among several other shack restaurants opposite the market area. Authentic mutton, chicken and vegetarian curries and biryanis, along with Indian specialties such as masala tea.

Corkers
INTERNATIONAL $$

(📋 822-0400; www.corkersbelize.com; Hibiscus Plaza, Melhado Pde; ⊙ 11am-9pm Mon-Wed, to late Thu-Sat; 🛜🍴) This breezy upstairs restaurant and bar has a 'Brit-pub in the tropics' feel with a welcoming atmosphere and a melange of seafood, meat and pasta dishes from tortillas and wraps to steak and veggies. There are good-value lunch dishes and snacks, share plates and happy hour at the bar is a generous 4pm to 10pm Thursday to Saturday.

Blue Moon
INTERNATIONAL $$

(📋 822-4433; 1533 Constitution Dr; mains BZ$16-56; ⊙ 11am-9pm; 🅿🛜🍴) Blue Moon is a welcoming family restaurant serving a wide range of international dishes from burgers to steaks and tacos to pasta. The ceviche and fried chicken are reliable, while the steaks (from BZ$45) push well into top-end price category.

Pasquale's
PIZZA $$

(📋 822-4663; Forest Dr; calzones from BZ$15, pizzas BZ$25-60; ⊙ 11am-9pm Mon-Sat, noon-9pm Sun; ✳🛜) In a log cabin just off Constitution Dr, this Chicago-style pizza joint has Belmopan's best range of pizzas, but if you're still not satisfied you can 'build-your-own'. Also great calzones, burgers, hot subs, pasta and draft beer.

 Drinking & Nightlife

For a capital city, nightlife is somnolent in Belmopan but Corkers and **Bull Frog Inn** (📋 822-2111; www.bullfroginn.com; 25 Half Moon Ave; mains BZ$12-30; ⊙ 7am-10pm; 🛜🍴) have reliably lively bars with occasional live music.

La Cabaña
CLUB

(📋 822-1577; Hummingbird Hwy; ⊙ 11am-3am) This Latin-themed dance club has Belmopan's liveliest nightlife most nights of the week. Tuesday, Friday and Saturday are dance nights, Thursday and Sunday see a bit of karaoke. It's a dingy bar and restaurant by day, out on the highway just south of the roundabout. Cover charge after 10pm is BZ$10.

☆ **Entertainment**

Screen on the Green
CINEMA

(N Ring Rd, Governor General Field; ⊙ 2nd Thu of month) **FREE** The US embassy hosts free outdoor movie nights once a month at Governor General Field. Movies start at dark; if it's raining the screening moves to the George Price Center from 6pm.

ℹ **Information**

Darah Travel (📋 822-3272; www.belizetravel services.com; 21 Moho St) This Belmopan-based travel agency can organise flights, transfers and adventure tours throughout Cayo and Southern Belize.

Immigration Office (📋 822-3860; Mountain View Blvd, Belmopan; ⊙ 8am-5pm Mon-Thu, to 3:30pm Fri) Cayo's big new immigration office offers 30-day visa extension stamps for BZ$50. It gets busy, so arrive early.

Western Regional Hospital (📋 822-0666; off N Ring Rd) Just north of the city center, this is the only emergency facility between Belize City and San Ignacio.

US Embassy (📋 822-4011; https://bz.usembassy .gov; Floral Park Rd; ⊙ 8am-noon & 1-5pm Mon-Fri) From visa and passport information to marriage advice and hurricane preparedness tips, the US embassy can help. The website is comprehensive and easy to navigate.

ⓘ Getting There & Away

Belmopan is 1 mile east of the Hummingbird Hwy, and 50 miles from Belize City.

AIR

Belmopan's tiny airstrip is just a few miles east of the city.

Tropic Air (⌨ 226-2012; www.tropicair.com) has three daily flights to San Pedro (BZ$260, 55 minutes), Belize City Domestic (BZ$142, 25 minutes) and two to Belize City International (BZ$190, 25 minutes).

BUS

Belmopan's **bus terminal** (⌨ 802-2799; Market Sq) is Cayo's main transit hub, and all buses (regardless of company) heading south or west from the Belize District, as well as north and west from Dangriga (and points south), stop in Belmopan. Along the George Price Hwy, buses head east to Belize City (BZ$6, one hour) and west to San Ignacio (BZ$3, one hour) and Benque Viejo del Carmen (BZ$4, 1½ hours) every half-hour from 6am to 7pm. Along the Hummingbird Hwy, buses go south to Dangriga (BZ$7, two hours) once or twice an hour from 6:45am until 7:15pm. From Dangriga, most buses continue on to Punta Gorda (BZ$20, 5½ hours).

Transfers to Hopkins- and Placencia-bound buses can be made in Dangriga.

AROUND BELMOPAN

West of the Belize District, the sealed George Price (Western) Hwy speeds along for about 50 miles to Belmopan – probably the country's most heavily trafficked road. This region gets busy with island-based tourists and cruise-ship passengers heading to inland adventures, such as cave-tubing, ziplining and horseback riding.

⊙ Sights & Activities

Guanacaste National Park   NATIONAL PARK
(George Price Hwy; BZ$5; ⊙ 8am-4:30pm) Belize's smallest national park was declared in 1990 and is named for the giant guanacaste tree on its southwestern edge. The tree survived the axes of canoe-makers but has now died naturally, though it still stands in its jungle habitat. The 51-acre park, off the highway at the Belmopan turnoff, is framed by Roaring Creek and the Belize River, with 2 miles of hiking trails that will introduce you to the abundant local trees and colorful birds.

Birding is best here in winter, when migrants arrive from North America. On the short Guanacaste Trail there's a timber deck leading down to the river where you can swim in a deep waterhole. Don't leave bags or valuables unattended here while swimming.

★ Nohoch Che'en Caves Branch Archaeological Reserve   CAVING
(park admission BZ$10; ⊙ 8am-5pm) This extensive network of limestone caves northwest of Belmopan is super-popular for cave-tubing, kayaking and spelunking. The Caves Branch River flows through nine caves, providing ideal conditions for floating through on a rubber tube or allowing for exploration of side passages, which lead to other caves, such as the spectacular Crystal Cave.

A number of operators run tours – you can only enter the caves with a licensed guide (minimum one guide per eight people).

The basic 1½-hour tour includes a jungle walk and a gentle float through the caves, witnessing (with the help of your headlamp), schools of eyeless cave fish, stalactites and strange Maya paintings high on the cave ceilings. The cost (from BZ$70) includes life vest and helmet, and the tubes are linked together for safety. Tours can be customized to explore further into the cave system – the ultimate full-day tour includes Crystal Cave.

The turnoff for Nohoch Che'en Caves Branch Archaeological Reserve is at Mile 37 on the George Price Hwy, then it's 6 miles down a sealed road to the reserve entrance. The reserve has toilets, snack shops and numerous tour operators.

Vital Nature & Mayan Tours   CAVING
(⌨ 602-8975; www.cavetubing.bz; per person from BZ$90, with ziplining BZ$140) One of the pioneers of cave-tubing in Belize, Vitalino Reyes is still a reliable and recommended operator. There are a variety of cave-tubing trips (including equipment and lunch), up to the full-day Crystal Cave (BZ$180) and 'sunset tubing' (last entry is at 4pm). Vital also has a zipline course and ATVs (quad bikes).

A combo with all three activities costs BZ$200 per person. Add BZ$40 per person for transfers from Belize City or Belmopan.

Butt's Up!   CAVING
(⌨ 605-1575; www.cave-tubing.com; tubing per person from BZ$100) This outfit runs cave-tubing trips as well as ziplining and ATV adventures. It specializes in cruise-ship passengers from Belize City. Lunch included.

Caves Branch Outpost ZIPLINING
(☑ 671-8823; www.cavesbranchoutpostbelize.com; ziplining from BZ$90, cave tubing from BZ$60) Located inside the entry to Nohoch Che'en Caves, Caves Branch Outpost operates a ziplining course and cave-tubing.

Banana Bank Lodge HORSEBACK RIDING
(☑ 820-2020; www.bananabank.com; Banana Bank Rd; 2/4hr jungle tour BZ$120/180) Set on a jungle- and pasture-covered property of more than 6 sq miles, Banana Bank has over 100 well-tended horses enjoying an extensive grazing area and state-of-the-art stables. Besides miles of jungle and riverside trails, facilities include a round pen and a large arena for training and exercising the horses. Combined accommodation and riding packages are available.

The turnoff to Banana Bank is at Roaring Creek, then it's 4 miles on a signposted dirt road. If you're not driving, inquire about the hand-cranked boat across the Belize River.

Zipline Canopy Tour ADVENTURE SPORTS
(☑ 602-8975; www.zipline.bz; per person from BZ$110) This zipline canopy tour, just outside Nohoch Che'en, is a professional operation where you zoom through the treetops from platform to platform on nine linked cable runs up to 200ft long. Ziplining can easily be combined with cave-tubing and ATV rides.

🛌 Sleeping

Banana Bank Lodge RESORT $$
(☑ 832-2020; www.bananabank.com; Banana Bank Rd; d/tr/q chalet with fan BZ$150/200/250, s/d/tr with air-con BZ$240/300/350, s/d/tr cabañas BZ$260/330/390; P❄🛜🏊) This old-fashioned lodge and equestrian center is ensconced in lush gardens on the banks of the Belize River, north of Belmopan, and offers mahogany-and-thatch cabañas with a unique two-bedroom design with a sitting room, ceiling fans and wrought-iron or carved-mahogany bedsteads. Suites and standard rooms have air-con, while the budget 'chalet' rooms sleep up to five people.

The lodge has a bird observation tower overlooking a lagoon, an orchid garden with over 50 species of orchids and some small Maya ruins onsite. To get here, turn off at Roaring Creek village and follow the signs for 4 miles.

Belize Jungle Dome RESORT $$$
(☑ 628-8550; www.belizejungledome.com; Banana Bank Rd; r BZ$190-330; P❄🛜🏊) ⊘ This

retreat is an architectural oddity, with a signature dome allowing sunlight to filter in, reflecting the polished mahogany interior. Standard rooms, suites and terraces are fully equipped with modern conveniences, such as air-con, cable TV and wi-fi, and have easy access to the central swimming pool.

There's also an organic fruit orchard and an enticing treetop cafe (meals extra) from which to survey the domain. Drive to Belize Jungle Dome via the village of Roaring Creek at Mile 47 on the George Price Hwy (follow the signs to Banana Bank Lodge).

🛍 Shopping

Art Box ARTS & CRAFTS
(☑ 822-2233; www.artboxbz.com; Mile 46 Western Hwy; ⊕ 8am-5:30pm Mon-Sat; 🛜) It's hard to miss this cube-like two-story building on the highway just before the Belmopan airstrip. It's a combination gallery, store and cafe, with locally made furniture, jewelry, crafts and stationery, as well as a bookstore heavy on bibles; the branching staircase to the mezzanine is a sight to behold. The attached cafe specializes in strong organic coffee and frappacinos.

HUMMINGBIRD HIGHWAY

The lyrically named Hummingbird Hwy is one of the prettiest drives in Belize, winding its way through jungle and citrus orchards and impossibly small villages as it skirts the northern edges of the Maya Mountain range between Belmopan and Dangriga. Passing caves and jungle adventures, on a clear day the road affords plenty of postcard-perfect vistas. You can drive the 55-mile length of it in two hours but along the way are some excellent ecolodges and budget accommodations, just begging for an overnight stay.

⊙ Sights

St Herman's Blue Hole
National Park NATIONAL PARK
(BZ$8; ⊕ 8am-4:30pm) The 575-acre St Herman's Blue Hole National Park contains St Herman's Cave, one of the few caves in Belize that you can visit without a guide. The visitors center (where flashlights can be rented for BZ$3) is 11 miles along the Hummingbird Hwy from Belmopan. From here

a 500yd trail leads to St Herman's Cave. A path leads 200yd into the cave alongside an underground river – to go any further you'll need a guide.

Return via the Highland Trail, steep in places but with rope guides, for some nice views. Carry a strong flashlight and good insect repellent. If you're keen on a longer hike, there's a three-hour trail from here via Crystal Cave.

The Blue Hole, a 25ft-deep swimming hole, is about a mile further along the highway. Drive there, or take the 45-minute jungle trek from the visitors center. Admission is with the same ticket as St Herman's Cave.

Any bus along the Hummingbird Hwy will drop you at the visitors center or the entrance to the Blue Hole.

Billy Barquedier Waterfall　　WATERFALL

(Hummingbird Hwy; BZ$8; ⊙9am-4pm) This magnificent waterfall cascades into a cool swimming hole located a 15-minute walk off the Hummingbird Hwy (signposted). A further one-hour walk brings you to a lovely viewpoint. If there are no volunteers there to take your entry fee, it may be risky leaving a vehicle unattended.

🏃 Activities

Angel Falls Belize
Xtreme Adventures　　ADVENTURE SPORTS

(☏615-6003; www.angelfallsbelize.com; ziplining BZ$170, waterfall rappelling BZ$300) Ziplining courses are not uncommon in Belize, but this new set-up in thick jungle off the Hummingbird Hwy claims to be among the fastest and most exhilarating around, with eight lines and 16 platforms. Even more adventurous is rappelling down 400ft Angel Falls – book ahead. Easier tours include birdwatching, nature trails and river tubing.

A very stylish ecolodge was due to open here at the time of writing; as part of the resort visitors can make use of the jungle restaurant, nature trails and swimming holes.

Lamanai Chocolate　　FOOD

(☏621-9127; www.lamanaichocolate.com; Hummingbird Hwy; chocolate tour BZ$25; ⊙8am-5pm) This small roadside chocolate factory and mini spice farm is run by expat Roger. Tours demonstrate the traditional Maya cacao chocolate-making process and include samples. Various cacao products and flavors are available for sale.

Tours

Caves Branch Adventures　　ADVENTURE

(☏610-3451; www.cavesbranch.com; Mile 41.5 Hummingbird Hwy; tours per person BZ$150-500) At Ian Anderson's the signature adventures include jungle treks, river cave and waterfall cave expeditions, and the Black Hole Drop. Adventure activities are exclusive, exciting and depart from the excellent lodge just off the Hummingbird Hwy.

Maya Guide Adventures　　TOURS

(☏600-3116; www.mayaguide.bz; caving from BZ$170, overnight jungle tours from BZ$300) Experienced Kekchí Maya guide Marcos Cucul runs jungle survival tours ranging from overnight to multiple nights. Tours feature trekking, leadership and survival skills with the night spent in Hennessy hammocks. With over a decade's experience as an area guide, Cucul enjoys an excellent reputation.

Belize Inland Tours　　ADVENTURE

(☏634-5384; www.belizeinlandtours.com; Mile 42 Hummingbird Hwy, Armenia) Based just out of Belmopan in Armenia, Belize Inland Tours runs cave-tubing trips, guided tours of St Herman's Blue Hole National Park and tours all over the Cayo District.

Belize True Adventures　　ADVENTURE SPORTS

(☏615-3156; www.belizetrueadventures.com; Hummingbird Hwy, Armenia) Caving, ruins, jungle tours and transfers around the Cayo District. Trips go as far as Tikal and Belize Zoo.

🛏 Sleeping

Some fine mountain and jungle lodges are complemented by a few excellent budget eco-guesthouses.

T.R.E.E.S　　CABIN $

(Toucan Ridge Ecology & Education Society; ☏669-6818, 665-2134; Mile 27.5 Hummingbird Hwy; bunkhouse BZ$40, s/d cabin BZ$125/140, without bathroom BZ$80/100; ☏) ✿ T.R.E.E.S is part field station and part ecofriendly lodge, welcoming research students, interns, birders and passing backpackers alike. The operation is nonprofit, with proceeds going into community conservation projects and ecotourism. There are lectures in biodiversity, field courses and guided activities, along with yoga, hiking and village tours.

Accommodation is in simple but comfortable cabins away from the main lodge, and meals are available (breakfast/lunch/dinner BZ$18/20/22).

CAYO DISTRICT HUMMINGBIRD HIGHWAY

Lost World Jungle Lodge LODGE $

(📞 668-0183, 423-1951; www.lostworldlodgebelize.com; Mile 20.5 Hummingbird Hwy; dm/r BZ$30/100, cabins/bungalows BZ$60/200; 🛜) Tucked away on a quiet property just off the Hummingbird Hwy, Lost World is a family-run backpacker haven with an offbeat choice of accommodations. The main lodge has a 12-bed dorm, lounge and kitchen but elsewhere you find rooms in a faux English castle, a small cabin and self-contained bungalow with air-con. Plenty of walks and activities in the area.

Hummingbird Haven Lodge & Hostel HOSTEL $

(📞 626-4599; Mile 29.5 Hummingbird Hwy; campsite BZ$20, dm/d BZ$30/80, 2-bedroom lodge BZ$150; P 🛜) 🍴 Hummingbird Haven enjoys a sublime location in a quiet patch of forest just off the highway and surrounded by a split in the creek. The 100-acre property features a double-story timber lodge with two large dorms, and a few private rooms in another building, as well as plenty of space to camp.

There are a couple of chill-out areas, a self-catering kitchen, eco credentials such as solar power and organic gardens, and plenty of opportunities for jungle hikes and swimming in the river.

Yax'che Jungle Camp CABAÑAS $

(📞 600-3116; www.mayaguide.bz; Hummingbird Hwy; campsites BZ$20, bunkhouse BZ$30, d cabañas BZ$140; P 🛜) 🍴 Adventure guide Marcos Cucul runs this little camp just off the highway. Spacious cabañas on stilts have sunken bathrooms and verandas. There's a communal dining area and a great range of jungle activities on offer.

Tree of Life Guesthouse HOMESTAY $$

(📞 602-6828; treeoflifeguesthouse@gmail.com; Agua Viva; r/cabañas BZ$110/150) 🍴 This eco-oriented farmstay/guesthouse about 2 miles west of the highway near Armenia village is the offbeat ecoproject of expats Jason and Natalie (aquaponics, solar power). There are two family rooms in the rustic farmhouse and two cabañas. It's a nice place to unwind with various farm animals and walking trails. Call for pickup from highway.

Kantara Ku CABAÑAS $$

(📞 in USA 818-903-1999; www.kantaraku.com; Mile 34 Hummingbird Hwy, St Margaret's; cabañas per person BZ$70, villas BZ$150-300, 3-bedroom cottages BZ$400; P 🛜 🖼) Kantara is an

intimate midrange resort, with just a few cabañas, villas and cottage rooms in grounds full of fruit trees, backed by verdant rainforest. There's an inviting little pool and bar area, and easy access to excellent jungle hikes.

★ Ian Anderson's Caves Branch Jungle Lodge LODGE $$$

(📞 in Belize 610-3452, in USA & Canada 866-357-2698; www.cavesbranch.com; Mile 41.5 Hummingbird Hwy; d cabañas & bungalows BZ$340-$492, d ste & tree houses BZ$588-$1182; P 🛜 🖼) 🍴 Hidden away in dense jungle off the Hummingbird Hwy, Ian Anderson's is a 90-sq-mile private estate that acts as a base for a variety of exclusive jungle activities on the property. Accommodations are superb jungle-chic, and guests can indulge themselves in the beautiful riverside pool and hot tub, and enjoy meals and cocktails at the family-style restaurant overlooking the river.

Most exclusive of the accommodations are the canopy tree houses overlooking the Caves Branch River, featuring beautifully carved four-poster beds, screened-in decks, outdoor tropical showers and views to die for. More humble but no less lovely are the wooden cabañas closer to the river, and there's a varying range of lodge rooms in between. The lodge also has an onsite artisanal cheese factory and organic soap-making facilities.

Most guests to the lodge book multi-day packages, including tours, accommodations, meals and more. Check the website for current deals.

Sleeping Giant Rainforest Lodge LODGE $$$

(📞 822-0037, toll free 888-822-2448; www.vivabelize.com/sleeping-giant; Mile 36.5 Hummingbird Hwy; r BZ$480-880, penthouse BZ$1120; P ❄ 🛜 🖼) 🍴 The swanky Sleeping Giant has 20 rooms either garden-facing in the main lodge or in vast individual cottages, *casitas* (small cottages) or suites scattered around a lush garden. They feature modcons such as air-con, espresso machine and local hardware furniture, while the best have gorgeous bathrooms with skylight tubs or Jacuzzis.

The property, split by the Sibune River, features mountain views, abundant birdlife and guided hikes, and there's a lovely two-story restaurant-bar and pool area as its centerpiece.

BELIZE WILDLIFE & REFERRAL CLINIC

With a mission statement including the goals of establishing and managing a state-of-the-art veterinary clinic for wildlife and domestic animals in Belize, the **Belize Wildlife & Referral Clinic** (☑615-5159; www.belizewildlifeclinic.org; ☉8:30am-5pm) provides educational opportunities and training for students, professionals and interested individuals. This nonprofit organization offers ongoing internships in wildlife medicine, rescue and rehabilitation.

Internships focus on wildlife medicine, rescue and emergency medicine and conservation, and are designed to provide students with real-world experience while supporting wildlife rescue and conservation in the field. Some interns are pre-veterinary or animal-science students, while others are veterinary students seeking clinical rotation credit in wildlife medicine.

Short-term internships ranging from two to six weeks for non-veterinary students are available from BZ$1900 per week (including lodging, breakfasts and airport pickup and drop-off), with reductions after the first two weeks. Various courses are available, and the clinic is interested in speaking with sincere potential interns and long-term volunteers.

Contact internship coordinator Justin Ford (jford@belizewildlifeclinic.org) or check out the website.

✗ Eating

Hibiscus

Fast Food　　　　　　　　　BELIZEAN $
(☑632-8271; Hummingbird Hwy, Armenia; mains BZ$2-7; ☉6am-2pm) This simple roadside shack in Armenia village serves just a few local dishes such as heaped plates of rice and beans with chicken stew, burritos and *salbutes*. Among the fresh juices, try the milky-white *horchata* juice, made from rice milk and cinnamon.

Country Barn　　　　　　　ICE CREAM $
(☑630-0031, Mile 31 Hummingbird Hwy; drinks & ice cream BZ$3-5; ☉7am-5pm Mon-Sat) Stop in at this roadside dairy and cafe situated near St Margaret's village for homemade ice cream, flavored milk and fresh yogurt. It's run by a Christian ministry, which employs local youth and trains them in farming skills.

Café Casita

De Amour　　　　　　　　　CAFE $
(Mile 16.5 Hummingbird Hwy; meals BZ$5-15; ☉8am-5pm Tue-Sun) Café Casita De Amour – the House of Love – is an architectural oddity and a worthwhile pit stop on the Hummingbird drive. Inside is a cafe with a simple menu of crepes, sandwiches, burgers, coffee and smoothies. It's a mile or so past the Barquedier waterfall, before the village of Pomona.

BELMOPAN TO SAN IGNACIO

The George Price Hwy continues for 22 miles from the Belmopan turnoff to San Ignacio through verdant, well-shaded countryside, with a number of villages, lodges and resorts strung along the road. The single main attraction out here is remote Actun Tunichil Muknal cave – best accessed on guided tours from San Ignacio or Belmopan. The dirt road to Actun Tunichil Muknal heads south at Teakettle Village, 8 miles west of Belmopan. At Mount Hope, a sealed road heads northwest to the industrious Mennonite community of Spanish Lookout, while at Georgeville, the unsealed Chiquibul Rd turns south off the highway, heading to Barton Creek and the Mountain Pine Ridge.

🏃 Activities

Belize Bird Rescue　　　　VOLUNTEERING
(☑610-0400; www.belizebirdrescue.com; Rock Farm Rd) This avian rescue and rehabilitation NGO has been taking in sick and injured birds for the past 15 years. There's a bird sanctuary here and the Rock Farm Guesthouse, so visitors are welcome to drop by or stay overnight. Internships and short-term volunteering programs are also available to interested bird-lovers. See the website for details.

DON'T MISS

ATM – CAYO'S ADVENTURE CAVE

Actun Tunichil Muknal (guided tour BZ$190) – the Cave of the Stone Sepulchre – is one of the most unforgettable and adventurous underground tours you can make in Belize. The guided trip into ATM takes you deep into the underworld that the ancient Maya knew as Xibalba. The entrance to the 3-mile-long cave lies in the northern foothills of the Maya Mountains. Most people arrive on a guided tour from San Ignacio, Belmopan or the coastal resorts, but it's also possible to arrange a guide and self-drive.

The experience is moderately strenuous, starting with an easy 45-minute hike through the lush jungle, crossing Roaring Creek three times (your feet will be wet all day). At the wide, hourglass-shaped entrance to the cave, you'll don your helmet, complete with headlamp. To reach the cave entrance, you'll start with a bracing swim across a deep pool (about 15ft across), so you must be a reasonably good swimmer (or request a life jacket). From here, follow your guide, walking, climbing, twisting and turning your way through the blackness of the cave for about an hour.

Giant shimmering flowstone rock formations compete for your attention with thick, calcium-carbonate stalactites dripping from the ceiling. Phallic stalagmites grow up from the cave floor. Eventually you'll follow your guide up into a massive opening, where you'll see hundreds of pottery vessels and shards, along with human remains. One of the most shocking displays is the calcite-encrusted remains of the woman whom Actun Tunichil Muknal is named for. In the cave's Main Chamber, you will be required to remove your shoes; wear socks to protect the artifacts from the oils on your skin.

The trip takes about eight hours from San Ignacio, including a one-hour drive each way. A number of San Ignacio–based tour companies do the trip for around BZ$190 per person, including transportation, admission, lunch and equipment. You must be accompanied by a licensed guide (of which there are around 30). Cameras are no longer allowed inside the cave due to an incident involving a clumsy traveler, a dropped camera and the breaking of priceless artifacts.

Hot Mama's   TOURS
(☎ 824-0444; www.hotmamasbelize.com; Mile 60 George Price Hwy, Unitedville; tour BZ$10; ☺ shop 8am-4pm Mon-Fri, tour Tue-Fri by appointment) Take a tour of the chili gardens and the factory producing hot sauces at Hot Mama's, not far out of San Ignacio. Or just visit the shop and pick up some sauce.

🎓 Courses

**Universal Healing
Institute & Retreat**   RETREAT
(☎ 677-7878; www.universalhealinginternational. org) 🌿 The unique Universal Healing Institute & Retreat is spread out over a 150-acre organic jungle farm near the village of Unitedville on the George Price Hwy. Operators Yosiah and Linda offer medium- and long-term retreats focusing on health and nutrition, yoga and spirituality, as well as courses in organic gardening and sustainability.

A 30-day workshop starts at BZ$1600 per person, a 30-day assisted healing retreat is BZ$5000, or just book one of the cabins and get a feel for the place. Check the website for more details.

🛏 Sleeping

**Lower Dover Field
Station & Eco Lodge**   CABIN **$**
(☎ 834-4200; www.lowerdoverbelize.com; Mile 59 Western Hwy; campsite per person BZ$10, bunk house per person BZ$35, cabañas BZ$118-128, air-con cabins BZ$170; 🅿 🛜) 🌿 Located on 99 acres of prime jungle and virtually on top of extensive and largely unexcavated Maya ruins, Lower Dover is an intriguing eco backpacker place where you can sleep cheap and explore some serious archaeological history. If you have your own tent you can camp, or take a bed in the bunkhouse.

The private cabañas range from basic with open-sky shower to extremely comfortable cabins on stilts. There are self-guided walks to Maya ruins (the dogs will help you find the way) or hire a guide for a BZ$10 donation. Other activities include canoeing, swimming in one of the seven river-fed swimming holes, fishing and birdwatching. There's also a house winery producing hibiscus wine.

Leslies' Private Paradise
RESORT $$

(☑822-2370; Mile 51.5 Western Hwy; cabins BZ$215-240; P 🛜 ≋) Situated on 60 acres of jungle-covered property a short drive from Belmopan, this welcoming retreat is run by Robert and Bernadette Leslie. The three timber cottages are well-separated for privacy and are self-contained with king-sized beds, kitchenette, modern bathroom and soothing verandas. There's a pool, bar area (BYO) and dining-barbecue area, or head up to the serene hilltop meditation hut.

Nina's Place
CABIN $$

(☑637-6701; www.explore-belize.com; Mile 57 Western Hwy, Blackman Eddy; cabañas BZ$120-170; 🛜) There are three cabañas and a bungalow on a hillside at this 1.5-acre resort in the Western Hwy village of Blackman Eddy. Cabins are well-furnished with queen-size beds, a futon and cold-water shower. The best is the 'Eco-cabaña', an octagonal cabin with wraparound screened windows offering a good view of the surrounding countryside.

Orange Gallery
GUESTHOUSE $$

(☑824-2341; https://orangegifts.com/guesthouse; Mile 60 George Price Hwy; s/d/tr/q BZ$196/236/256/276; P ✳ 🛜) The guesthouse behind the Orange Gallery gift shop offers simple but clean and comfortable en-suite rooms and easy access to the excellent Orange Cafe.

Dream Valley
RESORT $$$

(☑665-1000; www.dreamvalleybelize.com; Young Gal Rd, Teakettle Village; d/ste from BZ$400/700; P ✳ 🛜 ≋) The spectacular timber chalet–style rooms and suites overlook a broad section of the Belize River in the vast grounds of Dream Valley. Spacious cabins are rustic luxury, with hand-carved timber four-poster beds and furniture, private veranda, and mod-cons like air-con, flat-screen TV, fridge and wi-fi. The stunning split-level suites feature a Jacuzzi.

The property has a popular restaurant (open to nonguests), pool, day spa, nature trails and kayaks.

Amber Sunset
Jungle Resort
RESORT $$$

(☑824-3142, 824-3141; www.ambersunsetbelize.com; Mile 59 George Price Hwy; d/q treehouse cabañas BZ$350/600; P 🛜 ≋) 🥾 Set atop a mountain with brilliant views of the surrounding Cayo District, this ecoresort is spread over 28 hilly acres, with five unique cabañas (three doubles and two family cabañas), each named after one of the cultures that makes up the tapestry of Belizean life. Each cabaña is built and furnished with locally sourced and crafted materials.

The Garifuna features a king-sized bed suspended from ropes, indoor rock-tiled shower and an outdoor stone pool for bathing beneath the stars. Other rooms also have their own outdoor tubs and screened lounge areas that immerse you in the surrounding jungle. There's a beautiful onsite restaurant and a hilltop pool with an attached bar.

Pook's Hill Lodge
LODGE $$$

(☑832-2017; www.pookshilllodge.com; s/d cabañas from BZ$400/500; P 🛜) Off the dirt road that leads to Actun Tunichil Muknal, approximately 8 miles south of Teakettle Village, this is a gorgeous lodge on the site of a small Classic Period Maya residential complex. Round, thatch-and-stucco cabañas sport wraparound windows and immaculate natural-stone bathrooms. They are well spaced, allowing plenty of privacy. Breakfast (BZ$16), lunch (BZ$24) and dinner (BZ$40) are offered.

Set within a 300-acre private reserve, the grounds are lush with life, excellent for swimming, river-tubing, birdwatching and horseback riding.

🍴 Eating

Ham's Barbecue in a Bun
BARBECUE $

(Mile 60 George Price Hwy, Unitedville; mains $5-12; ⏲10am-4pm) This hole-in-the-wall highway diner, beside Hot Mama's hot sauce factory, does delicious pit-smoked pork, beef and chicken in rolls, as well as baked potatoes. A good place for a drive-by snack.

Casa Sofia
ITALIAN $$

(☑824-2161; www.casasofiainn.com; Mile 59 George Price Hwy, Unitedville; mains BZ$18-35; ⏲dinner Wed-Sat by appointment) Stop in at tiny Unitedville to savor the Italian delights of elegant Casa Sofia. Lovingly crafted antipasti, pizza and pasta feature on the menu, with homemade sauces and garden-fresh salads. It's all served in a uniquely quirky churchlike dining room or garden patio. There are also three rooms at the Inn. Reserve ahead.

🛍 Shopping

Orange Gallery
GIFTS & SOUVENIRS

(☑824-3296; www.orangegifts.com; Mile 60 George Price Hwy; ⏲7:30am-5:30pm) On the highway, east of Georgeville, Orange Gallery is a quality gift shop and gallery showcasing a wide selection of Belizean souvenirs and handicrafts, including fine hardwood furniture, kitchen wares and sculptures made in the family's own workshop. The owner and founder – Caesar Sherrard – designed the ergonomic folding 'clam chair' that now furnishes just about every resort in Belize.

Spanish Lookout

POP 2250

A well spread but thriving Mennonite community, Spanish Lookout is a fascinating place located about 5 miles north of the Western Hwy, and a good day trip from San Ignacio.

With its broad, ordered streets lined with transplanted palm trees, neat farmland, huge factories and modern stores (hardware is popular here!), Spanish Lookout appears a little incongruous in this part of Cayo, but it's a great place to see Mennonites' industriousness in action. They are the country's primary producers of dairy, meat, poultry and produce: here in Spanish Lookout you will find Quality Chicken, the biggest poultry producer, as well as Western Dairy, the only commercial dairy. They're also renowned builders – many of the cabins and cabañas you might stay in were probably built right here. Although Mennonites are known for eschewing modern conveniences, you will see more cars and tractors here than horse and carts.

✖ Eating

★Western Dairies   ICE CREAM $

(☑ 823-0112; www.westerndairies.com; Center Rd; scoop from BZ$2; ⊙ 7am-5pm Mon-Thu, to 7:30pm Fri & Sat) Famous for its ice cream but also producing cheese, flavored milk and other dairy products, this is the headquarters for Western Dairies in Belize and a must-stop situated on the main street in Spanish Lookout. It also does pizzas and burritos.

Sister's Diner   DINER $

(☑ 624-9436; Center Rd; dishes BZ$3.50-17; ⊙ 8am-8pm Mon-Sat) Styled like an American diner, open-air Sister's does a fine line in burgers, pizzas, wings, Tex-Mex and Philly cheesesteak.

🛍 Shopping

Reimers Health Food   FOOD

(☑ 823-0096; Bee Lane; ⊙ 8am-5pm Mon-Sat) Looking to stock up on vitamins or locally grown chia products? Reimers is a dedicated health-food store stocking a similar selection of vitamins, supplements and other health products as you'd find at a good American supermarket.

ℹ Getting There & Away

From the George Price Hwy at Mount Hope, a wide, sealed 8.5-mile road (built by the Mennonites) leads to Spanish Lookout. The alternative (old) route crosses the Belize River by hand-cranked vehicle ferry and joins the highway at Central Farm (though it was closed at the time of writing). Several buses a day go to Spanish Lookout from San Ignacio (BZ$6, one hour), via Bullet Tree Falls.

A taxi costs around BZ$50 one way.

SAN IGNACIO

POP 21,150

San Ignacio is the heart and soul of the Cayo District, a vibrant traveler center from where all roads and activities fan out. Together with twin-town Santa Elena, on the east bank of the Macal River, this is the main population center of Cayo, with lots of good budget accommodations, decent restaurants and frequent transport.

But as much as it is geared to travelers, San Ignacio is no inland San Pedro, existing only for tourism. It has a very positive and infectious vibe, with a market and a steady influx of immigrants, mainly from nearby Guatemala. Residents are mestizos, Maya and Garifuna, as well as free-spirited expats from Europe and North America.

Most travelers come to San Ignacio as a base for the adventures of Cayo or as a stepping stone to or from Guatemala; many stay longer than they expected.

Orientation

Pedestrianized Burns Ave has most of San Ignacio's tour operators and a good bunch of restaurants, so it's a good place to start exploring. The central plaza and market are a block to the east. San Ignacio is on the west bank of the Macal River, a couple of miles upstream from its confluence with the Mopan River – a meeting of waters that gives birth to the Belize River.

⊙ Sights

★ Green Iguana
Conservation Project   GARDENS
(☏824-2034; www.sanignaciobelize.com; 18 Buena Vista St; tour BZ$18; ⊘8am-4pm, tours every hour; ♿) ✐ On the lush Macal Valley grounds of the San Ignacio Resort Hotel, this excellent program collects and hatches iguana eggs, raising the reptiles until they are past their most vulnerable age. The iguanas are then released into the wild. On the guided tour you'll get plenty of opportunities to stroke and handle the adorable iguanas and learn much about their habits and life cycle. The tour also follows the medicinal jungle trail that winds through the forest.

Cahal Pech   RUINS
(☏824-4236; BZ$10, 2hr tours BZ$20; ⊘6am-6pm) High atop a hill about a mile south of San Ignacio, Cahal Pech is the oldest-known Maya site in the Belize River valley, having been first settled between 1500 and 1000 BC. Less impressive than Xunantunich and Caracol, it's still a fascinating example of a Pre-classic Maya architecture and an easy uphill walk from town. It was a significant Maya settlement for 2000 years or more. Drop into the small visitors center, which explains some of the history of Cahal Pech.

Cahal Pech (kah-hahl pech) is Mopan and Yucatec Mayan for 'Place of Ticks,' a nickname earned in the 1950s when the site was surrounded by pastures grazed by tick-infested cattle. Today it's a pleasantly shady site with plenty of trees and few tourists. Its core area of seven interconnected plazas has been excavated and restored since the late 1980s. Plaza B is the largest and most impressive complex; Structure A-1, near Plaza A, is the site's tallest temple. Two ballcourts lie at either end of the restored area.

The earliest monumental religious architecture in Belize was built here between 600 and 400 BC, though most of what we see today dates from AD 600 to 800, when Cahal Pech and its peripheral farming settlements had an estimated population of between 10,000 and 20,000. The place was abandoned around AD 850.

Branch Mouth   PARK
(Branch Mouth Rd) Branch Mouth is the meeting place of the Mopan River, coming from Guatemala, and the Macal River, flowing down from Mountain Pine Ridge. The confluence of these rivers forms the beginning of the Belize River, which flows northeast to the sea. It's a cool spot for a swim on a hot day. A cable swing bridge connects to the opposite bank. To get there, cycle or walk 1.5 miles north of town past Midas Resort.

House of Culture   MUSEUM
(☏824-0783; Simpson St; ⊘8am-noon & 1-5pm Mon-Fri) FREE In the former hospital behind the town hall, the House of Culture has regular art, history and cultural exhibitions, as well as being a local meeting place.

⚶ Activities

Most activities – and there are many – happen outside of San Ignacio but can be organised here. Swimming is possible in the Macal and Mopan Rivers, or head to the pools at Midas Resort (p175) or Cahal Pech Village Resort (p175).

Marie Sharp's Tourist
Center & Culinary Class   COOKING
(☏674-1984; www.rainforesthavens.com; 2 Victoria St; tastings BZ$10, cooking classes BZ$100; ⊘cooking classes 9am-noon & 4-7pm Mon-Sat) Although Marie Sharp's famous hot sauce factory is based out of Dangriga, this showroom at Rainforest Haven Inn is the next best thing. A wide range of hot sauces, jams and fruit wines are available for tastings (BZ$10 per person) and sale, but the highlight here is the half-day cooking class (BZ$100 per person) for lunch or dinner.

Classes include a market tour, and a hands-on introduction to Belizean food and culture, preparing (and eating) dishes such as fry-jacks, rice and beans, and stew chicken. Minimum two people, book a day in advance.

Travellers Maya Juice   RUM TASTING
(☏674-1984; www.rainforesthavens.com; 2 Victoria St; tours per person BZ$30; ⊘10:30am-7pm) Rum is the national drink of Belize and the Caribbean and this excellent little tasting room not only presents a range of six top-shelf rum drinks but also explains the history and culture of Belizean rum on a one-hour tour. Alternatively you can just pay per tasting.

★ Ajaw Chocolate   TOURS
(☏635-9363; ajawchocolatebze@gmail.com; 16 Benque Viejo Rd; demonstration only per person BZ$24, with farm tour BZ$50; ⊘9am-6pm Mon-Sat, tours hourly; ♿) Adrian and Elida, Kekchí Mayans from Toledo, bring their chocolate-making expertise to San Ignacio with excellent demonstrations that can be

San Ignacio

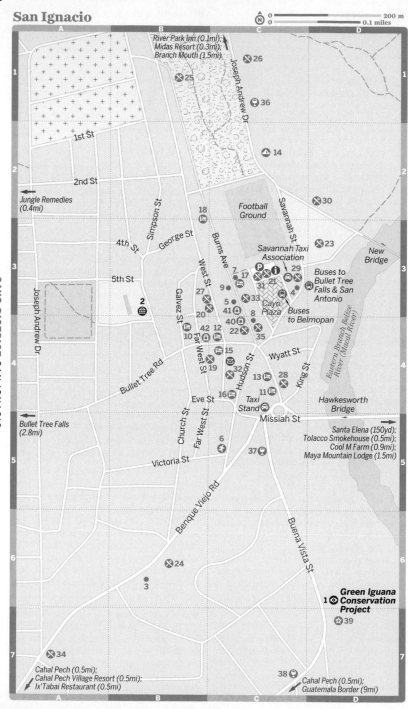

0   200 m
0   0.1 miles

River Park Inn (0.1mi);
Midas Resort (0.3mi);
Branch Mouth (1.5mi)

Joseph Andrew Dr

26

25

36

1st St

14

2nd St

Jungle Remedies
(0.4mi)

Savannah St

30

Football
Ground

New
Bridge

18

Simpson St

4th St   George St

West St

Burns Ave

Savannah Taxi
Association

23

5th St

Galvez St

7   17

27   9

5

29

31   21

33

Cayo
Plaza

Buses to
Bullet Tree
Falls & San
Antonio

4

Joseph Andrew Dr

2

Far West St

20

41

8

40
22

42   12

10

35

Buses to
Belmopan

Eastern Branch Belize
River (Macal River)

Bullet Tree Rd

15

19

32

Hudson St

Wyatt St

13   28

16

11

King St

Hawkesworth
Bridge

Church St

Far West St

Eve St

Taxi
Stand

Missiah St

Santa Elena (150yd);
Tolacco Smokehouse (0.5mi);
Cool M Farm (0.9mi);
Maya Mountain Lodge (1.5mi)

Bullet Tree Falls
(2.8mi)

Victoria St

6

37

Benque Viejo Rd

Buena Vista St

24

3

Green Iguana
Conservation
Project

1

39

34

38

Cahal Pech (0.5mi);
Cahal Pech Village Resort (0.5mi);
Ix'Tabai Restaurant (0.5mi)

Cahal Pech (0.5mi);
Guatemala Border (9mi)

San Ignacio

combined with a tour of their small cacao farm. The one-hour tour includes grinding and creating your own chocolate drink and chocolate bar from roasted beans.

☞ Tours

San Ignacio, or the lodges around it, are the natural base for visiting the cultural and natural riches of the Cayo region. There are numerous tour operators on Burns Ave and most hotels organize the same tours working with the same operators.

Trips to Actun Tunichil Muknal and Barton Creek Cave can only be done with a guide, while Caracol is usually visited by vehicle convoy.

Typical day-trip prices per person are BZ$190 for Actun Tunichil Muknal (p168), BZ$160 for a half-day trip to Barton Creek Cave (p179), BZ$190 to BZ$220 to Caracol (p186), BZ$180 for a cave-tubing trip to No-hoch Che'en (p163), BZ$160 for Mountain

Pine Ridge (p184) and BZ$300 (plus border fees) for Tikal in Guatemala.

David's Adventure Tour   ADVENTURE
(☎804-3674; www.davidsadventuretours.com; Savannah St; canoe tours BZ$60-90, Barton Creek BZ$150) Based just across the street from the Saturday market, David's is an experienced operator offering ecofriendly tours to sites throughout the area, specializing in river canoe trips, cave adventures and overnight jungle treks.

Pacz Tours   TOURS
(☎824-0536; www.pacztours.net; 30 Burns Ave; tours BZ$90-300) Offers reliably excellent service and knowledgeable guides to Actun Tunichil Muknal and Tikal, kayaking, river canoeing and horseback riding, as well as shuttle transfers all over Cayo.

Jungle Splash Tours   ADVENTURE
(☎824-0395; www.junglesplashtours.com; Burns Ave) Caving, Maya ruins, horseback riding

and waterfall trips. Guides are licensed to visit Che Chem Ha cave.

Maximum Adventure Tours ADVENTURE
(☑ 623-4880; www.sanignaciobelizetours.com; 27 Burns Ave) Runs tours to caves and Maya ruins, and offers hiking expeditions. Also operates shuttle services throughout Belize.

Carlos the Caveman CAVE TOUR
(☑ 669-7619; www.carloscaveman.com) Cayo native Carlos Panti has a high level of cave and cultural knowledge, and specializes in small-group spiritually themed journeys into the Actun Tunichil Muknal cave.

Belize Nature Travel CAVE TOUR
(☑ 824-3314; www.experiencebelize.com) Luis Godoy is an experienced guide specializing in cave tours to places such as Actun Tunichil Muknal and Barton Creek, birding and trips to Caracol. Check the website for other tour packages.

MayaWalk Tours ADVENTURE
(☑ 824-3070; www.mayawalk.com; 19 Burns Ave) One of San Ignacio's original tour companies and the most visible on Burns Ave, Maya Walk does recommended trips to Caracol (BZ$190), Actun Tunichil Muknal (BZ$190), Tikal (Guatemala) and many other adventure tours geared toward travelers of all levels and interests. Also operates a shuttle service all over Belize.

River Rat Expeditions ADVENTURE
(☑ 661-4562; www.riverratbelize.com) Specialist in kayaking, river-tubing and cave trips, including Che Chem Ha near Benque Viejo del Carmen.

🛏 Sleeping

San Ignacio has the best range of good-value budget accommodations (including camping) in Belize, with a few excellent midrange places as well. More luxurious options – some of the best in Belize – are the jungle and mountain lodges out of town.

Casa Blanca Guest House GUESTHOUSE $
(☑ 824-2080; www.casablancaguesthouse.com; 10 Burns Ave; s/d/tr BZ$50/70/90, with air-con BZ$75/100/120; ❄ 🛜) Intimate, immaculate and secure, Casa Blanca is everything you need from a budget guesthouse. Decent-sized rooms have clean white walls and crisp fresh linens. Guests have a comfy sitting area, a clean kitchen and a breezy balcony from which to watch the world go by.

Bella's Backpackers HOSTEL $
(☑ 824-2248; www.bellasinbelize.com; 4 Galvez St; dm BZ$25-30, d with/without bathroom BZ$90/60; 🛜) Bella's is a classic backpackers, with rustic charm, bohemian travelers of all ages floating about and a sociable rooftop chill-out area with hammocks and couches. Well-laid-out dorms with sturdy timber bunk beds and bathrooms are complemented by a few private rooms with screened-in windows and a rock-motif bathroom. Bella also has a jungle lodge at Cristo Rey.

Old House Hostel HOSTEL $
(☑ 623-1342; www.facebook.com/hostelbelize; 3 Buena Vista St; dm/d BZ$25/70) There's a lot to like about this hostel above the sometimes-happening Soul Project bar. The two eight-bed dorms are clean and spacious with lockers and wi-fi, and there's a neat common room, self-catering kitchen and street-view balcony. There's only one private double room so book ahead.

Western Guesthouse GUESTHOUSE $
(☑ 824-2572; www.westernguesthousebelize.com; 54 Burns Ave; s/d with fan BZ$60/70, with air-con BZ$70/90; 🅿 ❄ 🛜) The Urbina family's guesthouse is above a hardware store on San Ignacio's quiet west side. Big pluses are the family atmosphere and access to a fully furnished kitchen. The eight clean and comfortable guestrooms each have two beds, TV and hot shower.

Mana Kai Camping & Cabins CAMPGROUND $
(☑ 624-6538; www.manakaibelize.weebly.com; Branch Mouth Rd; campsite per person BZ$15, s/d cabins BZ$40/50, with bathroom BZ$50/60, with air-con BZ$100/110; 🅿 ❄ 🛜) Perhaps the best urban camping ground in Belize, Mana Kai is a big swath of flat grassy land with an open-air communal kitchen, *palapa* with hammocks and free wi-fi. Even if you're not camping there are several cottages, some with air-con. There's a great feeling of space here, a short walk from the town center.

River Park Inn CAMPGROUND $
(☑ 824-2116; www.riverparkinnbelize.com; Branch Mouth Rd; campsite per person BZ$14, RV site BZ$35, d cabins BZ$90, r BZ$100-130; 🅿 ❄ 🛜) This large property backs onto the Macal River just north of the town center, with plenty of space for campers and RVs. There are also two comfortable timber cabañas, and neat double rooms with bathroom, cable TV and air-con in the main building.

Venus Hotel
HOTEL **$**

(✆824-3202; 29 Burns Ave; d/tr BZ$93/115; 🅿✳️📶) The three-story Venus is something of a landmark on Burns Ave, drawing in wandering travelers. It's not flash but it's friendly, decent value and the rooms are clean and comfy – the best are the spacious rooms with shared balcony overlooking the marketplace. All rooms have air-con. A bonus is the free use of the large adjacent car park.

Hotel Mallorca
HOTEL **$**

(✆824-2960; mallorcahotel@gmail.com; 12 Burns Ave; s/d BZ$50/60, d with air-con BZ$95) Colorful quilts on firm beds in compact rooms with cable TV and hot showers are the main selling points of Hotel Mallorca. Management lives onsite and guests have access to a small kitchen, a pleasant lounge area and a tiny balcony overlooking Burns Ave.

Hi-Et Guest House
GUESTHOUSE **$**

(✆824-2828; thehiet@yahoo.com; 12 West St; s/d BZ$25/30, with bathroom BZ$50/55; 📶) Friendly, family-owned and budget-friendly, Hi-Et occupies two connected timber houses, each with its own veranda overlooking the busy street below. The cheaper rooms have shared bathrooms, but all are clean, comfy and good value for money.

Rosa's Hotel
HOTEL **$**

(✆804-2265; 65 Hudson St; s/d/tr incl breakfast BZ$75/92/120; ✳️📶) Rosa's is a little nondescript but it's friendly, central and decent value, especially if you value air-con. Close to a nightclub that gets loud on weekends.

Rainforest Haven Inn
HOTEL **$$**

(✆674-1984; www.rainforesthavens.com; 2 Victoria St; r BZ$130, 2-bedroom apt BZ$150; ✳️@📶) Rainforest Haven is a good find if you're looking for midrange comfort at an almost budget price. The five rooms have air-con, flat-screen TV with cable, fridge, wi-fi and hot-water showers. The two-bedroom apartment boasts a full kitchen – a steal for families or groups. There's a cool chill-out spot on the 2nd floor.

Midas Resort
HOTEL **$$**

(✆824-3172; www.midasbelize.com; Branch Mouth Rd; cottage/cabañas/casitas BZ$152/175/370, d/f BZ$235/370; 🅿✳️📶🏊) In a budget town, Midas stands out as one of San Ignacio's better midrange choices. The large pool, funky bar and friendly staff complement an interesting array of accommodations from hotel-style rooms in the main building to cottages, cabañas and a two-bedroom *casita* at the back of the property. It's in a quiet location a five-minute walk north of the market.

Martha's Guesthouse
HOTEL **$$**

(✆804-3647; www.marthasbelize.com; 10 West St; d BZ$180, ste BZ$200-225; ✳️📶) This family-run guesthouse has 10 bright, sparkling-clean rooms, each with a private balcony and a cut above most in the town center. Woven Maya tapestries accent the mahogany walls and furniture, while tile floors keep the rooms cool. Hotel amenities include a laundry, shuttle bus and a good restaurant.

Cahal Pech Village Resort
RESORT **$$**

(✆824-3740; www.cahalpech.com; Cahal Pech Hill; d/cabañas/ste BZ$215/270/330; 🅿✳️@📶🏊) Atop Cahal Pech hill, half a mile up from the town center, you can enjoy San Ignacio's finest views from this upscale family resort. The resort has 21 bright, tile-floored, air-con rooms, nine family suites and 27 dreamy thatch-roof cabañas dotted around the property. The amazing two-level cascading pool (nonguests BZ$10) is a great place to cool off.

The onsite restaurant serves good international, Belizean and Maya food with a view. The resort also has its own onsite tour service, booking trips to Caracol, Tikal, Xunantunich and anywhere else in Belize.

★San Ignacio Resort Hotel
HOTEL **$$$**

(✆824-2034; www.sanignaciobelize.com; 18 Buena Vista St; s/d from BZ$400/480, ste BZ$890-1320; 🅿✳️📶🏊) The most upscale hotel in San Ignacio by a considerable margin (Queen Elizabeth stayed here, as the photos in the lobby attest), this is boutique luxury but with welcoming, professional staff and a serene location just uphill from the town center. Beyond the pool area the property is backed by jungle and home to the excellent Green Iguana Conservation Project.

Rooms are understated but exquisite; family-sized suites comfortably house six, while standard rooms are more cozy but all have private balconies with views of the pool or the hotel's lush garden. If you're in the mood for an in-town splurge, this is the place (ask for the Queen's room).

🍴 Eating

San Ignacio's compact center is packed with eateries, street-food stalls and small supermarkets. True to its traveler vibe, most places are good value and a few open very early to feed adventurers heading out on tour.

Locals rave about Miss Deb's food truck that parks at the Victor Galvez sports stadium on Wednesdays from 6pm to 9pm (check the Facebook page at www.facebook.com/MissDebs2go).

★Cenaida's
BELIZEAN $

(☑631-2526; Far West St; mains BZ$7-12; ⊘11am-9pm Mon-Tue & Thu-Sat, to 5pm Wed) One of the best places in town for authentic traditional Belizean food, Cenaida's is a no-frills diner serving rice and beans, stew chicken and cow-foot soup, along with burritos and fajitas.

Pop's Restaurant
DINER $

(☑824-3366; www.popsbelize.com; West St; breakfast BZ$4-15; ⊘6:30am-3pm) You may feel like you're in a *Seinfeld* episode at this friendly diner with booth seating. Best omelets in town, along with waffles and good coffee make this San Ignacio's worst-kept breakfast secret and a cozy place to while away the morning. Good subs and burgers at lunchtime.

D'Stock Burger
BURGERS $

(☑667-6333; Cayo Plaza; waffles BZ$6-12, burgers BZ$9-22; ⊘6:30am-10pm Sun-Wed, to 11pm Thu-Sat) San Ignacio's best burgers are lovingly made here with interesting variations such as the jerk chicken, pesto or mushroom burgers right up to the gut-busting one pounder. It also does a great line in sweet and savory breakfast waffles.

STREET FOOD & FARMERS MARKET

To experience the true cultural tapestry of Belize firsthand, head down to the **Farmers Market** (⊘from 5am Sat) on Saturday, when San Ignacio's open-sided covered market draws farmers and food producers from all ends of Belize (culturally and geographically) to buy and sell all manner of fruits, vegetables, jams and dairy products. The food stalls here are superb – cheap, tasty, fast and offering a wide variety of choice. For street food when the market is not on, try the taco and *salbute* (mini-tortilla) stands on Savannah St or head over the bridge to Santa Elena.

Paradise Grill
LEBANESE $

(☑637-7777; Cayo Plaza; mains BZ$8-23; ⊘10am-10pm) Rounding out San Ignacio's multicultural dining scene, this Lebanese place serves up delicious shawarma, pita wraps, felafel and kebabs. Most meals come with Middle Eastern sides such as tabbouleh, baba ghanoush and hummus.

Tandoor
INDIAN $

(☑824-4444; Burns Ave; mains BZ$6-36) The obvious standout on the menu here is the Indian cuisine, from samosas to butter chicken and fish curry, but there's also a typical range of Belizean dishes, burritos, wings and burgers. Pizzas are available whole or by the slice. It's also a popular place for a drink at the busy end of Burns Ave.

Ice Cream Shoppe
ICE CREAM $

(☑634-6160; 24 West St; 1/2 scoops BZ$4/7; ⊘11am-9pm Mon-Thu, to 9:30pm Fri-Sun; 🛜♿) This is the place for excellent homemade ice cream with some deliciously offbeat flavors, such as pumpkin cheesecake, s'mores and fudge brownie.

Mike's
BREAKFAST $

(Savannah St; dishes BZ$3-10; ⊘5-9am) This unsignposted green shack opposite the market is a local legend for breakfast and fresh johnnycakes (cornmeal flatbread). Go early or miss out.

New French Bakery
BAKERY $

(☑804-0054; Joseph Andrew Dr; baked goods BZ$2-5; ⊘6:30am-6pm Mon-Sat) Best place in town for French bread, cinnamon rolls, croissants, apple turnovers and good coffee. It's in an open space just north of the market – get here early for the freshest, straight-out-of-the-oven stuff.

Sweet T'ing
BAKERY $

(☑610-4174; 96 Benque Viejo Rd; cakes BZ$2-5, coffee from BZ$2; ⊘noon-9pm) A tiny bakery at the top of the hill with an exceptional variety of local chocolates (including made-in-Belize favorites Cotton Tree and Goss) and coconut cream pie, Sweet T'ing is worth the walk.

★Guava Limb Cafe
INTERNATIONAL $$

(☑824-4837; www.guavalimb.com; 79 Burns Ave; mains BZ$16-45; ⊘11am-10pm Tue-Sat, to 5pm Sun; 🛜🌱) 🍃 One of San Ignacio's slickest restaurants, boutique Guava Limb is set in an adorable turquoise two-story building with a serene outdoor garden area. Fresh organic ingredients are sourced from the owners' farm or local providers to create an eclectic international menu that might include Indonesian *gado gado,* a Middle Eastern platter or conch ceviche.

Gourmet pizzas, burgers and quesadilla make for a filling lunch, and vegetarians will enjoy the wide range of fresh salads. There's a full bar and the garden is a fine place for a cold beer or cocktail. It's at the north end of Burns Ave.

Ko-Ox Han-nah   BELIZEAN, INDIAN $$
(☑623-0019; 5 Burns Ave; breakfast BZ$7-16, Belizean mains BZ$10-12, Asian mains BZ$22-32; ☺6am-9pm; ☑) The name means *let's go eat* in Mayan, but Han-nah's is far from just another Belizean restaurant. The eclectic menu features an intriguing range of Indian dishes, such as lamb curry and Burmese shrimp curry, with all food sourced from local farms. Breakfasts are good, while lunch and dinner are a mix of Mexican, burgers and Indo-Asian.

Eva's   BREAKFAST, BELIZEAN $$
(Burns Ave; mains BZ$12-35; ☺6am-10pm; ☎) Open early for breakfast, Eva's is a popular traveler hangout at the busy end of Burns Ave. The menu is pretty standard fare with Belizean and Western breakfasts, Belizean rice and beans, Creole curry, Tex-Mex, burgers, steaks and pasta. The street-side seating is a good spot for a cold beer and people-watching.

Hode's Place   BELIZEAN, AMERICAN $$
(☑804-2522; Branch Mouth Rd; mains BZ$6-30; ☺9am-10pm, ☑☑) Locals love this rambling barn-sized place just north of the city center. A large terrace restaurant opening onto a citrus orchard and kids' playground, it's a popular spot with families or for an evening drink. Friendly service and satisfying food – from burritos and fajitas to steaks, seafood and rice and beans – complete the recipe.

Tolacco Smokehouse   MAYA $$
(Cristo Rey Rd, Santa Elena; mains BZ$10-30; ☺4-10pm Mon-Sat) Across the river in Santa Elena, this family-run open-sided restaurant makes a welcome change from downtown San Ignacio. Pork ribs, chops and grilled chicken and fish are the specialties, along with juicy steaks. There's a bar and a friendly atmosphere. Dinner only.

Great Mayan Prince   BELIZEAN $$
(☑824-2588; 28 Benque Viejo Rd; mains BZ$12-28; ☺7am-11am, noon-3pm & 6-9pm; ☎☑)

Great Mayan Prince is worth the short hike up Benque Viejo Rd for the sweeping balcony view of San Ignacio and an honest (not overpriced) menu of Belizean and Mexican dishes. A good spot for breakfast and Sunday brunch. There were some crazy architectural additions going up when we visited.

Ix'Tabai Restaurant   BELIZEAN $$
(☑824-3740; Cahal Pech Village Resort, Cahal Pech Hill, mains BZ$15-30; ☺7am-10pm; ℗☎☑) If it's food with a view you're after, you won't get better than this unless you have your own chef and a zeppelin. From the dining room of the Cahal Pech Village Resort you can enjoy sweeping views over San Ignacio and Cayo while enjoying a menu of Belizean faves, such as Maya pork chops, or burgers and pasta.

Serendib   SRI LANKAN $$
(☑804-2302; Burns Ave; mains BZ$15-25; ☺11am-10pm) San Ignacio's only Sri Lankan restaurant serves excellent curries with a choice of yellow, fried or savory rice, spicy chicken tandoori, and other delicacies from the Indian subcontinent. Friendly owners and street side or peaceful courtyard dining areas, though diners complain of slow service.

Martha's Kitchen   BREAKFAST, INTERNATIONAL $$
(☑804-3647; 10 West St; mains BZ$8-30; ☺7am-10pm; ☎) Highlights run the gamut from tasty pizza and delicious fish burritos to juicy steaks and vegetarian kebabs. Take a seat inside the wood-accented dining room or outside on the foliage-fronted terrace. Good spot for breakfast.

★ Running
W Steakhouse   INTERNATIONAL, STEAKHOUSE $$$
(San Ignacio Resort Hotel, 18 Buena Vista St; mains BZ$24-65; ☺7am-9:30pm Mon-Thu, to 10:30pm Fri-Sun, 9am-2:30pm Sun brunch; ❋) One of San Ignacio's top dining splurges, the restaurant at the San Ignacio Resort Hotel is named for the owner's Running W ranch that supplies most of the best meat in western Belize. Steaks are a specialty, including Black Angus rib eye, but there's also a wide range of thoughtfully prepared international and Belizean dishes.

Dine in the air-conditioned restaurant or out on the romantic, candlelit balcony patio overlooking the pool and jungle. There's an attached bar with slick service.

Crave House of Flavour INTERNATIONAL $$$
(☎824-3707; 24 West St; mains BZ$16-45; ⏲6-9pm) A gourmet addition to San Ignacio's dining, Crave is a tiny and intimate restaurant with just a few tables inside and out. The changing menu is eclectic but has a strong Italian, steakhouse and barbecue flavor. Highlights include rib-eye, baby back ribs, oven roasted rabbit or spicy roasted lobster tail. Great for that romantic meal or splurge.

Drinking & Nightlife

Although low-key compared to beach resorts such as San Pedro, San Ignacio has the liveliest nightlife this side of Belize City, so enjoy it!

Soul Project BAR
(☎653-1855; Buena Vista Rd; ⏲6-11pm Wed & Fri; 📶) Soul Project is a sweet bar and venue where local artist, filmmaker and conservationist Daniel Velazquez works hard to create a space for local and visiting artists and musicians. And he makes his own herbal fruit wine. It's only open on Wednesdays and Fridays, so find out what's going on and definitely pencil in a night out here. It's sitiated below the Old House Hostel (p174).

Thirsty Thursdays CLUB
(☎824-2727; Buena Vista Rd; ⏲5pm-midnight Wed-Sun, to 4am Fri & Sat) The go-to place after (or before) other bars in town close, semi-open-air Thirsty Thursdays has regular live DJs, party nights, drink specials, bar food and a mixed crowd. Thursday is karaoke. It's up the hill past San Ignacio Resort Hotel.

CK Sports Bar BAR
(☎824-2996; Joseph Andrew Dr; ⏲4pm-midnight Wed-Fri, from noon Sat & Sun; 📶) Low-key sports bar with pool table, big screens and decent bar food.

Entertainment

Princess Casino CASINO
(Buena Vista St; ⏲noon-4am Mon-Fri, to 5am Sat & Sun) Belize isn't a big casino destination but you can spend your money here on a handful of live gaming tables (black jack, poker) or slot machines, or drink at the Next Lounge Bar till late. Security is tight – ID, webcam photo and bag checks.

Shopping

Baka Bush Books BOOKS
(☎608-0324; cnr Far West S & Bullet Tree Rd; ⏲11am-7:30pm Mon, Thu & Fri, 10am-8pm Sat) Good range of secondhand books to buy or trade.

Back to My Roots ARTS & CRAFTS
(☎824-2740; 30 Burns Ave) Offers cool handmade jewelry, including silver, amber and other semiprecious stones. The name of the place refers to the drums and other Rasta gear for sale.

Jungle Remedies HEALTH
(☎663-0248; Orange St; ⏲by appointment) From gastric distress and asthma to high blood pressure, gall stones and gout, Dr Harry Guy claims his jungle remedies can cure nearly any ailment. Many locals swear by his potions, made from locally harvested roots, barks and leaves. His place, off Bullet Tree Rd, is hard to find – call ahead for an appointment.

Arts & Crafts of Central America ARTS & CRAFTS
(☎824-3734; 24 Burns Ave; ⏲10am-8pm) This little shop below Central Otel sells a wide variety of handmade jewelry, handbags and textiles, mostly from Guatemala.

Information

MEDICAL SERVICES

La Loma Luz Hospital (☎804-2985, 824-2087; www.lalomaluz.org; Western Hwy; ⏲emergency services 24hr) This Adventist hospital in Santa Elena is one of the best in the country.

San Ignacio Hospital (☎824-2761; Bullet Tree Rd)

MONEY

Belize Bank (Burns Ave), **Scotiabank** (cnr Burns Ave & King St) and **Atlantic Bank** (Burns Ave) have ATMs that accept international Visa, MasterCard, Plus and Cirrus cards.

POST

Post Office (☎824-2049; West St)

TOURIST INFORMATION

Cayo Welcome Center (☎634-8450; Savannah St, Cayo Plaza; ⏲8am-5pm Mon-Fri, to 4pm Sat) The only tourist office in the Cayo District, this is a helpful, air-conditioned modern place in the central plaza. As well as some local exhibits, a short film about the region runs on a loop.

ⓘ Getting There & Away

AIR

The nearest airstrip is tiny Maya Flats on Chial Rd, about 7 miles from San Ignacio. Tropic Air has three daily flights to/from Belize City. A taxi to/from town costs around BZ$40.

BUS

San Ignacio (surprisingly) has no bus station. Buses stop in the market plaza en route to/from Belize City (regular/express BZ$9/10, two hours), **Belmopan** (Savannah St; BZ$4, one hour) and Benque Viejo del Carmen (BZ$2, 30 minutes). Buses run in both directions about every half-hour from 3:30am to 7pm, with a less frequent service on Sunday.

From a **vacant lot** (Savannah St) on Savannah St, buses leave for Bullet Tree Falls (BZ$1, 15 minutes) roughly hourly from 10:30am to 5pm Monday to Saturday. From the same spot, buses go to San Antonio (BZ$3, 35 minutes) five or six times a day, Monday to Saturday.

Several tour companies also run charter shuttle buses around Cayo and further afield. Sample fares include Guatemala border (BZ$50) and Belize City (BZ$150).

There are no direct government buses between Belize and Guatemala, but the Marlin Espadas shuttle runs daily between Chetumal (Mexico) and Flores (Guatemala) via Belmopan and San Ignacio.

CAR

To really explore Cayo, a car is useful, preferably with good off-road capabilities and high clearance. Local car-hire companies include **Cayo Auto Rentals** (☑ 824 2222; www.cayoauto rentals.com; 81 Benque Viejo Rd).

There is a convenient central gas station next to the bridge out of San Ignacio.

TAXI

Several taxi stands are dotted around the town center; **Savannah Taxi Association** (☑ 824-2155; Savannah St; ☺ 24hr) is San Ignacio's main central taxi stand. Sample fares are BZ$25 to the Guatemalan border (9 miles), BZ$60 round-trip to Xunantunich, and BZ$80 to BZ$100 one-way to the Mountain Pine Ridge lodges. Taxis to Bullet Tree Falls (colectivo (shared)/private BZ$4/20) go from **Wyatt St** (Benque Viejo Rd), just off Burns Ave.

For lodges around Cristo Rey village, the Cristo Rey shuttle (BZ$2) leaves regularly from the Cayo Plaza.

ⓘ Getting Around

San Ignacio is small enough that you can easily walk to most places of interest. If you're driving, note that parking can be difficult in the city center. Also pay attention to the one-way traffic system; Hawkesworth Bridge is one-way leaving San Ignacio while New Bridge enters town north of the market and a new ring road allows you to bypass the town center completely.

Short taxi rides around town cost BZ$5.

SOUTHEAST OF SAN IGNACIO

Forming a loop encircling a large, beautiful swath of the Cayo District and leading into both the Mountain Pine Ridge Forest Reserve and Caracol, unsealed Cristo Rey Rd winds southeast of San Ignacio (via Santa Elena), eventually linking up with Chiquibul Rd (sometimes called Pine Ridge Rd), which runs 9 miles up to Georgeville on the George Price Hwy.

The only major population center on the loop is **San Antonio** (population 2000). Settled by Maya from the Yucatán, the village gets its name from the statue of St Anthony in the town church.

Apart from the exhilarating forest drive, there are numerous cultural and adventure activities along the way.

⊙ Sights & Activities

Barton Creek Cave   CAVE
(guided canoe tour per person BZ$130; ☺ 7am-4pm) Barton Creek rises high in the Mountain Pine Ridge and flows north to join the Belize River near Georgeville. Along the way it dips underground for a spell, flowing through the Barton Creek Cave. During the Classic Period, the ancient Maya interred at least 28 people and left thousands of pottery jars and fragments and other artifacts on 10 ledges. Today the cave is only accessible by canoe on excellent guided tours.

Canoe trips take you (in groups of eight or fewer per guide) about 800ft into the cave so you can get a look at the limestone cave formations, as well as the spooky skulls, bones and pottery shards that remain from the Maya. Numerous tours operate out of San Ignacio, or head to Mike's Place (p181) just outside the cave entrance, where guides will take you out without prebooking.

Even if you don't tour the cave, you can swim here for free and there's a restaurant and bar at Mike's Place.

There are two routes to the cave, both very rough and both turning off Chiquibul

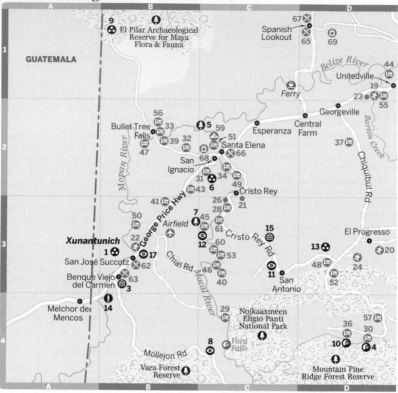

Rd. The main route on Upper Barton Creek Rd passes through the scattered traditional Mennonite farming community of Upper Barton Creek and fords Barton Creek itself, which means this route may be closed in high water. The second route along Seven Mile El Progresso Rd (follow the signs for Mike's Place) involves possibly the steepest road in Belize with a series of tight switchbacks descending into the valley – but no river crossings!

García Sisters' Place CULTURAL CENTER
(☏671-1753; artistmai1981@gmail.com; Cristo Rey Rd, San Antonio; ⊙7am-6pm) The García sisters display and sell a wide assortment of beautiful black-slate carvings. These five sisters developed this craft, which is now widely imitated around Belize. Their carvings, selling for between BZ$10 and BZ$200, depict a variety of subjects, including Maya deities and calendars. With advance notice the

sisters also offer Maya ceremonies, blessings, massage and herbal tours.

Today their home and gallery is part museum of Maya culture, part art center and shop, and part healing center. Various herbal and healing treatments cost from BZ$40. Outside is a garden where medicinal and herbal tours (BZ$20) are held, along with lectures and workshops on Maya culture, meditation and spiritual healing.

Sa'c Tunich MUSEUM
(☏662-1253; Cristo Rey Rd; tours BZ$5; ⊙8am-8pm) Many refer to Sa'c Tunich as 'the living Maya site' because at first glance it looks like an excavated ruin. However, Sa'c Tunich is actually the museum-workshop of Maya artists Jose and Javier Magaña, who create contemporary Maya artworks from stone and clay, both for exhibition and for sale. Tours of the site include the nearby *gibnut* (small, brown-spotted rodent similar to a

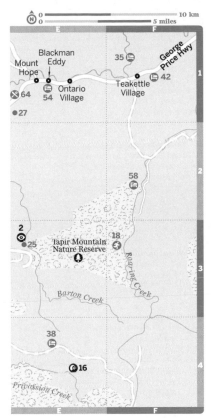

guinea pig) breeding program and the lookout tower.

Pacbitun
ARCHAEOLOGICAL SITE

Pacbitun, a small site, 12 miles south of San Ignacio via Cristo Rey Rd, near San Antonio, seems to have been occupied continuously through most of Maya history, from 900 BC to AD 900. Today only lofty Plaza A has been uncovered and partially consolidated. Structures 1 and 2, on the east and west sides of the plaza, respectively, are worth a look. You may find archaeologists and researchers working onsite.

Calico Jack's
ADVENTURE SPORTS

(☎832-2478; www.calicojacksvillage.com; 7 Mile Rd, El Progreso; per person BZ$80-175; ☺8am-4pm) This 365-acre property boasts the largest state-of-the-art ziplining setup in Western Cayo, a nine-run, 15-platform zipline; various packages take you on different runs ranging from a 45-minute 'explorer' to a 90-minute 'ultimate adventure'. Adventurous visitors can try the jungle swing (BZ$60), which offers a trip across a canyon combined with a 55ft free-fall, or the cable walk.

MET Outfitters & Lodge
HORSEBACK RIDING

(☎669-1124, in USA 800-838-3918; www.metbelize.com; Mile 8 Chiquibul Rd; half-/full-day horseback rides BZ$136/200) For equestrians, nothing beats exploring the area from the back of a horse. Mountain Equestrian Trails (MET) has highly professional half-day and full-day local rides to Big Rock Falls, Barton Creek and more, as well as multiday riding packages, including accommodation in rustic cabañas. Expert guides can also arrange birdwatching, caving and vehicle tours.

Mike's Place
TOURS

(☎670-0441; www.bartoncreekcave.com; Barton Creek Cave; cave tour per person BZ$130) Mike's is based near the entrance to Barton Creek Cave and offers guided canoe trips into the cave, as well as rock climbing and a short ziplining course. Discounts are offered for children and groups, and there's a welcoming restaurant and bar. Transfers available from San Ignacio for BZ$60. If self-driving, check road conditions and prepare for a hairy ride.

Mike's also has a bunkhouse and an entire two-story house for rent with rooms from BZ$50, or you can camp for BZ$20. There are lots of walks and birdwatching opportunities on the 11,000-acre property.

Chaya Garden Ashram
HEALTH & WELLBEING

(☎652-9642; www.chayagardenashram.com; ☺yoga 10am) Set on lush grounds next to a series of stunning natural waterfalls with an amazing swimming hole, Chaya Garden offers yoga classes, massage treatments, natural healing, and excellent vegan and vegetarian meals. Drop-in yoga classes are BZ$20, massage is BZ$100 for an hour treatment, and the ashram also hosts workshops and musical events.

Paradise Expeditions
BIRDWATCHING

(☎610-5593, 820-4014; www.birdinginbelize.com; Cristo Rey Rd, Crystal Paradise Resort) Run by the accomplished local bird guide Jeronie Tut, Paradise Expeditions does trips for both the casual and serious birder from its base at Crystal Paradise Resort (p183).

CAYO DISTRICT SOUTHEAST OF SAN IGNACIO

Around San Ignacio

🛏 Sleeping

Bella's Jungle Lodge HOSTEL **$**
(📞 663-5183; www.bellasinbelize.com; Mile 3.5 Cristo Rey Rd; campsites BZ$25, dm BZ$30, d BZ$40-60) Bella's has added a very cool riverside jungle location to its hostel world and it's a fine spot for budget travelers to commune with nature. Accommodation is simple but includes camping (tents and hammocks available for hire), dormitory beds and a tree house. Swim and kayak in the Macal River or just hang out by the camp fire.

The Cristo Rey shuttle from San Ignacio will drop you within easy walking distance of the lodge.

Cool M Farm
FARMSTAY **$**

(☑615-6206; cool.m.farm@gmail.com; Mile 0.25 Cristo Rey Rd; cabañas d/f BZ$100/110, per extra person BZ$20) 🏠 Cool M is an offbeat place to stay for a few days on a genuine Mennonite farm. The Löhr family's 75-acre garden-filled dairy farm, on Cristo Rey Rd about a five-minute drive from San Ignacio, has two lovely fan-cooled cabañas – one double and one family with two double beds – each with modern bathrooms and a sun porch overlooking the valley.

The welcoming family offers a light breakfast (BZ$5) and can provide farm-fresh dinners, boxed lunches and even babysitting on request. Minimum two-night stay.

García Sisters' Homestay
HOMESTAY **$**

(☑671-1753; Cristo Rey Rd; campsite per person BZ$15, r BZ$30) Just north of San Antonio village, the García Sisters offer rooms behind their Maya gallery and spots to pitch a tent. Traditional meals are BZ$15.

Calico Jack's Village
VILLA **$$**

(☑832-2478; www.calicojacksvillage.com; 7 Mile Rd, El Progresso; d/tr BZ$160/200, d/tr villas BZ$300/340; P❄🛜🏊) By day it's best known for its ziplining course, but Calico Jack's also has a range of comfortable loft rooms and two- and three-bedroom villas with kitchen facilities, wi-fi and cable TV. The onsite restaurant serves breakfast, lunch and dinner overlooking the pool.

Inn the Bush
CABIN **$$**

(☑670-6364; www.innthebushbelize.com; Macaw Bank; 1-/2-bedroom cabins BZ$280/450; P🛜) Sitting on a small hill near the Macal River, intimate Inn the Bush has two large cabins with massive four-poster mahogany beds, couches, full-sized bathrooms with hot showers and porches bigger than most hotel rooms, and a two-bedroom family cabin with living room. A large *palapa* bar and dining area overlooks a swimming-pool deck with jungle views.

Meals featuring locally sourced meats and vegetables are served all day, but advance notice is requested. It's signposted about 2 miles south of Cristo Rey Rd.

Maya Mountain Lodge
RESORT **$$**

(☑824-2164; www.mayamountain.com; Mile 0.75 Cristo Rey Rd; r BZ$138-258, cottages BZ$238-258; P❄🛜🏊) Lush gardens with a trail leading to a small, ancient Maya ceremonial site and the eight air-conditioned cottages with tile floors and porches hung with hammocks

keep visitors coming back. Family units are like apartments with complete kitchenettes, and all units have wi-fi. There's also a medicinal trail and a wellness center onsite.

Maya Mountain Lodge is easily reached (even on foot), less than 1.5 miles from San Ignacio on Cristo Rey Rd.

Macaw Bank Jungle Lodge
LODGE **$$**

(☑603-4825; www.macawbankjunglelodge.com; off Cristo Rey Rd, Macaw Bank; d cabañas BZ$220-260; P🛜) 🏠 Deep in jungle about 2 miles south of Cristo Rey Rd and spread out along the Macal River, Macaw Bank is a 50-acre wildlife wonderland, teeming with birds and other animals. The six rustic but spacious cabañas are decorated with hand-hewn furniture, mosaic-tile floors and woven tapestries. A restaurant serves locally sourced meals (order in advance).

Eco credentials are good, including solar power, recycling projects, organic gardening and water-conservation efforts.

Crystal Paradise Resort
RESORT **$$**

(☑834-4016, 820-4014; www.crystalparadise.com; Cristo Rey Rd; s/d/tr from BZ$146/190/235; P🛜) The Tut family's resort is spread out over well-tended gardens just above the Macal River, and offers utilitarian but comfortable cabañas. Most guests come here on packages that incorporate preplanned tours, including birdwatching, horseback riding, canoeing, Maya ruins and other activities. Breakfast and dinner are included.

Gumbolimbo Village Resort
RESORT **$$**

(☑650-3112; www.gumbolimboresort.com; Chiquibul Rd; d cabañas BZ$230-300; P❄🛜🏊) 🏠 Perched high atop a hillside covered in gumbo-limbo trees, this resort offers modern cabañas, as well as the romantic hexagon room with cool white interiors and large glass doors offering mountain and jungle views. The ecoresort runs completely on solar and wind power. Meals available.

Moonracer Farm
CABAÑAS **$$**

(☑667 5748; www.moonracerfarm.com; Mile 9 Mount Pine Ridge Rd; cabañas d/q BZ$120/230; P@🛜🏊) Intimate, rustic Moonracer occupies the former grounds of a wild feline rehabilitation center. There's one jungle cabin with two double rooms, each with two queen-size beds, bathroom with hot shower, and screened-in porches with hammocks. Kerosene lamps provide ambience for the rooms, but the communal *palapa* kitchen and dining room has electricity and wi-fi.

The location is good for bird-watchers and explorers looking to head out early to explore Caracol. It also has nearby Cohine Camping Casitas – raised cabins with running water but no electricity at BZ$70 a double.

Mystic River   CABIN $$$

([📱]834-4100; www.mysticriverbelize.com; Mystic River Rd; ste BZ$400-720; [P][📶]) This beautiful ecolodge on the east bank of the Macal River features nine beautifully furnished cabañas with Mexican-tiled floors and high wooden ceilings (four with private plunge pool), and a few one- and two-bedroom suites. All feature spacious living areas and bathrooms, and river-facing verandas.

Hang out on the river with tubes, boogie boards and canoes, or hike the jungle trails that wind through Mystic River's 180 acres. The lodge also has the new Jasmine Spa and a yoga deck, the open-sided restaurant serves organic foods, and there's an onsite artisanal cheese house. Turn south off Cristo Rey Rd at Mile 6.

Mariposa Jungle Lodge   LODGE $$$

([📱]670-2113; www.mariposajunglelodge.com; Cristo Rey Rd; d/tr/q from BZ$450/470/550, tree house BZ$850; [P][✳][📶][♨]) This luxurious jungle lodge is a cut above some of the more rustic nearby places in terms of comfort, with seven beautiful cabins featuring king-size canopy beds dressed with Egyptian linens and mosquito nets, hardwood furniture and hand-thatched roofs. Rooms also come with mini-fridge, optional air-con and hot showers.

With views of the rainforest or the mountain ridge, the screened porch is a perfect place to hang a hammock. There's a pool complete with barstools and a waterfall, and a full-service bar and restaurant. It's easily reached near the Chiquibul Rd junction 3 miles east of San Antonio.

Table Rock Jungle Lodge   RESORT $$$

([📱]834-4040; www.tablerockbelize.com; off Cristo Rey Rd; r & cabañas d BZ$350-450, Shamrock Bluff house BZ$800; [P][📶][♨]) [♿] This exquisite little resort boasts five classy cabañas, each furnished with custom-made four-poster beds, tile floors and thatched roofs, and equipped with 24-hour electricity and hot showers. Guests can make use of free activities, such as canoeing, cave-tubing and mountain biking, as well as organised tours throughout Cayo District.

The owners of Table Rock produce their own electricity, grow their own fruits and vegetables, and use purified rainwater. Nonguest diners are welcome at the Table Rock restaurant with 24 hours' notice. Minimum two-night stay.

MET Outfitters & Lodge   RESORT $$$

([📱]669-1124, in USA 800-838-3918; www.met belize.com; 5-night package d per person BZ$2800; [P][📶]) The accommodations here are mainly geared around horseback riding and bird-watching packages of between four and eight days. After a day of horseback riding, rest your weary body in the 10 spacious thatched-roof *cabañas*, decorated with beautiful Maya tapestries and boasting lovely forest views. Kerosene lamps light the way (no electricity), and meals are served in the *cantina* (canteen).

Mountain Pine Ridge Area

South of San Ignacio and the Western Hwy, the land begins to climb toward the heights of the Maya Mountains, whose arching ridge forms the border separating Cayo District from Stann Creek District to the east and Toledo District to the south.

In the heart of this highland area, 200 sq miles of submontane (ie on the foothills or lower slopes of mountains) pine forest is the **Mountain Pine Ridge Forest Reserve** [FREE]. The sudden switch from tropical rainforest to pine trees as you ascend to the Mountain Pine Ridge – a broad upland area of multiple ridges and valleys – is a little bizarre and somewhat startling. The reserve is full of rivers, pools, waterfalls and caves; the higher elevation means relief from both heat and mosquitoes.

⊙ Sights

Big Rock Falls   WATERFALL

The small but powerful Big Rock Falls on Privassion Creek are, for many, more impressive than the Thousand Foot Falls – not least because you can get up close and swim in the pools below. Take the road toward Gaïa River Lodge (signposted) and 1.5 miles past Blancaneaux Lodge turn along a track to the left marked 'Big Rock'. From the parking area it's a steep walk down (even steeper back up!), aided by timber steps.

Five Sisters Falls   WATERFALL

The pools at tranquil Five Sisters Falls are only accessible to guests or diners at Gaïa

River Lodge. A cable tram can take you down and back up.

Río On Pools   WATERFALL

Just off Chiquibul Rd, 2.5 miles north of Douglas D'Silva (Augustine), Río On Pools is a series of small waterfalls connecting pools that the river has carved out of granite boulders. It's a beautiful spot: the pools are refreshing for a dip and the smooth slabs of granite are perfect for stretching out on to dry off. It's remote but a popular spot for tour groups on their way back from Caracol.

Thousand Foot Falls   WATERFALL

(⊙lookout point 8am-6pm) Ten miles off Chiquibul Rd, the Thousand Foot Falls are reckoned to be the highest in Central America, a ribbon of water cascading down a mountainside that you can view from a distant lookout point. Access them by turning onto Cooma Cairn Rd (follow the Hidden Valley sign), then turn left after 7 miles at the '1000 Ft Falls' sign. Walk around the lookout area for views over the pine-covered valley out toward Belmopan.

Río Frio Cave   CAVE

In Douglas D'Silva (Augustine), on the way to or from Caracol, look for the signed turnoff to Río Frio Cave, less than 1 mile away. The river gurgles through the sizable cave, keeping it cool while you go off and explore.

🛏 Sleeping & Eating

There are no independent restaurants in the Mountain Pine Ridge area. Nonguests should reserve in advance for lunch or dinner at Blancaneaux Lodge or Gaïa River Lodge.

★ Blancaneaux Lodge   RESORT $$$

(☑824-3878, in USA 800-746-3743, in USA 866-356-5881; www.thefamilycoppolahideaways.com/en/blancaneaux-lodge; cabañas BZ$770-1200, 2-bedroom villas BZ$1470; P 🛜 🌊) 🍴 Owned by movie director Francis Ford Coppola (who keeps a personal villa, 'the Francis Ford Coppola Villa', complete with attendant and private pool, yours for BZ$1800 per night), this indulgent 78-acre lodge offers 20 thatched cabañas and luxury villas, spread around beautifully manicured gardens, with some looking right over the picturesque Privassion Creek.

The lodgings feature beautiful tiled bathrooms, with open-air living rooms in the villas, and handicrafts from Belize, Guatemala, Mexico and Thailand. Luxury cabañas feature their own plunge pools and outdoor showers, as well as indoor-style Japanese baths. There's also the Enchanted Cottage, a secluded one-bedroom stone cottage with fireplace, private pool, attendant and majestic view. Two onsite restaurants serve Italian and Guatemalan cuisine, nonguests are welcome with advance reservations.

Gaïa River Lodge   CABAÑAS $$$

(☑834-4005, 834-4024; www.gaiariverlodge.com; r & cabañas BZ$450, ste BZ$630, villas BZ$680; 🛜) Stylish Gaïa River Lodge is beautifully perched on a ridge above Privassion Creek. Luxurious cabañas and villas are well spaced out in the lodge grounds, creating a sense of privacy; the best are the waterfall-view rooms and the riverside lodge.

From the restaurant and bar, with its outdoor terrace, there are fine views down to horizontal Five Sisters Falls, which can be reached in style by the lodge's hydropowered tram. Nonguests are welcome to eat here with advance notice – lunch with a view is unbeatable – or just call in for a drink at the bar or on the rear deck.

Hidden Valley Inn   RESORT $$$

(☑822-3320, in USA 866-443-3364; www.hiddenvalleyinn.com; 4 Common Cain Rd; d/ste BZ$530/740; P 🛜 🌊) Secluded Hidden Valley Inn is set on 11 sq miles of Mountain Pine Ridge, all for the exclusive use of its guests. The grounds straddle pine and tropical forest ecosystems, and have access to 90 miles of signposted trails, waterfalls, swimming spots and spectacular lookouts. The 10 cottage-style estate rooms and two suites feature earth-toned tapestries, fireplaces and mahogany furniture.

The lodge also offers a plethora of amenities, including free mountain bikes, yoga classes and more. It is situated 4 miles off the Chiquibul Rd, along Cooma Cairn Rd.

Pine Ridge Lodge   CABAÑAS $$$

(☑661-8264; www.pineridgelodge.com; r & cabañas BZ$200-700; P 🛜) Beautifully designed eco-accommodation here ranges from rooms in cottages with screened-in porches and private bathrooms, to thatched Maya cottages and spectacular split-level family cabañas with Maya furnishings and artworks and king-sized beds. It's all set in a lovely garden, split by a burbling creek, with a communal restaurant bar area at its heart.

Considering the location and flashy lodges in the vicinity, Pine Ridge is a down-to-earth getaway.

Caracol

Beyond Mountain Pine Ridge, to the southwest, are the ruins of Belize's largest and most important Maya site, **Caracol** (BZ$30; ⊙8am-4pm, convoy departs 9am). Once among the most powerful cities in the entire Maya world, this ancient city now lies enshrouded by thick jungle near the Guatemalan border, a rugged 52-mile drive from San Ignacio that takes two to three hours. A multimillion dollar road upgrade will eventually make Caracol more accessible to independent travelers.

At the ticket office, a small **visitors center** outlines Caracol's history and has a helpful scale model, and a new museum houses much of the sculpture found at Caracol.

History

Sitting high on the Vaca Plateau, 1650ft above sea level, it's postulated that Caracol may have stretched over 70 sq miles at its peak (around AD 650). Nearly 40 miles of internal causeways radiate from the center to large outlying plazas and residential areas, connecting different parts of the city. At its height, the city's population may have approached 150,000, more than twice as many people as Belize City has today. Though they had no natural water source, the people of Caracol dug artificial reservoirs to catch rainwater and grew food on extensive agricultural terraces. Its central area was a bustling place of temples, palaces, busy thoroughfares, craft workshops and markets. Caracol is not only the preeminent archaeological site in Belize but also exciting for its jungle setting and prolific birdlife.

◉ Sights

A system of trails meanders through Caracol, but Plazas A and B are the most excavated. The highlight is **Caana** (Sky-Place), which rises from Plaza B, and at 141ft is still the tallest building in Belize! Caana underwent many construction phases until its completion in about 800. It supports four palace compounds and three temples. High steps narrowing up to the top probably led to the royal family's compound, where Structure B-19 housed Caracol's largest and most elaborate tomb. It contained the remains of a woman, possibly Lady Batz' Ek from Calakmul, who married into Caracol's ruling dynasty in 584. Climb to the top of Caana to feast upon one of the most magnificent views in all of Belize. On the way down, don't miss the hidden tombs around the back on the left side.

South of Plaza B, the Central Acropolis was an elite residential group with palaces and shrines. To its west, Plaza A contained many stelae, some of which are still in place. Atop Structure A-2 is a replica of a stela found here in 2003 that is engraved with the longest Maya inscription found in Belize. Structure A-6, the Temple of the Wooden Lintel, is one of the oldest buildings at Caracol. One of its lintels (the one to the left as you enter the top chamber) is original.

EXCAVATION HISTORY OF CARACOL

In 1937 a logger named Rosa Mai first stumbled upon the ruins. In 1938 commissioner of archaeology AH Anderson named the site Caracol (Spanish for snail), perhaps because of all the snail shells found in the soil. In 1950 Linton Satterthwaite from the University of Pennsylvania recorded the visible stone monuments, mapped the site core, and excavated several tombs, buildings and monuments. Many stelae were removed and sent to Pennsylvania.

Since 1985, Drs Diane and Arlen Chase have led the Caracol Archaeological Project (www.caracol.org), with annual field seasons conducting surveys and excavations that have revealed Caracol's massive central core and complex urban development. From 2000 to 2004, the Tourism Development Project carried out an excavation and conservation program led by Belizean archaeologist Jaime Awe, which also improved road access to the site.

Caracol

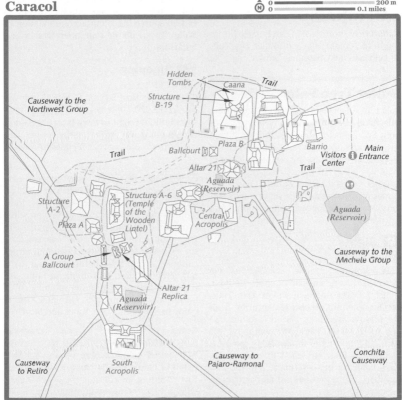

South of the Temple of the Wooden Lintel is the A Group Ballcourt, where the all-important Altar 21, telling us so much about Caracol's history, was found. A replica of the 'altar,' actually a ball-court marker, sits in the middle. Further south is one of Caracol's many *aguadas* (reservoirs), and beyond that the South Acropolis, a Classic Period elite residential complex where you can enter two tombs.

Getting There & Away

Most people come on a guided tour but it's possible to self-drive with a 4WD, or a high-clearance 2WD when it's dry – check road conditions in advance. Note that some car-hire companies prohibit driving this route. The road to Caracol, once the stuff of rugged travel legend, is now regularly graded and no worse (and in many places better) than other unpaved roads in the area. In 2018, an BZ$80 million road upgrading project was approved, meaning it will eventually be an all-weather paved road.

Most visitors – individuals and groups alike – travel to Caracol in a convoy that departs the park gate in the Mountain Pine Ridge area at 9am every morning. On the return trip, the convoy departs at 2pm. Each car must sign in and out here and at the Douglas D'Silva Ranger Station about 8 miles further on. The convoy is accompanied by two park ranger vehicles to ensure the safety of all passengers. This system was instituted after several reported incidents of tourist vehicles being stopped by armed robbers some years ago, but it also safeguards against breakdowns and accidents. The security situation has eased, however, and rangers have stated they will permit vehicles that miss the convoy to go in anyway.

The 52-mile drive from San Ignacio can be done in around two to three hours, depending on road conditions.

NORTHWEST OF SAN IGNACIO

A short drive northeast of San Ignacio brings you to the quaint village of Bullet Tree Falls and close to the Guatemala border.

Bullet Tree Falls

Bullet Tree Falls is a quiet and quaint little village on the Mopan River, only 3 miles from San Ignacio. Activities include hiking in the nearby forests, river-tubing down the Mopan and exploring the remote ruins of El Pilar.

Don't expect a raging waterfall here – the namesake falls are a gentle set of rapids, but the river is great for swimming, tubing and kayaking.

◉ Sights

El Pilar RUINS
(El Pilar Archaeological Reserve for Maya Flora and Fauna; BZ$10; ⊘8am-4pm) Remote El Pilar, about 7 miles north of Bullet Tree Falls, was occupied for at least 15 centuries, from the middle Preclassic Period (around 500 BC) to the late Classic Period (about AD 1000). Long before present-day political borders, El Pilar stretched to modern-day Pilar Poniente in Guatemala, and the two countries are now working as partners to preserve the area.

With 25 plazas and 70 major structures, El Pilar was more than three times the size of Xunantunich. Despite excavations since 1993, not much of El Pilar has been cleared; this has been to avoid the decay that often follows the clearing of ancient buildings. While appreciating El Pilar's greatness requires some imagination, this may help to give you the feeling that you're discovering the place rather than following a well-worn tourist trail.

Six archaeological and nature trails meander among the mounds. The most impressive area is Plaza Copal, which has four pyramids from 45ft to 60ft high. A partly visible Maya causeway runs 500yd west from here to Pilar Poniente.

The rough road to El Pilar heads off to the left, 400yd past the bridge in Bullet Tree Falls. Be prepared for a bumpy ride: if it's wet, a 4WD is required. If you have your own vehicle, it's an incredible, remote and rewarding place to wander on your own – you might have the entire site to yourself.

Otherwise, you can hire a taxi (BZ$50 from Bullet Tree Falls) or take a tour. Local guides can be sourced through accommodation in Bullet Tree Falls or tour operators in San Ignacio.

🛏 Sleeping

Hotel El Pilar HOTEL $
(☑824-3059; Main Rd; s/d BZ$60/95, with aircon BZ$95/120; P❄🖧) The yellow two-story building right in town is an utterly dull choice compared with nearby lodges and cabins but rooms are clean enough.

Parrot Nest Jungle Lodge CABAÑAS $$
(☑669-6068, 660-6336; www.parrot-nest.com; treehouses or cabins without bathroom BZ$110, d cabañas with bathroom from BZ$140; P🖧) Individually designed *cabañas* – some on stilts, some in trees, one in a 100ft guanacaste tree – all have sturdy wood construction, tin roofs and shared bathrooms; four larger cabañas have private bathrooms and inviting verandas. The lush jungle grounds are a relaxed haven for wildlife-watching, river swimming and hammock swinging. Guests enjoy free use of kayaks, tubes and bicycles.

Cohune Palms CABAÑAS $$
(☑664-7508; cabañas BZ$170-250; 🖧) The four well-spaced cabañas here occupy a lovely patch of jungle on the banks of the Mopan River. Getting into or onto the water is easy, with a rope swing, swimming deck, tubes and canoes available. The thatched cabañas are spacious and comfortable with private bath, hot-water showers and fans – the family cabaña features a loft and sleeps five.

There's a lovely open-sided restaurant overlooking the river, and helpful owners.

Casa del Caballo Blanco CABAÑAS $$
(☑667-5424, in USA 707-974-4182; www.casacaballo blanco.com; 3 Bullet Tree Rd; s/d/tr incl breakfast BZ$122/176/214; P🖧) 🖉 About a mile out of San Ignacio on the way to Bullet Tree Falls, the 'House of the White Horse' is a concrete yellow ecolodge set on 23 acres of rolling hills and forest overlooking the Mopan River valley. Guests stay in spacious thatched-roof cabañas that are sparingly decorated with hardwood furniture and Maya fabrics.

★ Mahogany Hall BOUTIQUE HOTEL $$$
(☑844-4047; www.mahoganyhallbelize.com; Paslow Falls Rd; d/ste from BZ$490/930; ❄🖧🖧) This beautiful three-story eight-room colonial mansion sits on the eastern bank of Mopan River, about a mile from Bullet Tree

Falls village. Rooms feature dark mahogany floors and beds, classic French doors, and bathrooms with exquisite brass fixtures. All rooms have air-con and LCD-screen TV with cable. There's even a small, chic pool and a patio overlooking the rushing river.

Onsite restaurant Rico's Restaurant and Bar offers breakfast, lunch and dinner, and cocktails with a traditional colonial West Indies feel.

❶ Getting There & Away

Bullet Tree Falls is 3 miles from San Ignacio on a good sealed road. Seven buses run daily (except Sunday) from San Ignacio (BZ$1, 15 minutes) and back. Alternatively, *colectivos* (shared taxis) run frequently between San Ignacio and Bullet Tree Falls (BZ$4). A private taxi costs BZ$20.

SOUTHWEST OF SAN IGNACIO

Southwest from San Ignacio, the George Price Hwy runs across rolling countryside toward Benque Viejo del Carmen and the Guatemalan border. There is a variety of places to stay along the highway and along diversions such as Chial Rd.

◉ Sights & Activities

Belize Botanic Gardens   GARDENS
(☑824-3101; www.belizebotanic.org; admission only BZ$16, per person self-guided/guided tour BZ$15/30; ☺7am-5pm, last entry 3pm) 🌿 The magnificent Belize Botanic Gardens, accessed from the grounds of Sweet Songs Jungle Lodge, hold samples of roughly one-quarter of the approximately 4000 species of plants in Belize. The bountiful 45-acre zone boasts 2 miles of trails, many fruit trees and four different Belizean habitats: wetlands, rainforest, Mountain Pine Ridge (with a lookout tower) and medicinal plants of the Maya.

Two ponds attract a variety of waterfowl; Hamilton Hide allows birders to spy on various species. The garden's native orchid house is the largest of its kind in Belize. The self-guided tour includes a 56-page guidebook, while specialty tours from Sweet Songs include Plants of the Maya (per person BZ$100), which starts at 6am and includes the entrance fee, shuttle from San Ignacio, a traditional knowledge tour, with lunch and lessons in cooking or crafting with a local Maya guide; or a Day at the Gardens (per person BZ$100), which includes transportation, guided tour and lunch.

Chaa Creek   NATURE RESERVE
Set along the banks of the Macal River, beautiful Chaa Creek is a 365-acre nature reserve offering extensive facilities to lodge guests and nonguests alike. Running through the jungle just above the river, the **Rainforest Medicine Trail** was established by Dr Rosita Arvigo. This project aims to spread knowledge of traditional healing methods and preserve the rainforest habitats, from which many healing plants come. It identifies about 100 medicinal plants used in traditional Maya and/or modern medicine.

Guided tours of the trail operate from 8am to 5pm and cost BZ$10.

Chaa Creek Natural History Center & Butterfly Farm   NATURE CENTER
(guided tours BZ$10; ☺tours hourly 8am-4pm) Hike up the tree-covered hillside above the Macal River to reach the Chaa Creek Natural History Center & Butterfly Farm, a small nature center with displays on Belize's flora and fauna, as well as the early Maya. The highlight is the butterfly farm, which breeds the dazzlingly iridescent blue morpho (*Morpho peleides*) for export. Tours are offered from the lodge.

Ix Chel Farms   FARM
(BZ$10; ☺8am-noon & 1-5pm) This herbal-cure research center is at Ix Chel Farms, 8 miles southwest of San Ignacio up Chial Rd.

Dr Eligio Panti, who died in 1996 at age 103, was a healer in San Antonio village who used traditional Maya herb cures. Dr Rosita Arvigo, an American, studied medicinal plants with Dr Panti, then began several projects to spread the wisdom of traditional healing methods and to preserve the rainforest habitats, which harbor an incredible 4000 plant species.

Hanna Stables   HORSEBACK RIDING
(☑661-1536; www.hannastables.com; Mile 71 George Price Hwy; adult/child from BZ$96/74) Long-running Hanna's offers horseback-riding trips ranging from a ride around San Lorenzo farm to the popular half-day tour to Xunantunich (adult/child BZ$144/96).

Spa at Chaa Creek   SPA
(☑824-2037; www.chaacreek.com; spa treatments BZ$56-210, massages BZ$190-240) The luxurious hilltop Spa at Chaa Creek overlooks the Macal River and the Lodge at Chaa Creek.

Treatments range from facials and manicures to aromatherapy massage.

🛏 Sleeping

Log Cab-Inn   CABAÑAS $$

(☎824-3367; www.logcabinn-belize.com; Mile 68 Western Hwy; d BZ$215, d cabañas BZ$260-325; P✳🛜🏊) The name says it all, with 20 well-designed cabañas built from mahogany logs and furniture crafted at the onsite carpentry workshop. All cabañas have air-con, hot showers and cable TV, and the whole property is set on a citrus- and palm-dotted hillside. Meals are served in an open-air restaurant and bar overlooking a pool area.

Macal River Camp at Chaa Creek   CABIN $$

(Macal River Camp; cabin per person BZ$130) ✐ A half mile from the Lodge at Chaa Creek, the Macal River Camp at Chaa Creek offers rustic screened-in wooden cabins on stilts with comfy cots inside and a shady veranda. The place is not landscaped, but rather inhabits the jungle without disturbing the environs. All cabins share clean bathrooms and hot showers. Rates include breakfast and dinner.

To reach the Camp at Chaa Creek, you'll have to park in the designated area and hike in through the jungle for about half a mile. Rates include canoeing, guided bird walks, and visits to the onsite rainforest medicine trail, natural history center and butterfly farm.

★ Black Rock Lodge   RESORT $$$

(☎834-4038, 834-4049; www.blackrocklodge.com; cabins BZ$280-430, ste BZ$490; P🛜) ✐ High up the Macal in beautiful Black Rock Canyon, this is a stunning setting for a jungle adventure. Slate-and-wood cabins are fan-cooled and have lovely verandas overlooking the river and up toward towering cliffs. Black Rock is all about the location and activities; you can hike pristine trails, ride a horse to Vaca Falls or canoe down the Macal River.

The inviting dining area and deck, covered by a *palapa*, is fantastic for birding, and you may also spot howler monkeys, otters and iguanas. An onsite organic farm provides produce for some of the meals served in the restaurant, and all electricity is solar and hydro powered. Black Rock Lodge is at the end of a rugged, well-signposted, 6-mile unpaved road that leaves Chial Rd 0.8 miles off the Western Hwy.

★ Lodge at Chaa Creek   ECOLODGE $$$

(☎824-2037; www.chaacreek.com; Chaa Creek Rd; d/tr cottages BZ$390/270, d ste BZ$860, d villas BZ$1120; P🛜🏊) ✐ Consistently rated among the best lodges in Belize, and with good reason, Chaa Creek's tropical gardens and beautifully kept thatched cottages are spread across a gentle slope above the Macal River. Chaa Creek blossomed from an overgrown farm more than 40 years ago. The cottages, decorated with Maya textiles and local crafts, have decks, fans and private bathrooms.

For the last word in luxury, check out the three-level treetop Jacuzzi suite, the amazing garden suite and the spa villa, which has three bedrooms and sleeps up to seven people. An array of tours and activities is offered, or just laze around the infinity pool in tropical bliss. A state-of-the-art hilltop spa (p189) provides all levels of pampering. Breakfast is included with all rates and other meals can be enjoyed in the open-sided Mariposa Restaurant.

Ka'ana Resort & Spa   RESORT $$$

(☎824-3350; www.kaanabelize.com; Mile 69 George Price Hwy; ste BZ$750, casitas BZ$1190, villas 1-/2-bedroom BZ$2140/3330; P✳🛜🏊) ✐ A touch of understated luxury, this unique boutique resort and spa (Ka'ana means 'heavenly place' in Kekchí Maya) offers luxurious rooms and *casitas* fully equipped with high-thread-count sheets, down comforters, LCD TVs and iPod docking stations. Decor is contemporary Maya, with artwork by local Belizean artists. The private pool villas offer the peak of both privacy and luxury.

Private terraces overlook the lush grounds. The gourmet restaurant offers innovative, organic local cuisine and is open to nonguests with advanced reservations. Equally tempting is the Caribbean Spa, with treatments including facials, pedicures, mud wraps and coffee massage.

Sweet Songs Jungle Lodge   RESORT $$$

(☎824-3101; www.sweetsongslodge.com; r/bungalows BZ$410/520, tree houses BZ$360, ste from BZ$700; P🛜) Family-run Sweet Songs occupies large and lovely grounds above the Macal River. One of the original Cayo lodges, It has a wide range of accommodations from breezy, spacious lodge rooms and private bungalows to a six-bedroom house sleeping up to 16 people. The secluded stilted tree house is perfect for honeymooners. Rooms are fan-cooled, with private verandas overlooking the jungle grounds.

The superbly located lodge restaurant and bar serves breakfast, lunch and dinner (a light breakfast is included with room rates); a raised timber walkway leads out to fine views of the river and jungle canopy. Guests can enjoy swimming and canoeing in the river, hiking along the jungle trails, horseback riding and free visits to the adjacent Belize Botanic Gardens.

San José Succotz & Around

San José Succotz is 6.5 miles west of San Ignacio on the way to the Guatemalan border. The main reason to stop here is to visit the exceptional ruins of Xunantunich across the Mopan River, but there are a handful of other nearby attractions. Though Xunantunich can easily be done as a day trip from San Ignacio, you may prefer to use this slow-paced barrio (district) as your base for exploring Cayo or along the way to Guatemala.

◉ Sights & Activities

★ **Xunantunich** RUINS
(San José Succotz; BZ$10; ☉ 7:30am-4pm) Set on a leveled hilltop, Xunantunich (shoo-nahn-too-neech) is one of Belize's most easily accessible and impressive Maya archaeological sites. Getting here is half the fun with a free hand-cranked cable ferry taking you (and vehicles) across the Mopan River. Xunantunich may have been occupied as early as 1000 BC but it was little more than a village. The large architecture that we see today began to be built in the 7th century AD.

From AD 700 to 850, Xunantunich was possibly politically aligned with Naranjo, 9 miles west in Guatemala. Together, they controlled the western part of the Belize River valley, although the population probably never exceeded 10,000. Xunantunich partially survived the initial Classic Maya collapse of about AD 850 (when nearby Cahal Pech was abandoned), but was deserted by about AD 1000.

The site centers on Plazas A-2 and A-1, separated by Structure A-1. Just north of Plaza A-2, Structure A-11 and Plaza A-3 formed a residential 'palace' area for the ruling family. The dominant El Castillo (Structure A-6) rises 130ft high at the south end of Plaza A-1. El Castillo may have been the ruling family's ancestral shrine where they

Xunantunich

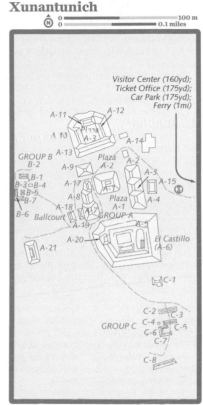

were buried and/or represented in sculpted friezes. Structures A-1 and A-13, at either end of Plaza A-2, were not built until the 9th century and would have had the effect of separating the ruling family from the rest of the population, possibly a response to the pressures that came with the decline of Classic Maya civilization at that time.

You can climb to the top of El Castillo to enjoy a spectacular 360-degree view. Its upper levels were constructed in two distinct phases. The first, built around 800, included an elaborate plaster frieze encircling the building; the second, built around 900, covered over most of the first and its frieze. The frieze on the east end of the building and part of the western one have been uncovered by archaeologists; these depict a series of Maya deities, with Chaac, the rain god, probably the central figure at the east end. The friezes you see today are replicas, with the originals underneath for safekeeping.

South of El Castillo is a partly overgrown area of lesser structures (Group C) that were abandoned as the city shrank after 900, leaving El Castillo (formerly at the center of the ancient city) on the southern edge of the occupied area.

There's a visitor center just past the ticket office. Inside are archaeological finds from the site, including pottery and jewelry, an interesting burial site and explanations of the El Castillo friezes.

To reach the ruins, take the ferry in San José Succotz village, then it's about 1 mile uphill to the parking lot and ticket office. Any bus from San Ignacio can drop you at the ferry point.

Tropical Wings Nature Center   GARDENS
(☑823-2265; www.thetrekstop.com; Mile 71 Western Hwy; adult/child BZ$10/5; ⊙8am-5pm; ♿) This interactive ecology exhibit is aimed at kids, but even adults will enjoy the butterfly house and medicinal gardens. It's on the grounds of The Trek Stop just outside San José Succotz.

Frisbee Golf   ADVENTURE SPORTS
(Mile 71 Western Hwy; per person BZ$6; ⊙8am-5pm) This nine-hole Frisbee golf course is on the grounds of The Trek Stop. The idea is to get your Frisbee into the basket in as few throws as possible – just like golf. Admission includes unlimited play for the day.

🛏 Sleeping & Eating

★Trek Stop   LODGE, CAMPGROUND $
(☑823-2265; www.thetrekstop.com; Mile 71 Western Hwy; camping per person BZ$14, d/tr/q with bathroom BZ$150/200/240, s/d without bathroom BZ$50/80; P@🛜🏊) 🌿 Trek Stop is a good option if you want to get out of San Ignacio on a budget and be close to Xunantunich. The backpackers' outpost consists of well-made timber cabins in a jungle setting just off the highway. There's an ecovibe but it has electricity and wi-fi. Plenty of hangout space, above ground pool and a cool little restaurant.

Maya Vista   RESORT $$
(☑in USA 609-828-1163, in USA 856-235-5826; www.mayavistabelize.net; Mile 70 Western Hwy; cabañas from BZ$200; P❄🛜) This family-run resort is set on 70 acres of working farm and garden-filled jungle savanna with a killer view of El Castillo in Xunantunich. Eight comfortable cabañas have tiled floors, aircon, private bathrooms with hot showers

and beautiful Maya carvings. Call ahead for pickup or to make sure that someone is there to meet you when you arrive.

Benny's Kitchen   BELIZEAN $
(☑823-2541; Mile 72 Western Hwy; meals BZ$10-18; ⊙8am-9pm Mon-Thu, to 11pm Fri & Sat, to 10pm Sun; 🛜♿) Benny's is a local institution in San José Succotz – the turnoff is opposite the Xunantunich ferry so it's convenient for a post-ruin meal. Local specialties include tangy *escabeche* (spicy chicken with lime and onions), fiery BBQ and cow-foot soup. The semi-open-air dining area has a bar, gift store and children's playground.

ℹ Getting There & Away

All buses between San Ignacio and Benque Viejo de Carmen stop at San José Succotz.

Benque Viejo del Carmen

POP 6700

About a mile from the Guatemalan border and 7 miles from San Ignacio, Benque Viejo del Carmen is a small town with some interesting cultural attractions in the vicinity.

The George Price Hwy passes through, becoming George Price Blvd through town. Most places of interest, including the bus terminal, market, hotels and Centennial Park, are west of the highway and south of the Mopan River.

◎ Sights

Poustinia Land Art Park   SCULPTURE
(☑822-3532; Mile 2.5 Mollejon Rd; admission by appointment only BZ$20) Created and managed by the Ruiz family, this highly unexpected avant-garde sculpture park is one of the hidden artistic gems of Western Belize. Set in 60 acres of rainforest (part of a 270-acre property) about 2 miles southeast of Benque, the park displays some 35 works by Belizean and international artists. Poustinia was conceived as an environmental art project, where, once in place, the exhibits – including a car, greenhouse and some parquet flooring – become subject to the action of nature.

One piece, *Stone Labyrinth,* is set on top of an unexcavated Maya mound with views to Xunantunich. Poustinia is best enjoyed if you have time to contemplate the art and the natural environment it's set in. Allow at least two hours. Buy your admission ticket at the Benque Viejo House of Culture in Benque Viejo del Carmen (if it's the weekend, when House of Culture is closed, call the park directly). The House of Culture can give directions or arrange a taxi (BZ\$25). Otherwise, turn south off George Price Blvd onto unpaved Mollejon Rd (beside the Long Luck Super Store), and drive 2 miles to the park (signposted but hard to spot).

It's possible to camp in the park (BZ\$20) or stay in the Artists Studio (BZ\$60).

Che Chem Ha   CAVE
(✆ 666-5816, 653-0799; chechemha@gmail.com; Mile 8 Mollejon Rd; tour per person BZ\$100) William Morales' dog was busy chasing down a *gibnut* on his lush property one day in 1989, when the dog seemingly disappeared into a rock wall. Morales pressed into the 'wall' and found it was a cave mouth; inside he came upon probably the largest collection of Maya pottery ever discovered. This was Che Chem Ha (Cave of Poisonwood Water). Morales' family has been farming this land since the 1940s, and today they also conduct tours through the cave.

The cave, about 800ft long, was used by the Maya for many centuries for food storage and rituals. Narrow passages wind past ceremonial pots, many of them intact, to a stela at the end of the tunnel. Short ladders enable you to climb up rock ledges. Bring strong shoes, water and a flashlight. There are usually two daily tours lasting about 90 minutes, following an uphill jungle walk of about 30 minutes to the cave mouth.

For cave tours, contact the Morales family directly. If you don't have your own transport, a number of tour operators and lodge-based guides offer this trip, including River Rat Expeditions (p174) and Jungle Splash Tours (p173).

Benque Viejo House of Culture   MUSEUM
(✆ 823-2697; 64 St Joseph St; ⊙ 9am-4pm Mon-Fri) On the southeast corner of Centennial Park, Benque Viejo House of Culture hosts regular traveling exhibits of art and music and provides a space for local artists and musicians to gather and perform. For travelers it's also a de facto tourist office and a good source of local information.

🛏 Sleeping & Eating

Benque Resort & Spa   HOTEL \$
(✆ 632-0688; www.benque-resort.com; 22 Riverside; dm BZ\$40-44, r BZ\$60-100, apt BZ\$200; ❉ 🐾) This three-story home on the south bank

---

ⓘ GETTING TO GUATEMALA: BENQUE VIEJO DEL CARMEN TO MELCHOR DE MENCOS

Getting to the border From San Ignacio *colectivos* run to Benque Viejo del Carmen (BZ\$4 per person, they leave when full). From Benque the same vehicles charge BZ\$2 to the Guatemala border – you can pick these up at the bus stand or simply flag them down on the George Price Hwy through town. There are no public buses to or across the border.

At the border Clear immigration and pay the BZ\$40 departure fee.

Moving On Once you've crossed the border, you'll need to walk about a mile or hop in a taxi to get to the *colectivo* stand in Melchor de Mencos for Q10 (Guatemalan quetzals), from where you can catch a ride to Flores or El Remate.

---

of the Mopan River offers unexpected B&B-type amenities, including beautiful woodwork and colorful tiled bathrooms with hot showers, as well as popular budget dorm accommodations. More expensive rooms have air-con. Call ahead as there is no onsite reception.

Tel-esh   CAFE \$
(✆ 628-5938; Churchill St; meals BZ\$5; ⊙ 8am-4pm; 🐾) This hole-in-the-wall cafe serves up cheap and tasty Belizean dishes, such as chicken, rice and beans, good coffee, fruit drinks and breakfasts.

Boulevard Bar & Grill   AMERICAN \$\$
(✆ 823-2633; 23 George Price Blvd; mains BZ\$10-32; ⊙ 10am-10pm) This open-sided bar and restaurant is a handy refueling pit stop on the highway. The menu is mainly burgers, wings, pizza and pasta.

ⓘ Getting There & Away

Buses depart for San Ignacio (BZ\$2, 30 minutes), Belmopan (BZ\$6, 1½ hours) and Belize City (BZ\$10, 2½ hours) about every half-hour from 7am to 5:30pm (and about every hour on Sunday). The bus terminal is just off the highway.

Colectivos or taxis to the Guatemala border will meet buses, or you can flag them down on the highway.

Southern Belize

POP 78,930

Best Places to Eat

➡ Rumfish (p222)

➡ Jungle Farm Restaurant (p234)

➡ Omar's Creole Grub (p222)

➡ Loggerheads Pub & Grill (p211)

➡ Chef Rob's (p211)

➡ Tuáni Garifuna (p199)

Best Places to Stay

➡ Copal Tree Lodge (p234)

➡ Thatch Caye Resort (p203)

➡ Beaches & Dreams (p210)

➡ Coconut Row Guesthouse (p207)

➡ Tobacco Caye Paradise (p202)

➡ Turtle Inn (p220)

Why Go?

Southern Belize is the country's most absorbing cultural melting pot, with a strong Garifuna influence around Dangriga and Hopkins, and Belize's largest Maya population down in Toledo. Nature is rich here too, where open savanna and citrus-filled farmland give way to forested hills dotted with Maya villages, ruins and national parks primed for adventurous jungle trekking.

The beaches of villagey Hopkins and chilled-out Placencia are inviting, with their opportunities for diving, fishing and slacking, while offshore is an alluring string of cays including Tobacco Caye and Glover's Reef. These are less well known than those in the north but here snorkeling, boating and diving enthusiasts can experience Belize's nautical reef wonders while avoiding the crowds and high costs of the Northern Cayes.

Southern Belize may be off the radar for many but you can't say you've truly seen Belize until you've been down south.

When to Go

Dec–Apr Blue skies and beach weather; high season on the coast.

May–Oct Rainy season but lower occupancy rates and prices (and you can eat lobster starting June 15).

May & Jun Chocolate Festival in Punta Gorda and Lobster Festival in Placencia respectively.

Southern Belize Highlights

1 Placencia (p215)
Eating, drinking, slacking and snorkeling at the mainland 'cay you can drive to.'

2 Mayflower Bocawina National Park (p201) Hiking, ziplining and waterfall rappelling in the jungle.

3 Tobacco Caye (p201) Hanging out on reef with backpackers at Belize's best budget cay.

4 Punta Gorda (p225) Basing yourself in town for explorations into Maya territory in remote Toledo District.

5 Hopkins (p205) Listening to Garifuna drumming under the full moon in this laid-back beach village.

6 Cockscomb Basin Wildlife Sanctuary (p213) Mountain biking or jaguar-spotting on the trails with a Maya guide.

7 Glover's Reef (p204) Kayaking and diving at this wonderfully remote atoll.

❶ Getting There & Away

AIR
Daily flights operate from Belize City (international and municipal airports) to Punta Gorda, via Dangriga and Placencia.

BOAT
Scheduled boat services link Dangriga and Placencia with Puerto Cortés in Honduras, and Punta Gorda with Puerto Barrios and Lívingston in Guatemala.

BUS
Clapped-out buses from Belize City and Belmopan head down the Hummingbird Hwy to Dangriga then on to the Southern Hwy to Independence and Punta Gorda. Less frequent services run from Dangriga to Hopkins and Placencia, and from Punta Gorda to the villages in the far south. Two main companies (James and Ritchie's) operate on the main routes and schedules fluctuate, but they are reasonably frequent and cheap.

CAR & MOTORCYCLE
Two roads connect Southern Belize to the Belize District and Northern Belize: the Hummingbird Hwy (which runs from Belmopan to the start of the Southern Hwy near Dangriga) and the Coastal (Manatee) Hwy, an unpaved road that stretches from the Belize District just south of the zoo to the Hummingbird Hwy west of Dangriga (along the way stretching the very definition of the term 'highway.') Though shorter in terms of miles, unless you're planning to visit Gales Point Manatee on your way down south, the Manatee isn't worth the chiropractic trauma and some hire-car companies prohibit customers traveling on it.

STANN CREEK DISTRICT

POP 42,230

Bordering the Belize District to the north, Cayo to the west and Toledo to the south, the Stann Creek District comprises the coastal towns of Dangriga, Hopkins and Placencia, some of Belize's least-visited cays and the amazing inland protected areas and jungle sanctuaries west of the Southern Hwy.

Dangriga

POP 10,200

Dangriga is the largest town in Southern Belize, and the spiritual capital of the country's Garifuna people. Despite sharing a similar ramshackle appearance and funky coastal vibe with Belize City, Dangriga doesn't have a big-city feel and is generally a safe place to explore. This is a proud, festive town, one that does its best to make the most of its vibrant Garifuna heritage, but apart from a handful of worthwhile cultural sights it's not a tourist hangout like Hopkins or Placencia – most travelers are either changing buses or getting a boat out to the central cays.

The name Dangriga comes from a Garifuna word meaning 'sweet water' – the town's name having been changed from Stann Creek Town in the 1980s. This is the birthplace of *punta* rock (a fusion of acoustic Garifuna and electric instruments), and home to a number of notable Garifuna artists, artisans and festivals.

◉ Sights

Central Dangriga is split by rivers and has the Caribbean coast to its east, but its best sights are a little way west of the town center.

Pen Cayetano Studio Gallery   GALLERY
(📲 628-6807; www.cayetano.de; 3 Aranda Cres; adult/student BZ\$5/3; ⊙ 9am-5pm Mon-Fri, Sat & Sun by appointment) Renowned throughout Belize for his art and music, Pen Cayetano's workshop and gallery displays Garifuna artifacts and crafts. It also has works of art and music by Pen, and the textile artwork of his wife, Ingrid, available for sale. Among the most unique items are drums made of turtle shells, which sell for around BZ\$50.

There are also occasional musical shows by Pen and drum workshops led by local drummers. The gallery is west of town down a small side street.

Gulisi Garifuna Museum   MUSEUM
(📲 669-0639; www.ngcbelize.org; Hummingbird Hwy, Chuluhadiwa Park; BZ\$10; ⊙ 10am-5pm Mon-Fri, 8am-noon Sat) This museum, operated by the National Garifuna Council (NGC), is a must for anyone interested in the vibrant Garifuna people. It brings together artifacts, pictures and documents on Garifuna history and culture, including an exhibit on the life and music of the late Garifuna musician Andy Palacio. A free guided tour is included with admission. The museum is 2 miles out of town; ask any bus heading out of Dangriga to drop you here.

Marie Sharp's Factory   FACTORY
(📲 532-2087; www.mariesharps.bz; 1 Melinda Rd; ⊙ 7am-4pm Mon-Fri) The super-hot bottled sauces that adorn tables all over Belize and beyond are made from habanero peppers here at Marie Sharp's Factory, 8 miles northwest of town on Melinda Rd. Free tours are

usually offered during business hours (by advance reservation), and the factory shop sells hot sauces and jams at outlet prices. If you can't make it to the factory, Marie Sharp's also has a store (p200) in Dangriga.

Drums of Our Father's
Monument   LANDMARK
(George Price Dr) This monument in the traffic circle south of Dangriga's main bus station underscores the importance of percussion in Garifuna (and Belizean) life, with its large bronze representations of ritual dügü drums and *sisira* (maracas). It was sculpted by Stephen Okeke, a Nigerian resident of Dangriga.

🏃 Activities

Belize Kayak Rentals   KAYAKING
(☑ 522-3328, in USA 800-667-1630; www.belize kayaking.com; Magoon St; single/double kayak per day BZ$70/110, per week BZ$420/700) If you want to go it alone on your kayaking expedition, this branch of Island Expeditions rents out kayaks from its base camp in Dangriga. Also offers weekly packages, which include a boat charter out to the cays.

Island Expeditions   WATER SPORTS
(☑ in USA 800-667-1630; www.islandexpeditions. com; Magoon St) 🏄 This ecologically minded Canadian company runs a variety of tours including week-long kayaking expeditions and inland trips, which include hiking in the jungle or visiting Maya ruins. Tours also depart from Belize City.

🎪 Festivals & Events

Garifuna Settlement Day   CULTURAL
On November 19 Dangriga explodes with celebrations to mark the arrival of Garifuna in Dangriga in 1832. Dangrigans living elsewhere flock home for the celebrations. Drumming, dancing and drinking continue right through the night of the 18th to the 19th, while canoes reenact the beach landing in the morning. Book ahead for accommodation.

Día de los Reyes   CULTURAL
(Three Kings' Day) On the nearest weekend to January 6, Dangrigans celebrate Día de los Reyes with the *wanaragua* or *jonkonu* (John Canoe) dance: male dancers wearing bright feather-and-paper headdresses, painted masks representing European men, and rattling bands of shells around their knees move from house to house dancing to Garifuna drums.

🛌 Sleeping

Decent accommodation choices are slim in Dangriga – this is not a holiday town. Book way ahead during festivals.

⭐ D's Hostel   HOSTEL $
(☑ 502-3324; 1 Sharp St; dm/d BZ$25/100; ❅ 🛜) Dangriga's one and only hostel is a local institution, kept in great condition by friendly owner Dana. The 8-bed dorm has individual fans and lockers, while the two spacious private rooms have either two or three double beds, air-con, kitchenette and private bathroom. The inflatable beds are unusual but comfy enough.

This is also the local laundry (bonus!) and the porch looks out to the water. There's a communal kitchen, wi-fi and luggage lockers for guests.

Ruthie's Cabanas   GUESTHOUSE $
(☑ 502-3184; 31 Southern Foreshore; s cabañas BZ$60, additional person BZ$15; 🛜) Ruthie's four tumbledown, seaside, thatched-roof huts on the north side of Havana Creek fit well into the gritty Dangriga mold. Cabañas have hot and cold showers, an earthy Garifuna ambience, plenty of coconut-tree shade and home-cooked meals for an additional charge.

Pelican Beach Resort   RESORT $$
(☑ 522-2044; www.pelicanbeachbelize.com; 1st St; s/d BZ$210/270, ste s/d BZ$260/330; 🅿 ❅ 🛜) The Pelican is the most 'upmarket' choice in Dangriga but still has a faded 1950s air about it. The hotel is on the northern fringe of town, close to the small airport and fronting the Caribbean Sea. Clean but uninspiring rooms come with TV, air-con (some have fans but sea-facing verandas) and colorful local artwork.

The beachside restaurant has a good vibe and sea views, though most of the dishes are pricey for Dangriga.

Chaleanor Hotel   HOTEL $$
(☑ 522-2587; 35 Magoon St; s/d/tr/q with bathroom BZ$126/180/216/248, without bathroom BZ$36/60/80/100; 🅿 ❅ 🛜) This old-style family-run hotel straddles the budget divide with clean air-con rooms of a midrange standard (upstairs rooms have views). The cheaper units without bathroom are fairly run-down but would suit committed budget travelers. The owners can help arrange any trips or boat charters.

Dangriga

0   500 m
0   0.25 miles

5th St
Football Field
6th St
7th St
8th St
9th St
10th St

Benguche Ave

(0.2mi);
Pelican Beach Resort (0.2mi)

Cemetery

CARIBBEAN SEA

Pen Rd
Gumaragu Rd
Sawai St
Yampa St
Front St

Starla Ferry

16

Church St

Melinda Rd

Ball Field

Main Channel

Ecumenical Dr

Coconut Rd

Ramos Rd

Plum St
Commerce St
Court House Rd

Doctor's Alley

14
13

8

Boats to Central Cayes
Captain Doggy's Water Taxi

N Riverside Dr
North Stann Creek
S Riverside Dr

9

Oak St
Chatuye St

11

Alejo Beni Ave

Canal St
Cedar St
St Vincent St

Moho Rd

Madre Cacao Rd

Salmwood Rd

Mahogany Rd

4
3

5

Sylvia Flores St

15
7

Aranda Cres

2

Tubroose St
Magoon St
Sharp St

Dangriga Tourist Information Center

Yemeri Rd

6
10

Southern Regional Hospital (0.4mi);
Gulisi Garifuna Museum (2mi);
Southern & Hummingbird Hwys (5mi)

Mangrove Rd

12

Havana Creek
Havana St

Isla Rd

Stann Creek Valley Rd

Unity St

Dangriga Bus Station

George Price Dr

1

Dangriga

◎ Sights

✦ Activities, Courses & Tours

🛌 Sleeping

✖ Eating

☕ Drinking & Nightlife

🛍 Shopping

Bonefish Hotel   HOTEL **$$**

(📞522-2243; www.bluemarlinlodge.com/bonefish-hotel; 15 Mahogany Rd; r BZ$170-200; P✳🛜) Upper floors are very spacious and not without charm, while the ones on the lower floor are a bit darker and somewhat less cheery, though no less functional. All rooms have two double beds, fan, air-con and cable TV. Breakfast is BZ$20.

✖ Eating

Some of Dangriga's main street restaurants appear a bit run-down, but the food is pretty good and even dodgy-looking streetside shacks on the main drag serve up decent stews, fish, rice and beans, barbecue and Garifuna dishes. Head to the central market for reliably good (and cheap) local food stalls.

Dangriga also has several Asian-run supermarkets as well as Chinese restaurants.

★Tuáni Garifuna   BELIZEAN **$**

(📞502-0287; 1734 Southern Foreshore; BZ$10-25; ⊙7am-10pm; 🛜) Belizean and Garifuna dishes such as *hudut* (fish with plantain in coconut curry), pigtail, fried plantain and stew beans are the specialty at this lovely little

waterfront restaurant and bar. Also good for a local breakfast of fry-jacks and johnnycakes or just a cold beer on a warm evening.

Riverside Café   SEAFOOD **$**

(South Riverside Dr; mains BZ$8-20; ⊙7am-9pm) Just east of the Stann Creek bridge, this cafe is the place to meet fishers and the boat captains who offer tours and transport to the outlying cays. The food is inexpensive, the fish is always fresh and the Belikin is cold.

King Burger   BELIZEAN **$**

(Commerce St; dishes BZ$4-18; ⊙7am-3pm & 6-10pm Mon-Sat) Serves reliably fresh breakfasts of eggs, beans and fry-jacks, as well as hamburgers and plates of fried shrimp. The coffee is instant, but juices are fresh.

Ivy's   CHINESE **$$**

(📞522-3922; Ecumenical Dr; mains BZ$8-25; ⊙10:30am-11pm, ✳) Next to the huge Family City Supermarket west of the center, this reliable Chinese place has a bright air-conditioned dining room and a popular takeout window on the side. Veg dishes, seafood, chow mein and noodle dishes are served in generous portions.

🍸 Drinking & Nightlife

Dangriga's main-street bars and 'cool spots' can get lively, especially during festivals when Garifuna drumming takes center stage but it's mostly a local scene – there are no tourist bars.

Island Breeze Bar & Grill   BAR

(South Riverside Dr; ⊙from 4pm) The location is unbeatable – this open-sided beach bar overlooks the mouth of Stann Creek and the Caribbean Sea. Hours can be unpredictable but it's open most nights, offering drinks, music and bar food such as wings, burgers and quesadillas.

Wadini Shed   BAR

(St Vincent St; ⊙noon-midnight) One thatched roof, no walls and a mainly local Garifuna clientele make this an intriguing spot to have a stout and get down with Dangriga culture.

🔒 Shopping

Dangriga Central Market   MARKET

(behind Doctor's Alley; ⊙6am-5pm) The Dangriga Central Market is a microcosm of Dangriga society with traders selling shoes, clothing, crockery and Maya crafts alongside farmers and fishmongers.

MARIE SHARP, HOT SAUCE MAKER

If there's one thing that defines Belize from a culinary perspective, it's Marie Sharp's hot sauces. On every table in every restaurant and cafe across the country you'll find at least two, maybe three, bottles of Marie's iconic habanero chili sauces. From mild green pepper to eye-watering 'Belizean Heat' and 'No Wimps Allowed', Marie has managed to occupy a national market more successfully than any product since Coca-Cola.

Marie started out in 1980 bottling peppers and preserves from her farm for friends and family. Encouraged by positive feedback and a high demand for good sauce, she went into business and the rest is history. Today, the factory (p196), about 1 mile off the Hummingbird Hwy and 8 miles from Dangriga, offers tastings and sales, and exports sauces and preserves around the world. Even if you curl your tongue at spicy hot sauce, it's a unique opportunity to see a family business that started around a cooking pot and turned into a national institution.

Marie Sharp's Factory Store FOOD
(☑ 522-2370; 3 Pier Rd; ⊘ 8am-noon & 1-5pm Mon-Fri) In an unassuming white building down a lane off the main street, this is Dangriga's outlet store for Marie Sharp's iconic hot sauces.

Austin Rodriguez ART
This master artisan carves Garifuna drums from mahogany, cedar and mayflower wood in his outdoor workshop by the water's edge (southeast of Dangriga Central Market). Though Austin's drums are sold all over Belize, you can buy them straight from the maker himself. Mr Rodriguez can usually be found working away and is happy to talk about the drum-making process.

Family Shopping Center SUPERMARKET
(Ecumenical Dr; ⊘ 8am-9pm Mon-Sat, to noon Sun) Dangriga's best-stocked supermarket also has a bakery and deli.

❶ Information

Immigration Office (☑ 522-3412; St Vincent St; ⊘ 8am-5pm Mon-Thu, to 4:30pm Fri) Offers 30-day visa extension stamps for BZ$50.

Tourist Information Center (Mahogany Rd; ⊘ 9am-noon & 1:30-5pm Mon-Fri, closed Wed afternoon)

❶ Getting There & Away

AIR
From Dangriga airport (DGA), **Maya Island Air** (☑ 522-2659; www.mayaislandair.com) and **Tropic Air** (☑ 226-2012; www.tropicair.com) fly direct to Belize City, Placencia and Punta Gorda several times daily.

BOAT
Starla Ferry (☑ 628-0976) between Belize City and Puerto Cortes (Honduras) stops at the main boat dock in Dangriga at 11am every Friday, departing at noon (BZ$120).

Dangriga is the departure point for trips to Belize's central cays, as well as for chartered trips up and down the coast. The best spot to arrange boat transport is just outside the Riverside Café on South Riverside Dr. Stop by before 9am, or the afternoon before, to check when boats will be leaving. The more people you can get for one trip (within reason), the cheaper it works out per person.

Boats usually go daily to Tobacco Caye (BZ$40 per person) but can also be chartered to Thatch Caye, South Water Caye and Glover's Reef. The upmarket lodges on these islands will also organize a boat for you but check if it's included with your accommodation; if not, it's cheaper to charter from the boatmen here.

The colorful Captain Doggy's 25ft **boat** (☑ 627-7443; captaindoggy@gmail.com) travels between Dangriga and all of the cays. He also does custom day trips with spearfishing, island stops and lunch for BZ$100.

BUS
A major transit point for all bus companies servicing Southern Belize, Dangriga's main **bus station** (Havana St) is near the roundabout at the southern end of town. There are frequent buses to Belize City (regular/express BZ$12/14, two hours), Belmopan (BZ$8, 1½ hours), Punta Gorda (BZ$14, 2½ hours) and San Ignacio (BZ$12, 2¼ hours), and a handful of direct services to Hopkins (BZ$5, 30 minutes) and Placencia (BZ$10, 1½ hours).

Mayflower Bocawina National Park

Easily reached from Hopkins or Dangriga, this beautiful 11-sq-mile park offers high-adrenaline adventure activities or plain old-fashioned DIY jungle hiking to mountains, waterfalls, swimming holes and small Maya sites. It's remote enough that you might find yourself alone (apart from the birdlife) on some spectacular walking trails.

◉ Sights & Activities

Mayflower Bocawina National Park   NATIONAL PARK

(BZ$10; ⊙6am-9pm) This beautiful 11-sq-mile park of jungle, mountains, waterfalls, walking trails, swimming holes and small Maya sites is located about 16 miles southwest of Dangriga and 12 miles northwest of Hopkins. The walks here are at least as good as the trails most people do at nearby Cockscomb Basin, and you'll encounter far fewer tourists. You will see lots of birds, and the park is home to troops of black howler monkeys.

A 4-mile unpaved access road heads west from the Southern Hwy, 2 miles north of Silk Grass village, to the park **visitors center** (⊙6am-5pm), where you pay the park fees. Rangers will happily explain the walks and show you a map. Here you'll also find the partly excavated **Mayflower Maya site**, with two pyramids and nine other structures, occupied in the late 9th and early 10th centuries. The **Antelope Trail** leads down over Silk Grass Creek to the larger, unexcavated, partly tree-covered **Maintzunun temple mound**, 250yd away (built around AD 800). Continue on a further 1.7 miles – steep and strenuous in places with steps – to the beautiful 100ft-high **Antelope Falls**, with great panoramas. There's a further rope-assisted climb to the top of the falls.

The less demanding **Bocawina Hill Trail** (1.4 miles) leads to the lower and upper **Bocawina Falls**: there's a cool swimming pool at the foot of the 50ft upper falls. Branch trails, for which a guide is recommended, lead to **Peck Falls** and **Big Drop Falls**.

Bocawina Adventures   ADVENTURE

(📋670-8019; www.bocawinaadventures.com) At the Mayflower Bocawina National Park this outfit, based at the Rainforest Resort, features Belize's longest zipline (BZ$130), and rappelling down either the 1500ft/457m Antelope Falls (BZ$250) or the smaller 125ft/38m Bocawina Falls (BZ$130). Also available are hiking, birdwatching tours, night flying (ziplining at night) or combination packages.

🛏 Sleeping & Eating

Bocawina Rainforest Resort   RESORT $$$

(📋670-8019, in USA 1-844-894-2311; www.bocawina.com; d BZ$238, cabañas BZ$358, ste BZ$438; P🕈) ✐ Within Mayflower Bocawina National Park, this ecoresort is the base for some of the most exciting adventure activities in Southern Belize. Accommodation ranges from six lodge rooms with timber floors and mountain views, to traditional thatch cabañas and spacious suites with separate lounge and jungle views. All have hot showers and wi-fi, and breakfast is included.

Wild Fig Restaurant   CAFE $$

(📋670-8019; BZ$8-25; ⊙6am-10pm; 🕈) This casual screened-in thatch restaurant and bar on the grounds of Bocawina Rainforest Resort is a good place to stop for lunch after walking in the national park or rappelling down local waterfalls. Lunch features tacos, burgers and sandwiches, while dinner is a changing menu of Belizean, Creole and BBQ grill dishes using locally sourced ingredients. Bar snacks and drinks are available in between lunch and dinner hours.

❶ Getting There & Away

Day tours to the park can be arranged from Hopkins or Maya Center. A taxi from Dangriga is about BZ$60 (one-way). Guests at the Rainforest Resort can arrange a pickup from Belize City, the airport, Dangriga, Hopkins or Placencia for a fee.

Central Cayes

Less crowded, lesser known and often less expensive than the cays in the north, the Central Cayes – most of them private islands – off Belize's central coast are smack in the middle of some of the country's most amazing diving, snorkeling and fishing sites.

❶ Getting There & Away

In most cases the resorts will arrange boat transfers. The central cays are best reached from Dangriga, but charters also run from Hopkins and Placencia.

Tobacco Caye

Sitting right on the barrier reef, 12 miles from Dangriga, tiny Tobacco Caye is the budget destination among the central cays, relative to other resort islands of course. It shows in the fairly basic array of cabañas and lodge rooms, but the setting and the surrounding azure waters are still dreamy. Mainly composed of sand, palm trees and guesthouses, just 200yd long and 100yd wide, the cay can be circumnavigated in 10 minutes.

Part of the South Water Caye Marine Reserve, Tobacco Caye is a fabulous place for snorkeling, diving, fishing or hanging out on a hammock. Sociable and friendly, it's ideal for travelers on a limited budget looking for that *Gilligan's Island* experience.

🛏 Sleeping & Eating

There are half a dozen places to stay on the island and it's best not to just show up looking for a bed, even in low season; book ahead.

Meal packages are available and obligatory at most lodgings, or you can usually dine at Reef's End Lodge restaurant. There's a small kiosk but no supermarkets, so bring your own snacks and alcohol from Dangriga.

Fairweather Place   HOTEL $
(☑ 660-6870, 802-0030; per person BZ$60) The cheapest of the Tobacco Caye guesthouses, Fairweather has four basic rooms in a rickety wooden building, each with one double bed and fan. There's a shared bathroom with a cold-water shower, and a sea-facing porch with a couple of chairs and hammocks out the front. The 1st-floor kitchen is open for use by guests; bring supplies.

Tobacco Caye Paradise   CABIN $$
(☑ 532-2101; www.tobaccocaye.com; d cabañas incl meals BZ$160; 🕸) This is the most romantic deal on Tobacco with the only overwater bungalows on the island. Paradise has six brightly painted cabañas perched on stilts over the water with private baths and cold-water showers. Verandas, with chairs and hammocks, look out towards the reef where the water is shallow enough to wade in.

Meal plan (breakfast, lunch and dinner) is mandatory, so the minimum rate per couple per night is BZ$320 (plus tax). Snorkeling gear and kayaks can be rented here.

Joe Jo's by the Reef   CABIN $$
(☑ 601-1647; www.joejosbythereef.com; r per person BZ$130, cabañas per person BZ$170-200, all incl meals; 🕸) Joe Jo's has the smartest and best-built bungalows on the island. The seven lemon-yellow cabins come with private bathroom, fans, balcony deck and, in most cases, clear ocean views. There are four more rooms just back from the beach in the main building. Hot and cold water, free wi-fi, kayak rental, transfer and three meals a day included.

Reef's End Lodge   LODGE $$
(☑ 676-8363; www.reefsendlodge.com; 3-night s/d BZ$600/860, beachfront cabañas BZ$695/995; 🕸) Situated at the south end of the island, Reef's End has lodge-style rooms plus a couple of beachfront ramshackle cabañas, available on all-inclusive packages for a minimum of three nights. It's pretty simple stuff for the price, but the overwater restaurant is the best on the island and the only dive shop is here. May close in the low season.

Windward Lodge   RESORT $$
(☑ 532-2033; www.tclodgebelize.com; r per person incl meals BZ$140; 🕸) This turquoise-green waterfront place (formerly Tobacco Caye Lodge) has six simple but clean, fairly spacious beach-facing rooms with private bathrooms, fans and inviting verandas. There's generator power in the evenings.

ℹ Getting There & Away

Boat transfers operate out of Dangriga every morning (BZ$40 per person), or ask your accommodation to arrange transport.

South Water Caye

Three times as big as Tobacco Caye, but with half as many resorts, the 15-acre South Water Caye has excellent sandy beaches and an interesting combination of palm and pine trees. Like Tobacco Caye, it's part of the South Water Caye Marine Reserve. A seemingly bottomless 8-mile-long underwater cliff on the ocean side of the reef makes for excellent wall-diving, usually with good visibility, and there's a dive resort on the island. Snorkelers will find healthy coral reefs in the lagoon. Trips to Belize's offshore atolls are possible from here and there's excellent fishing, too.

Bring insect repellent; the sand flies are voracious.

🛏 Sleeping & Eating

⭐**Pelican Beach Resort**   CABIN $$$
(☑ 522-2044; www.pelicanbeachbelize.com; s/d incl meals BZ$620/820, s/d cottages incl meals BZ$770/950; 🕸) 🍃 The solar-powered Pelican's eight comfortable wooden cottages at the south of the island are well spaced among the palms, giving a feeling of seclusion. Heron's Hideaway is the pick of the bunch, with a big porch and two hammocks looking out to the reef.

ⓘ THE CAY THAT'S RIGHT FOR YOU

Tobacco Caye

Pros Cheapest of the southern cays to get to and stay on. You'll never be lonely on Tobacco Caye and it won't bust your budget.

Cons With half a dozen accommodations in a small space, Tobacco can feel a bit cramped and cheap. Also, the coral around the island isn't as healthy as it once was.

South Water Caye

Pros Excellent diving and snorkeling opportunities and great space-to-resort ratio make this a good choice for visitors looking for a sublime island experience.

Cons Lack of cheap accommodations keeps South Water Caye off-limits to travelers on a budget.

Thatch Caye & Plum Caye

Pros Beautiful and ecofriendly, Thatch Caye is a good choice for honeymooners and families looking for exclusive luxury with a low carbon footprint.

Cons It's not cheap, and with only one resort on the island (plus neighboring Coco Plum), Thatch might not be the best place for singles looking to mingle.

Glover's Reef

Pros The best of both worlds, Glover's is surrounded by amazing coral, provides access to good dive sites, and the resorts along the atoll offer the full spectrum accommodations.

Cons The boat ride out takes between 1½ and three hours. Glover's remoteness makes it a less-than-ideal choice for those looking to spend just a couple of days – most packages are a minimum of one week.

Blue Marlin Lodge RESORT **$$$**
(☑ 522-2242, in USA 800-798-1558; www.blue marlinlodge.com; r & cabañas BZ$950-1200, 3-night all-inclusive per person BZ$2000-2350; ❀ ☎) At the northern end of South Water Caye, Blue Marlin is a popular dive destination with its own full-service PADI dive center. The resort has a series of cabañas and rather odd (but cool-looking) igloo-shaped 'dome cottages,' as well as free kayaks and an excellent overwater restaurant serving fresh seafood. Nonguests should call ahead for dining reservations.

The complicated rate sheet published on its website gives the lowdown on the dozens of offered packages, including longer stays, meals, transits and diving. The Dangriga office is at the Bonefish Hotel (p199).

IZE South Water Caye RESORT, CABIN **$$$**
(☑ 580-2000, in USA 1-508-655-1461; www.izebelize. com; s/d BZ$420/840, packages per person per night from BZ$350; ☎) Massachusetts-based IZE (International Zoological Expeditions) operates this site in the middle of the island with dorms (primarily for students) and beautiful, spacious log-cabin shoreline cottages for other guests. The main building incorporates a field station, an attractive wood-furnished dining room and bar.

The basic package (minimum three nights) includes meals, transfers to/from Dangriga, snorkeling and sightseeing boat trips, as well as use of kayaks and sports equipment.

Thatch Caye & Plum Caye

Thatch Caye, and neighboring Plum Caye, are stunning twin private islands with an air of exclusivity and a luxury-meets-castaway, sand-between-the-toes vibe.

Activities on offer at the resorts include swimming, diving, snorkeling, fishing and kayaking, or just hanging out on the islands' white sands.

🛏 Sleeping & Eating

★ **Thatch Caye Resort** RESORT **$$$**
(☑ 603-2414, 1-800-435-3145; www.thatchcaye belize.com; cabañas or bungalows BZ$400-790, overwater bungalows BZ$950; ❀ ☎ ✉) ✆ The most luxurious of the South Caye private island resorts, Thatch Caye has 13 beautiful thatched-roof, air-conditioned cabañas and overwater bungalows built from local hardwoods and

set on stilts, connected by paths winding through native mangroves. The resort features an excellent social-hub bar-restaurant (add BZ$300 per person for all-inclusive package), the overwater Starfish Bar and a dazzling array of activities.

For all its luxury, Thatch has a strong eco philosophy with power generated from solar and wind sources, with a single diesel generator kept as backup. Wi-fi is available only in the common lounge. Nonguests can dine here with 24 hours' notice.

Coco Plum Island Resort   CABIN $$$
(☑1-800-763-7360;   www.cocoplumcay.com; 4-night package incl meals & drinks per person BZ$3080-3680; ❋🐾🛜) Coco Plum is the laidback, but still luxurious little sister to flashy Thatch Caye, just a Frisbee throw away – you can wade across at low tide. The colorful Caribbean-style cabañas offer air-conditioning and sea views. All packages – and there are many variations from honeymoon to diving adventures – include meals, drinks, full use of the private island and transportation from Dangriga.

Glover's Reef

If you're serious about getting away from it all, Glover's Reef is the place. Named after the 18th-century English pirate John Glover (who attacked Spanish merchant ships from here), the atoll is 16 miles long and 7 miles wide, and is pretty much as far from mainland Belize as you can get. Lying like a string of pearls in a blue sea, Glover's consists of half a dozen small cays of white sand, palm trees, and a handful of low-key resorts, diving and kayaking bases.

Despite the remote location, weekly packages including transport make Glover's an affordable getaway.

🕴 Activities

The reef's unique position atop a submerged mountain ridge on the edge of the continental shelf makes it home to some of the world's finest dive sites. As a protected marine reserve, guests at all resorts pay a park fee of BZ$30 per week.

Diving & Snorkeling

Divers here regularly see spotted eagle rays, southern stingrays, turtles, moray eels, dolphins, several shark species, large groupers, barracudas and many tropical reef fish. In the shallow central lagoon, 700 coral patches

brim with marine life – brilliant for snorkelers. Turtles lay eggs on the beaches between June and August. Glover's Reef is included in the Belize Barrier Reef World Heritage listing, and it's also a marine reserve with a no-take zone covering most of the southern third of the atoll.

Kayaking & Fishing

All resorts rent sea kayaks and fishing gear.

Slickrock Adventures   WATER SPORTS
(☑in USA 800-390-5715; www.slickrock.com; 5-/6-/9-night package US$1525/1675/2425) These top-class water-sports holidays are based on Long Caye, Glover's Reef, and combine sea kayaking, surf kayaking, windsurfing, snorkeling and diving. Accommodations are in stilt cabañas (cabins), and packages include all meals and drinks.

🛏 Sleeping & Eating

Resorts have restaurants and meals are usually included in the package. For snacks and alcohol, stock up on the mainland.

★**Glover's Atoll Resort**   CABIN $
(☑532-2916; www.glovers.com.bz; per person per week campsite BZ$298, dm BZ$398, cabins BZ$498-698; 🛜🖥) Occupying the Glover's northeast cay, this little backpackers' island paradise is the perfect, affordable island getaway. The private 10-acre island has 16 cabins (overwater and on the beach), a basic dorm and eight private campgrounds. Most travelers take the weekly deal, which includes boat transfers from Sittee River, but nightly 'drop-in' rates are also available, starting from BZ$24 for camping.

There's an open-air thatched restaurant (breakfast/lunch/dinner BZ$24/24/36), or you can make your own meals – a few basic groceries plus fish, lobster and conch are available on the island, but the rest (including any alcohol) you must bring over yourself. Activities on the island include a PADI dive center, snorkeling, kayaking, catamarans and fishing, all at an additional cost. The free transfer leaves from Glover's Guest House (p212) in Sittee River at 9am every Sunday, returning the following Saturday, or you can charter a boat for BZ$700 one-way (up to four people) from Sittee River or Dangriga.

Off the Wall   RESORT $$$
(☑532-2929; www.offthewallbelize.com; Long Caye; per person per week from BZ$3200; 🛜) 🐾 On beautiful Long Caye, close to the reef, solar- and wind-powered Off the Wall is a small and

SOUTHERN BELIZE CENTRAL CAYES

intimate PADI five-star island resort offering a variety of weeklong packages. Rates include meals and non-alcoholic drinks, use of kayaks and stand-up paddleboards, a couple of snorkeling trips and transfer. Scuba diving and gear rental (for diving, fishing or snorkeling) are extra.

The five cozy oceanfront cabañas come with queen-size beds with Egyptian high-thread-count linens, verandas and hammocks. Other touches include yoga mats, and the owners strive to make this a personalized and intimate island experience. Boat transfers are from Dangriga every Saturday.

Isla Marisol Resort   RESORT $$$

(☑ 532-2399, 610-4204, in USA 866-990-9904; www.islamarisolresort.com; cabañas 3-/4-/7-night per person incl meals BZ$1750/2150/3250; ❄ ☎) The atoll's 18-acre southernmost island (called Usher Caye by some) is home to Glover's most upscale resort. Eleven sturdy and comfortably furnished wooden cabins with zinc roofs, hot showers, fans and air-conditioners are laid out along the island, while two family-size reef houses provide accommodations for six closer to the water.

There's also an excellent restaurant and a bar on stilts over the water. Prices include boat transfers to and from Dangriga, with boats running on Wednesday and Saturday. Activities at Marisol include snorkeling, kayaking, sunbathing, fishing and, of course, diving.

ⓘ Getting There & Away

Most travelers reach Glover's on a scheduled resort transfer or a dive boat, but you can charter a boat from Dangriga, Hopkins or Placencia for around BZ$450 one way. The trip takes anywhere from 1½ to three hours.

Hopkins

POP 1500

The friendly, slightly scruffy, coastal village of Hopkins attracts travelers looking to soak up sea breezes and Garifuna culture. It's an unpretentious place to meet other travelers or satisfied expats and makes a good base for explorations to the cays, reefs and islands to the east, and the jungles, mountains and parks to the west.

Hopkins was founded in 1942 by people from Newtown, a nearby Garifuna settlement that was destroyed by a hurricane. The village is named for Frederick Charles Hopkins, a Catholic priest who (perhaps as a cautionary tale to future travelers) drowned in the waters here in 1923. These days there's a vibrant Garifuna population in Hopkins but also a growing North American expat community.

Hopkins stretches about 1.5 miles along the coast and is divided by the 4.5 mile sealed Hopkins Rd from the Southern Hwy into North Side and South Side.

🏃 Activities

Hopkins is a fine place from which to access some of Belize's best dive sites. The barrier reef is less than a 40-minute boat ride away, and Glover's Reef is about 90 minutes on a fast skiff. Diving and snorkeling can be arranged through several outfits in Hopkins and nearby Sittee Point.

Lebeha   COURSE

(☑ 650-2318; Front St, North Side; lessons per person per hour BZ$20) Local Garifuna drummer Jabbar Lambey and his wife Dorothy run Lebeha both as an educational and cultural center for locals and as a general happening spot for travelers interested in Garifuna drumming. Lessons for individuals and groups are available, and there's drumming most nights from 7pm. Full-moon drumming parties are an especially great reason to visit.

Dum Bei Yurumein   MUSIC

(☑ 608-6592, 665-6291; Front St, North Side; drumming lessons per hour US$20) Garifuna drumming lessons from a local musician. Call into Blossoming Gift Shop to make a booking.

Outback Trails   HORSEBACK RIDING

(☑ 650-9083; www.outbacktrails.com; Mile 13 Southern Hwy, Kendal; ⊙ trail rides 8:30am & 2pm) Trail rides head out from this friendly ranch through the forest and make a stop at the Sittee River. Suitable for riders of all abilities from seven years old. It's just off the Southern Hwy about 10 miles from Hopkins.

Under the Sun   BOATING

(☑ in USA 970-270-3556; www.underthesunbelize. com; 8-day trip per person BZ$4400) The Lodge Hopper's Special is an outstanding eight days of Caribbean cruising on an 18ft Hobie Cat, with plenty of stops for snorkeling, fishing, kayaking and hammocking. Instruction is provided for novice sailors. Accommodations in lodges on the cays, food, guide and support boat are all included in the price.

Putt-in-Belize   MINIGOLF

(☑ 523-7249; Main St, South Side; 9-hole/unlimited play BZ$6/10; ⊙ 1-10pm Mon-Wed & Fri-Sat) It's fun to spend an hour or two at this homemade

Hopkins & Sittee Point

SOUTHERN BELIZE HOPKINS

Hopkins & Sittee Point

minigolf course at Windschief bar – it's flood-lit after dark. Occasional tournaments attract locals and expats.

⟲ Tours

Routes & Roots Tours ADVENTURE
(☑ 672-7218; www.belizerootstours.com; South Side; tours BZ$110-350) As the name suggest Routes & Roots offers a range of adventure and cultural tours from cave tubing and birding to chocolate making.

Happy Go Luckie Tours BOATING
(☑ 635-0967; www.hgltours.com; South Side; half-/full-day charters BZ$470/700) Happy Go Luckie offers custom half- and full-day boat charters for up to five people, including snorkeling, fishing and island-hopping. Also does transfers to the southern cays and Glover's Reef. The office is in Hopkins village but the boats leave from Sittee Point marina.

Seemore Adventures DIVING, SNORKELING
(☑ 602-4985, 667-6626; www.seemoreadventures. com; Main St, South Side; half-/full-day snorkeling BZ$160/200, 2-/3-tank dive BZ$320/400; ⊙ 7am-6pm) Run by local dive instructor Elmar 'Boo' Avila, Seemore offers customized snorkeling, fishing or just cruisey trips out to the reef, as well as scuba-diving trips.

Motorbike Rentals &
Alternate Adventures TOURS
(☑ 665-6292; www.alternateadventures.com; Main St, South Side; ⊙ 8am-5pm) MR&AA rents 200cc dirt bikes (BZ$118 per day, BZ $598 per week) and 250cc cruiser motorcycles (BZ$150 per day, BZ$750 per week) for self-guided motorcycle touring. The owners offers helpful suggestions for independent-minded travelers.

Hopkins Kulcha Tours TOURS
(☑ 661-8199; www.hopkinskulchatours.weebly.com; South Side; tours BZ$110-300) Charlton Castillo will take you birdwatching, hiking or on a tour of Maya ruins. Tours explore Stann Creek, Cayo and beyond.

Lloyd Nunez FISHING
(☑ 603-2970, 662-0873) Lloyd is a professional fly-fisherman who leads expeditions into both the inner and outer cays.

🛌 Sleeping

Guesthouses and hotels are spread out along the main street and the beaches north and south of the main road into the village. More upmarket lodges are further south in Sittee Point.

★Funky Dodo HOSTEL $
(☑ 676-3636; www.funkydodo.bz; Main St, South Side; d with bathroom BZ$69-86, dm/d without bathroom BZ$25/57; ☜) Hopkins' only hostel is indeed a funky place, with a tightly packed village of rustic timber cabin rooms and dorms inhabiting a leafy garden. Backpackers swing in hammocks reading books, while others roll out yoga mats. The best rooms are the upper level Tree Top rooms with their own deck. There's also a communal kitchen, tour desk and bike hire.

Kismet Inn & Cafe GUESTHOUSE $
(☑ 651-9368; www.kismetinn.net; Front St, North Side; camping BZ$10, dm BZ$30, r BZ$60-90, cabañas BZ$110) On a secluded patch of beach amid shady palms at the north end of Hopkins village, Kismet is an eccentric collection of rough-hewn cabañas and rooms designed, built and run by passionate owner Tricia. The array of rooms and communal areas, including a library and veg cafe, are quirky to say the least, but the beachfront location is a bargain.

Lebeha CABIN $
(☑ 650-2318, 665-9305; www.hopkinscabanas.com; Front St, North Side; cabañas BZ$30, cabins BZ$50-100; ☜) You'll get a warm welcome at these very basic North Side cabins attached to a Garifuna drumming school.

Windschief Cabanas CABIN $
(☑ 523-7249; www.windschief.com; Main St, South Side; small/large cabañas BZ$70/95; P ☜) There are just two basic, but comfy stilted cabanas (fan only) with private bathrooms and hot showers here in this seafront location. Oliver and Pamela's beachfront bar is a popular spot for expats and Oliver, a keen golfer and windsurfer, has constructed a neat little minigolf course.

Castillo Beach CAMPGROUND $
(☑ 660-2413; per tent BZ$15) You can pitch a tent on this bit of beach in front of a private residence between Hopkins and Sittee Point. Shared bathrooms and canoes available. Parties and events are held here in season.

★Coconut Row
Guesthouse GUESTHOUSE $$
(☑ 675-3000, in USA 518-658-3677; www.coconut rowbelize.com; Front St; d BZ$210-230, cabins BZ$230-250, apt BZ$280-300; P ☀ ☜) The colorfully painted Coconut Row boasts some of the finest beachfront rooms in Hopkins. The five main rooms are spacious and

spotless, and come with air-conditioning, fridge and coffee-maker and king-sized beds, while two of them are full two-bedroom apartments. In the adjoining property are three excellent free-standing beachfront log cabins. The latest addition is the Coconut Husk restaurant.

Whitehorse Inn
GUESTHOUSE $$

(2 651-7961; www.whitehorseguesthouse.com; Main St, South Side; r BZ$120-180, bungalows BZ$200; ❄ 🤝) This plush new beachfront guesthouse brings a level of space and comfort at a price that's probably unmatched elsewhere in Hopkins. The four rooms in the main house and two free-standing sea-facing cabañas are warmly furnished, air-con cooled and fitted with mini kitchens (fridge, microwave) and TV. Stay a week and get a night free. Highly recommended.

Buttonwood Lodge
GUESTHOUSE $$

(2 675-3000; Front St, North Side; r BZ$250-280, 2-bed apt BZ$270; ❄ 🤝) The four spacious suites and one two-bedroom self-contained apartment at Buttonwood all face the sea. This is high-quality boutique accommodation located at the North Side of town and run by the same folks at Coconut Grove. The superb rooftop deck has some of the best views in Hopkins.

All Seasons Guest House
GUESTHOUSE $$

(2 523-7209; www.allseasonsbelize.bz; Main St, South Side; r BZ$130-170, cabañas BZ$218-238; P ❄ 🤝) With its brightly painted two-bedroom cabañas and cozy guesthouse rooms, All Seasons has some of the cutest accommodations in the village. All rooms have air-con, coffee-makers and hot showers. There's a great patio out front with a grill and picnic area. The location is good, at the south end of town and a short walk to the beach.

Tipple Tree Beya
HOTEL $$

(2 615-7006; www.tippletreebelize.com; Main St, South Side; r BZ$90-110, 1-/2-bedroom apt BZ$206/350; 🤝) 🏖 This sturdy wooden beachside place features three cozy, clean, fan-cooled rooms sharing a sociable veranda beneath the owner's quarters upstairs. In an adjacent building are some excellent self-contained apartments that would suit a family or group. The owner implements a number of sustainable practices including composting, recycling and keeping the place as energy efficient as possible.

Latitude 17
CABAÑAS $$

(2 665-9929; www.latitude17.com; Main St; r/cabañas BZ$118/178; ❄ 🤝) This central pair of aqua-blue two-room cabañas are super comfortable and great value with living area, full country-style kitchen and separate bedroom. There are also two air-con rooms that are even easier on the budget. Cabañas and rooms have either a private deck or porch.

Latitude Adjustment
CABAÑAS $$

(2 670-1705; www.latitudeadjustment.bz; North Side; d BZ$210; 🤝 ❄) A block west of the main street, the five raised timber cabins here are beautifully finished with dark-wood interiors, king-size beds, kitchenettes, cable TV and immaculate bathrooms. The units orbit a small saltwater pool and there are security cameras and laundry facilities onsite.

Jungle Jeanie by the Sea
CABIN $$

(2 533-7047; www.junglejeaniebeachcabanas.com; Sittee River Rd; d cabañas BZ$120-240; 🤝) 🏖 About a 10-minute walk south of Hopkins village, Jungle Jeanie is a neat little ecoresort with beautiful hardwood single and duplex cabins on stilts, some with sea views and easy beach access. This is a place where serenity meets spirituality meets action – there's a yoga *shala* (studio) with regular classes (BZ$10), but also kitesurfing, kayaks and stand-up paddleboards for rent.

Hopkins Inn
HOTEL $$

(2 665-0411; www.hopkinsinn.bz; Main St, South Side; cabañas incl breakfast BZ$185-260; P 🤝) The four stylish and spacious cabañas (cabins) here are in a good location right by the beach. Owners also supply a hearty breakfast of fresh breads, fruit and johnnycakes.

Hopkins Bay Resort
RESORT $$$

(2 523-7284; www.hopkinsbaybelize.com; Front St, North Side; 1-/2-/3-bedroom villas incl breakfast BZ$500/890/1180; P ❄ 🤝 ❄) This flashy resort at the far northern end of Hopkins feels worlds away from the village life with two pools, an absolute beachfront position and luxurious villas. Take out a free kayak or relax under the Rum Shack, an inviting sea-facing *palapa* bar and restaurant. Significant discounts are available off-season or with promo rates.

🍴 Eating

Hopkins has a surprisingly good range of traveler-oriented restaurants and local Garifuna and Creole food shacks, mostly in the budget and midrange categories.

Kat's Coffee   CAFE $
(Main St, South Side; mains BZ$5-9, coffee BZ$2.50-5; ⊙7am-6pm; 🐕) Top spot for breakfast, this tiny main street shack offers bagels, fruit cups packed with granola and yogurt, smoothies, juices and, of course, filter and espresso coffee.

Jalapeno's BBQ & Grill   INTERNATIONAL $
(📷 671-3667; Main St; mains BZ$5-26; ⊙10am-9pm Fri-Tue; 🐕) In a prime corner position on Hopkin's main intersection, Jalapeno's does things a little differently, specializing in fluffy crepes (from BZ$5 plus fillings) and weekend specials of smoked brisket and pork ribs. The rest of the menu is standard burgers, pastas and salads and the bar is well stocked.

Sandy Beach Bar & Restaurant   GARIFUNA $
(📷 650-9183; South Side beachfront; meals BZ$10-15; ⊙11am-9pm Mon-Sat) The ladies of the Sandy Beach Women's Cooperative serve up daily Garifuna specials such as *hudut*, stew chicken, and rice and beans. It's also a cool beachfront bar.

Thongs Cafe   CAFE $$
(Main St; mains BZ$10-23; ⊙7am-3pm; 🐕) This cute Caribbean-meets-Euro-style cafe is a cool spot for breakfast or a light lunch of salad, wraps and specials such as quesadillas or meatballs. Smoothies are good – if you're detoxing try the Green Fusion with spinach, cucumber and pineapple. Service can be slow, so browse the gift shop with designer T-shirts and vintage clothing while you wait.

Gecko's   BELIZEAN $$
(📷 629-5411; Main St, North Side; mains BZ$15-30; ⊙noon-9pm Mon & Wed-Sat; 🐕📷) Gecko's gets ticks for cheap tacos; vegetarian, vegan and gluten-free dishes; an interesting range of specials and a breezy open-air dining space and bar just north of the main intersection.

Peer's Place   INTERNATIONAL $$
(📷 661-8768; Main St, South Side; mains BZ$15-29; ⊙4-10pm Sat-Wed) Peer's Place has a European flair with fresh seafood dishes, pasta, schnitzels, pork chops and some intriguing desserts such as chocolate chili cake. A good option for a relaxed but ambient dinner on the breezy open-air deck.

🍷 **Drinking & Nightlife**

Garifuna drumming and singing can be heard most nights in season. Tuesday is the big night at Driftwood Beach Bar – ask around for the action on other nights.

Hopkins has a few good beach bars that attract travelers, expats and locals.

⭐ **Driftwood Beach Bar**   BAR, LIVE MUSIC
(North Side; ⊙10am-10pm Thu-Tue, to midnight Sat & Tue) Ever-popular Driftwood has moved closer to the center of the village but still has a great beachfront location, Hopkins' best drumming nights and pizza (from BZ$16) and tacos (BZ$10). This is a popular social hub and party place: Tuesday is the big night with Garifuna drumming, but there are also weekend events and beach BBQs.

Windschief   BAR
(📷 523-7249; Main St, South Side; ⊙1-10pm Mon-Wed & Fri-Sat; 🐕) The small bar at this local beachfront place is one of the best spots in the village to meet expats and visitors. It serves light snacks, such as burgers and nachos, and there's a minigolf course out front.

Herbal Healer Tea Bar   TEAHOUSE
(📷 663-7218; South Side; ⊙8am-6pm) With 22 types of homegrown tea, smoothies, juices and even homemade wine (tea and drinks BZ$4 to BZ$12), this is a zen place to nurse a cuppa. There's a gift shop with herbal remedies and an organic garden out the back.

☆ **Entertainment**

Lebeha   LIVE MUSIC
(📷 608-3143; Main St, North Side; BZ$10) This drumming center is one of the coolest spots in Hopkins to be on any given evening from about 7pm, when local Garifuna drummer Jabbar Lambey hosts drum-ins for friends, students and travelers alike. Drop in during the day to see what's going on.

🔒 **Shopping**

Garimaya Gift Shop & Gallery   ARTS & CRAFTS
(📷 666-7970; Main St, South Side; ⊙8am-6pm) This excellent gallery and craft display is a one-stop shop for arts, crafts and souvenirs from the local area and all over Belize. Fabulous displays of wood carving, paintings, jewelry, textiles, drums and products such as hot sauces make it well worth a browse.

Sew Much Hemp   ARTS & CRAFTS
(📷 668-6550; ⊙daylight hours) Between Hopkins and Sittee Point, follow the signs toward the beach and stop at the old bus. This is Sew Much Hemp, a classic hippie outpost where Barbara makes and sells bags and clothing from hemp, as well as concocting various

balms, bug repellents and healers from natural ingredients including hemp oil, beeswax and citronella.

ⓘ Information

There's a solitary **Belize Bank ATM** (Main St; ⊙24hr) at the main intersection in the town center. If it's out of action the nearest banks are in Dangriga.

ⓘ Getting There & Away

There are two daily buses from Hopkins to Dangriga (BZ$5, 30 minutes) and Placencia (BZ$5, one hour). Many travelers hitch or take a taxi (BZ$20) the 4 miles to the Southern Hwy junction and pick up any passing bus going north or south from there. A taxi to Hopkins from Dangriga costs BZ$80.

ⓘ Getting Around

Hopkins is walkable but it's well spread out from north to south and it helps to have some form of wheels. You can rent bikes or golf carts at numerous places in the village. A taxi around Hopkins or to Sittee Point costs BZ$10.

Sittee Point

About 1.5 miles south of Hopkins, Sittee Point is a small community where high-end beachfront resorts and a few interesting independent restaurants gather. It's like the Paris end of Hopkins. Just where Hopkins ends and Sittee Point begins is the subject of mild debate locally, but it's generally considered to be at the junction with the Sittee River Rd. The *actual* Sittee Point is about 2.7 miles further south at the mouth of the Sittee River, while the marina is about 1.5 miles south.

🏃 Activities

Hopkins Stand-up Paddleboarding
WATER SPORTS
(☑650-9040; www.suphopkins.com; Sittee River Rd; paddleboarding tours BZ$140-270) This outfit offers stand-up paddleboarding (SUP) tours on the Sittee River with a mind-blowing two-hour evening bioluminescence paddle or a half-day paddle in search of wildlife. Combination paddle and snorkel tours are also available.

Belize Underwater
DIVING
(☑670-7298; www.belizeunderwater.com; Sittee River Rd; 2 dives BZ$270, 3 dives Glover's Reef BZ$470) This PADI-certified dive shop offers scuba instruction and trips to South Water Caye, Thatch Caye and Glover's Reef.

Sittee River Marina
TOURS
(☑533-7888; Sittee River Rd; ⊙6am-5:30pm) Boats head out to the reef and cays or on fishing trips from this full-service marina near the mouth of the Sittee River. Reef snorkeling and 4WD tours can also be arranged here, and there's a gas station and popular bar-restaurant.

🛏 Sleeping

Sittee Point is home to the most upmarket resorts in the region, as well as holiday rentals and the odd guesthouse.

Cosmopolitan Guest House
GUESTHOUSE $$
(☑673-7373; www.cosmopolitanbelize.com; Sittee River Rd; cabañas BZ$150, d BZ$170; ⓟ✳🛜🏊) This traditional guesthouse has four spotless rooms in the two-story main house and three, slightly smaller, private cabañas at the side, facing the tiny pool. All have air-con and verandas.

★Hamanasi Adventure & Dive Resort
RESORT $$$
(☑533-7073, in USA 877-552-3483; www.hamanasi .com; Sittee River Rd; r BZ$840-970, treehouse BZ$1140-1450; ⓟ✳🛜🏊) The premier resort of the area, Hamanasi (Garifuna for 'almond tree') combines the amenities of a top-class dive resort with an array of inland tours and activities, all on a gorgeous 400ft private beachfront. All of Hamanasi's rooms and suites face the sea, except for the popular wood-floored tree houses, which hide among the foliage behind the beach.

The best deals at this exclusively priced resort are available as packages including room, meals and tours. Hamanasi's professional PADI dive operation can carry divers out to all three of Belize's atolls (Lighthouse, Turneffe and Glover's), as well as the barrier reef's best dive spots; it is also equipped with the latest developments in nitrox dive technology.

★Beaches & Dreams
BOUTIQUE HOTEL $$$
(☑523-7259; www.beachesanddreams.com; Sittee River Rd; tree house BZ$300, d cabañas BZ$350, ste BZ$400; ⓟ✳🛜🏊) Beaches & Dreams is a sweet little family-run resort with direct beach access, an inviting pool area and the highly regarded Barracuda Bar & Grill. Rooms include the 'Bird's Nest,' with a loft area, while the beachfront cabañas have sea views and hammocks on the veranda. Bikes and kayaks are available for guests.

The three-story boutique hotel has six spacious suites each boasting sea-facing balconies, cable TV and air-conditioning, and sharing a pool and rooftop deck.

Parrot Cove Lodge RESORT $$$
(☑523-7225; www.parrotcovelodge.com; Sittee River Rd; s/d from BZ$200/450, apt BZ$520; P✳🖢🅢) This beachfront lodge has eight beautifully appointed rooms with air-con, full bathrooms with hot showers, TVs and coffee-makers. There's also a beach house next door with apartment suites sleeping up to six. The lodge has its own dock, a courtyard pool with a small waterfall, and an excellent beachfront bar. It's also the home of Chef Rob's restaurant.

Lodge at Jaguar Reef RESORT $$$
(☑822-3851, in USA 888-822-2448; www.vivabelize.com/jaguar-reef; Sittee River Rd; cabañas BZ$480-560, beachfront ste BZ$720-800; P✳🖢🅢) Part of the Viva Belize trio (along with nearby Almond Beach and Villa Margerita resorts) this 'cash-free' luxury resort has a long, sandy beachfront and ample amenities and activities on land and water. The breezy and beautifully furnished cabañas here feature king-size beds, full bathrooms with tiled tubs, and end tables made from traditional Garifuna drums.

🍴 Eating & Drinking

Even if you're staying in Hopkins, it's worth the trip down to Sittee Point to sample some fine waterfront restaurants and the region's best burgers.

Fat Mermaid Beach Cafe HEALTH FOOD $
(☑662-5550; Sittee River Rd; mains $BZ10-20; ⊙noon-8:30pm Wed-Sun; 🖢) Snugged up beside the beachside pool at Belize Underwater, Fat Mermaid is a new cafe specializing in whole foods and health-conscious plant-based food such as plantain buns with your mushroom burger, local fish, shawarma and healthy smoothies.

★Loggerheads Pub & Grill BURGERS $$
(☑650-2886; Sittee River Rd; burgers BZ$12-23; ⊙11am-10pm Thu-Mon) The best burgers in town are served here on homemade rolls. Try the gorgonzola-stuffed beef burger with bacon or the to-die-for surf and turf with garlic lobster and brie. Or build your own burger. The breezy upstairs dining area is the place for a cold beer while the rear courtyard regularly has live music.

Lucky Lobster SEAFOOD $$
(☑676-7777; Lot 6 Sittee River Rd; mains BZ$16-45; ⊙noon-10pm Wed-Sun) In season this is a good place to try out the local lobster but it's also a convivial midrange place for tacos, burritos and fish and chicken dishes. The brightly colored furniture, surfboard table and Western soundtrack give it an international-meets-tropical vibe. Good cocktail list and Chilean wines.

★Chef Rob's SEAFOOD $$$
(☑523-7225; www.chefrobbelize.com; Sittee River Rd; mains BZ$37-59, 4-course dinner BZ$59-79; ⊙noon-9pm Tue-Sat; 🖢) Well-known locally for his sublime seafood creations and steaks cooked over hot rocks, Chef Rob's changing menu here might include sautéed red snapper, grilled jumbo shrimp kebabs or rib-eye in rum sauce. Put together a four-course meal from BZ$59. The waterfront dining area at Parrot Cove is suitably romantic.

Barracuda Bar & Grill INTERNATIONAL $$$
(☑523-7259; Sittee River Rd; mains BZ$22-58; ⊙7am-9pm; 🖢) Attached to Beaches & Dreams, Barracuda is a long-running and highly regarded beachfront restaurant. Seafood is a specialty here, including local lobster, along with steaks and homemade pastries. Grab a pre- or post-dinner drink at the social Sea Bar.

Curve Bar BAR
(☑675-8525; Sittee River Rd; ⊙11am-9pm Tue-Sun) At Sittee River Marina, this lovely riverside thatch-roof restaurant and bar is worth the trip from Hopkins for the fine location, friendly atmosphere and bar snacks, such as nachos and sliders. Happy hour is from 4pm to 6pm. It's about 1.5 miles south of the Sittee Point junction.

ⓘ Information

Diversity Cafe (☑661-7444; Sittee River Rd; golf carts 2/5/24hr BZ$60/100/130; ⊙8am-5pm Mon-Tue & Thu-Fri, 9am-4pm Sat) Information, drinks and golf-cart rental.

ⓘ Getting There & Away

Sittee Point is closer to Hopkins than to Sittee River village (with which it should not be confused); it's about a 20-minute bike ride from Hopkins or BZ$10 in a taxi.

Sittee River

The tranquil, spread-out Creole village of Sittee River, with its increasing population of North American expats, stretches alongside the beautiful jungle-lined river of the same name, about 3 miles by unpaved road southwest of Hopkins. Sittee River is known for its spectacular river, plethora of birds and other wildlife, and notorious for its nigh-invisible and perpetually ravenous sand flies.

◉ Sights & Activities

Serpon Sugar Mill
Historical Park   HISTORIC SITE
(Sittee River Rd; BZ$10; ⊙8am-5pm) This well-kept riverside historical park is the preserved site of the Serpon Sugar Mill, which operated here from 1865 until 1910. There's a small interpretative center but the real attractions are the various pieces of machinery including a steam-powered engine and parts of the crusher and boiler scattered through the park and slowly becoming one with nature.

Belize by Horace   TOURS
(📱603-8358; www.belizebyhorace.com) Offers tours out to the cays and through the lagoons and rivers around Sittee River on a 26ft skiff, as well as land trips to Mayflower, Cockscomb and Red Bank.

🛏 Sleeping

Glover's Guest House   GUESTHOUSE $
(📱532-2916; Sittee River Rd; camping per person BZ$8, dm BZ$24, cabins BZ$40; P) Most visitors come to Glover's Guest House on Saturday night prior to catching the boat to Glover's

---

MAYA VILLAGE HOMESTAY PROGRAM

The Maya Village Homestay program, where you stay with a local family in the Maya Center area, is an excellent way to immerse yourself in the local community and learn about the modern Maya way of life. There are around 10 families in the program and the price is fixed at BZ$50 per person (usually limited to two people, but some homes may be able to accommodate a small family), including two meals. Contact the Saquis at Aurora & Ernesto's Nu'uk Che'il Cottages for information and bookings.

Atoll Resort (p204), but the riverside guesthouse is a peaceful, slightly isolated budget place with free kayaks and bikes for rent. It has one large bunkhouse and two cabins on stilts; bring insect repellent.

River House Lodge   HOTEL $$
(📱533-7799; www.riverhouselodgebelize.com; Sittee River Rd; r BZ$140-170; P❄@🛜🏊) With a lovely secluded riverside setting, River House Lodge has six comfortable air-con rooms with screened verandas in two-story wooden houses. There's also a quirky restaurant-bar with a small indoor pool. Bikes and kayaks are free for guests, and meals and tour information are available by request.

❶ Getting There & Away

Buses that serve Hopkins also go through Sittee River twice a day to the Southern Hwy and on to Placencia, or north to Hopkins and Dangriga. A taxi from Hopkins costs around BZ$25.

Maya Center

POP 300

Maya Center, at the junction of the Southern Hwy and the access road to Cockscomb Basin Wildlife Sanctuary, was established in the 1980s to relocate Mopan Maya villagers when the sanctuary was proclaimed. Many of the villagers now make their living from the sanctuary, running tourist accommodations or guiding tours, selling handicrafts or working as park staff.

If you're not staying in the sanctuary itself, this is the closest base.

🏃 Activities

Che'il Chocolate Factory   CULTURAL TOUR
(📱660-3903; juliosaqui@gmail.com; Southern Hwy; tours per person BZ$35; ⊙shop 7am-5:30pm, tours 9am, 11am, 1pm & 3pm or by appointment) Julio Saqui is a master chocolate maker who offers two-hour farm-to-factory tours including a trip to the cacao plantation. The full process is explained right through to the finished bar of dark chocolate. There's a shop selling cacao products and a separate Maya cultural museum. Call ahead to book a place on a tour.

Aurora's Herbal Clinic   HEALTH & FITNESS
(📱533-7043; Sanctuary Rd; private reading or group healing per person BZ$45) Niece and apprentice of the legendary Maya healer Eligio Panti, Aurora performs consultations at her clinic at Nu'uk Che'il Cottages using locally harvested herbal medicines, treating everything

from the common cold and gastric distress to spiritual and emotional issues. She also maintains a medicinal plant trail (BZ$5 per person with a self-guiding leaflet, BZ$25 per group for 30-minute guided tours).

Mayan Sky Canopy Tour   ADVENTURE SPORTS
(📞671-6533; www.mayanskybelize.com; Southern Hwy; zipline BZ$130, river tubing BZ$70) About 6 miles south of Maya Center a track leads into the jungle (you can't miss the entrance, marked by a replica Mayan statue). A relatively new ziplining course awaits with seven lines and 11 platforms, as well as river tubing and waterfall swims. This is the closest adventure course to Placencia.

🛏 Sleeping & Eating

There are two guesthouses in the village, as well as the Maya homestay program.

⭐**Aurora & Ernesto's**
Nu'uk Che'il Cottages   CABIN $
(📞670-7043; www.nuukcheilcottage.com; camping per person BZ$10, dm BZ$30-45, d & tr BZ$125; ⏰restaurant 7am-8pm; 🅿❄🛜) Spread around a verdant garden about 500yd (450m) along the sanctuary road, Nu'uk Che'il is owned by Ernesto and Aurora Saqui. There's camping and a range of rooms for varying budgets (all air-con), a *palapa* restaurant serving Maya meals, and lots of resident bird (and insect) life.

Among her many talents, Aurora is a great cook and has published a Maya cookbook. She offers farm-to-table cooking classes (BZ$25 per person). Ernesto is a knowledgeable guide who was director of the Cockscomb Sanctuary from 1988 to 2004. Taxis to the national park cost BZ$30 each way.

Tutzil Nah Cottages   CABIN $
(📞533-7045; www.mayacenter.com; s/d BZ$28/36, house BZ$110; 🅿🛜) On the Southern Hwy, 100yd (90m) north of the Maya Centre junction, the Chun brothers offer four clean rooms in houses on stilts decked out in basic Maya style. Rooms have shared bathrooms, but there is a fifth with its own bathroom (BZ$44). The brothers lead guided hikes throughout the area and sanctuary.

🛍 Shopping

Maya Center Women's
Craft Shop   ARTS & CRAFTS
(Southern Hwy; ⏰7:30am-5pm) At the junction of the Southern Hwy and the road to Cockscomb Basin Wildlife Sanctuary, this shop stocks locally made Maya arts and crafts including jewelry, carvings, baskets and textiles. You can arrange taxi transport, guides and buy sanctuary tickets here.

❶ Getting There & Away

Any bus heading north or south along the Southern Hwy will drop you at Maya Center. A taxi from Hopkins costs around BZ$80. It's 6 miles from here to the sanctuary entrance; a taxi costs about BZ$60 return

---

Cockscomb Basin Wildlife Sanctuary

The Cockscomb Basin Wildlife Sanctuary is Belize's most famous jaguar sanctuary; at 200 sq miles, it's also one of Belize's biggest protected areas.

Part of the eastern Maya Mountain range, most visits to the sanctuary are restricted to a small eastern pocket, which contains a visitors center, the sanctuary's accommodations and a network of excellent walking trails.

Early mornings are the best time for wildlife watching, as most animals seek shelter in the heat of the day. Many visitors come as part of large (and inevitably noisy) tours arranged through nearby lodges or travel agencies, but your best bet for viewing more elusive wildlife is to come alone or in as small and quiet a group as possible.

◎ Sights

The unpaved, 6-mile road to the sanctuary starts at the village of Maya Center, on the Southern Hwy, 5 miles south of the Hopkins turnoff. The sanctuary office, where you pay admission, is at the end of the road. The office has trail maps (BZ$5) plus a few gifts, soft drinks and chocolate bars for sale. You can also rent binoculars (BZ$5 per day).

The visitor sighting book records instances of people spotting jaguars (often on the drive in), so it is possible. But, despite its size, the sanctuary itself isn't big enough to support a healthy breeding population of jaguars. However, its position adjacent to other reserves and swaths of jungle make it part of a biological corridor that, many believe, offers promise for the jaguar's future in Central America.

Belize's four other wild cats, the puma, ocelot, margay and jaguarundi, also reside in and pass through the sanctuary, as do tapirs, anteaters, armadillos (the jaguar's favorite prey – crunchy on the outside, but soft and chewy on the inside), brocket deer, coatimundis, kinkajous, otters, peccaries, tayras iguanas, local rodents such as *gibnuts,* and other animals native to the area.

The sanctuary is also home to countless birds: over 290 feathered species have been spotted. Egrets, hummingbirds, the keel-billed toucan, king vulture, great curassow and scarlet macaw are just a few that live in or pass through the park.

There's also a thriving community of black howler monkeys living close to the visitors center. If you don't see them near the center, you'll definitely hear their eerie, cacophonous howling if you stay overnight. Large boa constrictors, small (and deadly poisonous) fer-de-lances and tiny coffee snakes are some of the snakes that call the sanctuary home.

🏃 Activities

The main activities in the park are hiking, including short nature walks, and wildlife viewing.

Hiking

Though a guide is useful, the well-maintained 12-mile network of trails that fans out from the park office is pretty user-friendly. Most of the walks are flat along the bottom of the basin, but the moderately strenuous **Ben's Bluff Trail** (1.25 miles and steep in parts) takes you up to a lookout point with fantastic views over the whole Cockscomb Basin and the Cockscomb Mountains.

An easy 1.4-mile self-guided nature walk, looping together the **Curassow Trail**, **Rubber Tree Trail** and **River Path**, can be fol-

IGNACIO'S BIKE TRAIL

Ignacio's Bike Trail (per person BZ$50, bike hire BZ$50; ☺ Jan-May) is a mountain-biking trail in Cockscomb Basin Wildlife Sanctuary, winding 7.5 miles from the park office to the campsite at the start of the Victoria Peak hiking trail. The ride takes about four hours return and is only accessible in dry conditions between January and May.

Serious riders should bring their own bike, but there are a limited number of bikes for hire at the park office. The trail is named for Ignacio Pop, a pioneer of the sanctuary and former warden who used to ride his bike 6.5 miles up from Maya Center to work, before the access road was fully constructed.

lowed with the trail map from the park office. The **River Path** (0.4 miles) and the **Wari Loop** (a 2.3-mile loop from the office) are good early-morning bets for seeing a variety of birds. Jaguar tracks are often spotted on the Wari Loop and the Victoria Peak Path. The **Antelope Loop** (a 3.4-mile loop from the office) rises and falls through a variety of terrain and vegetation, and offers walkers a good overview of the basin's geological features. The **Tiger Fern Trail** (4 miles return) leads to a two-tier waterfall and a wonderful swimming hole.

Victoria Peak (34 miles return) is a three- to four-day hike for experienced walkers and must be done with a licensed local guide. It's open only in the dry from February to May.

Tubing

The visitor center rents tubes (BZ$5) for hour-long river-tube floats down South Stann Creek from the River Overlook on Wari Loop.

☞ Tours

Villagers who formerly lived in the park area now make their living from the sanctuary, running tourist accommodations or tours, or working as park staff. A typical day tour to the sanctuary from Maya Center costs around BZ$100 per person and includes transportation, a couple of guided walks (usually including a waterfall), lunch and maybe river-tubing. An interesting option is a night tour (BZ$50 per person), which offers increased chances of seeing nocturnal animals.

🛏 Sleeping

To truly appreciate Cockscomb Basin Wildlife Sanctuary, especially its night-time jungle noises, you need to stay the night and there's a decent range of accommodation close to the park office. To make bookings, contact the **Belize Audubon Society** (☎ 223-5004; www.belizeaudubon.org; campsites & cabins BZ$20-164).

Campgrounds & Cabins

There are three campgrounds with raised tent platforms (one near the visitor center and two on park trails; per person BZ$20), a lodge with five six-bed dormitories (per person BZ$40) and various standards of cabins (from BZ$40 to BZ$109).

Cabins range from a basic hut (BZ$40) with composting toilet and shower, to the two-room 'Bird House' (BZ$164) and the self-contained two-story 'White House' (BZ$300) near the entrance gate. There's a functional self-catering kitchen and dining area close to the main lodge buildings.

❶ Information

Call into the **Cockscomb Basin Wildlife Sanctuary Office** (www.belizeaudubon.org; ☉7am-4:30pm, night warden on duty after hours) to register, buy your ticket, and peruse the displays and visitor book (for recent jaguar sightings). You can arrange park accommodation and hire river tubes here, but you can't hire guides – do that in Maya Center.

❶ Getting There & Away

Any bus along the Southern Hwy will drop you at Maya Center, but there is no public transportation into the sanctuary. Most of the Maya Center tour guides offer taxi services to the sanctuary for around BZ$60 return. Otherwise, it's a hot two-hour walk or you can try hitching in.

Placencia

POP 1500

Placencia, a true beach-holiday strip poking out from the mainland, is enduringly popular with North American expats and tourists. Perched at the southern tip of a long, narrow, sandy peninsula, the village has long enjoyed a reputation as 'the cay you can drive to' – a fully paved 27-mile road heads off the Southern Hwy via Maya Beach and Seine Bight to the tip of the peninsula.

Placencia can be a lot of fun, but how you feel about it really depends on what you're looking for. If it's laid-back ambience, varied accommodations, boat access to private islands and some of the best restaurants in Southern Belize, this beachfront hangout may be for you. During the full moons of May and June especially, divers and snorkelers are drawn here as whale sharks come to feed in the nearby waters.

Orientation

The village of Placencia occupies the southernmost mile of the peninsula. On the eastern side is a sandy beach; between the beach and the road is a narrow, pedestrian-only footpath known as the Sidewalk.

Placencia's airport is about 1 mile north of the village; 6 miles beyond that is Maya Beach. Between the village and the airport lie an increasing number of accommodations, including some of the swankiest in Belize and a growing number of luxury housing units.

🏃 Activities

Jaguar Lanes Bowling BOWLING

(☎664-2583; Maya Beach; per person per game BZ$7, shoe rental BZ$3; ☉2-10pm Wed-Mon) A cool distraction from the beach, this six-lane bowling alley is a lot of fun. Apart from knocking down the pins, there's a lively bar and cafe area serving pizzas, wings, burgers and fries (BZ$5 to BZ$8). It's about 55yd south of the Maya Beach Hotel and about 8 miles north of Placencia town.

Diving & Snorkeling

Placencia is close enough to a plethora of cays, reefs and dive sites to make it a good base for **diving** and **snorkeling**. The more distant the area, the more expensive the trip. Most operators will charge around BZ$250 to BZ$300 per person for a two-tank dive on an inner reef site such as Laughing Bird Caye. Longer outings to spots such as Glover's Reef or the Sapodilla Cayes should be around BZ$350.

For some sites you may need to add admission fees of between BZ$8 and BZ$30. March, April, May and June are especially good months to see whale sharks in the area, particularly either side of the full moon when plankton blooms are abundant. Most dive operators also run snorkeling trips. A snorkeling day trip to nearby cays, often with a beach BBQ included, costs from BZ$100.

★ Splash Dive Center DIVING, TOURS

(☎523-3058; www.splashbelize.com; Main St) Splash teaches PADI courses to divers of all levels, as well as offering diving and snorkeling tours to islands and reefs throughout the area. Owner Patty Ramirez is a patient and professional instructor, making her suitable for first-time divers and experts alike. As Quest Tours, Patty and partner Ralph also lead tours inland, including trips to Maya ruins and jungles.

Seahorse Dive Shop DIVING

(☎523-3166; www.belizescuba.com; snorkeling BZ$170, 2-tank dive BZ$280) Seahorse runs regular diving and snorkeling trips to the reef, South Water Caye, Glover's, Blue Hole and (in season) to see whale sharks. Also offers Discover Scuba courses (from BZ$350) and PADI open-water courses (BZ$900).

Go Sea DIVING

(☎523-3033; www.goseabelize.com; Main St; 2-tank dive BZ$290) Scuba diving and snorkeling trips to all the main sites, as well as fishing,

Placencia

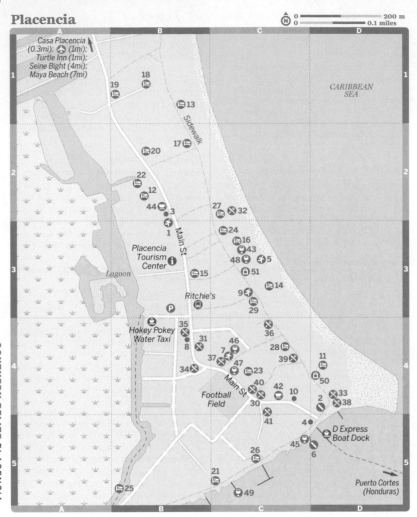

island-hopping and seasonal whale-shark snorkeling tours.

Fishing & Sailing

Opportunities for fishing are equally amazing, and in the waters off Placencia you can troll for barracuda, kingfish or tuna; spincast or fly-fish for tarpon, bonefish or snook; and bottom-fish for snapper or jack.

Sailing is also popular in the waters around Placencia. In addition to Belize's cays and other ports, Río Dulce in Guatemala and Honduras' Bay Islands are close enough to sail to.

Permit Pow   FISHING

(☏523-3132; www.permitangling.com) Renowned local fishing guide 'Pow' Cabral will take you fly-fishing or on customized trips in search of permit fish (among others).

Moorings   BOATING

(☏ in USA 888-952-8420; www.moorings.com) Luxury catamaran offering customized bareboat (self-charter) sailing from Placencia or you can hire a skipper. It's based at Laru Beya marina, which is located 4 miles north of Placencia.

Placencia

Watersports

Placencia Awesome Water Sports
WATER SPORTS

(☑ 608-7110) On the beach next to Tipsy Tuna, PAWS rents out kayaks (from BZ$20 per hour), stand-up paddleboards (BZ$25 per hour), snorkel gear, tubes and windsurfers.

Yoga & Massage

Eucalipto
YOGA

(☑ 615-7111; Main St; BZ$25; ⊙ 9:30am or 10am Mon-Fri) Drop-in morning classes in vinyasa and hatha yoga.

Secret Garden Massage & Day Spa
SPA

(☑ 523-3420; www.secretgardenplacencia.com; Main St; massage per hour from BZ$110; ⊙ by appointment) Beside the garden restaurant (p222) of the same name, US-trained and licensed massage therapist Lee Nyhus offers a soothing range of Swedish massages, hot-stone massages, facials, Reiki and physical therapy.

Tree of Life
MASSAGE

(☑ 624-5408; Sidewalk; massage BZ$150-180; ⊙ 9am-6:30pm) Pamper yourself with Swedish massage, hot-stone massage, wraps or facials at this beachfront studio.

 Tours

Placencia is a good base for inland exploration. Several tour companies offer full-day trips to the village of Red Bank to see the beautiful scarlet macaws (January to March), to Cockscomb Basin Wildlife Sanctuary and Mayflower Bocawina National Park, or to local banana and cacao plantations. You can also get as far as Toledo and Cayo district for ziplining, caving or trips to Maya ruins.

A popular trip is the boat ride to Monkey River, which includes a sea cruise to Monkey River Town, crocodile-spotting and bird-watching, as well as jungle walks and a swim or river-tube float, followed by a Creole lunch in the village.

★ **Taste Belize Tours** FOOD & DRINK
(Main St; day tours from BZ$250) Belize's premier culinary tours include Maya chocolate tours, Garifuna, Creole and Maya cooking tours and spice farm trips. You can also taste cacao chocolate the Placencia shop.

King Lewey's Island Resort ISLAND
(☑543-4010; www.kingleweysislandresort.com; day tour BZ$100-240) If you're after a bit of island time on a budget, this pirate-themed resort on a tiny island about 12 miles from Placencia is a fun place for a day trip. Naturally there's a restaurant and bar and water sports such as kayaks, paddleboards, fishing and snorkeling gear. Or just laze around in the hammock.

Boats leave daily at 8:30am from a booking office in Placencia village, returning at 4:30pm.

Seakunga Adventure ADVENTURE
(☑523-3644; www.seakunga.com; Mile 18 Placencia Rd; 1-/4-day kayaking tours BZ$160/2400) On the peninsula, just past Seine Bight, Seakunga runs fully supported multiday river and ocean kayaking tours and a range of adventure trips. It rents windsurfing equipment (per day BZ$80, lessons BZ$160) and it started Placencia's first kiteboarding school.

Cayequest Tours TOURS
(☑633-6330; www.cayequestadventures.blogspot. com) Cayequest, run by local guide Mark Leslie, runs some offbeat tours to an organic chocolate farm and banana plantations, as well as culinary-oriented trips to the cays.

Trip 'n Travel TOUR, FISHING
(☑660-7189; www.tripntravel.bz; Main St; tours BZ$140-250; ⊙8am-6pm Mon-Fri, to 2pm Sat) Reliable company offering all the usual tours, plus full-day trips into Maya country in Toledo and Cayo. Most tours will go with only two people.

Nite Wind Tours TOURS
(☑503-3487, 660-6333; Main St; tours BZ$45-385; ⊙8am-5:30pm) Offers a variety of land and nautical tours including snorkeling on nearby cays and day trips to Monkey River and Cayo District.

🎉 Festivals & Events

Lobsterfest FOOD & DRINK
(⊙last weekend of Jun) Celebrates the opening of the lobster-fishing season with music, boat races, a fishing contest, a huge variety of lobster dishes to eat and a lot of fun.

Mistletoe Ball DANCE
(⊙Dec) Organised by the Belize Tourism Industry Association (BTIA), this popular party of dancing and music takes place at one of Placencia's resorts each December.

Sidewalk Art Festival ART
(⊙mid-Feb) Features art, crafts and music, with scores of participants from all over Belize.

🛏 Sleeping

Many of Placencia's accommodations span the budget and midrange spectrum, while more upmarket resorts are further north around Maya Beach and the airport. Places fill up fast, especially in high season, so book ahead or expect to pay a premium. During low season some places close, but others offer discounts of 25% or more.

Placencia Village

The majority of budget and midrange accommodations are found at the far southern end of the peninsula, known as 'the village' of 'the point'.

★ **Placencia Hostel** HOSTEL $
(☑627-0104; colinbelize@yahoo.com; Main St; dm/d BZ$35/60) Backpackers have more options in Placencia now, with the opening of this excellent place. Run by welcoming local Chris, it's more like a guesthouse than a hostel with a range of private fan-cooled rooms. The doubles with private bathroom are a bargain, especially by Placencia standards. There's a small kitchen, laundry service and bikes for rent.

Anda Di Howse HOSTEL $
(☑631-1614, 523-3306; pandora_gaudino@yahoo. com; Sidewalk; dm BZ$25; 🕙) 'Under the House' was Placencia's first genuine hostel, with an absolute beachfront location, no less. Owner Pandora has designed a functional 10-bed dorm beneath her stilt home, with timber floors, spring mattresses, individual fans, lockers and spotless bathrooms. It's a cozy space with full kitchen and small veranda. Rent a tent or hammock and camp for BZ$15.

The house is right on the beach at the southern end of the Sidewalk.

Casa Placencia APARTMENT $
(☑630-7811; www.casaplacencia.com; Placencia Rd; r BZ$110, apt per week BZ$1300; P❋🕙🏊) On the quiet northern end of town, long-running Casa Placencia offers beautifully decorated

rooms with kitchenettes, cable TV and wi-fi. There's an organic garden with bananas, mangoes and papayas, and a chill-out spot with an above-ground pool and BBQ at the back. The one- and two-bedroom apartments come with full kitchen and are perfect for families. Free bikes.

Lydia's Guesthouse   GUESTHOUSE **$**
(☑ 523-3117; www.lydiasguesthouse.com; Sidewalk; r BZ$65, apt BZ$110-200; 🛜) Lydia's is a reliable budget option on a quiet stretch of Side walk on the northern side of town. The eight rooms share bathrooms and there's one studio and a two-bedroom apartment with full kitchens. Lydia also offers a laundry service, communal kitchen with purified drinking water and hammocks on the veranda.

Manatee Inn   HOTEL **$**
(☑ 523-4083; www.manateeinn.com; Harbour Pl; s/d/tr BZ$70/80/90; 🅿 🛜) Built by Slavek Machacka in 1999, this classical wooden hotel is still one of the best bets in the budget category. Down a lane in a quiet spot, the Manatee puts you close enough to the beach to feel a constant breeze. Rooms are airy with high ceilings, hardwood floors, refrigerators and private bathrooms with hot-water showers.

Deb & Dave's Last Resort   GUESTHOUSE **$**
(☑ 523-3207; debanddave@btl.net; Main St; s/d without bathroom BZ$50/60; 🛜) A reliable central cheapie in the town centre, D&D offers four compact rooms (two twins, two doubles) with fans, surrounded by a leafy garden. A screened-in space offers a communal chill-out spot with a coffee-maker, but no kitchen. The outdoor pool is not for guests!

Palma's Guesthouse   GUESTHOUSE **$**
(☑ 628-7922; www.casapalmaplacencia.com; Main Rd; d with/without air-con BZ$120/80; 🅿 ✳ 🛜) The distinctive yellow-and-blue guesthouse at the north end of the village is decent value in pricey Placencia, especially if you desire air-con. The compact rooms share bathrooms but each have a fridge and there's a well-equipped common kitchen leading to a front veranda. The owner also has more expensive apartments (from BZ$300) closer to the beach.

Sailfish Resort   RESORT **$**
(☑ 651-9885; www.sailfishbelize.com; Sunset Pointe; d with bathroom BZ$198, s/d without bathroom BZ$60/100; ✳ 🛜 🏊) Across the water from Sunset Pointe at the very southern edge of Placencia Village, Sailfish is something of a bargain if you don't mind the simple budget rooms with fan and shared bathroom, since you get to use the infinity pool and common rooms with cable TV. Or go for the hotel-style suites with air-con and private bathroom.

Placencia Villas   APARTMENT **$$**
(☑ 620-9975, 523-3103; www.placenciavillas.com; Main St; studios from BZ$130, cabañas BZ$180, apt from BZ$200; 🅿 ✳ 🛜) These clean, colorful, fully equipped studios and apartments come with kitchenettes, ample parking and a leafy central courtyard.

Serenade Hotel   HOTEL **$$**
(☑ 523-3113; www.serenadeplacencia.com; Sidewalk; d BZ$130-170; 🅿 ✳ 🛜) This big old two-story house on the Sidewalk has nine spacious brightly painted rooms and are very reasonable by Placencia standards with air-con, microwave, minifridge, cable TV and bathrooms with hot showers. The better upper-floor rooms have sea views and the beach is just steps away.

Cozy Corner   HOTEL **$$**
(☑ 523-3540; www.cozycorner-belize.com; Sidewalk; r/ste BZ$142/196; ✳ 🛜) There's nothing particularly flash about Cozy Corner, but the location on the beach makes it a good deal at this price. The hotel itself is behind an above-average beach bar and restaurant that's popular with locals and often overlooked by tourists. Clean rooms at the back come with air-con and hot water.

Seaview Suites   HOTEL **$$**
(☑ 523-3777; www.seaviewplacencia.com; Sidewalk; r BZ$170; ✳ 🛜) A great location at the southern end of the Sidewalk and six immaculate rooms makes this a good deal. Rooms have either a king or two double beds and come with air-con, fridge, microwave and coffee-maker.

Colibri House   APARTMENT **$$**
(☑ 605-0586; www.colibrihouseplacencia.com; Sidewalk; downstairs/upstairs apt BZ$190/240, per week BZ$1200/1500; ✳ 🛜 🏊) The one-of-a-kind, octagonal Colibri house is built from a mix of hardwoods and is fully furnished with treasures from Tibet, Bali, Italy and India. Of the two apartments, the upper suite features a bedroom and living room and a 2nd-floor loft space, while the downstairs studio is ideal for couples.

Paradise Resort   HOTEL **$$**
(☑ 523-3179; www.belize123.com; Sunset Pointe; r BZ$180-280; 🅿 ✳ 🛜) This semi-upmarket,

12-room hotel enjoys a peaceful location on the peninsula's southern edge, offering clean and comfortable rooms with air-con, flat-screen TVs and comfy beds – the best are the upper-floor sea-view rooms with balconies. The popular nautical-themed bar and restaurant is a good meeting place and there's an overwater burger bar in season.

Captain Jak's
CABIN $$

(628-6447; www.captainjaks.com; Main St; cabañas BZ$190, cottages BZ$250; P 🛜) The Captain offers three cabañas and two larger cottages surrounding a quiet garden (weekly rates are available). All rooms are fan-cooled and come with kitchenettes, hot water and private bathrooms. There is also an immaculately furnished two-story private villa that sleeps up to eight for BZ$630 a night.

Michelo Hotel
HOTEL $$

(523-3519; Harbour Place 21; d BZ$200-250; P ❄ 🛜) This small hotel on the north end of town has four spotless suites with queen-sized beds and futons, cable TV, wi-fi, and full kitchenettes with microwaves and fridges. The owners have built a beautiful circular temple and meditation space around the back, open to guests and non-guests alike.

Julia's Guesthouse
GUESTHOUSE $$

(503-3478; www.juliascabanas.com; Sidewalk; r BZ$138-250; 🛜) A beachfront place on the tightest packed part of the shore (next to Barefoot Bar), Miss Julia has three cabins, four duplexes and one apartment, all painted in Julia's signature tropical yellow and orange, and offering TVs, hot showers, private bathrooms and sea views. Laundry facilities are available, and guests can use the beachside hammocks and lounge chairs.

Seaspray Hotel
HOTEL $$

(523-3148; www.seasprayhotel.com; Sidewalk; r BZ$66-160, cabañas BZ$170; ❄ 🛜) Owned and operated by the Leslies (one of Placencia's most established families), this lovely hotel has seven grades of room in varying sizes, luxury and proximity to the ocean. All come with private hot-water bathrooms and fans; the economy rooms are cheap enough but can be pokey. De-Tatch Restaurant (p222) is next door.

Ranguana Lodge
CABAÑAS $$

(523-3112; www.ranguanabelize.com; Sidewalk; garden-/sea-view cabañas BZ$180/260; ❄ 🛜) Ranguana offers five good-sized mahogany cabins on a piece of happening beach (near Barefoot Bar). The garden cabins have kitchens; the smaller beachfront cabins have sea views and air-con. All have two double beds, hot-water bathrooms, cable TV and microwaves, not to mention lovely verandas. Prices are for up to three people.

Sea Glass Inn
HOTEL $$

(523-3098; www.seaglassinnbelize.com; Garden Grove; d/tr BZ$158/188; ❄ 🛜) The welcoming Sea Glass Inn offers unobstructed ocean views and endless sea breezes thanks to its position on Placencia's southern shore. Renovated rooms have coffee-makers, microwaves, fridge and air-con. The wide, wood-floored veranda has chairs and hammocks for long-term lounging.

Around Placencia

If laid-back Placencia town is too busy for you, a range of hotels and swish resorts line the beach on the peninsula north of the village towards Maya Beach.

Singing Sands Inn
BOUTIQUE HOTEL $$

(533-3022; www.singingsands.com; 714 Maya Beach Rd; r BZ$220-550, cabañas BZ$220-280; P ❄ 🛜 ➿) Tucked away in a beautifully landscaped garden at Maya Beach, Singing Sands offers an affordable oceanside tropical oasis. Choose from thatched-roof cabañas or garden-view rooms with hardwood floors, custom-designed doors and furniture made by local craftspeople. Dine in the poolside Bonefish Grill, and take a sunset cocktail at the bar on the end of the private pier.

★ Turtle Inn
LODGE $$$

(523-3486, in USA 800-746-3743; www.thefamily coppolahideaways.com/en/turtle-inn; Placencia Rd; cottages BZ$638-2038, villas BZ$1300-3858; P 🛜 ➿) The last word in ultra-chic luxury (with price tag to match), this Balinese-themed lodge is owned by the family of Francis Ford Coppola, where the director himself maintains his own Belizean villa. The thatch-roofed cottages and villas are a combination of opulence with a hint of the rustic, while signature Italian fine dining can be found at the Mare Restaurant.

Facilities include a private beach and jetty, two pools, a fully equipped PADI dive shop, and day spa staffed with Thai masseurs. The most exclusive accommodations, Francis' Family Pavilion and Sofia's Beach House, top out at BZ$6700 and BZ$7840 respectively! From January to April there's a three- or four-night minimum. It's just under 2 miles north of town.

★ Maya Beach Hotel   HOTEL $$$
(☑533-8040; www.mayabeachhotel.com; Maya Beach; r BZ$280-400, ste BZ$500; P❄☎☀) The Maya Beach has 10 delightful, individually furnished and decorated rooms facing the beach. The smallest is cozy but most are spacious and thoughtfully designed, all with air-conditioning, custom-made furniture, kitchenettes and balconies or verandas. There's a cool little pool and swimming off the private jetty, and guests have free use of kayaks and stand-up paddleboards.

Owners John and Ellen also manage a number of beautiful beachfront houses ranging from one to three bedrooms.

Naïa Resort Spa   SPA HOTEL $$$
(☑523-4600; www.naiaresortandspa.com; off Placencia Rd, Cocoplum; studios BZ$750-850, 1-/2-/3-bedroom villas from BZ$970/1600/1990) Naïa is the newest luxury resort on the Placencia peninsula with a full-service day spa and spectacular beachfront villas. The beach houses and villas, many with private plunge pools, are spacious, private and luxuriously appointed with kitchenettes, modern artworks and full-length French windows opening onto balconies or verandas.

Complementing the five spa suites is a gym and yoga *shala* (studios), while the main restaurant specializes in Belizean cuisine.

Ray Caye Resort   RESORT $$$
(☑533-4446; www.raycaye.com; Hatchet Caye; r/cabañas BZ$750/840, all-inclusive 3-day package per person BZ$2400/2600; ❄☎☀) This spectacular private island resort, about 18 miles east of Placencia, should fulfill all of your tropical island fantasies without completely breaking the bank. Luxurious oceanfront cabañas and rooms – with a maximum of 30 guests – are spaced among the palms, while the warm, shallow waters fringing the island are perfect for snorkeling, swimming and water sports.

Green Parrot Beach Houses   CABAÑAS $$$
(☑533-8188, in USA 734-667-2537; www.green-parrot-belize.com; 1 Maya Beach; d BZ$350; P☎) Green Parrot offers six quirky timber beach houses and two stilted thatched cabañas, all on the beach. All-wood interiors, high ceilings and huge screened-in windows maximizing breezes are features. Cabañas have thatched roofs and open-air showers with a tropical feel. Guests have free use of bicycles, snorkeling equipment, kayaks and glass-bottom

canoes, and the restaurant serves breakfast, lunch and dinner.

Robert's Grove Beach Resort   RESORT $$$
(☑523-3565, in USA 800-565-9757; www.roberts grove.com; Placencia Rd; r & ste BZ$400-560, villas from BZ$700; P❄☎☀) ♥ From the Grecian fountain in the front driveway to the beautiful beachfront patio bar and restaurant, Robert's Grove is classy all the way. Rooms range from studios with ocean or garden views to one- and two-bedroom suites or spacious three- and four-bedroom villas sleeping up to eight people. Eat at the fine-dining Seaside Restaurant or the more-casual Habanero Cafe.

✕ Eating

Placencia stands out as having the best restaurants and diversity of cuisine in Southern Belize, from street BBQs and Italian gelati to high-quality resort restaurants. If you're looking to stock up on supplies, there are a number of good Chinese-run supermarkets.

Look out for the numerous fast-food shacks doing Mexican street food or Belizean staples, such as Brenda's on the main waterfront.

★ Tutti Frutti   ICE CREAM $
(Main St; 1-/2-scoop BZ$4/5; ⊘9am-9pm Thu-Tue) If you don't like the ice cream here, you won't like ice cream anywhere. It's that simple. The Italian gelato is even better and the 18 flavors on display are constantly changing – from salted caramel to Ferrero Rocher.

Chachi's   ITALIAN $
(☑523-3305; Main Rd; pizza slice BZ$5-8; ⊘11am-11pm) Chachi's is a fine addition to Placencia's main street scene; a sociable pizza joint and cocktail bar downstairs and breezy live music bar upstairs. Pizzas are available by the slice or you can buy a whole one and build your own toppings, including housemade sausage or blue cheese. Sip a cocktail or sangria and see what's happening upstairs.

Mr Q   BARBECUE $
(☑653-3568; Main St; plates BZ$10; ⊘noon-9pm) One of several good Belizean BBQ places at the southern end of the peninsula, Mr Q serves up BBQ plates and fried chicken with rice and beans, along with ice-cold beer. Cheap and filling.

Shak   CAFE $
(☑523-3252; Placencia Point; smoothies BZ$8, mains BZ$10-26; ⊘7am-6pm Sun-Tue, to 9pm

Wed-Sat) This ocean-facing restaurant is one of the best places in town for a healthy smoothie – there are 30 varieties – or an all-day breakfast. It also serves seafood including lobster or conch fritters, tacos and other Mexican dishes. The vibe is mellow and the people-watching fine.

Friends Near the Pier
BREAKFAST $

(667-4805; Sidewalk; mains BZ$10-15; 6:30-11:30am Tue-Sat;) Locally famous for its breakfasts, this bright-yellow shack at the southern end of Sidewalk offers friendly service and a lavish menu of pancakes, waffles, French toast and lobster-and-cheese omelets, all served on a nice people-watching deck.

Sweet Dreams
BAKERY $

(Sidewalk; baked goods from BZ$5; 7am-noon;) Freshly baked mini pizzas, multigrain breads, cinnamon rolls and baked goods of all sorts are served all morning at this family-run Swiss bakery.

★ Omar's Creole Grub
SEAFOOD $$

(605-7631; Main St; mains BZ$10-45; 7am-9pm Sun-Thu, to 4pm Fri, to 6pm Sat) Omar's has been around a long time and still serves some of the freshest seafood in town. Step into the small and rustic streetside shack and choose from crab, lobster, shrimp or conch prepared as either traditional Creole, Caribbean curry or coconut curry. There's also burgers and burritos, and omelets for breakfast. BYO alcohol only.

Wendy's Creole Restaurant & Bar
CARIBBEAN $$

(523-3335; Main St; breakfast & lunch BZ$10-16, dinner mains BZ$15-45; 7am-9:30pm;) Wendy's is a traditional-style air-conditioned restaurant serving a wide range of dishes from burgers and burritos to seafood specialties such as Caribbean jerk snapper fillet and Creole fish. Full breakfast menu with Belizean and Mexican faves. There's a full bar and cheap beer.

Rick's Cafe
PIZZA $$

(Sidewalk; mains BZ$14-35; 11am-9:30pm Thu-Tue;) This cool little veranda cafe on the Sidewalk has just a few tables and is best known for its pizza and pasta, but Rick also whips up sandwiches, quesadillas and ceviche.

Secret Garden Restaurant
CARIBBEAN $$

(523-3617; mains BZ$22-40; 5-9pm Mon-Sat) In a lush patch of garden strung with fairy lights and hidden away from the main street, this low-key restaurant and bar offers up an eclectic menu with Caribbean gumbo, chicken Maya and spicy jambalaya.

Dawn's Grill
BELIZEAN $$

(602-9302; Main St; meals BZ$10-24; 7am-3pm & 5:30-9pm) Good food comes from a small kitchen at Dawn's Grill shack on Main St. Changing daily specials include fajitas, chicken, pork roast and fish fillets, while lobster is a seasonal specialty in sandwiches, ceviche or omelets. Saturday is BBQ day, while breakfast is a treat daily.

De-Tatch Restaurant
CARIBBEAN $$

(Sidewalk; breakfast & lunch dishes BZ$7-18, dinner mains BZ$20-45; 7am-10pm Wed-Mon;) This popular thatched-roof, open-air beachfront place specializes in tasty shrimp and seafood dishes in a range of styles: Caribbean, Belizean and North American food are De-Tatch signatures and service is snappy. The specials board might include coconut shrimp curry or whole fried snapper. It's also a good spot for breakfast and lunch.

★ Maya Beach Bistro
INTERNATIONAL $$$

(533-8040; www.mayabeachhotel.com; Maya Beach; lunch BZ$18-40, dinner BZ$14-58; 7am-9pm) Maya Beach Hotel's popular bistro is a Placencia landmark, offering excellent international dishes using fresh local ingredients. This is the place where restaurant folk come to eat seafood and coconut chowder, lobster bread pudding or cacao pork on their days off. The waterfront view is fine, service is friendly and you can swim in the small pool.

★ Rumfish
FUSION $$$

(523-3293; www.rumfishyvino.com; Main St; tacos BZ$9, small plates BZ$10-22, mains BZ$35-55; noon-midnight, kitchen closes at 10pm) Rumfish is a gastro-style wine bar a la Central American style. Head up to the balcony of the beautiful old timber building and sample starters such as Peruvian ceviche or specialty mains such as Yucatán chicken or Caribbean fish stew. Gourmet tacos are BZ$18 for two. Imported wines, beers and cocktails, and a breezy veranda complete the perfect picture.

 Drinking & Nightlife

Placencia is low key but still the best place in Southern Belize for partying, with some good beach bars and a nightclub.

SEINE BIGHT

Most visitors to Placencia just breeze through Seine Bight, the Garifuna village in the center of the peninsula, which – with its shacks, shanties and cheap restaurants – contrasts sharply with the resorts and condos either side of it. But as the home of many of the folks who keep the surrounding resorts running and with an obvious local flavor, Seine Bight is worth a stop. In addition to offering some of the cheapest food on the peninsula, Seine Bight is home to renowned artists, such as painter and sculptor Lola Delgado, who runs **Lola's Art** (☑523-3342; off Placencia Rd, Seine Bight). A Garifuna cultural museum has been under development in the village for some years.

Seine Bight is about 5.5 miles north of Placencia and 3 miles north of the airport. The same buses that ply the road between Placencia village and Dangriga will stop at Seine Bight on request. A taxi costs about BZ$20 from Placencia.

Brewed Awakenings   CAFE
(Main St; ⊘6am-9pm Mon-Sat, to 5pm Thu; ☜) The imaginative name extends to the drinks with perfectly brewed espresso coffee (BZ$3.50 to BZ$7) and a range of flavored seaweed shakes (BZ$7 to BZ$8; the seaweed acts as a thickener and is said to contain various healthy vitamins). Great for an early-morning caffeine fix.

Barefoot Bar   BAR
(☑523-3515; Sidewalk; ⊘11am-midnight; ☜) Occupying prime beach real estate, Placencia's most happening spot for drinking and entertainment has live music five nights a week, fire dancing on Wednesdays, full-moon parties, horseshoe tossing comps and more. Happy hour is from 5pm to 6pm, with discount beer and cheap rum. The menu has a big range of Mexican snacks, pizza and burgers.

Above Grounds   COFFEE
(☑634-3212; www.abovegroundscoffee.com; Main St; ⊘7am-4pm Mon-Sat, 8am-noon Sun; ☜) This coffee shop stilt shack offers great coffee drinks, bagels, muffins and people-watching from the raised wooden veranda deck (coffee from BZ$3 to BZ$7, snacks BZ$2 to BZ$9). All coffee is Guatemalan organic, sourced directly from the farmers. It also has organic chocolate drinks, fresh juice, free wi-fi and good tunes.

Sky Deck   BAR
(☑523-3305; Main St, Chachi's) Upstairs from Chachi's, Sky Deck is a slick bar and live music venue with regular live jazz, blues and DJs.

Street Feet   CLUB
(☑523-3515; Main St; ⊘11pm-4am Fri & Sat) Placencia doesn't party like San Pedro but this lounge and nightclub keeps things going on weekends after the beach bars close with DJs and dance parties.

Yoli's   BAR
(☑624-3807; ⊘7am-8pm, till late Fri) This sociable thatched bar over the water at the south end of the village is especially popular on Fridays, when there's a live band and Yoli's BBQ grill, and again on Sunday afternoons.

Pickled Parrot   BAR
(☑636-7068; Pompass Rd; ⊘11am-midnight Wed-Mon) This thatched-roof Caribbean-meets-Brit-pub-style bar and restaurant, tucked down a lane off the main street, is a sociable spot for a drink and the food is top notch. Head in for the bargain BZ$10 specials (meatloaf Monday, shrimp Saturday) or trivia on Thursday.

Tipsy Tuna Sports Bar   BAR
(www.tipsytunabelize.com; Sidewalk; ⊘11am-midnight) Brightening up the beach with its multicolored sun loungers, Tipsy Tuna provides occasional action with live music (Garifuna drumming on Wednesdays), along with sports on the big-screen TV, pool tables, rooftop deck and happy hour from 5pm to 7pm. Bar snacks include wings and cheese fries.

J-Byrds   BAR
(Main St; ⊘10am-midnight or later) This rustic-looking dockside bar can get pretty lively with locals and visitors, especially at the Friday dance party.

🛍 Shopping

Art 'n' Soul Gallery   ARTS & CRAFTS
(Sidewalk; ⊘9am-6pm) This cooperative of local artists displays arts and crafts for sale in a beachside gallery.

Made in Belize ARTS & CRAFTS
(📞 627-5125; Sidewalk; ⊘ 7am-9pm) Leo hand-crafts exquisite wooden sculptures from rosewood, mahogany and driftwood at his workshop on the Sidewalk and displays and sells them in his little shop. Birds (such as toucans) and marine life (dolphins and turtles) are featured. Small pieces start at BZ$50.

ℹ Information

MONEY

Belize Bank (Pompass Rd) and **Scotiabank** (⊘ 8:30am-2:30pm Mon-Thu, to 4pm Fri) are both on the main drag and have 24/7 ATM access. There's an Atlantic Bank branch on the far north end of town.

TOURIST INFORMATION

There's no shortage of info on Placencia, both on the web and around Belize. In town, head to the **Placencia Tourism Center** (📞 523-4045; www. placencia.com; ⊘ 9am-5pm Mon-Fri), down a lane opposite Scotia Bank (look for the sign). This private BTIA (Belize Tourism Industry Association) office has friendly staff who can offer local information such as transport info. Pick up a copy of the free monthly *Placencia Breeze*.

VISA EXTENSIONS

The **immigration office** (Independence; ⊘ 8:30am-5pm Mon-Fri) for visa extensions (BZ$50) is at the deep-water port in Independence. Take the Hokey Pokey Water Taxi from Placencia and it's a 2-mile taxi ride away (BZ$20 return).

ℹ Getting There & Away

AIR

Between them, from Placencia airport (PLJ), **Maya Island Air** (📞 523-3443; www.mayaisland air.com; Placencia Rd, Maya Island air terminal) and **Tropic Air** (📞 523-3410; www.tropicair.com; Placencia Rd) fly around 16 times daily to Belize City (one-way BZ$240, 35 minutes), and 10 times to Dangriga (BZ$120, 15 minutes) and Punta

Gorda (BZ$120, 15 minutes). The airstrip is just north of town.

BOAT

The **Hokey Pokey Water Taxi** (📞 665-7242; one-way BZ$10; ⊘ hourly from 6:45am to 6pm, or 5pm Sunday) is a great way to arrive or depart Placencia. The scenic 10-minute boat ride along Mango Creek brings you to the administrative town of Independence/Mango Creek; from Independence bus station you can connect with any of the buses that traverse the Southern Hwy.

The 45-passenger D Express sails from Placencia municipal pier to Puerto Cortés, Honduras (BZ$130, 4½ hours including immigration time) at 9am on Friday. Tickets are sold on board or ask at Nite Wind Tours (p218). The return trip leaves Puerto Cortés at 11am on Monday.

BUS

Ritchie's (📞 523-3806) bus line has one daily bus to Belize City at 6:15am (BZ$20, 4½ hours) and three buses to Dangriga (BZ$10, 1¾ hours) Monday to Saturday, from where you can transfer to Belmopan and points beyond. Buses to Dangriga leave at 7am, 12:45pm and 2:30pm (2:30pm only on Sunday) from the **bus stop** (Main St) on Main St opposite the Hokey Pokey Water Taxi.

Two Bebb Line buses between Placencia and Dangriga at 10:30am and 5:30pm stop at Hopkins. Alternatively, ask to be let off at the Hopkins junction and hitch or call a taxi from there.

Travelers heading to Toledo should take the Hokey Pokey Water Taxi to Independence; from the Independence bus stand (taxi BZ$5) you can connect with any of the James Line buses that traverse the Southern Hwy.

ℹ Getting Around

Many accommodations north of the village offer free airport transfers and free use of bicycles for guests.

Taxis meet flights. The ride to or from the village costs BZ$10. A taxi from the village costs around BZ$20 to Seine Bight or BZ$30 to Maya Beach.

HARVEST CAYE

Harvest Caye is a private island about 2.5 miles southwest of Placencia Point. Since 2016 it has been the exclusive cruise-ship port and resort owned by Norwegian Cruise Line. This US$50 million, purpose-built resort of lagoon swimming pools, beaches, adventure activities and shopping villages is very nice, but unless you're a cruise-ship passenger or an employee you're unlikely to set foot on it.

Likewise, the majority of cruise-ship passengers to the island don't see much point heading to the mainland, leading many Placencia locals to complain that the new port hasn't done much to boost the local economy. To be fair, Harvest Caye employs some 400 Belizeans and with the potential for up to 360 cruise-ship passengers to be tendered across to Placencia each day, the economic effects are bound to be felt.

Cars, motorbikes and golf buggies can be hired along the Placencia peninsula; try **Barefoot Services** (☑ 523-3066; www.barefootservicesbelize.com; Placencia Rd; ☉ 8:30am-5:30pm Mon-Fri) or **Captain Jak's Rentals** (☑ 628-6447; www.captainjaks.com; Main St; ☉ 7am-5pm).

Dangriga or Independence. Another option is to get off any bus heading along the Southern Hwy at the Red Bank turnoff and arrange transport through Scarlet Macaw Guesthouse (BZ$10).

Tour operators in Placencia and Hopkins run day tours to Red Bank when the macaws are in residence.

Red Bank

POP 1000

The Maya village of Red Bank, off the Southern Hwy just south of the Placencia turnoff, would be well off the tourist radar if not for one remarkable natural experience. The rare and spectacularly plumaged scarlet macaws gather in the trees surrounding the village for around four months of the year (December to March, though sometimes they will arrive as early as November) to feast on the fruits that grow in the area.

Lush and verdant, the surrounding jungles are filled with brooks, rivers and swimming holes. A group of villagers manage the area and lead guided tours deep into the surrounding jungles (with some strenuous hiking) to see not just the macaws, but other unique animals that inhabit the area, including tapirs, jaguars, *gibnuts* and agoutis.

☞ Tours

Florentino Tours   TOURS
(☑ 660-6320; scarletmacawb3b@gmail.com; tours BZ$45) Red Bank local Florentino arranges guided walking tours to visit the macaws (BZ$45 per person), as well as accommodations and meals.

🛏 Sleeping

Scarlet Macaw Guesthouse   GUESTHOUSE $
(☑ 660-6320; scarletmacaw3b@gmail.com; Red Bank; camping per person BZ$10, r with/without bathroom BZ$100/35) Red Bank's only real guesthouse, at the entrance to the village, is superbly set up as an ecoretreat for visiting the surrounding jungle and scarlet macaws. The original rooms in the main thatched building are pretty basic with shared bathrooms, but owner Florentino was putting the finishing touches on brand new en-suite rooms when we visited.

❶ Getting There & Away

Red Bank is just under 4 miles off the Southern Hwy along an unsealed road, and 14 miles from Independence (with easy boat access from Placencia). There are four daily local buses (mostly in the morning) between Red Bank and either

TOLEDO DISTRICT (DEEP SOUTH)

POP 36,700

Bordering Guatemala to the south and west and the Stann Creek and Cayo Districts to the north, the 1669-sq-mile Toledo District encompasses an area most Belizeans refer to affectionately as 'The Deep South.' The only major town is Punta Gorda, and about half the district is under protection as national parks, wildlife sanctuaries, forest reserves or nature reserves.

Toledo's attractions – jungle trails, lagoons, wetlands, rivers, caves, waterfalls, villages, countless birds – and its Maya archaeological and cultural heritage are much less trumpeted than those of Belize's other districts, which makes them all the more magnetic to those looking to get off the beaten path.

The sealing of the Southern Hwy through to Guatemala has made this area much more accessible and numerous Maya villages can be visited without leaving the main road, but you'll need to delve a little further to experience the best of the Deep South.

❶ Getting There & Away

Frequent James Line (p232) buses run along the Southern Hwy from Belize City and Dangriga to Punta Gorda. Less-frequent local buses connect villages.

Any north-bound bus leaving Punta Gorda will drop you off at the Dump or Lubaantun intersections, from where people often hitchhike to many of the villages.

Punta Gorda

POP 6030

Punta Gorda (or PG) is a slightly ramshackle coastal settlement down in the Deep South of Toledo. Once known to travelers mainly as a port to get the boat across to Guatemala or Honduras, it's increasingly attracting visitors looking to chill out in the south and as a base for exploring surrounding Maya villages and culture, and the remote southern cays.

Toledo District

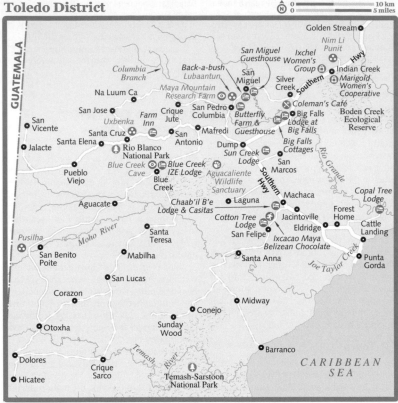

PG spreads along the Gulf of Honduras, its compact downtown area stretching lazily for several blocks just in from the coast. The town center is a triangular park with a distinctive blue-and-white clock tower; the airstrip is northwest, on the inland edge of town. Though it lacks the beaches of Placencia, there are plenty of docks from which to take a dip in the calm waters. A good part of PG's charm lies in its unassuming character.

🏃 Activities

Aside from swimming off various docks in town, the best of the region's activities are outside PG. Numerous tour operators in town can arrange a host of activities.

⭐ Cotton Tree
Chocolate Factory　　　FOOD & DRINK
(☑ 621-8776; www.cottontreechocolate.com; 2 Front St; ⊙ 8am-noon Mon-Sat & 1:30-5pm Mon-Fri) 🍴 **FREE** Cotton Tree is a good opportunity to

buy some local chocolate and learn a bit about the process. Beans are sourced from Toledo Cacao Growers Association, promoting both fair trade and local production. The owner happily offers tours of the small factory, and there's a gift shop selling only locally made handicrafts, including soaps, cacao-bean jewelry and, obviously, chocolate bars.

Ecotourism Belize　　　OUTDOORS
(☑ 722-0108; www.ecotourismbelize.com; Main St) 'Ranger for a Day' program enables travelers to experience the life and work of jungle rangers as they go about their daily activities in the Golden Stream Corridor Preserve, protecting the area from illegal activity and monitoring biodiversity. To the untrained eye, it's a pile of poop, but to a ranger, the scat tells many a tale.

Diving & Snorkeling
Offshore, some of the islands of the **Port Honduras Marine Reserve**, northeast of

Punta Gorda, offer good snorkeling and diving, especially the **Snake Cayes** (named for their resident boa constrictors), 16 miles out, with white-sand beaches. The beautiful **Sapodilla Cayes** on the barrier reef, some 38 miles east of Punta Gorda, are even better, with healthy coral reefs, abundant marine life and sandy beaches. A day trip for four costs around BZ$500 to the Port Honduras Marine Reserve or BZ$650 to Sapodilla Cayes.

Drum Lessons

Two of Belize's best drumming schools are here.

Maroon Creole Drum School   COURSE
(🖉 632-7841, 668-7733; methosdrums@hotmail.com; Joe Taylor Creek Rd; ⊙ by appointment) Those looking to study with a master will find the trip to Emmeth Young's drum school well worth it. When he's not touring the country performing, one of Belize's most respected Creole drummers hosts drum-making workshops and group presentations. It costs BZ$25 an hour for drum lessons, or BZ$250 for a few days learning both drumming and drum making. Open-hearth cooking classes can also be arranged here. Appointment only.

Warasa Garifuna Drum School   COURSE
(🖉 632-7701; www.warasadrumschool.com; New Rd; drum lessons BZ$25, half-day package BZ$125; ⊙ by appointment) Local drummer Ronald Raymond (Ray) McDonald teaches Garifuna beats at his Warasa Garifuna Drum School on New Rd (15 minutes' walk out of town). There are one-on one classes and group lessons. McDonald performs and lectures about Garifuna culture at Hickatee Cottages (p230).

Fishing

Fishing for bonefish, tarpon, permit, snook, barracuda, kingfish, jacks and snapper is superb in the offshore waters and some coastal lagoons and inland rivers: fly- and spin-fishing and trolling can be practiced year-round. Any of the tour operators in town can help you arrange fishing and sailing trips, as well as other activities.

**Garbutt's Marine &
Fishing Lodge**   FISHING, DIVING
(🖉 722-0070; www.garbuttsfishinglodge.com; Front St; fishing charters per half/full day US$350/550) Garbutt's is an experienced and highly professional fishing charter company and dive outfit, with exclusive access to private island Lime Caye in the Sapodillas, and accommodation and kayak rental in Punta Gorda.

Kayaking

Kayaking is increasingly popular, either on Joe Taylor Creek, which enters the sea at the eastern end of town, or around Port Honduras Marine Reserve. A number of operators, including TIDE Tours and Wild Thing have kayaks for rent.

🔗 Tours

Ideally located for exploring Belize's Deep South, Punta Gorda has a number of certified tour guides who lead day trips and longer expeditions, both terrestrial and nautical, as well as renting out canoes, kayaks and other gear.

TIDE Tours   TOURS
(🖉 722-2129; www.tidetours.org; Hopeville) 🖋 Ecofriendly TIDE Tours is a subsidiary of the Toledo Institute for Development and Environment (TIDE), running conservation and ecotours throughout the Toledo area, including inland adventures to caves and waterfalls, birding trips to Payne's Creek National Park and cultural tourism to local Maya villages. TIDE also does boating adventures out to the southern cays including snorkeling, fishing and diving tours.

All proceeds go back into conservation programs, sustainable tourism and training and development of local guides.

PG Tours   TOURS
(🖉 636-6162; www.pgtoursbelize.com; Front St) Run from a tiny Front St office by energetic English expat Jo, PG Tours is an excellent place to go for local information and advice. Tours throughout Toledo include birding, snorkeling in the Port Honduras Marine Reserve, Maya cultural tours and cooking classes. If you're interested in birding, ask here about the Toledo Belize Birding Club which meets monthly.

Toledo Cave & Adventure Tours   TOURS
(🖉 604-2124; www.tcatours.com) Bruno Kuppinger has been running adventure tours, caving excursions and cultural trips for more than 15 years. Ask about the trip to Tiger Cave, on private land near San Miguel.

Wild Thing   ADVENTURE
(🖉 636-1028; Snack Shack, Main St) Offers custom tours around the Toledo District, but specializes in kayaking expeditions in the southern cays – including outfitting for multiday trips. Head to the Snack Shack and ask for Roberto.

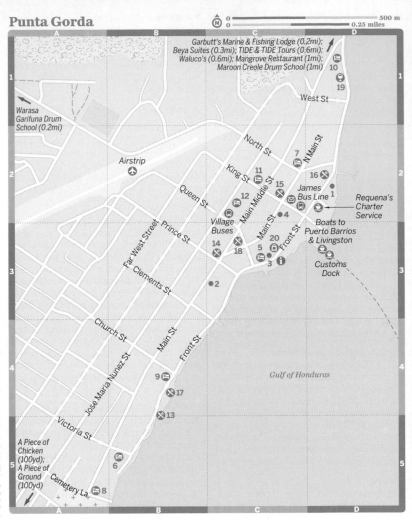

Punta Gorda

✨ Festivals & Events

Chocolate Festival of Belize FOOD & DRINK
(⊙ May) Celebrating all things to do with cacao and chocolate – the Maya food of the gods – this festival is held on the Commonwealth Day holiday weekend, mainly in Punta Gorda. As well as tastings, demonstrations and music, there's a street fair.

TIDE Fish Fest FOOD & DRINK
(⊙ Oct) The Fish Fest weekend celebrates the town's favorite natural resource with seafood feasts and live music.

🛏 Sleeping

There's a sprinkling of accommodations in PG's downtown but some of the best places are on the northern and southern fringes of town.

A Piece of Ground HOTEL $
(☑ 665-2695; www.apieceofground.com; 1050 Pelican St; dm/d BZ$38/78; ❄ 🕱) Also known locally as Backa Jama's, this funky, sociable four-story place has a ground-floor hostel with two dorms (one with air-con) and four spotless guesthouse rooms with attached bathroom on the second floor. Keep going up

Punta Gorda

🜲 Activities, Courses & Tours

🛏 Sleeping

🍴 Eating

🍷 Drinking & Nightlife

🛍 Shopping

the stairs to the popular restaurant, serving chicken dishes and American-style burgers and fries, and the rooftop bar with pool table.

It's at the southern end of town past the football field. Call ahead for directions.

Tate's Guest House   GUESTHOUSE $
(📞 722-0147; tatesguesthouse@yahoo.com; 34 Jose Maria Nunez St; r BZ$75-90, units BZ$125-150; 🅿 ❄ 🛜) Former postmaster Mr Tate keeps his guesthouse in immaculate condition and it's the best budget deal in the town center. The six rooms inside the mauve two-story facade, set in a little garden with a gazebo, are all air-conditioned and good value at these rates. Two are self-contained, with kitchenettes, and all come with cable TV and hot showers.

Nature's Way Guest House   GUESTHOUSE $
(📞 702-2119; natureswayguesthouse@hotmail.com; 82 Front St; s/d with bathroom BZ$45/60, s/d/tr/q without bathroom BZ$40/55/65/75; 🛜) Rustic and ramshackle, this place has been a long-time backpacker bolthole in Punta Gorda, though there are no dorm beds and it's not

the bargain it once was. Simple, screened-in, ocean-breeze–cooled wooden rooms are upstairs, and a large communal area with TV, music and free wi-fi is below. Nature's Way also rents bikes and kayaks for BZ$15 per day.

St Charles Inn   HOTEL $
(📞 722-2149; 23 King St; s/d/tr BZ$55/66/77, with air-con BZ$77/88/99; ❄ 🛜) Lilac-colored walls, verandas with hammocks, and clean budget rooms are the main draws of this aging guesthouse in downtown Punta Gorda. Rooms come with private bathrooms, coffee makers and cable TV.

Amaya Inn   GUESTHOUSE $
(📞 602-4251; Front St; r BZ$25) There are just four basic fan rooms with shared bath here above the PG Tours office. It's only steps away from the ferry dock so is a popular crash pad for backpackers coming from Guatemala.

Charlton's Inn   HOTEL $
(📞 722-2197; www.charltonsinn.com; 9 North Main St; s/d/tr BZ$80/100/110, apt s/d per month BZ$900/1000; ❄ 🛜) With 25 clean rooms with air-con and cable TV, not to mention a good location at the north end of town, Charlton's is a decent choice for those looking for a place in the upper level of the budget category. Triples are more like suites, with two stand-alone bedrooms. There are also five apartments for long-stayers.

★ Coral House Inn   BOUTIQUE HOTEL $$
(📞 722-28/8; www.coralhouseinn.com; d incl breakfast BZ$220-240, ste BZ$290; ❄ 🛜 🏊) This sublime seaside inn at the southern end of town boasts a lovely garden and in-ground swimming pool. Enormous rooms are stylishly designed, giving the place a classic (but not at all pretentious) colonial feel. A spacious veranda overlooks the sea on one side and a quaintly picturesque old cemetery on the other.

Chilling at the quiet poolside bar and exploring the area by bicycle (provided free) are just some of the bonuses for guests.

Garbutt's Marine & Fishing Lodge   CABIN $$
(📞 722-0070, 604-3548; www.garbuttsfishinglodge.com; Front St, Joe Taylor Creek; r BZ$200; 🅿 ❄ 🛜) Although primarily for guests on fishing or dive charters, Garbutt's lovely seafront rooms and stilt cabañas are available to anyone if they're available. It's a low-key setup, but this is the only absolute waterfront accommodation in PG, and the lodge rooms and private cabins with air-con, TV and over-water

TEA – TOLEDO ECOTOURISM ASSOCIATION

The **TEA** (☎ 722-2096; www.southernbelize.com/tea.html) is a well-meaning community organization that manages guesthouses in several Maya villages, but various bureaucratic battles have seen the program wind back in recent years. There are currently TEA guesthouses in San Miguel (managed by TIDE (p232)), San Antonio and Laguna. With a bit of luck, funding and good management, the program may pick up again and extend to more villages.

Although these are essentially basic guesthouses rather than homestays, you get the opportunity to mix with local families by having meals in village homes. Rates vary depending on the guesthouse, starting from BZ$25 per person, and meals are around BZ$10.

Most of the funds collected through the programs go directly to the villages themselves, benefiting local communities. Organised activity programs range from guided hikes, caving, canoeing and birdwatching to classes in textiles, basket weaving and cooking, as well as village tours and after-dinner storytelling.

To get specific contact information for key people in individual villages, call Reyes Chun or stop by Nature's Way Guest House (p229) in Punta Gorda, which has a booking desk.

balconies are excellent value. Also a dive shop and kayak rental.

Hickatee Cottages RESORT **$$**
(☎ 662-4475; www.hickatee.com; cottages BZ$170-230, d BZ$160, ste BZ$270-290; P 🏕🛜🌊) 🅿
Serene Hickatee Cottages is a beautiful and unique solar-powered resort that leaves as light an ecological footprint as possible. There are three fully furnished cottages, two spacious suites and the Hickatee Den, a small detached unit that sleeps two and overlooks the tiny plunge pool. The property features both garden and wild jungle space, and a 3-mile trail network.

Activities at Hickatee include nature walks and tarantula spotting, and Ronald Raymond McDonald gives drumming performances and lessons here at 6:30pm most Wednesdays. Hickatee has a remote feel, located down a rugged dirt road, but it's only 1¼ miles from town – call ahead for a free pickup.

Beya Suites HOTEL **$$**
(☎ 722-2188; www.beyasuites.com; Southern Hwy, Hopeville; s/d/tr from BZ$145/175/210; P ❄🛜)
The garish two-story pink building facing the sea about a mile north of PG, Beya is a good find for those looking to balance comfort with value. The eight rooms and two suites are well appointed and comfortable for this price. The cozy dining room serves breakfast and there's a small bar.

Sea Front Inn HOTEL **$$**
(☎ 722-2300; www.seafrontinn.com; 4 Front St; s/d/tr from BZ$140/170/190; P ❄🛜) One of the quirkiest looking hotels in Southern Be-

lize, this four-story gabled stone, wood and concrete construction is a comfortable and hospitable place. There are sea views from the front rooms and the well regarded Boneville cafe.

★**Blue Belize Guest House** B&B **$$$**
(☎ 722-2678; www.bluebelize.com; 139 Front St; ste BZ$170-340; @ 🛜🌊) 🅿 It's impossible not to feel a calming sense of space and relaxation at Blue Belize, with its waterfront location, lush garden and enormous rooms in a pair of connected two-story houses. The six breezy and beautifully decorated suites are more like serviced apartments than hotel rooms, offering well-furnished living rooms and kitchenettes, in addition to a comfortable master bedroom.

🍴 Eating

Punta Gorda has a number of good restaurants along Front St and tucked away in the town center.

★**Gomiers** VEGETARIAN **$**
(Southern Hwy, Hopeville; meals BZ$5-17; ⊙8am-10pm; 🛜🍴) Gormiers has moved from his little green shack to a new location across from the waterfront north of town. It's still the best place in PG for organic vegetarian and vegan cuisine, a variety of tofu-based creations, veg lasagna and a few fish dishes. Look out for live reggae nights on Fridays.

★**Snack Shack** CAFE **$**
(Main St; mains BZ$7.50-12; ⊙7am-3pm Mon-Fri, to noon Sat) With a breezy upper deck overlooking Main St, this is the best spot in town for

all-day Western or Belizean breakfasts, served alongside brain-freezing slushies, juices and shakes.

A Piece of Chicken
AMERICAN $

(1050 Pelican St; mains BZ$5-16; ⊘5-9pm) The main ingredient here is chicken – in burgers, sandwiches, wings or with rice and beans. Also hand-cut fries and nachos. The food is good and the 3rd-floor bar is a great place to hang out.

Marian's Bayview Restaurant
CARIBBEAN $

(☑722-0129; 76 Front St; mains BZ$10-16; ⊘11am-3pm & 5-9pm) This nondescript 3rd-floor outdoor eatery on the southern waterfront has a good local reputation and great views. Marian serves up excellent east Indian cuisine. Lunch and dinner are served buffet-style.

Grace's Restaurant
SEAFOOD $

(16 Main St; mains BZ$7-25; ⊘7am-10pm; 🐾) A longtime favorite of locals and travelers alike, Grace's offers a wide range of dishes, from Belizean specialties such as stew chicken, fry fish, and rice and beans, to more exotic seafood fare and good breakfasts. The decor is simple but breezy.

Express Diner
FAST FOOD $

(Main St; mains BZ$3-10; ⊘10am-10pm) The cheapest fast food in town – burgers, hot dogs, fries and shakes – is found at this central diner.

PG Clock Stop
ICE CREAM $

(Main St; snacks BZ$2-10; ⊘10am-2pm Mon-Wed & Fri-Sat, 3-9pm Wed-Mon) In the base of the central clock tower, this kiosk specializes in ice cream and shakes but also does fast food such as fish burgers and fries.

★ Asha's Culture Kitchen
SEAFOOD $$

(☑722-2742; 74 Front St; mains BZ$15-30; ⊘noon-10pm, closed Tue dinner) Twisted lobster, baked barracuda, cracked conch, whole snapper and lionfish fingers – and the best waterfront deck in PG. There's a lot to like about Asha's, where seafood is the specialty and the sea breezes are fine. A standard meal includes a choice of main from the blackboard menu and two sides (garlic mash potato is a winner). Service can be slow but it's worth the wait.

Leela's Bistro
CREOLE $$

(☑668-7548; 6 Front St; mains BZ$10-50; ⊘6am-10pm) This cozy little Creole restaurant and bar is a legacy of legendary PG *brukdown* (19th-century Creole music) singer Leela Vernon, who died in 2017. The menu is traditional Belizean with the likes of rice and beans, stew chicken, Creole lobster and breadfruit. Occasional live music on weekends. Don't forget to pop into the tiny adjoining Kriol museum dedicated to Leela Vernon.

Mangrove Restaurant
SEAFOOD $$

(☑623-0497; Milestone One, Cattle Landing; mains BZ$12-20; ⊘5-10pm Mon-Sat) Chef Iconie is well known locally for her fusion Belizean meals, incorporating locally caught seafood, curries, steak and pasta dishes. Choose from a small selection of mains and sides on the changing blackboard menu. It's across from the waterfront north of PG.

 Drinking & Nightlife

Punta Gorda has a number of bars along Front St and downtown. The town is also home to some top performers, such as the late *brukdown* queen Leela Vernon, and

---

FOOD OF THE GODS

The cacao plant, and the chocolate that derives from it, have always been important in Mayan society, known to the Maya as the 'food of the gods.' Traditional methods of fermenting, drying and roasting the cacao beans, then grinding them by hand, are still practiced in the Toledo District and chocolate-making cottage industries can be found in a number of places in Belize. The Chocolate Festival of Belize celebrates all things chocolate in Punta Gorda in May.

Cotton Tree Chocolate Factory (p226) in Punta Gorda is a good place to sample and buy local chocolate products, while Taste Belize Tours (p218) in Placencia offers culinary tours to chocolate factories.

Other chocolate-making enterprises open to tourists in Belize include Ixcacao Maya Belizean Chocolate (p233) and Eladio's Chocolate Adventure (p238) in Toledo, Che'il Chocolate Factory (p212) in Maya Center, Lamanai Chocolate (p165) near Belmopan and Ajaw Chocolate (p171) in San Ignacio.

SOUTHERN BELIZE PUNTA GORDA

local *punta* (traditional Garifuna dance) rock favorites, the Coolie Rebels.

To find out what's on, see the PG What's Happening Facebook page at www.facebook.com/groups/Whatshappeningpg.

Rainforest Reggae BAR
(Front St; ⊙3-11pm) This rather makeshift-looking waterfront bar is popular locally for its cocktails and laid-back soundtrack.

Waluco's BAR
(☑702-2129; Front St, Hopeville; ⊙11:30am-midnight Tue-Sun; 🛜) This big, breezy *palapa*, a mile northeast of town, is a popular weekend spot, especially for Sunday sessions when the BBQ fires up and everyone goes swimming off the pier opposite. There's cheap bar food and Garifuna drummers sometimes play here.

🛍 Shopping

Fajina Crafts Center ART
(Front St; ⊙8am-11:15am Mon, Wed, Fri & Sat) Operated cooperatively by a women's association with members from 13 villages around southern Toledo, the Fajina Crafts Center opens on market days selling handmade necklaces, belts, bracelets, baskets, clothing, bags, earrings, wood carvings and many other items made by Toledo's indigenous peoples.

ℹ Information

Customs & Immigration (☑722-2022; Front St; ⊙9am-5pm Mon-Fri) This is your first port of call when coming to Punta Gorda by boat from Guatemala or Honduras; it should also be your last stopping place when leaving by sea (there's a departure tax of BZ$40). Head here for visa extensions too.

Belize Bank (30 Main St) and **Scotia Bank** (1 Main St) both have 24-hour ATMs accepting most international cards.

Post Office (King St; ⊙8am-noon & 1pm-5pm Mon-Thu, to 4:30pm Fri)

Punta Gorda Tourism Information Center (☑722-2531; Front St; ⊙8am-5pm Mon-Fri) PG's little BTIA tourist office can answer general questions and has village bus timetables. If they have it, pick up a free copy of the local tourist paper *Toledo Howler*.

TIDE (☑722-2274; www.tidebelize.org; One Mile San Antonio Rd) The Toledo Institute for Development and Environment is responsible for a range of community conservation projects in the Deep South, both in the inland forests and the marine parks.

ℹ Getting There & Away

AIR
Tropic Air (☑722-2008; www.tropicair.com) has five daily flights to Belize City and Belize City International (BZ$370, one hour), and one to Placencia (BZ$150, 20 minutes) and Dangriga (BZ$226, 40 minutes). **Maya Island Air** (☑722-2856; www.mayaislandair.com) also flies four times daily to Belize City, Placencia and Dangriga for similar prices. Specials are often available, and ticket offices are at the **airstrip** (PND).

BOAT
At the time of writing there were two daily boat services to Puerto Barrios in Guatemala at 9am and 2pm. There was also one daily boat to Livingstone at 2pm (BZ$60). Boats depart from the municipal pier in front of the customs and immigration office, where you'll need to clear customs.

Requena's Charter Service (☑722-2070; 12 Front St) operates the *Mariestela*, departing Punta Gorda at 9am daily for Puerto Barrios, Guatemala (BZ$60, one hour), and returning at 2pm. Tickets are sold at the office and customs dock down the street.

At the time of writing, a shuttle boat between Punta Gorda, Barranco and Monkey River was under consideration.

BUS
James Bus Line (☑702-2049, 722-2625; King St) has hourly buses from Punta Gorda to Belize City (regular/air-con BZ$26/28, seven hours) from 4am to 4pm. Buses stop at Dangriga (BZ$14/15, 3½ hours) and Belmopan (BZ$20/22, 5½ hours). Another regular service runs to Independence (for Placencia). All buses leave from the main bus station on King St and cruise around PG a bit before heading north.

ℹ Getting Around

Aliram Auto Rental (☑610-1475; aliram@btl.net; 6th St) rents cars for use in the Toledo area.

Taxis congregate around Central Park.

The main stop for **buses** to villages around Punta Gorda is on the corner of Queen St and Jose Maria Nunez St. Timetables are available from the tourist office.

Around Punta Gorda

The Southern Hwy heads northwest from Punta Gorda to the intersection at Dump (we didn't name it!), where there's a gas station. Along the way are detours to some of the region's best ecolodges and there are several interesting places on the rugged road to remote Barranco village.

THE CAYES OF THE DEEP SOUTH

Unlike the northern or central cays the little-visited cays of the Deep South are truly off the beaten path, with no flashy resorts or regular boat transfers.

About a two-hour boat ride from Punta Gorda (and right on the barrier reef) is the **Sapodilla Cayes Marine Reserve**. A protected reserve (visitors pay a daily BZ$20 conservation fee), the Sapodillas offer superlative opportunities for swimming, snorkeling and diving. **Lime Caye**, the most popular of the Sapodillas, has wonderful white-sand beaches, a basic *Gilligan's Island* bunkhouse (BZ$40 per person), beach camping (BZ$30) and meals for BZ$20. A round-trip fare to Lime Caye is around BZ$600 per boat (maximum of six passengers). Trips to other cays in the chain are also available. Contact Garbutt's Marine & Fishing Lodge (p227) in Punta Gorda.

Closer to Punta Gorda, the **Port Honduras Marine Reserve** contains 130-plus mangrove cays and is managed by the TIDE in Punta Gorda. There's a daily fee of BZ$10. Snorkeling and kayaking tours to the reserve, run by TIDE and other local operators, can be organized from Punta Gorda. A charter boat from Punta Gorda with TIDE costs around BZ$700 a day (for up to six people).

Trips to the Port Honduras reserve begin at **Abalone Caye**, where a short presentation is given by the rangers in charge. Visitors will then be brought to different cays in the reserve, including **West Snake Caye** (known for its white-sand beaches), **East Snake Caye** (excellent snorkeling) and **Frenchman Caye** (a prime spot for manatee watching). Depending on the trip, you may also get to see **Wild Cane Caye**, an ancient Maya center of obsidian trade and production.

To arrange trips to either Sapodilla or Port Honduras, contact Garbutt's Marine & Fishing Lodge (p227). Garbutt's also arranges a variety of marine tours around the area, including fishing, scuba and snorkeling trips, with price dependent on distance.

⊙ Sights

Temash-Sarstoon
National Park   NATIONAL PARK
(☑ 626-7684, 604-8564; egbertvalencio@yahoo. com) The tiny Garifuna fishing community of Barranco (population 160), about an hour's drive from Punta Gorda, is the access point for Temash-Sarstoon National Park, a remote 64-sq-mile protected reserve of rainforest, wetlands, estuaries and rivers lined by towering mangroves and stretching all the way to Guatemala. The park harbors a huge variety of wildlife including jaguars, tapirs, ocelots, birdlife and manatees in the estuaries.

Two Barranco natives deeply involved in both local tourism and park conservation are Egbert Valencio and Alvin Loredo; both lead land and river tours (around BZ$200 per day) into the nearby park given at least a few days' notice.

Ask in Punta Gorda about the boat service to Barranco that was mooted when we visited.

Aguacaliente
Wildlife Sanctuary   NATURE RESERVE
(Laguna) About 13 miles northwest of Punta Gorda and 2 miles off the Southern Hwy, the village of Laguna is the starting point for the 8.6-sq-mile Aguacaliente Wildlife Sanctuary, an extensive wetland area. The lagoon, at the heart of the park, is home to flocks of ibis and woodstork, many raptors including ospreys, plenty of kingfishers and herons and the odd jabiru stork. There's a visitors center on the trail from the village.

The two-hour hike in can be wet and muddy and is sometimes impossible at the height of the rains.

⊙ Tours

Ixcacao Maya Belizean
Chocolate   FOOD & DRINK
(☑ 742-4050; www.ixcacaomayabelizeanchocolate. com; San Felipe village; tours per person BZ$60-100; ⊙ 9am-5pm) ◉ Learn all about the Maya chocolate-making process at Juan and Abelina's beautiful cacao farm and chocolate factory. There's a variety of tour options, including farm tours, factory tours and traditional Maya lunch (BZ$24). Juan will walk you through the traditional chocolate-making process – from harvest and fermentation to drying and roasting, and on to deshelling and grinding, tasting as you go.

Reserve a day in advance; group discounts are available.

The family also has a small homestay bunkhouse next to the factory (BZ$50 per person including breakfast and dinner) as well as camping (BZ$10) and farmstay (BZ$50).

🛏 Sleeping & Eating

Sun Creek Lodge
RESORT $$

(☑607-6363; www.suncreeklodge.de; incl breakfast d cabañas BZ$120-150, villas BZ$170-240) As jungle lodges in Belize go, Sun Creek is a real bargain. Thomas and Marisa run this rustic, eco-oriented lodge in a fine patch of jungle near the village of San Marcos about 13 miles from Punta Gorda. In the tropical garden are four thatched-roof cabañas, two with bathroom outside and open-sky shower, and two beautifully appointed family villas.

Villas are a comfortable blend of modern and rustic, with a spacious living area, kitchenette with fridge and private bathrooms with open-sky shower.

Chaab'il B'e Lodge & Casitas
RESORT $$

(☑666-3099, in USA 1-800-819-9088; www.chaabilbe.com; r & cabañas BZ$200-250; P❋🛜) A change of name and ownership has breathed new life into Chaab'il B'e Lodge & Casitas, just off the highway 8 miles from Punta Gorda. Three rustic, thatched-roof cabañas and four lodge rooms are set amid pretty gardens and jungle. Rooms are equipped with aircon and flat-screen TVs, while the thatched cabañas are big, breezy, fan-cooled and TV-free but very comfortable.

Meals are available in the screened lodge dining/lodge, and there's an excellent swimming hole on the property.

★ Copal Tree Lodge
LODGE $$$

(☑722-0051, in USA 1-844-238-0216; www.copaltreelodge.com; Wilson Rd; ste incl breakfast BZ$690-1490; P❋🛜🏊) Formerly Belcampo Belize, Copal Tree Lodge enjoys a superb hilltop setting overlooking miles of protected jungle stretching down to the Gulf of Honduras. This beautiful lodge offers 16 spacious and luxurious suites, including four Canopy Suites, with solid wood furniture, queen- or king-size beds, full-length windows and private verandas overlooking jungle and sea.

There's a day spa and two cable tramways, one leading down through the jungle to the Río Grande and hotel gym. The excellent restaurant serves food sourced from the lodge's own organic farm, which guests can visit by free guided tour. Other tours on offer

include fly-fishing, birding, snorkeling and trips to Maya ruins. Copal Tree feels remote but is only 2.5 miles off the Southern Hwy, and about 5 miles from Punta Gorda.

Cotton Tree Lodge
RESORT $$$

(☑670-0557, in USA 866-480-4534; www.cottontreelodge.com; r BZ$392, d cabañas BZ$415-700; P❋🛜🏊) 🌿 Luxury, environmentalism and intense beauty meet on the banks of the Moho River a few miles north of the village of San Felipe. All of Cotton Tree's 11 thatched-roof cabins on stilts are luxuriously furnished in a superb jungle/hardwood motif – while they're all screened in, there's an exhilarating feeling of sleeping in the open.

The resort's power is partially provided by solar panels, while most of the food served in the lodge's excellent restaurant is bought locally or sourced from the onsite organic garden. Activities include hiking, horseback riding, kayaking, canoeing, caving and birdwatching (included in all-inclusive packages, extra if you take room-only). The 100-acre property offers amazing views of the nearby Maya Mountain Range on the western horizon.

★ Jungle Farm Restaurant
INTERNATIONAL, BELIZEAN $$$

(☑722-0051; Wilson Rd, Copal Tree Lodge; lunch BZ$18-30, dinner BZ$42-60; ⏱6am-9pm) If you have only one dining splurge in Southern Belize, the restaurant at Copal Tree Lodge is the place to do it. The location, high on a jungle hilltop, is superb and the restaurant is a delight with its large deck, expansive views and attentive service. Food is expertly prepared with a farm-to-table philosophy combining uniquely Belizean and international flavors.

Most of the produce and ingredients come from Copal Tree's own farm and gardens or from local farmers and fishers. Light lunch might consist of tacos, salads or lionfish ceviche. Dinner is a daily changing menu that might feature fresh fish, homegrown chicken or vegetarian dishes. Downstairs is the sociable Rum Bar. Reservations recommended, especially for dinner.

❶ Getting There & Away

The Southern Hwy is sealed but you might need a 4WD to tackle side roads to Barranco and Laguna during the wet. At the time of writing, a boat service between Punta Gorda and Barranco was being planned.

Big Falls & Indian Creek

POP 1100 (BIG FALLS), 570 (INDIAN CREEK)

On the Southern Hwy, about 20 miles from Punta Gorda, Big Falls is a small village with a number of cultural and adventure attractions. This is a good starting point for the Toledo cultural circuit taking in San Miguel and San Pedro Columbia. The ruins of Lubaantun are 4.3 miles west on an unpaved road.

Further north up the highway are the Kekchí villages of Silver Creek (population 320), Indian Creek (population 570) and Golden Stream (population 320), each with their own roadside cultural attractions.

☉ Sights

★ **Living Maya Experience** CULTURAL CENTER

(☏ Chiacs 632-4585, Cals 627 7408; livingmaya experience@gmail.com; Big Falls; tours per person BZ$20-30; ☺ by appointment) Two Kekchí families in Big Falls village have opened up their homes as a cultural experience for visitors and both are excellent. The Cal family demonstrates ancient Maya lifestyle from tortilla- and chocolate-making to traditional instruments and an exploration of their self-sufficient garden. With the Chiac family, you can learn to make woven Maya crafts – baskets, hammocks or bags.

Nim Li Punit RUINS

(☏ 822-2106; BZ$10; ☺ 8am-5pm) The Maya ruins of Nim Li Punit stand atop a natural hill half a mile north of the Southern Hwy, near the village of Indian Creek. The site is notable for the 26 stelae found in the southern Plaza of the Stelae. Four of the finest are housed in the stela house beside the visitors center.

Stela 14, at 33ft, is the second-longest stela found anywhere in the Maya world (after Stela E from Quirigua, Guatemala). It shows the ruler of Nim Li Punit in an offering or incense-scattering ritual, wearing an enormous headdress which is responsible for the name Nim Li Punit ('Big Hat' in Kekchí Maya).

Rediscovered in 1976 by oil prospectors, Nim Li Punit was inhabited from some point in the middle Classic Period (AD 250–1000) until sometime between AD 800 and 1000. It was probably a town of 5000 to 7000 people at its peak, and likely was a political and religious community of some importance in the region.

The most interesting part of the site is the south end, comprising the Plaza of the Stelae and the Plaza of Royal Tombs. The

Nim Li Punit

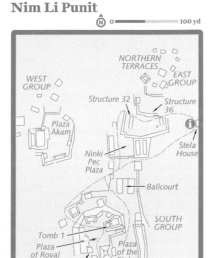

Plaza of the Stelae is thought to have acted as a calendrical observatory: seen from its western mound, three of the small stones in front of the long eastern mound align with sunrise on the equinoxes and solstices. The Plaza of Royal Tombs, with three open, excavated tombs, was a residential area for the ruling family. Archaeologists uncovered four members of this family in Tomb 1, along with several jadeite items and 37 ceramic vessels.

Nim Li Punit has a good visitors center where you can view various items preserved from earlier excavations, as well as hire tour guides or get general information. Buses along the highway will drop you off or pick you up at the turnoff.

🏃 Activities

Big Falls Extreme Adventures ADVENTURE SPORTS

(☏ 634-6979, 634-5185; www.bigfallsextreme adventures.com; Big Falls; ziplining & tubing BZ$120, with lunch BZ$140) The six-line ziplining course will have you flying through the jungle on a 45-minute adventure. It can be combined with tubing down the Río Grande, including a stop at hot springs and lunch at a riverside restaurant. Kayaks are also available. Reserve a day in advance.

MAYA CULTURAL TRAIL

A good short loop of the central Maya villages starts in Big Falls, where you can visit the Cal and Chiac families as part of the Living Maya Experience (p235). Next head north to Indian Creek, where Ixchel Women's Group and Marigold Women's Cooperative are two of a growing number of Maya arts-and-crafts cooperatives where you can see and buy traditional textiles and jewelry. Returning via Silver Creek it's about 4 miles to the village of San Miguel where there's a TEA guesthouse and a cacao chocolate-making enterprise. Stop in to visit the ancient Maya ruins of Lubaantun on the way to San Pedro Columbia, where you can tour another cacao farm with Eladio Pop (p238) and learn more about the art of chocolate making.

Belize Spice Farm FARM TOUR

(☑ 732-4014; www.belizespicefarm.com; Golden Stream; tours BZ$40; ⊙ tours on demand 8am-4pm) Spices more commonly associated with India and Asia – black pepper, nutmeg, vanilla, cardamom and clove – grow in abundance at this large farm. Take a 45-minute vehicle tour and learn the full spice story. The lovely open restaurant serves breakfast and lunch for BZ$22.50.

🛏 Sleeping & Eating

Big Falls Cottages GUESTHOUSE $

(☑ 605-9985; www.bigfallscottages.com; Esperanza Rd; s/d BZ$75/85; P 🛜) These two lovely, family-run cottages are set in a magnificent garden and come with a kitchenette and bathroom (with hot showers). They're tucked away just off the highway south of Big Falls.

Big Falls Extreme Adventures CABANAS $$

(☑ 634-5185; www.bigfallsextremeadventures.com; Southern Hwy; s/d cabañas BZ$190/240, r BZ$380; ❄ 🛜) These cabañas and family rooms on the banks of the Río Grande in Big Falls offer a comfortable stay with air-con, cable TV and spring mattresses. It's part of the Extreme Adventures resort with ziplining, river tubing, kayaking and an onsite restaurant. Packages are available including tours, meals and transfers.

Lodge at Big Falls RESORT $$$

(☑ 610-0126, 732-4444; www.thelodgeatbigfalls.com; Big Falls; s/d/tr cabañas incl breakfast BZ$346/442/508; P 🛜 ❄) On a bend in the jungle-clad Río Grande, 18 miles from Punta Gorda, Lodge at Big Falls is a meticulously maintained property where tiled-floor, palm-thatched cabins are spread around beautiful gardens. Popular with birdwatchers and butterfly enthusiasts, the lodge is also a fine place from which to enjoy a host of activities and tours including caving, kayaking and river tubing.

The hardwood cabañas come with air-con and kitchenettes, while the thatch cabañas are fan-cooled with screened windows catching the breeze. The lodge also has a fine restaurant and bar serving breakfast, packed lunches (BZ$24) and dinner (BZ$80). Transfers to or from Punta Gorda are BZ$100 for up to four people.

Coleman's Café BELIZEAN $$

(☑ 630-4069; Big Falls; buffet BZ$20; ⊙ 10:30am-4:30pm; P 🛜) Something of an institution for travelers driving the Southern Hwy, Coleman's offers a self-serve lunch buffet with three or four dishes plus rice, beans and salad. Pile up your plate! Dinner is by reservation and you can also get beer, soft drinks and local chocolate. It's signposted off the highway north of Big Falls.

🛍 Shopping

Marigold Women's Cooperative ARTS & CRAFTS

(☑ 620-6084; marigoldwomen@gmail.com; Southern Hwy, Indian Creek) In Indian Creek village, Marigold is a cooperative of local Kekchí Maya women working to preserve their culture through cooking. Traditional Maya food, including breads and cakes are available, along with arts and crafts and occasional traditional dance performances. Call ahead to check that it's open.

Ixchel Women's Group ARTS & CRAFTS

(☑ 632-7938; www.indiancreekvillage.info/ixchel.html; Indian Creek; ⊙ 7am-5:30pm) Operating from a hut in Indian Creek village, the Ixchel Women's Group is run by a small cooperative of Kekchí Maya women who produce traditional handicrafts and sell them throughout the area. Among the items you'll find here are bracelets, bags, necklaces and *kalaba* shakers (a local instrument). Free craft demonstrations are also given.

ℹ️ Getting There & Away

Big Falls is on the Southern Hwy, so any bus to or from Punta Gorda will let you off here (or at Indian Creek village). At least five local buses pass through here daily to/from Punta Gorda.

San Miguel

POP 620

Just up the road from San Pedro Columbia, this Kekchí village is on the unsealed loop road past the Lubaantun ruins and off the Southern Hwy. You can walk to Lubaantun (2 miles) or trek to Tiger Cave, 1½ hours' walk away, returning by canoe along the Río Grande.

🛏️ Sleeping

San Miguel offers the basic budget options of Back-a-bush and a TEA guesthouse.

San Miguel Guesthouse   GUESTHOUSE $
(📞 602-6240; ackmartin82@gmail.com; r per person BZ$25) This thatched TEA guesthouse has basic accommodation but it's a fine place to delve into Maya village life and home-style cooking (meals BZ$10 per person). The family that runs the guesthouse also has a small cacao chocolate-making operation.

Back-a-bush   HOSTEL $
(📞 631-1731; www.back-a-bush.com; camping per tent BZ$10, dm BZ$30, d withouth bathroom BZ$60; 📶) In the village of San Miguel, just a few miles from Lubaantun, is this simple, chilled-out jungle guesthouse and farm with a lovely Dutch owner. Accommodations are very rustic but peaceful and guests can enjoy meals made with cacao, coffee and vegetables grown on the farm.

San Pedro Columbia

POP 1500

San Pedro Columbia is the largest Kekchí Maya community outside Guatemala. Columbia (as locals call it) was established by Kekchí families who left Pueblo Viejo to look for new farmland around 1905. The village has seen boom and bust, with mahogany and cedar felling, chicle collection and, in the 1970s and 1980s, marijuana cultivation. There are several shops where handicrafts and food can be bought.

Two miles up the river is the source of the Columbia Branch of the Río Grande, where water bubbles out from beneath the rocks. Local guides can take you to see the source; it's a 45-minute walk from the center of town. Behind the village, up in the hills, is the Columbia Forest Reserve, which has thousands of acres of forest, sinkholes, caves and ruins hidden in the valleys. There are also local guides who can take you there.

◎ Sights & Activities

Lubaantun   RUINS
(BZ$10; ⏰ 8am-5pm) The Maya ruins at Lubaantun, 1.3 miles northwest of San Pedro Columbia, are built on a natural hilltop and display a construction method unusual in the ancient Maya world of mortar-less, neatly cut, black-slate blocks. Archaeologists postulate that Lubaantun, which flourished between AD 730 and 860, may have been an administrative center regulating trade, while nearby Nim Li Punit was the local religious and ceremonial center. The Maya site comprises a collection of seven plazas, three ballcourts and surrounding structures.

MAYA MOUNTAIN RESEARCH FARM

The 70-acre organic **Maya Mountain Research Farm** (📞 630-4386; www.mmrfbz.org) and registered NGO offers internships for those interested in learning about organic farming, permaculture, biodiversity and alternative energy. Located in a beautiful jungle valley 2 miles upriver from San Pedro Columbia, the farm is run by permaculture teacher Christopher Nesbitt, with the philosophy of promoting fully sustainable food production.

Accommodations in a series of rustic dorm-style cabañas and *palapas* cost BZ$350 a week, or BZ$1200 a month, all inclusive.

Interns take part in every stage of meal preparation, from harvesting fruits, vegetables, nuts and herbs to cooking over a wood-burning stove inside the farm's outdoor kitchen (hand-built with stones from the river). MMRF also offers short-term courses lasting between one and three weeks in both permaculture design and renewable energy. Rustic and beautiful in the extreme, the farm is pretty remote, with no road access. To get there you need to walk or take a *dory* (dugout canoe) from San Pedro Columbia village.

Lubaantun

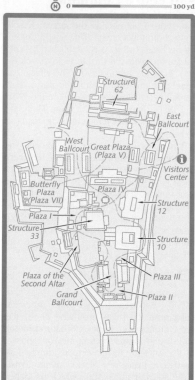

At the entrance is a small visitors center displaying pottery, ceramic figurines, maps and panels detailing the controversial 'crystal skull,' said to have been found here in 1926 by 17-year-old Anna Mitchell-Hedges. Lubaantun is known for the numerous mold-made ceramic figurines found here, many of which represent ancient ball players.

In 1924, Belize's then-chief medical officer Thomas Gann, an amateur archaeologist, bestowed the name Lubaantun (Place of Fallen Stones) on these ruins. More professional archaeological work has taken place since 1970 and much of the site is now cleared and restored.

There are two entry points to Lubaantun from the Southern Hwy, either via Silver Creek (signposted just north of Big Falls) or San Pedro Columbia. Either way it's around 23 miles from Punta Gorda along dirt roads once you leave the highway. Village buses running between San Pedro Columbia and

San Miguel can drop you at the turnoff to the site, then it's about half a mile further.

Chaos Oasis ARCHITECTURE
(www.facebook.com/TheChaosOasisBelize; Lubaantun Rd; by donation) One of the stranger things you're likely to see in Belize is this 'Earth Ship' structure, made even more incongruous because it's so close to the entrance of the Lubaantun ruins. It's made entirely from recyclable materials such as old tires and glass and plastic bottles (a lot of Crystal Head vodka was consumed in the process), all plastered together into a whimsical fantasy.

It's a labor of love for British expats Alisa and Richard; current uses include a juice bar, yoga *shala* (studio) and craft shop, and there's a butterfly house under construction. Stop in for a chat and admire their work. Donations go to help local communities.

Eladio's Chocolate Adventure FOOD & DRINK
(☑ 624-0166; eladiopop@gmail.com; per person BZ$60) In San Pedro Columbia village, passionate local Eladio Pop will take you on a tour of his cacao farm, followed by a traditional chocolate-making demonstration and Maya lunch.

🛏 Sleeping

Butterfly Farm & Guesthouse HOSTEL $
(☑ 632-5949; www.columbiarivercooperative.com; r BZ$30; 🛜) Lisa runs this offbeat farm and butterfly house just out of San Pedro Columbia. The four dorm-style rooms are in a large wooden bunkhouse with clean beds and one shared bathroom with cold shower. It's as basic as you would expect out here, but there's wi-fi and the butterfly house and farm are interesting. Meals are available (BZ$10).

ⓘ Getting There & Away

San Pedro Columbia is on the dirt road loop, 2.3 miles from San Miguel and about the same to the Southern Hwy turnoff. Five village buses from Punta Gorda, 20 miles southeast, stop here daily on the way to Silver Creek.

San Antonio

POP 1200

The largest Mopan Maya community in Belize, San Antonio was founded in the mid-19th century by farmers from San Luis Rey in the Petén, Guatemala. A wooden idol (of San Luis) was taken from the church in San Luis Rey by settlers who returned to Guatemala to retrieve their saint. The idol remains in the beautiful stone church in San Antonio, which has wonderful stained-glass windows with Italian and Irish names on them (because the glass was donated by parishioners from St Louis, Missouri).

San Antonio has a large concentration of cacao farmers growing cacao for export and use in Belizean-made chocolate products.

◉ Sights

Río Blanco National Park NATIONAL PARK
(BZ$10; ⊙ 7am-5pm) The 105-acre Río Blanco National Park, just west of Santa Elena village, is a compact protected wildlife area that's home to a variety of flora and fauna. The highlight for visitors is definitely Río Blanco Falls, a beautiful 20ft-high waterfall leading into a clear swimming hole just a five-minute walk in from the ranger station. Steps lead down to a platform for swimming and a concrete path has been constructed leading to a swing bridge across the river.

Other prime attractions here are birdwatching and hiking. There's also a basic dorm bunkhouse at the ranger station (BZ$20), which has a small stove for cooking, or you can camp in the park itself (BZ$10).

Uxbenka RUINS
FREE The Maya ruins of Uxbenka are close to the village of Santa Cruz on the road from San Antonio. The site is mostly undeveloped and the visible part is merely the center of a larger, yet-to-be-excavated city. Archaeologists believe Uxbenka dates back to the Classic Period, with stelae erected in the 4th century.

There is evidence that it had a close relationship with Tikal to the north. The open site has a large plaza with some excavated tombs and sweeping views to the sea. On a clear day it is possible to see the mountains of Honduras and Guatemala. There's no visitor center for Uxbenka – a local guide can take you, or you can make your own way there; look out for signs from the highway.

✪ Festivals & Events

Feast of San Luis RELIGIOUS
(⊙ Aug 15-25) The Feast of San Luis, a harvest festival where the famous Deer Dance is performed, is celebrated in town.

🛏 Sleeping

Bol's Hilltop Hotel HOTEL $
(r without bathroom BZ$25) This village guesthouse in San Antonio has very basic rooms.

CRYSTAL SKULL OF LUBAANTUN

Crystal skulls, usually carved out of white quartz, are not generally associated with Mayan history and culture. However, one of the more famous skulls was allegedly found at Lubaantun in 1926 by Anna Mitchell-Hedges, the teenage daughter of British writer and explorer Frederick Mitchell-Hedges. The veracity of the claim and the origin of the skull have long been controversial as its existence wasn't recorded until Frederick Mitchell-Hedges' memoirs in 1954. It has since been the subject of a 1990 documentary, *Crystal Skull of Lubaantun* and has been examined by the Smithsonian Institute among others.

Whether the skull came from Lubaantum or the story is a hoax (some claim Mitchell-Hedges bought it at an auction in London in the 1940s), Belizeans lay claim to the skull and would like it back. You can read the story of the skull in the visitor center at Lubaantun.

Meals can be obtained next door at Clara Bol's house.

Farm Inn FARMSTAY $$
(🖉 732-4781; www.thefarminnbelize.com; San Antonio; campsite BZ$20, d incl breakfast BZ$220-300; P 🛜 🖳) 🡪 On the highway between Santa Cruz and San Antonio, the family-owned Farm Inn is a little gem set on 52 acres of jungle and organic farmland (with 7000 cacao trees). Accommodation consists of a cabaña with two comfortable en-suite rooms and the superb four-room inn by the creek.

The double-story inn has spacious rooms with porch or balcony, kitchenette and lounge areas. The sociable restaurant and bar is open all day but reserve ahead for lunch or dinner; meals are Belizean with an African influence. Power is solar with a backup generator. It's about 2 miles west of San Antonio village.

❶ Getting There & Away

San Antonio is on the newly sealed section of the Southern Hwy around 22 miles northwest of Punta Gorda. Around six village buses stop here daily from Punta Gorda.

THE ROAD TO GUATEMALA

The Southern Highway in Belize is now sealed all the way to the Guatemalan border. But it abruptly ends there. The US$8 million, 23-mile road extension from Dump to the border began in 2011 and was due to be completed in 2014 but, in true Belizean style, it took a few more years. This continuation of the Southern Hwy has opened up the Deep South with villages such as Mafredi, San Antonio, Santa Cruz and Santa Elena now easily accessible. (Jalacte, which has long been an unofficial crossing point via a swing bridge, has been bypassed by the new road, but is still easily accessed just off it.)

This doesn't mean there's an official border crossing here yet. There is a vehicle inspection point at the Jalacte turnoff and a military presence at the actual border but the road on the Guatemalan side doesn't link up, so crossing is only possible on foot, as many cross-border locals do. It will happen eventually though, and it's difficult to say what changes the road will bring to these communities, and what effect an official border crossing will have on the flow of visitors in the south. But the Deep South's days as a quiet, dead-end backwater may be numbered.

Blue Creek

POP 450

Part Kekchí and part Mopan Maya, Blue Creek is split by the pretty, blue-green–tinted namesake river. Howler monkeys inhabit the surrounding hilly jungles, otters live along the creek and green iguanas are plentiful. For travelers Blue Creek is an appealing destination for its cave and jungle walks.

Near Blue Creek is the **Tumul'kin School of Learning**, a Maya boarding school that hosts students from throughout Toledo and other parts of Belize, providing a learning venue that inculcates pride in being Maya and gives students an education that values traditional knowledge.

⊙ Sights

Blue Creek Cave CAVE
(Hokeb Ha Cave; guided tours from BZ$30) About a 20-minute walk along a jungle path from the bridge is Blue Creek Cave, which you can only enter with a guide. The cave has a 'wet side,' where you swim and wade up to an underground waterfall (about one hour in the cave), and a 'dry side' where you can try a more difficult venture involving some climbing and emerge at a different entrance.

Guides and caving equipment can be hired in the village.

🛏 Sleeping

There's a cool riverside lodge that requires advanced bookings, or ask local guides about homestay rooms.

Blue Creek IZE Lodge LODGE $$
(☑ 655-1461; www.izebelize.com; d incl meals BZ$140) This IZE (International Zoological Expeditions) property enjoys a gloriously remote rainforest location on the banks of Blue Creek, deep in rural Toledo District but only a 10-minute walk from Blue Creek village. There are five rustic river-facing timber cabins and two tree houses, all with verandas, fans and shared bathroom.

It's primarily for school and study groups but travelers are welcome with advance reservation.

⊙ Getting There & Away

Blue Creek is 23 miles from Punta Gorda and 5 miles down a rough dirt road off the Southern Hwy. Two village buses (11:30am and noon) head to Blue Creek from Punta Gorda on Monday, Wednesday, Friday and Saturday, returning on the same day.

Tikal & Flores, Guatemala

Best Places to Eat

➜ Las Orquídeas (p251)

➜ Terrazzo (p255)

➜ Mon Ami (p251)

➜ Maple y Tocino (p255)

➜ Antojitos Mexicanos (p256)

Best Places to Stay

➜ Tikal Inn (p247)

➜ Jungle Lodge (p247)

➜ Alice Guesthouse (p250)

➜ La Posada de Don José (p253)

Why Go?

The glory and splendors of the ancient Maya world await you, just over the border in the lush rainforests of Eastern Guatemala. The region is especially important to the Maya people, being home to many temples, pyramids and ruins with significance to the alignment of 12/21/2012, which recently completed a major cycle of the Maya calendar and began another.

The most fabled (and easiest to reach) of Guatemala's slice of La Ruta Maya is Tikal. Larger and more completely restored than any of the Maya sites in Belize, Tikal offers visitors the unique opportunity to spend the night at the ruins, waking up in the middle of the jungle, thanks to its in-park campground and lodges. Alternatively, the nearby lakeside villages of Flores and El Remate are peaceful, picturesque places to recover from some intensive archaeological exploration.

When to Go

Feb–May Drier, less boggy, less mud, though May gets humid.

Jun–Aug Rainy season. Cooler but bring bug spray (and a mosquito net) for any outdoor activities.

Dec–Feb Cool nights and mornings, with temperatures moderate during the day. A pleasant time to visit El Petén.

Tikal & Flores, Guatemala Highlights

1 Tikal (p242) Watching at sunset, sunrise, or any time in between, there's nothing that beats this ancient city.

2 El Mirador (p248) Trekking through the jungle

to this huge, though still scarcely excavated, Maya ruin.

3 Flores (p251) Lounging lakeside over evening

cocktails on the *malecón* of this picturesque island town.

4 Yaxhá (p247) Viewing the lagoons from the highest pyramid is hard to beat.

Tikal

The most striking feature of **Tikal** (2367-2837; www.tikalnationalpark.org; Q150; 6am-6pm) is its towering, steep-sided temples, rising to heights of more than 44m, but what distinguishes it is its jungle setting. Its many plazas have been cleared of trees and vines, its temples uncovered and partially restored, but as you walk from one building to another you pass beneath a dense canopy of rainforest amid the rich, loamy aromas of earth and

vegetation. Much of the delight of touring the site comes from strolling the broad causeways, originally built from limestone to accommodate traffic between temples. By stepping softly you're more likely to spot monkeys, agoutis, foxes and ocellated turkeys.

Tikal is a popular day trip to take from Flores or El Remate, so it is much quieter in the late afternoon and early morning, which makes an overnight stay an attractive option.

◉ Sights

Gran Plaza

The entry path comes into the Gran Plaza around the Templo I, the Templo del Gran Jaguar (Temple of the Grand Jaguar). This was built to honor – and bury – Ah Cacao. The king may have worked out the plans for the building himself, but it was actually erected above his tomb by his son, who succeeded him to the throne in AD 734. The king's rich burial goods included stingray spines, which were used for ritual bloodletting, 180 jade objects, pearls and 90 pieces of bone carved with hieroglyphs. At the top of the 44m-high temple is a small enclosure of three rooms covered by a corbeled arch. The sapodilla-wood lintels over the doors were richly carved; one of them was removed and is now in the Basel Museum für Völkerkunde. The lofty roofcomb that crowned the temple was originally adorned with reliefs and bright paint. When it's illuminated by the afternoon sun, it is still possible to make out the figure of a seated dignitary.

Although climbing to the top of Templo I is prohibited, the views from Templo II just across the way are nearly as awe-inspiring. Templo II, also known as the Temple of the Masks, was at one time almost as high as Templo I, but it now measures only 38m without its roofcomb.

Nearby, the Acrópolis del Norte (North Acropolis) significantly predates the two great temples. Archaeologists have uncovered about 100 different structures, the oldest of which dates from before the time of Christ, with evidence of occupation as far back as 600 BC. The Maya built and rebuilt on top of older structures, and the many layers, combined with the elaborate burials of Tikal's early rulers, added sanctity and power to their temples. The final version of the acropolis, as it stood around AD 800, had more than 12 temples atop a vast platform, many of them the work of King Ah Cacao. Look especially for the two huge, powerful wall masks, uncovered from an earlier structure and now protected by roofs. On the plaza side of the North Acropolis are two rows of stelae. These served to record the great deeds of the kings, to sanctify their memory and to add power to the temples and plazas that surrounded them.

Acrópolis Central

South and east of the Gran Plaza, this maze of courtyards, little rooms and small temples is thought by many to have been a palace where Tikal's nobles lived. Others think the tiny rooms may have been used for sacred rites and ceremonies, as graffiti found within them suggest. Over the centuries the configuration of the rooms was repeatedly changed, suggesting that perhaps this 'palace' was in fact a noble or royal family's residence and alterations were made to accommodate groups of relatives. A hundred years ago, one part of the acropolis provided lodgings for archaeologist Teobert Maler when he worked at Tikal.

Templo III

West of the Gran Plaza, across the Calzada Tozzer (Tozzer Causeway) stands Templo III, still undergoing restoration. Only its upper reaches have been cleared. A scene carved into the lintel at its summit, 55m high, depicts a figure in an elaborate jaguar suit, believed to be the ruler Dark Sun. In front of it stands Stela 24, which marks the date of its construction, AD 810. From this point, you can continue west to Templo IV along the Calzada Tozzer, one of several sacred byways between the temple complexes of Tikal.

Templo V & Acrópolis del Sur

Due south of the Gran Plaza, Templo V is a remarkably steep structure (57m high) that was built sometime between the 7th and 8th centuries AD. It consists of seven stepped platforms and, unlike the other great temples, has slightly rounded corners. A recent excavation of the temple revealed a group of embedded structures, some with Maya calendars on their walls. Tempting as it may seem, you are not allowed to scale the broad central staircase.

Excavation is slow to progress on the mass of masonry just west of the temple, known collectively as the Acrópolis del Sur (South Acropolis). The palaces on top are from the Late Classic Period (the time of King Moon Double Comb), but earlier constructions probably go back 1000 years.

Plaza de los Siete Templos

To the west of the Acrópolis del Sur is this broad grassy plaza, reached via a path to its southern edge. Built in the Late Classic Period, the seven temples with their stout roofcombs line up along the east side of the plaza. On the south end stand three larger 'palaces'; on the opposite end is an unusual triple ballcourt.

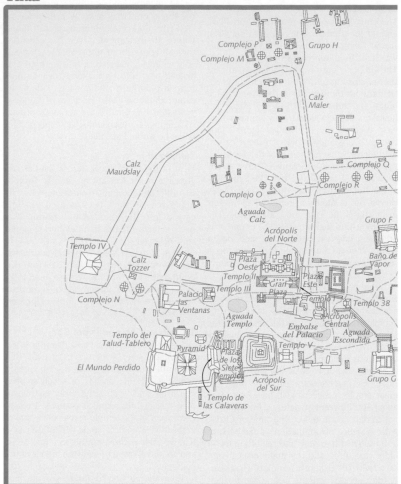

El Mundo Perdido

About 400m southwest of the Gran Plaza is **El Mundo Perdido** (Lost World), a complex of 38 structures with a huge pyramid in its midst, thought to be essentially Preclassic (with some later repairs and renovations). The pyramid, 32m high and 80m along the base, is surrounded by four much-eroded stairways, with huge masks flanking each one. The stairway facing eastward is thought to have functioned as a platform for viewing the sun's trajectory against a trio of structures on a raised platform to the east, a similar arrangement to the astronomical observatory at Uaxactún. Tunnels dug into the pyramid by archaeologists reveal four similar pyramids beneath the outer face; the earliest (Structure 5C-54 Sub 2B) dates from 700 BC, making this pyramid the oldest Maya structure at Tikal.

A smaller **temple** to the west, dating from the Early Classic Period, demonstrates Teotihuacán's influence, with its *talud-tablero* (stepped building) style of architecture.

Templo IV & Complejo N

Templo IV, at 65m, is the highest building at Tikal and the second-highest pre-Columbian building known in the western

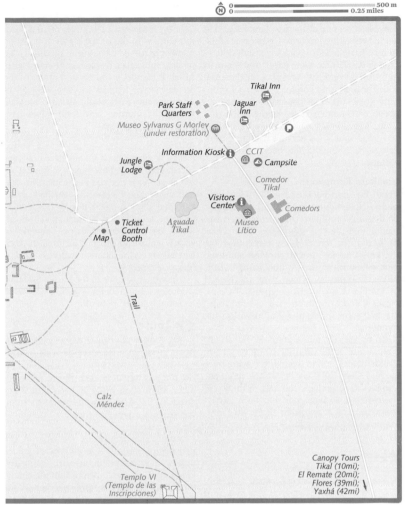

hcmisphere, after La Danta at El Mirador. It was completed about AD 741, probably by order of Ah Cacao's son, Yax Kin, who was depicted on the carved lintel over the middle doorway (now in a museum in Basel, Switzerland), as the western boundary of the ceremonial precinct. A steep wooden staircase leads to the top. The view east is almost as good as from a helicopter – a panorama across the jungle canopy, with (from left to right) the temples of the Gran Plaza, Temple III, Temple V (just the top bit) and the great pyramid of the Mundo Perdido poking through.

Situated between Templo IV and Templo III is **Complejo N**, an example of the 'twin-temple' complexes erected during the Late Classic Period. This one was built in AD 711 by Ah Cacao to mark the 14th *katun,* or 20-year cycle, of *baktún* 9. The king himself is portrayed on the remarkably preserved Stela 16 in an enclosure located just across the pathway. Beside the stelae is Altar 5, a circular stone that depicts the same king accompanied by a priestly figure in the process of exhuming the skeleton of a female ruler.

Templo de las Inscripciones (Templo VI)

Templo VI is one of the few temples at Tikal to bear written records. On the rear of its 12m-high roofcomb is a long inscription – though it will take some effort to discern it in the bright sunlight – giving us the date AD 766. The sides and cornice of the roofcomb bear glyphs as well. Its secluded position, about a 25-minute walk southeast of the Gran Plaza along the Calzada Méndez, makes it a good spot for observing wildlife. From here, it's a 20-minute hike back to the main entrance.

Northern Complexes

About 1km north of the Gran Plaza is Complejo P. Like Complejo N, it's a Late Classic twin-temple complex that probably commemorated the end of a *katun*. Complejo M, next to it, was partially torn down by the Late Classic Maya to provide building materials for a causeway, now named after Alfred P Maudslay, which runs southwest to Templo IV. Grupo H, northeast of Complexes P and M, with one tall, cleared temple, had some interesting graffiti within its temples.

Complejo Q and Complejo R, about 300m north of the Gran Plaza, are very Late Classic twin-pyramid complexes with stelae and altars standing before the temples. Complex Q is perhaps the best example of the twin-temple type, as it has been partly restored. Stela 22 and Altar 10 are excellent examples of Late Classic Tikal relief carving, dated to AD 771.

Museums

Museo Sylvanus G Morley MUSEUM
(Museo Cerámico; Museum of Ceramics; Q30, also valid for Museo Lítico; ⊙8am-4pm) This museum exhibits a number of superb ceramic pieces from excavations, including incense burners and vases, with descriptions of their uses and significance (in Spanish). The usual museum building is under restoration indefinitely, during which time the ceramics are displayed at the CCIT.

Two of the most highly prized items, the elaborately carved Stela 31 dedicated to the ruler Stormy Sky-Double Comb, and the simulated tomb of King Moon Double Comb with the precious items unearthed from his burial site beneath Temple I, remain inside the museum, and the guard can show them to you on request.

Museo Lítico MUSEUM
(Stone Museum; Q30, also valid for Museo Sylvanus G Morley; ⊙8am-4pm) The larger of Tikal's two museums is in the visitor center. It houses a number of carved stones from the ruins. The photographs taken by pioneer archaeologists Alfred P Maudslay and Teobert Maler in the jungle-covered temples in various stages of discovery are particularly striking. Outside is a model showing how Tikal would have looked around AD 800.

CCIT MUSEUM
(Centro de Conservación e Investigación de Tikal; ⊙8am-4pm) FREE This Japanese-funded research center is devoted to the identification and restoration of pieces unearthed at the site. The 1300-sq-meter facility has a huge cache of items to sort through, and you can watch the restorers at work. Though not strictly a museum per se, it features an excellent gallery on the different materials used by Maya craftspeople.

The center is home to the Museo Sylvanus G Morley for an indefinite period while that museum is under restoration.

☞ Tours

Family-owned, local **Gem Trips** (☑4051-3805, USA (530) 853-4329, cell 4214-9514; www.gemtrips.com; Tikal sunrise US$150) offers excellent sunrise tours as well as guided trips to Tikal and other Maya sites, while archaeologist **Roxy Ortiz** (☑5197-5173; www.tikalroxy.blogspot.com) has years of experience trekking throughout the Maya world.

Multilingual guides are available at the information kiosk. These authorized guides display their accreditation card, listing the languages they speak. Before 7am the charge for a half-day tour is Q100 per person for three to six people. After that you pay for a group tour (Q600).

Canopy Tours Tikal ADVENTURE
(☑5615-4988; www.tikalcanopy.com; tours Q240; ⊙7am-5pm) By the national-park entrance, this outfit offers a one-hour tour through the forest canopy, with the chance to ride a harness along a series of cables linking trees up to 300m apart, and to cross several hanging bridges. The fee does not include transport from Tikal or El Remate.

🛏 Sleeping & Eating

Campground CAMPGROUND $
(campsite per person Q50, hammock with mosquito net Q85) Located across the road from

the visitor center, the campground covers a large, grassy area and has a clean bathroom block and thatched shelters for hanging hammocks. Pay for your campsite at the main ticket booth. You don't need a reservation as there's plenty of room.

Tikal Inn
HOTEL $$

(☎7861-2444; www.tikalinn.com; s/d Q500/730, bungalow Q720; P❄️📶🏊) Built in the late '60s, this resort-style lodging offers rooms in the main building and thatched bungalows alongside the pool and rear lawn, with little porches out front. All are simple, spacious and quite comfortable. The most secluded accommodations are the least expensive, in a handful of cabins at the end of a sawdust trail through the forest.

Jungle Lodge
HOTEL $$$

(☎7861-0446; www.junglelodgetikal.com; s/d Q680/772, without bathroom Q359/423; P❄️📶) Nearest of the hotels to the site entrance, this was originally built to house archaeologists working at Tikal. Self-contained bungalows, plus a bank of cheaper units, are well spaced throughout rambling, jungle grounds. Some newer suites feature jungle-chic decor and outdoor rain-showers. The restaurant-bar (mains Q80 to Q100) serves veggie pastas, crepes and other international dishes in a tropical ambience. Wi-fi is in the pool and lobby only.

Jaguar Inn
HOTEL $$$

(☎7926-2411; www.jaguartikal.com; campsite per person Q50, with tent Q115; s/d/tr Q532/639/852; P❄️@📶) The inn of choice for youthful, independent travelers has duplex and quad bungalows with thatched roofs and hammocks on the porches, plus a smart little restaurant with a popular terrace out front. For those on a tight budget there are tents for rent on a platform.

❶ Information

Everyone (even those staying inside the park at one of the hotels) must purchase an entry ticket *in advance* at the initial gate on the road in (or at Banrural locations such as Flores or Guatemala City). Note that *tickets are no longer available anywhere inside the entry gate* – that includes sunrise tour tickets. You purchase in advance and then use them as needed at the time/day of your choice.

Seeing the sunrise from Templo IV at the west end of the main site is possible from about October to March, but to enter the park before or after visiting hours you must purchase an additional ticket for Q100, as this is not covered in the normal park entry. You must also have a guide.

The core of the ancient city takes up about 16 sq km, with more than 6000 structures, to which an additional 4000 have recently been identified by LIDAR technology, making this one of the largest Maya cities ever discovered. To visit all the major building complexes, you must walk at least 10km, so wear comfortable shoes with good rubber treads that grip well. The ruins here can be slick from rain and organic material, especially during the wet season. Bring plenty of water, as you'll be walking around all day in the heat.

Please don't feed the coatis (pisotes) that wander about the site.

❶ Getting There & Away

Eight **ATIM** (ATIM; ☎5905-0089) microbuses depart Flores between 6:30am and 3pm (Q30 to Q80, 1¼ hours), the last returning at 5pm. They return from Tikal at noon, 1:30pm, 3pm and 6pm. You could also take the Uaxactún-bound bus from the market of Santa Elena at 3:30pm, which goes a bit slower.

From El Remate, a collective shuttle departs at 5:30am for Tikal, starting back at 2pm (one way/round trip Q30/50). Any El Remate accommodations can make reservations.

If traveling from Belize, get a Santa Elena–bound microbus to Puente Ixlú, sometimes called El Cruce, and switch there to a northbound microbus for the remaining 36km to Tikal. Heading from Tikal to Belize, start early and get off at Puente Ixlú to catch a bus or microbus eastward. Be wary of shuttles to Belize advertised at Tikal: these have been known to detour to Flores to pick up passengers! And do not purchase any tickets for ruins (or anything else) from so-called vendors on the bus.

Yaxhá

The Classic Maya sites of Yaxhá, Nakum and El Naranjo form a triangle that is the basis for a national park covering more than 370 sq km and bordering the Parque Nacional Tikal to the west. Yaxhá, the most visited of the trio, stands on a hill between two sizable lakes, Lago Yaxhá and Lago Sacnab. The setting, the sheer size of the site, the number of excellently restored buildings and the abundant jungle flora and fauna all make it particularly worth visiting. There are also some stunning views from the tallest pyramid, which looks out over the lagoons. Not surprisingly, the foot traffic here is far less than at more popular, easy-to-reach sites.

The site is 11km north of the Puente Ixlú–Melchor de Mencos road, accessed via an

TIKAL & FLORES, GUATEMALA YAXHÁ

WORTH A TRIP

EL MIRADOR

Buried within the furthest reaches of the Petén jungle, just 7km south of the Mexican border, the Late Preclassic metropolis at **El Mirador** (Lookout; www.miradorbasin.com; ⊘24hr) contains one of the largest clusters of buildings of any single Maya site, among them the biggest pyramid ever built in the Maya world. Ongoing excavations have only scratched the surface, so many are still hidden beneath the jungle.

El Mirador (The Lookout), the name given to the site by *chicheros* (chicle harvesters) before its 'discovery' by archaeologists, is due to the excellent views provided by some of the pyramids. La Danta (the Tapir) looms some 70m above the forest floor. Another pyramid, El Tigre, measures 55m high and its base covers 18,000 sq meters – six times the area of Tikal's biggest structure, Templo IV. La Danta, El Tigre and the other temples erected here display the unusual 'triadic' style, in which three pyramids crown a large platform, with the one in the middle dominating the other two, which face each other at a lower level. The facades of these buildings were once embellished with carved masks.

You'll have to use your imagination to picture this city that, at its height, spread over 16 sq km and supported tens of thousands of citizens. It was the greatest Maya city of the Preclassic era, far exceeding in size anything built subsequently in the Maya world. Within the complex, more than a dozen internal causeways link the main architectural complexes.

Scholars are still figuring out why and how El Mirador thrived (there are few natural resources and no water sources save for the reservoirs built by ingenious, ancient engineers) and what led to its abandonment in 150 AD. Some five centuries after that date, El Mirador appears to have been resettled, as suggested by the existence of Classic architecture among the older structures. Pottery unearthed from this era displays the highly refined codex-style of decoration, in which calligraphic lines are painted on a cream-colored surface, with designs believed to resemble Maya codices.

Richard Hansen, a professor from Idaho State University, is leading the effort to map the Mirador basin, a vast swath of northern El Petén comprising dozens of interconnected cities, with funding from an assortment of international and Guatemalan foundations and private sources. In March 2009, Dr Hansen and his crew made a significant discovery when they excavated a 4m frieze at the base of La Danta, dating from 300 BC, which they surmise decorated a royal pool. The carved images upon it depict the twin heroes Hunahpú and Ixbalnqué swimming through the underworld domain of Xibalbá, a tale that is related in the *Popol Vuh* (the Maya 'Bible'). The finding underlines the importance of El Mirador in establishing the belief system of Classic-era civilizations.

unpaved road from a turnoff 32km from Puente Ixlú and 33km from Melchor de Mencos.

⊙ Sights

Occupied as early as 600 BC, Yaxhá (translated as 'blue-green water') achieved its cultural apex in the 8th century AD, when it counted some 20,000 inhabitants and 500 buildings, including temples, palaces and residential complexes.

It takes about two hours to wander round the main groups of ruins, which have been extensively excavated and reconstructed. Pick up an excellent map/information guide (Q20; in English) at the ticket booth. One approach is to cover the site in a clockwise fashion, traversing the original road network. The first group of buildings you come to, the

Lesser Astronomical Complex (Plaza C), is one of a pair of astronomical observatories. Take the Calzada de las Canteras to the **South Acropolis**, a complex of palatial structures from which Yaxhá's aristocracy could watch the games going on in the **Palace Ball Court** below. To the northwest stands one of Yaxhá's most ancient constructions, the **Greater Astronomical Complex (Plaza F)**. The arrangement is similar to the one at Uaxactún's Grupo E, with an observation tower (unexcavated) facing a three-part platform for tracking the sun's trajectory through the year. You can ascend the pyramidal tower (there's a wooden staircase alongside) for jaw-dropping views of the **North Acropolis** to the northeast, with a formidable temple rising above the jungle foliage. Far less impressive is the **Northeast Acropolis**, nearby. From here, take the Calzada de las Aguadas north to reach the **Plaza de las Sombras (Grupo Maler)**, where archaeologists believe throngs of citizens once gathered for religious ceremonies. Return toward the entrance along the Calzada Este to reach the high point of the tour (literally), **Structure 216** in the East Acropolis. Also called the Temple of the Red Hands, because red handprints were discovered there, it towers over 30m high, affording views in every direction. Though mostly unexcavated, the **Twin Pyramid Complex** is similar to a structure at Tikal.

A trail from the boat landing leads along the lake shore to a new **Interpretive Center**, which displays ceramic pieces, musical instruments and jewelry unearthed from the site, along with descriptions of its discovery and excavation.

On an island near the far (south) shore of Laguna Yaxhá is a Late Postclassic archaeological site, **Topoxté**, where the dense covering of ruined temples and dwellings harbor some 100 structures. Evidence shows two distinct periods of occupation here: the latter, as late as AD 1450, by a migrant group from the Yucatán Peninsula. At the bottom of the Calzada del Lago in Yaxhá is the **boat landing**, from where a boat operator might be willing to take you to Topoxté for around Q250.

🛏 Sleeping

El Sombrero Eco-Lodge (☑ 4147-6380, 5460-2934; www.ecolodgeelsombrero.com; s/d/tr Q380/750/940; 🅿 ➲ 🛜) 🐾 offers comfortable lodging 2km from the archaeological site. On the lakeshore below the Yaxhá ruins is **Campamento Yaxhá** FREE, where you can camp for free (you only pay the park entry fee) on raised platforms with thatched roofs.

❶ Getting There & Away

Agencies in Flores and El Remate offer organized trips to Yaxhá, some combined with Nakum and/or Tikal. **Horizontes Mayas** (☑ 5773 6193; www.horizontesmayas.com; Ruta a Tikal) in El Remate runs tours (Q125 per person, minimum three people), including guide and entrance fee, at 7am and 1pm, returning at 1pm and 6:30pm. Otherwise, take a Melchor de Mencos–bound microbus and get off at Restaurante El Portal de Yaxhá, opposite the Yaxhá turnoff; it can arrange transport to the site by pickup truck or motorcycle (Q200 return). *Colectivos* from Flores charge Q200 as well.

El Remate

This peaceful spot at the eastern end of Lago de Petén Itzá makes a good alternative base for Tikal-bound travelers – it's more relaxed than Flores and closer to the site, and its lakeside living has a ramshackle vibe all of its own. People come here to bask in life-affirming slowness, so don't expect pumping discos or craft cocktails. This is all about the *cerveza* and the view.

El Remate begins 1km north of Puente Ixlú, where the road to the Belize border diverges from the Tikal road. The village strings along the Tikal road for 1km to another junction, where a branch heads west along the north shore of the lake.

El Remate is known for its wood carving, which you can buy from stalls along the main road.

🏃 Activities

Most El Remate accommodations can book two-hour boat trips for **birdwatching** or nocturnal **crocodile spotting** (each Q150 per person). Try Hotel Mon Ami (p250), which also offers sunset lake tours with detours up the Ixlú and Ixpop rivers (Q200 per person).

🛏 Sleeping

Casa de Doña Tonita   HOSTEL **$**
(☑ 5767-4065; dm/r Q50/150) This friendly family-run place has seven basic, adequately ventilated rooms, each with two single beds and screened windows, in a two story clapboard *rancho* (small house), plus a dorm situated over a restaurant that serves tasty, reasonably priced meals. There's just one shower. Across the road at the end of a pier is a hut for sunset gazing.

Hotel Las Gardenias   HOTEL **$**
(☑ 5923-4338; www.hotelasgardenias.com; Ruta a Tikal; s/d Q80/160, with air-con Q150/250; 🅿 ➲ ❄ @ 🛜) Right at the junction with the north-shore road, this cordial hotel/restaurant/shuttle operator has two sections: the wood-paneled rooms at the front are bigger, while those in the rear are appealingly removed from the road. All feature comfortable beds with woven spreads, attractively tiled showers and some porches with hammocks. There's also an onsite restaurant.

Posada Ixchel   HOTEL **$**
(☑ 3044-5379; hotelixchel@yahoo.com; s/d/tr Q90/140/190) This family-owned place near

the village's main junction is a superior deal, with spotless, wood-fragrant rooms featuring fans and handcrafted mosquito nets. The cobbled courtyard has inviting little nooks with tree-log seats.

Hostal Hermano Pedro
HOSTEL $

(☑ 5164-6485; www.hhpedro.com; Calle Camino Biblico 8055; dm/s/d incl breakfast Q80/80/160; P ⊜ 🛜) About 150m from the north-shore junction, this two-level wooden structure has a relaxed environment, with plenty of hammocks in the patio and along the verandas. Recycled elements are cleverly incorporated into the decor of the spacious rooms, which feature big fans and lacy curtains. Guests can use the kitchen. Q50 for a dorm without breakfast.

★Alice Guesthouse
BUNGALOW $$

(☑ 3087-0654; www.facebook.com/aliceguesthouse guatemala; dm Q70, bungalow with/without bathroom Q230/200; P ⊜ 🛜) As in Wonderland, that is. Fruit of the budding imaginations of a Franco-Belgian pair, this slightly remote spread looks not at the lake but at a swath of jungle. Free-form, friendly and fun, it has dorms in fanciful huts with conical thatch roofs, a pair of neat colorful cabins and a tropical shower in a roundhouse, all connected by pebbly paths.

★Posada del Cerro
BUNGALOW $$

(☑ 5376-8722; www.posadadelcerro.com; Jobompiche Rd; dm/s/d/tr/apt Q100/220/330/450/550; P ⊜ 🛜) 🌿 This ecologically sound option blends into the jungle, close enough to Biotopo Cerro Cahuí to hear monkeys howl the evening in. Ten thoughtfully furnished rooms occupy stone-and-hardwood houses and solitary huts scattered over the hillside; one is open to the woods with its own lakeview deck. It also has an eight-bed hut and an apartment that sleeps four to five.

La Casa de Don David
HOTEL $$

(☑ 5949-2164; www.lacasadedondavid.com; Jobompiche Rd; s/d incl breakfast or dinner from Q248/468; ⊙ restaurant 6:30am-9pm; 🌸 @ 🛜) Just west of the junction, this full-service outfit has spotless, modern rooms decorated with Maya textiles. All feature verandas and hammocks facing the broad garden that's been cultivated into an incredible aviary. Whether or not you're staying here, don't miss the ceiba tree and Maya calendar arrangement in the rear garden designed by owner David Kuhn (the original Gringo Perdido).

Gringo Perdido Ecological Inn
RESORT $$

(☑ 2334-2305; www.hotelgringoperdido.com; Jobompiche Rd; campsite Q50, s/d with breakfast & dinner Q360/700; P ⊜ 🛜) 🌿 Ensconced in a paradisaical lakefront setting within the Cerro Cahuí biosphere reserve, this jungle-style lodge offers a bank of rooms with full-wall roll-up blinds to give you the sensation of sleeping in the open air. A few lakeside bungalows offer a bit more seclusion. It also has a grassy campground with thatched-roof shelters for slinging hammocks, and a large bookcase lending library.

Hotel Mon Ami
HOTEL $$

(☑ 3010-0284; Jobompiche Rd; dm/s/d Q75/150/200, s/d without bathroom Q100/150; 🛜) A 15-minute walk from the Tikal road, Santiago's place maintains a good balance between jungle wildness and Euro sophistication. Quirkily furnished cabins and dorms with hammocks are reached along candlelit paths through gardens bursting with local plant life. And the pier opposite is a delight. Fans of French cuisine will appreciate the open-air restaurant.

Pirámide Paraíso
HOTEL $$$

(☑ 2334-1967; www.hotelgringoperdido.com; Jobompiche Rd; s/d Q488/975; P 🛜) Built in time for the dawn of the new *baktún* (a *baktún* equals about four centuries) of the Maya calendar (in 2012) is this glitzy addition to the Gringo Perdido Ecological Inn, a smooth white structure that rises surreally from the forest like a Maya temple. Each of the eight huge, luxuriously decorated suites features its own exterior Jacuzzi.

La Lancha
RESORT $$$

(☑ 3045-0817; www.thefamilycoppolaresorts.com; Aldea Jobompiche; lakeview casitas/ste incl breakfast Q1638/3102; P ⊜ ❄ 🛜 🏊) Featuring his signature blend of exclusivity and adventure, film director Francis Ford Coppola has created a lodge of rustic luxury about 13km west of El Remate. Secluded casitas house exquisite furniture from native woods and wide verandas with amazing views of the surrounding rainforest or the blue-green waters. The grounds are alive with howling monkeys and squawking birds.

🍴 Eating

Desayunos El Árbol
CAFE $

(☑ 5950-2367; breakfast mains Q30-40, dinner mains 40-60; ⊙ 6am-2pm, 5-9pm Thu-Tue)

This gringo-friendly shack sports a lovely, lake-view terrace, a fine setting for healthy breakfasts, including granola, pancakes and omelets. Sandwiches come with a side of salad, and the smoothies are just grand. It's 50m south of the crossroads.

La Casa de Don David　　　INTERNATIONAL $
(📷5949-2164; mains Q45; ☺7am-8:30pm; 🥗)
This splendid open-air dining hall serves a good breakfast, including banana pancakes (Q30), fruit and granola, and boasts a collection of *National Geographic* articles on Maya sites to browse over coffee. Nightly *prix fixe* specials include vegetarian fare – reserve your meal by 4pm.

★Mon Ami　　　FRENCH $$
(📷5805-4868, 3010-0284; Jobompiche Rd; mains Q35-85; ☺6am-10pm) On Jobompiche Rd, this peaceful palm-thatched affair is the French jungle bistro you've dreamed of. Try the lake whitefish or the big *ensalada francesa* (French salad). Specials usually run Q35 to Q45, and change frequently.

★Las Orquídeas　　　ITALIAN $$
(📷5701-9022; Jobompiche Rd; pastas Q55-120; ☺noon-9pm Tue-Sun; 🅿) Almost hidden in the forest, a 10-minute walk along the north shore from the Tikal junction, is this marvelous open-air dining hall. The genial Italian owner-chef blends *chaya,* a local herb, into his own tagliatelle and *panzarotti* (smaller version of calzones). There are tempting desserts, too.

❶ Getting There & Away

El Remate is linked to Santa Elena by frequent minibus service (Q25) from 5:30am to 6pm daily.

For Tikal, a collective shuttle departs at 5:30am, starting back at 2pm (one-way/round trip costs Q30/50). Any El Remate accommodations can make reservations. Or catch one of the ATIM (p247) or other shuttles passing through from Santa Elena to Tikal from 5am to 3:30pm.

For taxis, ask at **Hotel Sun Breeze** (📷5898-2665; infosunbreezehotel@gmail.com; Main Rd; s/d Q150/200, with air-con Q200/250; 🅿🌀❄🛜). A one-way ride to Flores costs about Q250; a round trip to Tikal costs about Q350.

For Melchor de Mencos on the Belizean border, get a minibus or bus from Puente Ixlú, located 1km south of El Remate (Q60, 1¼ hours). Additionally, Horizontes Mayas (p249) offers private departures to Belize City (Q400) going via Melchor.

Flores & Santa Elena

POP 73,000 / ELEV 117M

With its pastel houses cascading down from a central plaza to the emerald waters of Lago de Petén Itzá, the island town of Flores evokes Venice or something Mediterranean. A 500m causeway connects Flores to its humbler sister town of Santa Elena on the mainland, which then merges into the community of San Benito to the west. The three towns actually form one large settlement, often referred to simply as Flores.

Flores proper is by far the more attractive base. Small hotels and restaurants line the streets, many featuring rooftop terraces with lake views. Residents take great pride in their island-town's gorgeousness, and a promenade (partly submerged now due to lake levels rising) runs around its perimeter.

Santa Elena is where you'll find banks, buses and a major shopping mall.

◉ Sights

Nuestra Señora de los Remedios　　　CATHEDRAL
(Map p252; Flores) The double-domed Nuestra Señora de los Remedios (the Spaniards' original name for the Isle of Flores) stands at the isle's summit, anchoring the Parque Central.

Cuevas de Ak'tun Kan　　　CAVE
(Q35; ☺7am-5pm) Try spelunking at the impressive limestone caverns of Ak'tun Kan, which translates from Q'eqchi' Maya as 'Cave of the Serpent.' The cave-keeper provides the authorized interpretation of the weirdly shaped stalagmite and stalactite formations, including the Frozen Falls, the Whale's Tail, and the Gate of Heaven, the last within a great hall where bats flutter in the crevices.

Museo Santa Bárbara　　　MUSEUM
(📷7926-2813; www.radiopeten.com.gt; Isle of Santa Bárbara; Q25; ☺8am-5pm) On an islet to the west of Flores, this little museum holds a grab bag of Maya artifacts from nearby archaeological sites, plus some old broadcasting equipment from Radio Petén (88.5 FM), which still broadcasts from an adjacent building. Phone ahead to get picked up (Q10 per person) at the dock behind Hotel Santana (p255).

🏃 Activities & Tours

Arcas　　　VOLUNTEERING
(Asociación de Rescate y Conservación de Vida Silvestre; 📷7830-1374, volunteer coordinator 5690-6762; www.arcasguatemala.org/volunteering; initial week

Flores

US$250, per week after US$200) This Guatemalan NGO has a rescue and rehabilitation center for wildlife on the mainland northeast of Flores, where volunteers can assist in feeding animals, such as macaws, parrots, jaguars and coatis, that have been rescued from smugglers and the illegal pet trade. The fee of US$200 a week covers food and accommodation.

Explore   TOURS
(Map p254; ☑ 7926-2375; www.exploreguate.com; 2a Calle 4-68, Santa Elena; ⊘ 7am-6pm Mon-Fri, to noon Sat) Professionally managed agency

offering custom-designed tours and its own accommodations in Santa Elena.

Mayan Adventure   ARCHAEOLOGICAL TOUR
(Map p252; ☑ 5830-2060; www.the-mayan-adventure.com; Calle 15 de Septiembre, Flores; ⊘ bookings Mon-Fri) Coordinated by a German Mayanologist, this outfit offers 'scientific' tours to sites currently under excavation, with commentary by archaeologists or architects. Some of these tours are available year-round – such as to Naranjo, a huge site being restored and excavated by more than 100 scientists – others only part of the year.

Flores

🛏 **Sleeping**

Hostel Los Amigos HOSTEL **$**
(Map p252; ☎ 7867-5075, 4495 2399, www.amigos hostel.com; Calle Central, Flores; dm Q100-120, r Q220; ⦿) Far and away the most popular backpackers haven in El Petén, this hostel has grown organically in its 15 years of existence and now includes various sleeping options, from six- and 10-bed dorms to a treehouse (Q200). An annex around the corner is quieter, with seven originally designed rooms.

La Posada de Don José HOTEL **$$**
(Map p252; ☎ 7867-5298; cnr Calle del Malecón & Calle Fraternidad, Flores; dm Q75, r with/without air-con Q250/175; ⊜❄🉡) Near the northern tip of the island, this is an old-fashioned establishment (check the lobby for a portrait of the founder) with rocking chairs scattered around a plant-laden patio and a friendly family that knows your name. The lake level has reclaimed the *malecón* (jetty) here, making the rear terrace infinitely more peaceful than further down.

Hotel Quinta Maya HOTEL **$$**
(Map p254; ☎ 7926-4976; www.hotelquintamaya. com; 6a Av & 4a Calle; s/d/tr Q275/390/490; 🅿⊜ ❄🉡🏊) Newly rebranded, this comfortable hotel offers large rooms arranged around a pleasant courtyard. There's a restaurant, airport transfers and a travel agent onsite.

Hostel Yaxha HOSTEL **$$**
(Map p252; ☎ 7867-5055; www.cafeyaxha.com; Calle 15 de Septiembre, Flores; dm/d/apt Q70/220/400; ⊜❄🉡) A haven for archaeologists, historians and fans of pre-Hispanic cuisine, Café Arqueológico Yaxha (p256) now offers a clean and simple place to lay your head. There are

four-, six-, and nine bed dorms, private rooms with bathroom, and an apartment – all with quality mattresses and ceiling fans. Air-con adds to the price.

Casazul BOUTIQUE HOTEL **$$**
(Map p252; ☎ 7867-5451; www.hotelesdepeten.com; Calle Unión, Flores; s/d/tr Q400/450/650; ❄🉡) As the name suggests, it's blue all over, from the plantation-style balconies to the nine individually decorated, spacious and comfortable rooms. A couple have their own balconies and everyone can enjoy the beautiful top-floor terrace.

Hotel La Mesa de los Mayas HOTEL **$$**
(Map p252; ☎ 7867-5268; mesamayas@hotmail. com; Av La Reforma, Flores; s/d Q125/200, with air-con Q150/250; ⊜❄🉡) Standing alongside a narrow alley, the Mesa is terrific value. Its 19 rooms are neatly furnished, with pyramidal headboards, checkered bedspreads and reading lamps; some feature plant-laden balconies. There's a restaurant on the 1st floor.

Casa Amelia BOUTIQUE HOTEL **$$**
(Map p252; ☎ 7867-5430; www.hotelcasamelia. com; Calle Unión, Flores; s/d Q350/450; ⊜❄🉡) Standing tall along Flores' western shore, the Amelia offers bright, stylish chambers with excellent lake views; rooms 301 and 302 are best, opening onto the superb balustraded roof terrace.

Hotel Villa del Lago HOTEL **$$**
(Map p252; ☎ 7867-5131; www.hotelvilladelago. com.gt; Calle 15 de Septiembre, Flores; r 545; ⊜❄🉡) Behind the odd Grecian columns there's a cool, breezy interior that's long on potted plants and patio furniture. Comfortable, airy rooms have bright decor and big

Santa Elena

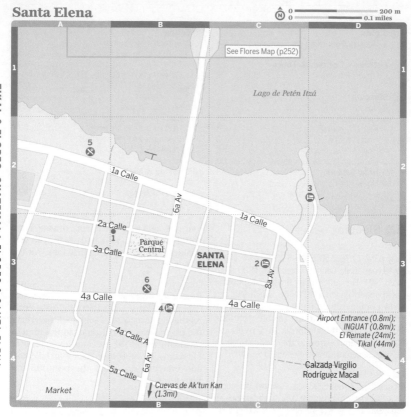

Santa Elena

🏃 Activities, Courses & Tours

🛏 Sleeping

🍴 Eating

ceiling fans. Breakfast (not included) is served on the delightful upper terrace.

Hotel Santa Bárbara　　HOTEL **$$$**
(📞7926-2813; http://radiopeten.com.gt; cabins incl breakfast Q750; 🅰🌡🛜) Part of a trio that includes a museum (p251) and a cafe, this is a perfect retreat from the hubbub of Flores on an islet just five minutes west by *lancha*

(small motorboat; included in price). Three comfy cabins with big beds and tile floors overlook the lake past a garden brimming with coconut palms and a ceiba tree.

Hotel Isla de Flores　　HOTEL **$$$**
(Map p252; 📞2476-8775; www.hotelisladeflores. com; Av La Reforma, Flores; s/d Q570/663; 🅰🌡@🛜🛳) This island hotel sports an understated tropical style that's highly appealing. Hardwood beams frame bone-white walls with floral motifs that are echoed on cool stone floors, and large firm beds back up on painted headboards. Though it doesn't stand on the lakeshore, the plank-deck roof terrace, with a small pool, commands fantastic views over the whole island.

Hotel Maya Internacional　　HOTEL **$$$**
(Map p254; 📞7926-2083; www.villasdeguatemala. com; 1a Calle, Santa Elena; s/d/tr Q738/927/1064; 🅿🅰🌡🛜🛳) One of the best reasons to stay in Santa Elena is this tropical-chic resort

spreading over a landscaped marsh by the waterfront. The big-top dining room is the center of activity; an adjacent wooden deck with a small infinity pool is great for sunset daiquiris. A boardwalk snakes through tropical gardens to reach the 26 thatch-and-teak rooms.

Hotel Santana
HOTEL $$$

(Map p252; ☑ 7867-5123; www.santanapeten. com.gt; Calle 30 de Junio, Flores; d/tr Q600/700; ☺✱@☎☒) A tropical fantasy, the Santana holds a commanding presence at Flores' southwest corner, with a popular terrace restaurant and its very own ferry dock. Rooms are generously sized with wicker furniture and lime-yellow walls, and if you get one out back, you'll have a great balcony facing Isla Santa Bárbara.

Hotel del Patio
HOTEL $$$

(Map p254; ☑ 7926-0104; http://hoteldelpatio. com.gt; cnr 8a Av & 2a Calle, Santa Elena; r Q780; P☺✱@☎☒) Shady corridors lined with terracotta floors wind around a stunning courtyard, centered on a gurgling fountain. Rooms are tasteful and comfortable, though not quite as luxurious as the courtyard. Wi-fi is decent, and the onsite restaurant serves food from 6am to 9pm.

✕ Eating

Maple y Tocino
CAFE $

(Mapp252; ☑ 7867-5294; www.facebook.com/mapley tocino; btwn Calle La Union & El Malecón; mains Q29-54; ☺ 7am-9pm Sun-Thu, to 10pm Fri & Sat) Amazing spot for breakfasts and lunches, ranging from smoothies and frappés (some topped with a fresh donut!) to waffles, pizza, sandwiches and wraps. Tasty coffee and espresso drinks and, to top it all, a view of the lake (and the now submerged *malecón*).

Cafe Uka
CAFE $

(Map p252; www.facebook.com/cafeukapeten; Calle Centroamérica; breakfast mains Q25-35; ☺ 7am-3pm Mon-Sat) Cheap, clean and tasty, the cheery turquoise- and peach-painted Cafe Uka won't win awards for fanciness, but the service is friendly and the food (a mix of Guatemalan and Western dishes) is fine.

Restaurante El Mirador
GUATEMALAN $

(Map p252; ☑ 7867-5246; Parque Central, Flores; set menu Q25; ☺ 7am-10pm Mon-Sat) Refreshingly not aimed at foreign travelers, this traditional eatery does toothsome home cookin'. You'll find such hearty options as

caldo de res (beef stew, only on Mondays), served with all the trimmings, and *fresco* (fruit drink) in the bright lunch hall that looks over the treetops.

Restaurante El Peregrino
GUATEMALAN $

(Map p252; ☑ 7867-5701; Av La Reforma, Flores; mains Q35-60; ☺ 7am-10pm) Part of the hotel of the same name, this humble *comedor* serves heaping helpings of home-cooked fare such as *caldo de panza* (beef belly stew, Q40) and breaded tongue. Ask for the daily lunch specials (Q30).

Cool Beans
CAFE $

(Map p252; ☑ 5571-9240, mobile 7867-5400; Calle 15 de Septiembre, Flores; breakfast Q25-35; ☺ 7am-10pm Mon-Sat; ☎) Also known as Café Chilero, this laid-back place is more clubhouse with snacks than proper restaurant, featuring salons for chatting, watching videos or laptop browsing. The lush garden with glimpses of the lake makes a *tranquilo* spot for breakfast or veggie burgers. Be warned – the kitchen closes at 9pm sharp.

Las Mesitas
GUATEMALAN $

(Map p252; El Malecón, Flores; mains Q10-20; ☺ 2-10pm) Every afternoon and evening the midpoint of the bridge to Flores turns into a cheap-eats paradise, as local families fix enchiladas (actually *tostadas* topped with guacamole, chicken salad and so on), tacos and tamales, and dispense fruity drinks from giant jugs. All kinds of cakes and puddings are served, too. Everyone sits on plastic chairs or low barrier walls.

Restaurante Mijaro
COMEDOR $

(Map p254; ☑ 7926-1615; www.restaurantemijaro. com; 6a Av, Santa Elena; meals Q25-40; ☺ 6:30am-10pm; ☜) You'll find good home cooking at this locally popular *comedor* a few blocks south of the causeway, with an airy garden area. Besides the grub, it does good long *limonadas* (lime-juice drinks). There's even a kiddie playground. Another branch, Mijares II, is nearby.

★ Terrazzo
ITALIAN $$

(Map p252; ☑ 7867-5479; Calle Unión, Flores; pasta Q70-90; ☺ 11am-10pm) Inspired by a chef from Bologna, this Italian gourmet restaurant covers a romantic rooftop terrace. The fettuccine is produced in house, the pizzas (made of seasoned dough) are grilled rather than baked, and the fresh mint lemonade is incredible. All this, and the service is the most attentive in town.

Antojitos Mexicanos
STEAK $$

(Don Fredy; Map p252; ☑3130-5702; Calle Playa Sur, Flores; grilled meats Q60-70; ☺7-10:30pm; ℗) Every evening at the foot of the causeway these characters fire up the grill and char steak, chicken and pork ribs of exceptional quality. Their specialty is *puyazo* (sirloin) swathed with garlic sauce. Sit outside facing the twinkly lights on the lake or, if it's raining, inside under a tin roof.

Café/Bar Doña Goya
CAFE $$

(Map p252; ☑7867-5774; El Malecón, Flores; mains breakfast Q40-50, lunch or dinner Q50-100; ☺6:30am-10pm; ☏) Doña Goya's is good for an early breakfast or sunset snack, with a pretty terrace facing the lake. Toward the weekend, it blends into the nightlife scene along this stretch of the promenade.

Raíces
STEAK $$

(Map p252; ☑7867-5743; Calle Playa Sur, Flores; mains Q90-270, pizzas Q70-160; ☺7am-10pm; ☏) A broad deck and a flaming grill are the main ingredients at this lakefront restaurant/bar, possibly the prettiest setting in Flores for dinner. Chargrilled meats and seafood are the specialty; it also does wood-oven pizzas.

Café Arqueológico Yaxha
CAFE $$

(Map p252; ☑7867-5055; www.cafeyaxha.com; Calle 15 de Septiembre, Flores; mains Q45-80; ☺6:30am-10pm) Part of the Hostel Yaxha (p253), this spot offers the usual egg-and-bean breakfasts, but what's special here are the pre-Hispanic and Itzá items – pancakes with *ramón* seeds (Q30), yucca scrambled with *mora* herbs (Q38), chicken in *chaya* sauce (Q60). There's also a 'Tight Ass Traveler' special that ranges from Q15 to Q35.

Restaurante El Puerto
SEAFOOD $$

(Map p254; ☑5510-5023, 4211-8668; 1a Calle 2-15, Santa Elena; mains Q90-130; ☺11am-11pm) Seafood is the star attraction at this breezy, open-air hall by the lakefront in Santa Elena, with a well-stocked bar at the front. It's an ideal setting to enjoy shellfish stews, popular *ceviches* or the famous *pescado blanco* – whitefish from the lake.

🍷 Drinking & Nightlife

Qué Pachanga
CLUB

(Map p252; El Malecón, Flores; ☺2pm-1am) One of a pair of lively nightspots round the west side of the island, this room gets heavy most evenings, when young Guatemalans decked out in their tightest possible jeans gyrate to a continuous barrage of throbbing reggaetón and *cumbia* (Colombian dance tunes).

El Trópico
BAR

(Map p252; Calle Playa Sur, Flores; ☺5pm-1am Mon-Sat) Longest running of the bars along the southern bank, El Trópico supplies tacos and *cerveza* (beer) to a mostly older Guatemalan clientele. It's quiet at sunset, but many *gallos* (tortilla sandwiches) later, the pulse picks up and DJs work the crowd.

❶ Information

Comisión de Turismo Cooperativa Carmelita Agency (Map p252; ☑4836-9423, 7867-5629; Calle Centroamérica, Flores; Tikal tour per person Q150, El Mirador 5-day/4-night per person Q1925; ☺8am-8pm) Flores agency for this Carmelita-based cooperative of trekking guides.

INGUAT (Map p252; ☑3128-6906; info-ciudad flores@inguat.gob.gt; Calle Centroamérica, Flores; ☺8am-4pm Mon-Fri, sometimes Sat & Sun) The official INGUAT office provides basic information. There's another **branch** (☑3128-6905, 7926-0533; info-mundomaya@inguat. gob.gt; Aeropuerto Internacional Mundo Maya; ☺7am-7pm Tue-Thu, 7-11am & 3-7pm Fri-Mon) at the airport.

❶ Getting There & Away

AIR

Aeropuerto Internacional Mundo Maya is on the eastern outskirts of Santa Elena, 2km from the causeway connecting Santa Elena and Flores. **Avianca** (www.avianca.com) has two flights daily between here and Guatemala City. The Belizean airline **Tropic Air** (☑7926-0348; www.tropicair. com; Aeropuerto Internacional Mundo Maya) flies once a day to/from Belize City, charging around Q1432 each way for the one-hour trip. It leaves at 8:30am daily.

BUS & MICROBUS

Long-distance buses use the Terminal Nuevo de Autobuses in Santa Elena, located 1.5km south of the causeway along 6a Av. It is also used by a slew of *aka expresos* (microbuses), with frequent services to numerous destinations.

SHUTTLE MINIBUS

Most hotels and travel agencies can book shuttles, and they will pick you up from where you're staying. Returns leave Tikal at 12:30pm, 3pm and 5pm. If you know which round-trip you plan to be on, ask your driver to hold a seat for you or arrange one in another minibus. If you stay overnight in Tikal and want to return to Flores by minibus, it's a good idea to reserve a seat when a driver when they arrive in the morning.

Understand
Belize

Belize Today

Belize is finally booming. After years in the shadow of its neighbors, Central America's youngest and least-populated nation is suddenly seen as the next big thing in Caribbean tourism. Add to this a stable, decade-old government offering laudable environmental policies and promising economic growth and you have the makings of a country that's spreading its wings. However, not everyone in Belize has seen the benefits of this progress, and poverty remains widespread.

Best in Print

Beka Lamb (Zee Edgell; 1982) A heart-wrenching novel about a girl's coming-of-age amid political upheaval.

The Last Flight of the Scarlet Macaw (Bruce Barcott; 2008) An unflinchingly honest account of Sharon Matola's fight against the construction of the Chalillo Dam on the Macal River.

Jaguar (Alan Rabinowitz; 1986) A first-person account of two years living among the Maya and the jaguars.

How to Cook a Tapir: A Memoir of Belize (Joan Fry; 2009) Fascinating memoir from an American woman who spent a year living among the Kekchí Maya with her anthropologist husband in 1960s British Honduras.

Best on Film

Mosquito Coast (1986) Harrison Ford and River Phoenix star as members of an American family in search of a simpler life in Central America.

Apocalypto (2006) Mel Gibson's visually arresting – if not historically accurate – Maya thriller.

Curse of the Xtabai (2012) Belizeans are quite proud of this feature-length horror film, the first to be 100% filmed and produced in Belize using local scenery, cast and crew.

Tourism & the Environment

Tourism is the country's major source of employment and investment (along with agriculture), with visitor numbers doubling in the past decade. The challenge moving forward is one of balancing the tourism industry's needs with Belizeans' desire to protect the environment and maintain the low-key lifestyle that makes their country so appealing. In 2018 Dean Barrow's UDP government made its most important environmental move to date – indefinitely banning offshore oil drilling and exploration in all its waters to protect the delicate barrier reef. The legislation was widely applauded by conservationists and the tourism industry, and was key to Unesco removing the World Heritage–listed reef from its endangered list.

While the benefits of tourism for the country as a whole are acknowledged by Belizeans at nearly every level of society, Belize does not yet have the infrastructure to support the increasing numbers of tourists that arrive each year. One of the most contentious tourism-related issues concerns cruise-ship passengers. Belize received more than one million cruise-ship visitors in 2017 (almost three times the national population), but many Belizeans believe these day visitors do not contribute enough to the local economy to justify their impact on environment and infrastructure. Norwegian Cruise Lines opened an exclusive cruise-ship port on Harvest Caye, near Placencia, in 2016; the island resort is so well-equipped that Placencia locals now complain not enough passengers bother to visit the mainland to spend their money.

Foreign investment is another growth industry and hot-button issue. Thanks to low property taxes and other retirement tax perks, North American expats are snapping up beachfront properties and whole islands are being developed for resorts. Good or bad for Belize?

Poverty & Crime

Despite the growth in tourism, economic prosperity remains elusive for most Belizeans. A few entrepreneurs have made big money, and a small middle class survives from business, tourism and other professions. But many more Belizeans live on subsistence incomes in rudimentary circumstances. In 2013 an estimated 41% of the population lived below the poverty line.

Unemployment was just under 10% in 2018. And labor is poorly paid when compared with the high cost of living. Although Belize has the second-highest per capita income in Central America, this does not reflect the huge disparity that exists between rich and poor.

Over the years Belize has developed an unfair reputation for violent crime, though much of this was confined to gang-related crime in Belize City. Several murders of foreigners – notably Canadian filmmaker Matthiew Klinck and Chicago journalist Anne Swaney within weeks of each other in 2016 – shone an unwanted light on the country. However, authorities, including the US State Department, agree there's no evidence that tourists are targeted in violent crime here. Indeed, Belize *feels* a safe country to travel in and the worst you're likely to experience is opportunistic theft.

Hurricane Earl

In August 2016, Hurricane Earl battered the Caribbean coast and Mexico, resulting in a state of emergency in Belize. Some 80% of homes were flooded or damaged across the country and numerous businesses, including tourist operators in San Pedro and the Northern Cayes, were destroyed. Resilient as ever in the face of nature's fury, Belizeans quickly rebuilt, despite a US$100 million-plus damage bill.

Petro Caribe & the Petroleum Economy

Since 2005 Belize has been the beneficiary of Petro Caribe, a regional development and socialist program founded by the late Venezuelan president Hugo Chavez, under which member countries receive fuel from Venezuela but only pay half the selling price up front, with the other half being converted into a low-interest long-term loan. The stated aim was to alleviate financial hardships on vulnerable Caribbean and Latin American countries due to rising oil prices. In Belize the profits from retailing the imported fuel were largely fed into government coffers, allowing the Barrow government to spend big on a range of major infrastructure projects around the country.

However, falling crude oil production and a shattered Venezuelan economy has cast doubt over the future of Petro Caribe and in mid-2018 it was reported that Venezuela had suspended the program. Although Belize has two low-production oil fields, it must still import the majority of its oil and the demise of Petro Caribe will likely have a significant impact on the national economy.

POPULATION: **388,000**

AREA: **8867 SQ MILES**

GDP: **US$1.765 BILLION (2016)**

INFLATION: **0.7%**

. . . .

population per sq mile

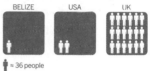

BELIZE USA UK

👤 ≈ 36 people

. . . .

languages
(% of population)

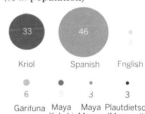

Kriol	Spanish	English
33	46	4

Garifuna	Maya Kekchi	Maya Mopan	Plautdietsch (Mennonite Low German)
6	8	3	3

. . . .

if Belize were 100 people

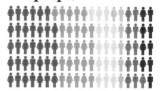

34 would be Mestizo 6 would be Garifuna
25 would be Creole 11 would be Maya
15 would be Spanish 9 would be other

History

Don't be fooled into believing that Central America's youngest independent nation is short on history. Though independence came only in 1981 (peacefully, we might add), many Belizean families trace their connection to the land back for many generations. Most Belizeans have a story to tell about the role played by their relatives in the creation of the nation they now proudly call home.

From Lordly Realm to Lost World: Ancient Maya

History Books

....

Thirteen Chapters of a History of Belize by Assad Shoman

....

Belize: A Concise History by PAB Thomson

....

The Caste War of the Yucatán by Nelson Reed

Belize hosted one of the great Mesoamerican civilizations of ancient times, the Maya. The Maya created vibrant commercial centers, monumental religious temples and exquisite artworks. They possessed sophisticated knowledge about their earthly and cosmological environments, much of which they wrote down. The Maya thrived from roughly 2000 BC to AD 1500, before succumbing to domestic decline and alien assault. The stone foundations of their lordly realm became a lost world submerged beneath dense jungle.

The Maya ranged across Central America, from the Yucatán to Honduras, from the Pacific to the Caribbean. They were not ethnically homogeneous but only loosely related, divided by kinship, region and dialect. The different communities sometimes cooperated and often competed with one another, building alliances for trade and warfare.

Archaeological findings indicate that Maya settlements in Belize were among the oldest. In the west, Cahal Pech, an important commercial center between the coast and interior, was dated to around 1200 BC. In the north, majestic Lamanai, a major religious site for more than 2000 years, was founded as early as 1500 BC. In Belize today, three distinct Maya tribes still exist: the indigenous Mopan in the north; the Yucatec, who migrated from Mexico, also in the north; and the Kekchí, who migrated from Guatemala, in the west and south.

The Maya were organized into kingdoms, in which social and economic life was an extension of a rigid political hierarchy. At the top were the king – or high lord – and his royal family, followed by an elite stratum

TIMELINE	2400 BC	2000 BC– AD 250	AD 250–1000
	The earliest known settlement in Belize is at Cuello in Orange Walk. It predates even the Preclassic period, and some archaeologists attribute the settlement to Maya predecessors.	The earliest sedentary Maya communities are formed during the Preclassic period. Among the earliest Maya settlements are Cahal Pech in Cayo and Lamanai in Orange Walk.	The Classic period of the Maya civilization is characterized by the construction of cities and temples and other artistic and intellectual achievements. The population reaches around 400,000.

of priests, warriors and scribes; next came economically valued artisans and traders; and finally, holding it all up were subsistence farmers and servant workers. The system rested on a cultural belief that the high lord had some influence with the powerful and dark gods of the underworld, who sometimes took the form of a jaguar when intervening in human affairs. This view was reinforced through the ruling elite's elaborately staged power displays, a temple theater of awe.

Even before the germ-ridden Europeans arrived, the cultural underpinnings of Maya society were already coming undone. A prolonged drought had caused severe economic hardship, leaving the impression that the kings and priests had somehow lost their supernatural touch. It was left to the Spanish, however, to officially cancel the show.

Possibly the most impressive of the Maya kingdoms in Belize was at Caracol, in the western Mountain Pine Ridge. At its height, in the 6th and 7th centuries, Caracol was a major urban metropolis, with more than 100,000 residents. It boasted first-rate jewelers and skilled artisans, an intricately terraced agriculture system, a prosperous trading market, and 40 miles of paved roads (considerably more than it has today). According to the story carved by Maya artists into commemorative stone, the king of Caracol, Water Lord, defeated his chief rival, Double Bird, king of Tikal, in a decisive battle in AD 562, ushering in a long period of Caracol supremacy in the central highlands. The pictographic stone inscriptions also suggest that Water Lord personally sacrificed Double Bird to further emphasize the Caracol triumph. Perhaps this had something to do with the still-simmering feud between Belize and Guatemala.

In the 1500s, the jaguar kings were forced to take cover in the rainforest when the sword-wielding Spanish arrived in Belize with the aim of plundering Maya gold and spreading the word of God. The Maya population of Belize at this time numbered about a quarter of a million, but their ranks were quickly decimated by as much as 90%, from the lethal combination of the disease and greed of the Spanish. In the 1540s, a conquistador force based in the Yucatán set out on an expedition through much of present-day Belize, down the coast and across to the central highlands. Disappointed by the lack of riches uncovered, they left a bloody trail of slaughtered victims and abandoned villages in their wake. Religious sites, such as Lamanai, were forcibly converted to Catholicism.

In the early 1600s, the Maya finally staged a counteroffensive that successfully drove out the few Spanish settlers and missionaries that had decided to stay. Weakened and fearful, the Maya did not return to the now desolate old cities, choosing instead to stay huddled in the remote interior.

Joyce Kelly's *An Archaeological Guide to Northern Central America* offers the best descriptions of the Maya sites of Belize, along with those in Guatemala and Mexico.

The virtually unexplored Glover's Atoll is named for the pirate John Glover, who hung out there in the 1750s; there are supposed to be pirate graves on Northeast Caye.

900–1000	1000–1600	1540s	1638
The great Maya civilization declines, possibly as a result of drought, disease or environmental disaster. Large urban centers come under stress and their populations disperse throughout the region.	During the Postclassic period, the Maya civilization continues to develop, although populations are not as concentrated. Political and cultural centers migrate to northern Belize and the Yucatán.	Spanish conquistadors sweep through Northern and Western Belize, attempting to establish strongholds in Chetumal near Corozal, Lamanai in Orange Walk, and Tipu in Cayo.	British Baymen 'settle' Belize when former pirate Peter Wallace lays the foundations for a new port at the mouth of the Belize River, on the site of today's Belize City.

Baymen of the Caribbean: British Settlement

When Columbus accidentally bumped into the continental landmass soon to be known as the Americas, his Spanish royal patrons Ferdinand and Isabella had it made. Soon, Aztec gold and Incan silver overflowed in the king's coffers, making Spain a transatlantic superpower. In 1494 the Treaty of Tordesillas established an exclusive Iberian claim on the region, declaring New World riches off-limits to old-world rivals. But the temptations were too great, and the hiding places too many. Spain's spoils were set upon by British buccaneers, French corsairs and Dutch freebooters. In times of war, they were put into the service of their Crown as privateers; at other times, they were simply pirates.

Belize emerged as one of several Caribbean outposts for Britain's maritime marauders. In the early 17th century, English sea dogs first began using the Bay of Honduras as a staging point for raids on Spanish commerce; henceforth the Brits in the region came to be known as Baymen.

The Belizean coast had several strategic advantages from a pirate's perspective. The land was both bountiful and uninhabited, as the Spanish had already driven the Maya out but never bothered to settle in themselves. It was just a short sail away from the heavily trafficked Yucatán Straits, where – if luck be with ye – the Treasure Fleet might be gathering in Havana or the Silver Train passing through on its way from Panama. And the shoreline, concealed behind thick mangroves

THE FIRST MESTIZO

In 1511 the Spanish ship *Valdivia* was wrecked at sea when a reef ripped through its hull. About 15 survivors drifted for several days before making it to shore in Northern Belize, where they were promptly apprehended by anxious Maya. Just to be on the safe side, the locals sent 10 to the gods and kept five for themselves.

One of the captives was conquistador Gonzalo Guerrero, a skilled warrior and apparently not a bad diplomat either. Guerrero managed to win his freedom and a position of status with the Maya chief at Chetumal. He became a tribal consultant on military matters and married the chief's daughter; their three children are considered the first mestizos (mixed-race Spanish and Amerindian) in the New World.

Eight years later, Hernán Cortés arrived in the Yucatán and summoned Guerrero to serve him in his campaign of conquest. But Guerrero had gone native, with facial tattoos and body piercings. He turned down the offer, saying instead that he was a captain of the Maya. Cortés moved on in his search for gold and glory. Guerrero, meanwhile, organized Maya defenses in the wars that followed. It would take the Spanish more than 20 years to finally defeat the Maya of Yucatán and Belize.

1638–40	1667	1724	1717–63
Maya rebellion finally drives out the Spanish for good, although they never relinquish their claim on the territory. The Maya population drops dramatically due to war, drought and disease.	Britain and Spain sign a treaty that grants freedom of trade, as long as Britain agrees to control piracy. The result is an increase in logging and the acceleration of settlement of Belize.	The first African slaves are recorded in Belize. Slaves are put to work cutting logwood and mahogany, as well as doing domestic work and farming.	Spanish attacks attempt to end British extraction of hardwoods. Finally, the Treaty of Paris gives Britain the right to cut and export logwood, but the Spanish still claim the land.

and littoral islands, offered protective cover, while the long barrier reef was a treacherous underwater trap that kept Spanish war galleons at a distance.

For the sake of historical record, the year 1638 was made the official founding date of a British settlement at the mouth of the Belize River. It was around then that a Scottish pirate captain, Peter Wallace, decided to organize the building of a new port town. Legend has it that he laid the first foundations of what became Belize City with woodchips and rum bottles, presumably empty.

Meanwhile, the Baymen found yet another activity to annoy the Spanish crown – poaching its rainforest. The settlement became a rich source of hardwoods, especially mahogany, much valued by carpenters, furniture-makers and shipbuilders back in Britain. In addition, the lowland forest was abundant in logwood trees, which provided a valuable dye extract used to make woolen textiles.

By the 18th century, Britain's monarch finally had a navy and merchant fleet to match Spain's. Privateers were no longer needed, and pirates were a nuisance. In 1765 Jamaican-based British naval commander Admiral Burnaby paid a visit to the rough-hewn Baymen and delivered a code of laws on proper imperial etiquette: thieving, smuggling and cursing were out; paying taxes and obeying the sovereign were in.

As the British settlement became more profitable, the Spanish monarch became more irritable. Spain's armed forces made several unsuccessful attempts to dislodge the well-ensconced and feisty squatters. With the Treaty of Paris, in 1763, Spain instead tried diplomacy, negotiating a deal in which the Brits could stay and harvest wood as long as they paid rent to the Spanish Crown and promised not to expand the settlement. The Baymen did neither.

Spain finally got the better of the Baymen in 1779, burning down Belize City in a surprise attack and consigning the prisoners to slavery in Cuba. The conflict reached a decisive conclusion in 1798 at the Battle of St George's Caye when a squadron of 30 Spanish warships was met and turned back by the alerted Baymen operating in smaller but faster craft. From this point, Spain gave up trying to boot the Brits from Belize. And the battle made such a good story that it eventually inspired a national holiday (Battle of St George's Caye Day).

Colonial Sights

Government House
(Belize City)

Museum of Belize
(Belize City)

St John's Cathedral
(Belize City)

In Living Color: British Honduras

In the 19th century, modern Belize began to take form, largely shaped by its economic role and political status in the British Empire, where it was officially dubbed British Honduras. At first it was administered from Jamaica, but later was made a Crown Colony with its own appointed royal governor. Belizean society was an overlapping patchwork of British,

1786	1798	1832	1838
The Convention of London gives loggers the right to fell the forest, but not to establish any agriculture or government. However, an informal group of magistrates governs and agriculture exists.	During the seven-day Battle of St George's Caye, British Baymen and Creole slaves defend their settlement from Spanish invasion, finally ending Spanish claims on the territory.	A group of Garifuna from Honduras settles in present-day Dangriga. This ethnic enclave was previously deported from the British-ruled island of St Vincent, after being defeated in the Carib Wars.	According to the Abolition Act, slavery is outlawed throughout the British Empire, including Belize. Former slaves are unable to own property and are dependent on their ex-masters for work.

African, Maya and Spanish influences. It was a haven for refugees and a labor camp for slaves, a multicultural but hierarchical Crown Colony in living color.

At the top of the colonial social order were the descendants of the Baymen. In earlier times, their outlaw ancestors comprised an ethnically mixed and relatively democratic community. But as the colony grew larger and ties with the empire stronger, an oligarchy of leading families emerged. They may have descended from anti-establishment renegades, but now they were all about aristocratic manners. They touted their white, cultured British lineage, and used the Crown's authority to reinforce their status. By order of His Majesty's Superintendent for British Honduras, they alone were given political rights in colonial affairs and private entitlement to the forest and land. This elite colonial cohort managed to hold sway until the early 20th century.

Emory King's *The Great Story of Belize* is a fun read, and quite detailed, even though it has come under criticism for glamorizing the swashbuckling ways of the early British settlers.

As the economy was centered on timber exports, strong bodies were needed to perform the arduous labor of harvesting hardwoods from the dense rainforest. As elsewhere in the Americas, African slaves provided the muscle, along with much sweat and pain. By 1800 the settlement numbered about 4000 in total: 3000 black slaves, 900 mixed-race and free blacks, and 100 white colonists. Slave masters could count, and acted shrewdly to stay on top. Male slaves were kept divided into small work teams based on tribal origins. They were forced to do long tours of duty in remote jungle camps, separated from other teams and from their families. Slave women performed domestic chores and farm work. Interracial separation, however, did not mean interracial segregation, as mixed-race Creoles (descendants of African slaves) would eventually make up nearly 75% of the population.

In 1838 slavery was abolished in the British Empire. The plight of Afro-Belizeans, however, did not much improve. They were forbidden from owning land, which would have enabled them to be self-sufficient, and thus remained dependent on the white-controlled export economy. Instead of slaves, they were called 'apprentices' and worked for subsistence wages.

When the timber market declined in the 1860s, landowners diversified their holdings by introducing fruit and sugarcane. One persistent historical narrative has it that slave life in Belizean logging camps was more benign than the harsh conditions that existed on Caribbean sugar plantations. While this may be so, the facts remain that Belize experienced four major slave revolts between 1760 and 1820, and recorded a high annual incidence of runaways, suggesting instead that repressive inhumanity may come in different packages.

Toward the mid-19th century, British colonists finally came into contact – and conflict – with indigenous Maya people. As loggers

1847	1854	1862	1865
Spanish, mestizo and Maya peoples engage in the War of the Castes in the neighboring Yucatán Peninsula. The violence sends streams of refugees into Belize.	A new constitution establishes a Legislative Assembly of 18 elected, property-holding members, thus consolidating British political control of the territory.	The settlement in Belize is declared a Crown Colony and named British Honduras. Initially it is administered from Jamaica, but a separate royal governor is appointed soon after.	The Serpon sugar mill – the country's first steam-powered mill – is built on the Sittee River, ushering in an era of economic development.

BELIZEAN STARS & BARS

At the end of the US Civil War, several thousand Confederate soldiers chose not to return to their defeated and occupied homeland. The rebels instead accepted an invitation to resettle under the British flag in Belize.

The white colonial elite of Belize sympathized with the Southern cause during the conflict. During the war, they supplied the Confederacy with raw materials and guns. After the war, colonial officials enticed the war veterans with promises of land grants and other economic incentives. It was hoped that these expatriate Americans could help rejuvenate the Belizean economy, which suffered from a decline in timber exports, by sharing their expertise of the plantation system.

As many as 7000 American Southerners made it to Belize in the 1860s, mostly arriving from Mississippi and Louisiana, with the dream of recreating the Old South in tropical climes. Their initial attempts to cultivate cotton, however, were dashed by the inhospitable steamy jungle climate. They had better luck with sugarcane. The Confederate contribution to the colonial economy was notable, as Belizean sugar exports between 1862 and 1868 increased four-fold, from 400,000lb to 1,700,000lb.

But the move did not go smoothly. The American newcomers had run-ins with the local white landowners, who resented their presence and privileges, and with the local black workforce, who refused to submit and serve. All but a couple of hundred of the Confederate contingent eventually cashed out and returned home.

penetrated deeper into the interior, they encountered the indigenous population, who responded with hit-and-run assaults on the encroaching axmen.

At this time in the neighboring Yucatán Peninsula, an armed conflict broke out among the Maya, second-class mestizos and privileged Spanish-descended landlords. The bloody War of the Castes raged for over a decade and forced families to flee. Caste War refugees more than doubled the Belize population, from less than 10,000 in 1845 to 25,000 in 1861.

The movement of peoples redefined the ethnic character of northern Belize. Mestizo refugees, of mixed Spanish-Indian stock, brought their Hispanic tongue, corn tortillas and Catholic churches to scattered small-town settlements. Yucatecan Maya refugees, meanwhile, moved into the northwestern Belizean forest, where they quickly clashed with the logging industry. In 1872 the desperate Maya launched a quixotic attack on British colonists at Orange Walk, in what was a fierce but futile last stand. Diminished and dispirited, the remaining Maya survived on the territorial and social fringes of the colony.

1871	1927	1931	1950
A new constitution establishes a nine-member Legislative Council, which governs the colony alongside the lieutenant governor.	Successful international trading ties give rise to a prosperous Creole elite, which gains formal means of power when several representatives are appointed to the Legislative Council.	The deadliest hurricane in Belizean history hits on September 10, when the country is celebrating the national holiday. Belize City is destroyed, as is most of the northern coast; 2500 people die.	A severe economic crisis sparks anti-British protests, and the pro-independence movement is launched under the leadership of George Price and the People's United Party (PUP).

Patience & Resistance:
Belizean Independence

Belize remained a British colony until 1981, rather late for the West Indies. Spain and France lost most Caribbean possessions in the early 19th century, while Her Majesty's island colonies were liberated in the 1960s. With its deep ethnic divisions, a unifying national identity formed slowly, and the Belizean independence movement displayed more patience than resistance.

As the 19th century closed, the orderly ways of colonial life in British Honduras showed signs of breakdown. The old elite was becoming more isolated and less feared. Its cozy connections to the mother country were unraveling. By 1900 the US surpassed Britain as the main destination of the mahogany harvest; by 1930 the US was taking in 80% of all Belizean exports.

The colonial elite's economic position was further undercut by the rise of a London-based conglomerate, the British Estate and Produce Company, which bought out local landowners and took over the commodity trade. Declining timber fortunes caused colonial capitalists to impose a 50% wage cut on mahogany workers in Belize City, which provoked riotous protests and the first stirrings of social movement.

During the first half of the 20th century, Belizean nationalism developed in explosive fits and starts. During WWI, a regiment of local Creoles was recruited for the Allied cause. The experience proved both disheartening and enlightening. Ill-treated because of their dark skin, they were not even allowed to go to the front line and fight alongside white troops. They may have enlisted as patriotic Brits, but they were discharged as resentful Belizeans. Upon their return, in 1919, they coaxed several thousand into the streets of Belize City in an angry demonstration against the existing order.

It was not until the 1930s that a more sustained anticolonial movement arose. It began as the motley 'Unemployed Brigade,' staging weekend rallies in Battlefield Park in Belize City. The movement fed on the daily discontents of impoverished black workers, and spewed its wrath at prosperous white merchants. It soon was organizing boycotts and strikes, and shortly thereafter its leaders were thrown into jail.

Finally, in the early 1950s, a national independence party, the People's United Party (PUP), became politically active. When WWII caused the sudden closing of export markets, the colony experienced a severe economic crisis that lasted until well after the war's end. Anti-British demonstrations spread all across Belize, becoming more militant and occasionally violent. Colonial authorities declared a state of emergency, forbidding public meetings and intimidating independence advocates.

1961	1971	1972	1975
Hurricane Hattie devastates Belize, killing hundreds of people and destroying Belize City. British naval troops arrive to control widespread violence and looting.	In response to the devastation wrought by Hurricane Hattie, a new inland capital is established at Belmopan. The new National Assembly building is designed to resemble a Maya temple.	Jacques Cousteau takes his research ship *Calypso* to the Blue Hole, bringing unprecedented publicity and kicking off its popularity as a destination for divers and snorkelers.	Young activist attorneys Said Musa and Assad Shoman begin an intensive campaign to obtain international support for an independent Belize.

In response, the PUP organized a successful general strike that finally forced Britain to make political concessions. Universal suffrage was extended to all adults and limited home rule was permitted in the colony. The imperial foundations of the old ruling elite crumbled, as the colony's ethnically divided peoples now danced to a common Belizean drum beat.

Full independence for Belize was put off until a nagging security matter was resolved. Spain never formally renounced its territorial claim to Belize, which was later appropriated by Mexico and Guatemala. In the 19th century, Britain signed agreements with both claimants to recognize the existing colonial borders, but the one with Guatemala did not stick.

Guatemala's caudillo (Spanish/Latin American military dictator) rulers remained very preoccupied with the perceived wealth of British Honduras. The 1945 Guatemalan constitution explicitly included Belize as part of its territorial reach. Britain, in turn, stationed a large number of troops in the west. Guatemala barked, but did not bite. By the 1960s, the border threat was stabilized and the demand for independence was renewed.

Belizeans waited patiently. In 1964 the colony became fully self-governing, installing a Westminster-style parliamentary system. In 1971 the capital was relocated to Belmopan (a portmanteau of Belize and Mopan), a geographic center symbolically uniting all regions and peoples, but mainly because Belize City was partly wiped out by Hurricane Hattie a decade earlier. In 1973 the name was officially changed from the colonial sounding British Honduras to the more popular Belize. And in September 1981 Belize was at last declared an independent nation-state within the British Commonwealth. Even Guatemala recognized Belize as a sovereign nation in 1991, although to this day it maintains its territorial claim.

Return of the Jaguar King: Contemporary Belize

Independence did not turn out to be a cure-all. The angry nationalists that led Belize to independence turned into accommodating capitalists. The country had a small economy whose fortunes were determined beyond its control in global commodity markets. Belizeans eventually discovered that rather than remain vulnerable to exports, they had something valuable to import: tourists. The rise of ecotourism and revival of Maya culture has reshaped contemporary Belize, and cleared the jungle overgrowth for a return of the jaguar king.

Belizean politics were long dominated by the founder of the nationalist People's United Party (PUP), George Price. His party won nearly

In 1984, 18-year-old David Stuart became the youngest person to receive a McArthur Genius Award for his work in cracking the Maya hieroglyphic code, which he had been working on since the age of 10.

In 1988 the Duke of Edinburgh and WWF head, Prince Philip, was on hand to celebrate the creation of the Cockscomb Basin Wildlife Sanctuary, the world's first wildlife sanctuary for the jaguar. By 1998 the protected realm of the Belizean jungle's king eventually reached more than half a million acres.

1981	1991	1994	1998
After years of anticolonial and pro-independence political movements, Belize receives formal international recognition of its independence. George Price (People's United Party; PUP) is the first prime minister.	Guatemala finally recognizes Belize as a sovereign, independent state. Tensions continue, however, as the neighbor to the west refuses to relinquish its territorial claim over parts of Belize.	The United Kingdom withdraws military forces, with the exception of the British Army Training & Support Unit, which is established to assist the new Belize Defence Force.	Promising to 'Set Belize Free,' PUP takes the national elections, winning 26 of 31 seats in the House of Representatives. Party leader Said Musa becomes prime minister.

TERRITORIAL DISPUTES

In 2008 the Belize and Guatemala governments signed a historic agreement to refer their territorial conflict to the International Court of Justice, pending approval from their electorates. Guatemala held its territorial dispute referendum in April 2018, with voters overwhelmingly agreeing to submit the claim to the ICJ. Belize has scheduled its referendum for April 2019.

every parliamentary election, consolidating political independence and promoting a new middle class. In 1996, at the age of 75, Price finally stepped down with his national hero status intact; the PUP, however, looked vulnerable.

The party was tainted by corruption scandals: missing pension funds, selling off of public lands and bribery. Supporters argue that other parties' politicians are guilty of similar crimes.

The frail economy inherited at the time of independence was slow to recover. Many Creoles began to look for work outside the country, forming sizable diaspora communities in New York and London. As much as one-third of the Belizean people now live abroad. Meanwhile, civil war and rural poverty in neighboring Guatemala and Honduras sent more refugees into Belize, whose demographic profile changed accordingly, with Spanish-speaking mestizos becoming the majority ethnic group. From the time of independence, the Belize nation has more than doubled in size, from 150,000 in 1981 to over 380,000 by 2017.

Belize was an ideal candidate for a green revolution. Wide swaths of lowland rainforest were unspoiled by loggers, while sections of the interior highland had never even been explored by Europeans. The jungle hosted a rich stock of exotic flora and fauna, feathered and furry, while just offshore was the magnificent coral reef and mysterious Blue Hole, which Jacques Cousteau had already made famous.

A Tourist Ministry was created in 1984, but it was not until the 1990s that the government began to recognize ecotourism as a viable revenue source and invested in its promotion and development. Infrastructure associated with various sites improved, small business loans became available, training programs were organized for guides, and a bachelor's degree in tourism was created at Belize University.

Over the next decade, more than 20 sites from the western mountains to the eastern cays were designated as national parks, wildlife sanctuaries, forest reserves and marine preserves. More than 40% of Belizean territory received some form of protective status, including 80% of its pristine rainforest. The number of visitors rose steadily, from 140,000

2002	2006	2008	2011
The purpose-built Tourism Village opens in Belize City to welcome cruise-ship passengers to Belize. The following year, the tiny country hosts more than half a million cruise-ship tourists.	Black gold. After more than four years of exploration around the country, oil is discovered in commercially viable quantities in the Mennonite village of Spanish Lookout.	Led by Dean Barrow, the United Democratic Party (UDP) overwhelmingly defeats the PUP in countrywide elections, capturing 25 out of 31 seats in the House of Representatives.	Under pressure from local residents and hotel owners, the Belize Tourism Board decides against the development of a new cruise-ship port on Placencia peninsula.

in 1988 to more than 1.4 million in 2017. By the end of the 1990s, tourism was Belize's fastest-growing economic sector, surpassing commodity exports.

The eco-craze coincided with archaeological advances to spur a revival of Maya culture. In the 1980s significant progress was made in cracking the Maya hieroglyphic code, enabling researchers to gain deeper insights into this once-shrouded world, while NASA satellite technology revealed over 600 previously unknown sites and hidden temples beneath the Belizean rainforest. In 2000 the government allocated nearly $30 million to support excavation projects. A lost culture became a live commodity. Maya descendants re-engaged with traditional ceremonies, craft-making, food preparation and healing techniques often in response to tourist curiosity. However, the commercial aspects of cultural revival can be controversial, and one doesn't have to look far for examples where tourism and sanctity clash. One example concerns Cayo's Actun Tunichil Muknal cave, which is at once a sacred spot to the Maya and a top tourist attraction. After one visitor dropped a camera, fracturing an ancient human skull, cameras were banned from the cave. This example, among others, begs the question of how to promote cultural tourism while avoiding a carnival atmosphere.

In contemporary Belize, the new understanding of the Maya past fostered a changed attitude in the Maya present. The Maya culture is no longer disparaged at the fringe of society, but now is a source of pride and a defining feature of Belizean identity.

Modern Belize

In modern politics, Belize is a parliamentary democracy within the Commonwealth, where the monarch of Britain is the head of state but executive power rests with the government. Since 2008 the government and ruling party has been the center-right United Democratic Party (UDP), led by Dean Barrow, with the opposition People's United Party (PUP) holding the remaining seats in parliament.

2012	**2015**	**2016**	**2018**
While the UDP loses several seats in the general election, it holds onto its majority with 17 seats. The bizarre antics of eccentric computer millionaire John McAfee in San Pedro put the nation briefly in the international spotlight.	Prime Minister Dean Barrow of the UDP wins an unprecedented third straight election after calling a snap early election.	Hurricane Earl causes widespread damage along the Caribbean Coast, particularly in Belize District and the Northern Cayes.	The Belize Barrier Reef is removed from Unesco's list of endangered World Heritage Sites after the government stops all exploration.

Ancient Maya

Though the Maya population of Belize is small (around 10% of the nation's population), imagining contemporary Belize without the Maya would be difficult. From the Cayo District's Caracol (which covers more area than Belize City and still boasts Belize's tallest structure) and Xunantunich to smaller archaeological sites stretching from the nation's far north into its deep south, remnants of ancient Maya glory abound.

Creation Story

Nearly all aspects of Maya faith begin with their view of the creation, when the gods and divine forebears established the world at the beginning of time. From their hieroglyphic texts and art carved on stone monuments and buildings, or painted on pottery, we can now piece together much of the Maya view of the creation. We can even read the precise date when the creation took place.

In AD 775, a Maya lord with the high-sounding name of K'ak' Tiliw Chan Yoat (Fire Burning Sky Lightning God) set up an immense stone monument in the center of his city, Quirigua, in Guatemala. The unimaginative archaeologists who discovered the stone called it Stela C. This monument bears the longest single hieroglyphic description of the creation, noting that it took place on the day 13.0.0.0.0, 4 Ahaw, 8 Kumk'u, a date corresponding to August 13, 3114 BC on our calendar. This date appears over and over in other inscriptions throughout the Maya world. On that day the creator gods set three stones or mountains in the dark waters that once covered the primordial world. These three stones formed a cosmic hearth at the center of the universe. The gods then struck divine new fire by means of lightning, which charged the world with new life.

This account of the creation is echoed in the first chapters of the *Popol Vuh*, a book compiled by members of the Maya nobility soon after the Spanish conquest in 1524, many centuries after the erection of Quirigua Stela C. Although this book was written in their native Maya language, its authors used European letters rather than the more terse hieroglyphic script. Thus the book gives a fuller account of how they conceived the first creation:

> This is the account of when all is still, silent and placid. All is silent and calm. Hushed and empty is the womb of the sky. These then are the first words, the first speech. There is not yet one person, one animal, bird, fish, crab, tree, rock, hollow, canyon, meadow or forest. All alone the sky exists. The face of the earth has not yet appeared. Alone lies the expanse of the sea, along with the womb of all the sky. There is not yet anything gathered together. All is at rest. Nothing stirs. All is languid, at rest in the sky. Only the expanse of the water, only the tranquil sea lies alone. All lies placid and silent in the darkness, in the night.

> All alone are the Framer and the Shaper, Sovereign and Quetzal Serpent, They Who Have Borne Children and They Who Have Begotten Sons. Luminous they are in the water, wrapped in feathers...

Preclassic Maya Sites

Cuello (Orange Walk)

Lamanai (Orange Walk)

Cerro Maya (Corozal)

Caracol (Cayo)

Altun Ha (Belize District)

For a lively discussion of Maya religion and the creation, pick up a copy of *Maya Cosmos* by David Freidel, Linda Schele and Joy Parker.

They are great sages, great possessors of knowledge...Then they called forth the mountains from the water. Straightaway the great mountains came to be. It was merely their spirit essence, their miraculous power, that brought about the conception of the mountains.

Popol Vuh: The Sacred Book of the Maya

The Maya saw this pattern all around them. In the night sky, the three brightest stars in the constellation of Orion's Belt were conceived as the cosmic hearth at the center of the universe. On a clear night in the crisp mountain air of the Maya highlands, one can even see what looks like a wisp of smoke within these stars, although it is really only a far-distant string of stars within the M4 Nebula.

Maya Cities as the Center of Creation

Perhaps because the ancient Maya of Northern Belize didn't have real mountains as symbols of the creation, they built them instead in the form of plaza-temple complexes. In hieroglyphic inscriptions, the large open-air plazas at the center of Maya cities are often called *nab'* (sea) or *lakam ja'* (great water). Rising above these plastered stone spaces are massive pyramid temples, often oriented in groups of three, representing the first mountains to emerge out of the 'waters' of the plaza. The tiny elevated sanctuaries of these temples served as portals into the abodes of gods that lived within. Offerings were burned on altars in the plazas, as if the flames were struck in the midst of immense three-stone hearths. Only a few elite people were allowed to enter the small interior spaces atop the temples, while the majority of the populace observed their actions from the plaza below. The architecture of ancient Maya centers thus replicated sacred geography to form an elaborate stage on which rituals that charged their world with regenerative power could be carried out.

Many of the earliest-known Maya cities were built in Belize. The earliest temples at these sites are often constructed in this three-temple arrangement, grouped together on a single platform, as an echo of the first three mountains of creation. The ancient name for the site known today as Caracol was Oxwitza' (Three Hills Place), symbolically linking this community with the three mountains of creation and thus the center of life. The Caana (Sky-Place) is the largest structure at Caracol and consists of a massive pyramid-shaped platform topped by three temples that represent these three sacred mountains.

The Belizean site of Lamanai is one of the oldest and largest Maya cities known. It is also one of the few Maya sites that still bears its ancient name (which means Submerged Crocodile). While other sites were abandoned well before the Spanish Conquest in the 16th century, Lamanai continued to be occupied by the Maya centuries afterward. For the ancient Maya the crocodile symbolized the rough surface of the earth, newly emerged from the primordial sea that once covered the world. The name of the city reveals that its inhabitants saw themselves as living at the center of creation, rising from the waters of creation. Its massive pyramid temples include Structure N10-43, which is the second-largest pyramid known from the Maya Preclassic period and represents the first mountain and dwelling place of the gods.

The Maya Creation of Mankind

According to the *Popol Vuh,* the purpose of the creation was to give form and shape to beings who would 'remember' the gods through ritual. The Maya take their role in life very seriously. They believe that people exist as mediators between this world and that of the gods. If

Book about Maya Art & Architecture

Maya Art & Architecture
by Mary Ellen Miller

The Ancient Maya
by Robert J Sharer

THE HERO TWINS

According to the *Popol Vuh*, the Lords of Xibalba (the underworld) invited Hun Hunahpu and his brother to a game in the ballcourt. Upon losing the game, the brothers were sacrificed and one of their skulls was suspended from a calabash tree as a show of triumph.

Along came an unsuspecting daughter of Xibalba. As she reached out to take fruit from the tree, the skull of Hun Hunahpu spat in her hand, thus impregnating her. From this strange conception would be born the Hero Twins, Hunahpu and Xbalanque.

The Hero Twins would go on to have many adventures, including vanquishing their evil half-brothers. Their final triumph was overcoming Xibalba and avenging the death of their father – first by fooling the Lords, and then by sacrificing them. After this, the twins ascended into the sky, being transformed into the sun and moon.

Mara Vorhees

The oldest known copy of the *Popol Vuh* was made around 1701–03 by a Roman Catholic priest named Francisco Ximénez in Guatemala. The location of the original *Popol Vuh* from which Ximénez made his copy, if it still survives, is unknown.

they fail to carry out the proper prayers and ceremonies at just the right time and place, the universe will come to an abrupt end.

The gods created the first people out of maize (corn) dough, literally from the flesh of the Maize God, the principal deity of creation. Because of their divine origin, they were able to see with miraculous vision:

> Perfect was their sight, and perfect was their knowledge of everything beneath the sky. If they gazed about them, looking intently, they beheld that which was in the sky and that which was upon the earth. Instantly they were able to behold everything... Thus their knowledge became full. Their vision passed beyond the trees and the rocks, beyond the lakes and the seas, beyond the mountains and the valleys. Truly they were very esteemed people.

> *Popol Vuh: The Sacred Book of the Maya*

In nearly all of their languages, the Maya refer to themselves as 'true people' and consider that they are literally of a different flesh than those who do not eat maize. They are maize people, and foreigners who eat bread are wheat people. This mythic connection between maize and human flesh influenced birth rituals in the Maya world for centuries.

Maya Kingship

The creation wasn't a one-time event. The Maya constantly repeated these primordial events in their ceremonies, timed to the sacred calendar. They saw the universe as a living thing. And just like any living thing, it grows old, weakens and ultimately passes away. Everything, including the gods, needed to be periodically recharged with life-bearing power or the world would slip back into the darkness and chaos that existed before the world began. Maya kings were seen as mediators. In countless wall carvings and paintings, monumental stone stelae and altars, painted pottery and other sacred objects, the Maya depicted their kings dressed as gods, repeating the actions of deities at the time of creation.

As in ancient Greece, there was no unified Maya empire. Each city had its own royal family and its own patron gods. Warfare was often conducted not for conquest, but to obtain captives who bore within their veins royal blood to be sacrificed.

A common theme was the king dressed as the Maize God himself, bearing a huge pack on his back containing the sacred bits and pieces that make up the world, while dancing them into existence. A beautiful example of this may be seen on the painted Buenavista Vase, one of the true masterpieces of Maya art. Discovered at Buenavista del Cayo, a small site in the Cayo District of Belize, right on the river (north side) close to the border with Guatemala, it is now one of the gems of the Maya collection housed in the Department of Archaeology, Belize City. These rituals were done at very specific times of the year, timed to match calendric dates when the gods first performed them. For the Maya, these ceremonies were not merely symbolic of the rebirth of the cosmos, but a genuine creative act in which time folded in on itself to reveal the actions of the divine creators in the primordial world.

In Maya theology, the Maize God is the most sacred of the creator deities because he gives his very flesh in order for human beings to live. But this sacrifice must be repaid. The Maya, as 'true people', felt an obligation to the cosmos to compensate for the loss of divine life, not because the gods were cruel, but because gods cannot rebirth themselves and need the intercession of human beings. Maya kings stood as the sacred link between their subjects and the gods. The king was thus required to periodically give that which was most precious – his own blood, which was believed to contain the essence of godhood itself. Generally, this meant that members of the royal family bled themselves with stingray spines or stone lancets. Males did their bloodletting from the genital area, literally birthing gods from the penis. Women most often drew blood from their tongues. This royal blood was collected on sheets of bark paper and then burned to release its divine essence, opening a portal to the other world and allowing the gods to emerge to a new life. At times of crisis, such as the end of a calendar cycle, or upon the death of a king and the succession of another, the sacrifice had to be greater to compensate for the loss of divine life. This generally involved obtaining noble or royal captives through warfare against a neighboring Maya state in order to sacrifice them.

Altar 23 from Caracol shows two captive lords from the Maya cities of B'ital and Ucanal, on the Guatemala–Belize border, with their arms bound behind their backs in preparation for sacrifice, perhaps on that very altar. If this were not done, they believed that life itself would cease to exist.

The beauty of Maya religion is that these great visions of creation mirror everyday events in the lives of the people. When a Maya woman rises early in the morning, before dawn, to grind maize for the family meal, she replicates the actions of the creators at the beginning of time. The darkness that surrounds her is reminiscent of the gloom of the primordial world. When she lights the three-stone hearth on the floor of her home, she is once again striking the new fire that generates life. The grains of maize that she cooks and then forms into tortillas are literally the flesh of the Maize God, who nourishes and rebuilds the bodies of her family members. This divine symmetry is comforting in a world that often proves intolerant and cruel.

The Maya hieroglyphic writing system is one of only five major phonetic scripts ever invented – the others being cuneiform (used in ancient Mesopotamia), Egyptian, Harappan and Chinese.

When the Spaniards arrived, Christian missionaries zealously burned all the Maya hieroglyphic books they could find. Only four are known to have survived and are held in Dresden, Madrid, Paris and Mexico City.

Maya Hieroglyphic Writing

More than 1500 years prior to the Spanish Conquest, the Maya developed a sophisticated hieroglyphic script capable of recording complex literary compositions, both on folded screen codices made of bark paper or deer

GUIDE TO THE GODS

The Maya worshiped a host of heavenly beings. It's practically impossible to remember them all (especially since some of them have multiple names), but here's a primer for the most powerful Maya gods.

Ah Puch God of Death

Chaac God of Rain and Thunder

Itzamma God of Priestly Knowledge and Writing

Hun Hunahpu Father of the Hero Twins, sometimes considered the Maize God

Hunahpu & Xbalanque The Hero Twins

Ixchel Goddess of Fertility and Birth

AMAZING MAIZE

No self-respecting Maya, raised in the traditional way, would consider eating a meal that didn't include maize. They treat it with the utmost respect. Women do not let grains of maize fall on the ground or into an open fire. If it happens accidentally, the woman picks it up gently and apologizes to it. The Maya love to talk and laugh, but are generally silent during meals. Most don't know why; it's just the way things have always been done. As one elder explained, 'For us, tortillas are like the Catholic sacramental bread: it is the flesh of god. You don't laugh or speak when taking the flesh of god into your body. The young people are beginning to forget this. They will someday regret it.'

If you are curious about how scholars unlocked the secrets of Maya hieroglyphics, read Michael Coe's *Breaking the Maya Code*. It reads like a detective novel.

skin, as well as texts incised on more durable stone or wood. The importance of preserving written records was a hallmark of Maya culture, as witnessed by the thousands of known hieroglyphic inscriptions, many more of which are still being discovered in the jungles of Belize and other Maya regions. The sophisticated Maya hieroglyphic script is partly phonetic (glyphs representing sounds tied to the spoken language) and partly logographic (glyphs representing entire words), making it capable of recording any idea that could be thought or spoken.

Ancient Maya scribes were among the most honored members of their society. They were often important representatives of the royal family and, as such, were believed to carry the seeds of divinity within their blood. Among the titles given to artists and scribes in Maya inscriptions of the Classic period were *itz'aat* (sage) and *miyaatz* (wise one).

Counting System

Maya arithmetic was elegantly simple: dots were used to count from one to four, a horizontal bar signified five, a bar with one dot above it was six, a bar with two dots was seven etc. Two bars signified 10, three bars 15. Nineteen, the highest common number, was three bars stacked up and topped by four dots.

The Maya didn't use a decimal system (which is based on the number 10), but rather a vigesimal system (that is, a system that has a base of 20). The late Mayanist Linda Schele used to suggest that this was because they wore sandals and thus counted not only their fingers but their toes as well. This is a likely explanation, since the number 20 in nearly all Maya languages means 'person.'

The Maya likely used their counting system from day to day by writing on the ground, the tip of the finger creating a dot. By using the edge of the hand they could make a bar, representing the entire hand of five fingers.

To signify larger sums the Maya used positional numbers – a fairly sophisticated system similar to the one we use today and much more advanced than the crude additive numbers used in the Roman Empire. In positional numbers, the position of a sign and the sign's value determine the number. For example, in our decimal system the number 23 is made up of two signs: a 2 in the 'tens' position and a 3 in the 'ones' position; two tens plus three ones equals 23.

In the Maya system, positions of increasing value went not right to left (as ours do) but from bottom to top. So the bottom position showed values from one to 19 (remember that this is a base-20 system so three bars and four dots in this lowest position would equal 19); the next position up showed multiples of 20 (for example four dots at this position would equal 80); the next position represents multiples of 400; the next, multiples of 8000 etc. By adding more positions one could count as high as needed.

Such positional numbers depend upon the use of zero, a concept that the Romans never developed but the Maya did. The zero in Maya numbering was represented by a stylized picture of a shell or some other object – but never a bar or a dot.

Calendar System

The Maya counting system was used by merchants and others who had to add up many things, but its most important use – and the one you will most often encounter during your travels – was in writing calendar dates. The ancient Maya calendar was a way of interpreting the order of the universe itself. The sun, moon and stars were not simply handy ways of measuring the passage of time, but living beings that influenced the world in fundamentally important ways. Even today, the Maya refer to days as 'he.' The days and years were conceived as being carried by gods, each with definite personalities and spheres of influence that colored the experience of those who lived them. Priests carefully watched the sky to look for the appearance of celestial bodies that would determine the time to plant and harvest crops, celebrate certain ceremonies, or go to war. The regular rotation of the heavens served as a comforting contrast to the chaos that characterizes our imperfect human world.

In some ways, the ancient Maya calendar – still used in parts of the region – is more accurate than the Gregorian calendar we use today. Without sophisticated technology, Maya astronomers were able to ascertain the length of the solar year as 365.2420 days (a discrepancy of 17.28 seconds per year from the true average length of 365.2422 days). The Gregorian calendar year works out to be 365.2425 days. Thus the Maya year count is 1/10,000 closer to the truth than our own modern calendar.

Maya astronomers were able to pinpoint eclipses with uncanny accuracy, a skill that was unknown among the brightest scholars in contemporary medieval Europe. The Maya lunar cycle was a mere seven minutes off today's sophisticated technological calculations. They calculated the Venus cycle at 583.92 days. By dropping four days each 61 Venus

Dr Allen J Christenson has an MA and a PhD in Pre-Columbian Maya Art and Literature, and works as a professor in the Humanities, Classics and Comparative Literature department of Brigham Young University in Provo, Utah. His works include *Popol Vuh: The Sacred Book of the Maya*, a critical translation of the *Popol Vuh* from the original Maya text.

ANCIENT MAYA CALENDAR SYSTEM

HOW THE MAYA CALENDAR WORKED

The ancient Maya used three calendars. The first was a period of 260 days, known as the Tzolkin, likely based on the nine months it takes for a human fetus to develop prior to birth. The second Maya calendar system was a solar year of 365 days, called the Haab. Both the Tzolkin and Haab were measured in endlessly repeating cycles. When meshed together, a total of 18,980 day-name permutations are possible (a period of 52 solar years), called the Calendar Round.

Though fascinating in its complexity, the Calendar Round has its limitations, the greatest being that it only goes for 52 years. After that, it starts again and so provides no way for Maya ceremony planners to distinguish a day in this 52-year Calendar Round cycle from the identically named day in the next cycle. Thus the Maya developed a third calendar system that we call the Long Count, which pinpoints a date based on the number of days it takes place after the day of creation on August 13, 3114 BC.

Let's use the date of Friday April 1, 2011 as an example. The Maya Long Count date corresponding to this day is 12.19.18.4.10, 3 Uayeb 11 Oc.

The first number, '12,' of this Long Count date represents how many *baktuns* (400 x 360 days or 144,000 days) that have passed since the day of creation (thus 12 x 144,000 = 1,728,000 days). The second number, '19,' represents the number of *katuns* (20 x 360 or 7200 days) that have passed, thus adding another 19 x 7200 = 136,800 days. The third number, '18,' is the number of *tuns* (360 days), or 6480 days. The fourth number, '4,' is the number of *uinals* (20 days), or 80 days. Finally the fifth number, '10,' is the number of whole days. Adding each of these numbers gives us the sum of 1,728,000 + 136,800 + 6480 + 80 + 10 = 1,871,370 days since the day of creation.

The Maya then added the Calendar Round date: the Haab date (3 Uayeb) and the Tzolkin date (11 Oc).

years and eight days at the end of 300 Venus years, the Maya lost less than a day in accuracy in 1000 years!

The ancient Maya believed that the Great Cycle of the present age would last for 13 *baktun* cycles in all (each *baktun* lasting 144,000 days), which according to our calendar ended on December 23, AD 2012, beginning a new cycle. The Maya saw the end of large cycles of time as a kind of death, and they were thus fraught with peril. But both death and life must dance together on the cosmic stage for the succession of days to come. Thus the Maya conducted ceremonies to periodically 'rebirth' the world and keep the endless march of time going.

The Maya never expected the end of this Great Cycle to be the last word for the cosmos, since the world regularly undergoes death and rebirth. Koba Stela 1 (the first stela from the site of Koba) records a period of time equivalent to approximately 41,341,050,000,000,000,000,000,000,000,000 of our years! (In comparison, the Big Bang that is said to have formed our universe is estimated to have occurred a mere 15,000,000,000 years ago.)

People of Belize

Belize is a tiny country, but it enjoys a diversity of ethnicities that is undeniably stimulating and improbably serene. Four main ethnic groups – mestizo, Creole, Maya and Garifuna – comprise 76% of the population. The remaining 24% includes East Indians (people of Indian subcontinent origins), Chinese, Spanish, Arabs (generally Lebanese), the small but influential group of Mennonites, and North Americans and Europeans who have settled here in the last couple of decades.

Mestizo

Mestizos are people of mixed Spanish and indigenous descent. Over the last couple of decades, mestizos have become Belize's largest ethnic group, now making up about 34% of the population. The first mestizos arrived in the mid-19th century, when refugees from the Yucatán flooded into Northern and Western Belize during the War of the Castes. Their modern successors are the thousands of political refugees from troubled neighboring Central American countries. While English remains Belize's official language, Spanish is spoken by more than half of the population; this has caused some resentment among Creoles, who are fiercely proud of their country's Anglo roots.

Creoles

Belizean Creoles are descendants of African slaves and British Baymen, loggers and colonists. In the 1780s, after much conflict, the Spanish and the British finally reached an agreement allowing Brits to cut logwood from the area between the Río Hondo and the Belize River (essentially the northern half of Belize). Three years later, according to the Convention of London, the area was extended south.

The convention also permitted the British to cut mahogany, a hardwood that was highly valued in Europe for making furniture. In return, Britain agreed to abandon the Miskito Coast of Nicaragua, prompting 2214 new settlers to come to Belize and quadrupling its non-Maya population. Three-quarters of the newcomers were slaves of African origin.

This influx of slave labor was convenient for the loggers. Mahogany is a much larger tree than logwood, and it is more scattered in the forest, meaning that its

WHO ARRIVED WHEN

2000 BC–AD 250
The oldest Maya sites in Belize – including Cahal Pech and Lamanai – date to the Preclassic period of this indigenous civilization.

16th Century
By now dispersed and depopulated, the Maya nonetheless resist the Spanish attempts to convert and conquer them. Early Spanish explorers do not stay.

17th Century
Belize becomes a popular hideaway for British Baymen, who eventually establish settlements along the coast and move inland.

1786
Britain cedes the coast of Nicaragua, bringing to Belize an influx of African slaves – the beginning of today's Creole population.

1832
After being deported from St Vincent and migrating from Honduras, a group of Garifuna settles in present-day Dangriga.

1847
Spanish, mestizo and Maya peoples engage in the War of the Castes in the neighboring Yucatán Peninsula, sending streams of refugees to settle in Belize.

1958
After being driven out of Mexico, the first group of Mennonites settles in Belize.

WHAT THEY BELIEVE IN BELIZE

Ethnicity is a big determinant of religion in Belize, with most mestizos, Maya and Garifuna espousing Catholicism as a result of their ethnic origins in Spanish- or French-ruled countries or colonies. Catholicism among Creoles increased with the work of North American missionaries in the late 19th and early 20th centuries. Approximately a quarter of Belizeans are Protestants, chiefly Anglicans and Methodists. Today the number of Pentecostalists and Adventists is growing due to the strength of their evangelical movements. Mennonites also constitute a small minority.

Among the Garifuna, and to a lesser extent the Maya and Creoles, Christianity coexists with other beliefs. Maya Catholicism has long been syncretized with traditional beliefs and rites that go back to pre-Hispanic times, while some Creoles (especially older people) have a belief in *obeah*, a form of witchcraft.

Belize's tradition of tolerance also encompasses Hindus, Muslims, Baha'i, Jehovah's Witnesses and a small (but eye-catching) number of Rastafarians.

Experts estimate that the number of Belizeans living overseas is roughly equal to the number of Belizeans living at home.

extraction required more labor. Thus it was that mahogany played a key role in the creation of the Afro-Belizean population. After several generations of mixing with the loggers and other colonists, the so-called Creoles became the most populous ethnic group in Belize.

Belizean Creoles now form only about 25% of Belize's population, but theirs remains a sort of paradigm culture. Racially mixed and proud of it, Creoles speak a fascinating and unique version of English: it sounds familiar at first, but it is not easily intelligible to a speaker of standard English. Most of the people you'll encounter in Belize City and the center of the country will be Creole.

Maya

The Maya of Belize make up almost 11% of the population and are divided into three linguistic groups. The Yucatec Maya live mainly in the north; the Mopan Maya in the southern Toledo District; and the Kekchí Maya in Western Belize and also in the Toledo District. Use of both Spanish and English is becoming more widespread among the Maya. Traditional Maya culture is strongest among the Maya of the south.

Garifuna

In the 17th century, shipwrecked African slaves washed ashore on the Caribbean island of St Vincent. They hooked up with the indigenous population of Caribs and Arawaks and formed a whole new ethnicity, now known as the Garifuna (plural Garinagu, also called Black Caribs).

Garifuna History, Language & Culture of Belize, Central America & the Caribbean, by Sebastian Cayetano, gives an easily understood overview of the Garifuna people and their culture.

France claimed possession of St Vincent in the early 18th century, but eventually ceded it to Britain according to the Treaty of Paris. After prolonged resistance, the Garifuna finally surrendered in 1796, and Britain decided to deport them. Over the course of several years, the Garifuna were shuffled around various spots in the Caribbean, with many dying of malnutrition or disease. Finally, 1465 of the original 4000-plus deportees arrived at the Honduran coastal town of Trujillo. From here, these people of mixed Native American and African heritage began to spread along the Caribbean coast of Central America.

The first Garifuna arrived in Belize around the turn of the 19th century. But the biggest migration took place in 1832, when, on November 19, some 200 Garifuna reached Belize in dugout canoes from Honduras. The anniversary of the arrival is celebrated as Garifuna Settlement Day, a national holiday.

Today the Belize Garifuna number around 20,000, about 6% of Belize's population, most of whom still live in the south of the country, from

Dangriga to Punta Gorda. The Garifuna language is a combination of Arawak and African languages with bits of English and French thrown in.

The Garifuna maintain a unique culture with a strong sense of community and ritual, in which drumming and dancing play important roles. The *dügü* ('feasting of the ancestors' ceremony) involves several nights and days of dancing, drumming and singing by an extended family. Its immediate purpose is to heal a sick individual, but it also serves to reaffirm community solidarity. Some participants may become 'possessed' by the spirits of dead ancestors. Other noted Garifuna ceremonials include the *beluria* (ninth-night festivity), for the departure of a dead person's soul, attended by entire communities with copious drumming, dancing and drinking; and the *wanaragua* or *jonkonu* dance, performed in some places during the Christmas-to-early-January festive season.

Garifuna culture has been enjoying a revival since the 1980s, due in no small part to the *punta* rock phenomenon. In 2001 Unesco declared Garifuna language, dance and music to be a 'Masterpiece of the Oral and Intangible Heritage of Humanity' – one of the initial selections for what has become the cultural equivalent of the World Heritage list.

The Mennonites

It almost seems like an aberration, an odd sight inspired by too much sun: women in bonnets and drape-like frocks; blond-haired, blue-eyed men in denim overalls and straw hats; the family packed onto a horse-drawn carriage, plodding along the side of the highway. In fact, it is not something your imagination has conjured up; you're looking at Belizean Mennonites.

The Mennonites originate from an enigmatic Anabaptist group that dates back to 16th-century Netherlands. Like the Amish of Pennsylvania, the Mennonites have strict religion-based values that keep them isolated in agricultural communities. Speaking mostly Low German, they run their own schools, banks and churches. Traditional groups reject any form of mechanization or technology (which explains the horse-drawn buggies).

Mennonites are devout pacifists and reject most of the political ideologies that societies have thrust upon them (including paying taxes). So they have a history of moving about the world trying to find a place to live in peace. They left the Netherlands for Prussia and Russia in the late 17th century. In the 1870s, when Russia insisted on military conscription, the Mennonites upped and moved to isolated parts of Canada. After WWI the Canadian government demanded that English be taught in Mennonites' schools and their exemption from conscription was reconsidered. Again, the most devout Mennonites moved, this time to Mexico. By the 1950s Mexico wanted the Mennonites to join its social security program, so once again the Mennonites packed up.

The first wave of about 3500 Mennonites settled in Belize (then called British Honduras) in 1958. Belize was happy to have their industriousness and farming expertise, and the settlements expanded.

Today Belize has many different Mennonite communities The progressives – many of whom came from Canada – speak English and have no qualms about using tractors or pickup trucks; other groups are strongly conservative and shun modern technologies.

Belize has been good to the Mennonites and in turn the Mennonites have been good to Belize. Mennonite farms now supply most of the country's dairy products, eggs and poultry. Furniture-making is another Mennonite specialty and you'll often see them selling their goods at markets. They are also accomplished house builders – constructing houses within their communities and then loading them onto massive tractor trailers to be delivered to clients around the country.

Conservative Mennonites

*Shipyard
(Orange Walk)*

*Little Belize
(Corozal)*

Progressive Mennonites

*Blue Creek
(Orange Walk)*

*Spanish Lookout
(Cayo)*

Rhythms of a Nation

Belize knows how to get its groove on. You'll hear a variety of pan-Caribbean musical styles, including calypso (of which Belize has its own star in Gerald 'Lord' Rhaburn), soca (an up-tempo fusion of calypso with Indian rhythms) and, of course, reggae (with Belize being represented by exceptionally talented Tanya Carter). But what's most special about the Belizean music here is the styles that are uniquely homegrown.

Punta & Punta Rock

Pen Cayetano is a polymathic figure who started the *punta rock* musical phenomenon, but he also does oil paintings portraying Garifuna culture.

Musicians and linguists speculate that *'punta'* comes from the word *bunda*, which means 'buttocks' in many West African languages. The word derivation is not certain, but it is appropriate. Heard at any sort of celebration or occasion, this traditional drumming style inspires Garifuna peoples across Central America to get up and shake their *bunda*.

The crowd circles around one couple, who gyrate their hips while keeping the upper body still. Traditionally, it is associated with death and ancestor worship, which explains why the dance is often performed at funerals and wakes.

Punta rock was born in the 1970s, when *punta* musician Pen Cayetano, a native of Dangriga, traveled around Central America and came to the realization that Garifuna traditions were in danger of withering away. He wanted to inspire young Garifuna people to embrace their own culture instead of listening to and copying music from other countries – and so he invented a style that is cool, contemporary but uniquely Belizean. He added the electric guitar to traditional *punta* rhythms and so was born *punta rock*.

Punta rock can be frenetic or it can be mellow, but at its base are always fast rhythms designed to get the hips swiveling. Like traditional *punta*, the dance is strongly sexually suggestive, with men and women gyrating their pelvises in close proximity to each other. The lyrics are almost always in Garifuna or Kriol, which differs from traditional *punta*.

After musician Andy Palacio's untimely death, an estimated 2500 people descended on his home village of Barranco, where he was laid to rest following a Catholic Mass, a Garifuna ceremony and an official state funeral.

Cayetano's Turtle Shell Band spread the word, and the rhythm, to neighboring Guatemala, Honduras (both with their own Garifuna populations), Mexico and even the USA (where there are sizable Belizean and Garifuna communities). Ideal Castillo, Mohobub and Mime Martinez are all members of the Turtle Shell Band who went on to enjoy success in their solo careers.

Andy Palacio was a leading ambassador of *punta rock* until his untimely death in 2008. Palacio was known for mixing the Garifuna sound with all sorts of foreign elements, including pop, salsa and calypso beats. He deserves the credit for widening the audience for *punta rock* and turning it into the (unofficial) national music of Belize.

One of Belize's biggest modern sensations is Supa G, who provides a fusion of *punta rock*, techno and even a spot of Mexican balladeering. His songs include amusing takes on Belizean society and culture.

Originally from Hopkins, Aziatic has blended *punta* with R&B, jazz and pop, earning him an international audience, particularly in the US, where he now lives.

Paranda

Shortly after the Garifuna arrived in Central America, they started melding African percussion and chanting with Spanish-style acoustic guitar and Latin rhythms. The resulting mix is known as *paranda,* named after a traditional African rhythm that is often at the root of the music. Unlike *punta rock, paranda* music is totally unplugged, played on wooden Garifuna drums, acoustic guitars and primitive percussion instruments, such as shakers and turtle shells. It combines fast rhythms and lyrical melodies.

Although musicians have been playing *paranda* since the 19th century, it was not recorded and therefore rarely heard outside Garifuna communities. It is another genre of folk music that is in danger of dying out, as very few young musicians are making new *paranda* music. In the mid-1990s, producers from Stonetree Records recognized the importance of making a recording before the great *paranderos* passed. The so-called Paranda Project resulted in an album that featured eight of the most esteemed *paranda* musicians from Belize and Honduras.

The Belizean master of *paranda* was the late Paul Nabor, who was born in Punta Gorda in the 1920s. The next generation of the genre is led by Honduran-born Aurelio Martínez, who also served as his country's first black congressman. The title of Martínez' album *Garifuna Soul* gives a good idea of what *paranda* is all about.

Top Albums

Best of Punta Rock, Pen Cayetano and Mohobub Flores

Bumari, Lugua Centeno

Garifuna Soul, Aurelio Martínez

Brukdown Reloaded, Mr Peters' Boom & Chime

Brukdown

In the 18th and 19th centuries, most of the hard labor of logging – the intensive cutting and heavy lifting of the massive mahogany trees – was carried out by African slaves and their descendants. Here, in the logging camps of the Belize River valley, workers soothed their weary bodies and souls by drinking, dancing and making their own unique music, known as *brukdown.*

Belize's most prominent Creole music, *brukdown* is deeply rooted in Africa, with layered rhythms and call-and-response vocals. Back in the camps, it was normally played by an ensemble of accordion, banjo, harmonica and a percussion instrument – usually the jawbone of a pig, its teeth rattled with a stick. Nowadays, modern musicians might add a drum or an electric guitar.

Like the Garifuna music, *brukdown* is predominantly a rural folk tradition that is rarely recorded. The exception is the so-called King of Brukdown, Wilfred Peters, and his band Mr Peters' Boom & Chime. Mr Peters made music for more than 60 years before his death in 2010, and became

GARI-FUSION

In contemporary Belize there has been a resurgence of Garifuna music, popularized by musicians such as Andy Palacio, Mohobub Flores and Adrian Martinez. These musicians have taken many aspects of traditional Garifuna music and fused them with more modern sounds. Andy Palacio's last album, *Watina,* was a collaboration with other musicians, known as the Garifuna Collective. Each track on the album is based on a traditional Garifuna rhythm, and all of the songs are in the Garifuna language, which is a novelty itself. Rooted in musical and folkloric tradition, the album exhibits remembrance of the past and hope for the future of the Garifuna people.

Umalali, which means 'voice' in the Garifuna language, is the name of an album created by the Garifuna Women's Project. In 2002 Garifuna women from all around Central America met in the village of Hopkins to record their most beloved songs and musical stories. Their voices were then layered on top of the rhythms and instrumentation of the Garifuna Collective, fusing many elements of the rich but endangered culture.

THREE KINGS OF BELIZE

Three Kings of Belize is a documentary by Katia Paradis (2007) that follows three pre-eminent musicians, each considered the 'king' of his genre. Paul Nabor was a legendary Garifuna *parandero* from Punta Gorda, Wilfred Peters was a Creole *brukdown* accordionist from Belize City, and Florencio Mess is a traditional Maya harpist living in the farming village of San Pedro Columbia. The film captures the artists in their homes, interacting with their families, recalling stories from their lives and, of course, making music.

The recurring theme – expressed by all three gentlemen – is a frustration, and perhaps a fear, that young people no longer make this music. There is a sense that when the original artists of traditional genres die, their music might die too. But *Three Kings* is not just about frustration or fear. It is wistful, perhaps, but ultimately accepts that nothing is eternal.

In June 2010, Wilfred Peters died at the age of 79. Hundreds of people attended his funeral, including the prime minister and the leader of the opposition – proof that music is greater than politics.

Another state funeral was held in Punta Gorda for Paul Nabor, who died in October 2014 at the age of 86.

a national icon and the country's best-loved Creole musician. In 1997 Queen Elizabeth II awarded him an MBE for his cultural contributions.

If Mr Peters was the King of Brukdown, the Queen of Brukdown was undoubtedly Leela Vernon MBE. A resident of Punta Gorda, Leela Vernon was a high-energy singer and dancer who was awarded National Hero status in 2016, prior to her death in early 2017. In addition to making four albums, she started a dance group to preserve traditional Creole dance.

Kungo Muzik

'This muzik is one of the heart beats felt out of Afrika coming by way of Belize.' So says Brother David Obi, better known in Belize as Bredda David. And he should know, as he created the fast-paced fusion of Creole, Caribbean and African styles known as *kungo muzik*.

Maya

The Maya have been making music for thousands of years. In contemporary Maya music, bones and rattles are used for percussion, while other instruments include whistles, flutes and horns made from conch shells. The ocarina is an ancient wind instrument that is something like a flute with a wider body and 10 to 12 finger holes. The same types of instruments have been found as artifacts at archaeological sites all around Central America.

Founded in Benque Viejo del Carmen in 1995 by producer Ivan Duran, Stonetree Records has long been at the forefront of producing and releasing Garifuna music and Belizean indie. Find latest releases at www. stonetreerecords. com.

Originally from Guatemala, Pablo Collado is a Maya flautist who now resides in Benque del Carmen. His new-age-style music is light and relaxing, often incorporating sounds that mimic nature, such as the gurgling of water or the calls of birds or insects.

Also popular among the Maya is the marimba, a percussion instrument that resembles a xylophone, except it is made of wood and so produces a mellower sound. Marimba music is used during Maya religious ceremonies.

Stringed instruments like the guitar, violin and harp are used in Maya ceremonial and recreational music. Crafted from native woods such as mahogany or cedar, harps were traditionally carved with animal symbols, representing the Maya gods. Florencio Mess not only plays the Maya harp, but also makes these instruments from hand in the traditional style. His music – based on age-old melodies and rhythms – has been called 'a living connection to ancient Maya culture.'

Belize Cuisine

A staple of Belizean cuisine, rice and beans comes in two varieties: 'rice and beans,' where the two are cooked together; and 'beans and rice,' where beans in a soupy stew are served separately in a bowl. Both variations are prepared with coconut milk and red beans, which distinguishes them from other countries' rice and beans. You're bound to eat a lot of rice and beans (or beans and rice) while you are in Belize, but Belizean cuisine has more depth than would first appear.

Seafood

When it comes to seafood in Belize, lobster plays the starring role. Distinguished from the American and European lobster by their lack of claws, the Caribbean crustaceans are no less divine, especially when grilled. Lobster is widely available in coastal towns, except from mid-February to mid-June, when the lobster season is closed.

Conch (pronounced 'konk') is the large snail-like sea creature that inhabits conch shells. Much like calamari, it has a chewy consistency that is not universally appreciated. During conch season, from October to June, it is often prepared as *ceviche* (seafood marinated in lemon or lime juice, garlic and seasonings) or conch fritters (and it's considerably cheaper than lobster).

Aside from the shellfish, the local waters are home to snapper, grouper, barracuda, jacks and tuna, all of which make a tasty filet or steak.

Belizeans really know how to prepare their seafood, be it barbecued, grilled, marinated, steamed or stewed. A common preparation is 'Creole-style,' where seafood, peppers, onions and tomatoes are stewed together.

Meat & Poultry

Seafood is popular on the coast (and especially in tourist towns), but most often the main course in Belize comes from a chicken. Poultry serves as an accompaniment for rice and beans, a stuffing for burritos and *salbutes* (a variation on the tortilla), and a base for many soups and stews.

Belizeans do not eat a lot of beef, but they do love cow-foot soup. This is a glutinous concoction of pasta, vegetables, spices – and an actual cow's foot. Cow-foot soup is supposed to be 'good for the back'; in other words, an aphrodisiac.

Pastries

Almost every town in Belize has at least one shop where the shelves are lined with sweet and savory pastries to make you drool. If you're looking for a quick, tasty and cheap snack, you can't go wrong at the local bakery. Grab a tray and a pair of tongs and make your selection from the delectable treats on display.

While these pastries are pretty to look at and delicious to eat, they are not the best in Belizean baked goods. That title belongs to fresh-baked johnnycakes, or biscuits, smothered in butter, beans or melted cheese. Johnnycakes are the quintessential breakfast in Belize, but they are also served throughout the day as a snack or side dish.

Food Festivals

Lobster Festivals
(Placencia,
Caye Caulker,
San Pedro)

Fish Fest
(Punta Gorda)

Cashew Festival
(Crooked Tree)

Chocolate Festival
of Belize
(Punta Gorda)

Cookbooks

Mmm... A Taste of Belizean Cooking, by Tracy Brown da Langan

Foods of the Maya, by Nancy and Jeffrey Gerlach

Flavors of Belize Features 120 recipes

Every cuisine in the world includes some version of fried dough, usually topped with fruit or sugar. In Belize they are stuffed then fried and are called fry-jacks. Again, they can be served sweet or savory, usually for breakfast but also throughout the day.

Maya Specialties

Maya meals are sometimes on offer in the villages of southern Belize and in Petén, Guatemala. *Caldo* is a hearty spicy stew, usually made with chicken (or sometimes beef or pork), corn and root vegetables, and served with tortillas. *Ixpa'cha* is steamed fish or shrimp, cooked inside a big leaf. The Maya also make Mexican stews such as *chirmole* (chicken with a chili-chocolate sauce) and *escabeche* (chicken with lime and onions).

Garifuna Specialties

Garifuna culinary traditions come from St Vincent. When the Garifuna people came to Belize, they brought their own traditions, recipes and even ingredients, meaning that cuisine is one more way that Garifuna culture is unique.

Taste Belize Tours (p218) is a boutique foodie tour company based in Placencia, offering Maya chocolate tours and cooking tours, among others.

One of the most important staples, cassava, is a starch, like a sweet potato, used to make cassava bread. A *varasa* is like a tamale, but it's made from a fruit that is a cross between a banana and a plantain, picked while it's still hard and cooked until it's soft.

A 'boil-up' is a stew of root vegetables and beef or chicken. This is the dish that is most common on restaurant menus, although it is traditionally prepared for Garifuna Settlement Day.

Other Garifuna specialties feature fresh fish, bananas or plantains, and coconut milk. *Alabundiga* is a dish of grated green bananas, coconut cream, spices, boiled potato and peppers, served with fried fish fillet (often snapper) and rice. *Sere* is fish cooked with coconut milk, spices and maybe some root vegetables. Possibly the most beloved Garifuna dish, *hudut* is made from plantain, cooked until tender, mashed with a big mortar and pestle, then cooked with local fish such as snapper and coconut milk.

JOHNNYCAKES

There is no more satisfying Belizean breakfast than a fresh-baked johnnycake with a pat of butter and a slice of cheese. These savory biscuits – straight from the oven – steal the show when served with eggs or beans.

Ingredients

2lb flour

6 teaspoons baking powder

½ cup shortening

½ cup margarine

1 teaspoon salt

2 cups coconut milk or evaporated milk

Method

Sift dry ingredients. Heat oven to 400°F (200°C). Use fingertips or knife to cut margarine and shortening into flour. Gradually stir in milk with a wooden spoon. Mix well to form a manageable ball of dough. Roll out dough into a long strip and cut into 1½in to 2in pieces. Shape into round balls and place on greased baking sheets. Flatten lightly and prick with a fork. Bake in hot oven for 10 minutes or until golden brown.

Snacks

Just like their Caribbean and Central American neighbors, Belizeans like to cook with habaneros, jalapeños and other peppers. Most restaurants have a bottle of hot chili sauce on the table next to the salt and pepper so guests can make their meals as spicy as they like.

In small towns, the best breakfast is usually found at the local taco vendor's cart, where tortillas stuffed with meat and lettuce are sold. Other Mexican snacks are also ubiquitous, including *salbutes, garnaches, enchalades* and *panades* – all variations on the tortilla, beans and cheese theme (*salbutes* usually add chicken, *panades* generally have fish). You'll also come across burritos and tamales (wads of corn dough with a filling of meat, beans or chilles).

Drinks

If you want to know what tropical paradise tastes like, sample the fresh fruit juices that are blended and sold at street carts and kiosks around the country. Usually available in whatever flavor is seasonal (lime, orange, watermelon, grapefruit, papaya and mango), they're delicious and refreshing – and healthy!

In recent years, Belize has started catering to coffee drinkers with its own homegrown beans, even though Belize lacks the high altitudes that benefit other Central American coffee-growing countries. On a *finca* (farm) in Orange Walk, a local company called Gallon Jug is producing shade-grown beans for commercial distribution. Caye Coffee in San Pedro and Above Grounds in Placencia support small coffee-growing cooperatives from Guatemala, but roast their beans, producing such popular blends as Belizean Roast and Maya Blend.

Belikin is the native beer of Belize, always cold and refreshing and available in several varieties, including a regular, a popular stout and a lower-calorie, lower-alcohol beer, called Lighthouse Lager. Look out for seasonal Belikin beers including chocolate and sorrel. Other widely available bottled beer brands include Red Stripe, Heineken and Guinness.

Beer (refrigerated), imported wine and spirits can be purchased at the ubiquitous (mostly) Chinese-run supermarkets or stores found throughout Belize.

In a Caribbean country that produces so much sugarcane, it's not surprising that Belize's number one liquor is rum. The country has four distilleries; the Travellers distillery in Belize City has won several international awards with its thick, spicy One Barrel rum. Visitors can take a tour of the factory and sample all the company's varieties.

Cuba libre (lime, rum and coke), rum punch and piña colada are the most popular ways of diluting your fermented sugarcane juice. But according to Belize bartenders, the national drink is in fact the 'pantyripper' or 'brief-ripper,' depending on your gender. This concoction is a straightforward mix of coconut, rum and pineapple juice, served on the rocks.

Restaurants for Foodies

Aji Tapas Bar
(San Pedro)

Running W
Steakhouse
(San Ignacio)

Hidden Treasures
(San Pedro)

Rumfish
(Placencia)

Hibisca by
Habaneros
(Caye Caulker)

Palmilla Restaurant
(San Pedro)

Wild Mango's
(Ambergris Caye)

Chef Rob's
(Sittee Point)

BELIZE CUISINE SNACKS

'Belikin' is Mayan for 'road to the east' and the main temple of Altun Ha is pictured on the label of Belize's national brew, Belikin beer.

Wildlife

Belize's sparse human population and its history of relatively low-key human impact have yielded a vast diversity of animal and plant species. The country has an admirable conservation agenda, pursued by governments and nongovernmental organizations (NGOs) since Belizean independence in 1981. This has led to the nation becoming a top destination for anyone interested in the marine life of the coral reefs, the vegetation and animal life of the forests, or the hundreds of bird species that soar, flutter and swoop through the skies.

Animals

Land Mammals

Felines

Everyone dreams of seeing a jaguar in the wild. Jaguars are found across the country, and live in large expanses of thick forest. The largest populations and most frequently reported sightings are near Chan Chich Lodge and at the Río Bravo Conservation & Management Area in Orange Walk. You also might see their tracks or the remains of their meals in Cockscomb Basin Wildlife Sanctuary, which was established in Stann Creek as a jaguar reserve in the 1980s. But although Belize has healthy numbers of the biggest feline in the western hemisphere (which measures up to 6ft long and 250lb in weight), your best chance of seeing one is still at the Belize Zoo.

Belize has four smaller wildcats, all elusive like the jaguar: the puma (aka mountain lion or cougar), almost as big as the jaguar but a uniform gray or brown color (occasionally black); the ocelot, spotted similarly to the jaguar but a lot smaller; the margay, smaller again and also spotted; and the small, brown or gray jaguarondi.

Wildlife Watching

Community Baboon Sanctuary

Río Bravo Conservation & Management Area

Shipstern Conservation & Management Area

Gales Point Manatee or Swallow Caye

Cockscomb Basin Wildlife Sanctuary

Monkeys

The endangered black howler monkey exists only in Belize, northern Guatemala and southern Mexico. Its population has made a comeback in several areas, especially in the Community Baboon Sanctuary in Belize District, established in the 1980s to protect this noisy animal. The sanctuary is now home to some 3000 individual monkeys. Other places to see and hear howlers include Lamanai in Orange Walk; Cockscomb Basin Wildlife Sanctuary in Stann Creek; Chan Chich and Río Bravo in Orange Walk; and Tikal National Park in Guatemala. The howler's eerie dawn and evening cries – more roars than howls – can carry 3 miles across the treetops.

Less common are the smaller, long-tailed spider monkeys, though you may still spot some in similar areas.

Other Land Mammals

Visitors and residents alike are often surprised to learn that the national animal of Belize is Baird's tapir (sometimes called the mountain cow). The tapir is related to the horse, but it has shorter legs and tail, a stouter build and small eyes, ears and intellect. Baird's tapir is a herbivore and – interestingly – a daily bather. It tends to be shy, so it's infrequently spotted and likely to run like mad when approached.

You have better chances of catching sight of a peccary, a wild pig that weighs 50lb or more. There are two types, whose names – white-lipped peccary and collared peccary – define their differences. Both types of peccaries are active by day and they travel in groups, making them relatively easy to check off your wildlife list. Be aware that these meanies can run fast. If you get in the way of a pack of wild peccaries, experts advise you to climb a tree (they can't catch you up there).

Resembling a large spotted guinea pig, the *gibnut* (or *paca*) is a nocturnal rodent, growing up to 3ft long and weighing up to 22lb, that often lives in pairs. You might see a *gibnut* in the wild, and you are also likely to see one on the menu at your local Belizean restaurant. The agouti is similar but diurnal and more closely resembles a rabbit, with strong back legs. The *tayra* (or tree otter) is a member of the weasel family and has a dark-brown body, yellowish neck and 1ft-long tail. The coatimundi (or *quash*) is a cute, rusty-brown, raccoon-like creature with a long nose and ringed tail that it often holds upright when walking. It's not uncommon to see coatimundi in daylight on the sides of roads or trails. Also in the raccoon family is the nocturnal kinkajou (or nightwalker), mainly a tree-dweller.

Marine Life

West Indian manatees inhabit the waters around river mouths, in coastal lagoons and around the cays. The sure-fire places to spot these gentle, slow-moving creatures are Southern Lagoon, near Gales Point Manatee village, and Swallow Caye, off Belize City. Manatees are the only vegetarian sea mammals in existence. Typically 10ft long and weighing 1000lb, adults eat 100lb to 150lb of vegetation each day (especially sea grass). Only a few hundred manatees survive in Belizean waters.

Belizean waters are home to the world's largest fish. Whale sharks grow up to a whopping 60ft (although the average length is 25ft) and weigh up to 15 tons. They hang out at Gladden Spit, near Placencia. Between March and June – usually during the 10 days after a full moon – these filter-feeding behemoths come in close to the reef to dine on spawn. Fun fact: whale sharks can live up to 150 years.

MIND THE MANATEES

Belonging to a unique group of sea mammals comprising only four species worldwide, manatees are thought to be distantly related to elephants. However, with at least 55 million years separating the two, their kinship is only apparent in a few fairly obscure anatomical similarities and a broadly similar diet. Like elephants, manatees are herbivores and require huge amounts of vegetation each day. Grazing on a wide variety of aquatic plants, a large adult can process as much as 110lb every 24 hours, producing a prodigious amount of waste in the process — fresh floating droppings (similar to a horse's) and almost continuous, bubbling streams of flatulence are useful ways to find them. (Not too appetizing, but it does make them easier to spot.) The best places for a chance to observe manatees are around 'blowing holes' or *sopladeros* (deep hollows where manatees congregate to wait for the high tide).

Manatees are reputed to have excellent hearing, but they're most sensitive to fairly high-frequency sounds, such as their squeaking vocalizations. Apparently, the engine of a motorboat is not a high-frequency sound, which means that quiet approaches are often rewarded with good viewing, although sadly it also makes them vulnerable to collisions with motorboats.

Other sharks – nurse, reef, lemontip and hammerhead – and a variety of rays often make appearances around the reefs and islands. Sharing the water with the larger animals is a kaleidoscope of reef fish, ranging from steely-eyed barracuda and groupers to colorful parrotfish, angelfish and butterfly fish. The fish frolic amid a huge variety of coral formations, from hard elkhorn and staghorn coral (named because they branch like antlers) to gorgonian fans and other soft formations. Belizean waters host more than 500 species of fish and 110 species of coral, plus an amazing variety of sponges.

Reptiles

The protected green iguana is a dragon-like vegetarian lizard that is often spotted in trees along riverbanks. You can also see them in iguana houses at Monkey Bay Wildlife Sanctuary in Belize District and at the San Ignacio Resort Hotel.

Belize is home to two species of crocodile: the American crocodile and Morelet's crocodile, both of which are on the endangered species list. The American usually grows to 13ft and can live in both saltwater and freshwater. The smaller Morelet's crocodile, which grows to 8ft, lives only in fresh water. Belizean crocs tend to stick to prey that's smaller than the average adult human. Still, it's best to keep your distance.

Hawksbill, loggerhead, leatherback and green sea turtles can be seen in the waters of Belize. They live at sea and the females come ashore only to lay their eggs. Sea turtles are victims of poaching and egg hunting, as their eggs are believed by some to be an aphrodisiac. However, while all sea turtles are endangered, the hawksbill, which was hunted for its shell, is the only one currently protected in Belize. Turtle-viewing outings are organized in the May-to-October laying season from Gales Point Manatee village.

Up to 60 species of snakes inhabit the forests and waters of Belize, but only a handful are dangerous. The nasties include the poisonous fer-de-lance (commonly known as the yellow-jaw tommygoff), which is earth toned and a particular threat to farmers when they're clearing areas of vegetation; the coral snake, banded with bright red, yellow and black stripes; the tropical rattlesnake; and the boa constrictor, which kills by constriction but can also give you a mean (but venomless) bite.

Birds

Ornithologists have identified 590 bird species in Belize, 20% of them winter migrants from North America. You're likely to see interesting birds almost anywhere at any time, although February to May are particularly good months. Wetlands, lagoons, forested riverbanks and forest areas with clearings (the setting of many jungle lodges and Maya ruins) are good for observing a variety of birds.

Best for Birds

Crooked Tree

Half Moon Caye

New River

La Milpa

Red Bank

Seabirds

Magnificent frigate birds constantly soar over the coastline on pointed, prehistoric-looking wings which have a span of up to 6ft. They have difficulty taking off from the ground, so their method of hunting is to plummet and catch fish as they jump from the sea. They often hang out around fisherfolk and other birds so that they can swoop in on discarded or dropped catches. Males have red throats that are displayed during courtship.

Swooping and soaring with the frigate birds are neotropic cormorants, brown pelicans, nine species of heron, eight species of tern and six species of gull. The rare red-footed booby bird lives at Half Moon Caye.

Raptors & Vultures

Raptors are predators that usually hunt rodents and small birds. The most common species in Belize include the osprey (look for their huge nests atop houses and telephone posts), peregrine falcon, roadside hawk and American kestrel. Most of these birds of prey are territorial and solitary. The majestic harpy eagle is rarely seen in the wild, but is a resident at the Belize Zoo, as is the ornate hawk eagle, which is a beautiful large raptor with a black crest, striped tail and mottled breast.

Inland along the sides of the road and flying overhead you'll see large turkey, black and king vultures. Their job is to feast on dead animals. The turkey vulture has a red head, the king has black-and-white plumage with a red beak, and the black vulture appears in black and shades of gray.

Other Well-Known Birds

The national bird of Belize is the keel-billed toucan. This is the species of Toucan Sam, the hungry bird who knows to 'follow your nose' to find the fruit loops. A black bird with a yellow face and neck, it has a huge multicolored bill. The 'keel bill' is actually very light and almost hollow, enabling the bird to fly with surprising agility and to reach berries at the end of branches. Toucans like to stay at treetop level and nest in holes in trees. They are surprisingly aggressive and are known to raid other birds' nests for breakfast.

The beautiful scarlet macaw, a member of the parrot family, is highly endangered. Belize's small population of the bird – possibly under 200 – lives most of the year in remote jungles near the Guatemalan border, but from January to March they can be seen at the southern village of Red Bank, where they come to eat fruit.

The jabiru stork is the largest flying bird in the Americas, standing up to 5ft tall and with wingspans of up to 12ft. Many of the 100 or so remaining Belizean jabirus gather in Crooked Tree Wildlife Sanctuary in April and May.

You'll also have the chance to see (among others) many colorful hummingbirds, kingfishers, motmots, parrots, woodpeckers, tinamous, tanagers and trogons.

The best all-in-one wildlife guide is *Belize & Northern Guatemala: The Ecotravellers' Wildlife Guide*, by Les Beletsky, offering helpful descriptions along with full-color drawings and photographs.

BELIZE'S WORLD HERITAGE SITE

In 1996 Unesco designated the Belize Barrier Reef Reserve System a World Heritage Site. The World Heritage listing covers seven separate reef, island and atoll areas, not all of which include bits of the barrier reef. The seven sites were recognized for demonstrating a unique array of reef types (fringing, barrier and atoll) and a classic example of reef evolution; for their exceptional natural beauty and pristine nature; and for being an important habitat for internationally threatened species, including marine turtles, the West Indian manatee and the American crocodile. In 2009 the reef was put on Unesco's endangered list due to environmental threats, but this was lifted in 2018. The following list outlines the sites:

➡ Bacalar Chico National Park & Marine Reserve (Ambergris Caye)

➡ Blue Hole Natural Monument (Lighthouse Reef)

➡ Half Moon Caye Natural Monument (Lighthouse Reef)

➡ Glover's Reef Marine Reserve (Central Cayes)

➡ South Water Caye Marine Reserve (Central Cayes)

➡ Laughing Bird Caye National Park (Central Cayes)

➡ Sapodilla Cayes Marine Reserve (Punta Gorda)

Plants

Belize is home to more than 4000 species of flowering plants, including some 700 trees (similar to the total of the USA and Canada combined) and 304 orchids. Nonspecialists can usually distinguish three chief varieties of forest in the country: coastal forests (19%), moist, tropical broadleaf forests (68%), and pine and savanna (13%).

Coastal Forests

Coastal forests comprise both the mangrove stands that grow along much of the shoreline and the littoral forests slightly further inland. Mangroves serve many useful purposes as fish nurseries, hurricane barriers and shoreline stabilizers, and they are credited with creating the cays: when coral grows close enough to the water surface, mangrove spores carried by the wind take root on it. Mangrove debris eventually creates solid ground cover, inviting other plants to take root and eventually attracting animal life. There are four common species of mangrove: red, buttonwood, white and black.

Trees of the littoral forests typically have tough, moisture-retaining leaves. They include the coconut palm, the Norfolk Island pine, the sea grape and the poisonwood, the sap of which causes blistering, swelling and itching of the skin, as well as (happily) the gumbo-limbo, with its flaky, shredding bark that acts as an antidote to poisonwood rashes. The sandy bays off the coast are covered in sea grass, including turtle grass, manatee sea grass and duckweed sea grass.

The tropical broadleaf is often called rainforest, although technically only far southwestern Belize receives enough rain to officially support rainforest.

Tropical Broadleaf Forest

Tropical broadleaf grows on thin clay soils where the principal nutrients come not from the soil but from the biomass of the forest – that is, debris from plants and animals. Buttressed trunks are a common phenomenon here. These forests support a huge diversity not only of plants but also of animal life.

One of the fascinating elements of these forests is their natural layering. Most have at least three layers: ground cover (a ground or herb layer); a canopy layer formed from the crowns of the forest's tallest trees;

MAYA MEDICINE

The Maya have not only long depended on the forest for food and shelter, but also for hygiene and healing. These days in Belize, tour guides are quick to recommend a herbal remedy for everything from stomach ills to sexual failures. But there are only a few remaining healers who are skilled and knowledgeable in the science of Maya medicine. If you are curious about this holistic and natural approach to medicine, consult a professional (eg at the Chaa Creek Rainforest Medicine Trail in Cayo).

Among the natural remedies used by Maya are the bark of the Guava tree (Psidium guajava), which is made into a tea that is used to treat diarrhea and dysentery. Another useful bark tea used as a remedy for stomach complaints is that of the Bay cedar (Guazuma ulmifolia). Stomach ulcers are treated with a tea made from Skunk root (Petiveria alliacea).

Maya medicine goes well beyond stomach complaints. Oil from the Cohune palm (Orbignya cohune) is used to moisturize the skin. A tea made of thorns from the Cockspur tree (Acacia cornigera) is a natural remedy for acne, while healers use the bark of the tree to relieve some snake bites.

One traditional Maya remedy that has become mainstream knowledge throughout Belize is that of the gumbo-limbo tree (Bursera simaruba), which is usually found growing near the nasty poisonwood. While poisonwood can cause an itchy rash, the inner bark of the gumbo-limbo tree provides rapid relief.

and, in between, shorter subcanopy or understory trees. Throughout the layers grow hanging vines and epiphytes, or 'air plants,' which are moss and ferns that live on other trees but aren't parasites. This is also the habitat for more than 300 species of orchids, including the national flower, the black orchid.

The national tree in Belize is the majestic mahogany, known for its handsome hardwood. Also important is the ceiba (the sacred tree of the Maya), with its tall gray trunk and fluffy kapok down around its seeds. The broad-canopied guanacaste (or tubroos) is another tree that can grow more than 100ft high, with a wide, straight trunk and light wood used for dugout canoes (its broad seed pods coil up into what look like giant, shriveled ears). The strangler fig has tendrils and branches that surround a host tree until the unfortunate host dies. The flowering calophyllum, sometimes called the Santa Maria tree, is used for shipbuilding, while its resin has medicinal uses.

Pine & Savanna

The drier lowland areas inland from Belize City and the sandy areas of the north are designated as lowland savanna and pine forest. Growth here is mostly savanna grasses and Honduran and Caribbean pine, as well as Paurotis palm, giant stands of bamboo, and some oak and calabash.

The Mountain Pine Ridge is a fascinating phenomenon. As you ascend these uplands, the forest changes abruptly from tropical broadleaf to submontane pine, due to a transition to drier, sandier soils. Predominant species include Mexican white pine, Pino amarillo (or Mexican yellow pine) and Hartweg's pine.

Jaguar: One Man's Struggle to Establish the World's First Jaguar Preserve is the story of American zoologist Alan Rabinowitz' efforts to set up what has become the Cockscomb Basin Wildlife Sanctuary.

WILDLIFE PLANTS

Land & Environment

Happily, the Belize government and the populace have recognized that their country's forests and reefs are natural treasures that need to be preserved – not only for their intrinsic ecological value, but also for attracting tourism. Early on, the government developed a large network of national parks and reserve areas; however, these areas are only as inviolable as the degree to which the community is able to protect them.

National Park & Protected Areas

About 44% of Belizean territory, a little over 4062 sq miles, is under official protection of one kind or another. Belize's protected areas fall into six main categories:

Forest reserve Protects forests, controls timber extraction, and conserves soil, water and wildlife resources.

Marine reserve Protects and controls extraction of marine and freshwater species; also focuses on research, recreation and education.

National park Preserves nationally significant nature and scenery for the benefit of the public.

Natural monument Protects special natural features for education, research and public appreciation.

Nature reserve Maintains natural environments and processes in an undisturbed state for scientific study, monitoring, education and maintenance of genetic resources; not usually open to the general public.

Wildlife sanctuary Protects nationally significant species, groups of species, biotic communities or physical features.

Ecotourism

Belize practically invented the concept of ecotourism. Its ecolodges allow guests to live in luxury but also in harmony with the creatures and plants in their midst, while its educational tours and activities allow travelers to learn about the forest and the reef without harming the fragile ecosystems. Conscientious enterprises minimize their environmental impact by employing alternative and renewable energy sources; avoiding destruction of surrounding habitats; effectively managing waste and employing recycling programs; and using locally grown produce whenever possible. Dedicated entrepreneurs also give back to the community by employing local people and investing in local causes, thus sharing the wealth.

Ecotourism depends on a precarious balance: welcoming tourists, but not too many of them; allowing access to natural sights, but not too much access; maintaining an infrastructure to support the visitors, but not having too much infrastructure. Belize is constantly struggling to maintain this balance, with varying degrees of success.

There is no doubt about the economical boon of tourist dollars flowing from visiting cruise liners; however, the increase in cruise-ship traffic in Belizean waters in the past decade has worried many conservationists and citizens, who view the large numbers of tourists as disturbing wildlife and overwhelming the infrastructure.

Tourist Numbers

Number of cruise-ship tourists in 2017: 1,014,231

Number of overnight tourists in 2017: 427,076

Development along the coast caters to the growing demands of tourists and entire islands are bought and sold for the construction of resorts. Construction of buildings and pavement of the roads on Ambergris Caye has dramatically changed the aesthetics and the atmosphere of that island, once a sleepy outpost and now a destination for package-tourists and partyers. San Pedro developers petitioned to eliminate the protected status of the southern portion of Bacalar Chico National Park & Marine Reserve – to the relief of many, the petition was rejected.

Of course, there is no hard and fast rule about how many tourists are too many or how much development is too much. Many Belizeans compare their country to Cozumel or Cancún and they are proud of the way that ecotourism is preserving their paradise. On Ambergris, few locals would stop the construction of condos and resorts that is taking place up and down the coast. It's predominantly the expats – who came to Belize to 'escape civilization' – who complain about the rampant level of development. Locals, by contrast, appreciate the influx of cash into the economy – the jobs, the roads, the restaurants – not to mention the constant flow of tourists who keep bringing money to spend.

The highest peak in the Maya Mountains is Doyle's Delight (3687ft), named after Arthur Conan Doyle, author of The Lost World.

Deforestation

Despite the impressive amount of protected territory, and having the highest relative forest cover in Central America, deforestation in Belize has been slow and steady since independence. Agriculture and aquaculture, development and illegal harvesting all contribute to the felling of the forests, which is taking place at a rate of 0.6% per year.

This contradiction is a result of poor management and monitoring. Protection requires money and even at the best of times Belizean governments are short of cash. Underfunding means understaffing, which impedes the fight against poaching and illegal extraction.

There is a perception in Belize that illegal Guatemalan immigrants are responsible for many of these incursions into protected areas. The ongoing territorial dispute between Guatemala and Belize exacerbates the situation, as some Guatemalan peasants are taught to believe they have a right to hunt and harvest there.

Forest Cover

Forest cover in 1980. 75.9%

Forest cover in 2014: 60.3%

Energy Management

The problem of power is certainly not unique to Belize. Like many other countries, Belize consumes more than it can produce, and its consumption is increasing by 10% to 15% per year. Historically, Belize has imported much of its electricity from Mexico, although the country is implementing a multi-prong strategy to reduce this dependency.

Hydro

Two plants harness the power of the Macal River in Cayo to produce hydroelectric power. Built in 1995, the Mollejon Dam is limited by the storage capacity of its reservoir, but since 2006, the huge Chalillo Dam has

---

ENVIRONMENTAL NGOS

➡ Belize Audubon Society (www.belizeaudubon.org)

➡ Oceanic Society (www.oceanic-society.org)

➡ Programme for Belize (www.pfbelize.org)

➡ Toledo Institute for Development & Environment (www.tidebelize.org)

➡ Wildlife Conservation Society (www.wcs.org)

BELIZE'S PROTECTED AREAS AT A GLANCE

PROTECTED AREA	FEATURES
Actun Tunichil Muknal	spectacular cave with ancient Maya sacrificial remains
Bacalar Chico National Park & Marine Reserve	northern Ambergris Caye barrier reef and surrounding waters
Blue Hole Natural Monument	400ft-deep ocean-filled sinkhole home to sharks
Caracol Archaeological Reserve	Belize's biggest and greatest ancient Maya city
Caye Caulker Marine Reserve	barrier reef reserve with plentiful marine life
Cockscomb Basin Wildlife Sanctuary	large rainforest reserve for jaguars, with huge range of wildlife
Community Baboon Sanctuary	forest sanctuary for black howler monkeys
Crooked Tree Wildlife Sanctuary	wetland area with huge bird population
Gales Point Wildlife Sanctuary	inland lagoons with Belize's largest colony of manatees
Gladden Spit & Silk Cayes Marine Reserve	barrier reef and island reserve visited by whale sharks
Glover's Reef Marine Reserve	beautiful atoll with coral-filled lagoon and seas swarming with marine life
Guanacaste National Park	small forest park centered on huge guanacaste tree
Half Moon Caye Natural Monument	lush bird-sanctuary atoll island with spectacular underwater walls offshore
Hol Chan Marine Reserve	waters off Ambergris Caye with the famous Shark Ray Alley Protected Area
Laughing Bird Caye National Park	island on unusual faro reef in waters full of marine life
Mayflower Bocawina National Park	rainforest park with hills, waterfalls, howler monkeys and hundreds of bird species
Mexico Rocks	marine reserve covers a vibrant area of reef just offshore from Ambergris Caye
Monkey Bay Wildlife Sanctuary	small private sanctuary on savanna and tropical forest
Mountain Pine Ridge Forest Reserve	upland area with rare pine forests and many waterfalls
Nohoch Che'en Caves Branch Archaeological Reserve	stretch of Caves Branch River running through caverns
Port Honduras Marine Reserve	inshore islands and coastal waters important for marine life
Río Bravo Conservation & Management Area	large rainforest reserve with great wildlife diversity
Sapodilla Cayes Marine Reserve	beautiful barrier reef islets with healthy coral and abundant marine life
Shipstern Conservation & Management Area	wetlands and rare semideciduous hardwood forests with diverse wildlife, including wood-stork colony
South Water Caye Marine Reserve	large reserve encompassing parts of barrier reef and inshore islands
St Herman's Blue Hole National Park	small rainforest park with cave and swimming hole
Swallow Caye Wildlife Sanctuary	small island with permanent manatee population
Temash-Sarstoon National Park	rainforests, wetlands and rivers with huge variety of wildlife
Turneffe Atoll Marine Reserve	Protects one of the most pristine areas of the Mesoamerican reef system

ACTIVITIES	BEST TIME TO VISIT	PAGE
caving	year-round	p168
diving, snorkeling, birdwatching, wildlife-watching	year-round	p85
diving, snorkeling	Dec-Aug	p130
exploring ruins, birdwatching	year-round	p186
diving, snorkeling	year-round	p112
hiking, wildlife and plant observation, river-tubing	Dec-May	p213
wildlife-watching, birdwatching, horseback riding	year-round	p71
birdwatching, walking, canoeing, horseback riding	Feb-May	p73
manatee and turtle observation, birdwatching, fishing, sailing	year-round	p81
diving, snorkeling, kayaking	Mar-Jun	p36
diving, snorkeling, swimming, fishing, sailing, kayaking	Dec-Aug	p204
birdwatching, swimming, plant identification	year-round	p163
diving, snorkeling, birdwatching, kayaking	Dec-Aug	p130
diving, snorkeling	year-round	p86
diving, snorkeling	Dec-Aug	p36
hiking, birdwatching, swimming	year-round	p200
diving, snorkeling	year-round	p90
birdwatching, wildlife-watching, canoeing, caving	year-round	p78
walking, swimming, birdwatching, horseback riding	year-round	p184
river-tubing	year-round	p163
diving, snorkeling	Dec-May	p226
birdwatching, wildlife-watching, trail hikes, canoeing	year-round	p144
diving, fishing, kayaking, snorkeling, swimming	Dec-May	p233
wildlife observation	year-round	p153
diving, snorkeling, birdwatching, kayaking	Dec-May	p202
swimming, caving, hiking, birdwatching	year-round	p164
manatee observation	year-round	p113
wildlife observation, walks, boat trips	Dec-May	p233
diving, snorkeling	year-round	p128

BLACK GOLD

Early in the millennium, the possibility of sweet crude oil in Belize caused dollar signs to start flashing inside the minds of Belizean officials and international prospectors. Eighteen oil companies obtained licenses for exploration all around the country, sometimes without conducting an environmental impact survey or campaigning for community involvement.

After several years, the Irish-owned Belize Natural Energy (BNE) found what they were looking for in Spanish Lookout: oil fields with commercially viable quantities. In 2010 BNE discovered another oil field near Belmopan.

Conservationists fear the environmental degradation that may result from further oil exploration and extraction. There is also significant overlap between the petroleum map and the protected-areas map, threatening the sanctity of these spots. In the wake of the 2010 oil spill in the Gulf of Mexico, an umbrella group of NGOs called for a ban on all off-shore drilling, especially in the Belize Barrier Reef, which has been designated as a World Heritage Site.

Under pressure from local communities and conservationists, in 2007 the government of Belize instituted a 40% tax on oil production profits, declaring that the 'petroleum fund' would be used to improve education, fight poverty and strengthen the Belizean dollar. Several years down the line, however, there are concerns about the success of this fund, with the local press asserting the revenues – estimated to be in the hundreds of millions of dollars – have been 'absorbed by the government for its day-to-day operating expenses.'

fed both plants. The dam has the advantage that it can generate power in the evening (peak consumption hours), when the imported electricity is more expensive. The construction of the Chalillo Dam sparked massive controversy, as critics voiced concerns about the damage inflicted on wildlife habitats in the river valley, as well as the financial viability of the project.

Cogeneration

Bruce Barcott investigates the construction of the Chalillo Dam and the efforts of Sharon Matola (founder of the Belize Zoo) to stop it, in his fascinating book *The Last Flight of the Scarlet Macaw*.

A byproduct of the processing of sugarcane, *bagasse* is also a fuel. In 2009 the sugar industry opened a cogeneration facility that would supply 13.5 megawatts to the national grid, in addition to powering the sugar mill and other industry facilities.

Solar

Solar power is becoming more viable on a small scale, but it does not yet offer a feasible solution for the energy needs of the country. Solar power is still relatively expensive and – significantly – it can't produce power at night. That said, it has become a popular alternative for some ecolodges and even some villages that are off the grid. In 2011 the government of Belize signed an agreement with the University of Belize to construct photovoltaic panels, which generate solar electricity. Proponents of alternative energy are hopeful that the so-called Photovoltaic Project might lead to a long-term, large-scale commitment to solar energy.

Survival Guide

Directory A–Z

Accessible Travel

Belize lacks accessibility regulations and many buildings are on stilts or have uneven wooden steps. You won't see many ramps for wheelchair access and there are very few bathrooms designed for visitors in wheelchairs.

More difficulties for wheelchair users come from the lack of footpaths, as well as plentiful rough and sandy ground. With assistance, bus travel is feasible, but small planes and water taxis might be a problem.

Not to put too fine a point on it – Belize is a very challenging destination for visitors with limited mobility. But while Belize definitely lacks accessible travel facilities it has no shortage of extremely helpful locals who are generally more than willing to lend a hand to assist travelers with special needs in getting around.

Accommodations

In the main tourist areas, Belize has a fair range of accommodations in most categories. Away from the coast, options become more limited. Book ahead in high season.

Most establishments have high- and low-season prices, often with extra-high prices for the peak weeks.

Low season May to November

High season December to May

Peak season December 15 to January 15, plus Easter week

Prices listed by Lonely Planet do not include the 9% hotel room tax or the (sometimes obligatory) service charges that might be added at some top-end places. Some midrange and top-end places add on a further 12.5% service tax as standard.

Booking Services

Belize Tourism Board (www.travelbelize.org/accommodation) The Belize Tourism Board has a helpful accommodations page.

Lonely Planet (lonelyplanet.com/belize/hotels) Recommendations and bookings.

Cabañas & Cabins

These two terms are pretty well interchangeable and can refer to any kind of free-standing, individual accommodations structure. You'll find cabins in every class of accommodations: they can be made of wood, concrete or brick, and be roofed with palm thatch, tin or tiles. They may be small, bare and cheap, or super-luxurious and stylish, with Balinese screens, Japanese bathrooms and Maya wall hangings. Locales vary from beachside, riverside or jungle to on the grounds of a hotel alongside other types of accommodations.

Camping

Belize does not have many dedicated camping grounds (though San Ignacio has two), but some (mainly budget) accommodations provide camping space on their grounds for tents and RVs, and some national parks such as Cockscomb Basin offer camping.

Guesthouses

Guesthouses are affordable, affable places to stay, with just a few rooms and usually plenty of personal attention from your hosts. Most are simply decorated but clean and comfortable. Rooms usually have a private bathroom with hot water. You'll find guesthouses in towns or on the coast or cays. Some guesthouses (also called B&Bs) provide breakfast.

BOOK YOUR STAY ONLINE

For more accommodations reviews by Lonely Planet authors, check out http://lonelyplanet.com/hotels/. You'll find independent reviews, as well as recommendations on the best places to stay. Best of all, you can book online.

SLEEPING PRICE RANGES

The following price ranges refer to a double room with bathroom during high season. Unless otherwise stated, a tax of 9% is added to the price.

$ less than BZ$120

$$ BZ$120–BZ$350

$$$ more than BZ$350

In the southern Toledo District, the **Toledo Eco-tourism Association** (TEA; Map p228; ☑722-2096; www.southernbelize.com/tea.html) runs an excellent village guesthouse program that enables travelers to stay in the area's Maya villages, and there's a similar program at Maya Center.

Hotels

A hotel is, more or less, any accommodation that generally doesn't give itself another name (although some smaller hotels call themselves inns). You'll find hotels in villages and towns of all sizes. Some offer lovely rooms and extra amenities such as a restaurant or a pool.

Lodges

In Belize the term 'lodge' usually means an upmarket resort-style hotel in a remote location, be it in the Cayo jungles or the offshore cays. Most lodges focus on activities such as diving, fishing, horseback riding or jungle or river adventures, aiming to provide comfortable accommodations and good meals to sustain their guests between outings. Many lodges have gorgeous island, beach or forest settings, and they tend to be on the expensive side, due mainly to their high standards and wide range of amenities.

Rental Accommodations

In main tourist destinations such as San Pedro, Caye Caulker and Placencia, there are houses and apartments for rent for short stays or by the week or month. If you plan a long stay, you'll certainly cut costs by renting your own place. Look out for real estate or rental offices but the easiest way to book ahead is to go online. Sites such as Airbnb (www.airbnb.com) and Flip Key (www.flipkey.com) have listings.

Resorts

Resorts have a great deal in common with lodges – again they tend to be among the more expensive options and can be found both inland and by the sea. If there is any real distinction, it's that the emphasis in resorts tends to be marginally less on activities and slightly more on relaxation.

Green Accommodations

Ecotourism means big business in Belize, and sometimes it seems like every hotel, hostel, lodge, resort and guesthouse is a friend and protector of Mother Earth. But attaching 'eco' to the front of a name does not necessarily make it so. This prefix may mean that the enterprise is taking serious steps to reduce its environmental impact, whether by practicing recycling, implementing alternative energy, participating in conservation programs or educating its guests. On the other hand, it may mean nothing more than a remote location or rustic accommodations. Most likely, the truth is somewhere in between.

BEST ACCOMMODATIONS

For Backpackers

➡ Sandbar (p96)

➡ Placencia Hostel (p218)

➡ Old House Hostel (p174)

➡ Bella's Backpackers (p174)

➡ Yuma's House Belize (p120)

Resorts

➡ Black Rock Lodge (p190)

➡ Belize Boutique Resort & Spa (p75)

➡ Matachica Beach Resort (p101)

➡ Chan Chich Lodge (p145)

➡ Turtle Inn (p220)

➡ Sea Dreams Hotel (p122)

On the Reef

➡ Glover's Atoll Resort (p204)

➡ Turneffe Island Resort (p129)

➡ Thatch Caye Resort (p203)

➡ Itza Lodge (p132)

➡ Hatchet Caye Resort (p221)

➡ Tobacco Caye Paradise (p202)

Customs Regulations

Duty-free allowances on entering Belize:

➡ 1L of wine or spirits

➡ 200 cigarettes, 250g of tobacco or 50 cigars
It is illegal to leave the country with ancient Maya artifacts, turtle shells, unprocessed coral and fish (unless you have obtained a free export permit from the Fisheries Department). It is also illegal to take firearms or ammunition into or out of Belize.

Electricity

Type A
120V/60Hz

Embassies & Consulates

A few countries have embassies in Belize. Many others handle relations with Belize from their embassies in countries such as Mexico or Guatemala, but may have an honorary consul in Belize to whom travelers can turn as a first point of contact.

Australian Embassy The Australian embassy in Trinidad & Tobago handles relations with Belize.

Canadian Honorary Consulate (☎223-1060; belize-city@ international.gc.ca; Newtown Barracks 8, Rennaisance Tower; ◷8:30am-3pm Mon-Thu, to noon Fri)

German Honorary Consulate (☎223-0896; kay@karl menzies.com; 104 Barrack Rd)

Guatemalan Embassy (☎223-3150; embbelice1@gmail.com; 8 A St, Kings Park; ◷8:30am-5pm Mon-Fri)

Honduran Embassy (☎224-5889; embahn.embajada belize@gmail.com; 6 A St, Kings Park; ◷appointments 9am-noon Mon-Fri)

Mexican Consulate (☎223-0193; consular@embamex. bz; cnr Wilson St & Newtown Barracks Rd; ◷8am-noon & 3-4pm)

Mexican Embassy (☎822-0406; https://embamex.sre. gob.mx/belice; Embassy Sq, Belmopan; ◷8am-5pm Mon-Fri)

Netherlands Honorary Consulate (☎223-2953; mchulseca@gmail.com; cnr Baymen Av & Calle Al Mar)

UK High Commission (☎822-2146; http://ukinbelize.fco.gov. uk; Embassy Sq, Belmopan; ◷8am-noon & 1-4pm Mon-Thu, 8am-2pm Fri)

US Embassy (☎822-4011; https://bz.usembassy.gov; Floral Park Rd; ◷8am-noon & 1-5pm Mon-Fri)

Food & Drink

See p283 for more information on the cuisine of Belize.

Health

Travelers to Central America need to be concerned about food- and mosquito-borne infections. While most infections are not life-threatening, they can certainly ruin your trip. Besides getting the proper vaccinations, it's important that you pack a good insect repellent and exercise great care in what you eat and drink.

Before You Go
HEALTH INSURANCE

Medical facilities in Belize are not of the highest standard – make sure to check your travel insurance covers major medical emergencies, hospitalization and evacuation.

In Belize
AVAILABILITY & COST OF HEALTH CARE

Not surprisingly for a small, developing country, medical care in Belize is not of the highest standard. It is also fairly expensive compared to neighboring countries – expect to pay around US$70 for a visit to a private doctor and around US$500 per night for hospitalization in a private clinic.

The cheapest health care can be found at the network of public hospitals and clinics throughout the country, but they are often overcrowded and sometimes have issues with supplies and equipment. Many visitors and expats with insurance prefer to go directly to private clinics, the best of which are located in Belize City.

EATING PRICE RANGES

The following price ranges refer to a standard meal – rice, beans, meat or fish and a side. Only the fanciest places tend to have service charges, but tipping is always appreciated.

$ less than BZ$15

$$ BZ$15–35

$$$ more than BZ$35

RECOMMENDED VACCINATIONS

Since many vaccines don't produce immunity until at least two weeks after they're given, visit a physician four to eight weeks before departure. Note that some of the recommended vaccines are not approved for use by children and pregnant women; check with your physician.

VACCINE	RECOMMENDED FOR	DOSAGE	SIDE EFFECTS
Hepatitis A	all travelers	one dose before trip with booster six to 12 months later	soreness at injection site; headaches; body aches
Hepatitis B	long-term travelers in close contact with the local population	three doses over a six-month period	soreness at injection site; low-grade fever
Chickenpox	travelers who've never had chickenpox	two doses one month apart	fever; mild case of chickenpox
Measles	travelers born after 1956 who've had only one measles vaccination	one dose	fever; rash; joint pain; allergic reaction
Tetanus-diphtheria	all travelers who haven't had a booster within 10 years	one dose lasts 10 years	soreness at injection site
Typhoid	all travelers	four capsules by mouth, one taken every other day	abdominal pain; nausea; rash
Yellow fever	required for travelers arriving from yellow-fever-infected areas in Africa or South America	one dose lasts 10 years	headaches; body aches; severe reactions are rare

Another option, popular with expats in Belize, is to head across the border to Chetumal in Mexico where quality health care is far cheaper.

For emergency situations it's recommended to have comprehensive insurance that covers evacuation to medical facilities outside Belize.

ENVIRONMENTAL HAZARDS

The major annoyance that almost all travelers are likely to encounter is biting insects, with sand flies (no-see-ums) being a real problem on some islands and mosquitoes pretty much everywhere. Bring quality repellent from home.

MOSQUITOES & TICKS

To avoid mosquito and tick bites, wear long sleeves, long pants, hats and shoes or boots (rather than sandals). Use insect repellent that contains DEET, which should be applied to exposed skin and clothing, but not to eyes, mouth, cuts, wounds or irritated skin. In general, adults and children over 12 years should use preparations containing 25% to 35% DEET, which last about six hours. Children between two and 12 years of age should use preparations containing no more than 10% DEET, which will usually last about three hours. Products containing lower concentrations of DEET are as effective, but for shorter periods of time.

For additional protection, you can apply permethrin to clothing, shoes, tents and bed nets. Permethrin treatments are safe and remain effective for at least two weeks, even when items are laundered. Permethrin should not be applied directly to skin.

TRAVELER'S DIARRHEA

To prevent diarrhea, avoid tap water unless it's been boiled, filtered or chemically disinfected (with iodine tablets); only eat fresh fruit or vegetables if cooked or peeled; be wary of dairy products that might contain unpasteurized milk; and be highly selective when eating food from street vendors.

If you develop diarrhea, be sure to drink plenty of fluids, preferably an oral rehydration solution containing salt and sugar. A few loose stools don't require treatment, but if you start having more than four or five stools a day, you should start taking an antibiotic (usually a quinolone drug) and an antidiarrheal agent (such as loperamide). If diarrhea is bloody, persists for more than 72 hours or is accompanied by fever, shaking chills or severe abdominal pain, you should seek medical attention.

TAP WATER

In major urban areas tap water in Belize is considered safe to drink. Outside larger cities and towns, hotels may use wells or rainwater collection tanks in which case water should be boiled or treated.

Many hotels will provide drinking water for guests.

Insurance

Travelers should take out a travel insurance policy to cover theft, loss and medical problems. Some policies specifically exclude 'dangerous activities,' which can include scuba diving, motorcycling and even trekking. Check that the policy you are considering covers ambulances as well as emergency flights home.

You may prefer a policy that pays doctors or hospitals directly rather than requiring you to pay on the spot and claim later. If you have to claim later, make sure you keep all documentation.

Worldwide travel insurance is available at www.lonely-planet.com/travel-insurance. You can buy, extend and claim online anytime – even if you're already on the road.

Internet Access

With plenty of wi-fi and affordable 4G, internet cafes are virtually nonexistent these days. Even remote hotels and lodges will usually have limited wi-fi where guests can access the internet, but occasionally you'll be completely off-grid.

For those traveling with laptops and smartphones, most accommodations have wireless access in the rooms or in common areas, as indicated by the 🛜 icon. This access is fairly reliable, but is easily overburdened if there are several people working simultaneously.

Public wi-fi hotspots have not really taken off in Belize but getting hooked up to the 4G network with a local SIM card is a reliable way of getting online when there's no wi-fi around.

Legal Matters

Drug possession and use is officially illegal, though in 2017 marijuana possession was decriminalized – possession of 10g of marijuana is legal.

Anyone found having sex with a minor will be prosecuted; the age of consent for both sexes is 16. Travelers should note that they can be prosecuted under the law of their home country regarding age of consent, even when abroad.

You are not required to carry ID in Belize but it's advisable to do so. If arrested, you have the right to make a phone call. The police force does not have a reputation for corruption as in many countries in Central America, and it is highly unlikely that you will be stopped and hassled or asked for a bribe.

For detailed information on the Belize legal code, check out the Belize Legal Information Network (www.belizelaw.org).

LGBT+ Travelers

Male homosexuality only became legal in Belize in 2016, when the Supreme Court found the anti-sodomy laws to be unconstitutional. The country's first official Pride march was held in 2017. Generally speaking, Belize is a tolerant society with a 'live and let live' attitude. But underlying Central American machismo and traditional religious belief mean that same-sex couples should be discreet. Some useful resources:

International Gay & Lesbian Travel Association (www.iglta.org) General information on gay and lesbian travel in Latin America.

Purple Roofs (www.purpleroofs.com) Includes some listings in San Pedro and Cayo District.

Undersea Expeditions (www.underseax.com) Gay and lesbian scuba-diving company that sometimes offers live-aboard trips to the Blue Hole.

PREVENTING CHILD SEX TOURISM IN BELIZE

Tragically, the exploitation of local children by tourists is becoming more prevalent throughout Latin America, including Belize. Various socioeconomic factors make children susceptible to sexual exploitation, and some tourists choose to take advantage of their vulnerable position. Sexual exploitation has serious, lifelong effects on children. It is a crime and a violation of human rights.

Belize has laws against sexual exploitation of children. Many countries have enacted extraterritorial legislation that allows travelers to be charged as though the exploitation happened in their home country.

Responsible travelers can help stop child sex tourism and exploitation by reporting it to websites such as the CyberTipline (www.cybertipline.com). You can also report the incident to local authorities and, if you know the nationality of the perpetrator, to their embassy.

Travelers interested in learning more about how to fight sexual exploitation of children can find more information through End Child Prostitution & Trafficking (www.ecpat.net).

Maps

Lonely Planet maps will enable you to find your way to many of the listed destinations, but if you'd like a larger-scale, more detailed travel map, you cannot beat the 1:350,000 *Belize* map, published by International Travel Maps of Vancouver.

Another high-detail map is German firm Dorch's laminated 1:500,000 *Belize* road map, which also includes Ambergris Caye and Caye Caulker at 1:250,000 and individual maps of all the main Maya ruins.

Divers should check out Franko Maps' laminated dive side map, which has a full-colored tropical fish identification card on the back.

Money

ATMs are widely available; credit cards are accepted at most hotels, restaurants and shops.

Currency

The Belizean dollar (BZ$) is pegged to the US dollar at two to one (BZ$1 = US$0.50). Nearly every business in Belize accepts US dollars and prices are often quoted in US dollars at resorts and hotels – always check in advance whether you're paying in Belize dollars or US dollars.

Tipping

Tipping is not obligatory but is always appreciated if guides, drivers or servers have provided you with genuinely good service. Some hotels and restaurants add an obligatory service charge to your check (usually 10%).

Hotels Not needed but baggage porters appreciate a small gratuity.

Restaurants Round up the check between 5% and 10%.

Taxis Tips are not expected.

PRACTICALITIES

Newspapers Belize's most-read paper is *Amandala*, a twice-weekly publication with a left-wing slant.

Radio Love FM is Belize's most widely broadcast radio station, with spots at 95.1MHz and 98.1MHz, while KREM FM (www.krembz.com) plays a modern selection of music at 91.1MHz and 96.5MHz.

TV There are two main commercial TV stations, Channel 5 (http://edition.channel5belize.com/) and Channel 7 (www.7newsbelize.com).

Weight & Measures The imperial system is used. Note that gasoline is sold by the (US) gallon.

Smoking Banned in many public indoor spaces such as government buildings, banks and bus stations, but it's still permitted in bars and restaurants with designated smoking and nonsmoking areas.

Tour Guides In high-volume areas, tour guides are used to receiving tips.

Taxes & Refunds

Hotel room tax is 9%. Restaurant meals are subject to a 12.5% sales tax. Some hotel owners quote prices with taxes already figured in.

Opening Hours

Outside of banks, phone companies and government offices, you'll generally find most opening hours to be flexible. Restaurants and bars tend to keep longer hours during high season, but will also close early if they wish (if business is slow etc).

Banks 8am to 3pm Monday to Thursday and 8am to 4pm or 4:30pm Friday

Pubs and Bars Noon to midnight (or later)

Restaurants and Cafes 7am to 9:30am (breakfast), 11:30am to 2pm (lunch) and 6pm to 8pm (dinner)

Shops 9am to 5pm Monday to Saturday, some open Sunday

Post

The Belize postal service has branches all over the country and offers fairly slow normal mail and a far better express service. Express mail sometimes needs to be sent from a different counter or office.

Public Holidays

Many of Belize's public holidays are moved to the Monday nearest the given date in order to make a long weekend. You'll find banks and most shops and businesses shut on these days. Belizeans travel most around Christmas, New Year and Easter, and it's worth booking ahead for transportation and accommodations at these times.

New Year's Day January 1

Baron Bliss Day March 9

Good Friday March or April

Holy Saturday March or April

Easter Monday March or April

Labor Day May 1

Sovereign's Day May 24

National Day September 10

Independence Day September 21

Day of the Americas October 12

Garifuna Settlement Day November 19

Christmas Day December 25

Boxing Day December 26

Safe Travel

Belize has fairly high levels of violent crime but most areas frequented by travelers are safe and by taking basic precautions visitors are unlikely to experience any serious problems. The most likely issues for travelers involve opportunistic theft, both while out and about and from hotel rooms.

In order to minimize risks:

➡ Keep your bag in the overhead rack or under your seat on long-distance buses rather than at the back of the bus.

➡ Make sure windows and doors lock correctly in your room, especially in remote beachside huts, and use hotel safes where provided.

➡ Ask hotels and restaurants in major urban areas to phone a trusted taxi.

Government Travel Advice

Official information can make Belize sound more dangerous than it actually is, but for a range of useful travel advice (including information on healthy traveling) you should consult the travel advisories provided by your home country's foreign-affairs department.

Australian Department of Foreign Affairs (www.smart traveller.gov.au)

British Foreign Office (www.gov.uk/foreign-travel-advice)

Canadian Department of Foreign Affairs (www.voyage.gc.ca)

German Foreign Office (www.auswaertiges-amt.de)

New Zealand Ministry of Foreign Affairs & Trade (www.safetravel.govt.nz)

US State Department (www.travel.state.gov)

Telephone

Belize has no regional, area or city codes. Every number has seven digits, all of which you dial from anywhere in the country. When calling Belize from other countries, follow the country code with the full seven-digit local number.

Country code ☑501

Directory assistance ☑113

Emergency ☑90, ☑911

International access code ☑00

Operator assistance ☑115

Mobile Phones

International cell phones can be used in Belize if they are GSM 1900 and unlocked. You can buy a SIM pack for US$10 from DigiCell distributors offices around the country. A typical DigiCell data plan valid for seven days and with 1GB of data costs BZ$11.25; a 5GB plan valid for 30 days costs BZ$45.

If your cell phone is not compatible with the local network or is locked to your phone company, you'll need to activate international roaming, which is expensive – around US$2.50 to US$3 per minute of calls. Check with your service provider back home about coverage in Belize.

If you're staying for more than a week or two, a cheap phone with a prepaid SIM card can be had for less than BZ$80. Many car-rental companies provide free phones with vehicles.

Time

Belize uses North American Central Standard Time (GMT/UTC minus six hours), same as in Guatemala and central Mexico. The Mexican Caribbean state of Quintana Roo, which shares its southern border with Belize, is one hour ahead (UTC minus five hours), which is important to note if flying in or out of Cancún.

Belize and Guatemala do not observe daylight saving, so there is never any time difference between them, but Mexico – with the exception of Quintana Roo – does observe daylight saving from the first Sunday in April to the last Sunday in October, so Belize is one hour behind central Mexico during that period.

When it's noon in Belize, it's 10am in San Francisco, 1pm in New York, 6pm in London and 4am the next day in Sydney (add one hour to those times during daylight saving periods in those cities).

Toilets

Public toilets are rare in Belize, although many businesses will lend you their services without a fuss.

Airports and museums generally have toilets, but not all bus terminals have facilities.

Tourist Information

Belize Tourism Board (BTB; Map p62; ☑227-2420; www.travel belize.org; 64 Regent St, Belize City; ⊗8am-5pm Mon-Thu, to 4pm Fri) The official tourist agency has information offices in Belize City and San Pedro.

Belize Tourism Industry Association (BTIA; Map p62; ☑227-1144; www.btia.org; 10 Taiwan St; ⊗8am-noon & 1-5pm Mon-Thu, to 4pm Fri) An independent association of tourism businesses, actively defending 'sustainable ecocultural tourism.' The Belize City office provides information about the whole country and it also runs small information offices in some key destinations. The website has a plethora of information.

Visas

For most nationalities, visas are issued upon entry for up to 30 days.

Information on visa requirements is available from Belizean embassies and consulates, and the Belize Tourism Board (www.travel-belize.org). At the time of writing, visas were not required for citizens of EU, Caricom

(Caribbean Community) and Central American countries, nor Australia, Canada, Hong Kong, Israel, Mexico, New Zealand, Norway, Singapore, Switzerland and the USA. A visitors permit, valid for 30 days, will be stamped in your passport when you enter the country. In most cases this can be extended by further periods of one month (up to a maximum of six months) by applying at an immigration office (there's at least one in each of Belize's districts). For further information contact the **Immigration & Nationality Department** (☑822-3860; Mountain View Blvd, Belmopan; ☺8am-5pm Mon-Thu, to 3:30pm Fri) in Belmopan.

Volunteering

There are a lot of volunteering opportunities for in Belize, especially on environmental projects. In some cases, you may have to pay to participate.

Belize Audubon Society (Map p62; ☑223-4987, 223-5004; www.belizeaudubon.org; 16 Taiwan St) Invites volunteers who are available to work for at least three months to assist in the main office or in education and field programs. Divers can volunteer for marine research projects. For rural sites, volunteers should be physically fit and able to deal with rustic accommodations.

Belize Wildlife & Referral Clinic (Map p180; ☑615-5159; www.belizewildlifeclinic.org; ☺8:30am-5pm) Offers short-term internships in wildlife medicine for veterinary and non-veterinary students. Various scholarships and work exchanges are available for students with sincere interests and skills, and the clinic is flexible and always interested in speaking with potential interns and long-term volunteers.

Oceanic Society (☑in USA 800-326-7491; www.oceanicsociety.org; St. George's Caye; family education program per person BZ$5000, voluntourism/snorkeling program per person BZ$6400) Paying participants in

the society's expeditions assist scientists in marine research projects on St George's Caye and around the Turneffe Atoll.

Cornerstone Foundation (www.cornerstonefoundationbelize.org) This NGO, based in San Ignacio, hosts volunteers to help with AIDS education, community development and other programs. Most programs require a two-week commitment, plus a reasonable fee to cover food and housing.

Monkey Bay Wildlife Sanctuary (☑664-2731, 822-8032; www.monkeybaybelize.com; Mile 31.5 George Price Hwy; ☺7am-5pm) ✐ Monkey Bay's programs provide opportunities in education, conservation and community service. It also has many links to other conservation organizations in Belize.

Earthwatch (www.earthwatch.org) Paying volunteers are teamed with professional scientific researchers to work on shark conservation projects.

Maya Mountain Research Farm (☑630-4386; www.mmrfbz.org) ✐ The 70-acre organic farm and registered NGO in Toledo offers internships for those interested in learning about organic farming, biodiversity and alternative energy.

Plenty International (www.plenty.org) Opportunities for working with grassroots organizations (such as handicraft cooperatives) and schools, mostly in Toledo District.

ProWorld Service Corps (www.proworldvolunteers.org) Like a privately run Peace Corps, ProWorld organizes small-scale, sustainable projects in fields such as healthcare, education, conservation, technology and construction mostly around San Ignacio in Cayo.

Volunteer Abroad (www.volunteerabroad.com) A sort of clearing house for volunteer opportunities around the world. The database includes a few dozen organizations that work in Belize.

T.R.E.E.S (Toucan Ridge Ecology & Education Society; ☑669-6818, 665-2134; Mile 27.5 Hummingbird Hwy; bunkhouse BZ$40, s/d cabin BZ$125/140,

without bathroom BZ$80/100; ☏) ✐ Internships and volunteer placements are available at this nonprofit conservation organisation on the Hummingbird Hwy.

Women Travelers

Women can have a great time in Belize, whether traveling solo or with others. Of course, you do need to keep your wits about you and be vigilant, as does any solo traveler. Keep a clear head, and keep in mind that excessive alcohol will make you vulnerable.

If you don't want attention, consider wearing long skirts or trousers and modest tops when you're using public transportation and when on solo explorations. Some men can be quite forward with their advances or even aggressive with their comments. Such advances are rarely dangerous: be direct, say no and ignore; they're likely to go away. A bicycle can be an asset in this scenario: you can just scoot.

Avoid situations in which you might find yourself alone with unknown men at remote archaeological sites, on empty city streets, or on secluded stretches of beach. For support and company, sign up for group excursions or head for places where you're likely to meet people, such as guesthouses that serve breakfast, backpacker lodgings or popular midrange or top-end hotels.

Work

Unemployment and under-employment is rife in Belize so visitors should think twice before taking on paid work that could be filled by a local.

In order to legally work in Belize, a work permit must be obtained from the Labor Department in the district where the business offering employment is located. There's a US$100 permit fee (US$750 for professional and technical workers).

Transportation

GETTING THERE & AWAY

Overland, travelers can enter Belize from Guatemala or Mexico. Boats also bring travelers from Honduras and Guatemala. Air carriers service Belize from the USA, Panama and El Salvador. Flights, cars and tours can be booked online at lonely planet.com/bookings.

Entering the Country

Entering Belize is a simple, straightforward process. You must present a passport that will be valid for at least three months from the date of entry. Officially, visitors are also required to be in possession of an onward or return ticket from Belize and funds equivalent to BZ$120 per day for the duration of their stay in the country but it's rare for tourists to be required to show these.

AIR DEPARTURE TAX

Non-Belizeans pay fees that total US$55.50 when flying out of Belize City on international flights. This includes the US$3.75 Protected Areas Conservation Trust (PACT) fee, which helps to fund Belize's network of protected natural areas. Most major carriers include this tax in the price of the ticket.

Air

Airports & Airlines

Philip Goldson International Airport (BZE; ☏225-2045; www.pgiabelize.com), at Ladyville, 11 miles northwest of Belize City center, handles all international flights. With Belize's short internal flying distances it's often possible to make a same-day connection at Belize City to or from other airports in the country.

The following airlines fly to and from Belize:

Air Canada (www.aircanada. com) Toronto to Belize City weekly.

American Airlines (www. aa.com) Direct flights to/from Miami, Charlotte, Dallas and Los Angeles.

Avianca (www.avianca.com) Direct flights to/from El Salvador.

Copa Airlines (www.copaair. com) Flights twice weekly to Panama.

Delta Airlines (www.delta.com) Direct flights to/from Atlanta and Los Angeles.

Southwest Airlines (www. southwest.com) Direct flights to Houston Hobby, Denver and Fort Lauderdale.

Transportes Aeros Guatemaltecos (www.tag.com.gt) Regular flights between Belize and Guatemala City via Flores.

Tropic Air (www.tropicair.com) Flights to Flores, Guatemala; Cancún in Mexico; Roatán in Honduras.

United Airlines (www.united. com) Direct flights to/from Houston.

Land

Border Crossings

There are well-traveled land border crossings between Belize and Mexico to the north and Guatemala to the west. Border formalities are straightforward between both countries.

MEXICO

There are two official crossing points on the Mexico–Belize border. The more frequently used is at Subteniente López–Santa Elena, 9 miles from Corozal Town in Belize and 7 miles from Chetumal in Mexico. The all-paved Philip Goldson Hwy runs from the border to Belize City.

The other crossing is at La Unión–Blue Creek, 34 miles southwest of Orange Walk Town near the Río Bravo Conservation and Management Area. A new highway

CLIMATE CHANGE & TRAVEL

Every form of transport that relies on carbon-based fuel generates CO_2, the main cause of human-induced climate change. Modern travel is dependent on airplanes, which might use less fuel per mile per person than most cars but travel much greater distances. The altitude at which aircraft emit gases (including CO_2) and particles also contributes to their climate change impact. Many websites offer 'carbon calculators' that allow people to estimate the carbon emissions generated by their journey and, for those who wish to do so, to offset the impact of the greenhouse gases emitted with contributions to portfolios of climate-friendly initiatives throughout the world. Lonely Planet offsets the carbon footprint of all staff and author travel.

runs between Blue Creek and Orange Walk.

If you are crossing from Mexico to Belize, you will have to hand in your Mexican tourist card as you leave and pay a US$30 tourist tax (payable in US dollars or Mexican pesos).

Bus

Mexican bus company **ADO** (www.ado.com.mx) runs excellent air-conditioned express bus services twice daily from Cancún (M$840, 10 hours) to Belize City via Corozal and Orange Walk. The Cancún bus stops in Playa del Carmen and Tulum and can drop passengers directly at Cancún airport on the return leg. The buses do not enter Chetumal town in either direction. Note that the overnight bus arrives at the border in the early hours of the morning, when you'll need to leave the bus, hand in your Mexican tourist card and pay a US$30 exit fee before entering Belize.

Many regular Belizean buses ply the Philip Goldson Hwy between Belize City and Chetumal. In Chetumal, buses bound for Corozal Town (BZ$4, one hour), Orange Walk Town (BZ$8, two hours) and Belize City (BZ$14 to BZ$16, four hours) leave from the north side of Nuevo Mercado, about 0.75 miles north of the city center. Leaving from Belize, buses mostly depart in the morning; from Chetumal, afternoon departures are more common.

Additionally, an air-conditioned tourist bus

(BZ$50, three hours) runs daily between the San Pedro Belize Express Water Taxi Terminal and Chetumal.

Car & Motorcycle

To bring a vehicle into Belize, you need to obtain a one-month importation permit at the border. This obliges you to take the vehicle out of Belize again within the validity of the permit. To get the permit you must present proof of ownership (vehicle registration) and purchase Belizean motor insurance (available for BZ$60 for one month from the insurance office at the border). Permit extensions can be obtained by applying to the **Customs Department** (227-7092) in Belize City. If you've rented a car in Mexico, the rental agency will need to supply you with the necessary rental documents showing permission to take the vehicle to Belize.

Although not specifically related to the permit, a fee of BZ$30 is charged to bring the vehicle in and you'll need to pay BZ$10 for the quarantine wash.

It's not unusual to see US license plates on cars in Belize, as driving from the USA through Mexico is pretty

straightforward and car rental in Belize is expensive. The shortest route through Mexico to the crossing point between Chetumal and Corozal is from the US–Mexico border points at Brownsville–Matamoros or McAllen–Reynosa, a solid three days' driving.

You are required to obtain a temporary import permit for your vehicle at the border when you enter Mexico; as well as the vehicle registration document you'll need to show your driver's license and pay a fee of around US$50. You'll also have to buy Mexican motor insurance, also available at the border.

GUATEMALA

The only land crossing between Belize and Guatemala is a mile west of the Belizean town of Benque Viejo del Carmen at the end of the all-paved George Price Hwy from Belize City. The town of Melchor de Mencos is on the Guatemalan side of the crossing. The border is 44 miles from the Puente Ixlú junction (also called El Cruce) in Guatemala, where roads head north for Tikal (22 miles) and southwest to

LAND DEPARTURE TAX

When departing Belize by land, non-Belizeans are required to pay fees that total BZ$40 (US$20) in cash (Belizean or US dollars). Of this, BZ$7.50 is the Protected Areas Conservation Trust (PACT) fee, which helps to fund Belize's network of protected natural areas.

Flores (18 miles). The road is fully paved.

The Southern Hwy now extends to the Guatemalan border in the south but there is no official border crossing here.

Bus

Two companies run express buses to/from Guatemala. From the San Pedro Belize Express Water Taxi terminal in Belize City, you can go to Flores (BZ$50 to BZ$55, five hours) at 10am and 1pm. From Flores there are frequent connections to Guatemala City.

You can also take any of the frequent westbound Belizean buses to Benque Viejo del Carmen and then use the local service to the border.

Sea

It's possible to arrive in Belize by boat from three neighboring countries.

GETTING AROUND

Air

Airlines in Belize

Belize's two domestic airlines, Maya Island Air and Tropic Air, provide an efficient and reasonably priced service in small planes on several domestic routes, with plenty of daily flights by both airlines on the main routes.

Maya Island Air (www.mayaislandair.com) Serves Corozal, Dangriga, Orange Walk, Placencia, Punta Gorda, San Pedro.

Tropic Air (www.tropicair.com) Serves Belmopan, Corozal, Dangriga, Orange Walk, Placencia, Punta Gorda, San Ignacio, San Pedro.

Belize City flights use both the Philip Goldson International Airport and the Municipal Airstrip, about 12 miles from the international airport; flights using the Municipal Airstrip are usually significantly cheaper than those using the international airport. At the time of writing, the airstrip on Caye Caulker was closed for upgrading but may reopen for regular flights in future.

Bicycle

Most of Belize, including all three of the main highways, is pretty flat, which makes for pleasant cycling, but traffic on the main highways does tend to travel fairly fast; make sure you're visible if riding along these roads. Belizeans use bicycles – often beach cruiser–type bikes on which you brake by pedaling backward – for getting around locally, but you don't see them doing much long-distance cycling unless they're into racing.

Bikes are available to rent in many of the main tourist destinations for around BZ$20 per day. You don't usually have to give a deposit. It may be possible to purchase a used bike from one of these rental companies for longer-term use.

Boat

There are several boat services operating between the mainland and the islands (mainly Caye Caulker and Ambergris Caye). Lodges

BOATS TO/FROM BELIZE

FROM	TO	FREQUENCY	DURATION	PRICE (BZ$)
Chetumal, Mexico	Caye Caulker	daily	2½hr	110
Chetumal, Mexico	San Pedro	daily	2hr	100
Lívingston	Punta Gorda	daily	30min	50
Puerto Barrios, Guatemala	Punta Gorda	twice daily	45min	50-60
Puerto Cortés, Honduras	Placencia	weekly (Fri)	4hr	130
Puerto Cortés, Honduras	Belize City	weekly (Fri)	5½hr	270
Puerto Cortés, Honduras	Dangriga	weekly (Fri)	5hr	120

and resorts on the smaller islands usually arrange transportation for their guests.

Otherwise, getting to and around Belize's islands and reefs is a matter of taking tours or dive-and-snorkel trips, using boats organized by island accommodations or chartering a launch. As a rough rule of thumb, launch charters cost around BZ$200 per 10 miles. They're easy to arrange almost anywhere on the coast and on the main islands.

Regular services include the following:

Belize City–Caye Caulker–San Pedro Two companies handle this route nearly a dozen times a day, so there are plenty of options.

Corozal–Sarteneja–San Pedro The **Thunderbolt** (☏631-3400) has a monopoly on this route, with a daily service in each direction.

Dangriga–Central Cayes A handful of water taxis make the run frequently. It's easy to arrange and cheaper to share.

Placencia–Independence The **Hokey Pokey Water Taxi** (☏665-7242) travels between Placencia and Independence, saving travelers a long road detour between Placencia and Punta Gorda.

River boats are an efficient way to get to some inland destinations, including the Maya ruins at Lamanai.

Bus

To the untrained eye, the Belize bus system seems to be in chaos. However, all you need to know is that there are regular buses plying the regular routes, and that they charge – more or less – the same prices.

Following are the three main bus routes, all of which originate in Belize City:

Philip Goldson Hwy (Northern Hwy) From Belize City to Orange Walk and Corozal (and on to Chetumal, Mexico). There are half a dozen companies servicing this route, and between 25 and 30 buses a day going in each direction.

George Price Hwy (Western Hwy) From Belize City to Belmopan, San Ignacio and Benque Viejo del Carmen. Several companies service this route, resulting in a regular service that runs in both directions every half-hour throughout the day.

Hummingbird and Southern Hwys Buses from Belize City and Belmopan head down the Hummingbird Hwy every hour or so, stopping in Dangriga then continuing on to the Southern Hwy to Independence and Punta Gorda. Other regular services run from Dangriga to Hopkins and Placencia.

Most Belizean buses are old US school buses. Regular-service buses stop anywhere to drop off and pick up passengers. Express buses have limited stops and are usually less crowded. They cost a bit more but they save a lot of time, especially on longer trips, so it's worth the extra few dollars.

A variety of smaller bus companies serve villages around the country. They often run to local work and school schedules, with buses going into a larger town in the morning and returning in the afternoon.

Occasional breakdowns and accidents happen with Belizean buses but their track record is at least as good as those in other Central American countries. Luggage pilfering has been a problem on some buses in the past. Carry valuables with you on the bus and give your stored baggage to the bus driver or conductor only, and watch as it is stored. Be there when the bus is unloaded to retrieve your luggage.

Car & Motorcycle

Having a vehicle in Belize gives you maximum flexibility and enables you to reach off-the-main-road destinations and attractions (of which there are many) without having to depend on tours and expensive transfers. Though car rental is costly in Belize, it doesn't look so exorbitant when you consider the alternatives, especially if there are three or four people to share the expenses.

Belize has four paved two-lane roads: the Philip Goldson Hwy between Belize City and the Mexican border north of Corozal; the George Price Hwy (formerly Western Hwy) between Belize City and the Guatemalan border near Benque Viejo del Carmen; the Hummingbird Hwy from Belmopan to Dangriga; and the Southern Hwy, which branches off the Hummingbird Hwy a few miles from Dangriga and heads south to Punta Gorda and the southern Guatemala border. Connecting the George Price Hwy just south of Belize City with the Southern Hwy just west of Dangriga, the unpaved Manatee Hwy will save you a few miles but isn't recommended for cars without 4WD and actually takes longer.

DRIVING DISTANCES BETWEEN BELIZE & THE USA

From Subteniente López–Santa Elena border crossing to US–Mexico border points:

Brownsville–Matamoros 1257 miles

McAllen–Reynosa 1267 miles

Laredo (Texas)–Nuevo Laredo 1413 miles

El Paso–Ciudad Juárez 1988 miles

Nogales (Arizona)–Nogales 2219 miles

MAIN DRIVING ROUTES

In 2012 the Belizean government renamed the country's two main highways. The Northern Hwy was changed to Philip Goldson Hwy and the Western Hwy to George Price Hwy. Note that many locals still use the old names when giving directions.

Philip Goldson Hwy Belize City to Orange Walk Town (1½ hours, 57 miles), Corozal Town (2¼ hours, 86 miles) and Santa Elena (Mexican border; 2½ hours, 95 miles).

George Price Hwy Belize City to Belmopan (1¼ hours, 52 miles), San Ignacio (1¾ hours, 72 miles) and Benque Viejo del Carmen (Guatemalan border; two hours, 80 miles).

Hummingbird and Southern Hwys Belmopan to Dangriga (1½ hours, 55 miles), Hopkins (two hours, 63 miles), Placencia (3½ hours, 98 miles) and Punta Gorda (4½ hours, 148 miles).

Most other roads are one- or two-lane unpaved roads. The most oft-used roads are kept in fairly good condition, but heavy rains can make things challenging. Off the main roads you don't always need a 4WD vehicle but you do need one with high clearance.

Driver's License

If you plan to drive in Belize, you'll need to bring a valid driver's license from your home country.

Fuel & Spare Parts

There are plenty of fuel stations in the larger towns and along the major roads. At last report, regular gasoline was going for around BZ$11 per US gallon. Premium (unleaded) is a few cents more. Spare parts and mechanics are most easily available in Belize City, although San Ignacio, Belmopan and Orange Walk Town also have parts suppliers and tire repairs. Check the Belize Yellow Pages (www.yellowpages.bz).

Car Rental

Generally, renters must be at least 25 years old, have a valid driver's license and pay by credit card.

Most car-rental companies have offices at Philip Goldson International Airport as well as in Belize City; they will often also deliver or take return of cars at Belize City's Municipal Airstrip or in downtown Belize City. Rental possibilities are few outside Belize City, but it is possible to rent cars in San Ignacio and Placencia.

Rental rates, including taxes, insurance and unlimited mileage, generally start at around BZ$90 a day for an economy vehicle with air-con or BZ$140 for a 4WD. If you keep the car for six days, you'll often get the seventh day free.

Most rental agencies will not allow you to take a vehicle out of the country. One agency that allows cars to be taken into Guatemala is **Crystal Auto Rental** (☎223-1600; www.crystal-belize.com; Philip Goldson Hwy; ☺7am-5pm) in Belize City.

Insurance

Liability insurance is required in Belize. There are occasional police checkpoints on the main highways, where you may be required to produce proof of it – you face possible arrest if you can't. You won't be able to bring your own vehicle into Belize without buying Belizean insurance at the border, but rental companies always organize the necessary insurance for you.

Road Conditions & Hazards

Outside Belize City, traffic is wonderfully light throughout the country, but there are some potential hazards to be aware of:

➡ On the main roads, watch out for erratic and dangerously fast driving by others. Drive defensively.

➡ Watch for speed bumps (also known as sleeping policemen): these are sometimes well signed, but sometimes not signed at all.

➡ Off the major highways, most roads are unpaved: be careful of potholes.

➡ After a lot of rain, some roads may become impassable; make inquiries before you set out, and if you're in doubt about whether you'll get through a stretch, don't risk it.

➡ Always have water and a spare tire, and always fill your tank before you head off into the back country as gas stations can be few and far between, and off-road driving can use more fuel than expected.

Road Rules

➡ Driving in Belize is on the right.

➡ Speed limits are 55mph on the open highway, and either 40mph or 25mph in villages and towns.

➡ Seat belts are compulsory for drivers and front-seat passengers.

➡ Mileposts and highway signs record distances in miles and speed limits in miles per hour, although many vehicles have odometers and speedometers that are calibrated in kilometers.

Golf Carts

If you're spending some time at the beach and you can't fathom being dependent on your own leg power, you might consider renting a golf cart. It's relatively inexpensive (compared to a car) but it still gets you to the beach and back without causing you to break a sweat. The golf cart is a popular form of transportation in Placencia, San Pedro and – to a lesser degree – Caye Caulker. Both gas-powered and battery-powered golf carts are available: gas goes further and faster, but battery is better for the planet. Expect to pay about BZ$100 to BZ$130 per day for a four-seater.

Hitchhiking

Hitchhiking is never entirely safe and we don't recommend it. In Belize, like anywhere, it's imperative that you listen to your instincts and travel smart. Travelers who decide to hitchhike should understand that they are taking a small but potentially serious risk. You're far better off traveling with another person, and never hitchhike at night. Also keep in mind that buses in Belize are cheap and fairly efficient; you might decide that a bus is a safer and more comfortable bet.

Hitchhiking is a fairly common way for Belizeans to get around, especially off the main highways. In a country where vehicle owners are a minority and public transportation is infrequent to places off the main roads, it's common to see people trying to catch a lift at bus stops or at speed bumps, where traffic slows down. If you too are trying to get someplace where there's no bus for the next three hours, it's likely that you'll soon get a ride if you hold out your hand and look friendly. Offering to pay a share of the fuel costs at the end of your ride never goes amiss.

Local Transportation

All of Belize's towns, including the parts of Belize City that most visitors frequent, are small enough to cover on foot, although for safety reasons you should take taxis for some trips within Belize City. Taxis are plentiful in all mainland towns and are also an option for getting to places out of town, although asking taxis to venture beyond their normal work area can be fairly expensive.

Bicycling is an enjoyable way of getting around local areas and bikes can be rented at around BZ$20 per day in many tourist haunts (and are free for guests at some accommodations). On the cays, of course, you get around by boat if you're going anywhere offshore.

Behind the Scenes

SEND US YOUR FEEDBACK

We love to hear from travelers – your comments keep us on our toes and help make our books better. Our well-traveled team reads every word on what you loved or loathed about this book. Although we cannot reply individually to your submissions, we always guarantee that your feedback goes straight to the appropriate authors, in time for the next edition. Each person who sends us information is thanked in the next edition – the most useful submissions are rewarded with a selection of digital PDF chapters.

Visit **lonelyplanet.com/contact** to submit your updates and suggestions or to ask for help. Our award-winning website also features inspirational travel stories, news and discussions.

Note: We may edit, reproduce and incorporate your comments in Lonely Planet products such as guidebooks, websites and digital products, so let us know if you don't want your comments reproduced or your name acknowledged. For a copy of our privacy policy visit lonelyplanet.com/privacy.

OUR READERS

Many thanks to the travelers who used the last edition and wrote to us with helpful hints, useful advice and interesting anecdotes: Andy Proctor, Carol Malko, Chris Bandy, Mark van Laarschot, Nils Macharis, Nirmala Singh-Brinkman, Paul Spizman Shane McCarthy, Thomas Huettner

WRITER THANKS
Paul Harding

It was a pleasure to meet many wonderful people on my travels in Belize. Thanks for chats and advice to (among others) Deborah in Corozal, Jo and Caz in Punta Gorda and Daniel in San Ignacio. Thanks at Lonely Planet to Alicia Johnson and to my co-writer Ashley Harrell. Most of all thanks and hugs to Hannah and Layla at home for their patience and love.

Ray Bartlett

Thanks first and always to my family and amazing friends, for letting me go on these adventures and still remembering me when I get back. To the incredible Alicia J, for the editorial wisdom and for speedy answers when I needed them. To all people I met or who helped along the way, especially Virginia, Mereja, Nathalie, Valerie, Peggy, Marlon, Ismael, Jane, Kelsey, Stuart, Rachna, Flor, and so many others. Thanks so much. Can't wait to be back again soon.

Ashley Harrell

Thanks to editor Alicia Johnson and co-author Paul Harding for being lovely to work with, Stacey Auch for the best road trip ever, David Roth for becoming a scuba diver, Richard Harrell for braving the Blue Hole, Ronni Harrell for letting Dad visit, Kat Marin for the good company and the help, Tacogirl for the invites and the floaties (sorry!), Kelly Samuels for the cookies and the good times, and Joanne Edwards for being a riot and pleasure to know.

ACKNOWLEDGEMENTS

Cover photograph: Tobacco Caye, Belize, Duarte Dellarole/Shutterstock ©

THIS BOOK

This 7th edition of Lonely Planet's *Belize* guidebook was researched and written by Paul Harding, Ray Bartlett and Ashley Harrell. This guidebook was produced by the following:

Destination Editor
Alicia Johnson

Senior Product Editor
Saralinda Turner

Regional Senior Cartographer Corey Hutchison

Product Editor
Alison Ridgway

Book Designer Fergal Condon

Assisting Editors Katie Connolly, Bruce Evans, Jodie Martire, Sarah Stewart

Assisting Cartographers Alison Lyall, Katerina Pavkova

Cover Researcher Naomi Parker

Thanks to Gwen Cotter, Bailey Freeman, Jenna Myers, Kirsten Rawlings

Index

Map Legend

Sights
- Beach
- Bird Sanctuary
- Buddhist
- Castle/Palace
- Christian
- Confucian
- Hindu
- Islamic
- Jain
- Jewish
- Monument
- Museum/Gallery/Historic Building
- Ruin
- Shinto
- Sikh
- Taoist
- Winery/Vineyard
- Zoo/Wildlife Sanctuary
- Other Sight

Activities, Courses & Tours
- Bodysurfing
- Diving
- Canoeing/Kayaking
- Course/Tour
- Sento Hot Baths/Onsen
- Skiing
- Snorkeling
- Surfing
- Swimming/Pool
- Walking
- Windsurfing
- Other Activity

Sleeping
- Sleeping
- Camping
- Hut/Shelter

Eating
- Eating

Drinking & Nightlife
- Drinking & Nightlife
- Cafe

Entertainment
- Entertainment

Shopping
- Shopping

Information
- Bank
- Embassy/Consulate
- Hospital/Medical
- Internet
- Police
- Post Office
- Telephone
- Toilet
- Tourist Information
- Other Information

Geographic
- Beach
- Gate
- Hut/Shelter
- Lighthouse
- Lookout
- Mountain/Volcano
- Oasis
- Park
- Pass
- Picnic Area
- Waterfall

Population
- Capital (National)
- Capital (State/Province)
- City/Large Town
- Town/Village

Transport
- Airport
- Border crossing
- Bus
- Cable car/Funicular
- Cycling
- Ferry
- Metro station
- Monorail
- Parking
- Petrol station
- Subway/Subte station
- Taxi
- Train station/Railway
- Tram
- Underground station
- Other Transport

Routes
- Tollway
- Freeway
- Primary
- Secondary
- Tertiary
- Lane
- Unsealed road
- Road under construction
- Plaza/Mall
- Steps
- Tunnel
- Pedestrian overpass
- Walking Tour
- Walking Tour detour
- Path/Walking Trail

Boundaries
- International
- State/Province
- Disputed
- Regional/Suburb
- Marine Park
- Cliff
- Wall

Hydrography
- River, Creek
- Intermittent River
- Canal
- Water
- Dry/Salt/Intermittent Lake
- Reef

Areas
- Airport/Runway
- Beach/Desert
- Cemetery (Christian)
- Cemetery (Other)
- Glacier
- Mudflat
- Park/Forest
- Sight (Building)
- Sportsground
- Swamp/Mangrove

Note: Not all symbols displayed above appear on the maps in this book

OUR STORY

A beat-up old car, a few dollars in the pocket and a sense of adventure. In 1972 that's all Tony and Maureen Wheeler needed for the trip of a lifetime – across Europe and Asia overland to Australia. It took several months, and at the end – broke but inspired – they sat at their kitchen table writing and stapling together their first travel guide, *Across Asia on the Cheap*. Within a week they'd sold 1500 copies. Lonely Planet was born.

Today, Lonely Planet has offices in Franklin, London, Melbourne, Oakland, Dublin, Beijing and Delhi, with more than 600 staff and writers. We share Tony's belief that 'a great guidebook should do three things: inform, educate and amuse'.

OUR WRITERS

Paul Harding

Southern Belize, Cayo District, Northern Belize As a writer and photographer, Paul has been traveling the globe for the best part of two decades, with an interest in remote and offbeat places, islands and cultures. He's an author and contributor to more than 50 Lonely Planet guides to countries and regions as diverse as India, Belize, Vanuatu, Iran, Indonesia, New Zealand, Iceland, Finland, Philippines and – his home patch – Australia. Paul also wrote the Plan, Understand and Survival Guide sections.

Ray Bartlett

Guatemala Ray has been travel writing for nearly two decades, bringing Japan, Korea, Mexico, Tanzania, Guatemala, Indonesia, and many parts of the United States to life in rich detail for top industry publishers, newspapers and magazines. His acclaimed debut novel, *Sunsets of Tulum,* set in Yucatán, was a Midwest Book Review 2016 Fiction pick. Among other pursuits, he surfs regularly and is an accomplished Argentine tango dancer. Ray Bartlett currently divides his time between homes in the USA, Japan and Mexico.

Ashley Harrell

Belize District, Northern Cayes After a brief stint selling day-spa coupons door-to-door in South Florida, Ashley decided she'd rather be a writer. She went to journalism grad school, convinced a newspaper to hire her, and starting covering wildlife, crime and tourism, sometimes all in the same story. Fueling her zest for storytelling and the unknown, she traveled widely and moved often, from a tiny NYC apartment to a vast California ranch to a jungle cabin in Costa Rica, where she started writing for Lonely Planet. From there her travels became more exotic and farther flung, and she still laughs when paychecks arrive.

Published by Lonely Planet Global Limited
CRN 554153
7th edition – July 2019
ISBN 978 1 78657 492 3
© Lonely Planet 2019   Photographs © as indicated 2019
10 9 8 7 6 5 4 3 2 1
Printed in China